# Issues for Debate in American Public Policy

# Issues for Debate in American Public Policy

Selections from *The CQ Researcher*
Sandra L. Stencel, editor

A Division of Congressional Quarterly Inc.
Washington, D.C.

1414 22nd Street, N.W., Washington, D.C. 20037
(202) 822-1475; (800) 638-1710

http://books.cq.com



Printed and bound in the United States of America

**A CQ Press College Division Publication**

| | |
|---|---|
| Director | Brenda Carter |
| Associate editor | Gwenda Larsen |
| Marketing manager | Julianne C. Rovesti |
| Managing editor | Ann Davies |
| Project editor | Christopher Karlsten |
| Project editor | Jerry Orvedahl |
| Cover designer | Ed Atkeson, Berg Design |
| Indexer | Deborah Patton |
| Print buyer | Jason Holloway |
| Sales | Carrie Hutchison |

Photos and illustrations: p. 1: © Bobby Neel Adams; p. 5: © Ericka McConnell; p. 8: BISON; p. 13: Austin CEO Foundation; pp. 19 and 29: NEA; pp. 79 and 91: Bob Hulsey, Missouri Dept. of Social Services; p. 106: AARP; p. 110: © Bettmann/UPI; pp. 137-139, 142, 144, 147, 148, 150: Environmental Justice Resource Center; p. 155: Smith and Wesson; p. 175: © AP; p. 187: © AP/Callie Lipkin; p. 193: © AP; p. 215: Microsoft Corporation; p. 233: © Barbara Sassa-Daniels; p. 253: Northern Virginia Community College.

"At Issue" pieces: p. 33: Reprinted with permission from *Insight.* Copyright 1998, News World Communications Inc. All rights reserved. p. 113: Reprinted with permission of Edward H. Crane and *Vital Speeches of the Day*; p. 207: Reprinted with the permission of *HR News,* published by the Society for Human Resource Management, Alexandria, VA. p. 227: Copyright © 1998 by *The New York Times.* Reprinted by permission; Copyright © 1998 by *The Denver Rocky Mountain News.* Reprinted with permission. p. 247: Reprinted with permission from *Insight.* Copyright 1996, News World Communications Inc. All rights reserved.

LIBRARY OF CONGRESS CATALOGING-IN-PUBLICATION DATA

Issues for debate in American public policy : selections from The CQ Researcher / Sandra L. Stencel, editor.
p. cm.
Includes bibliographical references and index.
ISBN 1-56802-463-0 (alk. paper)
1. United States--Social policy--1993- 2. Social problems--United States. 3. United States--Politics and government--1993-
I. Stencel, Sandra L.
HN65.I848 1999
361.6′1′0973--dc21 99-10539

# Contents

## ENVIRONMENT



## CIVIL LIBERTIES, CIVIL RIGHTS, AND JUSTICE

## BUSINESS AND THE ECONOMY



## FOREIGN POLICY

# Preface

*Issues for Debate in American Public Policy* is a collection of 16 issues of *The CQ Researcher*, a weekly policy brief that brings into focus the often complicated and controversial issues that make their way onto the public agenda. Each *Researcher* offers in-depth, objective, and forward-looking reporting on a specific topic. This compilation is designed to encourage discussion, to help readers think critically and actively about these vital issues, and to facilitate further research.

These issues of *The CQ Researcher* encompass some of the most prominent topics of the day. The collection we have compiled is organized into seven subject areas that span a range of important public policy concerns. We hope it will appeal to several audiences. It is an attractive supplement for introductory public policy and American government courses, where it can be used to introduce real-world examples that bring policy-making to life and help students appreciate what is at stake in everyday policy debates. In addition, we hope that interested citizens, journalists, and business and government leaders will turn to this collection to familiarize themselves with key issues, actors, and policy positions; to jump-start research; or to help in making informed judgments about the likely outcome of current controversies.

Each *Researcher* offers a variety of special features to aid learning and understanding. They are discussed in more detail in the introduction, but they also deserve mention here. The articles begin with an overview of the key questions or controversies that are driving the policy debate. Next, the history of that debate is examined, and then the current situation is assessed. Each article closes with an "Outlook" section that helps readers judge what might happen in the future. Sidebars in each article, including easy-to-read charts and graphs, add depth to the discussion. A full-page chronology summarizes the developmental milestones for each issue. An "At Issue" page airs a pro–con debate between experts who weigh in on opposing sides. And finally, each reading includes an annotated bibliography to guide further research. In addition, the book includes a "Topical Guide to the Chapters," which places all of the articles in the context of the public policy-making process.

**Acknowledgments**

We wish to thank many people for helping make this collection a reality. First is Sandra Stencel, editor of *The CQ Researcher*, who gave us her enthusiastic support and cooperation as we developed this project. She and her talented staff of editors and writers have amassed a first-class library of *Researcher* articles, and we are privileged to have access to that rich cache. David Masci, who wrote three of the articles in this collection, graciously wrote the book's introduction as well. Sarah Magner aided us at every step as the book took shape. We also gratefully acknowledge the advice of several scholars who commented on our plans for this book and helped us shape the content. In particular we thank Michael Kraft and Scott Furlong, both at the University of Wisconsin—Green Bay; Christopher Soper at Pepperdine University; Frank Kessler at Missouri Western State College; and John D. Cranor at Ball State University.

Some readers of this collection may be learning about *The CQ Researcher* for the first time. We expect that many readers will want regular access to this excellent weekly research tool. Anyone interested in subscription information or a no-obligation free trial of the *Researcher* can contact Congressional Quarterly via the Web at www.cq.com, or by phone toll-free at (800) 432-2250, ext. 279, or (202) 887-6279.

We hope that you are as pleased with *Issues for Debate in American Public Policy* as we are. We welcome your feedback and suggestions for future editions. Please direct any comments you may have to Gwenda Larsen, in care of CQ Press, 1414 22nd Street, N.W., Washington, D.C. 20037, or by e-mail at glarsen@cq.com.

— The Editors of CQ Press

# Introduction

by David Masci, staff writer, *The CQ Researcher*

Germany's first chancellor, Otto von Bismarck, once said that law was like sausage: People were better off not knowing what went into making it. Of course, the purpose of studying public policy is to repudiate this maxim. Today, people want to know the recipe for policymaking in its entirety, even if the ingredients are not always pure.

Much of what goes on in the halls of government, be it in legislatures, courts, or executive mansions, is transparent. We can identify and describe in great detail certain processes used to formulate and implement public policy. Yet boiling something complicated, like policymaking, down to its elements is bound to leave an incomplete picture of how the process really works. Indeed, even the most sound theoretical structure should be accompanied by clear, real-world examples, illustrations that add color and depth to our understanding of how things work in the public arena.

This book aims to add that color and depth to the study of policymaking by reprinting 16 recent articles from *The CQ Researcher,* a weekly magazine that focuses on issues of public concern. Each *Researcher* examines a single topic, like drug testing or the school choice debate. The article gives the reader a broad overview of a subject, from its historical background to a discussion of the current controversies and debates that surround it.

*The CQ Researcher* brings often complex issues down to earth. Difficult concepts are not oversimplified, but they are explained in plain English. At the same time, each piece is scrupulously nonpartisan, advancing no agenda and drawing no major conclusions. Instead, experts with differing viewpoints speak for themselves throughout the text, giving the reader a variety of perspectives.

The 16 *Researcher* articles reprinted in this book do not focus on one area of public policy. Indeed, the pieces were chosen purposely to expose students to a wide range of subjects, from civil rights to foreign policy. And yet the articles share much in common. To begin with, every issue examined in these pieces is currently very important and is likely to remain so in the future. Topics like social security reform, U.S.-Russian relations, and gun control will probably be on many policymakers' agendas in the years to come.

In addition, all of these articles, without exception, provide a window into how public policy is actually made and implemented by government institutions, interest groups and others. In every issue, the tough questions and controversies surrounding the subject at hand are aired and debated by key players. Moreover, past legislative and judicial action is chronicled and analyzed thoroughly. Finally, each piece looks at current and possible future political maneuvering, whether at the local, state or federal level.

These features make *The CQ Researcher* ideal for readers who are interested in understanding the process, politics and people behind the important issues of the day. No publication can match these pieces for breadth of knowledge or erudition.

### *The CQ Researcher*

*The CQ Researcher* began life in 1923 under a different moniker: *Editorial Research Reports.* ERR was sold primarily to newspapers, which used it as a research tool. The magazine was given its current name and a design overhaul in 1991.

Today, *The CQ Researcher* is still sold to many newspapers, some of which reprint all or part of each issue. But the market for the magazine has shifted significantly over the years. Currently, many more libraries subscribe than do newspapers. And now it is primarily students, not journalists, who use the publication for research.

People who write *Researchers* often compare the experience to that of drafting a college term paper. Indeed there are many similarities. Each article is as long as many term papers—running about 11,000 words—and is written by one person, without any significant outside help.

Like students, staff writers begin the creative process by choosing a topic. Working with the publication's editors, the writer tries to come up with a subject that has public policy implications and for which there is at least some existing controversy. A topic like Social Security would make a good *Researcher* since it is an issue of great import that policymakers are currently grappling with. On the other hand, something like "Recent Developments in Astronomy" would probably not be appropriate, because it is largely devoid of public policy implications.

After a topic is set, the writer embarks on a week or two of intense research. Articles are clipped, books ordered, and information gathered from a variety of sources, including interest groups, universities and the government. Often, the writer is approaching the subject for the first time and knows little or nothing about it. In these cases, research is especially important, since it helps the writer determine what is and is not worth putting into the article.

Once a writer feels well informed about the subject, he or she begins a series of interviews with experts—academics, officials, lobbyists, and people actually working in the field. Each piece usually requires a minimum of 10 to 15 interviews. Some especially complicated subjects call for more.

After much reading and interviewing, the writer begins to put the article together. Writing a *Researcher* usually takes more than a week. Often work is halted, as the writer discovers that more research or interviews are needed to fill an unexpected gap in the piece.

**Chapter Format**

Each chapter in this book is structured in the same way, beginning with an introductory overview of the topic. This first section briefly touches on the areas that will be explored in greater detail in the rest of the chapter.

Following the introduction is a section that chronicles the important debates currently going on in the field. The section is structured around a number of questions, known as "Issue Questions," such as: "Should the Federal government set privacy standards for the Internet?" or "Does the FDA take too long to review drugs and medical devices?"

This section is the core of each chapter, because the questions raised are often highly controversial and usually the object of much argument among those who work in and think about the topic. Hence the answers provided by the writer are never conclusive. Instead, each answer details the range of opinion within the field.

Following these questions and answers is the "Background" section, which provides a history of the issue being examined. Most often this look back includes important legislative and executive actions and court decisions from the past. Readers will be able to see how the current policy evolved.

An examination of existing policy (under the heading "Current Situation") follows the background section. Current Situation provides an overview of important developments that were occurring when the article was originally published. And in most cases, for instance the examination of rising teen drug use in the "Drug Testing" chapter, the issues are still current as this compilation goes to press.

Each chapter ends with an "Outlook" section, which gives a sense of what might happen in the near future. Often, as in the "Internet Privacy" chapter, this part of the piece looks at whether there will be new regulation over a certain industry. In other chapters, this section might anticipate what the courts or the White House could do in the coming years.

All chapters also contain other features that are not part of the main text. Each chapter has two or three sidebars that examine issues related to the topic. In addition, all chapters have what is known as an "At Issue" section, where two outside experts have been invited to provide brief opposing answers to a relevant question. Also included is a chronology that cites important dates and events.

Finally, all chapters have a bibliography, which details some of the sources used by the writer in the article. Unlike most bibliographies, which simply list books and articles used, this section includes a short paragraph detailing the reasons why each source was useful.

**An Overview of the Chapters: The Issues**

The 16 *CQ Researcher* articles reprinted in this book have been reproduced essentially as they appeared when first published. In a few cases where important new developments have occurred since an article came out, these developments are mentioned in the following overviews of the pieces, which highlight the principal issues that are examined.

**School Choice Debate:** Supporters of choice predict that private school tuition vouchers will become more widely used in the coming years as lawmakers, educators and parents realize that only radical reform can fix the nation's failing public schools. And school choice, these advocates argue, must be the cornerstone of this reform because it empowers parents to choose the best schools for their children. In addition, they say, vouchers will inject a healthy dose of competition and thereby improve a public education system that is monopolistic and resistant to change. But opponents say that vouchers will siphon money away from schools that are already woefully underfunded. Moreover, they argue that using taxpayer dollars to send children to sectarian schools violates the constitutional prohibition on government support for religion, in spite of a number of recent court decisions at the state level upholding the constitutionality of vouchers.

**Teacher Education:** An influential 1996 report presented a blistering indictment of public education in America, especially the quality of teacher training. The National Commission on Teaching and America's Future said that bold steps were needed to professionalize the nation's 2.7 million public school educators. Supporters of that view, including lawmakers, education experts and national teachers' unions, are pushing initiatives ranging from strengthening licensing standards to eliminating poorly performing teachers. Advocates hail the new emphasis on teaching as unique in the long history of attempted education reforms. But some skeptics say that reforming teaching without making more fundamental changes in the nation's public schools won't accomplish nearly enough. Others question where funding for this new training would come from.

**Patients' Rights:** The continuing growth of managed-care health plans is provoking a powerful backlash. Many patients say managed care makes it harder simply to see a doctor, let alone get insurance coverage for needed treatment. Doctors are also chafing under restrictions that limit the way they treat patients. The managed-care industry insists, however, that it is improving the quality of health care and slowing the rise in costs. Between 1996 and 1998, more than 30 states passed laws strengthening patients' rights in dealing with insurers. Congress is considering imposing new regulations on managed-care companies. Patient and consumer groups are pushing for these reforms, but insurers' and employers' groups warn that the result may be higher premiums and more uninsured workers.

**Reforming the FDA:** The Food and Drug Administration rarely has a shortage of critics. That's not surprising considering the agency's extraordinary role in American life: 25 cents of every consumer dollar is spent on FDA-regulated products. Much of the criticism leveled at the agency in recent years centered on its activist chief, David Kessler, who resigned in 1997 to head the Yale University Medical School. Just before leaving, Kessler refocused the spotlight on the FDA with his bid to regulate tobacco, an issue that continues to grab headlines. Kessler was not replaced until November 1998, when former FDA deputy commissioner Dr. Jane E. Henney was confirmed by the Senate and formally took charge.

**Welfare, Work and the States:** In one bold stroke, the federal government terminated its 61-year-old welfare program in 1996 and gave the states the leading role in charting welfare policy. But Washington also made it clear that it expects the states to help many more welfare recipients get to work. This has been an enormous challenge for states. Welfare-to-work efforts and public employment traditionally have cost more than simply writing benefit checks to recipients. But federal spending for training and welfare has been declining since the new law went into effect. And while welfare rolls have dropped significantly in the past few years, states face the prospect that some recipients could eventually lose welfare benefits completely, even though they may be unable to find jobs that pay enough for them to become self-sufficient.

**Social Security:** America's 76 million baby boomers pose a catastrophic threat to the nation's social safety net. Simply put, the social security system will not take in enough money to pay all of the boomers' guaranteed benefits as they retire over the next 30 years. To meet these obligations, the government will have to raise workers' payroll taxes, cut benefits or take more drastic steps, such as raising the retirement age. Increasingly, policymakers are embracing calls to "privatize" the system and shift some payroll taxes to private retirement accounts. But a consensus is proving elusive.

**Population and the Environment:** At the dawning of the 20th century, there were 1.6 billion people on Earth. Now, at century's end, there are nearly 6 billion. The phenomenal population growth has renewed a long-standing debate about how many people Earth can support. Thomas Robert Malthus launched the debate 200 years ago, predicting that global population would eventually overwhelm food supplies. Technological advances thus far have enabled agricultural productivity to outpace population growth. But the rekindled debate over human survival is about more than food supplies: Population growth causes environmental problems from water shortages to global climate change.

**Environmental Justice:** Toxic-waste dumps, sewage treatment plants and other pollution sources rarely are found near middle-class or affluent communities. Inner city neighborhoods, rural Hispanic villages and Indian reservations are far more likely to suffer. But a burgeoning new movement is helping poor communities across the country close the door on unwelcome dumps and factories. Charging that they are victims of environmental racism, activists are winning court battles on the ground that siting polluting facilities among disadvantaged people violates Title VI of the 1964 Civil Rights Act. But business representatives and residents of some affected minority communities say that the movement is stifling their opportunities for economic development and growth.

**Gun Control:** Gun control continues to inflame public opinion three decades after passage of the first broad federal firearms law, the Gun Control Act of 1968. Gun control supporters blame the high rate of violent crime and the large number of gun accidents and suicides on the easy availability of firearms and lax licensing and safety rules. Opponents argue that access to firearms deters crime and note that gun homicides are decreasing and fatal gun accidents are at a record low rate. Gun control supporters have begun pushing safety initiatives. They scored a partial victory in October 1997, when gun manufacturers in the United States agreed to include trigger locks on handguns. But they suffered a defeat the following month when voters in Washington state rejected a measure to require safety training for all gun users.

**Internet Privacy:** Privacy advocates warn that many Web sites try to collect personal information from on-line users, but few guarantee how that data will be used. They say the federal government should establish standards to protect privacy on-line. But Internet businesses and others contend that they can safeguard users' privacy without resorting to government interference. Law enforcement agencies, meanwhile, favor government limitations on the use of sophisticated encryption technology, which makes on-line communications secure—even from the police. They fear that strong encryption software will aid criminals in hiding their activities. But privacy advocates argue that encryption technology assures companies and consumers that their on-line communications are not being tampered with.

**Drug Testing:** Testing for illegal narcotics has become a major weapon in the war on drugs. Nearly three-quarters of America's biggest companies require job applicants to undergo urinalysis—up from 21 percent in 1988. Proponents say drug testing protects public safety and deters drug use, but opponents say neither claim can be proved. Until recently, most companies only tested job applicants and public-safety employees. Some state and local governments require random testing of public employees, high school students participating in after-school activities, prisoners and welfare recipients. Civil libertarians see such expanded drug testing as a dangerous erosion of Americans' constitutional right to privacy.

**Antitrust Policy:** For more than a century, federal law has sought to encourage competition by prohibiting monopoly behavior and other anticompetitive business practices. Now the government is accusing giant software maker Microsoft of illegally trying to stifle competition in computer markets. Microsoft says it has done nothing wrong and argues that the parallel suits by the federal government and coalition of 20 states will stifle innovation and hurt consumers. The high-stakes court action comes as the Justice Department and the Federal Trade Commission are also more closely scrutinizing corporate mergers that may restrict competition. With a record wave of mergers, including the late 1998 combining of oil giants Exxon and Mobil, some people are cheering the more aggressive policy and are urging the government to do even more. But others say the government should let the marketplace alone.

**Privatizing Government Services:** Many Americans—average citizens and policy experts alike—think government would cost less and run more smoothly if private-sector business operated troublesome public programs. In recent years, privatization efforts in many cities, notably Indianapolis and Phoenix, have lent support to the idea. Advocates of "contracting out" argue that government functions more efficiently when it is exposed to the competitive pressures faced daily by the business world. However, public-employee unions generally oppose the idea, claiming that privatizers cut costs by trimming workers' pay. So far, privatization in the United States has occurred mainly at the state and local levels. Now though, policymakers are talking about privatizing all or part of two of the largest federal programs—Social Security and the Postal Service.

**High-Tech Labor Shortage:** American employers say that a severe shortage of skilled high-tech workers is delaying projects and reducing expansion plans. To avoid economic disaster, they want Congress to admit more foreign workers into the country each year. But critics, including the Clinton administration, say employers are simply seeking more foreign workers because they will accept less pay. These critics say the answer to a shortage of skilled workers is training or retraining Americans already in the labor pool and hiring more women, minorities and unemployed or underemployed technical workers. But many employers say that the globalization of high-tech jobs is inevitable, and that U.S. borders eventually should be open to any skilled worker.

**Promoting Democracy in Asia:** Democracy has not fared well in Asia, through history or in recent times. Today, most Asians live under communist governments, military regimes or virtual one-party states. But Asia also includes two big, long-established democracies: India and Japan. And with the fall of Indonesia's autocratic and long-time president, Suharto, the world's fourth-most-populous country could be on its way to joining the ranks of democratic nations. But the country's new president, B.J. Habibie, faces a dire economic crisis and volatile political situation. Many reformers also doubt the new president's commitment to real political change. In addition, some Asians continue to debate whether democracy conflicts with Asian values. At the same time, U.S. policymakers are often at odds with interest groups on how best to promote democracy in Asia.

**U.S.-Russian Relations:** After the breakup of the Soviet Union, friendship blossomed between Russia and the United States. But relations have cooled in recent years, and the decision to admit Poland, Hungary and the Czech Republic into NATO over Russian objections added new tensions to the relationship. While NATO enlargement is seen by many as a step toward permanent peace in post-Cold War Europe, others argue that including old Soviet allies in the alliance will only antagonize Russia. Moreover, many enlargement opponents say the days of antagonism between Russia and the United States are over, making NATO unnecessary. But NATO boosters argue that Russia is growing increasingly hostile to U.S. interests and that other dangers, including Moscow's lack of control over its nuclear arsenal, make NATO enlargement vital to U.S. and European safety.

### The Policymaking Process

In his book *Public Policymaking: An Introduction,* professor James E. Anderson of Texas A&M University notes that, given the "complexity and diversity" of the policymaking process, "it is not now possible to develop a 'grand theory' of policy formation." Still, as Anderson points out, it is possible to create a general "framework" that can be used to better understand how public policy is made and implemented.

The policymaking process begins with the recognition of a problem. In other words, government officials and others recognize that something is wrong in our society and that it requires the attention of public institutions. For instance, in the chapter on school choice, those people who are for or against vouchers agree that public education is failing many of the nation's students, especially in poor areas. All understand that some action is necessary, even though they disagree on what that action should be.

Once a problem is articulated, the question then becomes What is to be done? In this next phase, proposals for solving the problem are formulated. Using the school choice chapter again as an example, we see that vouchers are presented by some as at least a partial solution to the problem of failing schools. Choice advocates argue that providing parents of public school children with government vouchers to pay for private school tuition will improve public education by injecting a measure of competition into the system.

But while some policy advocates may put forth a solution, it is meaningless unless it is championed and adopted by the appropriate government policymakers. In the case of school choice, a number of states established pilot voucher programs after difficult legislative battles between supporters of choice and teachers unions and civil liberties groups who oppose spending public money on private, especially sectarian, schools.

The next step involves implementing or applying the solution to the problem. At this stage we look at what is involved in putting the plan into action. Again, returning to the school choice example, we find that two cities, Cleveland and Milwaukee, have offered vouchers to a limited number of poor students chosen by lottery.

Finally, the policy must be evaluated for its effectiveness. Studying evaluation is more than just looking at the impact of a policy; students need also to examine who is evaluating the project and what are the consequences of the evaluation. In the school choice example, both supporters and opponents have marshaled studies to prove that the program either works or does not. Anecdotal evidence suggests that vouchers help at least those students who receive them, if not the local public school system, but even this assertion is hotly disputed.

There is no one way to look at the policymaking process, although the framework outlined here offers a simple, commonsensical approach. Regardless of which system a reader uses, these 16 issues of *The CQ Researcher* should be suitable for almost any theoretical template. With their accuracy, attention to detail, and clear examination of the policy issues and process, these readings should prove a valuable tool for anyone interested in understanding how public policy is made and implemented.

# Topical Guide to the Chapters

| | Chapter | | | | | | | | | | | | | | | |
|---|---|---|---|---|---|---|---|---|---|---|---|---|---|---|---|---|
| | 1 | 2 | 3 | 4 | 5 | 6 | 7 | 8 | 9 | 10 | 11 | 12 | 13 | 14 | 15 | 16 |
| **Level of Government** | | | | | | | | | | | | | | | | |
| National | T | T | M | M | S | M | M | M | S | M | M | M | S | M | M | M |
| State | M | M | S | — | M | — | — | S | M | — | T | T | S | — | — | — |
| Local | S | S | — | — | T | — | — | T | T | — | S | — | M | — | — | — |
| **Branch of Government** | | | | | | | | | | | | | | | | |
| Legislative | M | S | S | S | M | S | M | T | M | M | S | S | T | S | T | S |
| Executive | T | M | M | M | S | M | S | M | S | M | S | S | M | M | M | M |
| Judicial | T | — | — | T | — | — | — | S | S | — | M | M | — | — | — | — |
| **Policy Process Stage** | | | | | | | | | | | | | | | | |
| Agenda Setting and Formulation | M | M | M | M | T | M | M | S | S | M | M | M | S | T | S | M |
| Adoption | S | S | S | S | T | S | T | T | M | — | T | T | T | T | — | T |
| Implementation | T | T | — | S | M | — | T | M | T | — | T | S | T | S | M | S |
| Impact, Evaluation, Change | T | T | — | S | M | — | S | S | M | — | S | M | M | M | T | T |

M = main focus     S = secondary focus     T = tangential focus

Chapter titles: 1, School Choice Debate; 2, Teacher Education; 3, Patients' Rights; 4, Reforming the FDA; 5, Welfare, Work and the States; 6, Social Security; 7, Population and the Environment; 8, Environmental Justice; 9, Gun Control; 10, Internet Privacy; 11, Drug Testing; 12, Antitrust Policy; 13, Privatizing Government Services; 14, High-Tech Labor Shortage; 15, Promoting Democracy in Asia; 16, U.S.-Russian Relations

# 1 School Choice Debate

DAVID MASCI

For Rachgina Jeff and Brenda Ewart of Cleveland, Ohio, school choice is more than a matter of public policy. It's personal.

State-funded tuition vouchers enable Jeff's son Charles and Ewart's son Brandon to attend St. Adalbert's Roman Catholic elementary school.

"Charles already has two strikes against him — living in the inner city and being an African-American male," Jeff says. "I just wanted to give him a chance to get a decent education." To Jeff, that means keeping Charles out of the neighborhood public school.

"With the drugs, the gangs and the violence, it's hard for kids to learn in that environment," Ewart adds.

At St. Adalbert's, with its emphasis on core curricula, discipline and parental involvement, kids learn.

"Charles is really doing well there," Jeff says, noting that he recently scored in the 99th percentile on a standardized test.

Jeff and Ewart also are pleased that their children are receiving religious and moral instruction. "They're reinforcing the values I teach at home," Ewart says.

But St. Adalbert's is more than just a good school — it is affordable.

"The voucher is a blessing," says Jeff, a full-time student at Case Western Reserve University. "I would have to get a second job" without it, says Ewart, who works in a bank.

For school choice advocates, there are too few such success stories. Milwaukee is the only other city that offers publicly funded tuition vouchers. As pilot projects, however, the Cleveland and Milwaukee programs only offer assistance to a few thousand students. Moreover, the state laws that created the programs are being chal-

From *The CQ Researcher,* July 18, 1997.

lenged and may not survive judicial scrutiny. (*See story, p. 4.*)

Still, school choice proponents say that support for vouchers has been rising and will continue to increase as more and more Americans come to believe that public schools, especially in low-income areas, are failing. As evidence, they point to a Gallup Poll showing that 36 percent of Americans favored school choice in 1996, compared with 24 percent in 1993. [1]

In addition, voucher advocates say, school choice, over the last decade, has been transformed from a fringe issue dear to some conservatives and religious groups into a major part of the national education debate. For instance, vouchers were a major plank in Republican Bob Dole's 1996 presidential campaign.

Proponents say that vouchers are getting more attention because they make sense, especially for inner-city children like Charles and Brandon.

First and foremost, they argue, vouchers empower parents by giving them the freedom to choose what they believe to be the best school for their children. The power of choice, they say, would especially benefit the poor, who unlike Americans in higher income brackets often have no alternative but to send their children to the local public school.

"Choice is already in the hands of parents with money," says Nina Shokraii, an education policy analyst at the Heritage Foundation. "We have to extend that choice to parents without money."

Proponents also argue that vouchers will ultimately make the public schools better by injecting a healthy dose of competition into what is currently a stagnant and monopolistic system. Under the existing system, they say, public schools have no incentive to undertake real reform measures because, no matter what they do, their budgets won't shrink. But allowing parents to remove their children — as well as some of the money allotted to educate them — will force public schools to stop taking their students for granted, voucher advocates say.

Opponents of vouchers agree that as an issue, school choice is more visible than it once was. But that is where agreement ends between the two sides in the debate. And, they point out, a solid majority of Americans still oppose vouchers, a fact borne out by more than just polls. For instance, they say, every time school choice has come before voters in state referenda, it has been rejected, usually by overwhelming majorities.

As for the growing attention vouchers are getting, opponents say, it is due in part to legitimate anger over the inadequacy of public education in some areas. In particular, they say, school choice supporters are gaining ground by exploiting the frustrations of poor and minority parents, like Jeff and Ewart, who feel that neighborhood public schools are inadequate.

## States Where School Choice Is Being Considered

*School choice programs have been considered, or are being considered, by lawmakers in at least 20 states, but only two legislatures — in Wisconsin and Ohio — have actually enacted voucher programs.*

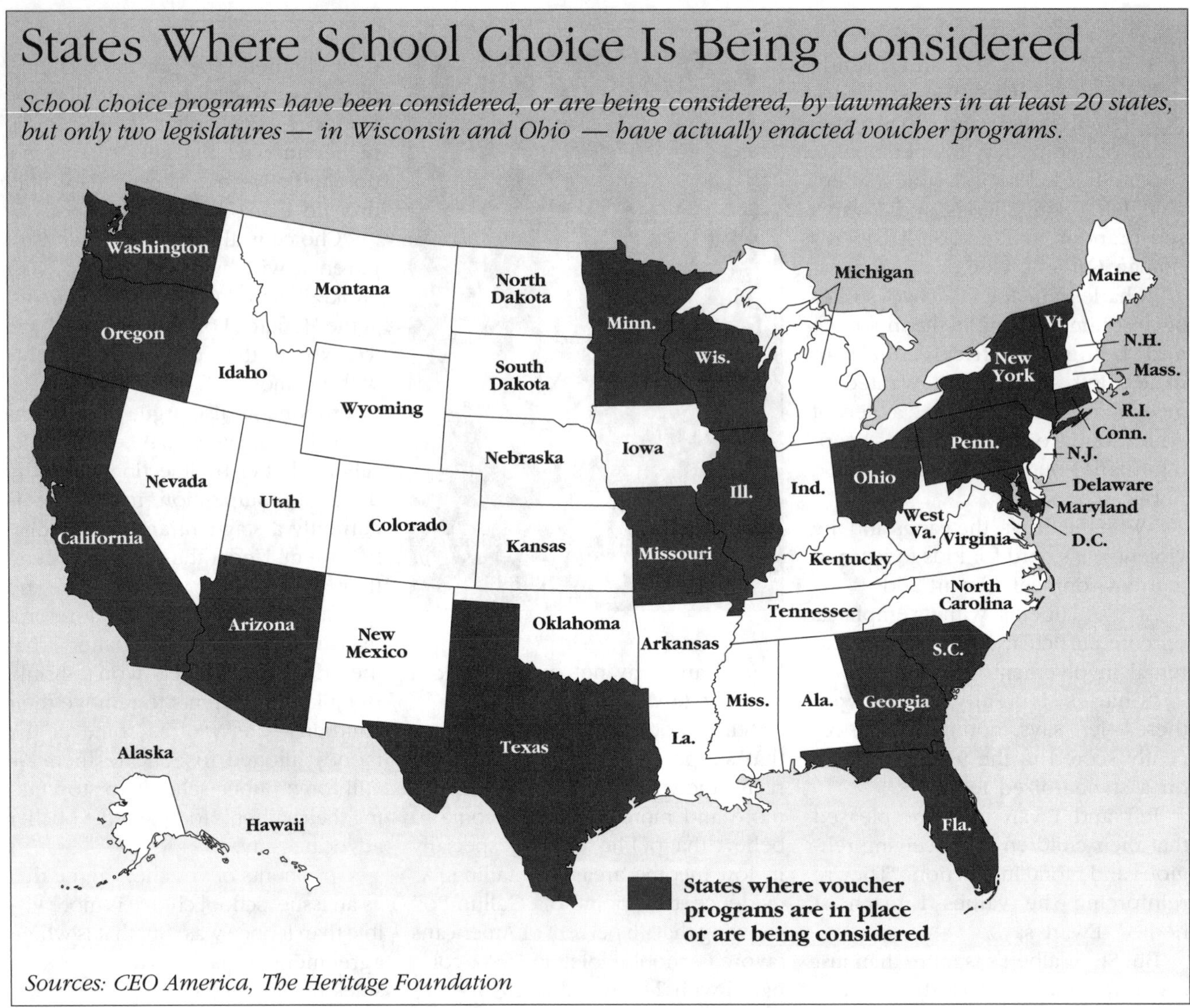


*Sources: CEO America, The Heritage Foundation*

"For them to say to poor people that [vouchers are] the answer is unfortunate because of course people in difficult situations are going to be more likely to listen," says Bob Chase, president of the National Education Association (NEA), the nation's largest teachers' union.

But Chase and other opponents say that school choice offers little more than a false, cruel hope to desperate parents. Vouchers, they point out, rarely amount to more than a few thousand dollars, not nearly enough to pay tuition at most top private schools.

"No one's going to go to Sidwell Friends," Chase says, referring to the expensive private school Chelsea Clinton began attending in Washington, D.C., after Bill Clinton won the presidency in 1992.

In addition, Chase and others argue, school choice actually will make public education worse, not better. For one thing, they say, instituting a voucher plan will take resources away from public school systems that in many cases are already desperately in need of additional funds. In addition, presenting vouchers as the solution to a school district's problems will only help to delay needed reforms.

"Where there are dysfunctional [school] systems, we need to correct those systems — expeditiously," Chase says, adding that the solution isn't to divert money to private schools.

Moreover, opponents say, it would still be the public schools that ultimately would have to educate the vast majority of the nation's children, even if vouchers were initiated nationwide. It's simply a question of size, they say. The public school

# School Choice Battles Embroil Many States

Voucher programs have only been instituted in a few places, but battles over school choice have touched many states. Proposals have been considered in at least 20 state legislatures over the years, and since 1990 vouchers have been the subject of referenda in California, Oregon, Colorado and Washington state.

The most recent vote occurred last November in Washington, where citizens decisively rejected a proposal to allow parents to receive tuition scholarships for non-religious private schools.

The fight over vouchers in Washington was typical of recent school choice campaigns. Both sides spent significant sums of money — about $2 million each — to get their message to the voters. The debate was contentious and at times even rancorous, with each side accusing the other of distorting the truth and representing interests other than educational improvement. By the time voters went to the polls, Initiative 173 was receiving almost as much attention in the state as the contest for president and governor.[1]

Voters in Washington rejected the initiative by a sizable majority, as they did in the other three states where referenda were held recently. For example, California's widely watched 1993 ballot initiative (Proposition 174) was defeated by a 2-1 margin.[2]

Voucher opponents say that the results in the recent referenda are further evidence of public opposition to school choice. "When voters have had the opportunity to vote on it, they've rejected it every time because they understand that it's counterproductive," says Bob Chase, president of the National Education Association, the nation's largest teachers' union.

But voucher proponents argue that the results are a testament to the power of groups like the NEA. For example, they claim, in California, opponents outspent supporters of school choice by 10-1.

And, the advocates say, the cause for vouchers has fared much better in state legislatures. Wisconsin and Ohio have voucher plans up and running. Other states, among them Iowa, have created tax credits that parents can use for educational expenses, including private school tuition.

The most recent legislative success for voucher advocates has come in Arizona, where on April 7 Republican Gov. Fife Symington signed into law a measure that allows residents to take a tax deduction of up to $500 for contributions to nonprofit foundations that provide scholarships to send children to private schools.[3]

The bill's sponsor, Republican state Rep. Mark Anderson, considers it a step toward a full voucher program.[4] Quentin L. Quade, director of the Blum Center for Parental Freedom in Education at Marquette University in Milwaukee, agrees: "This is a uniquely and distinctly important development."

Voucher proponents also are buoyed by recent events in Minnesota. On June 4, Republican Gov. Arne Carlson vetoed an education spending bill because it did not contain his proposal to give low- and middle-income families a $1,000 per child educational tax credit. Carlson has pledged to veto any new school spending bills that do not contain the tax credit provision.

School choice opponents also have had recent successes at the state level. In addition to their victory in the Washington referendum, they have beaten back a variety of tuition tax credit and voucher proposals in legislatures in Louisiana, Connecticut, Texas, New Jersey, New York and California.

In California, voters defeated a proposal that would have given vouchers to students scoring in the lowest 5 percent on state standardized tests. The plan passed the Republican-controlled Assembly only to stall in the Democratic-controlled Senate.

Both sides say that the real battle over vouchers will continue to be at the state level. "It's the states that really count," Quade says. "After all, 94 percent of all education spending comes from the states."

[1] Kerry A. White, "Choice Plans Face Big Statewide Test in Wash.," *Education Week*, Oct. 30, 1996.

[2] Barbara Kantrowitz, "Take the Money and Run," *Newsweek*, Oct. 11, 1993.

[3] From "Educational Freedom Report," Quentin L. Quade (ed.), April 25, 1997.

[4] *Ibid.*

system is almost eight times larger than its private counterpart, and vouchers would not be able to help more than a small percentage of public school students to attend private schools.

Finally, opponents say, even if vouchers are good education policy, they are barred by the Establishment Clause of the U.S. Constitution, which prohibits state support for religion.[2] They point out that courts in Wisconsin and Ohio have recognized that school choice leads to massive state subsidies for religious institutions, because the vast majority of private schools are sectarian. In Cleveland, for instance, 31 of the 48 schools participating in the voucher program are Roman Catholic.[3]

But school choice supporters argue that vouchers do not violate the Constitution because the funds go to the parents of the children, not directly to the schools. They also point out that the federal government and the states already are supporting

## Key Voucher Cases in the Courts

The U.S. Supreme Court has yet to consider the constitutionality of using publicly funded vouchers to send children to private, sectarian schools. At the state level, however, several school choice cases are working their way through the courts. Any one of these cases could form the basis for a future Supreme Court ruling. Here are the main voucher cases currently before state courts:

**Wisconsin** — The state Supreme Court deadlocked when it first considered Wisconsin's 1995 law expanding Milwaukee's existing voucher program to include religious schools. The 3-3 decision, which was handed down on March 29, 1996, was only possible because the court's seventh justice had recused herself from the case, citing a conflict of interest. [1]

The case was remanded back to the trial court, which ruled on Jan. 15, 1997, that including religious schools in the voucher program violated the state constitution's prohibition on government support of sectarian institutions. The law expanding the program to include sectarian schools has not been implemented. [2]

The trial court decision has been appealed and is once again before the state Supreme Court. Although only six judges will rule on the case, leaving open the possibility for another tie vote, voucher supporters are heartened by the recent retirement of one of three justices who voted against their position the first time. The new justice was appointed by Republican Gov. Tommy G. Thompson, an ardent supporter of vouchers.

**Ohio** — Cleveland's one-year experiment with school choice was put on hold on May 1, when Ohio's 10th District Court of Appeals ruled that the program violated the federal and state constitutions, which prohibit direct government support for religion. The case has been appealed to the state Supreme Court, which has yet to decide on the issue.

Even though the law in question allows parents to use vouchers to send their children to any private school participating in the choice program, the district court was troubled by the fact that 80 percent of these schools were sectarian. "The only real choice available to most parents is between sending their children to a sectarian school and having their child remain in the troubled Cleveland city school district," wrote Judge John C. Young. Hence the voucher program essentially provided assistance to religious schools, the judge concluded. [3]

The appeals court decision followed a trial court ruling the year before that allowed the voucher law to be implemented. In this earlier decision, Judge Lisa L. Sadler wrote that the vouchers were constitutional because the benefit to religious schools flowed through the parents (who choose how to use the voucher) and hence was indirect.

**Vermont** — The school board of tiny Chittenden, Vt., has filed a lawsuit against the state. The conflict centers around Chittenden's intention to pay tuition for 15 high school students to attend a local Roman Catholic school. The practice, known as "tuitioning," is common in Vermont, where many rural towns have no high school. All of Chittenden's 100 high school-age children are sent to outside public and private schools. The town pays the cost of tuition.

Citing a 1961 Vermont Supreme Court ruling outlawing tuitioning at sectarian schools, the state has threatened to deny Chittenden its share of education funding if it pays for students to attend the parochial school.

The town has sued the state, citing a 1994 Vermont Supreme Court decision allowing tuition reimbursement for parents who send their children to sectarian schools. Chittenden, and its attorneys at the Washington-based Institute for Justice argue that the more recent decision essentially overturns the earlier ruling.

[1] Mark Walsh, "Court Deadlocks on Vouchers," *Teacher*, May/June, 1996.

[2] Rene Sanchez, "In Wisconsin, Vouchers for Religious Schools are Handed Legal Setback," *The Washington Post*, Jan. 15, 1997.

[3] Paul Souhrada, "Court: Cleveland Vouchers Program Unconstitutional," The Associated Press, May 2, 1997.

thousands of religiously affiliated organizations such as hospitals, universities and social service providers with billions of dollars each year. Much of the state money assists K-12 students in parochial schools by providing them with textbooks, standardized tests, transportation and remedial education.

In addition, supporters say, recent Supreme Court decisions, including *Agostini v. Felton,* handed down in June (*see p. 5*), have steadily expanded the definition of what is permissible when it comes to government assistance for religious schools. These decisions, supporters argue, clearly indicate that vouchers will be adjudged constitutional by the Supreme Court.

As lawmakers, policy-makers, educators and parents continue to debate school choice, these are some of the questions being asked:

### *Does a voucher program that includes religious schools violate the constitutional separation of church and state?*

The First Amendment states that "Congress shall make no law respecting the establishment of religion, or prohibiting the free exercise thereof. . . ." On its face, the Establishment Clause is clear: The state cannot support one denomination or faith over others; nor can it inhibit citizens' practice of their religion.

But, like many parts of the Constitution, the Establishment Clause can be interpreted in a variety of ways when applied to more narrowly tailored, practical situations.

According to many legal scholars, the question of state support for religious schools has been especially perplexing because the Supreme Court has produced what some say are a host of confusing and contradictory decisions.

The question is simple: How far can the state go in supporting schools that are religiously affiliated? Some assistance is clearly allowed. For example, state governments have long been permitted to provide transportation and textbooks to students who attend parochial schools. The logic is that the assistance is going directly to the student, not the school, and hence is not supporting religion.

But the question becomes harder to answer when the assistance benefits the school more directly. While the Supreme Court has never ruled on the constitutionality of vouchers, it has looked at other schemes aimed at helping parents with educational expenses.

In 1973, for example, the court ruled in *Committee for Public Education and Religious Liberty v. Nyquist* that a New York state law granting parents reimbursements and tax credits for private school tuition was unconstitutional. The court said that even though the law was neutral on its face (allowing the benefit for any kind of private school tuition), it had the effect of subsidizing religious education because roughly three-quarters of parents receiving the reimbursements or credits sent their children to sectarian schools. Hence, regardless of its intent, the law resulted in advancing religious education and violated the Establishment Clause.

But over the next two decades, the court handed down several rulings that many regard as contradictory, including *Mueller v. Allen* in 1983. The court ruled in *Mueller* that an Ohio law offering a parental tax deduction for educational expenses was constitutional even though 93 percent of those claiming the deduction had children in religious schools. The court distinguished this case from *Nyquist* because the tax deduction also was available to parents with children in public schools. In addition, the justices argued that the deduction was a much less direct subsidy of religious schools than were the tuition reimbursements available under the New York law struck down in *Nyquist.* [4]

© Ericka McConnell

*The privately funded School Choice Scholarships program in New York City awarded 1,300 three-year tuition grants to enable poor children to attend private schools.*

In other cases in the 1980s and early '90s, the Supreme Court allowed various forms of state assistance for students enrolled in religious schools. For example, in *Zobrest v. Catalina Foothills School District* the court ruled in 1993 that a state could provide a sign language interpreter for a deaf student in parochial school, even when that student was in religion class.

And on June 23, in *Agostini,* the court ruled that remedial education teachers supplied by New York state could assist parochial school children on school property. Previously, such teachers had worked in buses parked off the grounds of the religious schools as a result of a 1985 Supreme Court ruling, *Aquilar v. Felton.* Voucher supporters were heartened by the fact that in *Agostini* the court reversed itself, overturning *Aguilar v. Felton.* [5]

Supporters of vouchers see cases like *Mueller, Zobrest* and *Agostini* as part of a trend within the Supreme Court away from what they say is the more restrictive view of the Establishment Clause put forth in *Nyquist.*

"This is just the court's way of moving from one position to another without actually admitting that they are changing the law," says Michael McConnell, a professor at the University of Utah's College of Law and an expert on the Establishment Clause.

According to McConnell, the court's shift is long overdue. "*Nyquist* was the product of the kind of separationist thinking that is really disguised hostility toward religion," he says. McConnell and others contend that there are a host of reasons why voucher programs would be constitutional.

First, they argue, the benefits go to the parents and children who receive them, not the school. "It's up to the parents to decide whether they want

# Privately Funded Vouchers Aid Students in 18 States

When the School Choice Scholarships Foundation offered tuition vouchers to 1,300 low-income children in New York City early this year, the response was an unanticipated — and overwhelming — 16,000 applications.

"It shows that the perception of need for the program is high," said Bruce Kovner, chairman of Caxton Corp., a New York investment firm, and head of the foundation. [1]

Kovner and other New York businessmen have already raised $7 million, enough to guarantee the recipients of the vouchers (who were chosen by lottery) up to $1,400 a year for three years. Kovner hopes to raise another $3 million in the near future in order to increase the number of scholarships and begin making a dent in the waiting list, which has swelled to 23,000 hopefuls. [2]

Amid the hoopla over publicly funded vouchers, efforts to privately finance school choice have gone almost unnoticed. But New York is just the latest in what has become a long list of cities where private philanthropists, usually in the business community, are establishing charities to pay for tuition vouchers.

**Cities With Private Voucher Programs**

*The number of voucher programs funded by nonprofit business and citizen groups has grown steadily since the first program was started in Indianapolis in 1991.*

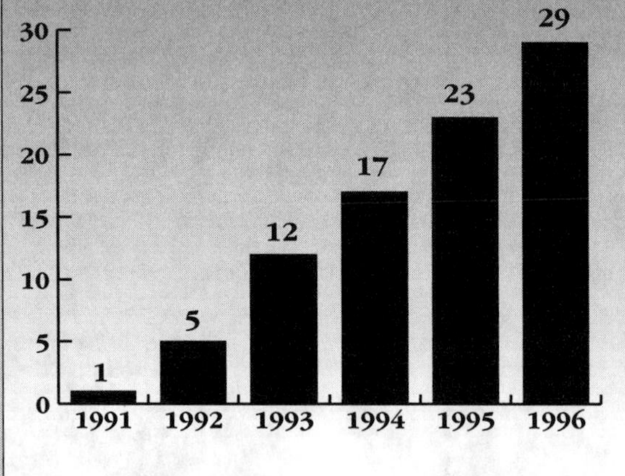


*Source: CEO America*

The first privately financed voucher program was created in Indianapolis in April 1991 by J. Patrick Rooney, then-chairman of the Golden Rule Insurance Co., who put up $1.2 million for 746 vouchers.

The following year, Jim Leininger a physician and businessman in San Antonio, Texas, decided to duplicate Rooney's efforts in his hometown. At roughly the same time, programs were being established in Atlanta, Milwaukee and Battle Creek, Mich.

Today, there are at least 30 programs in 18 states, including Dallas, Buffalo, N.Y., and Oakland, Calif. Some of the programs have just a few benefactors. Others are supported by large groups of well-to-do individuals. A few, like the group in Milwaukee, solicit funds from the general public.

The smallest group, in Midland, Texas, spent $6,000 on four students during the 1996-97 school year. The largest program is in Milwaukee, where $4.2 million provided vouchers for 4,127 children during the same period. Currently, all of the programs combined are serving 13,648 students, more than twice the number receiving privately funded vouchers two years ago.

"As time has gone on, this idea has really grown," says Fritz Steiger, president of Children's Educational Opportunity (CEO) of America, a group that supports local efforts to privately finance vouchers.

Founded in 1992, CEO America offers information and training to people interested in creating an organization to provide privately funded vouchers. In 1994, Steiger's group received a $2 million grant from the Walton Family Foundation. The money was used to help start nine programs. "We've gone in and said, "We'll give you $50,000 [for each of three years] if you can raise $50,000 to get the program started," Steiger says.

One reason these programs have proliferated so quickly, Steiger says, is that they can be relatively inexpensive to establish. The average voucher totals about $1,100, so a program can often serve 100 students with an annual budget of little more than $100,000.

Not surprisingly, new programs are being established each year. According to Steiger, new organizations have been or are being founded in San Francisco, Chicago, New Orleans, Miami, Baltimore and other cities.

"I think that by the year 2000, we'll have 60 programs and 30,000-40,000 students," he says.

But those who are starting these groups are not trying to build permanent charities. "The people who are funding this are not in it for the long haul," Steiger says. "These are transitional organizations that are models for public policy."

The hope, Steiger says, is to show politicians and the public at large how vouchers work and what they can do.

And what if the Supreme Court eventually rules that taxpayers' money cannot be used to finance vouchers that send children to religious schools? "Then many of these groups might become permanent," Steiger says.

---

[1] Jeff Archer, "16,000 N.Y.C. Parents Apply for 1,300 Vouchers to Private Schools," *Education Week*, April 30, 1997.

[2] Susan Lee and Christine Foster, "Trustbusters," *Forbes*, June 2, 1997.

to send their child to a religious school or not," says Nicole Garnett, a staff attorney at the Institute for Justice, a public advocacy law firm that has assisted voucher supporters in a number of school choice cases. "If an unemployment check winds up in a church collection plate, does that matter?" she asks. No, Garnett and other supporters answer, because the recipients of the benefit can spend it any way they please.

Advocates also point out that the federal government already supports religious institutions in a variety of ways. For instance, each year, tens of thousands of students use Pell grants and GI Bill benefits to attend religious colleges and universities. "You could use your Pell grant to go to a university where there is a prayer before every class," Garnett says, adding that this is no different than a voucher.

Howard Fuller, Milwaukee's school superintendent from 1991-95, agrees. "I find it strange that we are able to do it with higher education," he says, "but when that logic is applied to K-12, people start coming up with reasons why that can't be."

But opponents of school choice see big differences between Pell grants and vouchers. For one thing, they argue that children are more easily influenced by religious teaching than adults in college or graduate school, a fact recognized by the Supreme Court.

The court's "concern over [government] endorsement [of religion] is especially acute in the area of primary and secondary education, where many of the citizens perceiving the governmental message are children in their formative years," writes Steven K. Green, legal director of Americans United for the Separation of Church and State. [6]

In addition, Green and others argue, unlike primary and secondary schools, most colleges and universities with a religious affiliation are not overtly religious. "Let's face it, there's a big difference," he says.

School choice opponents also dismiss the argument that vouchers benefit parents and children and not religious schools. "They say [voucher laws] are neutral because they are based on the independent choices of the parents," says Bob Chanin, general counsel of the NEA. But, Chanin argues, in Milwaukee and Cleveland, which have voucher programs, "75-80 percent of [private] schools are sectarian." Hence, giving parents public money to send their children to private school amounts to a de facto subsidy for religious schools, he says.

Green agrees. "You cannot wash money through the hands of a third party when it is basically going to an entity that wouldn't get the money otherwise."

Opponents also dispute the idea that the legal winds of change are blowing against them. According to Chanin, *Nyquist* clearly invalidates current voucher schemes since it struck down tuition reimbursements, which are not a direct subsidy for religious schools. In addition, he says, despite what McConnell and others say about a trend toward allowing similar types of state aid in subsequent decisions like *Mueller*, *Nyquist* has not been overruled. "In fact, in *Mueller* the court specifically said it was not overturning *Nyquist*," he says.

Finally, those against vouchers dismiss the recent hoopla over the recent *Agostini* decision. "To imply that this is opening the door to vouchers is a misreading of this decision," says NEA President Chase. "They made very careful distinctions in this case, saying that the [public] money could only be used for public school teachers and for remedial education." In other words, Chase explains, *Agostini* is not a sign that the court is about to allow states to pay private school teachers to teach subjects like religion.

### *Can vouchers really offer poor children better educational opportunities?*

A recent poll commissioned by the American Education Reform Foundation found that 61 percent of all low-income residents of Washington, D.C., would send their children to private school if money were not an issue.

According to school choice advocates, the poll and others like it show that regardless of what many educators and scholars say, poorer Americans favor choice for their children. "Of course they do," Fuller says. "It's in the best interests of parents and children to have the widest range of options available when it comes to education."

Fuller and others say that having options is especially important when children are caught in poorly functioning school systems that fail to provide even basic remedial skills.

"Kids at the bottom are almost guaranteed to go to the scrap heap," says Diane Ravitch, a senior fellow at the Brookings Institution and an assistant secretary of Education in the Bush administration. "They need another option."

Voucher advocates argue that having options would provide a host of benefits for poor children. First, it would empower parents to get more involved in their child's school. [7] "There's this myth that low-income parents don't care about their kids' education," says Shokraii of the Heritage Foundation. She argues that private schools, and especially parochial schools, generally are more successful at tapping into parental concerns than public schools. "They do a better job of attracting parents and keeping them engaged in their kids' education," she says.

In addition, supporters of school choice say, many of the private schools that would take children with vouchers have a better track record of succeeding with poor students than their public counterparts, particularly Catholic schools in inner-city areas. For proof, they point to a 1990 RAND Corporation report showing that 95 percent of all students who attended Catholic schools in New York City graduated. Many of these students were from disadvantaged backgrounds. By contrast, only 25 percent of New York's public school students received their high school diploma.[8]

Various reasons are given for the success of Catholic and other parochial schools. Some voucher supporters acknowledge that private schools can be selective when it comes to whom they choose to admit.

But advocates also say that other more important factors lie behind the success. "Catholic schools . . . never went through the rights revolution of the 1960s, which eroded the order-keeping authority of schools and discouraged teachers and principals from disciplining disruptive students by establishing elaborate due-process procedures," writes Sol Stern.[9] Others point to parochial schools' emphasis on core curriculum and parental involvement.

Many of those who oppose school choice agree that some children in public schools might do better in a private school. "But you can't just help a few kids at the expense of everyone else," Green says.

In addition, Green and others say, it is counterproductive to compare public schools with their private counterparts. "If [public schools] could pick and choose the students who do not have discipline problems or special needs," Green says, "you'd see real improvement there."

James Coomer, a political science professor at Mercer University in Macon, Ga., agrees. "The public schools are asked to do too much," he says. "They are asked to take students who don't want to learn, students with disabilities and students who are disruptive."

Opponents of school choice also worry that vouchers might be used to subsidize private school tuition for those who can already afford it. In Cleveland, for example, 27 percent of the first vouchers awarded by the city went to students already enrolled in private schools.

BISON

*The privately funded Buffalo Inner-city Scholarship Opportunity Network (BISON) enabled more than 200 children from low-income families in Buffalo, N.Y., to attend private school last year.*

Moreover, opponents say, existing and proposed voucher programs do not offer enough money to give poor parents much of a choice outside of the public system. In Cleveland, vouchers provide up to $2,250 per pupil per year. And the school choice plan put forth by Dole during last year's election campaign would have offered students a maximum of $1,500.

"Many [poor families] would not be able to afford the extra tuition, transportation and related costs of using a voucher," says Kweisi Mfume, president of the NAACP, which opposes vouchers.[10]

In addition, opponents ask: How many students can actually be accommodated in a private school, even if every child in America were eligible to receive a voucher? The answer: not many. Gerald Tirozzi, assistant secretary of Education for elementary and secondary education, points out that 6 million pupils attend private school today, a far cry from the 46 million students enrolled in public schools.

"A simple mathematical exercise will immediately point out that the numbers don't work," he writes. "A voucher system, regardless of the amount of money provided, can only accommodate a minimal number of public school students."[11]

Given the very limited and brief use of vouchers in the United States so far, it is too soon to tell whether school choice will benefit students, poor or otherwise, who transfer from public to private school. Still, both sides in the debate have pointed to studies indicating that vouchers either do or don't make a difference in the performance of the students who use them.

According to voucher opponents, a series of studies of students in Milwaukee concludes that those who used vouchers performed no better on standardized tests than public school students. The state-sponsored studies by University of Wisconsin Professor John Witte focused on test scores from 1991-1995. [12]

But another evaluation of the same test data by Paul E. Peterson and Jiangtao Du of Harvard University and Jay P. Greene of the University of Houston discovered that voucher students performed better in key subjects than children who had applied for but had not been given vouchers. The voucher students scored 3-5 percent higher in reading and 5-12 percent higher in math, the researchers found. [13]

Different methodologies could explain why the two studies differed. For example, while Witte compared voucher students with all children in the same grades, Peterson and his colleagues used only those who had tried unsuccessfully to get a voucher.

Many experts believe that neither study should be used as a rationale for making decisions on school choice. "It's going to take a lot more analysis than this to figure out what's going on in these choice programs," says Richard Elmore, a professor of education at Harvard. [14]

### *Will vouchers lead to increased educational competition and improve the public schools?*

In a sense, voucher advocates say, public schools are like the automobile industry in the 1970s. Like Detroit's Big Three automakers 25 years ago, public schools today can afford to put out a shoddy education product because they have a virtual lock on the market.

"The auto industry was arrogant until it lost 25 percent of the market to the Japanese," Fuller says.

Fuller and others believe that like the auto industry or any other business, public education will only improve if it is subjected to outside competition. "When there is a captive audience," Ravitch says, "there is no incentive to change anything."

The idea is to unshackle that audience by giving them the option of taking some or all of the public money spent on their education with them to another school. "If children can get vouchers, public schools will begin treating them like customers," says Heritage's Shokraii.

Joe McTighe, executive director of the Council for American Private Education, agrees. "The opportunity to take your business someplace else is a powerful inducement to improve," he says.

As evidence, Shokraii, McTighe and others point to actions taken in those school districts that have had limited voucher programs. In Milwaukee, McTighe says, educators have opened a charter school and given principals in all schools more autonomy since vouchers were made available in 1990. According to McTighe, these innovations were a response to the competition posed by the new school choice program. [15]

But opponents of vouchers say that it is not school choice that is nudging public schools to make necessary reforms. "Those things happening in Milwaukee are going on all over the country," says Deanna Duby, director of education policy at People for the American Way, a First Amendment rights advocacy group. Duby argues that charter schools, principal autonomy and other innovations are part of a broad nationwide reform movement that has nothing to do with vouchers.

Instead, Duby and others argue, vouchers would simply take away money from already underfunded public school systems, especially in poor, inner-city areas. "You would drain badly needed money from public schools that already can't do what they need to," she says, adding that unlike a private institution, which can select the students it wants to admit, public schools must admit all children, including those who are disruptive or have special needs.

In addition, opponents argue, vouchers take more than much-needed money away from public schools. "The choice system is a system of segregation because it removes the most motivated kids and parents from the public system and puts them in private schools," says Richard Rothstein, a research associate at the Economic Policy Institute. Highly motivated parents would take a large share of any vouchers offered, he says, because they "are the most interested in their child's education" and thus more likely to take advantage of new opportunities. The resulting exodus, he says, would be disastrous for the students left behind, because these more-committed parents are often the impetus for positive change. "Everybody who has been involved in a public school knows that if you have a teacher who is not doing well, it only takes one or two parents in that classroom to complain to the principal to get a change," he says.

Opponents also dismiss the idea that you can treat a school district like a business and parents like consumers. "This market theory of competition assumes that people have good information on the choices they are making," Rothstein says, "but we really don't have any information on school quality. So if parents don't know what schools are good, there's no reason to believe they will choose the best school."

In addition, opponents say, there really is a difference between business and government. "To assume that market modalities will have an impact in the government sector is wrong," Green says. "What's good for selling cars is not necessarily good for schools."

But Fuller dismisses the argument that schools are unique institutions. "They are organizations just like any other," he argues, "and many of the principles that apply to business will apply to them." For example, Fuller says, the important issues in school districts, as in businesses, revolve around money. "People know that for all of the yakking, the key is how to allocate resources," he says.

In addition, voucher supporters say, private schools don't always just take the best students.

"We take the low achievers," says Lydia Harris, principal of St. Adalbert's, which has 47 voucher students. "It's a myth that we only take the cream of the crop," she says, adding: "We put our own cream on the crop."

Choice advocates also challenge the notion that vouchers will drain needed money from public schools. "There would not be a net loss of per-pupil funding because the fewer students you have the less it's going to cost," McTighe says.

In fact, McTighe and others say, most proposed vouchers are worth much less than the per-pupil amount spent by the school district. For example, in Cleveland, vouchers are worth a maximum of $2,500 per year, less than half of what the city spends for every pupil in public school. "So [the public school] actually does better [financially] with this," McTighe says.

But voucher opponents argue that the overall cost of education won't necessarily drop every time a student leaves the school system. "A lot of the cost of having the student in the school would still be there," Duby says. For example, she points out, the building would still need to be maintained and the teachers paid. "If a third of the students left an elementary school, almost all of the costs would remain," she says. ■

# BACKGROUND

## Rise of Public Schools

The proper role of government in education has been debated for more than 200 years. But public schools, as they exist today, are a relatively new phenomenon.

During the Enlightenment, thinkers like Thomas Jefferson, called for increased taxation to support a public school system that would educate "common people." Jefferson believed that only through education could citizens understand and exercise their rights. Indeed, he said, an educated populous was essential to the functioning of the new American republic. [16]

But others were more wary of using the public purse to finance education. Scottish economist Adam Smith, whose landmark work, *The Wealth of Nations,* was published the same year as Jefferson's Declaration of Independence, believed that the "invisible hand" of the market could not adequately provide enough incentives for universal education. But the father of laissez-faire economics also said that an educational system administered by the government would be inefficient and would fail to create a literate population.

By the early 19th century, the debate over public education had become one of the most important social questions in the United States. Trade unions and other advocates for workers' rights said that universal education was needed to fight social injustice and poverty. But business leaders in the North and slaveholders in the South worried that universal literacy could stoke the fires of revolution among the lower classes. [17]

The nation's leading proponent of public education was Horace Mann, secretary of the Massachusetts Board of Education and one of the most well-known social reformers of the last century. Mann argued that a public school system would inculcate the native-born poor and newly arrived immigrants with "American values." [18]

Over time, Mann's idea that education could mold disparate social and ethnic groups into good citizens gained currency around the country. By the time the Civil War broke out, most states had public elementary schools. And yet, while free, they were not compulsory. Moreover, public high schools were rare and would remain so throughout the 19th century. In fact, as late as 1920, only one-third of all eligible Americans attended high school. [19]

During the first half of the 20th century, public school attendance and respect for the nation's educational institutions grew at a rapid pace. By the 1950s, most American children were in school and, according to polls of their parents' attitudes, were receiving quality educations.

It was at this time, nonetheless, that the case for vouchers was first put forward. In 1955, libertarian economist Milton Friedman published a highly influential essay proposing vouchers as a way to give parents greater flexibility in choosing their child's school as well as an antidote for what he said was an increasingly inefficient and ineffective public education system.

Friedman advanced what has become the classic school choice argument: Vouchers will allow parents more choice when it comes to their children's education, which will in turn improve all schools, public and private, by injecting competition into the system. Friedman argued that this scheme would prove especially beneficial for the poor, who have no choice but to send their children to the local public school, even if it offers an inferior education. [20]

Friedman might have seemed an alarmist in the 1950s, but his ideas made sense to many more people two decades later. By the 1970s, the national consensus on public education had changed, with most Americans believing that public schools were failing. Statistics seemed to bear them out. In one key measure of education quality, SAT scores dropped steadily from the mid-1960s

# Chronology

## *1950s-1980s*

***The perception that public schools are inadequate in many parts of the country gathers momentum, giving birth to the school choice movement.***

***1955***
Libertarian economist Milton Friedman publishes an essay proposing tuition vouchers as a means to expand educational opportunity and improve public schools.

***1973***
The U.S. Supreme Court strikes down a New York state law granting parents reimbursements and tax credits for the cost of private school tuition.

***1979***
The Department of Education is created.

***1980***
Studies show a steady decline in Scholastic Aptitude Tests (SATs) over the previous 15 years.

***1983***
The Education Department's *A Nation At Risk* report charts what it sees as a decline in discipline and standards in the country's public schools.

———•———

## *1990s* ***The push for school choice is transformed into a national movement. The first voucher plans are created on a small scale.***

***April 1990***
Wisconsin establishes a voucher program to allow students in Milwaukee to go to non-sectarian private schools.

***April 1991***
The nation's first privately financed voucher program is created in Indianapolis, by J. Patrick Rooney, chairman of the Golden Rule Insurance Co. Rooney's action sparks dozens of similr programs in cities around the country.

***September 1993***
A pilot voucher plan is signed into law in Puerto Rico, and more than 1,800 vouchers are awarded.

***November 1993***
Voters in California overwhelmingly reject Proposition 174, which would have entitled every student enrolled in public or private school to a tuition voucher equal to half of the state's per pupil spending, or about $2,600.

***November 1994***
Puerto Rico's Supreme Court strikes down the commonwealth's voucher law, ruling that it violates a constitutional ban on transferring public funds to private schools.

***June 1995***
Ohio creates a pilot voucher program for the Cleveland public school system. Under the plan, vouchers can be used in both sectarian and non-sectarian private schools.

***July 1995***
Wisconsin legislators expand the Milwaukee voucher program to include religious schools.

***February 1996***
A proposal creating a $5 million voucher program for the District of Columbia is defeated in the Senate.

***May 1996***
The 10th District Court of Appeals for the State of Ohio strikes down the voucher plan in Cleveland on the grounds that the program violates federal and state constitutional Establishment clauses. The case is appealed to the state Supreme Court.

***July 1996***
Republican presidential candidate Bob Dole announces a proposal to spend $2.5 billion annually to fund a nationwide voucher program.

***November 1996***
Voters in Washington state reject Initiative 173, which would have created tuition vouchers for non-religious private schools.

***January 1997***
A Wisconsin trial court rules that state efforts to expand the Milwaukee voucher program to include sectarian institutions violates the Establishment Clause in the state's Constitution.

***June 1997***
In *Agostini v. Felton,* the U.S. Supreme Court overturns a 1985 ruling that barred public school remedial education teachers from entering parochial schools to help students there.

## Teachers' Choice

*In cities throughout the country, a large percentage of public school teachers whose household income is $35,000-$70,000 opt for private school for their own children, though teachers' groups uniformly oppose school choice.*

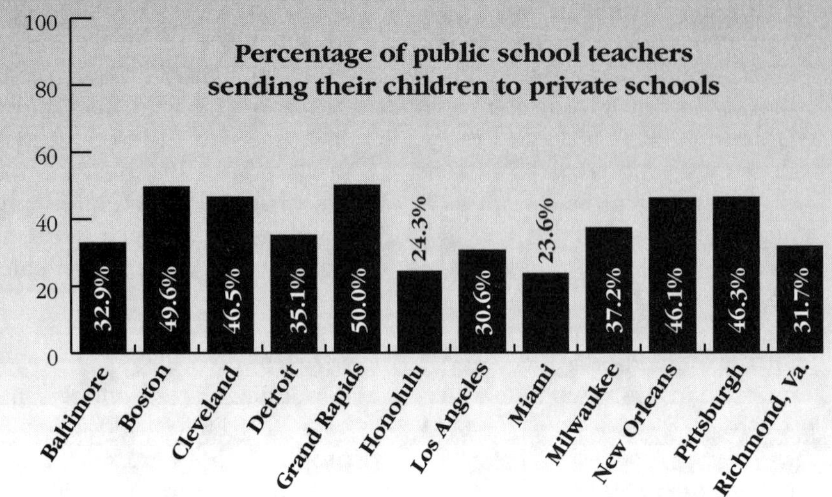


*Source: Compiled from 1990 Census data by Denis Doyle,* The American Enterprise, *September/October 1996*

to the early '80s. [21]

In 1983, an influential Department of Education report seemed to confirm the public's worst fears. Commissioned by Education Secretary Terrel H. Bell, *A Nation at Risk* painted a bleak picture of the state of learning in America. Among other things, it criticized schools for a marked decline in discipline and academic standards. [22]

When *A Nation at Risk* was published, the school choice movement already had a dedicated following in conservative circles. Over the next decade, the choice movement broadened its base of support significantly. Today, vouchers are still largely rejected by the Democratic Party and most liberal groups. But school choice has developed substantial support among a growing number of African-American political leaders and others who are normally identified with the left, though the NAACP remains opposed to choice, in large part, voucher proponents say, because of its traditional alliance with labor unions.

## Voucher Programs

School choice has never been established on a grand scale. Voucher plans have been carried out as pilot programs and have impacted very few students. The most significant school choice plan to date was created in Milwaukee in 1990, where the state provides up to $3,209 to some 1,100 mostly low-income children. The vouchers can only be used to send students to non-religious private schools. [23]

In the summer of 1995, the Wisconsin Legislature voted to include religious schools in the voucher program. The law also expanded the current program significantly, increasing the number of eligible students to 7,000 in 1996 and 15,000 the following year. But the expansion has not been carried out due to a court challenge filed by the state affiliates of the NEA and the American Civil Liberties Union (ACLU). [24]

Although the voucher program in Milwaukee has received the lion's share of national media attention, it does not represent the first or most recent attempt to experiment with school choice.

Indeed, since 1869, Vermont has allowed parents in sparsely populated districts without a high school to send their children to a public or private alternative at state expense. Until 1961, "tuitioning," as the practice is known, included parochial schools. That year, the state Supreme Court ruled that using government funds to pay tuition at parochial schools, in this case three Catholic schools, violated Vermont's Constitution.

An attempt last year to send 15 Vermont students from tiny Chittenden to a nearby Roman Catholic high school has reopened the debate over religious schools. Although the Chittenden case has not yet reached the state Supreme Court, a 1994 high court ruling allowing tuition reimbursement for a man who sent his son to a sectarian school is an indication that the tribunal may be willing to overturn its 1961 decision. [25]

Puerto Rico has also experimented, albeit briefly, with school choice. In 1993, the commonwealth's legislature created a pilot voucher program for children whose parents earn less than $18,000 per year. The program offered students up to $1,500 toward tuition at the school of their choice, including religious institutions. One year and 1,181 vouchers later, the commonwealth's Supreme Court struck down the program on the grounds that the Puerto Rican Constitution prohibits the use of public funds to support private schools, sectarian or otherwise.

Almost two years after vouchers were struck down in Puerto Rico, a similar school choice plan was instituted in Cleveland. The program, which began in September 1996, allows up to 2,000 elementary-age students to receive up to $2,500 annually to attend the school of their choice. As in Puerto Rico, a challenge to the plan is pending before the Ohio Supreme Court. ■

Austin CEO Foundation

*Scholarships to private schools in Austin, Texas, are provided by the private Austin Children's Educational Opportunity Foundation.*

# CURRENT SITUATION

## Politics of Choice

During the 1996 presidential campaign, school choice became a major issue for the first time in a national election. The issue rose to prominence after Republican nominee Bob Dole announced a plan to spend $2.5 billion annually to give lower-income children vouchers. Dole's plan offered students up to $1,000 a year for elementary school and $1,500 for high school.

On Oct. 6, in the first of Dole's two debates with President Clinton, Clinton came out against vouchers. Clinton's victory a month later assured that school choice would likely be off the White House agenda until at least the year 2000.

Still, voucher advocates say, the fact that school choice was in the spotlight during the campaign is evidence that the issue has now become an integral part of the national debate on education.

"When Bob Dole started talking about school choice and took on the teachers' unions ... we realized that it had become a mainstream issue," says Fritz Steiger, president of Children's Educational Opportunity of America (CEO America), which helps private groups that raise money to fund tuition vouchers.

Indeed, vouchers have become a top priority for many Republican politicians, who are supported by many religious groups and some education reformers.

On Capitol Hill, Republicans and a few Democrats have made frequent and concerted efforts since the early 1990s to create pilot voucher programs.

Last year, for instance, an attempt to establish a $5 million voucher program in the District of Columbia failed after Democrats in the Senate blocked action on the D.C. spending bill to which the proposal was attached. [26]

This year, a number of voucher plans are pending before Congress. A proposal sponsored by Sen. Paul Coverdell, R-Ga., would authorize $50 million in fiscal 1998 to establish school choice demonstration projects in 20-30 school districts.

Another measure, sponsored in the House by Majority Leader Dick Armey, R-Texas, and in the Senate by Daniel R. Coats, R-Ind., would authorize $7 million in fiscal 1998 to provide vouchers of up to $3,200 for 2,000 poor children in Washington, D.C.

Leading the charge against these and other attempts to create school choice programs are several labor and civil rights groups. By far the most powerful and notable of these organizations is the NEA. Other important players include the American Federation of Teachers (AFT), the NAACP, People for the American Way and the ACLU.

These and other groups claim that proponents of vouchers are not interested in finding new ways to provide a better education for poor children. Instead, they say, they are interested in subsidizing children already attending private schools at the expense of public education. Some even suggest that many school choice advocates, especially religious groups, want to do away with public schools entirely. "Their goal is to end public education," Chase says.

Supporters of school choice, among them the Institute for Justice, the Heritage Foundation and the Christian Coalition, contend that teachers' unions are only interested in protecting their members' jobs, regardless of performance or qualifications. "They protect teachers who have no business being with children," Fuller says.

Choice advocates also say that opposition by civil liberties groups actually reflects a thinly disguised fear of religion as much as an effort to guard constitutional principles.

"Their primary concern is what they take to be the undue influence of religion, in particular the Roman Catholic Church," says Quentin L. Quade, director of the Blum Center for Parental Freedom in Education at Marquette University in Milwaukee. ■

# OUTLOOK

## Momentum Building?

Proponents of vouchers believe that, despite recent setbacks in state courts, overall momentum is with them.

"This issue is on a roll because the alternatives have been tried for years and are failing," McTighe says.

Ravitch agrees, adding: "There's a growing interest because there's a growing sense of desperation, especially in the black community."

Indeed, choice advocates can point to a number of recent converts to the cause, among them Rep. Floyd H. Flake, D-N.Y., and *Washington Post* columnist William Raspberry, who are not only national figures with impeccable liberal credentials but also African-Americans.

But while well-known black voucher advocates are important to the school choice movement, it is at the grass-roots level where African-Americans are having the greatest impact.

For instance, proponents say, black community leaders and parents have been the driving force behind the school choice movements in Cleveland and Milwaukee. "The battle for parental choice [in Milwaukee] began in the church basements and meeting halls of the Near North Side," writes scholar Daniel McGroarty in his recent book *Break These Chains: The Battle for School Choice*. McGroarty, a fellow at the Institute for Contemporary Studies, says that the language used to advance school choice was reminiscent of the civil rights movement. "Their rhetoric was more redolent of Martin Luther King than the free-market pronouncements favored by conservative voucher proponents," he says. [27]

What McGroarty says is happening in Milwaukee and Cleveland is spreading to more and more cities and towns around the country, choice proponents say. Some of these movements are sure to succeed in bringing school choice to their communities, they say.

"I think it's going to start happening soon in the states," Steiger says. "In five years, we'll see three or four significant choice programs, and in 10 years a significant number of states will have vouchers."

Opponents of school choice concede that the movement has built up a head of steam. "There's a certain amount of momentum," says Duby of People for the American Way. But, she argues, the movement reflects parents' legitimate frustration, not necessarily the validity of vouchers as a public policy. "I understand when people say, 'I don't care about everyone else, I need to get my kid out of these schools,' " she says.

Duby and others fear that frustration may lead people to embrace choice as a panacea while avoiding more concrete reform efforts. "I think we could do a lot of damage with school choice," she says, adding that "if nothing else, choice could delay the work we need to do."

Chase agrees, saying that the NEA and other groups need to educate people adequately so that they understand that private school is not a "magic bullet." Still, Chase disputes the notion that there is a grass-roots groundswell for vouchers all over the country.

"This is not something that is being seriously discussed in most school districts," he says. "There is such a thing as the public good, and for [the American people] the public good means public schools for all children."

Chase and other voucher opponents, including many African-Americans, also reject the notion that school choice is akin to the fight for civil rights, noting that organizations like the NAACP firmly oppose choice.

In fact, they point out, many African American leaders think that school choice will be a huge step backward, and not only in education. "Choice is a subterfuge for segregation" as it existed in the South before the civil rights movement, says Felmers Chaney, head of the Milwaukee NAACP. [28]

### *Supreme Court to Rule?*

But whether school choice is embraced as a policy initiative or not, it may not be the most important immediate question facing those on both sides of the debate. Many supporters and some opponents of vouchers predict that the Supreme Court is likely to rule on the issue in the next two or three years.

# At Issue:

## *Is meaningful school choice possible within the public school system?*

**RICHARD W. RILEY**
***Secretary of Education***

**WRITTEN FOR *THE CQ RESEARCHER***

yes

As changes in our economy expand and transform our educational needs, America's public schools must become more flexible and offer students and parents more choices with higher standards and accountability. School districts are responding by creating new types of schools — charter schools, magnet schools, "schools within schools." They are letting parents pick among schools from across the district, even the entire state. This growing menu of choices is improving education by creating new models for learning, and we must do more to promote such advancements.

The Clinton administration is encouraging this trend with a significant effort to expand charter schools. Charter schools are public schools operated by teachers, parents or others in the community who enter into an agreement with the school district or another chartering agency authorized by the state. Since start-up capital is the primary obstacle to starting a charter school, President Clinton requested $100 million in his fiscal 1998 budget to provide seed money for up to 1,100 charter schools.

The progress achieved by charter schools and other innovations is threatened, however, by those who seek to funnel public tax dollars to private schools. More than any public institution, public schools unite citizens from all walks of life and pass on our democratic ideals to each generation. Any voucher program for private schools would drain much-needed resources from public schools and accommodate a limited number of students. Further, private school vouchers would make parochial schools less parochial and private schools less private, subjecting them to public supervision and compromising their independence.

There are several reasons for keeping publicly financed school choice within the public school domain. A public school is held in the public trust by local voters who select the 16,000 local boards that govern their schools. A private school is not required to be open to all students that live within a district, which means that it can choose to turn away students. A successful public school offers the potential to serve as a model that can be replicated elsewhere, while a school that fails to create a quality learning environment can be held accountable to the public and closed if necessary.

The nation's public schools educate close to 90 percent of America's 52 million schoolchildren. At a time of increasing enrollments and growing demands on the public schools, our limited resources should be focused on giving students and parents as many high-quality options as possible within the schools that serve the vast majority of America's students.

**JOE MCTIGHE**
***Executive Director, Council for American Private Education***

**WRITTEN FOR *THE CQ RESEARCHER***

no

As beauty is in the eye of the beholder, meaningful choice is in the mind of the selector. When it comes to schools, the selectors, of course, are parents, a child's primary educators. For many parents, the options already at play within public education constitute meaningful choice, but others can find such choice only outside the realm of public schools.

A growing number of parents, for example, desperately desire schools whose primary purpose is to provide youngsters with a sound moral and spiritual education — schools that touch the soul and call children to a life of love. Private schools are the only schools we have that can address the religious development of children — a sphere beyond the proper reach of public education.

And then there are the parents whose children are trapped in chronically failing and sometimes unsafe schools. They don't have the money to move to communities where the schools are better, and they don't have the time to see if the latest promise of improvement proves any more trustworthy than its predecessors. For those parents, an immediate alternative would be neighborhood private schools where high expectations, caring communities and remarkable records of success are the rule.

The same rationale that drives proposals for tax reductions, Pell grants and Hope scholarships to help low- and middle-income students attend the public, private or religious college of their choice applies to K-12 education. How can one argue that aid to the parents of a 12th-grader is taboo while the same aid a year later is laudable? We need a unified plan of parent aid in America — one that guarantees meaningful choice to needy parents across all grade levels.

There are some who say that choice within the public school system is sufficient. They consider such choice the silver bullet of school reform. But let's face it: The difference between the P.S. 8 and P.S. 9 is often inconsequential. And while some charter schools offer parents genuine alternatives, the truth is that many are nothing more than standard public school clones in a prettied-up package.

A single system of government schooling cannot possibly meet everyone's needs. Fortunately, our country is blessed by a rich diversity of schools that collectively serve a noble purpose: the education of our nation's children. Why not a comprehensive program of school choice that truly respects and promotes the right of all parents to choose the kind of education their children shall receive?

# FOR MORE INFORMATION

**Americans United for the Separation of Church and State,** 1816 Jefferson Pl. N.W., Washington, D.C. 20036; (202) 466-3234; www.au.org. The group opposes federal or state aid to parochial schools and other religious institutions.

**Council for American Private Education,** 18016 Mateny Rd., Suite 140, Germantown, Md. 20874; (301) 916-8485; cape@impresso.com. The council is a coalition of private-school associations that seeks greater access to private schools for American families.

**Institute for Justice,** 1001 Pennsylvania Ave. N.W., Suite 200S, Washington, D.C. 20004; (202) 457-4240; www.instituteforjustice.org. The institute is a conservative public interest law firm that litigates cases involving parental school choice.

**National Education Association,** 1201 16th St. N.W., Washington, D.C. 20036; (202) 833-4000; www.nea.org. The NEA is the nation's largest teachers' union with more than 2 million members. It is opposed to vouchers and works to defeat school choice proposals through lobbying and litigation.

"Without a question, the Ohio case will go to the U.S. Supreme Court," Quade says, referring to the Cleveland voucher case currently working its way through the state court system. Duby at People for the American Way agrees. "At some point in the next five years, we will have a voucher case before the Supreme Court," she says.

But others are not so sure about the Ohio case, or any other for that matter, making it to the nation's highest court. According to the NEA's Chanin, if voucher proponents lose the Ohio or another state case based on the court's reading of the state's constitution, there will be no grounds for an appeal to the Supreme Court because there will be no federal constitutional issue to decide

Still, if a voucher case does reach the nation's highest court, school choice supporters are confident the justices will rule that publicly financed tuition vouchers do not violate the Establishment Clause.

"In the long run, the Supreme Court will uphold a properly drafted voucher program," says the Institute for Justice's Garnet, citing *Mueller* and the other cases that school choice supporters say shrink Establishment Clause restrictions on government support for religion.

But Chanin thinks otherwise. "I'm confident we would win," he says, adding that the Supreme Court has gone out of its way not to overturn *Nyquist,* which is the closest existing case on the voucher question.

Either way, a high court decision would have a tremendous and possibly decisive impact on the school choice debate. A ruling in favor of allowing vouchers would undoubtedly give a huge boost to school choice advocates and lead to a frenzy of new activity on federal, state and local levels.

But if the court struck down a school choice law, the drive for publicly funded vouchers could diminish and even die. With the exception of funding from private sources, says CEO America's Steiger, "there would be no alternatives." ■

## Notes

[1] Richard Lacayo, "Parochial Politics," *Time,* Sept. 23, 1996. See "Attack on Public Schools," *The CQ Researcher,* July 26, 1996, pp. 649-672.
[2] For background, see "Religion in Schools," *The CQ Researcher,* Jan. 7, 1994, pp. 145-168.
[3] *Ibid.*
[4] Lawrence H. Tribe, *American Constitutional Law* (1988), pp. 1217-1218.
[5] Linda Greenhouse, "Court Eases Curb on Providing Aid in Church Schools," *The New York Times,* June 24, 1997.
[6] Steven K. Green, "The Legal Argument Against Private School Choice," *University of Cincinnati Law Review,* summer 1993. Green is quoting *Grand Rapids School District v. Ball.*
[7] For background, see "Parents and Schools," *The CQ Researcher,* Jan. 20, 1995, pp. 66-89.
[8] Sol Stern, "The Invisible Miracle of Catholic Schools," *City Journal,* summer 1996, published by the Manhattan Institute.
[9] *Ibid.* Stern is a *City Journal* contributing editor.
[10] Quoted in a recent letter to NAACP members.
[11] Gerald Tirozzi, "Vouchers: A Questionable Answer to an Unasked Question," *Education Week,* April 23, 1997.
[12] Lynn Olson, "New Studies on Private Choice Contradict Each Other," *Education Week,* Sept. 4, 1996.
[13] Jay P. Greene, Paul E. Peterson and Jiangtao Du, "The Effectiveness of School Choice in Milwaukee: A Secondary Analysis of Data from the Program's Evaluation," Aug. 14, 1996, p. 3.
[14] Olson, *op. cit.*
[15] For background, see "Private Management of Public Schools," *The CQ Researcher,* March 25, 1994, pp. 265-288.
[16] Bernard Mayo (ed.), *Jefferson Himself* (1942), p. 89.
[17] Peter Carrol and David Noble, *The Restless Centuries* (1979), pp. 220-221.
[18] *Ibid.*
[19] Daniel J. Boorstin, *The Americans: The Democratic Experience* (1973), p. 500.
[20] Milton Friedman, "The Role of Government in Education," in Robert A. Solo (ed.), *Economics and the Public Interest* (1955), pp. 127-134.
[21] John E. Chubb and Terry M. Moe, *Politics, Markets and America's Schools* (1990), p. 8.
[22] *Ibid.,* pp. 9-10.
[23] Mark Walsh, "Court Deadlocks on Vouchers," *Teacher,* May/June 1996.
[24] Dorothy B. Hanks, "School Choice Programs: What's Happening in the States," Heritage Foundation, 1997.
[25] Sally Johnson, "Vermont Parents Ask State to Pay Catholic School Tuition," *The New York Times,* Oct. 30, 1996.
[26] David A. Vise, "In a Win for Teachers Unions, Senate Rejects D.C. Tuition Vouchers; City Budget Stalled," *The Washington Post,* Feb. 28, 1996.
[27] Daniel McGroarty, *Break These Chains: The Battle for School Choice* (1996), p. 73.
[28] Nina Shokraii, "Free at Last: Black America Signs Up for School Choice," *Policy Review,* November/December 1996.

# Bibliography

## *Selected Sources Used*


### *Books*

**Lieberman, Myron, *Privatization and Educational Choice,* St. Martin's Press, 1989.**
Lieberman, an education policy consultant, covers the entire sweep of the school choice debate, from the effect of competition to the constitutionality of vouchers. He also examines the political landscape, describing the groups and interests lined up on both sides of the issue.

**McGroarty, Daniel, *Breaking These Chains: The Battle for School Choice,* Prima Publishing, 1996.**
McGroarty, a fellow at the Institute for Contemporary Studies, chronicles the efforts of parents and community leaders in inner-city Milwaukee to establish and sustain a voucher program. McGroarty argues that for many of these mostly black residents, the fight for school choice is akin to the civil rights battles of the 1960s.

**Moe, Terry M., and John E. Chubb, *Politics, Markets and America's Schools,* The Brookings Institution, 1990.**
Moe and Chubb look at the recent history of education and education reform in the United States and the problems that have plagued America's schools in the last three decades. The authors come to the conclusion that the institutions governing the nation's schools hamstring them and prevent real reform from taking hold. Moe and Chubb argue that vouchers are a way to break this institutional vise grip.

### *Articles*

**Goldberg, Bruce, "A Liberal Argument for School Choice," *The American Enterprise,* September/October, 1996.**
Goldberg criticizes public schools in the United States, arguing that they are "fundamentally at war with individuality." Only by allowing families to be education consumers will the public schools begin to respond to their needs, he says.

**Green, Steven, "The Legal Argument Against Private School Choice," *University of Cincinnati Law Review,* summer 1993.**
Green, legal director for Americans United for Church and State, examines Establishment Clause case law. He concludes that optimism on the part of school choice advocates over recent Supreme Court decisions is misplaced. Green points out that the high court has never considered the constitutionality of vouchers and that many legal questions remain unanswered.

**Hawley, Willis D., "The Predictable Consequences of School Choice," *Education Week,* April 10, 1996.**
Hawley, dean of the College of Education at the University of Maryland, argues that among other things, school choice will drive up the tuition at private schools and reduce diversity and funding at public institutions.

**Lacayo, Richard, "Parochial Politics," *Time,* Sept. 23, 1996.**
Lacayo gives a good overview of the current school choice debate, focusing on the voucher program in Cleveland, Ohio.

**Peterson, Bob, "Teacher of the Year Gives Vouchers a Failing Grade," *The Progressive,* April 1997.**
Peterson, a teacher in the Milwaukee public school system, says that in his hometown school choice has been a failure. Among the problems that followed the issuance of vouchers was massive fraud on the part of some private schools that participated in the program.

**Tirozzi, Gerald, "Vouchers: A Questionable Answer to an Unasked Question," *Education Week,* April 23, 1997.**
Tirozzi, assistant secretary of Education for elementary and secondary education, picks apart the arguments for vouchers and concludes that they are specious. Among other things, Tirozzi says that even if they were effective, vouchers would not impact more than a small fraction of the students currently enrolled in public schools because the private school system is just not big enough to accommodate many more students.

### *Reports*

**Hanks, Dorothy B., *School Choice Programs: What's Happening in the States,* The Heritage Foundation, 1997.**
The report gives an exhaustive state-by-state rundown of existing and proposed school choice programs and related news.

# 2 Teacher Education

**Thomas J. Billitteri**

Kay Shrewsbery, a 26-year veteran of the Toledo public schools, always considered herself a good teacher. Now she has the credentials to prove it.

Last year, Shrewsbery became the first board-certified elementary school teacher in Ohio, a distinction once reserved for physicians and other highly skilled professionals. After months of evaluations by her peers — including a critique of her teaching — Shrewsbery was designated as an "accomplished" teacher by the National Board for Professional Teaching Standards.

"Teachers get a bad rap," Shrewsbery says. "It was a chance for me to demonstrate that there are people in the teaching profession who are intellectually competent and excellent at what they do."

Certification, which in Ohio entitles Shrewsbery to an annual $2,500 salary bonus for 10 years, is part of a constellation of reforms aimed at reinvigorating and professionalizing the nation's 2.7 million public school teachers. Besides board certification, innovations include rigorous proficiency tests for new teachers, peer review of classroom veterans and new approaches to teacher training.

"A quiet revolution has been occurring within the ranks of the teaching profession," says Arthur Wise, president of the National Council for Accreditation of Teacher Education (NCATE). "There has never been a reform effort of this nature before."

In the past, Wise says, reformers focused "on schools, curriculum, technology, decentralization, vouchers, and so forth. But these were all efforts to improve education despite the teacher. This movement says we will only improve education if we improve the teaching force." [1]

From *The CQ Researcher*, October 17, 1997.

Linda Darling-Hammond, a professor at Columbia University's Teachers College in New York, agrees. "What distinguishes the era we're in now is that there are really dramatic, radical reforms of the teaching profession going on."

That includes an unprecedented vow of cooperation from teachers' unions.

For the first time, the 2.3-million-member National Education Association (NEA) this year endorsed peer review — what many see as a challenge to the hoary tradition of tenure. To the chagrin of unbending unionists, NEA President Bob Chase also advocated a "new unionism" in which teachers would play a collaborative role with school administrators in improving public education.

At the rival American Federation of Teachers (AFT), President Sandra Feldman says she recently called on her union "to get out front in closing down failing schools." "When you've got failing schools," Feldman says, "teachers and very often parents still rebel" when you propose to close them. "I have stood in front of faculties [at failing schools] and taken a lot of lumps."

Feldman says the AFT also vows to increase its support of peer review. "Teachers do not want incompetent people working with them," she says.

The tide of reformist sentiment has induced a measure of skepticism. Some observers fear that rigorous competency standards will create teacher shortages. Others wonder where the money for reforms will come from. [2] Still others question the motives of the unions, saying they are more concerned with survival than improvement. And many observers point to the long history of attempted education reforms and caution against moving too fast.

"One thing we all have to guard against is not to go for simple answers," says Thomas F. Warren, chairman of the Department of Education at Beloit College in Wisconsin and president-elect of the Association of Independent Liberal Arts Colleges for Teacher Education. "Obviously, education has a history of leaping on the bandwagon," sometimes in "blatantly farcical" ways. "We're talking about complicated issues. . . . How can we both be sensitive to what the past has taught us and to what's new?"

Yet many activists say it's time to take some bold steps into the future. The first move, they argue, is to bring strict professional standards to teaching. "Educators in this country are working in a system that is dysfunctional," Darling-Hammond argues. "We've got to look at how to transform that system."

Darling-Hammond was the primary author of a landmark report last September — "What Matters Most: Teaching for America's Future" — that presented a blistering indictment of American public education — especially teacher training. [3]

"Although no state will allow a

## Many New Teachers Are Unlicensed

*More than a quarter of the new public school teachers hired in 1990 were not fully licensed.*

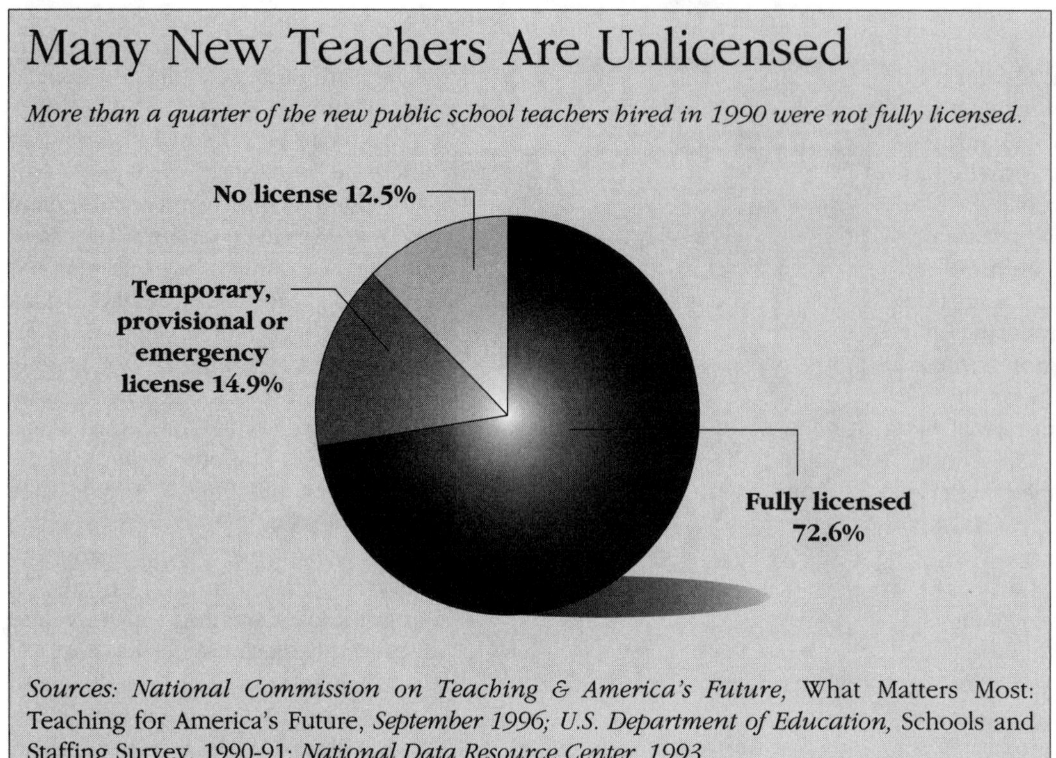


*Sources: National Commission on Teaching & America's Future,* What Matters Most: Teaching for America's Future, *September 1996; U.S. Department of Education,* Schools and Staffing Survey, 1990-91; *National Data Resource Center, 1993.*

person to write wills, practice medicine, fix plumbing or style hair without completing training and passing an examination, more than 40 states allow school districts to hire teachers who have not met these basic requirements," declares the report from the National Commission on Teaching & America's Future. [4]

Among the commission's findings:

• More than 25 percent of new public school teachers in 1991 were either untrained or had not fully met state standards.

• Almost one-fourth of secondary teachers — and more than 30 percent of math teachers — lack even a minor in their main teaching field.

• More than half of the high school students taking the physical sciences are taught by teachers without a minor or major in the subject, as are 27 percent of math students.

• Students in schools with high minority enrollments have less than a 50-50 chance of getting science or math teachers with a degree or a license in the field they teach.

In fact, the report notes that only 500 of the nation's 1,300 schools of education are accredited. * "Although some schools of education provide high-quality preparation, others are treated as 'cash cows' by their universities, bringing in revenues that are spent on the education of doctors, lawyers and accountants rather than on their own students." [5]

Advocates of teacher reform say the commission's findings are all the more compelling when read against the backdrop of the "baby-boom echo" — the surge of new pupils whose parents were born after World War II. Over the next decade, the commission noted, more than 2 million new teachers will be needed, and they will account for more than half of the nation's teaching force in 2006.

What is required to shore up American teaching, the commission said, is nothing short of a radical reformation of the education establishment, including:

• tougher standards for colleges of education;

• strict licensing standards for new teachers;

• rigorous procedures to certify "accomplished" teachers;

• innovative clinical experience for beginning and experienced teachers; and

• peer review to weed out poor performers.

"We pay teachers substantially less than any other college-educated worker, and we educate them unevenly," says Darling-Hammond, who serves as the commission's executive director. "Then we hope to control them with textbooks and training developed outside the classroom, and we rely on a huge administrative infrastructure to regulate teachers because we don't trust them to make good decisions."

Many of the commission's proposals already are being implemented. A dozen states have independent boards to set standards for teacher licensing and education. At least 20 states have — or are planning — mentoring programs for new teachers.

And there are signs that toughen-

* Most states do not require schools of education to be accredited, and several major education schools have not sought accreditation, including Columbia University Teachers' College in New York City.

ing standards for teachers can get results, as the Connetquot school district in Long Island's Suffolk County recently discovered. When it gave applicants for teaching jobs a reading-comprehension test designed for high school juniors, only one-fourth of the applicants answered at least 40 of the 50 questions correctly. [6]

Yet the reforms occurring nationwide are piecemeal and vulnerable to budget pressures and bureaucratic shakeups. And in many locales, school officials are struggling simply to find enough teachers — classroom veterans or not. In Texas, schools must accommodate 80,000 new students in each of the next three years.

While much of the ongoing debate over teacher training focuses on practical questions — training regimens, certification standards and so on — the climate of reform also raises difficult ideological questions. For example, is teaching indeed "what matters most" in public school reform, as the title of the commission report suggests? Or should policy-makers pursue more fundamental changes in public education?

Many conservative policy analysts argue that mandating training and testing standards for teachers will take education reforms only so far. More important, they argue, is changing the very nature of schooling through such options as government-funded vouchers, charter schools and other mechanisms of parental "choice." [7]

"Standards play a role," says John Berthoud, president of the National Taxpayers Union in Alexandria, Va. "But the danger I see is that these kinds of reforms can be a distraction from much more profound changes that should be happening in our schools."

Chester E. Finn Jr., a senior fellow at the conservative Hudson Institute, is skeptical of reports like "What Matters Most."

"It's like the dairy industry telling us we should drink more milk," he says of the report's heavy input from educators. "I don't give a damn about teacher performance unless it leads to student performance."

Wilmer S. Cody, Kentucky's commissioner of education, says focusing on teacher preparation and training is important, but that "those looking for a silver bullet are going to be disappointed if that's the only thing they work on." Equally important, he says, are such issues as the culture of school systems and administrative policies. Good teachers can be worn down "very quickly by a bad school environment," he warns.

Still, the appetite for teacher reform is growing keener across the nation. President Clinton recently announced a new effort to attract teachers to tough urban settings. And he backs federal funding support for the National Board for Professional Teaching Standards. Meanwhile, legislation to enhance teacher professionalization is percolating on Capitol Hill.

As education-reform efforts increasingly focus on teachers, here are some of the key questions being asked:

### *Will rigorous standards lead to a teacher shortage?*

Every year as summer comes to an end, school administrators across the country scramble to find enough teachers.

The Department of Education predicted a record public and private school enrollment of 52 million students in fall 1996 — and 54.3 million by 2007. In the West, public school enrollment will climb 17 percent, more than double the national average.

Under such circumstances, it might seem that raising teacher-performance standards will only exacerbate the teacher shortage. But many experts argue that elevating standards will ultimately attract more teachers, and improve student performance in the process. Some advocates see the need for new teachers as a golden opportunity to infuse the profession with a new crop of well-trained, highly motivated educators.

"We have a shortage of qualified teachers now, so I don't think raising standards will exacerbate the problem of finding good teachers," says Marilyn Scannell, executive director of the Indiana Professional Standards Board. "I know people usually associate raising teacher standards with shortages, but part of our problem is credibility for the profession anyway."

"What's the alternative? Lower the standards?" asks Timothy J. Dyer, executive director of the National Association of Secondary School Principals. "We can't do that. The bait has to shift to a reward system. What does industry do when it can't find people?"

In the late 1980s, Connecticut raised teacher salaries but also imposed rigorous new competency standards on beginning teachers. Even so, there have been no shortages in Connecticut, says Raymond Pecheone, the state's curriculum and teacher standards chief. Connecticut's higher-than-average teacher salaries no doubt have helped, as has its mentoring program for young teachers. But Pecheone credits the state's strict expectations with attracting teaching talent. "If you raise the standards and are very clear," he says, "it's more of a magnet."

On the other hand, lowering the bar can have serious policy and cultural consequences, notes Michigan State University education professor David F. Labaree. The need for teachers is so acute that, "Approximately one in every five college graduates every year must enter teaching in order to fill all the available vacancies," he notes. "If education schools do not prepare enough teacher candidates, state legislators are happy to authorize alternative routes into the profession . . . and school boards are quite willing to hire such prospects in order to place

## Poor Children Get Least-Prepared Teachers

*In secondary schools with a high percentage of minority students, less than half of the science and math teachers have a degree and certification in the field they teach.*

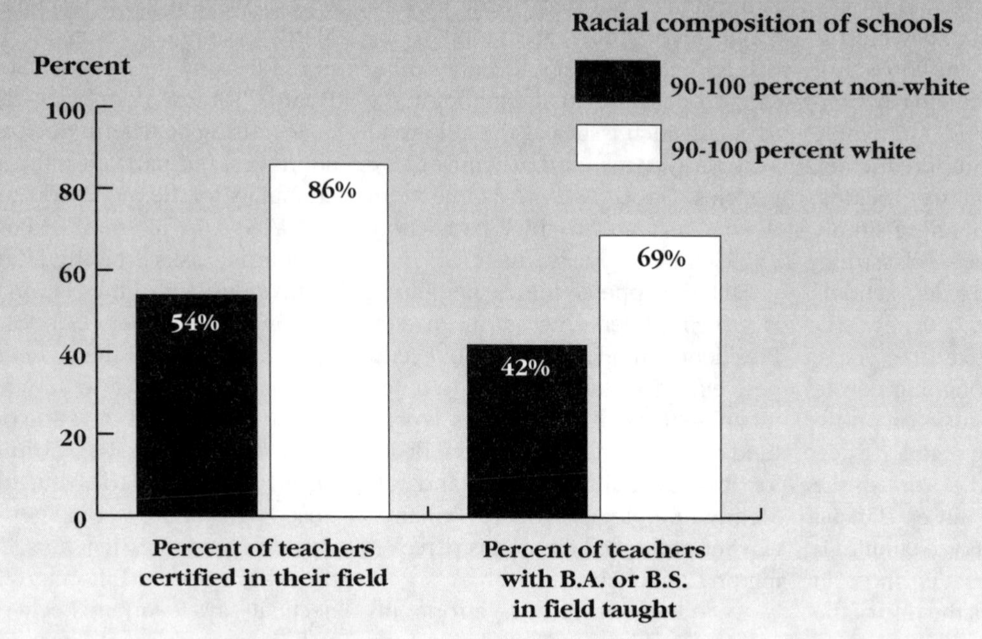


*Sources: National Commission on Teaching & America's Future,* What Matters Most: Teaching for America's Future, *September 1996; Jeannie Oakes,* Multiplying Inequalities: The Effects of Race, Social Class, and Tracking on Opportunities to Learn Mathematics and Science, *RAND Corp., 1990.*

warm bodies in empty classrooms." [8]

According to "What Matters Most," more than 12 percent of all newly hired teachers are untrained, and another 14 percent enter the profession without having fully met state standards. "Our schools' most closely held secret amounts to a great national shame," the report said. "Without telling parents they are doing so, many districts hire unqualified people as 'teachers' and assign them full responsibility for children." [9]

Of course, a dearth of qualified teachers can occur for a variety of reasons, especially in rural and small-town school districts. Dyer tells of a principal in the Midwest who had no one to teach Spanish last summer and wound up hiring a Spanish-speaking resident with no formal teaching experience. "You've got to get someone in that room when the door opens the day after Labor Day," Dyer says. "To say a principal isn't picking good people — well, you can't pick apples off a maple tree."

Hiring unqualified teachers can be "a function of genuine shortages in fields of short supply," "What Matters Most" acknowledges. But, the report adds, such decisions often result from "shortsighted hiring procedures, administrative convenience, efforts to save on teacher costs in favor of more 'important' areas and plain old-fashioned patronage." [10]

In California last year, serious classroom overcrowding prompted lawmakers to give financial incentives to schools that cut class sizes in lower grades. [11] The $1.5 billion program brought swift results. By this fall, nearly every public elementary school in California had reduced classes to 20 or fewer pupils in at least one or two early grades. But as schools have trimmed class size, they've had to hire more teachers — leading to a shortage of qualified candidates. A fifth of the candidates for new teaching slots do not have appropriate teaching credentials, and many are beginners with little or no classroom experience. [12]

The state has taken steps to ameliorate its shortage of competent teachers, including allowing retired teachers to return to the classroom for up to three years without sacrificing their retirement benefits. But that's done little to assuage critics, who see in California a rich example of the danger of pursuing reform before laying the proper groundwork.

"As a parent and as a taxpayer, I applaud California's effort to reduce classroom size, but frankly I am deeply troubled by the extent to which the state has compromised standards for teacher quality to meet this goal," says Rep. George Miller, D-Calif. He has sponsored a bill that would make it easier for parents to know the qualifications of their children's teachers. "Recruiting, preparing and supporting competent and qualified teachers is the single most important thing we can do to ensure that all students achieve to the utmost of their abilities."

Darling-Hammond contends that California policy-makers did not think enough about reorganizing the schools to lure back teachers who had fled the classroom for non-teaching posts. "Like other states, probably half the certified teachers in California are in non-teaching jobs in the school system," she says. True, she acknowledges, "the way we structure teaching is so grueling that many people do look longingly at the possibility of becoming specialists, or guidance counselors so they can see one student at a time." But in a restructured environment, "teaching can become interesting, enjoyable work again."

Stung by criticism, especially in wealthy areas such as Orange County near Los Angeles, California now is recruiting widely and enhancing teacher-training efforts, Darling-Hammond notes. "Maybe sometimes it takes a crisis to get the public's attention," she says.

If California raises troubling questions about the methods of reform, one thing is certain: Maintaining low standards is no guarantee of a surplus of teachers.

Consider Texas, where 12 percent of newly hired teachers were uncertified in their main subject area in 1990-91. [13] Yet this past summer, Texas was among the states facing a severe shortage of teachers. Up to 10,000 teaching posts throughout the state remained vacant in August, and some school districts had "all but given up trying to find accredited teachers," according to National Public Radio (NPR). [14]

Some argue that improving benefits and pay would go a long way toward solving Texas' teacher shortage. But Cindy Clegg, director of personnel services at the Texas Association of School Boards, told NPR the solution isn't that simple. Teachers need to have a career path that keeps them in the classroom while they advance in both pay and status, she said. "We could also compensate teachers differently for advanced skills and knowledge, advanced degrees and multiple certifications," she said.

Right now in Texas, she said, "the only career path is out of the classroom."

### *Does teacher training need to be radically overhauled?*

To advocates of education reform, one of the most pernicious popular myths is that "anyone can teach." Meeting the challenges of the classroom takes not only caring and charisma, they argue, but also rigorous training in pedagogy — the art and science of teaching — plus expertise in the subjects being taught and plenty of "professional development" throughout a teacher's career.

Yet critics claim that many schools of education do a poor job of training aspiring teachers.

The National Commission on Teaching & America's Future faulted traditional teacher training on a number of counts. *(See box, p. 920.)* "Until recently," the report states, "most teacher-education programs taught theory separately from application. Teachers were taught to teach in lecture halls from texts, and [by] teachers who frequently had not themselves ever practiced what they were teaching. Students' courses on subject matter were disconnected from their courses on teaching methods, which were in turn disconnected from their courses on learning and development. . . . When they entered their own classrooms, they could remember and apply little of what they had learned by reading in isolation from practice. Thus, they reverted to what they knew best: the way they themselves had been taught." [15]

There is also the widespread perception that education schools no longer attract the best and brightest students. "What Matters Most" seeks to rebut that notion, but clearly many other good students are indeed gravitating to better-paying or more prestigious fields.

Student test scores in Massachusetts tend to perpetuate the perception that the good ones get away. State lawmakers in 1993 agreed to help pay off the college loans of aspiring teachers — if they graduated in the top 25 percent of their class. But in Massachusetts, most new teachers graduate at the bottom half of their high school and college classes. [16]

While criticism of education schools isn't new, it has reached a crescendo lately. In 1995, the deans of 100 top education schools, as part of a decade-long education-reform initiative known as the Holmes Group, lambasted their own institutions. Putting on what they called "the hair shirt of self-criticism," they said that education schools strive so much for academic prestige and credibility within the university that they ignore the real-world needs of teachers and pupils. Schools of education must change "or surrender their franchise," the deans declared. [17]

Moreover, the deans said that many education professors make "hardly a nod toward the public schools, seldom if ever deigning to cross the thresholds of those 'lowly' places. Such attitudes transmit an unmistakable message: The people most intimately responsible for children's learning in elementary and secondary schools are not sufficiently valued by the education school. Schoolteachers and young learners, who should be the focus of the education school's concern, are kept at arm's length. They are a sideshow

## What's Wrong With Teacher Training

*In its landmark 1996 report,* What Matters Most: Teaching for America's Future, *The National Commission on Teaching & America's Future called for dramatic changes in teacher recruitment, preparation and professional development. The report faulted traditional teacher training on a number of counts, including:*

- *inadequate time devoted to mastering core subject matter, child-development and learning theory and effective teaching strategies;*
- *fragmentation of education coursework and practice teaching;*
- *"uninspired teaching methods" within education schools themselves;*
- *"superficial" education-school curriculum; and,*
- *failure to train aspiring teachers to work in teams and use technology in the classroom.*

to the performance in the center ring, where professors carry out their work insulated from the messiness and hurly-burly of elementary and secondary education." [18]

To improve teacher training, the National Commission on Teaching & America's Future proposed linking the practical with the theoretical in schools of education. It also recommended that poorly performing education schools be shut down and that universities and local school districts join forces to expand the number of "professional development schools" for training beginning and veteran teachers.

When it comes to accreditation, the National Commission on Teaching & America's Future says every education school should have NCATE's imprimatur or be closed by 2006. "On college campuses, all professional schools are expected to be accredited — except for education," Wise says. "Colleges of education charge the same tuition as the rest of the university, and when you look at how much is spent in the college of education vs. other disciplines, you find out education students are supporting the education of doctors, business people, lawyers and others."

Yet many education-school deans disagree that accreditation is crucial, and some resist it, sometimes because of NCATE itself. When Drake University withdrew from NCATE's accreditation process in 1992, university officials said it was expensive, unwieldy and concentrated on the structure of teacher-training programs rather than the quality of graduates. Wise concedes NCATE's process is "paper-intensive" but "so is accreditation in every other field."

Dissatisfaction with NCATE has spawned a rival accrediting organization — the Teacher Education Accreditation Council. Marilyn J. Guy, assistant dean for faculty life at Concordia College in Moorhead, Minn., says the group is looking at new ways to accredit education schools to enhance their accountability. One aim is to "encourage differences and diversity" among education schools rather than a uniform standard of teacher training. The new group will focus on "what students learn and what they're able to do as a result of a program of higher education."

There also is debate about the value of professional development schools — lab schools where beginning teachers spend a semester or two with pupils, veteran teachers coach the neophytes and upgrade their own skills and education professors work as mentors and conduct real-world research.

Advocates argue that without such programs, many teachers would get minimal mid-career training — perhaps an occasional one- or two-day seminar conducted by outside "experts" hired by the school district, but little else. Much of what passes for teacher professional development is a "joke," argues "What Matters Most."

Yet some education scholars hesitate to embrace professional development schools, calling them expensive and unproven. To Andy Hargreaves, director of the International Center for Educational Change at the University of Toronto, they're "the EPCOT Centers of educational change. Not in all cases, but in some, [proponents] find a little jewel on which they can focus their innovative energies. By saying they have this school in this place, they've solved the problem of teacher education."

Hargreaves favors partnerships between a university education department and an entire school district, or even several neighboring districts, as a way of involving professors in the full range of challenges facing public schools. The University of Toronto's education school participates in such an arrangement. In the United States, however, some professional develop-

## Teacher Quality Varies Widely Around the Nation

*At least 10 percent of the newly hired teachers in 1996 were unlicensed in nearly a quarter of the states. And in a majority of the states, at least 20 percent of the math teachers had neither a major nor a minor in math.*

| State | Unlicensed Hires | Out-of-Field Math Teaching | State | Unlicensed Hires | Out-of-Field Math Teaching |
|---|---|---|---|---|---|
| Alabama | 9% | 21% | Montana | 5% | 14% |
| Alaska | 7% | 63% | Nebraska | 8% | 26% |
| Arizona | 2% | 31% | Nevada | 7% | 37% |
| Arkansas | 9% | 20% | New Hampshire | 5% | — |
| California | 13% | 51% | New Jersey | 0% | 34% |
| Colorado | 4% | 35% | New Mexico | 8% | 47% |
| Connecticut | 0% | 11% | New York | 5% | 34% |
| Delaware | 0% | — | North Carolina | 3% | 24% |
| District of Columbia | 53% | — | North Dakota | 0% | 21% |
| Florida | 17% | 39% | Ohio | 0% | 17% |
| Georgia | 7% | 35% | Oklahoma | 3% | 34% |
| Hawaii | 10% | 51% | Oregon | 2% | 33% |
| Idaho | 4% | 25% | Pennsylvania | 0% | 14% |
| Illinois | 8% | 28% | Rhode Island | 0% | — |
| Indiana | 2% | 30% | South Carolina | 14% | 29% |
| Iowa | 2% | 18% | South Dakota | 3% | 20% |
| Kansas | 0% | 13% | Tennessee | 0% | 28% |
| Kentucky | 1% | 17% | Texas | 12% | 30% |
| Louisiana | 23% | 31% | Utah | 10% | 44% |
| Maine | 9% | 33% | Vermont | 0% | — |
| Maryland | 29% | 40% | Virginia | 15% | 34% |
| Massachusetts | 11% | 37% | Washington | 1% | 46% |
| Michigan | 4% | 33% | West Virginia | 10% | 16% |
| Minnesota | 0% | 14% | Wisconsin | 0% | 17% |
| Mississippi | 9% | 23% | Wyoming | 3% | 25% |
| Missouri | 0% | 15% | | | |

*Source: National Commission on Teaching & America's Future,* What Matters Most: Teaching for America's Future, *September 1996.*

ment schools have tended to be less integral to a region's public education.

If the education community is divided on accreditation and professional development, it also differs on even more fundamental issues — such as whether reform efforts should focus on new-teacher training or on the performance of veterans.

"If you are reforming teacher education, the worst place to start is with [pre-employment] education," Hargreaves says. "Even when new teachers are prepared at a high level of skill, the sociological reality is that they will tend to adapt to whatever workplace they find themselves in. So you're losing a lot of investment in [pre-employment] training."

Besides, he says, "New teachers are a very small portion of the overall teacher population. So if you're looking to change the system by changing new teachers who enter it, it's a very, very slow change process."

### *Should tenure for teachers be eliminated?*

Last summer, six teachers at Elsie Roberts High School in suburban Dallas handed out a math quiz that stirred a coast-to-coast storm of outrage. Presumably to make the quiz more appealing, they asked such questions as: "Rufus is pimping for three girls. If the price is $65 for each trick, how many tricks will each girl have to turn so Rufus can pay for his $800 per day crack habit?" [19]

While the teachers were all suspended without pay for at least 30 days, such episodes lead many critics to wonder whether public schools are willing — or able — to exert proper control over teachers.

Across the nation, state lawmakers, school administrators and even teachers' unions are studying ways to weed out bad teachers and put the laggards on notice that in the new climate of teacher reform, no job is guaranteed.

At the heart of the issue is the informal system of public school tenure, which traditionally has made it difficult, expensive and time-consuming to dismiss poor performers. "Basically now, the model is that after a few years, you're a teacher for life" unless a big removal effort is launched, Berthoud says. "In New York City, it took a year plus 100 days and $175,000-to remove a bad teacher. "With appeal costs, it was over $300,000."

Some conservative state lawmakers have moved to eliminate tenure, but with little success. It seems unlikely that tenure will be eliminated altogether, if for no other reason than the politically powerful teachers' unions continue to defend it. "The key purpose of tenure laws is to protect teachers' due-process rights — *not* to protect incompetent teachers from dismissal," declares the AFT.

Don Cameron, executive director of the NEA, says "tenure exists because traditionally teachers have been political pawns and have been dismissed unfairly for a whole lot of reasons. You don't have to go very far back in this country to find a time when teachers were dismissed because a spot had to be found for a school board member or a superintendent's relative or because 'men needed jobs more than women,' according to somebody."

Yet the unions' growing movement toward self-policing — most notably the NEA's new support of peer review for local NEA affiliates that want it — seems to signal a revision in the thinking about tenure. "There are lots of ways and means of getting rid of teachers once they're placed on tenure," Cameron says. "The problem is that it has taken too long for a whole variety of reasons, one of which is the role of the teachers' unions," including defending the rights of teachers to a hearing under the tenure laws.

"There are other things too — administrators who don't want to deal with these issues, and school districts that don't follow the process laid down in the law and end up with egg on their face."

Still, "If it's taking two or three years to get rid of somebody who's bad, that's an abuse of the system that all of us — school boards, administrators and teachers' unions — need to make sure doesn't happen."

Cameron is quick to differentiate between tenure reform and peer review, though he concedes the latter can be a first step toward ousting a poor performer. "Before any teacher is dismissed, we need to enter into a cooperative venture with school districts to try to help those teachers."

The AFT has supported peer review since the late 1970s, and a limited number of affiliates — including those in Toledo, Rochester, Cincinnati and New York City — have used it.

Some representatives of school management advocate an overhaul of tenure rules, and they are taking a wait-and-see stance on union peer review.

Anne Bryant, executive director of the National School Boards Association, argues that tenure should be a bargaining issue for local teachers' unions. Some locals "might come up with a variety of things they would prefer over tenure," she says.

Currently, however, "many state laws don't give flexibility to school districts to make it a bargaining issue," and that runs "counter to everything we say we want to be as a nation," Bryant says.

"It's pretty tough to hold teachers and superintendents and administrators accountable for raising student achievement when at the same time we limit that district's ability to get rid of poor teachers. "We would never say to business, 'Create a better car, but we're going to dictate the rules by which you hire, fire and discipline workers,' " she says.

Bryant welcomes the NEA's new support of peer assistance and review, but she warns, "The proof is in the pudding. When we say peer review, we have to have good evaluation measures, and teachers have to be really tough when it comes to evaluating each other. And that can be really hard."

Even groups that are solidly in the teachers' camp are approaching tenure and peer review with caution.

The attitude that "tenure is the problem" in American education is a "myth," according to "What Matters Most." In the view of the authors, "tenure is useful in protecting teachers from political hiring and firing," Darling-Hammond says.

But, she continues, "It should not be a cover for incompetent teachers."

Acknowledging the unions' highly visible embrace of peer review at a time when tenure is under fire, Darling-Hammond says: "I think for both of the unions this is a moment in history. If they can't make the idea of a professional union more than an oxymoron, they will have no claim to be part of the discourse about educational improvement. So they're biting the bullet." ■

# BACKGROUND

## Teacher Factories

Since the nation's beginnings, teaching typically has been a second-class occupation. Most teachers had minimal skills in reading, writing and arithmetic. It was common for a youngster to finish one grade

# Chronology

## 1800s As the nation's school systems grow, advocates press for better training of teachers.

***1839***
Horace Mann establishes the first "normal" school, in Massachusetts, to train teachers.

***1857***
The National Teachers' Association, predecessor of the National Education Association (NEA), is founded to advocate for improved working conditions for teachers and "promote the cause of popular education."

## 1910s-1930s

***Market demands force teachers' colleges to broaden their curriculum and ease standards to accommodate the growing number of students seeking a college education.***

***1916***
American Federation of Teachers (AFT) is founded with the help of John Dewey. The organization's growth accelerates in the early 1960s after an affiliate becomes the bargaining agent for teachers in New York City.

***1933***
Although 85 percent of high school teachers have a bachelor of arts degree, only 10 percent of elementary school teachers do.

## 1960s Reform fever is fueled by concern over scientific advances of the Soviets and later by worries that American children are falling behind in basic learning skills. But competing ideologies stymie many efforts at meaningful reform.

***1963***
James Koerner's *The Miseducation of American Teachers* is published.

## 1970s-1980s

***Concern about education quality leads to new reforms.***

***1970s***
California, Oregon and Minnesota become the first of a dozen states to create autonomous boards to control standards for teachers.

***April 26, 1983***
"A Nation at Risk," a report by the Education Department's National Commission on Excellence in Education, warns of a "rising tide of mediocrity" in American schools.

***May 1986***
The Carnegie Forum on Education and the Economy issues "A Nation Prepared: Teachers for the 21st Century," which helps launch a "second wave" of educational reform, with the intent of making teaching a full-fledged profession.

***1986***
The Holmes Group, an organization of deans from about 100 research-oriented education schools, issues the first of three reports, "Tomorrow's Teachers," arguing that education schools should take a scholarly, research-based approach to pedagogical study and that teaching should be professionalized, much like law or medicine.

***1989***
Governors gather in Charlottesville, Va., to launch America 2000, a plan for national education standards.

## 1990s State and federal policy-makers take an increasingly aggressive stance in setting standards for teachers and calling for the reshaping of teacher education.

***1990***
In its second report, "Tomorrow's Schools," the Holmes Group advocates the formation of professional development schools.

***1994***
Congress passes Goals 2000 legislation launching a standards movement.

***1995***
The Holmes Group's third report, "Tomorrow's Schools of Education," says education schools should become more involved in local schools.

***September 1996***
National Commission on Teaching & America's Future issues report critical of teacher education, "What Matters Most: Teaching for America's Future."

***July 1997***
Delegates to the NEA's 135th annual meeting approve peer assistance and peer review in local affiliates that want it.

# Introducing the New, Collaborative NEA

For decades, the National Education Association (NEA) has bargained collectively in the interests of public school teachers, often engaging in acrimonious brinkmanship with administrators who didn't want to budge on teacher salaries, working conditions and other labor issues.

The NEA will continue to represent teachers at the bargaining table. But now, adopting what NEA President Bob Chase calls a "new unionism," the NEA says it will seek a collaborative — rather than adversarial — relationship with management in decisions about school budgets, staffing and other issues.

"America's children desperately need an organization that cares about them, the quality of their education and the quality of their lives," Chase told the union's 135th annual meeting last summer. "NEA *is* that organization."

For many in the union, talk of a "new unionism" signals a move into unfamiliar — and controversial — territory.

"It's very scary," Don Cameron, the NEA's executive director, says of the new collaborative posture. "Bob Chase has really gone out on a limb."

Cameron says he believes that limb is "pointing in the right direction," but he acknowledges that many in the NEA don't feel that way. "There are many unionists within the NEA who don't believe we can be both professional and a union — that we can collaborate with administrators on the one hand and collectively bargain against them on the other."

The NEA, Cameron says, "has been focused inwardly for the last quarter-century. We devoted time and effort to members' needs, and we espoused and championed [issues] directly related to job protection and other union kinds of activities. To go into a totally different direction now, where we are facing outward, it means we have to change direction, programs, policies, our budget — that's scary because it's difficult. We are now turning outward and engaging the public and the world outside the NEA."

Cameron admits that "part of" the NEA's strategy is to shore up its bruised public image, made worse by a lashing from former GOP presidential candidate Bob Dole, who singled out the union in a speech to the 1996 Republican National Convention. "If education were a war," Dole said, referring to the NEA, "you would be losing it."

But overcoming a bad image isn't "the most important" impetus for the new union strategy, Cameron says. Rather, he says, it's a desire to help public education to "get better. If it was just a question of public relations, the NEA could go on another 25 years with a reputation that might not be totally positive but that is still successful with our members."

In a speech last February to the National Press Club, Chase said the NEA seeks to "reinvent" itself in as fundamental a way as it did in the 1960s, when it went from being a "rather quiet, genteel professional association of educators" to an "assertive" and sometimes "militant" labor union.

While defending the NEA's record, Chase said its gains "too often have been won through confrontation at the bargaining table or, in extreme cases, after bitter strikes. These industrial-style, adversarial tactics simply are not suited to the next state of school reform. It's time to create a new union, an association with an entirely new approach to our members, to our critics, and to our colleagues on the other side of the bargaining table. In some instances we have used our power to block uncomfortable changes — to protect the narrow interest of our members, and not to advance the interests of students and schools. We cannot go on denying responsibility for school quality. Too often, NEA has sat on the sidelines of change, nay-saying, quick to say what won't work and slow to say what will.

"A growing number of NEA teachers argue that it's not enough to cooperate with management on school reform. Quality must begin at home — within our own ranks. If a teacher is not measuring up in the classroom — to put it baldly, if there is a bad teacher in one of our schools — then *we* must do something about it."

The "new collaboration is not about sleeping with the enemy," Chase added.

"It is about waking up to our shared stake in reinvigorating the public education enterprise. It is about educating children better, more effectively, more ambitiously."

Sandra Feldman, president of the 940,000-member American Federation of Teachers (AFT), echoes Chase's sentiment that unions can be both labor advocate and engine of reform. "We have played the role of defense counsel" for teachers, she says, but "we don't see it as contradicting or precluding our ability to also be very involved in raising the quality issues."

The AFT, she says, has been a "new union for a very long time. We were sort of born that way, in a tradition of believing that the quality of education our members provide is part and parcel of [the other issues] we have to take care of."

Even so, no one is predicting that a familiar site in many communities — schoolteachers walking a picket line at bargaining time — will disappear from the American scene. Feldman says AFT locals have been in an "adversarial position much to often" in bargaining with school districts. But, she adds, that's happened "not because we wanted to but we had to fight to get basic dignity and decent economic security for our members. One thing people do not understand is that it takes two to tango."

and teach it the next year.

By the early to mid-1800s, as the nation expanded, demand for public education grew stronger. Social reforms were erasing the tradition of indentured servitude, making formal education necessary to train young people for jobs. Not only that, some social reformers saw compulsory schooling as a way to curb juvenile delinquency, especially in impoverished urban areas.

As public education expanded, reformers began to press for improvements in teacher training. Horace Mann (1796-1859), a champion of free public education, fought for establishment of a state school to train teachers in Massachusetts. He also agitated for higher teacher salaries, curriculum revisions and acceptance of women teachers. Henry Barnard (1811-1900) took up similar causes in Rhode Island and Connecticut and also served as the nation's first commissioner of education.

"During the whole 19th century, there was a chronic shortage of teachers," says Labaree of Michigan State. Mann, Barnard and other reformers worried that teacher recruitment was little more than an exercise in "finding warm bodies to fill classrooms. Right at the very beginning [of public education] you see a tension that has never gone away — local school districts having to have somebody there on Sept. 1 and being willing to take someone even if they're unprepared."

In the mid-to-late 1800s, states built so-called "normal" schools at a rapid pace, conceiving of them as elite institutions whose sole mission was to educate young people for classroom careers. But soon, the schools became victims of their own success.

The problem with normal schools was that they turned out relatively few teachers, and as the demand for teachers grew, they soon were under pressure to increase their output. It wasn't long before the typical normal school was lowering its standards and becoming what Labaree calls a "teacher factory."

National Education Association

*Many educators cite the increasing demand for new teachers as a primary reason why schools of education tend to function more as "teacher factories" than elite professional academies.*

In the early 20th century, normal schools — then evolving into "teachers' colleges" — were feeling a new set of market demands. Growing numbers of young people, many raised in the city, saw college as a ticket to prosperity and decent employment. Yet many private or state institutions were expensive or remote. The teachers' colleges — accessible and cheap — presented an alternative. Soon, they were under new pressure to broaden their curriculum and admit students not headed for classroom work.

"Very soon, teachers' colleges were looking like regular liberal-arts colleges," Labaree says. One result, he writes, "was to reinforce the already-established tendency toward minimizing the extent and rigor of teacher education." [20]

The homogenizing and minimizing continued. By the 1930s many teachers' colleges had become state liberal arts colleges. By the 1960s and '70s, many of those had evolved into regional state universities, with science and humanities departments garnering more status and resources than education departments.

"In part, these [former teachers' colleges] may have acquired — and earned — their universal disrepute by successfully adapting themselves to all of the demands that we have placed on them," Labaree asserts. [21]

Today's education departments, the descendants of the normal schools and teachers' colleges, still produce the largest share of America's teachers. Yet the question remains: Why has teacher preparation been shunted to the margins of higher education when teaching itself remains one of the most important occupations in the nation?

One reason is the incessant demand for new teachers, which keeps many

## Critics Warn Against Using Computers . . .

The computer software is called SuccessMaker, and it is designed to help elementary and middle-school students improve in basic skills such as math and reading. A growing number of school districts are using SuccessMaker, among them sprawling Fairfax County, in Northern Virginia.

But this past spring, Fairfax officials rejected a proposal to install SuccessMaker in all 45 elementary schools on the county's eastern side, which has a large number of children who need special help with schoolwork.

"Some Fairfax school administrators say they like the software but are concerned about its cost — about $55,000 to buy and install SuccessMaker in a lab with 10 computers," *The Washington Post* noted. "Other administrators question SuccessMaker's educational value. . . . Students can't interact with a computer as they could with a teacher, and schools should use computers to help students find and understand information rather than to teach basic skills, these educators contend." [1]

Along with the skeptics in Fairfax, a growing number of experts are concerned that schools are becoming too reliant on glitzy technology to replace the time-honored approach of one-on-one interaction between pupil and teacher.

"If computers make a difference, it has yet to show up in achievement," Samuel G. Sava, executive director of the National Association of Elementary School Principals, wrote in *The New York Times*. "What studies there are — many financed by computer companies — are not much help. In one New Jersey middle school, widely cited for raising achievement scores, the improvement occurred before computers were introduced and could be attributed to other changes: longer class periods, new books, after-school programs and an emphasis on student projects." [2]

Sava went on to note that in the 26-nation Third International Mathematics and Science Study this year, U.S. students were bested in math by fourth-graders from seven other countries. "Teachers in five of the seven countries reported that they 'never or almost never' have students use computers in class," Sava wrote.

To be sure, computerized learning has plenty of backing in education, policy and industry circles, to say nothing of voter support. President Clinton wants to connect every school to the information superhighway by the year 2000. "I want to get the children of America hooked on education through computers," he has said. [3] The Education Department wants one computer for every five students. [4]

Meanwhile, industry giants such as Microsoft and Oracle are speeding the move to technology, making big donations of hardware or software to computerize libraries and schools. And a survey this year by the Milken Foundation found that six in 10 registered voters would support a $100 increase in federal taxes to hasten the trend toward technology in schools. [5]

Computer advocates claim technology improves learning, enhances the competitiveness of young people entering the labor force, boosts business investment and interest in education and connects students to a global network of educators and research resources.

Yet traditionalists are calling for caution and moderation. Some say widespread computer use in schools will widen the gap between rich and poor because students in low-income regions don't always have the same access and cyber-skills as those in wealthier locales. And many say there is no proof that computers make a significant difference in learning, especially if teachers lack training in integrating technology into classroom activities.

education departments in the mode of teacher factories rather than elite professional academies. Another problem, critics say, is that because state universities receive funding based on enrollment, there is an incentive to pull as many students as possible into relatively low-cost programs — such as education schools — and use the surplus revenue for more prestigious departments like law and medicine.

What's more, while many education schools "would blow your socks off" with their "dedicated faculty and intellectual grounding," adequate federal commitment to teacher training is missing, argues David Imig, executive director of the American Association of Colleges for Teacher Education. "The thing we have lacked in teacher education is the kind of investment or capacity-building that all other professional schools have had."

Education schools also labor under stigmas that give teacher training a bad name. One such stigma is that unlike "hard" sciences like biology, pedagogy lacks rigorous research protocols and a scientifically based body of knowledge. Darling-Hammond vehemently disagrees. "There are about 30 years of extraordinarily productive research on learning and teaching, and it's very well grounded," she says. "It tells us a lot more than we ever knew before about how people learn, how different people learn differently and how to teach effectively."

### 'A Nation at Risk'

Whatever the arguments, the decades-long controversies over the quality of public schooling in

# . . . to Take the Place of Teachers

"There is no good evidence that most uses of computers significantly improve teaching and learning, yet school districts are cutting programs — music, art, physical education — that enrich children's lives to make room for this dubious nostrum," declared *The Atlantic Monthly* in its July cover story. [6]

The Washington-based Benton Foundation concluded in a study released this year that technology alone is no panacea: "For it to work well for students and schools, we must build 'human infrastructure' at the same pace we are installing computers and wiring. . . . [T]echnology is not an end in itself, and . . . any successful use of technology must begin with clearly defined educational objectives." [7]

The Benton report further stated that "even the staunchest advocates of computer networking in education concede that in most places technical problems, inadequate training and insufficient time for teachers to figure out ways to integrate technology with the curriculum have combined to thwart the dreams of reformers for a technology-driven overhaul of the education system."

The report noted the results of a poll last February in which only 13.4 percent of surveyed teachers said they believe Internet access had helped pupils do better.

"The big problem I see is literacy — not computer literacy, but the simple ability to read and write," the report quoted Princeton, N.J., teacher Ferdi Serim. "If you put the Internet in the hands of somebody who can neither read, write, nor think well, you aren't giving them much. But for kids who are equipped with language and learning skills, it's like a rocket."

In his op-ed piece, Sava acknowledged that his organization of elementary-school principals supports Clinton's call for widespread computer use in the classroom. "Part of the grants from his 'technology literacy' program can be used for teacher training," Sava explained. But he noted the complexity and expense of equipping schools with computers on a large scale.

Providing a computer for one in every five students would require an annual investment of $8 billion to $20 billion, which includes the wiring of schools and teacher training, according to Rand Corp. figures cited by Sava. The Benton report cited a 1995 McKinsey & Co. analysis estimating that connecting schools to the Internet could cost as much as $47 billion over 10 years, plus $14 billion a year in operating costs.

While computers in America's classrooms are surely here to stay, critics like Sava want to go slowly enough to ensure that teachers are prepared to use them effectively.

"We must have the courage to resist the public's enthusiasm for sexy hardware and argue for the money to train our teachers," he wrote. "We cannot send them into the computer room with nothing but a user's manual." [8]

---

[1] Victoria Benning, "In Fairfax Schools, Hard Questions on Software Program," *The Washington Post*, Sept. 30, 1997.

[2] Samuel G. Sava, "Maybe Computers Aren't Schools' Salvation," *The New York Times*, Sept. 6, 1997.

[3] Speech in California Sept. 21, 1995, quoted in "Networking the Classroom," *The CQ Researcher*, Oct. 20, 1995.

[4] Sava, *op cit.*

[5] *Ibid.*

[6] Todd Oppenheimer, "The Computer Delusion," *The Atlantic Monthly*, July 1997.

[7] Christopher Conte, "The Learning Connection: Schools in the Information Age," Benton Foundation, 1997.

[8] Sava, *op. cit.*

America reached a crescendo in the late 1970s and early '80s.

A major source of concern was the declining number of young people entering the teaching profession. Teaching has always been a predominantly female occupation, especially at the elementary level. In the past few decades, expanding career opportunities and better pay in non-teaching fields have diverted many students away from education schools, leading to acute shortages of qualified educators.

By the early 1980s, a combination of problems — shortages of qualified teachers, declining test scores, infighting over curriculum reforms, budgetary pressures, to name a few — elevated national concerns about education to stratospheric heights.

### *"Rising Tide of Mediocrity"*

In 1983, "A Nation At Risk," an influential Education Department report, asserted that U.S. schools were sinking under a "rising tide of mediocrity," in part because of a shortage of qualified teachers in math, science and other key disciplines. "If an unfriendly foreign power had attempted to impose on America the mediocre educational performance that exists today," the report declared, "we might well have viewed it as an act of war."

The report drew bitter criticism from public school advocates. Some saw it as a blatant misreading of the evidence on American education. They argued that while some schools — mainly underfunded inner-city schools facing deep social problems — were indeed in trouble, most schools were good and improving. Other critics accused the Reagan White House of using alarmist tactics to press for federal funding of private education.

Accurate or not, "A Nation At Risk"

helped spawn a decade of reformist zeal in public education, one that transcended think tanks and government commissions to include education school deans, teachers' unions and rank-and-file educators and administrators.

In 1986. the Carnegie Forum on Education and the Economy issued a report, "A Nation Prepared: Teachers for the 21st Century," which helped launch a second wave of educational reform aimed at making teaching a full-fledged profession. [22] One outgrowth of the Carnegie study is the National Board for Professional Teaching Standards.

In 1989, President George Bush convened an education summit with the National Governors' Association, headed by then-Gov. Bill Clinton, D-Ark. The summit laid the groundwork for what became "Goals 2000," an ambitious series of education goals and proposed standards that have become the centerpiece of the Clinton administration's education strategy.

Another important outgrowth of the 1980s was the Holmes Group, a convocation of deans from about 100 research-oriented education schools that has issued a series of reports on teacher preparation. In 1986, the Holmes Group argued that education schools should take a scholarly, research-based approach to pedagogical study and that teaching should be professionalized, much like law or medicine. In 1990, the group advocated the formation of professional development schools.

But in 1995, in what some view as a disavowal of the 1986 position, the Holmes Group said education schools should drop their ivory tower pretensions and become more involved in the nitty-gritty of local school problems.

The Holmes Group and other research efforts have helped to shape the current generation of thinking on teacher preparation and set the stage for a number of new initiatives in the education community and the policy arena.

"People have tried to find ways of integrating teacher education more effectively back into the schools," Hargreaves says of initiatives like the Holmes Group. Adds Pecheone, the Connecticut curriculum chief, "There's an active movement to restructure teacher preparation so it's more relevant to teachers and prospective teachers." ■

# CURRENT SITUATION

## 'Rigorous' Standards

Few American school districts are ignoring the popular mandate to improve teacher quality. Fairfax County, Va., near Washington, D.C., recently reshaped its teacher-hiring process so that an arcane, paper-intensive process — typical of many school districts — doesn't scare off good prospects. [23] East Carolina University's Peer Coaching Project Consortium lets teachers in some North Carolina districts mentor other teachers. [24] In Ohio, the University of Cincinnati has joined with the public schools and local teachers' union to improve teacher training. [25]

But along with such local programs, two national groups — the Interstate New Teacher Assessment and Support Consortium (INTASC) and the National Board for Professional Teaching Standards — are mounting far-reaching reform initiatives.

INTASC, a 10-year-old consortium of 31 states and a variety of professional organizations, has developed standards for licensing beginning teachers and is creating new ways to gauge how well a beginning teacher can plan, teach and guide pupils, including slow-learners. The idea, says Linda Wurzbach, senior project associate, is to make licensing decisions based on "what people show they can do rather than showing solely what they know in a multiple-choice format."

INTASC draws on the work of the National Board for Professional Teaching Standards, which aims to set "high and rigorous" voluntary standards for certifying "accomplished" teachers. A select group of experienced teachers assesses the candidates, and the hurdles are high. Only about 600 teachers — a third of the applicants — have emerged as board-certified, says Philip Kearney, senior program director of the Southfield, Mich.-based organization.

"In effect we have a national, but not a federal, set of standards," he says. "It's very much teacher-driven. Nobody has ever done this before."

In his State of the Union address in February, President Clinton expressed support for the board's work, calling for federal spending to help it complete its task of shaping standards and to provide money to states to aid teachers who want to apply for certification. "We should reward and recognize our best teachers," the president said.

Clinton wants to see 100,000 applicants seeking board certification. Some observers are skeptical of such goals. The University of Toronto's Hargreaves calls them "worthy but probably exaggerated." He expects that enthusiasm for the rigorous evaluation regimen will wane after the first wave of teachers wins certification.

Kearney remains optimistic. "It is a very large and demanding task in front of us," he says, "but the board has received very strong support from the profession. One of our tasks is to

# At Issue:

## *Do teachers' unions have a positive influence on the educational system?*

# yes

**Bob Chase**
***President, National Education Association; former social studies teacher for 25 years.***

**FROM *INSIGHT ON THE NEWS*, OCT. 21, 1996.**

**F**or true believers, the evil influence of teachers' unions is an article of faith. But for those who prefer empirical data to hunches, let's look at the record. As it happens, there are 16 states in the United States that do not have collective-bargaining statutes governing public-school employees. In seven of those states, there virtually is no collective bargaining by public school employees. In short, no teachers' unions. It hardly is a coincidence that these seven states — all but one, West Virginia, located in the South — have been notorious for their underfunded education systems. . . .

In recent years, pro-education Southern governors . . . have striven to energize their states' academic performance by, in effect, doing the job that teachers' unions perform elsewhere: insisting on decent pay to attract and retain quality teachers, pushing for higher academic standards and prodding state legislatures to boost investments in education.

And what about the superb public-school systems Americans envy in countries such as Germany, France and Japan? You guessed it: They all benefit from strong teachers' unions.

Yet despite this evidence, it would be foolish to claim that teachers' unions guarantee educational excellence. To do so would be the flip side of our critics' foolish claim that teachers' unions control America's public schools. For the record, the NEA's local affiliates do not certify teachers, hire or fire them, write curricula, determine graduation requirements or set funding levels. . . . In the last analysis, the only thing NEA members control is their individual professional commitment to making public education work. . . .

More significantly, unions are good for education because they give teachers a strong, unified . . . voice within their local school systems. Our members and affiliates have fought not just for decent pay . . . but also for issues more directly related to school quality, including smaller class sizes and stricter . . . classroom discipline. . . .

The NEA's bedrock commitment is to quality public education. This in no way entails a defense of the status quo, especially in school districts that are underperforming. To the contrary, in state after state, it has required the NEA to take the lead in instigating and implementing change.

Ultimately, this is what separates public school teachers from their critics: Most critics stand on the outside and blow spitballs. Teachers — supported by their unions — stand in the classroom and courageously confront the challenges of public education in the 1990s. The good news is that, in most of America's schools, the teachers are winning.

# no

**Myron Lieberman**
***Adjunct scholar, Social Philosophy and Policy Center, Bowling Green State University; author,* The Teachers' Unions: How the NEA and AFT Sabotage Reform and Hold Parents, Students, Teachers and Taxpayers Hostage to Bureaucracy.**

**FROM *INSIGHT ON THE NEWS*, OCT. 21, 1996.**

**I**f your child does not have a qualified mathematics or science teacher, you can thank the NEA and American Federation of Teachers [AFT] for the salary policies that are to blame. Teachers' unions advocate single-salary schedules — paying all teachers the same salary regardless of subject. Under single-salary schedules, teachers are paid solely on the basis of their years of teaching experience and their academic credits. . . .

Higher-education administrators know it would be practically impossible to operate a university by paying all professors, regardless of subject, the same salary. Universities would be unable to employ qualified medical professors if their salaries were the same as those for English professors. Similarly, people who can teach mathematics and science can earn more in occupations outside of teaching. Thus, when the teachers' unions insist that all teachers be paid the same regardless of subject, they help create shortages of qualified teachers of math and science.

Needless to say, the teachers' unions claim that their collective goals contribute to academic achievement. Higher salaries are supposed to attract more talented teachers and reduce turnover. Tenured positions for teachers are supposed to protect competent teachers. More preparation time during the regular school day should result in better-prepared teachers. . . .

The unions' arguments have a superficial plausibility but cannot withstand scrutiny. Take, for example, the unions' claim that smaller classes are the key to improving student achievement, since they allow individualized instruction. Actually, class size largely is overrated as a factor in student achievement. In many nations whose students outperform ours, classes are much larger than those in the United States. Of course, smaller classes mean that more teachers are needed, and more teachers mean more union revenues.

The question policy-makers should be asking, however, is whether the expenditures required to lower class size are the most productive way to use the money. In many cases, they are not. The funds used to lower class size often could be more productively spent for laboratory equipment or textbooks or supplies. In most situations, reductions in class size benefit the union and teachers much more than they benefit pupils. The same point applies to the other union objectives that allegedly help students. . . .

The union litmus test is not whether a policy benefits students; it is whether it benefits teachers or unions.

figure out how we can scale this thing up, handle the sorts of numbers we've been talking about, maintain the quality of the program and continue to make it attractive for teachers to pursue voluntarily."

## State Efforts

Individual states have made varying degrees of progress in upgrading teacher standards, with some far along the reform spectrum and others barely moving. Among the most aggressive are Indiana and Connecticut.

In the Hoosier State, the vehicle for change is the five-year-old Indiana Professional Standards Board, an autonomous group of classroom teachers, administrators, school board members, business people and education professors. It has legal authority to set teacher training, hiring, certification and relicensing standards.

The board's aim, says Executive Director Scannell, is to "establish the credibility of teaching as a profession. Only by describing what teachers ought to be able to do can the public understand what makes teachers special. Until now, they kind of thought teachers were born and not made."

In many states, legislatures or bureaucrats have held sway over teacher standards. Only about a dozen states have independent boards that set licensing rules, and few state boards are as ambitious and far-reaching as Indiana's. [26]

In 1994, the Indiana board decided to adopt a rigorous performance-based licensing system that it hopes to implement fully early in the next century. The board modeled the system on the new-teacher protocols of INTASC, the rigorous regimen of the National Board for Professional Teaching Standards, NCATE's standards for ed schools and the spirit and goals of the "What Matters Most" study. Working with Indiana education schools to reshape teacher-training programs means crafting "standards for what teachers should know and be able to do, rather than a prescriptive list of course and credit hours to be received for licensure," Scannell says.

Reform advocates are watching the Indiana board closely. "They are at the forefront of figuring out the proper relationship between accreditation and licensing and what colleges of education need to provide to teacher candidates," said Wise of NCATE. [27]

In Connecticut, besides providing for peer mentoring and other forms of professional development, the state requires beginning teachers to produce a portfolio of work demonstrating classroom competency. The benchmarks, similar to those adopted by the National Board for Professional Teaching Standards, now cover new and recently hired middle- and high-school teachers. By 2000 they also will apply to elementary school teachers, principals and other administrators.

Those who don't pass muster within three years of employment will be "out of the profession" in the state, Pecheone says.

Part of Connecticut's focus is to ensure that teachers are experts not only in pedagogy but also the field they teach. The state used to have "a one-size-fits-all type of evaluation system, based on generic understandings of teacher competence," says Pecheone. "We moved to subject-specific standards about what a teacher should know and be able to do."

Kentucky also is moving to improve teacher competency. But there, the results have stirred controversy. The state is working with INTASC and NCATE to develop strict, performance-based teacher certification standards. It also is exploring new ways to grant advanced certification to veteran teachers, based not only on their college credits but also on classroom demonstrations of their skill.

In September, however, *The Wall Street Journal* noted in a front-page story that Kentucky teachers are rewarded with cash bonuses if their school test scores rise, a policy that "has spawned lawsuits, infighting between teachers and staff, anger among parents, widespread grade inflation — and numerous instances of cheating by teachers to boost student scores." [28]

Even Jack Foster, the former Kentucky education secretary who helped design the program, conceded it needed work. "We tried to do too much, too fast," Foster said. [29] ■

# OUTLOOK

## Legislative Initiatives

Along with the states and local school districts, the federal government also is moving to reshape policies affecting classroom educators.

Much of the focus is on reshaping Title V of the Higher Education Act, an initiative authorized for funding at nearly $600 million in 1993 that was designed to improve elementary and secondary teaching. Only one of the measure's 16 programs — to recruit minority teachers — was funded in fiscal 1997, and only five have ever received money. *

Sen. Bill Frist, R-Tenn., wants to streamline Title V to focus on initial training of teachers. In September he submitted a bill that would cut Title V funding to $250 million and consolidate its programs. He would retain mi-

* The five programs that were funded previously were minority recruitment, early childhood violence counseling, Paul Douglas scholarships for high school students who want to be teachers, the Christa McAuliffe fellowship for working teachers and the National Board for Professional Teaching Standards.

nority recruitment and strengthen teacher preparation.

Noting that school enrollments are climbing and that a third to a half of current teachers are 45 or older, Frist argues that a supply of new, well-trained teachers is necessary to meet future demand. He also argues that while schools have mechanisms to improve skills of current teachers, federal support of new-teacher training is lacking. "There has been virtually no federal commitment to help institutions of higher education upgrade future teacher training programs," he said.

Miller, the California Democrat, also addresses teacher training in his proposed Teaching Excellence for All Children Act of 1997, which would require school districts to make teacher qualifications available to parents. "Teachers are among the hardest-working people in our country, and they certainly have one of the most important jobs in our country," Miller says. "Unfortunately, our public policies have not always reflected this reality."

Miller wants education schools that get federal money to be either nationally accredited or show that at least 90 percent of graduates pass state licensing exams on the first try. In addition, he wants to establish local community partnerships with accredited education schools to help recruit and retain qualified teachers. And Miller wants the federal government to forgive college loans of those who teach in high-poverty areas.

Sen. Jack Reed, D-R.I., wants to amend Title V to create a five-year competitive grant program for teacher training that would be administered by the Education Department. Building on the professional development school concept, Reed introduced a bill Sept. 11 that would direct $100 million to be used for partnerships between elementary and secondary schools and institutions of higher education as well as other educational agencies and organizations.

"These partnerships would operate like teaching hospitals, with university faculty and veteran teachers working with current and prospective teachers on how to improve and enhance their skills by offering supervised classroom experience and mentoring," Reed said. Up to 50 percent of new teachers leave the profession within three to five years, mainly because of lack of preparation and training provided for new teachers, according to Reed's office.

The Department of Education wants to replace Title V's myriad programs with the Lighthouse Partnerships for Teacher Preparation and an enhanced program to recruit minority teachers. Legislation calling for the changes was introduced Sept. 23 by Sen. Edward M. Kennedy, D-Mass.

Last summer, in a speech to the NAACP national convention in Pittsburgh, Clinton supported minority recruitment, proposing to spend $350 million over five years on tuition and training aid for up to 35,000 new teachers who agree to work in inner-city and rural schools for at least three years. "A third of our students are minority," he said, but "only 13 percent of their teachers are.

"Students in distressed areas who need the best teachers often have teachers who have had the least preparation," the president said. "For

## FOR MORE INFORMATION

**National Association of Secondary School Principals,** 1904 Association Drive, Reston, Va. 22091; (703) 860-0200; www.nassp.org. The association represents the interests of high school principals.

**The National Commission on Teaching & America's Future,** Teachers College, Columbia University, Box 117, 525 West 120th St., New York, N.Y. 10027; (212) 678-3204. The commission produced a landmark report last year, "What Matters Most: Teaching for America's Future."

**National Board for Professional Teaching Standards,** 26555 Evergreen Road, Suite 400, Southfield, Mich. 48076; 248-351-4444. The board sets rigorous standards for certifying expert teachers.

**Interstate New Teacher Assessment and Support Consortium (INTASC),** a program of the Council of Chief State School Officers, 1 Massachusetts Ave. N.W., Suite 700, Washington, D.C. 20001-1431; (202) 336-7048. The consortium crafts model standards for licensing new teachers.

**National Education Association,** 1201 16th St. N.W., Washington, D.C. 20036-3290; (202) 833-4000; www.nea.org. The NEA is the nation's largest teachers' union.

**American Federation of Teachers,** 555 New Jersey Ave N.W., Suite 10, Washington, D.C. 20001; (202) 879-4400; www.aft.org. The AFT, along with the NEA, represents the interests of American teachers.

**National School Boards Association,** 1680 Duke St., Alexandria, Va. 22314-3493; (703) 838-6225; www.nsba.org. This federation of school board associations is interested in such issues as local governance and quality of education programs.

**American Association of Colleges for Teacher Education,** 1 Dupont Circle, Suite 610, Washington, D.C. 20036-1186; (202) 293-2450; www.aacte.org. The association represents those responsible for teacher education, including schools, colleges and departments of education.

example, right now 71 percent of students taking physical science courses like chemistry and physics, and 33 percent of English students in high-poverty schools, take classes with teachers who do not even have a college minor in their field."

Such figures are familiar to those who deal with the challenges of inner-city education on a daily basis. Improving the quality of instruction is important, they agree. But so is mandating greater equity in spending on school buildings and other physical facilities in poor neighborhoods.

"As few as 40 percent of our youngsters even have higher-level math and science offered in their buildings," says Ramona H. Edelin, president of the National Urban Coalition. "There are great discrepancies in the quality of the teaching force in the hardest-hit inner cities and their suburban counterparts." And, she adds, inequities in "the rates of spending on facilities up and down the line are just a moral outrage."

While public officials wrestle with reshaping policy on teacher competence and recruiting, unionized teachers, mainly in the NEA, find themselves at a crossroads. Will they adopt a meaningful strategy of self-policing, or will the slogan of a "new unionism" become a hollow PR gimmick?

"There has been significant interest expressed by local associations in moving in the direction" of adopting peer review since the union approved it last summer, Cameron says. But it may be months before it is known whether NEA locals will embrace it on a wide scale.

Clearly, though, the delegates' embrace of peer review marks a watershed for a labor organization that frequently has been at bitter odds with school administrators. "This is a defining moment," said Lea Schelke, a Trenton, Mich., high school teacher who chairs the NEA's professional standards and practice committee. The union's endorsement of peer assistance and review "shifts the world for our new members. They appreciate all of us old workhorses who got the salaries and protections they don't want to walk away from — but they want more." [30]

Even if the unions do bend more in the future, they also will expect something in return from local school districts and national policy-makers — support and resources to make the teachers' jobs easier and more meaningful.

"If we're moving toward a situation where we want to have much higher standards — and of course we do — and we have to compete in a global marketplace and want to be a high-wage, high-skill society, we're going to have to make sure our schools are world-class," says AFT President Feldman. "We're asking a lot more of teachers than we ever have before. We must make sure they get the training and support to do the job." ■

## Notes

[1] For background, see "Attack on Public Schools," *The CQ Researcher,* July 26, 1996, pp. 649-672, and "Education Standards," *The CQ Researcher,* March 11, 1994, pp. 217-240.

[2] For background, see "School Funding," *The CQ Researcher,* Aug. 27, 1993, pp. 745-768.

[3] National Commission on Teaching & America's Future, *What Matters Most: Teaching for America's Future,* September 1996. The 26-member commission chaired by Gov. James B. Hunt Jr., D-N.C., includes educators and political, union, corporate and community leaders.

[4] *Ibid.*

[5] *Ibid.*

[6] *The New York Times,* July 8, 1997.

[7] For background, see "School Choice Debate," *The CQ Researcher,* July 18, 1997, pp. 625-648.

[8] David F. Labaree, "The Trouble With Ed Schools," *Educational Foundations,* summer 1996, p. 32.

[9] National Commission on Teaching & America's Future, *op. cit.,* p. 14.

[10] *Ibid.,* p. 15.

[11] The average elementary school class in California had 28.8 students in 1995, the highest in the nation, according to the Department of Education, National Center for Education Statistics, *Digest of Education Statistics,* 1995.

[12] *EdSource Report,* April 1997. EdSource is a nonprofit education information center for California public schools based in Palo Alto.

[13] National Commission on Teaching & America's Future, *op. cit.,* p. 149.

[14] National Public Radio, "All Things Considered," Aug. 21, 1997.

[15] National Commission, *op. cit.,* p. 31.

[16] Leslie Harris, "Recruiting the Best and Brightest," *Teacher Magazine,* January 1996.

[17] "Tomorrow's Schools of Education," Holmes Group, 1995, p. 5, quoted in Labaree, *op. cit.,* p. 29.

[18] Quoted in Labaree, *op. cit.*

[19] *The Washington Post,* Aug. 20, 1997.

[20] Labaree, *op. cit.,* p. 31.

[21] *Ibid.,* p. 30.

[22] "Should Teaching Be Made Into a Profession?" *Editorial Research Reports,* May 4, 1990, pp. 253-268.

[23] *Education Week,* Feb. 26, 1997, p. 1

[24] National Commission, *op. cit.,* p. 87

[25] *Education Week,* April 23, 1997.

[26] Marilyn Scannell and Judith Wain, "New Models for State Licensing of Professional Educators," *Phi Delta Kappan,* November 1996, p. 211.

[27] Quoted in *Education Week,* March 26, 1997, p. 6.

[28] *The Wall Street Journal,* Sept. 2, 1997.

[29] *Ibid.*

[30] Quoted in *Education Week,* Aug. 6, 1997.

# Bibliography

## Selected Sources Used


### Books

**Berliner, David C., and Bruce J. Biddle, *The Manufactured Crisis: Myths, Fraud, and the Attack on America's Public Schools,* Addison-Wesley, 1995.**

The authors, both university professors, question critics of American education. They argue that SAT scores are rising for many groups, figures on illiteracy are skewed and public schools deliver a quality education.

**Kramer, Rita, *Ed School Follies: The Miseducation of America's Teachers,* Free Press, 1991.**

Kramer visited 15 university education schools and talked to students, faculty and administrators. She concludes that most teachers believe their job isn't to transfer a specific body of knowledge to students, but to prepare them to live in a multicultural society.

**Goodlad, John I., *Educational Renewal: Better Teachers, Better Schools,* Jossey-Bass, 1994.**

Goodlad, director of the Center for Educational Renewal at the University of Washington in Seattle, expounds on his vision for "centers of pedagogy" that link schools and universities in a strong relationship. "Unfortunately, teacher education has come to be associated only with training and the mechanistic ways we teach dogs, horses, and humans to perform certain routinized tasks," he writes.

**Finn, Chester E. Jr., *We Must Take Charge: Our Schools and Our Future,* Free Press, 1991.**

Finn advocates a radical reorganization of American education, arguing that "public education in the United States is . . . a failure." He calls for a national curriculum of core subjects and a clear standard of achievement.

### Articles

**Bronner, Ethan, "End of Chicago's Education School Stirs Debate," *The New York Times,* Sept. 17, 1997.**

For the first time in more than a century, there are no doctoral candidates at the University of Chicago's department of education. The department, founded in 1895 by John Dewey, has been closed. "In recent months, a . . . complex discussion has emerged . . . about the nature of educational research, notably about the links between educational theory and practice, and how they fit into a traditional academic setting," Bronner writes.

**Oppenheimer, Todd, "The Computer Delusion," *The Atlantic Monthly,* July 1997.**

"Schools around the country are dropping traditional subjects to lavish scarce time and money on computers and computer education — with results that may be at best negligible and at worst harmful," the author argues.

**Schrag, Peter, "The Near-Myth of Our Failing Schools," *The Atlantic Monthly,* October 1997.**

While some criticisms of America's education system are correct, Schrag argues that misleading assumptions and incorrect conclusions persist. "Without a more realistic sense of what is going on — a better understanding of the myths — the country will never get beyond the horror stories and ideological set pieces that seem endlessly to dominate the educational debate," he writes.

**Stanfield, Rochelle L., "Good-Bye, Mr. Chips," *National Journal,* Oct. 10, 1996.**

"Talented teachers are tough to find and even harder to keep," declares this story on teacher competence.

**Stecklow, Steve, "Apple Polishing: Kentucky's Teachers Get Bonuses, but Some Are Caught Cheating," *The Wall Street Journal,* Sept. 2, 1997.**

Stecklow writes that a popular "carrot-and-stick" approach to motivating Kentucky teachers — paying cash bonuses if their schools' test scores rise — has led to grade inflation, lawsuits, "numerous instances of cheating by teachers to boost student scores" and other problems.

### Reports

**National Commission on Teaching & America's Future, *What Matters Most: Teaching for America's Future,* September 1996.**

Chaired by North Carolina Gov. James B. Hunt Jr., the commission calls for dramatic changes in teacher recruitment, preparation and professional development practices.

**National Association of Secondary School Principals, *Breaking Ranks: Changing an American Institution,* 1996.**

The report, done in partnership with the Carnegie Foundation for the Advancement of Teaching, says "the high school of the 21st century must be much more student-centered and above all much more personalized in programs, support services and intellectual rigor."

**Christopher Conte, with research and editorial contributions by Jon Berroya, Susan Goslee, Jillaine Smith and Kevin Taglang, Benton Foundation, *The Learning Connection: Schools in the Information Age,* 1997.**

The report argues that while school districts are spending $4 billion a year on new technology, the computers and other devices they are buying are not worth the price if they are adopted in a vacuum.

# 3 Patients' Rights

KENNETH JOST

Minnesota computer executive Patrick Shea thought he should see a cardiologist. He had been experiencing shortness of breath and dizzy spells. And heart disease ran in his family.

But Shea's physician assured him a specialist wasn't necessary and refused to give him the written referral required by his health plan. Instead, he told Shea that his problems were stress-related and that he was too young to have heart problems.

Later, while on an overseas business trip, Shea suffered chest pains so severe that he was hospitalized and had to return home. But his doctor still dismissed his concerns.

Shea never saw a specialist. He died in March 1993, less than a year later, leaving his wife, Dianne, with two young children and troubling questions. He was 40. An autopsy disclosed that Shea had suffered from arteriosclerosis — blocked arteries — which might have been corrected with cardiac bypass surgery.

"We repeatedly asked for referral to a cardiologist," Dianne later told a Minnesota legislative committee. "Not only were our pleas ignored, we were assured time and time again that our fears were unfounded."

In the months that followed, Dianne sought to discover how a man who had always followed his doctor's advice could die of an undiagnosed disease. What she found shook her confidence not only in their own doctors but also in the health care that more than 150 million Americans receive today from so-called managed-care systems: health maintenance organizations (HMOs) and similar network health-care plans. [1]

Supporters say managed care helps provide affordable, high-quality health care at a time when patients, health-care providers, insurers and employers are all straining to keep down costs. But Dianne became convinced from the inquiry she and her lawyers made that cost controls helped kill her husband.

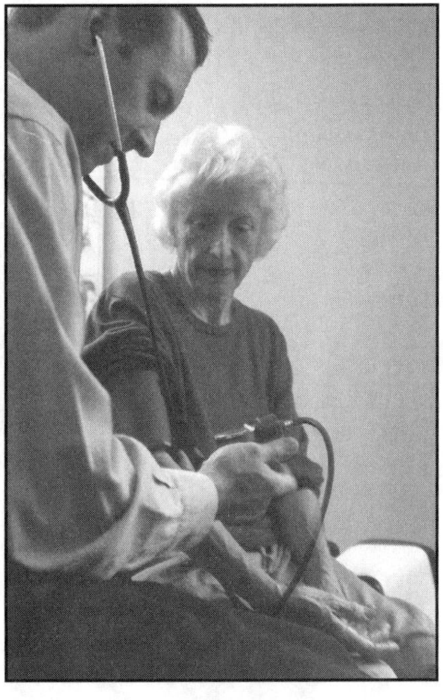

She claims in a wrongful death lawsuit that Shea's doctor had an undisclosed financial conflict of interest in refusing to refer him to a cardiologist because he received extra compensation from their HMO, Medica, for not sending patients to specialists.

The defendants in the federal court suit — Shea's doctors, their HMO clinic and Medica — deny that the doctors' compensation in any way depended on rejecting Shea's request to see a specialist. "Sheer speculation," Medica's lawyers say. The defendants also deny they were negligent in failing to diagnose Shea's heart disease. A trial in the case is expected later this year. [2]

Dianne Shea, meanwhile, has begun advocating reform of managed care. She urged the Minnesota Legislature to require health insurers to disclose their "payment methodology" — information she says that might have prompted Shea to ignore his doctor's advice and see a cardiologist. "People have to understand that health care is a business," she says. "Just as we would never buy an investment blindly, we just cannot trust our doctors blindly."

The state Legislature last year passed a weakened version of Shea's proposal, requiring disclosure of the financial arrangements only on the patient's request. Minnesota thus became one of more than 30 states to pass legislation in the past three years aimed at strengthening the rights of patients enrolled in managed care — by far the dominant form of health care in the United States. *(See chart, p. 42.)*

Congress is also set to consider legislation that would impose far-reaching regulations on managed-care systems and possibly make it easier to sue health insurers for malpractice. Consumer and patient advocacy groups as well as the American Medical Association (AMA) are generally backing the proposals, which are strongly opposed by health-care insurers and employers.

The reform efforts reflect a widespread belief that patients are being harmed in the shift away from traditional "fee-for-service" health insurance, which gave consumers greater freedom in choosing their own doctors and doctors greater freedom in prescribing treatment that insurers would pay for.

"Patients feel less personally taken care of, that they have interactions with too many health-care providers, that there's too much red tape in getting access to the specialists," says Myrl Weinberg, president of the National Health Council, a coalition of more than 40 patient advocacy

From *The CQ Researcher,* February 6, 1998.

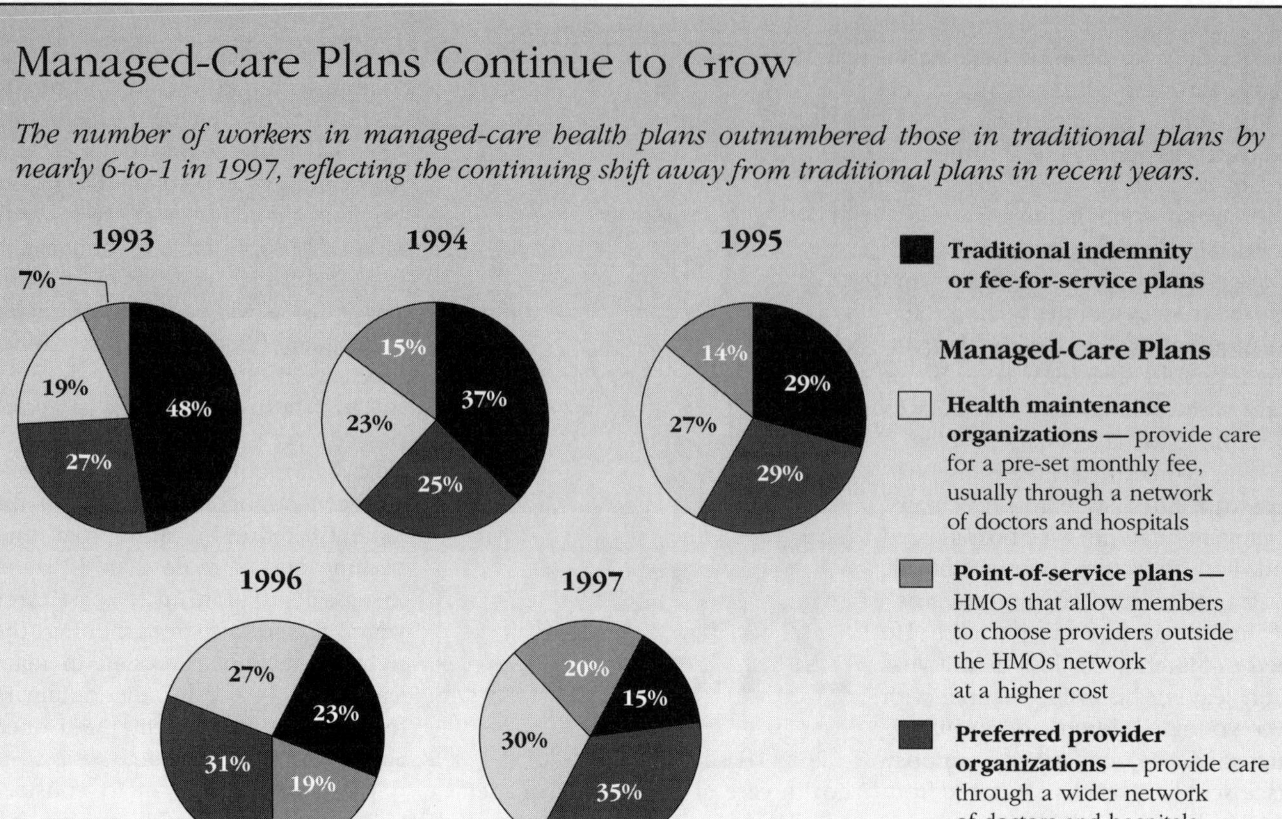


groups, such as the American Cancer Society and American Heart Association, as well as major drug manufacturers and health insurers.

But health insurance industry officials insist that patients actually receive better care under managed-care plans.

"There's a tremendous possibility [with HMOs] to receive better, more integrated care," says Karen Ignagni, president of the American Association of Health Plans (AAHP). She says greater coordination among health-care providers also enhances accountability. "We've put in place the beginnings of quality measurement so that we can ensure significant improvements," she says.

Critics of managed care generally stop short of blaming it for an overall decline in the quality of health care. "For the most part, the studies have shown that the care is relatively the same," says Thomas Reardon, an Oregon physician and chairman of the AMA's Board of Trustees.

But the critics cite cases like Shea's to argue that managed-care plans have an incentive to skimp on care at the patient's expense. "There are pluses and minuses," says Adrienne Mitchem, legislative counsel for Consumers Union. "Some of the minuses are the overriding cost pressures. With traditional fee-for-service, you had the financial incentives to overtreat. With managed care, you have the financial incentives to undertreat."

Managed-care advocates indeed take credit for helping contain health-care cost increases — and now feel unjustly blamed for the difficulties that patients and providers face in adjusting to the changes.

"The public said to do something about health-care inflation, and we've been largely successful in doing that," says former Rep. Bill Gradison, R-Ohio, president of the Health Insurance Association of America (HIAA), which includes companies offering both managed care and fee-for-service insurance.

"Now, patients are saying, 'Hold on, we don't like the way you're doing it,' " Gradison continues. "The pace of change is bewilderingly fast and off-putting to a lot of people, and I mean not just the patients but the providers as well."

Gradison warns that new regulations "run the risk of increasing the cost of health plans and discouraging innovation." But critics say some changes are needed. "Managed care can do a lot of things well, but it needs to be regulated differently than we're now regulating it," says Lawrence Gostin, a health-law expert at Georgetown University Law Center.

The proposal with the greatest support in Congress is the Patient Access to Responsible Care Act (PARCA), sponsored in the House by Rep. Charlie Norwood, a Georgia Republican, and in the Senate by New York Republican Alfonse M. D'Amato. Norwood, a dentist, says he wants to "reverse what's going on in this country in health care."

"We've gone from patients having the right to choose their own doctors to patients being denied care and being denied the right to choose their own doctors to save money," Norwood says. "I don't oppose managed care, but I think there needs to be rules and regulations."

President Clinton also strongly endorsed managed-care reform in his State of the Union address on Jan. 27. "Medical decisions ought to be made by medical doctors, not insurance company accountants," Clinton said. The line drew bipartisan applause from lawmakers that continued as Clinton spelled out his proposal:

"I urge this Congress to reach across the aisle and write into law a consumer bill of rights that says this: 'You have the right to know all your medical options, not just the cheapest. You have the right to choose the doctor you want for the care you need. You have the right to emergency room care, wherever and whenever you need it. You have the right to keep your medical records confidential.' Now, traditional care or managed care, every American deserves quality care."

Clinton's plea covered the main parts of a "Patients' Bill of Rights" issued in November by a 34-member commission he created last March. But he made no specific reference to one of its most contentious recommendations: a proposal to give patients greater ability to contest decisions by health plans to deny coverage for medical treatment.

Earlier, the administration also proposed separate legislation aimed at protecting patients' medical information. The privacy issue has become increasingly worrisome as computers have become more capable of accessing the most personal information. But the administration's proposals were widely criticized as too weak — in particular for giving law enforcement agencies broad discretion to obtain medical records without a patient's consent *(see p. 44)*.

When Congress and state legislatures tackle managed-care reform this year, these are some of the questions likely to be considered:

### *Should managed-care health plans be required to make it easier for patients to see specialists outside the plan's network of physicians?*

The most visible difference between managed-care health plans and traditional fee-for-service insurance involves choosing a doctor and deciding when to seek treatment. Traditional insurance plans leave those choices to the patient; managed-care plans limit the patient's options.

Typically, a patient who enrolls in an HMO, like Patrick Shea, selects a "primary-care provider" from its network of doctors. That doctor then functions as a "gatekeeper" — overseeing the patient's health care and deciding when the patient needs to be referred to a specialist. [3]

The earliest group-health plans, in the 1920s and '30s, centralized medical decisions both to improve health care and lower costs. But since the federal government began promoting HMOs in the '70s, and later as for-profit managed-care plans came to dominate the industry, the emphasis increasingly has been on cost.

Critics, including patients, doctors and some outside observers, say the result has been to deny patients needed care in some cases. "Obviously, you can cut costs by cutting services," says George Annas, a professor of health law at Boston University, "but that wasn't the idea."

Managed-care health plans do take credit for helping hold down costs, but they insist that the quality of care has not suffered. "I don't know of many physicians who are devoted more to controlling costs than to care delivering," says AAHP President Ignagni.

Access to specialists is the most frequent source of friction between patients and health plans. Health plans control costs by limiting the number of specialists in the plan and the number of referrals to specialists outside the plan; they may pay their primary physicians in ways that create incentives to minimize the number of referrals. For patients, those incentives may create minor burdens — for example, a woman's need to get a referral for routine obstetric care — or more serious disputes.

Critics say the industry has been making it more difficult for health-plan subscribers to see specialists. "Managed-care plans are increasingly using payment systems that discourage providers from referring patients

## States Where Patients Get Special Treatment

**Specialist care** — *Thirty states make it easier for people in managed-care health plans to see certain specialists; all but Kentucky allow women either to designate an obstetrician-gynecologist as their primary-care provider or see an ob-gyn without a referral:*

*Alabama, Arkansas**, California, Colorado, Connecticut, Delaware, Florida**, Georgia***, Idaho, Illinois, Indiana, Kentucky****, Louisiana, Maine*****, Maryland, Minnesota, Missouri, Mississippi, Montana, Nevada, New Jersey, New Mexico, New York, North Carolina, Oregon, Rhode Island, Texas, Utah, Virginia and Washington*

**External review** — *Eleven states allow health-care patients to appeal coverage decisions to outside bodies:*

*Arizona, California, Connecticut, Florida, Minnesota, Missouri, New Jersey, Rhode Island, Texas, New Mexico and Vermont*

**Post-mastectomy care** — *Thirteen states require coverage of post-mastectomy inpatient care:*

*Arkansas, Connecticut, Florida, Illinois, Maine, Montana, New Jersey, New Mexico, New York, North Carolina, Oklahoma, Rhode Island and Texas*

**Gag-rule ban** — *Thirty-six states bar insurers from limiting doctors' communications with patients about treatment options:*

*Arkansas, California, Colorado, Connecticut, Delaware, Florida, Georgia, Idaho, Illinois, Indiana, Kansas, Maine, Maryland, Massachusetts, Minnesota, Missouri, Montana, Nebraska, Nevada, New Hampshire, New Jersey, New Mexico, New York, North Carolina, Ohio, Oklahoma, Oregon, Rhode Island, South Carolina, Tennessee, Texas, Utah, Vermont, Virginia, Washington and Wyoming*

** also covers optometrist or ophthalmologist; ** also covers chiropractor, podiatrist, dermatologist; *** also covers dermatologist; **** only covers chiropractor; ***** also covers nurse-practitioner, nurse-midwife*

*Sources: American Association of Health Plans, National Conference of State Legislatures.*

to specialized care," John Seffrin, president of the American Cancer Society and chairman of the National Health Council, told the president's patients' rights commission last year.

"For the patient, it is difficult to know what they need to do" to see a specialist, agrees Weinberg, the council's president.

Industry officials, however, say that managed care — with its "gatekeeper" physician and network of specialists — actually simplifies decisions for patients. "Unlike the old days, where you went to the phone book, now you have the ability to seek care through a network of professionals working together," Ignagni says.

Moreover, she points out that many plans in recent years have given consumers more options — for example, "point-of-service" (POS) plans that allow enrollees to see physicians outside the plan's network if they pay part of the cost through a higher deductible or a percentage of the fee. "We recognize that [a closed-plan HMO] doesn't meet the needs of all consumers," she says, "and that's why these other products have been developed."

Still, state and federal legislators are seeking ways to assure patients easier access to specialists. Some 30 states require health plans to give women the option of selecting an obstetrician as their primary-care provider. *(See table, at left.)* A number of states are considering bills to establish a procedure for a "standing referral" to a specialist for patients with chronic or life-threatening diseases or conditions. In Congress, Norwood's bill includes a similar provision.

Annas says health plans should be required to pay specialists whenever a subscriber must go outside the network. "I don't think that would happen very often," he says. "But it's not really a health plan if it doesn't offer the full range of medical services."

Norwood's bill, as well as some bills in the states, also includes a provision requiring health plans to offer a "point-of-service" option. Some critics say that would harm patients by undercutting the ability of HMOs to control costs and reduce premiums.

"The way HMOs keep costs down is by hiring physicians who practice conservatively" and don't order a lot of tests, says John Goodman, president of the National Center for Policy Analysis, a free-market think tank in Dallas. "You can lower your premiums by joining an HMO that employs doctors who practice conservative medicine. If you take away the HMO's ability to do that, you take away one of the options that people have."

For their part, industry officials argue against any regulatory requirements, saying that market forces will drive health plans to give patients more choices for getting to a doctor of their choice. "Many plans are moving in that direction," Gradison says. "The question is whether the law should require that in every case, and my answer would be no."

But Paul Starr, a professor of sociology at Princeton University and author of a well-regarded history of the medical profession, says the industry cannot be counted on to give patients adequate choices for health care.

"We need legislation because whatever they're doing today doesn't guarantee what they'll do tomorrow," says Starr, who was an adviser for President Clinton's unsuccessful national health-care initiative in 1993 and '94. "They can just as easily withdraw access as provide it."

***Should health plans be subject to medical malpractice liability?***

When Ron Henderson died in a Kaiser Permanente hospital in Dallas in 1995, his family sued the HMO and several of its doctors for not diagnosing his heart disease.

Kaiser denied any wrongdoing and depicted Henderson as an overweight smoker who had ignored doctors' instructions. But the family's lawyers turned up embarrassing evidence of Kaiser's efforts to control costs by limiting hospital admissions in cardiac cases. In December 1997, Kaiser settled the case for $5.3 million. [4]

Kaiser was subject to a malpractice suit because, unlike most HMOs, it directly employs the physicians and nurses in its clinics. Courts have held that HMOs that contract with individual doctors or medical groups are shielded from malpractice suits on the theory that the doctor rather than the health plan is actually providing the care. But a new Texas law seeks to erase that distinction. [5]

"I can see no reason why a private, very profitable enterprise ought not be held accountable for mistakes that are made when everybody else is," says Texas state Sen. David Sibley, a conservative Republican and oral surgeon.

The new Texas law, which took effect on Sept. 1, was strongly pushed by the state medical association but vigorously opposed by health insurers. Geoff Wurtzel, executive director of the Texas HMO Association, called the law "bad policy" and blamed its enactment on what he termed "medical politics."

"In 1995, the Legislature overwhelmingly agreed that the threat of being sued didn't produce a better standard of care," Wurtzel said, referring to a restrictive malpractice law passed that year. "But all of a sudden, if it was HMOs, liability was OK."

Texas is so far the only state to directly subject health plans to malpractice liability. But Missouri has opened the door to malpractice suits against HMOs by repealing a law that gave health plans a defense against malpractice. And Rhode Island and Washington last year created commissions to study the issue.

The Texas law is being challenged in federal court by the Aetna insurance company on the grounds that it is pre-empted by the federal law that governs employee benefits, including health insurance.

That law — known as ERISA, short for the Employee Retirement Income Security Act — is also now at the center of the legislative debate in Congress. Norwood's bill would provide that ERISA does not pre-empt state laws dealing with malpractice liability, as some federal courts have held. Those courts have held that health-plan subscribers who feel they were wrongly denied medical care can sue the plans only for reimbursement of the value of the care they did not receive. [6]

Norwood says there is no justification for shielding health plans from malpractice suits. "If you're a health-plan accountant or administrator and you want to make decisions about medical necessity," Norwood explains, "then you have to be responsible about those decisions in a court of law."

The AMA, a strong supporter of limiting medical malpractice suits in the past, supports the change. "When I make a decision, I as a physician accept accountability and liability," says Reardon. "When the plan makes a decision to provide or not to provide treatment, they should have the same responsibility and liability, especially when they're overriding a recommendation from the treating physician."

But the health insurance industry is adamantly opposed. "That's a perfect example of raising the costs of insurance with little, if any, discernible effect on the quality of the care," says the HIAA's Gradison. "It's a boon for the trial lawyers; I don't think it's a boon for the patients at all."

"All of the data suggest that consumers are not the beneficiaries of the current system," says AAHP President Ignagni. "We don't do families very much good if we provide them in the end with a situation that is designed to maybe provide compensation, maybe not, vs. trying to set up a situation that is built on quality improvement in which injuries don't occur in the first place."

One patients' group voices a similar interest in improving medical care without resorting to litigation. "We feel [litigation] is not necessarily the most productive way to resolve problems," says Weinberg of the National Health Council. Instead, Weinberg says her group favors strong complaint-resolution procedures, such as the use of ombudsmen.

Other consumer groups go further and call for some independent external review of treatment decisions. "When a

## The Downside to Managed Care

*A majority of Americans believe health maintenance organizations (HMOs) and other managed-care plans have had some adverse effects on health care, according to a 1997 survey. Overall, though, two-thirds of the respondents in managed care gave their plans an A or B, compared with three-fourths of the people with traditional health insurance coverage.*

**Percent of Americans who say HMOs and other managed-care plans have . . .**

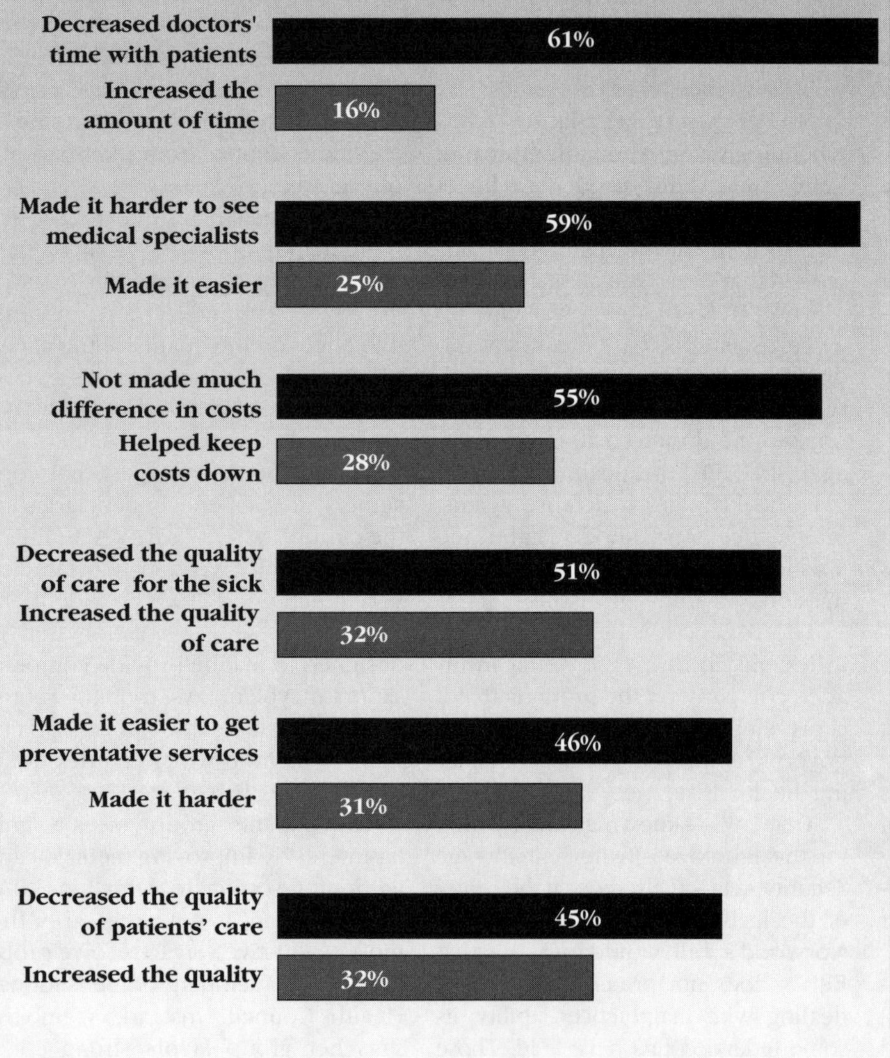


*Note: Percentages do not add up to 100 because "No effect" and "Don't know" responses are not shown.*

*Source: "Kaiser/Harvard National Survey of Americans' Views on Managed Care," November 1997.*

patient is denied coverage, it's ludicrous to think that they can appeal to the same system that denied them," says Mitchem of Consumers Union. But her group also favors malpractice liability for health insurers. "We want to ensure that there's some type of remedy that consumers can have access to," she says.

Health insurers are balking at any requirement for outside review procedures. "Some plans are doing this," Gradison says. "The question is whether it should be required by law."

Experts differ sharply on the potential effects of subjecting HMOs to malpractice liability. "If you apply tort liability to HMOs, you'll force them to do things that are not cost-effective," Goodman says. "You'll force them to waste money."

But Barry Furrow, a professor of health law at Widener University School of Law in Wilmington, Del., says that the threat of liability would result in better medical care by forcing managed-care administrators to focus more on quality than on costs. "You want to shift the competition more away from price and toward quality," Furrow says.

### *Are stronger safeguards needed to protect the privacy of patients' medical records and information?*

The Clinton administration unveiled its proposal to protect the privacy of patients' medical information after a media buildup that began with a speech at the National Press Club by Health and Human Services Secretary Donna E. Shalala in late July. "The way we protect the privacy of our medical records right now is erratic at best and dangerous at worst," Shalala said. When she presented the administration's proposal to the Senate Labor and Human Resources Committee on Sept. 11, Shalala declared: "With very few exceptions, health-care information about a consumer should be disclosed for health purposes and health purposes only." [7]

The administration won little praise for its proposal, however. Senators in both parties criticized the proposal at the hearing. Afterward, experts and interest groups said it left wide discretion for disclosing medical information to public-health and law enforcement officials without patients' consent.

"Would the administration proposal make things better or worse?" commented Denise Nagel, a Boston psychiatrist and executive director of the National Coalition for Patient Rights. "I think it would really make things worse." [8]

In fact, the administration's 81-page recommendation spends nearly 40 pages detailing and justifying exceptions to the general rule prohibiting disclosure of patient records without the patient's consent. The list includes exceptions to disclose information necessary for the patient's health care, for payment and for internal oversight of the patient's treatment. The recommendation also calls for permitting disclosure of individually identifiable information to public health authorities for "disease or injury reporting, public health surveillance or public health investigation or intervention."

Most controversially, the administration also said that law enforcement or intelligence agencies should be able to obtain such information, without a court order, if needed for "a legitimate law enforcement inquiry" or — in the case of intelligence agencies — if needed for "a lawful purpose."

Shalala disputed advance reports that the proposal broadened law enforcement access to patient information. [9] She said the provision simply restated existing law. But Sen. Tim Hutchinson, an Arkansas Republican, said the proposal gave patients less privacy than existing federal law for bank records, cable television and video store rentals. Sen. Patrick J. Leahy of Vermont, the committee's ranking Democrat, was also critical. "There is divided opinion in the administration," Leahy said, "and right now the anti-privacy forces are winning on the key issue of law enforcement access to medical records." [10]

"HHS completely dropped the ball" on the issue, says Georgetown's Gostin. "They made an unforgivable mistake."

Gostin also faulted the privacy recommendations from the president's commission, issued two months after Shalala's testimony on Capitol Hill. The report called for permitting disclosure of patient information for purposes of "provision of health care, payment of services, peer review, health promotion, disease management and quality assurance." It addressed law enforcement only obliquely, saying law enforcement agencies "should examine their existing policies to ensure that they access individually identifiable information only when absolutely necessary."

"Everybody's in favor of privacy," Gostin says. "But the devil's in the details, and these don't provide any details. It basically does nothing."

For their part, however, health industry and business groups saw the administration's proposals as unduly restrictive. "The industry is very concerned about interrupting the flow of health information," said Heidi Wagner Hayduk, a consultant on privacy issues for the Healthcare Leadership Council, a coalition of major insurers, hospitals and drug companies. Medical innovation would be "stifled," she warned, if health-care providers and researchers were required to obtain patient authorization "every time information changes hands." [11]

Health-care industry groups also said federal legislation should pre-empt any state laws setting stricter protections for patient privacy. The administration's proposal would leave state laws unaffected, as would a stricter bill introduced by Leahy. But Sen. Robert F. Bennett, a Utah Republican, has introduced a bill that would set a single federal standard on the issue.

The administration also has endorsed a separate privacy proposal affecting the health insurance industry: a bill to bar health insurance companies and managed-care plans from discriminating against people on the basis of their genetic make-up. [12] The proposal has been pushed by a number of bioethics and privacy-advocacy groups, which point to studies documenting instances of genetic discrimination by, among others, employers and insurers.

The genetic privacy bill has languished in Congress for several years. Clinton endorsed the measure in July. Last month, Vice President Al Gore announced the administration's support for also banning genetic discrimination in the workplace. [13]

The administration's medical-records privacy proposal drew additional criticism at a second Senate Labor Committee hearing on the issue on Oct. 28. Two medical groups, the AMA and the American Psychiatric Association, both called for stronger protection than the administration supported, while witnesses representing drug manufacturers and the American Hospital Association said the proposal went too far.

Such praise as the administration received for its proposal has been typically begrudging, at best. Boston University's Annas says the administration deserved credit for proposing a federal law guaranteeing patients the right to see their own records.

And Robert Gellman, a privacy consultant who led Shalala's outside advisers on the recommendations, stressed that the package would be "stronger than any comparable state law." [14] But both men also faulted the law enforcement provisions, among other exceptions. "The administration," Annas concludes, "has a long way to go." ■

# BACKGROUND

## Health Insurance

Health care became widely available to most Americans, and a financially secure profession for most doctors, only in the recent past. [15] Well into the 20th century, routine health care was a luxury available only to well-to-do Americans. And many doctors had only modest incomes, since they did not see enough patients often enough to have a lucrative practice.

Two 20th-century developments changed the face of health care in the United States: widespread private health insurance and government-funded medical programs. Together, the two developments produced the mythic image that forms the backdrop of today's debate over medical care. In that idealized vision, most Americans enjoyed the services of a family doctor, a Marcus Welby figure who gave skilled and compassionate care from birth to death with little concern about fees. And the government stepped in to provide care for those few who could not afford medical services. But the two developments also contained the germs of the cost problems that beset the health-care system today.

Private insurance entered the health field tentatively, limited at first to covering accidental injury and death. By the late 19th and early 20th centuries, however, many employers were providing limited medical care for their workers — motivated as much to reduce absenteeism caused by illnesses as to promote their employees' welfare.

The labor scarcities of World War II prompted some employers to begin offering health insurance as a benefit for workers. Labor unions, strengthened by New Deal legislation in the 1930s, included demands for health benefits in contract negotiations. And the postwar economic boom allowed major U.S. corporations to grant the demands.

Through the 1950s, more and more big corporations were including health benefits in union contracts; other employers followed suit. By the end of the decade, around two-thirds of the population at least had hospitalization insurance. [16]

The bill for these benefits was largely invisible. The expense was not a big cost item for employers, at least initially. For employees, the benefits were not taxed: In fact, the amounts did not even appear on pay stubs. As a result, many critics and observers contend, no one — neither business, labor, insurers nor health-care providers — had much incentive to watch the bottom line.

A second problem — access to care — was also somewhat obscured. With so many Americans sharing in the widened availability of health care, it was easy to overlook those who were not: the elderly, the poor and the uninsured.

## Government's Role

The government's initial moves to help provide health care were also tentative and limited. Some local governments began including medical benefits for the poor in general welfare programs in the early 20th century, and a New Deal program helped bring health care to some rural areas during the Depression. Throughout the century, progressives and labor interests called for compulsory national health insurance, but the efforts were blocked by business interests and, most important, the medical profession.

The two big federal health programs, Medicare and Medicaid, were enacted over the continuing opposition of the medical profession in the brief moment of liberal triumph in the 1960s. Congress had passed a limited bill to provide health insurance for the elderly poor in 1960, but the program proved to be unpopular. President Lyndon B. Johnson put the issue of health care for the elderly at the top of his Great Society agenda and pushed legislation through the overwhelmingly Democratic Congress in 1965.

As enacted, Medicare included the original idea of a contributory insurance program to cover hospitalization for the elderly (Part A) plus a similar plan for doctors' services (Part B). In addition, the legislation established the framework for Medicaid, the federal-state health-care program for the poor and the disabled.

Some doctors talked of boycotting Medicare, but they quickly realized that the program was — as Starr writes — "a bonanza," guaranteeing payment for medical services that many doctors had previously provided for free or for reduced fees. [17] Medicare and Medicaid closed the biggest gaps in health-care access, but liberals still said health care was too costly and favored broader national health insurance to ensure access for all.

Under President Richard M. Nixon, however, the federal government took a different approach in dealing with the intertwined issue of access and costs. It

# Chronology

## Before 1950

***Earliest forms of managed care are organized; employers begin to offer hospitalization insurance to workers.***

## 1960s

***Federal government establishes free health insurance for the elderly (Medicare) and a joint state-federal program to provide health care for low-income persons (Medicaid).***

## 1970s

***The Nixon administration backs the creation of health maintenance organizations (HMOs) to control health-care costs.***

***1973***
The Health Maintenance Organization Act provides funds and regulatory support for HMOs, but also includes some coverage mandates that slow their growth.

***1976***
Congress eases some regulations on HMOs; two years later, Congress votes increased funding.

## 1980s

***HMOs grow rapidly, gaining support from employers and consumers worried about spiraling increases in health-care costs.***

***1985***
Supreme Court rules that Employee Retirement Income Security Act (ERISA) supersedes state laws regulating private employers' health plans *(Massachusetts Mutual Life Insurance Co. v. Russell)*; some lower federal courts interpret decision as barring malpractice suits against managed-care plans.

## 1990s

***Backlash against managed care grows.***

***1993***
President Clinton proposes National Health Security Act, aimed at providing health insurance for all Americans; plan is assailed by business interests, medical lobby and Republicans.

***1994***
Clinton health-care plan dies in Congress.

***1995***
Many states pass laws requiring managed-care plans to allow women to designate ob-gyns as their primary-care provider.

***Aug. 21, 1996***
Clinton signs law making it easier for people to keep their health insurance when they lose or change jobs, start their own business or get sick; bill includes provision to facilitate sharing of patient information among health-care providers, but also requires government to develop privacy-protection guidelines by 1999.

***September 1996***
Congress responds to criticism of "drive-through deliveries" by requiring health insurance plans to cover at least 48 hours of hospital care for new mothers.

***May 1997***
Texas enacts legislation subjecting health maintenance organizations to medical malpractice liability; Aetna insurance company challenges law in federal court as pre-empted by ERISA.

***July 1997***
House and Senate conferees agree on provision in budget bill to bar Medicare-eligible HMOs from imposing "gag rules" on doctors by preventing them from discussing treatments or specialists that the plan would not pay for.

***Sept. 11, 1997***
Health and Human Services Secretary Donna E. Shalala presents medical-information privacy legislation to Congress; proposal is faulted by lawmakers, advocates and experts.

***October 1997***
Two House subcommittees hold hearings on Patient Access to Responsible Care Act sponsored by Rep. Charlie Norwood, R-Ga.

***Nov. 19, 1997***
Proposed "Patients' Bill of Rights" is issued by President Clinton's Advisory Commission on Consumer Protection and Quality in the Health Care Industry.

***January 1998***
Managed-care plans continued to grow in 1997 despite complaints about their services; coalition of health insurance and business lobbies announces plans for advertising campaign against managed-care reform legislation; Clinton urges Congress to pass consumer bill of rights.

## Are Elderly Americans 'Trapped' by Medicare?

Lawmakers and rival interest groups are clashing over the ability of senior citizens to see the physician of their choice outside the federal Medicare system. [1]

Conservatives want to get rid of a policy that largely prevents doctors and patients from arranging for Medicare-covered services outside the system's reimbursement scheme. They view the issue as a simple question of patients' rights.

"When you're sick, the federal government should not stand in the way of your getting the medical treatment you want," says Sen. Jon Kyl, an Arizona Republican who took up the issue after a constituent's complaint last year and forced a limited amendment to the law through Congress.

But the Clinton administration, Democratic lawmakers and the nation's largest senior citizens' group all argue that totally lifting the restriction would create the risk of gouging senior citizens and threaten the viability of the federal government's 33-year-old health insurance program for the elderly.

Seniors "would lose much of the financial protection that they are currently provided under Medicare" if the policy were eliminated, according to Rep. Pete Stark, a California Democrat and veteran legislator on health-care issues.

The dispute stems from a policy adopted by the Health Care Financing Administration (HCFA), the Health and Human Services agency that administers the Medicare program. For many years, the HCFA has prohibited doctors participating in the Medicare program from letting patients pay them out of their own pockets for services covered by Medicare.

Defenders of the policy say Medicare is acting just like any other insurer by requiring participating doctors to limit their fees to its schedule for reimbursements. Medicare reimbursements are sometimes markedly lower than prevailing fees for some services.

"Private payment would undermine the whole rationale for the Medicare fee schedule," says John Rother, legislative director of the American Association of Retired Persons (AARP). The 30-million-member organization strongly opposes lifting the ban.

Critics say the ban is bad for senior citizens and also bad for the Medicare program. They say it prevents senior citizens who can afford it from picking a particular doctor, for example, or from getting treatment without going through government red tape.

As for Medicare itself, these critics say that letting well-off seniors pay for some services themselves would strengthen the financially beleaguered insurance program. Supporters counter that lifting the ban would result in a two-tiered system — with one group of doctors for well-to-do seniors and another for Medicare patients.

Kyl won Senate passage on a party-line vote of an amendment to narrow the policy last summer as part of the Medicare reform provisions of the balanced-budget bill. [2] But the Clinton administration reportedly threatened to veto the entire bill over the issue. The result was a limited compromise that allows physicians to accept private payments for Medicare-covered services if they "opt out" of the Medicare program for two years. Critics say that few doctors could afford to drop out of the Medicare program.

A conservative senior citizens' organization is challenging that law in federal court in Washington. [3] United Seniors Association, a 60,000-member group founded in 1992, claims the law violates senior citizens' constitutional rights.

United Seniors President Sandra Butler says the new law makes health care less accessible for senior citizens. "Because seniors will be barred from contracting privately, many health- and life-saving services will be difficult for them to obtain, if they could obtain them at all," Butler says.

But Rother says few seniors agree. "I don't think I have a single letter in my file asking for the privilege of paying more for the services that Medicare already covers," he says. "This is not a patient-driven concern."

Medical groups are also divided on the issue. The American Medical Association (AMA) strongly supports Kyl's effort this year to repeal the restriction on private payments. "Medicare patients deserve the same rights as other patients to purchase health care directly from their physicians — without interference from the federal government," the AMA says.

But the American College of Physicians, which represents about 100,000 internists, opposes Kyl's bill. It says the measure "could threaten the viability of Medicare as an insurance program that offers accessible, affordable high-quality care."

[1] For background, see *USA Today*, Nov. 26, 1997, p. A6 and "Retiree Health Benefits," *The CQ Researcher*, Dec. 6, 1991, pp. 930-953.

[2] See *Congressional Quarterly Weekly Report*, June 28, 1997, p. 1529.

[3] The case is *United Seniors Association v. Shalala*, pending before U.S. District Judge Thomas F. Hogan.

backed a free-enterprise solution to the problems: a proposal being suggested by a physician-turned-health-care reformer in Minnesota that came to be called a "health maintenance organization," or HMO.

## Rise of Managed Care

Managed care had its origins in ideas pushed by socially conscious health-care reformers in the early 20th century. [18] In one form — known as cooperative or prepaid group health plans — consumers paid a modest annual fee to one or more doctors to cover their families' preventive and sick care. The medical profession opposed the idea, however, and succeeded in getting laws passed in many states to bar consumer-controlled cooperatives.

Then during World War II, California industrialist Henry J. Kaiser set up two prepaid group health plans for his company's employees, known as Permanente Foundations. Unlike the health-care cooperatives, Kaiser's plans flourished — and served as the forerunner for what is today the country's largest HMO, Kaiser Permanente.

The Nixon administration saw in HMOs an appealing alternative to the liberal-backed national health insurance plans. Administration officials were sold on the idea by Paul M. Ellwood, today regarded as the father of managed care. Ellwood, a Minneapolis physician, argued that the traditional fee-for-services system penalized health-care providers who returned patients to health. He met with the administration's key health policy-makers on Feb. 5, 1970, to make his case for organizations to provide members comprehensive care for prepaid amounts. At that meeting Ellwood coined the phrase "health maintenance organizations." [19]

Financial and regulatory help were needed to put the idea into effect. The administration initially found money to help launch HMOs beginning in 1970, without specific congressional authorization, even as it was asking Congress to pass a law to promote the plans. The law enacted three years later — the Health Maintenance Organization Act of 1973 — provided more money, $375 million over five years, for grants and loans to help start up HMOs. [20] More important, the law required all businesses with more than 25 employees to offer at least one HMO as an alternative to conventional insurance if one was available.

At the same time, though, the act established requirements that proved to be regulatory obstacles to the growth of HMOs. It required HMOs to offer not only basic hospitalization, physicians' services, emergency care and laboratory and diagnostic services but also mental health care, home health services and referral services for alcohol and drug abuse.

These requirements, combined with the government's delay in promulgating regulations to implement the law, stunted the growth of HMOs, according to Starr's account. At the same time, the medical profession viewed the idea with skepticism or hostility. But Congress eased some of the burdens in 1976, and then provided another shot of money in 1978: $164 million over three years. [21] By then, HMOs were starting to take off in the market. At the end of the decade, HMOs had enrolled 7.9 million members — double the figure in 1970. Still, the number represented only 4 percent of the population and — as of the early 1980s — was expected to grow only to 10 percent of the population by 1990. [22]

In fact, enrollment in HMOs more than tripled over the next decade, reaching about 25 million in 1990. Despite a decade of rapidly rising health-care costs, HMOs had to keep fees down and provide good service in order to attract customers. Most faced business losses, and some went bankrupt. But they were generally regarded as successful in containing cost increases, enough so that traditional fee-for-service health plans began copying some of their practices, such as utilization review, where insurers scrutinized doctors' fees and practices.

Meanwhile, the once comfortable relationship between patients and doctors had become badly frayed. The growth of specialized medicine had weakened the bond with the old-style family doctors — who now likely as not called themselves "internists." The rise in doctors' income created a distance between an increasingly well-to-do profession and its patient-customers. And the increase in malpractice litigation led many physicians to adopt "defensive-medicine" practices to guard against the threat.

## Managed-Care Backlash

The 1990s saw managed care reach a dominant position in the health insurance market. By 1993, most workers covered by employer-provided health insurance were enrolled in some form of managed care — either an HMO, a preferred provider organization (PPO) or a "point-of-service" (POS) plan. As of 1995, industry figures estimated a total of 150 million people nationwide were in a managed-care plan. Managed care was also credited with helping to bring down the rate of increase in health-care costs. But the decade also witnessed a growing backlash against managed care as many doctors chafed under cost-cutting pressures from HMO administrators, and many patients complained of delays in receiving — or outright denials of — needed medical care.

The consumer backlash against HMOs manifested itself most dramatically in court. A small number of HMO enrollees won whopping verdicts or settlements in suits claiming that their health plans had wrongfully denied or delayed necessary medical care. In California, the family of Helene Fox, who died of breast cancer after her HMO, Health Net, refused to pay for a bone marrow transplant, collected a $5 million settlement after a jury awarded her $89 million. In Georgia, Lamona and James Adams won a $45 million jury award in a suit that blamed Kaiser Permanente for the botched handling of a bacterial infection that forced doctors to amputate their infant son's arms and legs; the company later settled for an undisclosed sum. [23]

A mid-decade survey produced statistical evidence of the consumer dissatisfaction with HMOs, at least in comparison with traditional fee-for-service health plans. The survey, conducted for the Robert Wood Johnson Foundation by researchers at Harvard University and Louis Harris and Associates, found that significantly more HMO subscribers than fee-for-service plan subscribers complained about their medical care.

The complaints came only from small minorities: For example, 12 percent of HMO subscribers said their doctors provided incorrect or inappropriate medical care, compared with 5 percent of fee-for-service plan subscribers. Still, the higher levels of dissatisfaction with HMOs prompted a cautionary note from the survey's director. "Consumers need to be aware that all health plans don't treat you the same way when you are sick," said Robert Blendon, chairman of the department of health policy management at Harvard's School of Public Health. [24]

Health-care providers were also voicing dissatisfaction with managed care. In one incident, Massachusetts internist David Himmelstein attacked the HMO that he worked for, U.S. Healthcare, in an appearance on Phil Donahue's nationally syndicated television program in November 1995. Himmelstein charged that the company rewarded doctors for denying care and forbade them from discussing treatment options with patients. The company — later acquired by Aetna — responded by terminating its contact with Himmelstein just three days after the TV show. But it reinstated him in February 1996 after a storm of criticism and also modified its contracts to permit doctors to discuss payment methods with patients.

Himmelstein's comments reflected the concerns that many doctors and hospital administrators had about managed care. "This is all about cost, not improving patient care," a doctor told *Wall Street Journal* reporter George Anders in a 1994 interview. "You survive in managed care by denying or limiting care," William Speck, chief executive of Presbyterian Hospital in New York, told Anders in June 1995. "That's how you make money." [25]

As the complaints escalated, state and federal lawmakers took up the issues. By mid-decade, hundreds of bills were being introduced in state legislatures around the country. The earliest legislation dealt with specific problems — like allowing women to select an ob-gyn physician as their primary-care provider, or prohibiting health-care plans from imposing "gag clauses" on physicians. Congress in 1996 passed a provision requiring health insurance plans to cover at least 48 hours of hospital care for new mothers — prohibiting so-called "drive-through maternity stays." [26]

By 1997, more comprehensive reform packages were being put together, both in state capitals and in Washington. Health insurers opposed most of the proposals. But they also responded in the market — for example, by making access to specialists easier, though typically for an added cost. [27] In addition, managed-care administrators and advocates sought to take credit for the continuing progress in taming the health-care-cost-increase monster. In a study released last summer, the AAHP claimed that the lower costs due to managed care had allowed more than 3 million people to have health insurance than would have had coverage without managed care.

"By driving down health-care inflation, health plans have provided a safety net, assuring more families access to affordable, high-quality coverage," AAHP President Ignagni said. [28] ■

# CURRENT SITUATION

## Reform Efforts

The managed-care revolution that Kaiser started in California for his workers now provides health insurance for around 70 percent of the state's residents. Predictably, Californians have also led the backlash against managed care — first in the courts and, for the past three years, in the political arena. But regulatory proposals have failed at the polls or been vetoed by the state's Republican governor, Pete Wilson.

Today, the fate of efforts to rein in managed-care companies in California remains uncertain even after a special task force appointed by the governor and legislators spent eight months trying to develop a consensus package of regulatory changes for the industry.

The 30-member task force — representing health-care providers, insurers, patients' groups, consumers, business and labor — issued a report in early January recommending the creation of a new state agency to regulate HMOs and the enactment of some 60 changes in the way managed-care plans operate. [29] Among the major steps endorsed by the panel:

- An "unbiased, independent, third-party" review process for resolving HMO members' complaints involving denials of medical care.
- Mandatory, standardized procedures for resolving consumer complaints, including a member's right to appear in person at a grievance hearing.
- Collection and publication of detailed information on members' complaints.

• Standard descriptions of HMO products to facilitate comparison-shopping among plans.

Many outside observers described the task force's recommendations as fairly modest. In fact, it rejected the idea of subjecting managed-care companies to malpractice liability. Even so, a leading industry representative on the task force has stopped short of endorsing them, while a consumer representative on the panel believes enactment is not likely.

"The thing I would first ask the Legislature to do is to look at how the private sector has addressed the issue and decide whether the system is addressing the problem in a public-private partnership," says Ron Williams, president of Blue Cross of California. "In most situations," he adds, "I believe the market will suffice."

"The industry representatives have already said that this is too costly," says Jeanne Finberg, a senior attorney with Consumers Union and a task force member. As for Wilson, Finberg says, "He has an opportunity to embrace the package, but I'm not confident that he will."

Wilson, in fact, cited the task force's deliberations in deciding last summer to veto all but one of some 85 HMO reform bills passed by the Democratic-controlled Legislature during the year. Wilson called the bills "piecemeal" changes and said he wanted to wait for the task force's recommendations for comprehensive reform.

Wilson's decision — making an exception only for a bill to require 48-hour coverage for maternity stays — startled task force members and industry officials. Anthony Rodgers, a Los Angeles HMO executive, told the *Los Angeles Times* that Wilson had assured the task force it would not be used as "a graveyard" for legislation. [30]

The rejection of the legislatively approved changes marked the second defeat in two years for managed-care reform. In November 1996, Cali-

## Managed-Care Reforms Get Qualified Support

*Most Americans support several of the frequently mentioned proposals to make managed care more user-friendly. But their support drops when they are asked to consider potential consequences of the changes such as higher premiums.*

**Percentage of Americans who want health plans to . . .**

| | Favor | Oppose |
|---|---|---|
| **Provide more information about how health plans operate** | **92%** | **6%** |
| If higher premiums result | 58% | 34% |
| If the government gets too involved | 55% | 38% |
| If employers drop coverage | 54% | 43% |
| **Allow appeal to an independent reviewer** | **88%** | **9%** |
| If higher premiums result | 63% | 32% |
| If the government gets too involved | 51% | 41% |
| If employers drop coverage | 49% | 45% |
| **Allow a woman to see a gynecologist without a referral** | **82%** | **16%** |
| If higher premiums result | 63% | 34% |
| If the government gets too involved | 51% | 43% |
| If employers drop coverage | 48% | 47% |
| **Allow people to see a specialist without a referral** | **81%** | **18%** |
| If higher premiums result | 58% | 39% |
| If the government gets too involved | 47% | 48% |
| If employers drop coverage | 46% | 51% |
| **Pay for an emergency room visit without prior approval** | **79%** | **18%** |
| If higher premiums result | 62% | 33% |
| If the government gets too involved | 52% | 41% |
| If employers drop coverage | 48% | 47% |
| **Allow people to sue health plan directly** | **64%** | **31%** |
| If higher premiums result | 58% | 34% |
| If the government gets too involved | 55% | 38% |
| If employers drop coverage | 54% | 43% |

*Note: Percentages do not add up to 100 because all respondents did not answer.*

*Source: Kaiser/Harvard "National Survey of Americans' Views on Managed Care," January 1998.*

fornia voters decisively rejected two ballot initiatives that called for a variety of new regulations on HMOs, including the right to a second opinion when medical care is denied. Proposition 214 received about 42 percent of the vote, while Proposition 216, which included new fees on managed-care companies, garnered only 39 percent. [31]

The continuing divisions among task force members indicate the difficulty of getting any changes enacted. In transmitting the report to the governor and the Legislature, task force Chairman Alain Enthoven, a professor of business management at Stanford University, emphasized that the panel had not had time to assess the cost implications of its recommendations.

But Enthoven, widely regarded as the nation's leading expert on managed care, stressed that he "fully" supports the panel's recommendations, which he said "would lead to a greatly improved managed-health-care system in California."

For his part, Williams says he expects some legislation to pass this year, but he, too, faults the task force for failing to consider costs. He warns that some changes could drive up premiums and force small businesses to drop health insurance for their employees.

"We are essentially spending other people's money," Williams says. "Every change that costs one more cent in premiums has to come out of somebody's pocket."

But Finberg minimizes the potential cost increases and says the task force did not go far enough to protect consumers. As for the fate of the recommendations, she says Wilson holds the key.

"If it's not taken seriously by the governor," she says, "then I will have wasted a lot of time, and California consumers will have a lot to be angry with the governor about."

## Proposed Legislation

In his 15 years in Congress, Rep. John R. Kasich, R-Ohio, has been a leading spokesman for anti-Washington, anti-regulatory sentiment among House Republicans. But late last year, the powerful House Budget Committee chairman bluntly warned the managed-care industry that Congress will impose "comprehensive regulations" on the industry unless it takes "direct and responsible actions" to address consumers' complaints.

"Too often, cost control has been achieved at the expense of patients' legitimate interests," Kasich wrote in a Dec. 31 letter to Ignagni of the AAHP. He said the industry should "develop and implement" a code of ethics, allow doctors to be "the advocate" for the patient and make sure that health plans deliver "quality care" even while controlling costs. "Simply stated," Kasich concluded, "you must put the patient first." [32]

Kasich's letter exemplifies the surprisingly wide support that managed-care-reform proposals have attracted among conservative Republicans along with the more customary support for consumer-protection plans from Democratic lawmakers. Republicans are pushing the major reform bills in both chambers of Congress: Norwood's bill in the House and the companion measure introduced in the Senate by New York's D'Amato. Norwood's bill currently has 218 cosponsors, including 89 Republicans, 128 Democrats and one independent.

Norwood says he introduced the bill despite his aversion to federal regulation. "It turns my stomach to turn this over to the Labor Department," he said, referring to the agency that would have principal responsibility for implementing the bill's provisions. "But it makes me even more nervous not to do anything."

Among its major provisions, Norwood's bill would require health plans to give consumers an option to buy "point-of-service" coverage — allowing them to select their own doctor for an additional cost. It would also require adequate access to specialists and emergency care, require internal grievance procedures and subject managed-care companies to medical malpractice liability for negligent treatment decisions.

Despite professed support from a majority of the House, prospects for Norwood's bill are uncertain. The House Republican leadership is divided on the issue. In November, House Majority Whip Dick Armey of Texas wrote a strongly worded letter to GOP members urging opposition to the forthcoming recommendations from President Clinton's health-care commission. Even though Armey did not refer to Norwood's bill, he called for restricting rather than expanding medical malpractice liability and recommended medical savings accounts rather than regulatory changes to give consumers more health-care choices. [33]

For its part, the health insurance industry is gearing up for an all-out lobbying campaign to defeat Norwood's proposal or anything much like it. "It's our No. 1 issue," says HIAA's Gradison. "It's very bad public policy."

In a two-page lobbying flier, the AAHP warns that Norwood's bill would represent "the single, largest expansion of tort liability in memory," establish "federal price controls" and make it harder for families to get "affordable" health coverage. But Ignagni also hints at the possibility of supporting some legislative changes. "We intend to be very involved and will provide whatever information that we can," she says.

Democratic lawmakers have their own managed-care reform bills in both chambers, similar to the GOP-sponsored measures in thrust but different in detail. The main bill — introduced by Rep. John D. Dingell of Michigan and Sen. Edward M. Kennedy of Massachusetts — includes provisions aimed at ensuring access to specialists. Among its differences with

# At Issue:

## *Has the rise of managed care hurt patients' rights?*

**Adrienne Mitchem**
***Legislative counsel, Consumers Union***

**yes**

Americans are experiencing a true crisis in confidence in today's managed-care industry. Consumers' faith is shaken because of signs that managed care may be sacrificing quality health care to boost profits.

As managed care replaced the old fee-for-service system, the financial incentives driving the health-care industry have turned upside down. This revolution, replacing incentives to overtreat patients with incentives to undertreat, has provoked a strong backlash. Nearly three in five Americans in a recent poll believe managed-care plans make it harder for people who are sick to see a specialist.

But this revolution also creates an opportunity to reintroduce a simple and old-fashioned idea: consumer protection laws. Responding to grass-roots uprisings, states have passed laws giving consumers tools to help them be smart shoppers, ensure accountability when costly mistakes are made, provide more access to specialist and emergency care and guarantee a fair system to review patient disputes.

A presidential advisory commission has developed a "Consumer Bill of Rights," spurring a flurry of bill introductions on Capitol Hill and the promise of a healthy debate about nationwide reform. On one side is a multimillion-dollar scare campaign, funded by industry, designed to preserve the status quo. On the other, a coalition of consumer groups and individual Americans who have been burned by the current system and want change.

A scorecard of principles for reform from Consumers Union will help measure who wins:

- The linchpin for consumers is an appeals system that gives patients access to an independent entity to settle disputes over medically necessary care when benefits are denied, terminated or delayed. The current system, where the managed-care company serves as both judge and jury for every appeal, is stacked against patients.
- Another vital component is full disclosure. Plans should be required to provide consumers with information to help them understand all of their alternatives for treatment, not just the cheapest.
- Consumers also want assurance that they will not be holding the bag for medical mistakes. Families shouldn't shoulder the financial burdens of medical negligence because industry is unaccountable for its actions.
- Finally, a consumer bill of rights should set minimum standards for all managed-care plans. Voluntary provisions won't suffice. When you get sick, doctors, not accountants, should call the shots.

Congress can restore consumer confidence in the managed-care system by passing enforceable and loophole-free legislation that includes a fair review process, full disclosure and accountability. Anything less falls short of true reform.

**Karen Ignagni**
***President, American Association of Health Plans***

**no**

Health plans have advanced the cause of patients' rights with important patient protections that weren't available under the old system. Health-care practices and procedures have been made far more accountable — ensuring that the great majority of patients get the right care, at the right time and in the right setting — and appeals systems are in place to make sure that any patient who disagrees with a coverage or treatment decision has effective recourse.

Discussions of patients' rights should start with the fact that, from a patient's perspective, all other rights are meaningless without access to care. Under the old system, health care was being priced beyond reach. So one of the most important victories that health plans have won for patients' rights is to make health coverage more affordable for millions of working Americans.

Once assured of coverage, you should have the right to be protected against inappropriate care. Health plans promote quality care by emphasizing prevention and early diagnosis and monitoring practice patterns in order to do away with the wide variations in quality that did so much to make the old system not just costly but often downright dangerous. This commitment to accountability represents a major advance in patient protection.

But what if a conflict arises about what's covered or whether a particular treatment is in order? Despite critics' claims, disputes are rare and are usually resolved satisfactorily. Still, there's room for improvement — and health plans are participating in a nationwide initiative to continually improve care by identifying consumer concerns and developing patient-centered solutions. This, too, represents an unprecedented commitment to patients' rights.

Consumers should be wary of much that is being touted today as "consumer protection." For example, efforts to make health plans liable for individual practitioners' actions would simply clog the courts (at taxpayer expense) and enrich trial lawyers (not patients). At the same time, such efforts would adversely affect care by forcing health plans to act defensively, causing higher costs without producing better outcomes. Does that protect patients' rights? No — it just turns back the clock.

And we can't afford that. The health-care revolution that's in progress today was a necessary answer to the costly flaws of the old system. If the revolution has imperfections, the answer is to correct them — not to roll back progress or micromanage plans. Health plans are fully committed to making sure consumers are informed and their concerns met. That way, we can protect patients' rights without smothering innovative health care under layers of inflexible regulations and unproductive litigation.

## Estimated Costs of Reform Vary Widely

Two recent studies — one funded by an industry group, the other by a patient-consumer coalition — reached dramatically different conclusions about the likely cost impact of the leading managed-care reform proposal. But the industry's substantially higher estimate depends on interpretations of the bill, the Patient Access to Responsible Care Act (PARCA), that its sponsor says are wrong.

A report prepared for the insurance-business Health Benefits Coalition by the Washington consulting firm of Milliman & Robertson projected the bill would raise health insurance premiums by 23 percent. [1]

A study prepared for the Patient Access to Responsible Care Alliance — also known as PARCA — by Muse & Associates predicted a rate increase of between 0.7 to 2.6 percent. [2]

The reports made strikingly similar predictions about the effects of some provisions. Both reports, for example, predict little if any effect from provisions requiring emergency care coverage, easing referrals to specialists or giving consumers a choice between types of managed-care plans.

The industry-funded study, however, predicted substantially higher costs for three provisions in the bill:

- No payments to providers as an inducement to reduce or limit medically necessary services. Milliman & Robertson assumed the provision would prevent health plans from negotiating discount rates with providers and projected a 9.5 percent cost increase as a result. Muse & Associates noted that newly drafted report language specifically denied any intention to bar discounts; on that basis, it predicted no cost impact. Difference: 9.5 percent.
- Equal reimbursement for out-of-network providers. Milliman & Robertson say the provision could have no impact if interpreted to apply only to doctors' fees, but could raise premiums by 11 percent if it prevented point-of-service (POS) plans from requiring enrollees to pay a higher deductible for using an out-of-network provider. The firm then averaged the two figures to produce a "best estimate midpoint" of 5.5 percent. Muse & Associates says the bill would not bar higher deductibles for using a doctor outside the network. Difference: 5.5 percent.
- No discrimination against health professionals. Milliman & Robertson says the provision could require health plans to cover services of professionals not now covered, such as chiropractors or acupuncturists. Muse & Associates said new report language stipulates the bill will not have that effect. Difference: 5.5 percent.

In addition, the industry-funded study predicted that because of its projected increases, some customers would drop their coverage — raising rates still further for consumers still in plans. The consumer-funded study predicts a much smaller effect. Difference: 4.5 percent. [3]

The Muse study predicted only a slight increase from a provision subjecting group health plans to medical malpractice liability; the Milliman-Robertson study did not analyze the provision.

Milliman & Robertson qualified its study by stating that several of its projections "depend heavily on interpretation of PARCA." For its part, Muse & Associates noted that its study took account of legislative changes made after the Milliman & Robertson study was completed.

Rep. Charlie Norwood, R-Ga., the main sponsor of PARCA, says the industry-funded study is based on a misreading of his bill. "The assumptions made are neither reasonable nor honest," he says.

But the Health Benefits Coalition, the business group that released the study, is standing by its predictions. "We have other studies that show that mandates at the state level have raised rates," a spokeswoman says, "and we expect federal regulation to be even more costly."

[1] Milliman & Robertson Inc., "Actuarial Analysis of the Patient Access to Responsible Care Act (PARCA)," released Jan. 21, 1998.

[2] Muse & Associates, "The Health Premium Impact of H.R. 1415/S.644, the Patient Access to Responsible Care Act (PARCA)," Jan. 29, 1998.

[3] Milliman & Robertson says its individual cost estimates total more than its "composite" prediction of 23 percent because some PARCA provisions overlap.

Norwood-D'Amato is a provision — also included in the Clinton commission's recommendations — for external grievance-review procedures.

Clinton led a White House pep rally with House and Senate leaders on Jan. 14 to drum up support for the proposals — and take partisan credit for the issue. Health industry opponents will be "surprised at how many Republicans come over and join our side in this battle," Clinton said.

Norwood says the tone of the White House session could hurt his bill's prospects. "You need to be a little less partisan on this, a little less demagoguery," he says.

Procedurally, Norwood's bill went through the first of the legislative hurdles in October with hearings by the two subcommittees with jurisdiction over managed-care health plans — the Commerce Subcommittee on Health and the Environment and the House Education and the Workforce Subcommittee on Employer-Employee Relations. Today, he says he is optimistic that he can get the bill out of both committees after markups.

Norwood is also working on the House leadership. He says Armey assured him that the November memo was not intended to signal opposition to his bill. As for House Speaker Newt Gingrich, R.-Ga., Norwood says the two Georgians often talk about the issue when flying back to their home districts. Gingrich "clearly understands something has to be done with this," Norwood says. ■

# OUTLOOK

## Weighing the Costs

With Congress poised to start its new session, a coalition of health insurance and business lobbies unveiled plans in January for a $1 million-plus advertising campaign aimed at convincing the public that managed-care reform proposals will be bad medicine for patients. Their theme: Government mandates will drive up premiums and force some small businesses to drop health insurance coverage for their employees.

"The White House and some in Congress are proposing mandates that will drive up costs, forcing millions of Americans to lose their health insurance," one of the planned ads proclaims. The message appears alongside a picture of Dr. Frankenstein's monster: "Be careful how you play doctor," the ad warns in big type. "You might mandate a monster." [34]

The formation of the coalition by the two major health insurance groups, AAHP and HIAA, along with such big-business lobbies as the U.S. Chamber of Commerce, National Association of Manufacturers and National Federation of Independent Businesses, had been expected by opposing advocacy groups and by Norwood, the lead congressional sponsor of managed-care reform.

"This is pretty normal," he says. "The insurance companies stay in the background and try to push the Chamber of Commerce into the front. Yes, that will be formidable opposition. The problem is that they don't have the people on their side, and we do."

The coalition's Jan. 21 news conference came on the same day that a health policy study group released the results of a new public opinion poll that indicated widespread but conditional support for many of the provisions included in managed-care bills in Congress and in state legislatures. The survey by the Kaiser Family Foundation and Harvard University found substantial majorities in favor of such proposals as allowing people to appeal to an independent reviewer, to see a specialist or to sue health plans directly.

The survey also indicated, however, that public support for those ideas drops significantly if people are asked about the consequences forecast by opponents: higher premiums and reduced health insurance coverage. (*See poll, p. 51.*)

"Support may fall if the public comes to see [the proposals] as part of a larger government health-reform plan that could result in employers dropping coverage of higher health insurance premiums," Drew Altman, president of the Kaiser Family Foundation, told reporters.

Many of the major companies in the industry have been very profitable during the past decade, but last year some of the biggest — including Kaiser, Aetna and Oxford Health Plans Inc. — reported losses. [35] The pressure on the industry has eased somewhat because of the slowing pace of health-care inflation; the government estimates that health-care costs rose a modest 4.4 percent in 1996 — the lowest increase since the annual survey began in 1960. [36]

Even so, some insurers are starting to raise premiums now in anticipation

## FOR MORE INFORMATION

**American Association of Health Plans,** 1129 20th St., N.W., Suite 600, Washington, D.C. 20036; (202) 778-3200; www.aahp.org. The trade association represents health maintenance organizations (HMOs) and similar network health-care plans.

**American Medical Association,** 1101 Vermont Ave., N.W., 12th Floor, Washington, D.C. 20005; (202) 789-7400; www.ama-assn.org. The AMA, with 300,000 members, is the nation's largest physicians' group; it supports some managed-care reform proposals.

**Consumers Union,** 1666 Connecticut Ave., N.W., Suite 310, Washington, D.C. 20009; (202) 462-6262; www.consumersreport.org. Consumers Union, publisher of *Consumer Reports,* lobbies on health issues in Washington and in state capitals.

**Health Benefits Coalition,** 600 Maryland Ave., S.W., Washington, D.C. 20004; (202) 554-9000. The ad hoc coalition, comprising 31 business trade associations, opposes managed-care reform bills in Congress.

**Health Insurance Association of America,** 555 13th St., N.W., Suite 600E, Washington, D.C. 20004; (202) 824-1600; www.hiaa.org. This trade association represents 250 of the country's major for-profit health insurance carriers.

**Patient Access to Responsible Care Alliance,** 1111 14th St., N.W., Suite 1100, Washington, D.C. 20005; (202) 898-2400. The ad hoc coalition of 70 patient, provider and consumer-advocacy groups supports the major managed-care reform bill in Congress — the Patient Access to Responsible Care Act (PARCA).

of accelerating increases in health-care costs over the next few years.[37]

The cost debate will turn in part on which side manages to convince the public that it has "credible experts" on its side, according to Altman and Blendon. The debate has also produced the first set of dueling studies on the issue. *(See story, p. 54.)* One study prepared for the insurance-business coalition projected a 23 percent increase in health insurance premiums if the Norwood-D'Amato bill were enacted. But a rival study for the Patient Access to Responsible Care Alliance forecast a "slight increase" in managed care premiums of from 0.7 to 2.6 percent.[38]

"We're about to engage in the latest of our great wars of spin," Altman says. "The debate at this stage is very much up for grabs."

In Minnesota, however, Dianne Shea believes that the debate over patients' rights should not turn on costs. "This is the richest country in the world, and we're arguing about how to provide health care for everyone," she says. "Isn't it the right of every American to have health care?"

"We've come up with a solution to every problem in this country," Shea concludes. "I know we can come up with a way to provide good health care to people." ■

## Notes

[1] The American Association of Health Plans reported that nearly 150 million Americans belonged to managed-care plans at the end of 1995, the most recent year surveyed: 58.2 million in HMOs and 91 million in preferred provider organizations (PPOs). See "1995 AAHP HMO and PPO Trends Report." An annual survey of employer-provided health-benefit plans released last month shows that the percentage of employees enrolled in managed-care plans rose in 1996 and 1997. See Mercer/Foster Higgins's "National Survey of Employer-Sponsored Health Plans." In his State of the Union address on Jan. 27, President Clinton said that 160 million Americans are in managed-care plans today.

[2] The 8th U.S. Circuit Court of Appeals ruled on Feb. 26, 1997, in *Shea v. Esensten* that the suit could proceed. The court ruled that Shea could sue her HMO under the federal benefits protection law known as ERISA for failing to disclose its system for reimbursing doctors.

[3] For background, see "Managed Care," *The CQ Researcher*, April 12, 1996, pp. 313-336.

[4] See *The Dallas Morning News*, Dec. 23, 1997, p. 1C and *The Washington Post*, Dec. 20, 1997, p. D1.

[5] For background on the debate over medical malpractice litigation, see "Too Many Lawsuits," *The CQ Researcher*, May 22, 1992, pp. 433-456.

[6] For background, see Barry R. Furrow, "Managed Care Organizations and Patient Injury: Rethinking Liability," *Georgia Law Review*, Vol. 31, winter 1997, pp. 419-509, and Clark C. Havighurst, "Making Health Plans Accountable for the Quality of Care," *ibid.*, pp. 587-647.

[7] For background, see *Congressional Quarterly Weekly Report*, Nov. 1, 1997, pp. 2682-2684.

[8] PBS, "The NewsHour With Jim Lehrer," Sept. 16, 1997.

[9] See *The New York Times*, Sept. 10, 1997, p. A1.

[10] See *The New York Times*, Sept. 12, 1997, p. A24.

[11] PBS, "The NewsHour With Jim Lehrer," Sept. 16, 1997.

[12] For background, see "Medical Screening Raises Privacy Concerns," *The CQ Researcher*, Nov. 19, 1993, p. 1023. For opposing views on the issue, see *USA Today*, April 19, 1996, p. 13A.

[13] See *USA Today*, Jan. 20, 1998, p. 1A.

[14] Quoted in *The Washington Post*, Sept. 12, 1997, p. A1.

[15] Some background is drawn from Paul Starr, *The Social Transformation of American Medicine: The Rise of a Sovereign Profession and the Making of a Vast Industry* (1982).

[16] See *ibid.*, p. 334.

[17] *Ibid.*, pp. 369-370.

[18] Some of this material can also be found in "Managed Care," *The CQ Researcher*, April 12, 1996, pp. 324-327.

[19] Starr, *op. cit.*, p. 395.

[20] See 1973 *Congressional Quarterly Almanac*, pp. 499-507.

[21] See 1976 *Congressional Quarterly Almanac*, pp. 544-548, and 1978 *Congressional Quarterly Almanac*, pp. 576-580.

[22] Starr, *op. cit.*, p. 415.

[23] Details of the Fox and Adams case, along with citations to contemporaneous news accounts, can be found in George Anders, *Health Against Wealth: HMOs and the Breakdown of Medical Trust* (1996). Health Net had argued in the Fox case that the bone marrow transplant was not covered because it was an experimental procedure; Kaiser contended that it provided proper care in the Adams case.

[24] See "Sick People in Managed Care Have Difficulty Getting Services and Treatment," Robert Wood Johnson Foundation, June 28, 1995.

[25] Anders, *op. cit.*, pp. 42, 47.

[26] See 1996 *Congressional Quarterly Almanac*, pp. 10-85. The provision was included in the fiscal 1997 appropriations bill for the Veterans Administration, Department of Housing and Urban Development and other agencies. For a critical view of the impact of the law, see *Newsweek*, Aug. 4, 1997, p. 65.

[27] See *The New York Times*, Feb. 2, 1997, p. A1.

[28] Lewin Group, "Managed Care Savings for Employers and Households: 1990 through 2000," June 24, 1997.

[29] The task force's report can be found on its home page at http://www.chipp.cahwnet.gov/mctf. For background, see *Los Angeles Times*, Dec. 31, 1997, p. A1, and *The New York Times*, Jan. 6, 1998, p. A1.

[30] See *Los Angeles Times*, Aug. 6, 1997, p. A3; Aug. 7, 1997, p. A22.

[31] For background on the initiatives, see *Los Angeles Times*, Nov. 1, 1996, p. D1; Oct. 7, 1996, p. A1.

[32] Kasich's letter was first publicized in *Congress Daily*, Jan. 6, 1998.

[33] For background, see *Congressional Quarterly Weekly Report*, Nov. 22, 1997, pp. 2909-2911.

[34] See *The New York Times*, Jan. 22, 1998, p. A18, and *The Wall Street Journal*, Jan. 22, 1998, p. A20.

[35] See *The Wall Street Journal*, Dec. 22, 1997, p. A1 (Kaiser) and *The Washington Post*, Jan. 4, 1998 (Aetna, Oxford).

[36] *The Washington Post*, Jan. 13, 1998, p. A1. The figures are from the Health Care Financing Administration's National Health Statistics Group; *The Wall Street Journal*, reporting the same study, described the increase as "an inflation-adjusted 1.9 percent."

[37] See *The New York Times*, Jan. 11, 1998, p. A1.

[38] Milliman & Robertson, Inc., "Actuarial Analysis of the Patient Access to Responsible Care Act (PARCA)," released Jan. 21, 1998; Muse & Associates, "The Health Premium Impact of H.R. 1415/S.644, the Patient Access to Responsible Care Act (PARCA)," Jan. 29, 1998.

# Bibliography

## Selected Sources Used


### Books

**Anders, George, *Health Against Wealth: HMOs and the Breakdown of Medical Trust*, Houghton Mifflin, 1996.**
Anders, a reporter for *The Wall Street Journal*, provides a strongly written, critical account of the impact of health maintenance organizations on patients' rights. The book includes detailed source notes.

**Annas, George J., *The Rights of Patients: The Basic ACLU Guide to Patient Rights* [2d ed.], Humana Press, 1989.**
This American Civil Liberties Union handbook, updated in 1989, gives an overview of patients' rights in such areas as informed consent, medical records, privacy and confidentiality and medical malpractice. The book includes source notes and an eight-page list of organizations and other references. Annas is a professor of health law at Boston University's schools of medicine and public health.

**Goodman, John C., and Gerald L. Musgrave, *Patient Power: Solving America's Health Care Crisis*, Cato Institute, 1992.**
Goodman and Musgrave argue strongly that the country's health-care "crisis" calls for free-market solutions — reducing government regulation, diminishing the role of insurance and giving individual consumers and patients greater responsibility for paying for their health care. Goodman is president of the National Center for Policy Analysis, a free-market think tank in Dallas; Musgrave is president of Economics America Inc., a consulting firm in Ann Arbor, Mich.

**Patel, Kent, and Mark E. Rushefsky, *Health Care Policies and Policy in America*, M.E. Sharpe, 1995.**
The book gives an overview of contemporary health-care issues. It also includes a brief chronology (1798-1995) and a 23-page bibliography. Patel and Rushefsky are professors of political science at Southwest Missouri State University.

**Starr, Paul, *The Social Transformation of American Medicine: The Rise of a Sovereign Profession and the Making of a Vast Industry*, Basic Books, 1982.**
This widely praised study traces the history of the U.S. medical profession and health-care system from the 1700s through the birth and emerging growth of managed care in the 1970s and early '80s. Starr, a professor of sociology at Princeton University, has been an adviser to President Clinton on health-care policy. The book includes detailed source notes.

**White, Joseph, *Competing Solutions: American Health Care Proposals and International Experience*, Brookings Institution, 1995.**
White compares the U.S. health-care system with those in other countries, including Australia, Canada, France, Germany, Great Britain and Japan. He is a research associate in governmental studies at the Brookings Institution.

### Articles:

**Langdon, Steve, "Critics Want More 'Management' of Managed Care Industry," *Congressional Quarterly Weekly Report*, March 15, 1997, pp. 633-640.**
The article provides an overview of legislative developments on managed care at the start of the 105th Congress, along with summaries of major bills, legislative activity in selected states and a glossary.

### Reports and Studies

**Advisory Commission on Consumer Protection and Quality in the Health Care Industry, *Consumer Bill of Rights and Responsibilities: Report to the President of the United States*, November 1997.**
The 72-page report by the 34-member commission appointed by President Clinton contains recommendations dealing with such issues as choice of providers and health plans, complaints and appeals and confidentiality of health information. A list of references and selected readings are included.

**Computer Science and Telecommunications Board, National Research Council, *For the Record: Protecting Electronic Health Information*, National Academy Press, 1997.**
This book-length report details a scientific panel's findings and recommendations on protections for electronic health information. The book includes an 11-page bibliography as well as detailed source notes.

**Kaiser Family Foundation/Harvard University, "National Survey of Americans' Views on Managed Care," Nov. 5, 1997; "National Survey of Americans' Views on Consumer Protections in Managed Care," Jan. 21, 1998.**
The first survey found that majorities of the public are concerned about key aspects of managed health care. The second found majority support for many of the major reform proposals currently being debated, but support dropped when people were asked about potential consequences of changes, such as higher insurance premiums.

# 4 Reforming the FDA

RICHARD L. WORSNOP

The new drug was called thalidomide. Thousands of pregnant women in Europe who took the anti-nausea/sleeping medication in the late 1950s and early '60s gave birth to babies with flipperlike limbs and other deformities. But American women were spared. A skeptical U.S. government inspector refused to approve the drug for use in the United States.

Back then, Frances O. Kelsey helped win plaudits for the Food and Drug Administration. (*See story, p. 69.*) In recent years, however, the FDA's drug-approval process has not fared so well.

"Industry grouses that it over-regulates," *Fortune* noted. "Consumers complain that it under-protects. Victims of unsafe drugs and medical devices howl that it approves products willy-nilly, while AIDS activists agonize over its glacial testing procedures." [1]

Strictly from an economic standpoint, the spotlight on the FDA is understandable: Americans spend an extraordinary 25 cents of every U.S. consumer dollar on FDA-regulated products — chiefly drugs, medical devices, foods and cosmetics.

David A. Kessler, who recently stepped down as FDA chief to become dean of the Yale University Medical School, did much to focus intense scrutiny on FDA performance. During Kessler's controversial six-year tenure, his activism helped restore agency morale, but it also made the agency a lightning rod for anti-regulatory sentiment.

Because Kessler alienated many key figures in Congress and FDA-regulated industries, the appointment of a successor sharing his activist proclivities could provoke fierce opposition. Indeed, some lawmakers have vowed to block the confirmation of any nominee from the FDA.

Kessler himself received mixed reviews. "He made some good moves, and some not-so-good moves," says Louis Lasagna, dean of Tufts University's Sackler School of Biomedical Sciences. "He deserves a lot of credit for meeting the goals of the Prescription Drug User-Fee Act, which shortened the time required for approval of new-drug applications. That's a plus.

"Also, the role he played in bringing about mandatory nutrition labeling — secondary though his role was — made a lot of Americans feel grateful to him. However, I think his handling of the breast implant issue was a negative — probably the worst thing he did as commissioner." (*See story, p. 63.*)

It still may be too early to pass judgment on another hotly debated Kessler effort — his claim that the FDA had authority to regulate tobacco. A federal district judge in North Carolina recently upheld the agency's tobacco initiative. However, he rejected FDA proposals to control youth-oriented advertising and marketing of tobacco products (*see p. 72*).

Cynthia A. Pearson, executive director of the National Women's Health Network, applauds Kessler's decision to go after tobacco. "It shows that the FDA is not a pushover," she says. "It's willing to take on a tough issue and try to act in the best interests of the public. And that's what my group wants. The tobacco initiative was great for the FDA's future. It showed that they're keeping themselves alive as an important and respected consumer watchdog."

But Lasagna sees the tobacco initiative as "a burden that was needlessly assumed by the FDA" because cigarettes don't fit the standard drug profile. "Traditionally, drugs are [substances] that can harm you on occasion, but that also deliver good effects. I don't look on cigarettes as being in that category." Tobacco regulation, he believes, "will just distract the FDA from tasks I'd rather see it concentrate on."

Under legislation now pending in Congress, those tasks could include faster evaluation of new products, especially medical devices. Many of the proposals would require the FDA to allow experts employed by outside organizations to participate in the review process. But critics contend outside review would raise conflict-of-interest problems without necessarily saving the agency any time or money.

The FDA launched a pilot program last year to test the feasibility of using third parties to streamline agency reviews of medical devices. If successful, the program could be extended to drugs and food additives, both for humans and animals. The agency already has more than 40 advisory committees of outside experts that provide policy and technical assistance linked to product development and evaluation. The committees have no independent decision-making power, and their recommendations are not binding on the FDA.

From *The CQ Researcher,* June 6, 1997.

## Approval Time Dropped for New Drugs

*The FDA's average approval time for new drugs dropped by nearly half from 1987 to 1992, according to the General Accounting Office. **

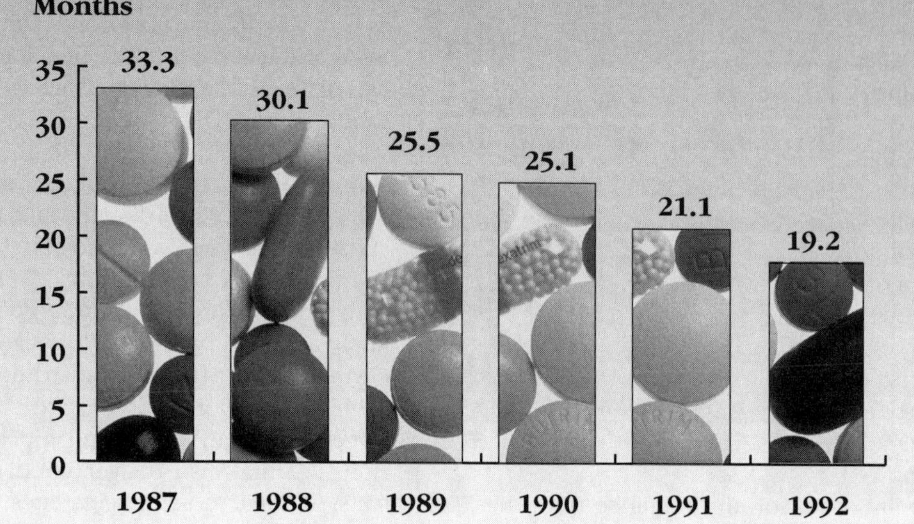


** Number of approved new drug applications: 1987 (80), 1988 (70), 1989 (65), 1990 (53), 1991 (64), 1992 (53).*

*Source: General Accounting Office, "FDA Drug Approval: Review Time Has Dropped in Recent Years," October 1995.*

Kessler urged lawmakers to go slowly before allowing third-party reviews, based on the agency's past performance.

"Unfortunately, too many of our critics justify the call for 'reform' based on how the FDA did its job in the 1980s, or earlier," he told a House subcommittee last year. "They have missed the substantial progress that the dedicated doctors, nurses, engineers, chemists, microbiologists, biostatisticians, nutritionists and others at the FDA have achieved over the past several years. . . . Those who fail to recognize the agency's performance and achievements threaten to undermine the real progress the agency has made." [2]

As debate on third-party review and other FDA-related issues continues, these are some of the questions being asked:

### *Does the FDA take too long to review drugs and medical devices?*

Industry critics contend the agency takes far too long to evaluate new products, thus blocking the public's access to advances in health care. The agency concedes that its performance in reviewing applications for medical devices needs upgrading. But it notes substantial reductions in the average time required to approve or disapprove new-drug applications in recent years.

Most observers credit the reductions to the Prescription Drug User-Fee Act of 1992 (PDUFA), which requires producers of brand-name pharmaceuticals to pay fees to the FDA to expedite federal safety and efficacy reviews. Under the law, which expires Sept. 30, companies must pay the FDA a fee for each drug submitted for evaluation. Moreover, companies making prescription drugs for which no generic copies are available must give the FDA an additional yearly fee.

But FDA argues that streamlining was well under way before PDUFA, a claim supported by a 1995 report by the General Accounting Office (GAO). "It took an average of 33 months for NDAs [new-drug applications] submitted in 1987 to be approved but only 19 months on average to approve NDAs submitted in 1992," the GAO found. [3]

The GAO also looked into claims by FDA critics that drug reviews conducted by Britain's Medicines Control Agency are equivalent in quality to the FDA's and performed more quickly. Although comparisons of the two regulatory bodies were hard to make, the GAO stated, "overall approval times are actually somewhat longer in the United Kingdom than they are in this country." [4]

Kessler and four FDA colleagues came to similar conclusions in a study published last December focusing on four major drug-manufacturing countries — the United States, Britain, Germany and Japan. The study examined marketing approval dates for 214 drugs that entered the world market between January 1990 and December 1994.*

* The four countries account for 60 percent of worldwide pharmaceutical sales.

The study contends "that no single country gets all drugs [approved] first, but that the United States and Great Britain have similar patterns of availability and that the United States is faster than either Germany or Japan in approving 'global' drugs — those important enough ultimately to be approved in more than one of the countries under study." [5] (*See graphs, p. 64.*)

"The results of FDA efforts to speed drug development and availability are most dramatically apparent for priority drugs," the study added. "The United States approved the first major antiviral drug available for use against HIV at the same time as Great Britain and approved all seven other anti-HIV drugs well ahead of every country in the world." [6]

The study went on to note that, "None of these accomplishments would be impressive if the FDA were not ensuring that approved drugs are safe and effective. Keeping products whose benefits do not outweigh their risks off the market is as important as ensuring that the U.S. public have access to significant therapies." [7]

Lasagna is less impressed with the FDA's record on reducing drug-approval times than Kessler. "While it's true that, on average, the U.S. patient is about as likely as the British patient to get useful new drugs," Lasagna says, "that means we're ahead of the British half of the time and the British are ahead of us the rest of the time. So we haven't completely solved the drug lag, as far as I'm concerned."

Lasagna also wishes Kessler had devoted more time as FDA commissioner "to what, if anything, the agency can do to cut the long period between drug discovery and drug approval. It's true that the time for handling new-drug applications has been shortened. But as far as the pharmaceutical industry is concerned, or patients are concerned, the important thing is how long it takes from discovery to getting the drug on the market."

FDA

*An FDA investigator inspects an ice cream-manufacturing plant during an on-site visit, required at least once every two years.*

Lasagna adds that "it's not at all clear to anybody, including me, how much of that time lag is due to unreasonable FDA requirements or unreasonable judgments on the part of FDA staff. But somebody ought to be looking into what could be fixed to make drugs available more quickly and at less expense to the sponsors."

Experts generally agree that medical-device manufacturers have more reason for complaining about FDA review, especially compared with reviews by the 15-country European Union (EU). "The U.S. and EU medical-device regulatory systems share the goal of protecting public health, but the EU system has the additional goal of facilitating EU-wide trade," GAO noted in a report issued last year. "Another distinction between the two systems pertains to the criteria for reviewing devices. Devices marketed in the EU are reviewed for safety and performing as the manufacturer intended; devices marketed in the United States are reviewed for safety and effectiveness. Effectiveness includes the additional standard of providing benefit to patients." [8]

The proof-of-efficacy requirement means that the FDA has more testing before passing judgment on a particular device. Consequently, review times are considerably longer than in the EU. Indeed, a study issued last year by the Health Industry Manufacturers Association (HIMA) found that higher-risk, breakthrough medical devices were approved in Europe up to three times as fast as in the U.S. [9] (*See graphs, p. 62.*)

As a result, U.S. device makers increasingly are shifting their operations to Europe. "This is an industry in which 98 percent of the manufacturers employ less than 500 people, and many are leaving the industry or moving production overseas because of the regulatory system in the United States," said Stephen L. Ferguson, CEO of the Cook Group Inc., a major

## U.S. Lags on Medical Device Approvals

*New medical devices are approved in Europe up to three times faster than in the United States, according to a study released by the Health Industry Manufacturers Association.*

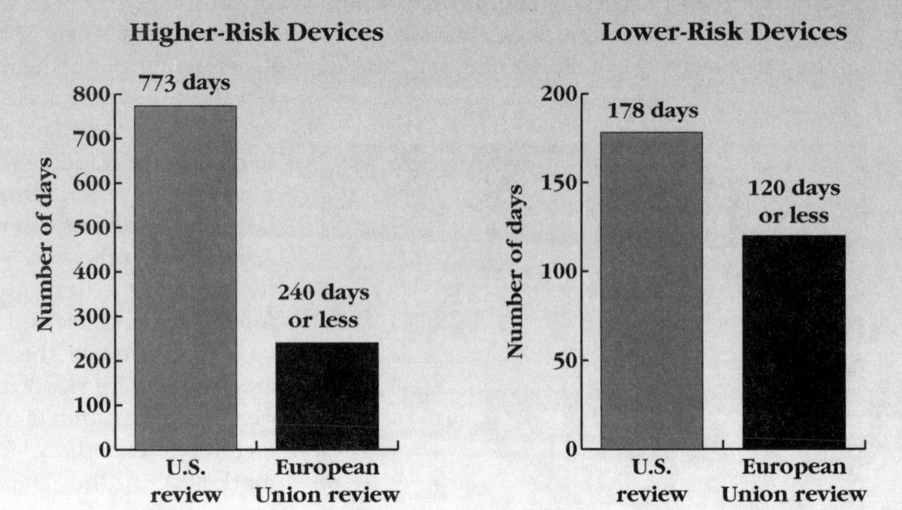


*Source: Medical Technology Consultants Europe Ltd./Health Industry Manufacturers Association, February 1996.*

U.S. medical-device company. "Many small, innovative companies cannot withstand the long waiting periods with attendant costs and the lack of predictability that result from the regulatory process in the United States. As they go out of business, Americans are losing the benefits of new technologies that come from their creativity." [10]

According to Jeffrey J. Kimbell, executive director of the Medical Device Manufacturers Association (MDMA), the ongoing trend "creates a really scary scenario for the future of the device industry in the United States. First of all, our companies are introducing their most innovative products in Europe. Affluent Americans can go there to make use of these state-of-the-art technologies, but Medicare and Medicaid patients won't have access to them."

However, a survey conducted last fall by *Medical Device & Diagnostic Industry,* a trade journal, indicated that industry executives are bullish about current and future marketing prospects. Editor John Bethune cited "the impact of FDA's internal reforms and review-time improvements" as a key factor. "The agency has not only reduced the product approval delays that slowed new product introductions, but perhaps more importantly, has also 'greatly reduced both executives' and investors' uncertainty about the timeliness of future product introductions."

Bruce Burlington, director of the FDA's Center for Devices and Radiological Health, credits improvements in the agency's medical-device review times to an internal program that is called "process improvement." He defines it as an attempt to make medical-device evaluation "accommodate budget reality and position us to do the right job for consumers, health professionals and the device industry. Process improvement is something we need to build into our way of doing business for the indefinite future." [11]

### *Should medical-device and generic-drug companies pay "user fees" to the FDA?*

Since PDUFA slashed the average time taken by the FDA to review applications for new brand-name drugs, some public-health activists have suggested that user fees also could expedite the processing of applications for generic drugs, as well as medical devices.

Broadening PDUFA to cover generics would be "a natural extension of this successful legislation," argues the Patients' Coalition, a national network of more than 100 patient and consumer-advocacy groups. In addition, the coalition noted, "Many concerns voiced by the medical device industry regarding FDA performance would be resolved through the implementation of a similar [user-fee] program for medical devices." [12]

The generic-drug and medical-device industries, however, are not interested. "We don't want to be part of PDUFA," says Diane E. Dorman, vice president for public affairs at the Generic Pharmaceutical Industry Association. "That's strictly a brand-name thing. What we're fighting for is full [congressional] funding for FDA's Office of Generic Drugs [OGD]. That's our biggest concern right now."

Kimbell of MDMA also is cool to the user-fee idea. "Drugs and medical devices are very, very different in terms of both average company size

# David Kessler's Wild Ride at FDA

David A. Kessler, who recently stepped down after six years as commissioner of the U.S. Food and Drug Administration (FDA), was unusually qualified for the job. He is both a doctor and a lawyer. Indeed after graduating from Amherst College in 1973, Kessler studied at Harvard Medical School for two years, and then at the University of Chicago Law School for two years. He completed his third year of both law and medical school simultaneously at Harvard. He later worked on food and drug legislation for Sen. Orrin G. Hatch, R-Utah, chairman of the Senate Labor and Human Resources Committee.

This background gave Kessler insights into Americans' ambivalent feelings about government regulation in general — and by the FDA in particular. "Ask whether government should get off the backs of business, get out of our lives, and the answer is a resounding yes," he told an interviewer. "Then ask whether government has a role to play in protecting the food supply and the blood supply, and you get a resounding yes. That's the American way." [1]

Scott Ferrell

Former FDA Commissioner David A. Kessler

Kessler took command of the FDA at a low point in the agency's history. In November 1989, Commissioner Frank Young had resigned during a scandal in which generic-drug manufacturers were found to have tampered with test results and to have bribed FDA employees to expedite drug approvals. Five agency officials were convicted of bribery as a result.

In April 1991, after just two months on the job, Kessler ordered U.S. marshals to seize 24,000 gallons of Citrus Hill Fresh Choice orange juice from a warehouse outside Minneapolis. Kessler said he acted because Procter & Gamble, the producer of Citrus Hill, had labeled the juice "fresh" even though it was made from concentrate. Within days, he also forced the maker of Ragu tomato sauce to remove the word "fresh" from its label because it was heat-processed.

Kessler's hard-nosed approach to food labeling set the tone for his stewardship of the FDA. In June 1991, for example, he launched a crackdown on drug companies that promote and advertise their products for non-approved uses — a practice known as "off-label" marketing. After a drug wins FDA approval, doctors may prescribe it for any purpose. But drug companies may promote it solely for the use sanctioned by the FDA.

In this connection, it should be noted that the FDA's initial decisions on drug use are open to revision. Last November, for instance, the agency said Prozac, the world's top-selling antidepressant, also could be used to treat the eating disorder bulimia. The decision allowed Eli Lilly Co. to advertise Prozac for that purpose.

The most common complaint against the FDA, whether under Kessler or his predecessors, is that it takes too long to process applications for promising new drugs. But the agency blunted some of that criticism early in Kessler's tenure by giving conditional approval to experimental drugs for Alzheimer's disease and AIDS. Manufacturers of the drugs were required to continue research on their effectiveness.

Occasionally, the FDA is accused of acting prematurely. In January 1992, for example, critics claim the agency acted too quickly in calling for a voluntary moratorium on the use of silicone breast implants. The FDA acted, officials said, because of evidence that the implants were linked to immune-system and connective-tissue disorders. But the agency lifted the moratorium three months later, saying limited use of the devices would be permitted for women who agreed to take part in clinical studies on their safety. The action echoed an earlier recommendation by an agency advisory panel.

Asked last December about the FDA's flip-flop on breast implants, Kessler noted that they "were one of the devices that came to market before the Medical Devices Act of 1976" made them subject to federal regulation. As a result of studies conducted since then, "We now know that although the implant may cause local pain, swelling or deformity, the patient is not at significant risk for systemic tissue disease." [2]

Kessler leaves the FDA without regrets. "The one thing I discovered about Washington is that while it's important to serve, it's also important to leave. I didn't want to spend my entire career within the Beltway." [3]

In a sense, Kessler added, his new post is a continuation of his former one. "At the FDA, we were only as good as the applications that came into the agency. Medical schools like Yale are where the real work gets done. Over the next 10 to 15 years, we'll see staggering advances in medical knowledge. We will know more in the next 10 years about human biology than we learned in decades — and that knowledge will result in new therapies that will help people." [4]

---

[1] Quoted by Jeffrey Goldberg, "Next Target: Nicotine," *The New York Times Magazine*, Aug. 4, 1996, p. 25.

[2] Quoted in "FDA Commissioner Sees No Special Deal Ahead for Tobacco Companies," *Barron's*, Dec. 30, 1996, p. 29 (interview with David A. Kessler).

[3] Quoted by Katherine S. Mangan, "Controversial FDA Chief Moves to Yale," *The Chronicle of Higher Education*, May 2, 1997, p. A9.

[4] *Loc. cit.*

## U.S. Approved More New Drugs First, 1990-1994

*The United States outpaced three big foreign drug producers in approving major, new drugs from 1990-1994.* Compared with Germany, for example, the U.S. was first to approve 31 of the 44 new drugs available to both countries, while 13 new drugs were available first in Germany.*

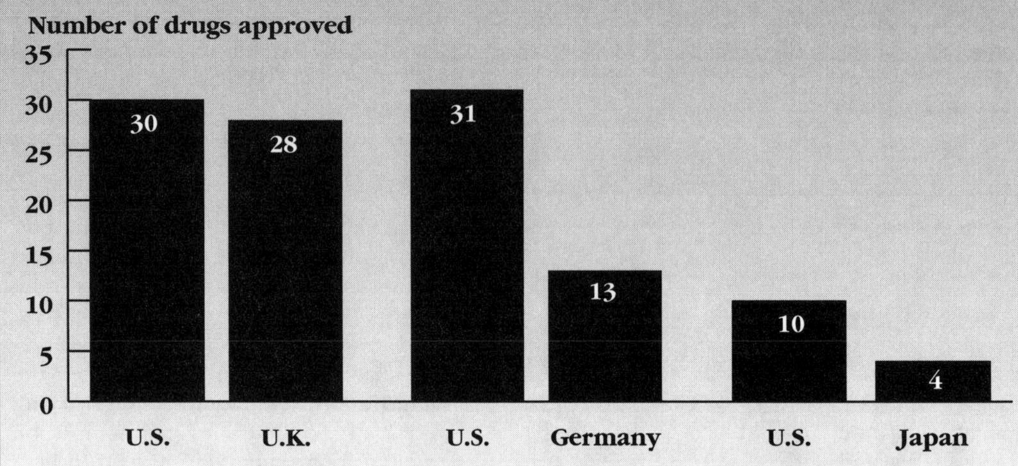


** A total of 214 new drugs were newly introduced to world markets from 1990-1994.*

*Source: David A. Kessler, et al., "Approval of New Drugs in the United States,"* The Journal of the American Medical Association, *Dec. 11, 1996.*

and the nature of the product," he says. "Eighty percent of the companies in our industry have fewer than 50 employees. They are entrepreneurial, innovative firms with a few product lines and a few million dollars in annual sales. The drug industry, on the other hand, is mainly composed of multinational, multibillion-dollar corporations. Those corporations can easily afford user fees, but most of our members can't."

Moreover, Kimbell notes, a manufacturer that wins FDA approval of a new brand-name drug receives a patent giving it 17 years of exclusive marketing rights. During that period, the makeup of the drug never changes.

"But with medical devices," he says, "as soon as a company gets FDA approval for a new or improved device, it may start tinkering with the technology with a view to improving it still further — something as simple as shortening the length of a syringe needle."

These kinds of improvements can put device manufacturers at a disadvantage, Kimbell says: "Under any user-fee proposal, device makers would have to pay additional money to the government every time they sought FDA approval of a product that was modified even slightly." The marketing life of a typical medical device, industry officials say, is only two to three years.

Pearson of the Women's Health Network says she understands why generic-drug and medical-device companies oppose user fees, but she still feels "consumers would benefit" from such an arrangement. "It works on the pharmaceutical side, so why not give it a try on the device side?" she reasons. The women's network wants new medical products to "go to market every bit as quickly as the industry does. We want FDA to have enough funding to do a thorough job and not miss anything they should have found during the review process."

Opinion within the generic-drug and device industries on user fees is by no means monolithic. "It's essentially a big business vs. small business issue," Kimbell says. "There are some multinational, multibillion-dollar medical-device companies that might actually welcome user fees." That's because a fee system "would eliminate a lot of the ankle-biters that are eating away at their market share in each particular product area."

Similarly, generic-drug producers also might accede to user fees under certain conditions, says Bruce Downey, president and CEO of Barr Laboratories, in Pomona, N.Y.

"Ultimately, to be embraced by the generic pharmaceutical industry, any user-fee proposal would have to be based on two essential assumptions," Downey told a House subcommittee in April. "First, the [Office of Generic Drugs] budget would have to be fully funded, and the FDA would have to provide services that meet all statutory requirements.

"Second, user fees would have to be clearly tied to some incremental improvements in timeliness of the review and approval process, such as making available additional or higher-

## The Drug-Approval Process

Drugs go through a painstaking approval process before reaching American consumers.

When a company develops a new drug, it first conducts "preclinical testing," during which the compound is given to animals to determine whether it would be safe for human consumption. If the tests are successful, the company drafts a plan for clinical trials on humans, known as a protocol.

**Preapproval process** — With animal test data and its protocol in hand, the company files an investigational New Drug Application with the FDA. If the agency accepts both the test results and the protocol, the company conducts a three-phase clinical trial.

During the first phase, the drug is tested on 20-80 healthy volunteers to determine its safety, dosage range and how it is absorbed, metabolized, distributed and excreted by the body.

The second phase uses 100-300 volunteers afflicted with the disease targeted by the proposed drug. The aim is to evaluate effectiveness and monitor side effects.

The third phase is similar, but involves some 1,000-3,000 patients in clinics and hospitals. Doctors try to verify effectiveness and track reactions to long-term use. The developmental and preapproval stages typically last six or more years.

**Approval process** — After the third phase, the drug company assembles its data and presents its case to the agency in a New Drug Application, asserting that the new product is both safe and at least as effective as comparable drugs already on the market.

The FDA is required by law to review new drug applications within six months, but usually takes much longer. If the application is approved, the drug goes to market and the agency continues to monitor it.

Adapted from Steve Langdon, "Drug Approval Process," *CQ Weekly Report*, Jan. 27, 1996, p. 224.

level reviewers or statisticians for particularly complex applications. In this way, additional fees would provide clearly defined benefits for the generic industry, in the same way that PDUFA benefits the brand companies, rather than simply replacing appropriations from previous years." [13]

### *Should the FDA turn to third parties for review of new-product applications?*

One of the most hotly debated FDA reform issues is product review by third parties — standard practice in much of Europe. FDA-regulated industries argue that outside experts could accelerate the review process without sacrificing thoroughness or integrity. FDA officials tend to be skeptical, mainly citing the potential for conflicts of interest.

But the "monopolized and centralized" review system in place now is hopelessly overburdened, the MDMA's Kimbell argues. "Essentially, Congress has asked FDA to do the impossible — maintain the best expertise in every product area in the medical device field," he says. "It's absolutely impossible for any institution in the world to do that."

Instead, he contends, companies should have the option of submitting their product-approval applications to a "leading, independent, scientific review organization," possibly based at a top-flight university. The FDA itself would accredit those institutions and prescribe conflict-of-interest safeguards, Kimbell says, adding that violations could bring loss of accreditation.

In congressional testimony last year, Kessler said he found third-party review "problematic for a number of reasons." For instance, "FDA's reviewers have extensive knowledge about all of the similar products that are made by different companies around the country. When a reviewer looks at all of the drugs for arthritis and other inflammatory diseases, or all of the heart valves, what that reviewer learns . . . increases his/her understanding of that group of drugs or devices and their effect on the body. As a result, FDA reviewers see problems that [independent] reviewers with less information might not see."

Kessler also addressed the conflict-of-interest issue. "[B]ecause there is a risk that only third parties that err on the side of approving applications and petitions will succeed in this market, there is a risk that the incentive will be for third parties to approve applications and petitions — not to critically review them." [14]

Advocates of third-party review claim it would be more economical than the present system. For instance, the National Electrical Manufacturers Association says it "will result in a competitive framework for the review of new-product submittals, thus leading to greater efficiency in the product-review process and a reallocation of FDA resources to focus on those products most likely to pose the greatest risk to the public safety and health." [15]

Pearson, for one, dismisses the association's argument. "There is no proof that third-party review is more timely or cost-efficient or even feasible," she told lawmakers in April. "Indeed, this system could well prove more expensive, slower and less safe. Additionally, even if direct conflict of financial interest is prohibited, indirect conflicts may be equally detrimental. Many universities or their staffs, who could serve as third-party reviewers, have significant financial and academic links to industry. Will such parties be willing to act independently and potentially risk losing a source of significant funds?" [16]

Gordon M. Binder, chairman and CEO of Amgen Inc., a biotechnology firm in Thousand Oaks, Calif., says that third-party testing actually is widespread, if not widely acknowledged. "For example, Amgen's toxicology studies for . . . Epogen and Neupogen were primarily conducted in Japan," he told lawmakers in 1996. "These products were approved in Europe and here in the United States by the FDA based in part upon these third-party toxicology studies. Furthermore, every clinical trial in the United States is conducted by third parties in collaboration with the sponsor and FDA."

Binder emphasized, however, that third-party involvement occurs before submission of a product-review application to the FDA. "The third parties have no authority to approve a drug or device, and no one in industry is suggesting they should have such authority." [17]

Carl B. Feldbaum, president of the Biotechnology Industry Organization, believes that the FDA now would accept third-party review in cases where it lacked in-house expertise — provided it retained the power of final approval.

"Judging from our talks late last year and early this year," he says, "I think there's consensus between FDA and industry that third-party review should be in place without any further ado. There doesn't seem to be any disagreement at all on that." ■

# BACKGROUND

## 'Embalmed Beef'

Food regulation in the United States dates from 1785, when Massachusetts approved the nation's first food-adulteration law. More than a half-century later, in 1848, Congress passed the Drug Importation Act, requiring U.S. Customs inspectors to block the entry of adulterated drugs from overseas.

Some historians date the birth of modern U.S. food and drug regulation to President Abraham Lincoln's naming of Charles M. Wetherill to head a Division of Chemistry in the new Department of Agriculture in 1862. The appointment eventually led to the formation of the department's Bureau of Chemistry, which was the forerunner of the FDA.

A bill introduced in 1879 by Rep. Hendrick Bradley Wright, D-Pa., was the first to seek federal regulation of the entire field of food and drugs. The measure was never reported out of committee, however. Indeed, only eight of approximately 190 bills proposing to regulate specific commodities were passed by Congress between 1879 and 1906. Among them was a law requiring inspection of meat intended for export and barring the importation of adulterated food and beverages. Other commodities subjected to some degree of federal control during this period included glucose, cheese, canned fish and baking powder.

Before 1900, proposals for federal regulation of food and drugs were widely dismissed as unnecessary. Moreover, Southern Democrats in Congress charged that such measures intruded on the autonomy of the states. Not surprisingly, manufacturers of the targeted products also were strongly opposed.

In the 19th century, families generally grew their own produce, chemicals were little used in foodstuffs and the effects of bacteria and common chemicals on human health were only dimly understood. It was assumed that consumers were capable of detecting filth, impurities, poisonous ingredients and other adulterants in food and medicines without government intervention.

However, popular opinion began to shift around the turn of the century. U.S. soldiers in the Spanish-American War claimed that the canned meat issued to them was "embalmed beef" that had been in storage since the Civil War.* The meatpacking industry also came under fire in *The Jungle,* the muckraking 1906 novel by journalist Upton Sinclair. In a celebrated passage, he described sausage-making in a typical Chicago packinghouse:

"There would be meat stored in great piles in rooms; and the water from leaky roofs would drip over it, and thousands of rats would race about on it. . . . These rats were nuisances, and the packers would put poisoned bread out for them, they would die and then rats, bread and meat would go into the hoppers together."

Sinclair was hardly alone in his crusade to expose industrial abuses. Other muckrakers assailed companies that used harmful chemicals to preserve food; produced "rectified" whiskey from artificially flavored and colored alcohol; made patent medicines; and misbranded and mislabeled food and drug products.

## Congress Acts

The public outcry that greeted such exposés prompted Congress to en-

* After the war, a presidential board of inquiry exonerated the War Department of the charge that it had supplied troops with contaminated beef.

# Chronology

## 19th Century

***The nation's concern about wholesome foods and drugs predates the Civil War.***

***1848***
Congress passes the Drug Importation Act, directing U.S Customs to block entry of adulterated drugs from overseas.

***1850***
The first federal law to protect consumers against unwholesome foods excludes certain brands of imported tea.

***1862***
President Abraham Lincoln taps chemist Charles M. Wetherill to head the Division of Chemistry, forerunner of the Food and Drug Administration (FDA).

## 1900s

***Abuses uncovered by muckraking journalists inspire legislation.***

***1902***
The Biologics Control Act is passed to ensure the purity and safety of serums and vaccines.

***1906***
Congress enacts the Food and Drug Act, barring interstate commerce in misbranded and adulterated foods and medicines, and the Meat Inspection Act.

## 1930s-1950s

***During the Depression, new safeguards protect against unsafe foods and drugs.***

***1938***
President Franklin D. Roosevelt signs the Food, Drug and Cosmetic Act. The law extends federal regulatory control to cosmetics and therapeutic devices and requires manufacturers to show new drugs to be safe.

***1954***
The Pesticide Chemical Amendments details procedures for setting safety standards for pesticide residues on raw produce.

***1958***
The Food Additives Amendments require manufacturers to demonstrate the safety of additives. The Delaney Clause bars any food additive shown to induce cancer in humans and animals.

## 1960s-1970s

***New food and drug products necessitate additional laws.***

***1960***
President Dwight D. Eisenhower signs the Color Additive Amendments, which require manufacturers to establish the safety of color additives in foods, drugs and cosmetics.

***1962***
Europe is hit by birth defects caused by thalidomide, an anti-nausea and sleeping medicine taken by many pregnant women. The tragedy prompts Congress to pass the Drug Amendments, requiring manufacturers to prove the effectiveness — not just the safety — of new drugs before marketing them.

***1976***
Congress enacts the Medical Device Amendments, which are designed to ensure the safety and effectiveness of medical devices.

## 1980s-1990s

***Though often criticized by industry and consumer groups, the FDA continues to gain more responsibilities.***

***1985***
The FDA approves an AIDS blood test, its first major action to protect patients from donors infected with fatal diseases.

***1990***
Congress approves the Nutrition Labeling and Education Act, which requires packaged foods to carry nutrition labeling and health claims. The Safe Medical Devices Act requires hospitals and nursing homes to report any incidents that suggest a medical device caused a patient's death or serious injury.

***1992***
President George Bush signs the Prescription Drug User-Fee Act (PDUFA), requiring makers of drugs and biologics to pay fees for drug and biologics applications and supplements.

***1994***
President Clinton signs the Dietary Supplement Health and Education Act, authorizing the FDA to issue good manufacturing practice regulations for dietary supplements.

act the landmark Federal Food and Drug Act in 1906.* Covering products shipped in foreign or interstate commerce, it sought to eliminate adulteration and misbranding. The law also required labels on medicines to indicate the presence of narcotics, stimulants or other such potentially dangerous ingredients.

Although the Food and Drug Act initially seemed far-reaching, it soon proved inadequate. The legislation "was, in fact, quite weak," writes reporter Philip J. Hilts of *The New York Times*. "Manufacturers did not have to prove that their drugs were safe in order to get them on the market; rather, the FDA had to prove they were unsafe before they could be taken *off* the market." [18]

To toughen the law, Congress in 1912 added penalties for "false and fraudulent" statements about the curative qualities of drugs, and in 1913 it required labels on packaged foods to indicate the net weight. In 1923, Congress revised the law yet again to prohibit the interstate shipment of "filled" milk — skim milk whose fat content had been increased by the addition of vegetable oils.

### FDA's Powers Expanded

In 1938, Congress greatly expanded FDA's powers and responsibilities by passing the Federal Food, Drug and Cosmetic Act (FDCA).** The law brought cosmetics and medical devices under federal regulation for the first time and applied to both fresh and processed foods, including poultry and fish. (Meat was largely regulated by the Agriculture Department under the 1906 Meat Inspection Act.)

The FDA could prevent the sale of adulterated or misbranded food through seizure and condemnation and through federal injunctions against the manufacturer, shipper or seller. Criminal penalties were provided for violations of the act.

These enforcement provisions fell short of what was needed, many commentators said. Except for coal-tar dyes and drugs introduced after the 1938 act, FDCA did not provide for the automatic establishment of safety standards, or require inspection or testing, before individual products could be placed on the market. Thus, drugs introduced before the law was passed were allowed to remain on store shelves unless the FDA could prove they were dangerous.

After World War II, Congress moved to strengthen federal controls over food additives, as well as controls over drugs and pesticides. The Food Additives Amendments of 1958 shifted the burden of proof from FDA to manufacturers, who were ordered to submit additive formulas to the agency along with evidence of their safety. In 1960, color additives in food, drugs and cosmetics were made subject to the same procedure.

### The Delaney Clause

The 1958 amendments contained the famous Delaney Clause, named for Rep. James J. Delaney, D-N.Y., which stated: "No additive shall be deemed to be safe if it is found to induce cancer when ingested by man or animal." The clause stipulated that any substance found in laboratory tests to cause cancer in humans or animals was to be banned — even if a "safe" level for human food could be established.

The clause resulted from concern in the 1950s about the rising incidence of cancer and its possible causes. It sparked controversy at the time among some scientists and food-industry spokesmen, who said it was not valid scientifically to bar use of a food additive at safe levels merely because the same substance at much higher levels of use could cause cancer in laboratory animals. Debate over the clause's merit continues today.

Another controversial aspect of the 1958 amendments concerned additives that were already in use. The food industry asked that they be exempt from licensing. When backers of the legislation protested that hazardous products might be left untested, a compromise was reached. Additives previously approved under old procedures were exempted, but they could be forced off the market through the courts if the FDA later found them to be dangerous. Additives designated in 1958 as "generally regarded as safe" (GRAS) included sugar, salt and spices that had been used for centuries. But some of the items originally on the GRAS list, such as the artificial sweetener cyclamate, were later found to be carcinogenic and were banned by the FDA. *

### Response to Thalidomide

A medical tragedy that swept Western Europe in the early 1960s, but spared the U.S., inspired legislation that significantly strengthened the FDA's drug-regulation powers. The incident centered on thalidomide, the generic name for a sleeping and anti-nausea medication developed in West Germany and put on the market there in 1957. Doctors liked to prescribe it because clinical trials had shown no risk of accidental death from an overdose. But Frances O. Kelsey, an FDA medical officer, refused to approve the drug for the U.S. market, suspecting that it might have some

---

* The act is also known, incorrectly, as the Pure Food and Drug Act. A comparable law, the Biologics Control Act of 1902, was designed to ensure the purity and safety of serums, vaccines and similar products used to prevent or treat diseases in humans.

** FDCA was enacted a year after 107 people died from ingesting an untested drug, sulfanilimide.

* In 1977, Congress passed the Saccharin Study and Labeling Act, which stopped the FDA from banning the chemical sweetener. But the law also required product labels warning that saccharin had been found to cause cancer in laboratory animals.

# A Stubborn FDA Inspector Saves the Day

In the late 1950s and early '60s, an anti-nausea and sleeping medication came on the market that quickly developed the aura of a wonder drug. Thalidomide not only did what it was supposed to do, but it carried no risk of death from overdose. European doctors enthusiastically prescribed the new drug to their patients, including thousands of pregnant women.

Eager to get in on the action, Cincinnati-based William S. Merrell Co. asked the Food and Drug Administration (FDA) in September 1960 for permission to market thalidomide in the United States under the trade name Kevadon. Merrell's application was assigned to Frances O. Kelsey, a physician who had been working at the agency for less than a month. Under FDA regulations, she had 60 days to evaluate the request.

Dr. Frances O. Kelsey

While poring over data supplied by the company, Kelsey, who specialized in pharmacology, was struck by the fact that thalidomide did not put animals to sleep, and that it acted differently than drugs it chemically resembled. With the backing of her FDA superiors, she withheld approval of the application and asked Merrell for more information on how thalidomide worked.

Then, in February 1961, Kelsey happened to see a letter in the *British Medical Journal* from a doctor who suggested that thalidomide might be causing numbness in the arms and legs. Kelsey promptly notified Merrell, which in turn alerted doctors who were testing the drug in the United States to watch out for side effects.

At that time, Kelsey had no reason for suspecting that thalidomide could cause deformities. Nonetheless, she informed Merrell in May 1961 that she thought it might have some effect on unborn babies. Still convinced of the drug's safety, Merrell continued to press for approval of its application. Meanwhile, reports of Kelsey's reluctance to certify thalidomide began to appear in the press, which generally portrayed her as a stubborn bureaucrat.

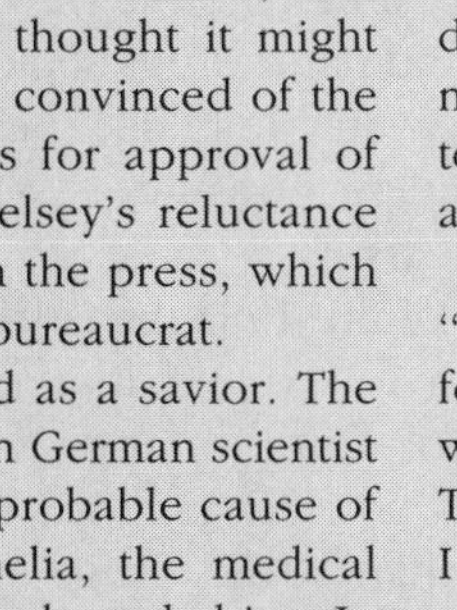

Six months later, she was being hailed as a savior. The turnaround came in November 1961, when German scientist Widukind Lenz cited thalidomide as the probable cause of an epidemic in his country of phocomelia, the medical term for malformed arms and legs in newborn babies. In some severe cases, the limbs resembled rudimentary flippers. Similar birth-defect reports soon surfaced in other countries where thalidomide had been widely used.[1]

Kelsey, meanwhile, had become a celebrity. In a July 1962 floor speech, Sen. Estes Kefauver, D-Tenn., praised her "great courage and devotion to the public interest" and suggested she be given the Award for Distinguished Federal Civilian Service. President John F. Kennedy presented her with the gold medal the following month, accompanied by a citation stating that her refusal to certify thalidomide had "prevented a major tragedy of birth deformities in the United States."

Galvanized by the thalidomide scare, Congress approved legislation requiring manufacturers to prove to the FDA the effectiveness — not just the safety — of new drugs before marketing them. Kennedy invited Kelsey to the White House signing ceremony that October. Two months later, she was named to head a new investigational drug branch within the agency.

Kelsey, who will be 83 in July, still works for the FDA — as deputy director for science and medicine in the Office of Compliance. Looking back, she credits the 1962 Drug Amendments for a number of improvements, including "better communications and better adverse-action reporting" within the agency, as well as "advances in the science of teratology," the study of malformations.

"A few human teratogens were recognized in 1962," Kelsey says, "but thalidomide really made people familiar with the problem. Quite a lot of research work got under way as a result. And it is still being done now."

Kelsey's FDA career spans a period of explosive growth. When she joined the agency in 1960, she recalls, only a dozen or so persons reviewed new-drug applications. Today, there are hundreds.

At the same time, the reviewing process has become vastly more complex. "Applications weren't nearly so detailed back then, since sponsors only had to show safety, not efficacy. A lot of sophisticated clinical trials are needed to demonstrate efficacy. So the information we were looking at then wasn't nearly as extensive as it is now."

Drugs themselves also have grown more complex. "When I joined the FDA, really exciting new drugs were few and far between," Kelsey says. "Many of them actually were mixtures of old drugs with minor modifications. Tranquilizers and antibiotics still were relatively new, and I don't think antiviral agents even existed."

Though Kelsey will always be remembered for having kept a particular drug off the market, that isn't a characteristic posture for the FDA, she says. "There's an eagerness here to get new drugs into the marketplace as quickly as possible. And I'm sure that effort won't relax."

[1] Thalidomide was developed in West Germany in the early 1950s and marketed there since 1957.

effect on unborn babies. (*See story, p. 69.*)

Congress responded to the thalidomide tragedy by passing the Drug Amendments of 1962, which extended the FDA's time limit for deciding whether to grant "new drug" applications to at least a year in most cases.* The amendments also permitted the secretary of Health, Education and Welfare to bar any drug from the market, even if already approved, if it was thought to pose an imminent danger to public health; and effectiveness, not just safety, was made a criterion for approving a new drug application. **

### *Medical Devices*

During the 1970s, the FDA took on additional duties, while a number of existing ones were shifted to other agencies. In 1971, for example, the Bureau of Radiological Health, which regulates human exposure to radiation, was transferred to the FDA. The FDA's National Center for Toxicological Research was established the same year in Pine Bluff, Ark., to monitor the biological effects of chemicals in the environment. In 1972, the FDA assumed responsibility for regulating biologics, including serums, vaccines and blood products.

Congress focused on medical devices in 1976, the first time it had addressed the subject in depth since approving FDCA 38 years earlier. Lawmakers enacted a bill giving the federal government clear-cut power to regulate the safety and effectiveness of medical devices ranging from tongue depressors to heart pacemakers. Key provisions of the law barred the sale of life-supporting devices, including implants, until they received FDA approval. Existing law had empowered the FDA to regulate medical devices only if they were misbranded or adulterated.

Two federal regulatory agencies created in the 1970s took control of functions previously handled by the FDA. The Environmental Protection Agency, founded in 1970, was put in charge of pesticide research and standards. Three years later, Congress gave the newly established Consumer Product Safety Commission control of programs pioneered by the FDA under the 1927 Caustic Poison Act, the 1960 Hazardous Substances Labeling Act and the 1966 Child Protection Act.

## Sweeping New Laws

After months of difficult negotiations between drug companies and public-interest groups, Congress in 1984 approved landmark legislation aimed at making generic drugs, or cheaper versions of many widely prescribed brand-name drugs, available to consumers while giving manufacturers additional patent protection for new brand-name pharmaceuticals. The FDA estimated that under the 1984 law, more than 150 brand-name drugs could be quickly made available in cheaper generic form, saving consumers $1 billion over 12 years. [19]

A key section of the 1984 measure directed the FDA to expand its use of a fast-track procedure for approving generic drugs, which retail for 50-80 percent less than brand drugs in many cases.

Until 1984, FDA had been using the expedited procedure only for drugs approved before 1962. This meant that so-called "post-1962" drugs still could be marketed exclusively, even after their patents had expired, largely because the expense of the regular FDA approval procedure generally discouraged generic versions of post-1962 drugs.

A second section of the 1984 measure, intended to reward pharmaceutical innovation, gave manufacturers up to five additional years of patent protection for new drugs, as well as certain other exclusive marketing rights. Companies had complained that a significant part of the standard 17-year patent period was lost to time-consuming regulatory reviews.

### *Crackdown on Claims*

In 1990, Congress responded to consumer groups' calls for a crackdown on advertising claims about the health benefits of processed foods. Lawmakers enacted legislation that for the first time ordered manufacturers to display detailed nutritional data on most packaged food items and some seafood. The measure required labels listing such information as calorie content and levels of fat and cholesterol.

In addition, the Nutrition Labeling and Education Act barred manufacturers from making certain nutritional claims on product labels — such as promoting a product as "high-fiber" or "low-sodium" — when other equally important nutritional information had not been mentioned. Companies also were prohibited from making health claims about a product — for instance, saying that high-fiber diets prevented cancer — if the claim had not been fully tested or endorsed by the FDA.

A second 1990 law sought to overhaul federal regulation of medical devices. The Safe Medical Devices Act required hospitals and nursing homes to report promptly to the FDA any incidents suggesting that a medical device caused or contributed to a death or serious illness or injury. In addi-

---

* Under the 1938 FDCA, an application for a "new drug" approval became effective automatically in 60 days (the FDA could extend the limit to 180 days if it needed more time), unless disapproved.

** To be certified as "effective" by the FDA, a drug must be shown to be equal to or better than comparable drugs already on the market.

tion, it directed manufacturers to monitor devices that are permanently implanted in the body and whose failure could cause serious health impairment or death. For its part, the FDA was authorized to order product recalls of suspect medical devices.

### *Prescription Drug User-Fees Act of 1992*

One of the most successful drug-regulation laws of recent years has been the Prescription Drug User-Fees Act of 1992 (PDUFA), which required producers of brand-name pharmaceuticals and biologics to pay a separate fee for each drug submitted to the FDA for approval. The law is credited with substantially reducing the average length of FDA review by enabling the FDA to hire more personnel.

After two years of intense lobbying, manufacturers and consumers of vitamins, minerals and herbal remedies persuaded Congress in 1994 to curtail the federal government's power to regulate dietary supplements. Passage of the Dietary Supplement Health and Education Act created an independent commission to set labeling guidelines for vitamins and other health supplements. However, the measure allowed the FDA to enforce existing regulations while the commission completed its work. [20]

In an unanticipated development last year, food industry representatives and environmental activists overcame their longstanding impasse over the 1958 Delaney Clause, which had barred processed food from containing even minute amounts of cancer-causing chemicals. Under the Food Quality Protection Act, they agreed to change the "no risk" Delaney standard to one based on "a reasonable certainty of no harm." Applying to raw as well as processed food, the revised standard meant there could be as much as one chance in a million that pesticide residue would cause cancer. ■

*At least once every two years, the Federal Food, Drug and Cosmetic Act requires the FDA to inspect each of the approximately 15,000 U.S. facilities that manufacture, test, pack and label drug products for humans.*

# Current Situation

## 'Reforms' Fizzle

Efforts to pass legislation "reforming" the FDA fizzled in 1996, despite seemingly broad bipartisan support. The proposed Food and Drug Administration Performance and Accountability Act, approved in March 1996 by the Senate Labor and Human Resources Committee, sought to speed up the review process for drugs, food products and medical devices. It reduced the amount of supporting data that manufacturers had to submit with their applications. The measure also would have required the agency to use third parties to help with product reviews.

Three reform bills were introduced in the House, dealing separately with pharmaceuticals, medical devices and food. All took the same general approach as the Senate bill, but none advanced beyond committee. Although Republicans had enough votes to move the House bills, they chose to negotiate with Democratic lawmakers and the Clinton administration before proceeding. Industry support weakened as Republicans made concessions to Democratic concerns, with the result that time ran out before Congress adjourned in early October.

Efforts to streamline FDA operations have resumed in the current session of Congress. Amgen's Binder told lawmakers in April that the drug industry had trimmed its legislative wish list to make it more politically palatable. The industry "dropped provisions that would have expedited FDA action on [new-drug applications] that had been approved abroad, required mandatory third-party reviews and established a Policy and Performance Panel to oversee agency activities," he said. [21]

## FDA Funding

At the same time, Binder stressed that "industry believes it is essential that FDA be funded in fiscal year 1998 at the level of appropriations enacted for the current fiscal year [$820 million], adjusted for inflation, and designating similar-level funding for the human drug development and review process." He added that drug manufacturers are "concerned" that the administration's fiscal 1998 budget proposal for the FDA "would reduce budget authority by over $68 million — an 8 percent reduction in federal appropriations and a 13 percent cut in the budget for human-drug approvals." [22]

The FDA funding issue also troubles public-interest groups. Bruce Silverglade, director of legal affairs for the Center for Science in the Public Interest, told another Senate panel in late April that the FDA's Center for Food Safety and Applied Nutrition (CFSAN) is seriously overburdened.

"[T]he size of the food industry has been increasing while the FDA's staffing levels for food programs have been decreasing," he said. "From 1989-1994 alone, the value of food products under FDA's jurisdiction grew by almost $50 billion. That means that although CFSAN staff levels have declined, there are more facilities for the FDA to inspect, more food labels for the FDA to check and more food standards to issue and update. . . . By failing to halt, and then reverse, this trend, Congress and the administration are seriously jeopardizing the health and welfare of the American people." [23]

Funding worries also figure in the debate over reauthorization of the Prescription Drug User-Fee Act. According to Binder, FDA and the drug industry "have developed a legislative framework for Congress to consider that would renew PDUFA for five more years and not only continue to reduce the FDA review times but also for the first time address the drug-development phase, in exchange for which the industry would pay at least 21 percent more in user fees." This arrangement, he said, "would allow the agency to continue PDUFA without interruption and implement new performance goals, enabling patients to receive medicine 10 to 16 months earlier." [24]

But these prospective gains could be jeopardized, Binder warned, unless funding for the FDA remains at the current level, adjusted for inflation. "[W]ithout level funding," he said, "the [user] fees would just be used for general deficit reduction — not to benefit patients. . . . With industry spending $19 billion on R&D to develop new cures and U.S. taxpayers providing $13 billion to [the National Institutes of Health] for biomedical research, it makes no sense to cut FDA's budget . . . and slow down approval of these new cures." [25]

## Kessler's Successor

Kessler's departure for the Yale Medical School means the FDA needs to fill a leadership void. The agency's acting commissioner is Michael Friedman, who Kessler persuaded in 1995 to become deputy commissioner for operations and to energize the FDA science board, which coordinates in-house research. In Friedman's view, the FDA would benefit from more frequent consultations with experts in other government agencies and academic institutions.

"We need more effective linkages with scientists outside the agency," he said. [26] Friedman and FDA deputy commissioners Mary K. Pendergast and William B. Schultz have been cited in media reports as leading candidates to succeed Kessler.

However, some observers feel it is much more likely that the job will go to someone with no current ties to the agency. Possibilities include Myron Weisfeldt, a former American Heart Association president who heads the Medical Department at Columbia University's Presbyterian Hospital; Gilbert Omenn, dean of the University of Washington's School of Public Health; and Randy Juhl, dean of the University of Pittsburgh's School of Pharmacy. All three reportedly have been interviewed by Health and Human Services Secretary Donna E. Shalala.

Administration officials also are said to have talked with Janet Woodcock, director of the FDA's Center for Drug Evaluation and Research, and Steven Phillips, an Iowa heart surgeon whose candidacy is backed by Sen. Tom Harkin, D-Iowa, a member of the Senate Labor and Human Resources Committee.

## Taking on Tobacco

Whoever succeeds Kessler may well be preoccupied with the consequences of his decision to assert FDA's authority to regulate tobacco. The initiative dates from Aug. 2, 1994, when an agency advisory panel rejected claims by the tobacco industry that its products were not addictive, asserting that the nicotine content of cigarettes produced and marketed by the companies was sufficient to cause addiction in most smokers.

A year later, on Aug. 10, 1995, the FDA published proposed regulations in the *Federal Register* curbing tobacco advertising and promotional activities directed at youngsters and requiring manufacturers to establish a $150-million-a-year education campaign to discourage children and

# At Issue:

## *Should the FDA privatize its product-review process?*

NATIONAL ELECTRICAL MANUFACTURERS ASSOCIATION

***FROM TESTIMONY SUBMITTED TO THE SENATE LABOR AND HUMAN RESOURCES COMMITTEE, APRIL 11, 1997***

yes

Specific elements of FDA modernization for which NEMA believes a statutory remedy is necessary include empowering the agency to expand upon its existing enterprise by making use of its independent scientific review organizations as a means of enhancing the product review process. . . . Fundamentally, delegating product review to independent scientific review organizations will result in a competitive framework for the review of new product submittals, thus leading to greater efficiency in the product review process and a re-allocation of FDA resources to focus on those products most likely to pose the greatest risk to the public safety and health.

Moreover, delegating FDA's product review functions to independent scientific review organizations will enhance the scientific and technical expertise available to the agency. . . . This, in turn, holds the potential to re-focus the product review process on product safety and performance. Finally, delegating product review and inspection responsibilities to independent scientific review organizations would result in considerable savings to the taxpayer. . . .

Although the agency's third-party pilot program represents a positive initial step toward the utilization of independent scientific-review organizations, NEMA continues to maintain that the scope and structure of the third-party pilot is insufficient, and that additional statutory changes are necessary to promote greater agency reliance on independent scientific review organizations. . . .

Second, just as the FDA needs the statutory authority to delegate its product review process to independent scientific review organizations, so does the agency need the statutory authority to utilize independent scientific experts to conduct good manufacturing practices inspections. Currently, FDA inspectors are required to inspect not only medical device manufacturing facilities but also factories engaged in the manufacture of foods, biologics, pharmaceuticals and animal drugs. As a result, oftentimes FDA inspectors lack the expertise necessary to offer constructive suggestions on improving the quality of the manufacturing process. . . .

Third, FDA needs the authority to recognize and permit manufacturer certifications of compliance to consensus standards as a means of expediting the product review process. Consensus standards, developed with the input of industry, government and medical professionals, represent state-of-the-art norms for ensuring the safety and performance of safety devices. . . .

Fourth, FDA needs to be provided with the flexibility to streamline reporting requirements so that the emphasis is on product safety, rather than paperwork. . . .

DAVID A. KESSLER
*Commissioner, Food and Drug Administration (FDA)* *

***FROM TESTIMONY BEFORE THE HOUSE COMMERCE SUBCOMMITTEE ON HEALTH AND THE ENVIRONMENT, MAY 1, 1996.***

no

The concept of privatization of product application reviews is problematic for a number of reasons. First, FDA's scientific and clinical experts are charged with exercising independent unbiased judgment. They comply with stringent financial disclosure and conflict-of-interest requirements designed to protect the decision-making process against bias. It is not clear how or whether this independence can be maintained with the private sector, particularly since the sponsor gets to choose and pay the private party, and repeat business may depend on the sponsor's satisfaction with the private party's decision.

Second, FDA's reviewers have extensive knowledge about all of the similar products that are made by different companies around the country. When a reviewer looks at all of the drugs for arthritis and other inflammatory diseases, or all of the heart valves, what the reviewer learns from each review increases his/her understanding of that group of drugs or devices and their effect on the body. As a result, FDA reviewers see problems that reviewers with less information might not see.

The third problem with privatization is the lack of continuity. For example, FDA's reviewers are able to work with the same drug over time. By staying involved in a drug's development, reviewers can build on what they already know. Third-party reviewers may have little knowledge of the specific development process for the product and/or of the development agreements made during the process.

We believe that contracting out product review to third parties should be done only if there is evidence that it can be done safely. A pilot study is essential to determine if that can be done. That is why FDA is conducting its pilot program for low-risk medical devices. We are trying to determine whether third parties can accomplish the goal of getting safe and effective products to the American public.

Finally, because there is a risk that only third parties that err on the side of approving applications and petitions will succeed in this market, there is a risk that the incentive will be for third parties to approve applications and petitions — not to critically review them.

* Kessler stepped down in February as FDA commissioner to become dean of the Yale University School of Medicine.

## FOR MORE INFORMATION

**Biotechnology Industry Organization (BIO),** 1625 K St. N.W., Suite 1100, Washington, D.C. 20006-1604; (202) 857-0244; www.bio.org. Members are manufacturing and research companies. BIO favors the contracting out of many FDA activities.

**Generic Pharmaceutical Industry Association,** 1620 I St. N.W., Suite 800, Washington, D.C. 20006; (202) 833-9070. The association represents the generic pharmaceutical industry in legislative, regulatory, scientific and health-care policy matters.

**Grocery Manufacturers of America,** 1010 Wisconsin Ave. N.W., Suite 900, Washington, D.C. 20007; (202) 337-9400; www.gmabrands.org. The GMA comprises companies that manufacture products sold in retail groceries. Many of the products are regulated by the FDA.

**Health Industry Manufacturers Association,** 1200 G St. N.W., Suite 400, Washington, D.C. 20005; (202) 783-8700; www.himanet.com. HIMA represents manufacturers of medical devices, diagnostic products and health-care information systems.

**Medical Device Manufacturers Association,** 1900 K St. N.W., Suite 100, Washington, D.C. 20006; (202) 496-7150; www.medicaldevices.org. MDMA represents about 130 mostly small- and medium-sized U.S. device manufacturers.

**National Women's Health Network,** 514 10th St. N.W., Suite 400, Washington, D.C. 20004; (202) 347-1140; www.aoa.dhhs.gov/aoa/dir/203.html. The network acts as an information clearinghouse on women's health issues. It also is a member of the Patients' Coalition, a national network of more than 100 patient and consumer advocacy groups, (202) 347-1140.

**Pharmaceutical Research and Manufacturers Association of America,** 1100 15th St. N.W., Suite 900, Washington, D.C. 20005; (202) 835-3400; www.phrma.org. The association's members are companies that develop and manufacture prescription drugs.

adolescents from smoking. Coalitions of tobacco companies and national advertisers quickly sued in U.S. District Court in Greensboro, N.C., to block implementation of the FDA's rulemaking package.

Because North Carolina is the nation's largest tobacco-producing state, some observers said the industry might get a more sympathetic hearing there than elsewhere. But the court's ruling, issued this April 25 by Judge William L. Osteen Sr., was widely seen as a sharp setback for tobacco producers. Osteen agreed that the FDA had authority to regulate tobacco as a drug, since nicotine alters bodily functions, and cigarettes are expressly designed to deliver it to smokers. At the same time, however, he held that the FDA lacked authority to regulate youth-oriented tobacco advertising.*

Osteen's ruling left intact FDA proposals to ban tobacco sales nationwide to persons under 18, require photo identification checks of all cigarette purchasers under 27, restrict the placement of cigarette vending machines and bar free samples or single cigarette sales. But Osteen rejected proposals to restrict the placement and format of print advertising and outdoor signs and billboards; prohibit giveaways of clothing and other products bearing tobacco brand names or logos; and require that entertainment or sporting events be sponsored under the corporate rather than cigarette brand name.

"It's a victory for the nation, for the public health," Kessler said. "A small group of very committed people at the agency took on the impossible. The president of the United States supported them and a federal judge in North Carolina in very large measure agreed. . . . It will change forever the way tobacco products are viewed." [27]

Indeed, a product recently approved by the FDA could be regarded as an indirect form of tobacco regulation. On May 5, the agency cleared for prescription sale the Nicotrol Inhaler, a device manufactured by McNeil Consumer Products Co., a unit of Johnson & Johnson.

According to McNeil, the inhaler is the first form of nicotine replacement therapy to help control a smoker's cravings for cigarettes while satisfying the need for a key behavioral aspect of smoking, the hand-to-mouth ritual. The device delivers nicotine to the user, but at a lower level than cigarettes.

## Pilot Programs

The FDA is approaching the midpoint of a two-year pilot program that could improve relations with the companies it regulates. The program, which began last Aug. 1, seeks to determine whether third-party review of medical devices will trim review times and whether strong conflict-of-interest safeguards can be maintained throughout the process.

"The program applies only to low- and moderate-risk devices for which the FDA does not require clinical data on safety and effectiveness — products such as electronic thermometers and surgical gloves," an article in the *FDA Consumer* explained. "A manufacturer

* In another blow to the tobacco industry, the Federal Trade Commission charged on May 28 that the R.J. Reynolds Tobacco Co. illegally aimed its Joe Camel advertising campaign at minors in violation of federal fair trade practice laws.

must show in a premarket notification application that such a product's safety and effectiveness are comparable to a device already legally marketed." [28]

The FDA receives about 1,500 applications a year from makers of devices eligible for the pilot program. Participation is voluntary. A firm may choose to have a third party conduct most of the review, or turn the entire job over to the agency.

A second FDA pilot program changes the ground rules for inspections of firms with a good history of compliance with agency regulations. During the experiment, targeted firms are to receive advance notice from the FDA, presumably giving them ample time to prepare for the visit. Ordinarily, FDA inspectors arrive at a plant unannounced.

### *FDA Under Fire*

Two recent incidents demonstrated yet again that FDA decisions on new-drug applications often create hard feelings, either immediately or years later. On May 8, for instance, an agency advisory panel voted to reject a new drug for treating amyotrophic lateral sclerosis (ALS), or Lou Gehrig's disease, which kills about 10,000 Americans a year. More than 20 ALS sufferers, some in wheelchairs, tearfully pleaded with panel members to recommend FDA approval of the drug, Myotrophin. [29] But a majority of panelists concluded that the manufacturer, Cephalon Inc., had failed to present persuasive evidence that Myotrophin was effective against ALS. The next day, Cephalon stock lost $7 a share, or 35 percent of its value, in trading on the Nasdaq exchange.

Also on May 8, FDA came under heavy fire for deciding in 1990 to let the Defense Department require U.S. troops in the Persian Gulf War to take an experimental drug intended to protect them against exposure to nerve gas. The drug, pyridostigmine bromide, is now suspected as a possible cause of the array of disorders called Gulf War Syndrome. Consequently, the FDA is now being assailed for allowing the Pentagon to administer the drug without first telling those who took it about potential side effects and obtaining their informed consent.

"It was feasible to inform them, and that's the least they could do," said Rep. Christopher Shays, R-Conn. "I have no sympathy whatever that they could not inform the soldiers." FDA Deputy Commissioner Pendergast acknowledged that the agency had extended "considerable deference" to the Defense Department. She added, "This was war. This was the first time, and it didn't work out particularly well." [30] ■

# OUTLOOK

## Era of Cooperation?

With a new commissioner waiting in the wings, and reform legislation unclear, the agency's future remains uncertain. But one thing is clear: The torrent of data pouring into the FDA will continue.

Pearson says she has listened to agency officials "discuss what they need to do over the next 10 years, and they talk about information management — getting on the electronic superhighway. They're wondering, as many business people are, how to take advantage of the ability to communicate more quickly and access huge amounts of information?"

Years ago, Pearson notes, "that was real easy. The agency handled only food, drugs and cosmetics. Then Congress gave it authority over medical devices, radiological health and other areas. But I don't think the agency adapted its thinking to the evolving product mix. FDA reviewers are now dealing with more medical devices than they used to, as well as genetically engineered foods. And I foresee even more dramatic changes down the road."

Changes to date in this area already are dramatic. "It's not unusual for [a new-drug application] to run to hundreds of thousands of pages," Hilts noted. "Drug companies used to deliver their applications to the FDA in trucks; now they're sent on CD-ROMs." [31]

Feldbaum of the Biotechnology Industry Organization expects continuation of formal and informal contacts between the FDA and industry representatives. These meetings "have proven to be very useful for both the regulators and the regulated," he says, because medical technology "changes kaleidoscopically." And since the situation is so fluid, Feldbaum says, "it requires a great deal of responsiveness from the regulating agencies — on an almost monthly basis, in fact. The idea is to acquaint the regulators with changes that are occurring in the science."

Tufts University's Lasagna agrees with Feldbaum on the desirability of more frequent FDA-industry communication. He adds, however, that "a lot will depend on the new commissioner — how supportive he or she will be of attempts to improve relationships between the regulators and the regulated." Lasagna believes there is evidence "suggesting that where early and collegial relations exist between the agency and sponsors, new-drug applications would turn out to be self-reviewing. The reason is that all the important questions would have been asked and answered in the course of the product's development."

But so far, Lasagna says, no "systematic and agencywide approach" to bilateral contacts has been established. "To my knowledge, no drug has ever benefited, all the way through its history, from this kind of early and continuing relationship between the regulator and the regulated."

Some sort of continuing relationship may be emerging, however, between the FDA and the medical-device industry. At MDMA's May 16 annual meeting, several company representatives voiced appreciation for the work done by Burlington of the FDA Center for Devices and Radiological Health to improve agency-industry relations in recent years. Burlington, in turn, acknowledged industry's help in bringing about change at the center and expressed hope that future contacts would remain cordial and productive.

The unyielding reality that government agencies face today, Burlington said, is that "discretionary domestic spending is not headed up. You're lucky if you're getting constant dollars. Everybody in business knows constant dollars get eroded by inflation. It's just as true in the government."

To cope with the fund squeeze, Burlington says, the center examined several options. User fees and higher funding from Congress were discarded as "rescue fantasies." The most promising approach, it was agreed, was to "refocus priorities to match resources and re-engineer processes for efficiency."

That means, Burlington says, that "FDA is going to be more involved in high-risk, high-consumer-benefit areas" in coming years. "We're going to redirect work where it can optimize consumer benefits. Conversely, our direct role in low-risk products will be greatly decreased." And that may open the way to third-party review of FDA-related products, with the FDA retaining overall direction of the process.

Change could come as early as the current session of Congress. But, he cautions, "Legislative reform takes time to develop," and experience "tells us that if we're going to do it this year, we ought to make sure we do it right." ■

## Notes

[1] Andrew E. Serwer, "SOS for the FDA?" *Fortune*, April 4, 1994, p. 142.

[2] Testimony before House Commerce Subcommittee on Health and the Environment, May 1, 1996.

[3] U.S. General Accounting Office, "*FDA Drug Approval: Review Time Has Decreased in Recent Years*," October 1995, p. 4.

[4] *Ibid.*, pp. 10-11.

[5] Kessler, David A., et al., "Approval of New Drugs in the United States: Comparison With the United Kingdom, Germany, and Japan," *The Journal of the American Medical Association*, Dec. 11, 1996, p. 1826.

[6] *Ibid.*, p. 1831.

[7] *Loc. cit.*

[8] U.S. General Accounting Office, "*Medical Device Regulation: Too Early to Assess European System's Value as Model for FDA*," March 1996, pp. 5-6.

[9] Gordon R. Higson, Medical Technology Consultants Europe Ltd., "*Medical Device Approval Times in Europe*," February 1996.

[10] Testimony before Senate Labor and Human Resources Committee, April 11, 1997.

[11] Remarks at the annual meeting of the Medical Device Manufacturers Association, Washington, D.C., May 16, 1997.

[12] The Patients' Coalition, "Agenda for Effective Change at FDA" (undated policy paper).

[13] Testimony before House Commerce Subcommittee on Health and the Environment, April 23, 1997.

[14] Testimony before House Commerce Subcommittee on Health and the Environment, May 1, 1996.

[15] Statement submitted to Senate Labor and Human Resources Committee, April 11, 1997.

[16] Testimony before Senate Labor and Human Resources Committee, April 11, 1997.

[17] Testimony before House Commerce Subcommittee on Health and the Environment, May 1, 1996.

[18] Philip J. Hilts, "Doing Drugs," *George*, September 1996, p. 81.

[19] See "Generic Drug Legislation Cleared by Congress," *1984 CQ Almanac*, pp. 451-453.

[20] For background, see "Dietary Supplements," *The CQ Researcher*, July 8, 1994, pp. 577-600.

[21] Testimony before Senate Labor and Human Resources Committee, April 11, 1997. Binder testified on behalf of the Biotechnology Industry Organization and the Pharmaceutical Research and Manufacturers of America.

[22] *Loc. cit.*

[23] Testimony before Senate Appropriations Subcommittee on Agriculture, Rural Development and Related Agencies, April 29, 1997.

[24] Testimony before Senate Labor and Human Resources Committee, April 11, 1997.

[25] *Loc. cit.*

[26] Quoted by Richard Stone, "Kessler's Legacy: Unfinished Reform," *Science*, Dec. 6, 1996, p. 1604.

[27] Quoted by John Schwartz, "Judge Rules That FDA Can Regulate Tobacco," *The Washington Post*, April 26, 1997, p. A14.

[28] Dixie Farley, "Agency Changes Include Medical Device Review," *FDA Consumer*, November 1996, p. 30.

[29] The FDA is not bound to accept the findings of its advisory panels, but it usually does so.

[30] Quoted by Sheryl Gay Stolberg in *The New York Times*, May 9, 1997, p. A26. Shays and Pendergast spoke at a May 8 hearing of the House Committee on Government Reform and Oversight.

[31] Hilts, *op. cit.*, p. 82.

# Bibliography

## Selected Sources Used


### Books

**Burkholz, Herbert, *The FDA Follies*, Basic Books, 1994.**
Burkholz revisits some of the FDA's misadventures of the 1980s, which included its hesitant response to the AIDS crisis, its fumbling of the Shiley heart valve and silicone breast implant cases and a generic-drug bribery scandal. He concludes on a hopeful note, however, citing reforms instituted by Commissioner David A. Kessler, then relatively new on the job.

**Morgenthaler, John, and Steven Wm. Fowkes, eds., *Stop the FDA: Save Your Health Freedom*, Health Freedom Publications, 1992.**
Making no claim to evenhandedness, the editors of this collection of articles lash out at the FDA for being "alone among federal institutions in its anti-vitamin, anti-nutrient and anti-health agenda." The authors include Sen. Orrin G. Hatch, R-Utah, and Linus C. Pauling, the late Nobel Prize-winning chemist and Vitamin C enthusiast.

### Articles

**Annas, George J., "Cowboys, Camels and the First Amendment — The FDA's Restrictions on Tobacco Advertising," *The New England Journal of Medicine*, Dec. 5, 1996.**
The author, a lawyer with a master's degree in public health, analyzes the main legal issues involved in the FDA's challenge to the tobacco industry.

**Farley, Dixie, "Agency Changes Include Medical Device Review," *FDA Consumer*, November 1996.**
Farley describes an FDA pilot program allowing private organizations to take part in the agency's evaluation of medical devices.

**Goldberg, Jeffrey, "Next Target: Nicotine," *The New York Times Magazine*, Aug. 4, 1996.**
Goldberg, a regular contributor to the Times magazine, uses the FDA's thus-far successful bid to regulate tobacco as the focal point of an analysis of the many controversies surrounding the agency.

**Kessler, David A., et al., "Approval of New Drugs in the United States: Comparison With the United Kingdom, Germany, and Japan," *The Journal of the American Medical Association*, Dec. 11, 1996.**
Kessler and four of his FDA colleagues present the results of a study of 214 new drugs introduced into the world market from January 1990 through December 1994. They found that the United States outpaced both Germany and Japan in approving important new drugs and that it ranked slightly ahead of Britain.

**Mahar, Maggie, "FDA Commissioner Sees No Special Deal Ahead for Tobacco Companies" (an interview with David A. Kessler), *Barron's*, Dec. 30, 1996.**
Noting that morale at the FDA "was rock-bottom" when he assumed command in 1992, Kessler reviews the highlights of his stewardship, including the confrontation with the tobacco industry and streamlining of the process for reviewing proposed new drugs.

### Reports and Studies

**U.S. General Accounting Office, *FDA Drug Approval: Review Time Has Decreased in Recent Years*, October 1995.**
GAO, the investigative arm of Congress, concludes that it took FDA an average of 33 months to approve new drug applications in 1987, but only 19 months in 1992.

**U.S. General Accounting Office, *Medical Devices: FDA Review Time*, October 1995.**
Surveying FDA review times for medical device applications between 1988 and 1995, GAO finds that median review times were stable from 1989 to 1991, rose sharply in 1992 and 1993 and then dropped in 1994.

**U.S. General Accounting Office, *Medical Device Regulation: Too Early to Assess European System's Value as Model for FDA*, March 1996.**
According to the GAO, "Meaningful comparison of the length of review time in the United States and the EU [European Union] is not possible because there are no data documenting review times under the new EU system comparable to data describing FDA's experience."

**U.S. General Accounting Office, *Blood Supply: FDA Oversight and Remaining Issues of Safety*, February 1997.**
GAO finds that the blood industry "has made many positive changes in collecting and processing blood in response to FDA initiatives." But it recommends that blood facilities be required to take several additional steps, including viral testing of all blood given for the donor's exclusive use.

**U.S. Senate Committee on Labor and Human Resources, Assessing the FDA's Performance, Efficiency and Use of Resources (published proceedings of hearing held April 11, 1997).**
Industry officials and representatives of public-interest groups present their views on proposed FDA reform legislation. Also examined is reauthorization of the expiring Prescription Drug User-Fee Act (PDUFA), which is credited with substantially trimming the time it takes for FDA review of new drug applications.

# 5 Welfare, Work and the States

CHRISTOPHER CONTE

It's a cold, blustery morning in Des Moines, and a group of welfare applicants are attending a rather chilling orientation session at the state Department of Employment Services.

"Don't confuse the state with big-hearted, warm, kind individuals," Todd McGee, an interviewer for the department, tells them. "Welfare reform means nothing else but 'Get off welfare and get a job.' "

That may oversimplify Iowa's Family Investment Program, one of the nation's longest-running and most comprehensive welfare-reform efforts. But it does capture the spirit of welfare reform in the 1990s. Across the country, policy-makers of all political stripes have come to agree that welfare recipients not only *can* but *must* work — and without a great deal of delay.

Now, the federal government has raised the stakes. The new Personal Responsibility and Work Opportunity Reconciliation Act of 1996, which President Clinton reluctantly signed in August, requires that in six years at least half of each state's adult welfare recipients must be working. States that fail could lose up to 21 percent of their federal welfare funding.

Individual recipients also will feel the heat. They generally will be expected to work — either in paid employment or community service — within two years of the time they go on welfare. And no one will be allowed to collect welfare for more than five years over a lifetime.

States must meet the new work requirements in the context of a fundamentally changed relationship with the federal government — one that poses some opportunities, but also considerable risks. In the past, Washington set most of the rules for welfare and then helped states pay benefits to all eligible

recipients. But now, states will receive federal money in the form of block grants, which will remain essentially unchanged for the next six years, regardless of what happens to welfare caseloads. While fewer strings will be attached to the federal money, states will have to bear the burden if, for any reason, they fail to contain costs and trim the welfare roles.

They also will have to bear much of the cost of any additional job training and counseling required to make welfare recipients more employable. That's because the federal government, even while requiring more welfare recipients to go to work, hasn't increased its support for job training. In fact, spending on the basic training programs that could benefit welfare recipients has declined steadily over the last several years, according to the Congressional Budget Office (CBO).

In 1994, the federal government provided $5 billion for job training under the Job Training and Partnership Act (JTPA), plus another $1.1 billion for the basic welfare-to-work program, the Job Opportunity and Basic Skills (JOBS) program. In fiscal 1997, which began Oct. 1, the government is providing just $4.7 billion for the JTPA, and the new welfare-reform law eliminated the JOBS program altogether.

How will states react? Will they feel emboldened to take advantage of their new flexibility, or will they become reluctant to take chances because of their greater fiscal exposure? Will they invest in efforts to make welfare recipients more employable, or will they slash benefits and services in a "race to the bottom" designed to make sure that they don't attract welfare families from other, less generous states?

Nobody knows for sure. Reform advocates hope most states will follow the lead of Iowa and others who have converted welfare into more of a jobs program. But there is no guarantee all will follow this course. "There are real questions about whether states will convert their welfare programs to work," concedes a House aide who worked on the legislation. "It's hard to do, and for some states, the money will be tight."

Indeed, money will be a pivotal issue. So far, the most successful welfare-reform efforts have required states to increase spending, at least initially. When Iowa launched its reform program, for instance, it more than doubled its outlays for employment programs, from $9.7 million in fiscal 1993 to $25.7 million in fiscal 1996. The additional funds paid for more counselors to help welfare recipients seek — and prepare for — work.

The hope, of course, is that this up-front investment eventually will pay off. Again, there are indications that it can — at least modestly. In Iowa, the welfare caseload dropped from 39,536 to 33,800 in the first two years after the reform program went into effect, and the portion of welfare recipients who work jumped to 35 percent, compared with 18 percent for a control group. With the caseload down, and more of those who remain on welfare earning

From *The CQ Researcher*, December 6, 1996.

## Welfare Block Grants Vary Greatly From State to State

*The 1996 welfare reform law creates block grants for Temporary Assistance for Needy Families to replace Aid to Families with Dependent Children (AFDC) and several related programs. States must convert to block grants no later than July 1, 1997. Money will be distributed to each state based on its federal funding for AFDC and related programs in fiscal 1995, fiscal 1994 or the average of fiscal 1992-94, whichever is higher.*

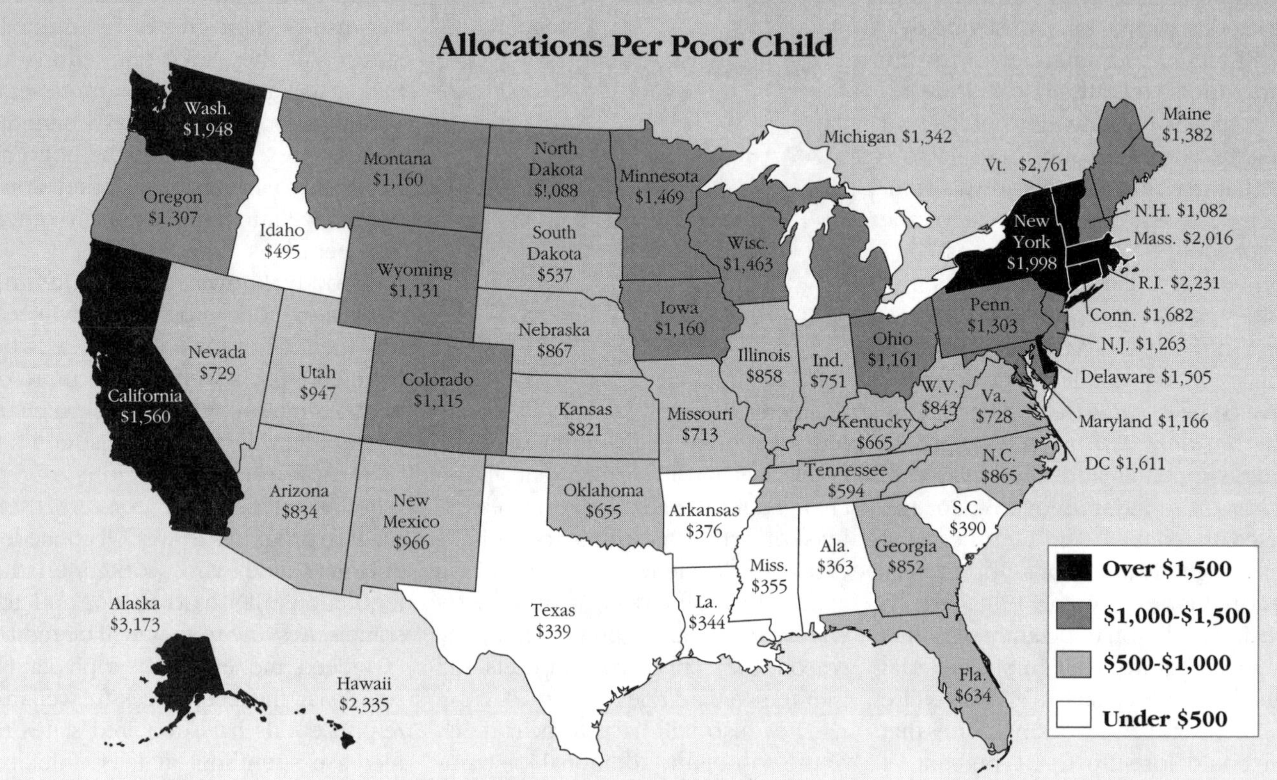


*Source: Center for Law and Social Policy, citing Congressional Research Service calculations based on data from Census Bureau March Current Population Surveys (CPS). Numbers of children in poverty were computed using 3-year averages for 1992-94. Estimates for smaller states are of lower reliability due to sample sizes.*

outside income, monthly cash assistance payments dropped from $14.1 million in January 1994 to $11.2 million two years later.

Still, Iowa had to curtail some training options — for instance, it limited the number of postsecondary education slots — to contain its costs. While some reform advocates argue that education hasn't proven to be an effective tool for reducing the welfare rolls anyway, critics of the work-no-matter-what approach say the lack of post-high school training opportunities consigns many welfare families to dead-end jobs that don't pay enough for them to achieve self-sufficiency.

To some, the debate over how much to provide in the way of training points to a fundamental contradiction in the goals of welfare reformers. "We want to reduce dependency on welfare and reduce poverty — and we want to do it all at low cost," says David Butler, a welfare analyst at Manpower Demonstration Research Corp. (MDRC) in New York. "We can't have it all."

If helping welfare families climb beyond the bottom rung of the career ladder would require increased spending, some alternatives for handling welfare recipients who won't be able to find private-sector jobs or won't be able to support themselves when their benefits run out won't be cheap either. Workfare — that is, requiring welfare recipients to perform community services — costs about $6,000 a year more per recipient than simply handing out benefit checks, according to Wendell Primus, who resigned as deputy assistant secretary of the Department of Health and Human Services when President Clinton decided to sign the tough, new welfare law.

The extra cost includes $3,000 for child care, about $700 for transportation and $2,000-$2,500 to arrange and supervise the jobs. And that investment wouldn't make welfare recipients any better off financially than when they were simply receiving welfare checks. To create a full-time public-sector job that would provide health and other benefits and offer a chance of economic advancement probably would cost $3,000-$6,000 more per recipient than a workfare job, Primus says.

Few people expect Washington or the states to come up with that kind of money. Indeed, far from increasing spending, the new law will cut federal welfare outlays by $54.2 billion, according to the CBO. While the bulk of those cuts reflects reductions in food stamps and a controversial provision making legal immigrants ineligible for most federal welfare benefits, the CBO estimates that the states will have to spend $13 billion more than Congress has authorized for welfare-to-work programs over the next six years to meet the employment targets set by the new law.

The $13 billion doesn't count child-care costs. Even though the new law increases federal spending for child care by $3.5 billion, to a total of $14 billion, the CBO says that still falls about $1.8 billion short of what would be needed if states are to meet the law's work targets. In light of those projections and the strong public pressure to reduce, rather than increase, spending on welfare, "We don't think states will meet the work requirements," says CBO analyst Sheila Dacey.

On top of the federal spending cuts, the new law will allow states to reduce their own welfare spending by $40 billion between 1997 and 2002 without penalty.

Balancing a desire to restrain welfare spending against the needs of many welfare recipients isn't the only tough choice states face. They also will have to reconcile the public's insistence that welfare recipients work with its desire to make sure that children are sheltered from severe poverty.

Unfortunately for reformers, "children and their parents are a package," notes MDRC President Judith M. Gueron. "You cannot help one without helping the other." [1]

The Urban Institute concluded that the new law will push 1.1 million more children below the poverty line, in addition to the 9.7 million already there. About 20 percent of all families with children would lose an average of $1,300 a year, it said. [2] Proponents of the new law argue that this analysis underestimates how many adults will be prompted by the work requirements to find jobs. And, they say, it fails to recognize the demoralizing effect of welfare dependency on children.

Only time will tell who is right. Meanwhile, the key issue in welfare reform for the years ahead will be whether states can achieve the ambitious work objectives set by the new law — and whether welfare families can become self-sufficient in the process.

### *Can states meet the work targets the new law sets for welfare recipients?*

At first glance, there appear to be plenty of jobs. For decades, the U.S. economy has been an impressive job-creation machine. In the 1960s, for instance, employment grew 19.6 percent, or by 12.9 million jobs, even though the population grew just 16.9 percent. In the 1970s, employment increased 26.2 percent, while the population rose 22.4 percent. And in the 1980s, the total number of jobs jumped 18.7 percent, again outstripping the 12.1 percent growth in population. [3] This pattern has continued in the 1990s; the unemployment rate in October stood at 5.2 percent, a rate that most economists consider at or near "full employment" given normal turnover in the work force.

But Rebecca Blank, an economist at Northwestern University, argues that "the aggregate numbers are very deceptive." For one thing, there is relatively less demand for poorly educated workers than for people who have had more schooling. The unemployment rate among people who don't have high school degrees is double that of people who graduated from high school, and five times that of people with college degrees, according to Blank. [4]

Those figures suggest welfare recipients may face tougher going in the labor market than most people. Almost 47 percent of the people on welfare have less than a high school education, and 39 percent had amassed no work experience at all for a year before they first began receiving assistance. [5] Besides lacking the basic skills needed for many jobs today, many welfare recipients don't have the necessary "soft" skills, such as knowledge about personal grooming, basic language abilities and an ability to function smoothly in workplace settings. Others face chronic health or emotional problems, are victims of violence or sexual abuse, or have histories of drug or alcohol abuse.

Given these problems, what can welfare reformers realistically expect to achieve? Iowa, which has been working at moving welfare recipients into jobs longer and harder than most states, hasn't been able to get more than 35 percent of its adult welfare caseload working. Doug Howard, administrator of the state Division of Economic Assistance, says there seems to be a "cellophane ceiling" — perhaps not as hard to break as a glass ceiling, but still a barrier — that has prevented the state from going

# Reforms Target Food Stamp Users, Immigrants ...

President Clinton has vowed to seek changes in two controversial provisions of the Personal Responsibility and Work Opportunity Reconciliation Act of 1996 that he says "have nothing to do with welfare reform." But his task will be complicated because the two provisions have much to do with the $54.2 billion the new law is expected to save the federal government over the next six years.

As signed by Clinton Aug. 22, the law will cut spending on the food stamp program by $23.3 billion. It will save almost $24 billion by making legal immigrants ineligible for most welfare benefits, including food stamps, Medicaid and Supplemental Security Income (SSI), a cash benefit program for the low-income aged, blind and disabled.

Critics say the changes will seriously fray the federal safety net — simply to save the government money. Sandy Clark, a policy analyst at the Urban Institute, says that "unlike the major fundamental changes in AFDC [Aid to Families with Dependent Children], changes in the food stamp program amount to cutting benefits, plain and simple."

**Projected Cuts in Welfare Spending**

*The 1996 welfare overhaul law will cut federal spending by $58.4 billion over six years, mainly by scaling back food stamps and making legal immigrants ineligible for most welfare benefits. The law also includes modest increases in family support payments and other programs, bringing the net savings to $54.2 billion.*

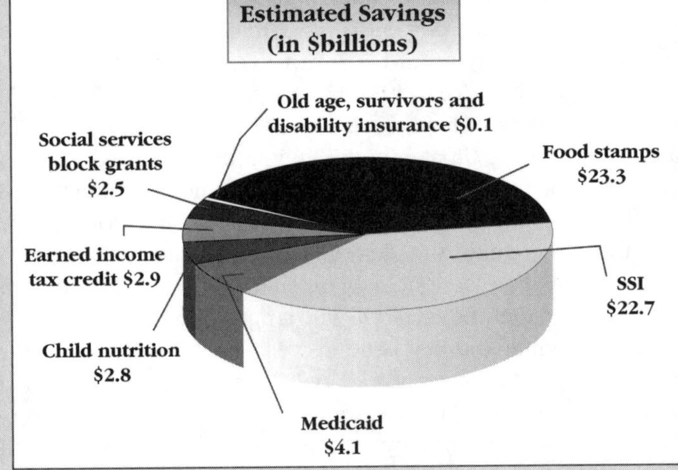


But reformers argue that the food stamp program was shot through with waste, fraud and abuse. They insist that welfare reform, not just budget cuts, was at the heart of reductions in both food stamps and benefits for immigrants.

The Center on Budget and Policy Priorities estimates that food stamp benefits will be reduced almost 20 percent — from the current 80 cents per person per meal to 66 cents per person per meal. According to the center, 6.7 million families with children (the primary beneficiaries of food stamps) will lose, on average, $435 in 1998, the first year that cuts take effect. The very poorest families — those with annual incomes at or below $6,250, or one-half the official poverty level for a family of three — will lose $655 each in 1998. By 2002, the cuts will cost them $790 a year.

In what the center calls "probably the single, harshest provision written into a major safety net program in at least 30 years," the law allows unemployed adults between 18 and 50 who have no dependent children to receive food stamps for just three months every three years, unless they are working at least half-time. Despite imposing this requirement, the bill provides no new money for workfare or training slots.

The Congressional Budget Office predicts that in an average month 1 million unemployed Americans who are willing to work but cannot find a job or a slot in workfare or job training programs will be affected. About 40 percent of them will be women, and nearly one-third will be over 40, an age at which it is particularly difficult for unskilled workers to find jobs. Because people in this group have no dependent children, they don't qualify for other welfare benefits.

Rep. Pat Roberts, R-Kan., chairman of the House Agriculture Committee, defends the cuts, arguing that the food stamp program has been on "automatic pilot" for too long, more than doubling in cost over the past 10 years. He says that under the new law, adjustments in benefits will be tied to increases in the actual cost of food. The law also tightens controls on waste and fraud while increasing penalties for illegal trafficking in food stamps. And, to help promote private-sector jobs for people moving from welfare to work, the law allows states to transfer food stamp allotments to private employers who can use them to supplement salaries for welfare recipients who take jobs.

Roberts, who declared July 31 on the House floor that "food stamps must not be a disincentive to work," says only a handful of food stamp recipients will be affected by the three-month restriction on benefits for the unemployed. For those who cannot find work because there are no jobs available, and for areas where the

beyond that.

Utah, which has been even more aggressive about moving welfare recipients into the labor force, reports similar results, although officials there appear a bit more optimistic. "About one-third [of the welfare caseload] can be moved into the job market fairly easily," says Connie Cowley, program specialist for the state's Family Employment Program. "A middle third have more difficult issues to resolve, but we think we can

# . . . But Clinton Vows to Seek Changes

unemployment rate is 10 percent or higher, the states will have flexibility to make exceptions to the three-month rule, he contends.

The immigration provisions of the welfare-reform law are contested just as vehemently as the food stamp ones. The National Immigration Law Center in Los Angeles says that legal immigrants are "by far the biggest losers in the final bill." Even though most legal immigrants to the U.S. pay taxes, have the right to vote and can join — or be drafted into — the armed forces, the law denies them eligibility for all welfare benefits except emergency medical treatment.

According to the National Conference of State Legislatures, approximately 600,000 legal immigrants may lose access to Medicaid, 1 million will be ineligible for food stamps and 500,000 elderly, blind and disabled legal immigrants will lose SSI benefits if the new law is enforced to the letter. [1]

That seems fair enough to those who support the change. "There ought to be meaningful distinctions between citizens and non-citizens, and this [welfare reform] can be one of them," says John J. Miller, vice president of the Center for Equal Opportunity, which says it is dedicated to establishing a color-blind, pro-assimilation society. Miller argues that welfare is destructive because it breeds dependency. "You want [immigrants] to come here and stay and succeed, and I don't think welfare helps them do that," he argues. "It may help them stay, but it does not help them succeed."

The old welfare system bred dependency and the presumption that entitlements are a natural part of the family budget, says Daniel Stein, executive director of the Federation for American Immigration Reform. New Chinese immigrants in California, for example, have "acculturated and assimilated into welfare and have evolved an understanding that [SSI] is part of a family entitlement," Stein says.

According to Stein, elderly Chinese immigrants who come to the United States commonly transfer their assets to children already here so that they can qualify for welfare benefits as indigents. Stein says the General Accounting Office has identified a 500 percent increase in the use of SSI by elderly aliens in the last 15 years. "We cannot be the retirement home for the world's indigent elderly," Stein argues.

He also contends America can't afford to continue letting a relatively uneducated, unskilled and more dependent immigrant population move to the U.S. just because some businesses want cheap labor. This is especially so because average taxpayers, not employers, cover the cost of welfare for such immigrants when they fall upon hard times, he says.

Jana Mason, a government liaison for Immigration and Refugee Services of America, argues that the law does an injustice to many of the immigrants and refugees whom the organization helps to settle in this country. Even though working-age immigrants are among the least likely welfare beneficiaries, she says, they can encounter the same difficulties and setbacks that any native-born or naturalized worker faces. "They can have an illness or they can have abuse in their families," she notes. "They also can have a falling out with people who sponsored them" and who are responsible for helping them stay off welfare if they are injured, lose their jobs or can't find work.

In the absence of any changes in the law, states may use their own funds to help legal immigrants living below the poverty line. In Maryland, for instance, Democratic Gov. Parris N. Glendening has pledged that the state will allocate almost $8 million to continue some welfare benefits to immigrants. [2]

Clinton, for his part, already has issued a directive saying that the administration will grant waivers to encourage extending the period that legal immigrants are eligible for food stamps to the maximum time allowed by law. He also said that legal immigrants should not be denied access to soup kitchens or emergency medical and child protection services. And to ensure access to full benefits as quickly as possible, Clinton directed Attorney General Janet Reno and the Immigration and Naturalization Service to "remove the bureaucratic roadblocks to citizenship to all eligible, legal immigrants." Partly as a result of the months-long debate over welfare reform, nearly 1.1 million immigrants were naturalized during fiscal 1996, more than double the record-breaking number of naturalizations in fiscal 1995. [3]

The welfare bill is "a great inducement to naturalize," Stein concludes. "In this sense, [it's] the greatest civics education we've had in 50 years. Suddenly, citizenship means something again."

---

[1] Most of the other savings in the SSI program will come from a provision that makes it harder for children to be considered disabled to qualify for SSI. The Congressional Budget Office estimates that about 300,000 children — or 22 percent — who would be receiving SSI in 2002 would lose their eligibility as a result of this change. See *CQ Weekly Report*, Aug. 3, 1996, p. 2193.

[2] See Jon Jeter, "Md. to Continue Some Welfare for Legal Immigrants," *The Washington Post*, Sept. 17, 1996, pp. D1, D6.

[3] The Associated Press, "Clinton Moves to Protect Legal Aliens' Welfare Benefits," *The Washington Post*, Aug. 24, 1996, p. A6; and Sam Howe Verhovek, "Immigrants' Anxieties Spur a Surge in Naturalizations," *The New York Times*, Sept. 13, 1996.

[get them working] with some short-term intervention."

But the final third have "multiple barriers" to employment — including alcohol or drug-abuse problems, family members who require regular care, histories of physical and sexual abuse and low IQs — that will greatly complicate efforts to move them from welfare to employment, Cowley says. Because the federal law allows states to exempt only 20 percent of welfare

## Welfare Cases Began to Drop Before Welfare Reform

*After rising for more than three decades, the number of families receiving Aid to Families with Dependent Children (AFDC) fell 13 percent between 1994 and August 1996 — the month Congress passed a welfare reform bill replacing AFDC with a system of block grants to the states. The total number of welfare recipients, including children, dropped 14 percent in the past two years, reflecting a continuing decline in the average size of families on welfare.*

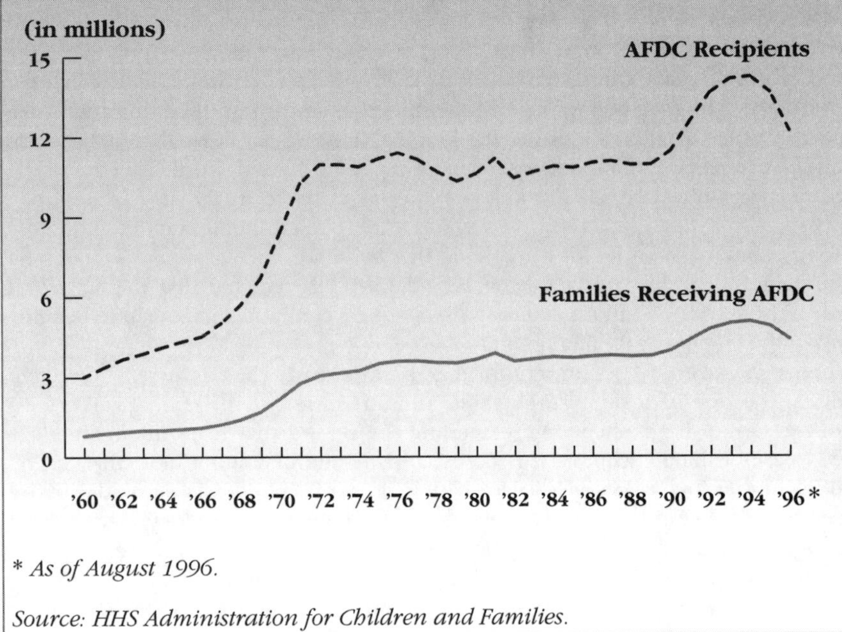


* *As of August 1996.*

*Source: HHS Administration for Children and Families.*

recipients from time limits, that suggests some people could be cut off from welfare even though they have serious obstacles to finding work.

There also are geographic pockets where jobs are particularly hard to find even in today's strong economy. In parts of West Virginia, for instance, the unemployment rate exceeds 17 percent; faced with such labor market conditions, Susan Sergi, commissioner of the state's Bureau for Children and Families, told *The Wall Street Journal* in August that she doubted the state will meet the employment targets in the new law. [6]

Inner cities, where many welfare recipients live, are an even tougher problem. For them, the long-term exodus of manufacturing jobs to the suburbs makes the welfare-to-work transition appear particularly daunting. Philadelphia, which has a welfare caseload of 70,000 adults, would have to put 15,000 welfare recipients to work in 1997 under the new law. But it actually lost 32,000 jobs between 1993 and 1996, according to Mark Alan Hughes, vice president of Public-Private Ventures, a public policy research organization in Philadelphia.

Hughes notes that other cities face similar challenges. New York, which has 285,000 adults on welfare, gained just 46,000 jobs between 1993 and 1996. Chicago picked up 12,000 jobs between 1993 and 1996, but it has 100,000 adults on welfare. Detroit, which has a welfare population of 65,000 adults, added just 14,000 jobs during the three-year period.

"The need is so great that unless we come up with some kind of public-sector employment and stop deluding ourselves that we can make a transition to private-sector employment, [welfare reform] won't work," says Hughes. In a recent op-ed article in *The Washington Post,* he predicted that time limits on welfare could create a "welfare dust bowl" in major American cities. [7]

Harvard sociologist William Julius Wilson describes the dismal labor market many urban blacks face in a new book, *When Work Disappears: The World of the New Urban Poor.* "For the first time in the 20th century," Wilson writes, "most adults in many inner-city ghetto neighborhoods are not working in a typical week." In 1950, according to Wilson, 69 percent of all males 14 and over who lived in three of Chicago's predominantly black South Side communities worked in a typical week. In 1960, the figure was still 64 percent. But by 1990, it had plummeted to just 37 percent. [8]

According to Wilson, the disappearance of high-paying manufacturing jobs from these inner-city areas was a major contributor to their social decline. Inner-city ghetto residents who continue to be employed — primarily in the kind of low-wage, service-sector jobs that remain in these neighborhoods — "are, in effect, working against all odds," Wilson argues. "They somehow manage to work steadily despite the lack of work-support networks (car pools, informal job information networks), institutions (good schools and training programs), and systems (child care and transportation) that most of the employed population of this country rely on. Moreover, the travel costs, child care costs and other employment-related expenses consume a significant portion of their already meager incomes." [9]

Many of Wilson's critics counter that he has mistaken the chicken for the egg — that the loss of manufacturing jobs in the inner cities was a response to social decline, rather than a cause of it. [10]

But whoever is right, there's no doubt that addressing the widespread joblessness in inner cities will be a crucial challenge for state welfare programs. Consider the case of Wisconsin, a state considered in the vanguard of welfare reform. Between 1990 and 1994, its welfare rolls dropped 6.3 percent statewide. But the number of welfare recipients actually climbed 0.4 percent in predominantly urban Milwaukee County. [11]

***Will the new welfare law lead to a permanent reduction in dependency?***

It's one thing to get a welfare recipient a job. But it may be something else altogether to help that person become truly self-sufficient.

"The presumption that a transition from welfare to work represents a move toward self-sufficiency or economic well-being ignores the fact that low-wage jobs neither pay enough to remove a family from poverty nor guarantee future access to better paying jobs," writes sociologist Kathryn J. Edin of Rutgers University. [12]

In a study of 214 recipients of Aid to Families with Dependent Children (AFDC) and 165 low-wage workers in four U.S. cities, Edin found frustration among welfare mothers. Most generally are eager to work, but the only jobs they can find — mostly in the fast-food business — pay very low wages, seldom offer benefits, often don't even guarantee a regular number of hours of work per week and are subject to frequent layoffs.

"Most of the welfare mothers interviewed believed they could eventually get a job if they tried, particularly if they were willing to do minimum-wage work," Edin writes. "However, they also believed that a minimum-wage job would get them nowhere." [13]

Edin estimates that a single mother would have to hold a full-time job paying between $8-$9 an hour to cover all her expenses — including the additional cost of clothing, transportation and day care associated with working — to be better off than when she was on welfare. Yet many welfare mothers can only find work at $5-$6 an hour, and often for less than 40 hours a week.

Faced with these realities, a significant number of women see welfare as part of a "broader strategy to improve their human capital," according to Edin. They opt for welfare in place of low-wage work, she explains, in the hope it will buy them the time and resources to receive training that will qualify them for jobs that will pay enough for them to become self-sufficient.

In spite of the obvious demand, critics of past welfare-to-work programs argue that financing education or training hasn't proven a cost-effective way to reduce welfare rolls. "Education and training are very ineffective because this population is not good at learning new skills," says Lawrence Mead, a professor of politics at New York University. "They accomplish more with work experience."

The new federal law, reflecting this view, says states can't count welfare recipients who are enrolled in post-secondary education toward satisfying their obligation to enroll a growing portion of their caseload in work programs. Further, it allows states to count only a limited number of people enrolled in vocational education classes.

Even if the lack of training opportunities consigns welfare families to low-wage jobs with little hope, Mead contends that this is an improvement over being on welfare. Having a job confers on a person a certain respectability and a right to claim other social benefits, such as earned-income tax credits and unemployment and disability insurance, he says.

While many analysts agree the welfare system can't be expected to solve the problem of declining wages for unskilled workers, they concede it is a serious concern. Between 1979 and 1995, according to a new study from the Economic Policy Institute, wages for people with less than a high school education fell a stunning 23 percent after adjustment for inflation — to an average of just $8.16 an hour. High school graduates saw their wages drop 11.8 percent, to $10.46 an hour. While people with college or advanced degrees didn't fare particularly well by historical standards either, their wages at least rose somewhat — 4.3 percent and 12.1 percent, respectively. [14]

Brookings Institution economist Gary Burtless adds a worrisome footnote to the well-documented deterioration in wages for low-skilled workers. If welfare reform succeeds in pushing 2 million more unskilled workers into the labor force, the likely result, he says, would be a further decline in wages. According to Burtless, "With fierce competition for unskilled and semiskilled jobs, wage rates would be driven down, at least modestly, and [welfare] recipients would face worse job prospects than those . . . who left the rolls during the 1980s." [15] ■

# BACKGROUND

## From Welfare to Work

It wasn't always assumed that welfare mothers should work. When Congress enacted the first modern welfare program in 1935, most mothers stayed home with their children, and Aid to Dependent Children, as the program established by Title IV of the Social Security Act of 1935 was then known, provided cash benefits to help needy widows care for their children at home.

As late as 1962, when Congress amended the Social Security Act at the behest of President John F. Kennedy, work was not a particular focus of welfare-reform strategies. The amendments approved that year instead stressed providing more social services to needy families. In particular, they provided funds to send welfare caseworkers into the neighborhoods and homes of welfare recipients.

Mary Jo Bane and David Ellwood, welfare experts at Harvard University who later would serve in the first Clinton administration, describe in their book *Welfare Realities* how the rising cost of welfare quickly led policy-makers to grow disenchanted with the social services approach. Conservatives, including Gov. Ronald Reagan of California, complained that caseworkers were driving up welfare costs by overlooking violations of welfare rules and advocating more services to address problems such as inadequate housing and child care, alcoholism and domestic violence. [16]

As a result of such criticism, welfare agencies were encouraged to concentrate on determining eligibility and processing welfare payments, rather than on providing services. Neighborhood visits were stopped, and standards for proving eligibility were toughened.

At the same time, with more and more women entering the work force, policy-makers increasingly began seeking ways to encourage welfare mothers to work. In 1967, House Ways and Means Committee Chairman Wilbur D. Mills, D-Ark., bemoaned a rising welfare caseload in terms that would be echoed almost 30 years later. "For five years, this load has gone up and up and up, with no end in sight," Mills said. "We are not going to put federal funds into states for the benefit of parents when they refuse to get out of the house and try to earn something." [17]

Mills helped steer one of the first welfare-to-work efforts through Congress that year. Under the Work Incentive (WIN) program, AFDC recipients with no preschool children were required to register for state work-training and employment services. The program was a disappointment, though. In 1986, according to Bane and Ellwood, 1.6 million AFDC recipients were registered with the program, but only about 220,000 actually were receiving services. And only 130,000 had worked their way off welfare — most of them without help from WIN. [18]

Bane and Ellwood attribute the lackluster results partly to inadequate funding. But they also cite a lack of coordination between state welfare and employment programs. "Welfare workers typically felt no obligation to require or encourage more active employment-directed activity," they said. "Employment service workers found welfare clients difficult to place, and saw no reason not to focus their activities on more promising clients." [19]

### *Family Support Act*

By the 1980s, politicians were becoming increasingly adamant that welfare recipients should be required to work — or at least participate in activities that would prepare them for jobs. President Reagan and the Democratic-controlled Congress agreed in 1988 to a new version of welfare reform that combined some of the social service concepts of the 1960s with tougher work requirements.

In the Family Support Act of 1988, conservatives won language stating that adult welfare recipients were to be "encouraged, assisted and required to fulfill their responsibilities to support their children by preparing for, accepting and retaining such employment as they are capable of performing."

But liberals won support for provisions that required states to offer welfare recipients, in addition to job readiness and placement services, opportunities to attain both basic literacy and high school or equivalent degrees, job skills training and help with child care and transportation expenses. States also could help pay for postsecondary education for welfare recipients interested in improving their skills, as well as provide community work experience slots — essentially public service employment — for those who otherwise couldn't find work. And the new law extended child-care and medical benefits to families of people who left the welfare roles for jobs.

"In return for having a work requirement and work as a goal, the government would provide support for education, training, health care and child care," said A. Sidney Johnson III, then-executive director of the American Public Welfare Association. "There was a concept of a reciprocal agreement." [20]

The grand left-right compromise failed to quell demands for welfare reform, however. States, free to determine for themselves which welfare recipients would be required to participate in the JOBS program, came up with widely differing figures. As late as fiscal 1994, Arizona exempted all but 19 percent of its AFDC adults, while Rhode Island said 70 percent of its adult caseload were eligible.

Nationwide, only 43.5 percent of AFDC recipients were designated as able to participate. But only a small portion of that group actually was required to participate. That's because sponsors of the new law, aware that JOBS would be more difficult and expensive than simply passing out benefit checks, set very low participation targets. Even when the law was fully phased in, states were required to enroll just 20 percent of eligible adults in work activities.

To make matters worse, the Family Support Act was staggered at the outset by a recession that sent welfare rolls surging 25 percent between 1989 and 1992. The weakened economy also drained state coffers, further undermining the new law. In fiscal 1992, for instance, states were able to claim only $750 million of the $1 billion in federal JOBS funds available, according to the Department of Health and Human Services.

## State Experiments

From its inception, welfare had been a shared responsibility between the federal government and the states. But beginning in the 1980s, as federal officials battled over welfare reform — and frequently came up with

# Chronology

## *1930s* ***The Depression throws millions of Americans into poverty, with no comprehensive policy in place for delivering aid and services to the needy.***

***1935***
Title IV of the landmark Social Security Act creates Aid to Dependent Children (ADC) program, giving states matching federal funds "to assist, broaden and supervise existing mothers' aid programs."

## *1960s* ***The nation focuses anew on poverty with the goal of helping Americans get off welfare and become self-sufficient.***

***1962***
President John F. Kennedy persuades Congress to amend the Social Security Act to fight poverty with larger welfare payments and to encourage more vocational training for welfare recipients. The ADC program is renamed Aid to Families with Dependent Children (AFDC). States are permitted to require unemployed adults to participate in community work and training programs as a condition to receiving AFDC benefits.

***1967***
Concerned about rising welfare caseloads, Congress enacts the Work Incentive (WIN) program, which requires states to offer worker training and work incentives to AFDC recipients.

## *1970s* ***States curtail efforts to bring social services to welfare recipients and focus instead on controlling costs by reducing fraud and policing eligibility more closely. Some states initiate demonstration programs that require AFDC recipients to work in exchange for welfare benefits.***

***1971***
WIN is amended to require all able-bodied AFDC recipients to register for the program.

## *1980s* ***President Reagan advocates strict work requirements for AFDC recipients. A number of states start experimenting with welfare-to-work programs.***

***1981***
Congress rejects Ronald Reagan's proposal to require states to operate Community Work Experience Programs as a condition of receiving AFDC. But lawmakers give states greater latitude in administering WIN and in imposing work requirements.

***1988***
Reagan and the Democratic-controlled Congress agree to the Family Support Act. The law creates the Job Opportunities and Basic Skills (JOBS) program, which offers welfare recipients a variety of options for work and training designed to lead them to self-sufficiency, and it requires that only 7 percent of eligible adults participate initially.

## *1990s* ***A recession hinders state efforts to implement the new JOBS program. States begin exploring new options for reforming welfare, ranging from letting welfare recipients keep more of their earnings before losing benefits to time limits on benefits to "family caps" limiting benefits to people who have more children while on welfare.***

***1992***
President George Bush pledges in his State of the Union address to support state experimentation on welfare. The Department of Health and Human Services grants nine waivers from AFDC rules for state reform experiments.

***Jan. 21, 1993***
Sen. Daniel Patrick Moynihan, D-N.Y., proposes legislation to provide full federal funding for the JOBS program, but it fails to advance.

***June 14, 1994***
President Clinton unveils his $9.3 billion welfare-reform proposal limiting welfare recipients to two years but providing community jobs for those who can't find work in the private sector. The plan gets a lukewarm reception from congressional Democrats and opposition from Republicans.

***November 1994***
Republicans vow to enact their "Contract with America," including a proposal to end entitlement status for AFDC.

***Aug. 22, 1996***
Following his earlier veto of two Republican welfare-reform bills, Clinton signs the Personal Responsibility and Work Opportunity Reconciliation Act of 1996.

## Recent Studies Offer Clues . . .

Advocates of the new welfare reform law say it will end welfare dependency, substitute work for passivity, reduce the size of welfare families, discourage out-of-wedlock births and teenage parenthood and reduce government costs. While it will take some years to test these theories, there are substantial data that may provide clues to what the future may bring.

The Twentieth Century Fund, a nonpartisan foundation that sponsors research on economic, social and political issues, summarized much of these data in a 1995 report, *Welfare Reform: A Twentieth Century Fund Guide to the Issues*. In addition, LaDonna Pavetti, a research associate at the Urban Institute and an authority on welfare dynamics, has summarized her research in the institute's 1996 report, *Welfare Reform: An Analysis of the Issues*.

Here are some of their findings:

***How many people will be affected by the two-year work requirement and the five-year time limit on welfare benefits?***

Advocates of time limits contend that welfare should provide temporary assistance, rather than be a way of life. In fact, half of all welfare recipients already stop receiving public assistance within a year, 70 percent leave within two years and almost 90 percent leave within five years. [1]

"It is commonly imagined that there is a large, stagnant Aid to Families with Dependent Children (AFDC) population for whom welfare has become a way of life," the Twentieth Century Fund report says. "But the data show a very dynamic welfare population, with many different women entering and leaving [and] only a small percentage remaining on welfare continuously."

There is, however, a difference between *getting* off welfare and *staying* off. While 30 percent of welfare recipients stop receiving welfare permanently in less than two years, fully 42 percent return within that time frame. That's partly because the earnings of many who escape remain so low, and their foothold in the labor market is so tenuous, that relatively minor problems — loss of a car or the breakdown of a day-care arrangement, for instance — can send them back to the welfare office. Some 40 percent of the women who leave welfare because they get jobs don't earn enough to escape poverty, according to the Twentieth Century Fund.

With so many people cycling on and off welfare, how many people are likely to bump up against the five-year lifetime limit on federal welfare benefits?

Only about one-third of the women who ever use welfare spend more than five years on it, according to Pavetti. Still, she estimates that if past patterns continue, 1.4 million families will hit the five-year time limit in 2001, the first year anybody could be thrown off welfare as a result of the controversial new provision. By 2005, she says, just under 2 million families could be affected. [2]

***What distinguishes welfare recipients who are likely to use up their lifetime welfare benefits from those who give up public aid relatively quickly?***

According to Pavetti, most long-term welfare recipients are women with limited job prospects. "Recipients who first receive welfare when they are young, have never married, have low levels of education and have no recent work experience are all overrepresented among recipients with longer stays on welfare," she told the House Ways and Means Subcommittee on Human Resources last May. "When these factors are considered simultaneously, the strongest predictors of whether a recipient will leave welfare for work in a given month are recent work experience and educational attainment, including mastery of basic skills." [3]

Fully 62.8 percent of long-term welfare recipients have less than a high school education, compared with 34.8 percent of those who spend two years on public assistance. Half of the long-term recipients had no work experience in the year before they first received welfare, compared

compromise solutions that seemed to please nobody — they began unleashing the states to try their own reform experiments. [21]

In 1981, for instance, President Reagan battled with Congress to require states to operate Community Work Experience Programs as a condition to receiving AFDC. Opponents of the idea ultimately succeeded in thwarting it, but its advocates managed to win for the states greater latitude in administering WIN and imposing work requirements of their own.

Several notable experiments were launched by state welfare departments under federal waivers of WIN rules. The Massachusetts ET (education and training) Program, for instance, used case managers to work with welfare recipients to develop plans for becoming self-sufficient. Clients were exposed to job listings and recruiters and were offered opportunities for basic education, skills training, job search assistance or subsidized employment. The voluntary program claimed modest successes in increasing employment.

In 1988, the Reagan administration launched a new phase in welfare reform experimentation by granting Wisconsin a waiver from federal AFDC rules to reduce welfare benefits to parents who failed to prevent truancy among their teenage children. Reagan's successor, George Bush, granted Ohio a waiver in 1989, allowing it to require all teen parents on AFDC to attend school.

But the idea of waiving AFDC rules really caught on in 1992, when Bush touted the idea in his State of the Union address. "States throughout the country

# . . . About Future Impact of Welfare Reform

with 30.2 percent of the short-stayers.

The number of children a welfare mother has is a poor predictor of how long she will stay on welfare, however. Although many believe that welfare mothers tend to have large families, Pavetti's figures show that 57.2 percent of all welfare mothers had just one child at the time they first went on welfare. Even among mothers who stayed on welfare five years or more, 59.1 percent have just one child. By the same token, just 9.7 percent of welfare mothers had three children when they first went on welfare, and just 10.4 percent of long-term recipients did. [4]

***Did AFDC encourage women to have more children?***

A few states, including New Jersey, have approved "family caps," which limit benefits to women who have children while on welfare. But the Twentieth Century Fund concluded from its review of research data that there is no evidence that welfare encourages women to have more children.

"Ten major studies on welfare and non-marital childbearing have been done over the past six years, and not one has found a direct effect of welfare-benefit levels on subsequent births to women on welfare," it says. Overall, the fund reports, 72.7 percent of all AFDC families have two or fewer children. And the average size of a family on AFDC decreased from 4.0 to 2.9 persons between 1969 and 1992. [5]

The evidence is more ambiguous on the correlation between welfare and out-of-wedlock births generally. White women appear to be more likely to have children out of wedlock if they live in high-benefit states, although illegitimacy among black and Hispanic women doesn't seem to rise as welfare benefits go up, the Twentieth Century Fund reports. Out-of-wedlock births are rising among all women, not just those on welfare, though. In 1960, just 5.3 percent of unmarried women of childbearing age gave birth; by 1990, that figure had risen fivefold, to 28 percent.

Still, the fund reports that welfare mothers who have never married tend to stay on welfare much longer than those who have married. Some 39 percent of welfare mothers who never married receive welfare payments during a 10-year period or longer, compared with just 14 percent of divorced mothers, 24 percent of separated mothers and 10 percent of widowed mothers. [6]

***Does welfare encourage teenage pregnancy?***

Finally, while teenage pregnancy is a particular concern of welfare reformers, the data show that it is a relatively small part of the welfare problem — and thus successes in averting it will have only a minor impact on the welfare system overall.

In 1992, only 7.6 percent of AFDC mothers were teenagers, the Twentieth Century Fund reports. And, contrary to widespread belief, teenage motherhood has *declined,* not increased, over the past 30 years. In 1960, 89 out of every 1,000 teenagers ages 15-19 bore a child; but in 1992, only 61 out of every 1,000 teenagers in that age bracket bore a child.

At the same time, however, far fewer teenagers are getting married now than 20 years ago. In 1960, 14 percent of all girls ages 15-19 were married, while in 1992, just 5 percent were. [7]

---

[1] LaDonna Pavetti, "Time on Welfare and Welfare Dependency," testimony before House Ways and Means Subcommittee on Human Resources, May 23, 1996. Available online at http://www.urban.org/welfare/pavtes.html

[2] LaDonna Pavetti, "Who is Affected by Time Limits?" in *Welfare Reform, An Analysis of the Issues* (1996), p. 32.

[3] Pavetti, "Time on Welfare and Welfare Dependency," *op. cit.*

[4] Pavetti, "Who is Affected by Time Limits?" *op. cit.*, p. 33.

[5] Twentieth Century Fund, *Welfare Reform, A Twentieth Century Fund Guide to the Issues* (1996), p. 6.

[6] *Ibid.*, p. 7.

[7] *Ibid.*, p. 5.

are beginning to operate with new assumptions: that when able-bodied people receive government assistance, they have responsibilities to the taxpayer, a responsibility to seek work, education or job training, a responsibility to get their lives in order; a responsibility to hold their families together and refrain from having children out of wedlock — and a responsibility to obey the law," Bush said. "We are going to help this movement."

Waiver requests came flooding in — a process that gained momentum when Bill Clinton, himself a former governor and vigorous welfare-reform advocate, took office in 1993. The waivers reflected a wide range of ideas about how best to reform welfare. A majority of states, hoping to increase incentives to work, received permission to allow families to earn more before having their AFDC benefits reduced. But many also won approval to impose time limits on welfare benefits.

Numerous states were allowed to begin experimenting with the idea of using AFDC grants to subsidize wages, employ welfare recipients to rehabilitate public housing, help welfare families set up their own small businesses and to create subsidized jobs. But a handful also were trying "family caps," which seek to prevent families from receiving additional cash grants — or even cut the grants they receive — if they have additional children while on welfare.

By 1996, waivers had become so widespread that states effectively had seized the initiative in setting welfare policy. Douglas Besharov, a resident scholar at the American Enterprise In-

## Big Companies See Big Profits in Welfare

If the era of big government is over, then the era of big welfare contracts for private companies is ready for takeoff.

"I see this as the future of welfare reform," said Gerald H. Miller, former director of the Michigan Family Independence Agency and former president of the American Public Welfare Association. "The private sector will ultimately run these programs," added Miller, who announced in September that he would leave his post to direct for-profit welfare initiatives for the $30 billion defense company Lockheed Martin. "The era of big government is over." [1]

Along with other large companies, such as Electronic Data Systems (EDS), IBM and the Arthur Andersen accounting firm, Lockheed Martin has positioned itself to become a major player in the competition for what promise to be lucrative welfare contracts with states and counties across the country.

Advocates of more private-sector involvement in welfare reform contend that corporations are quicker than government bureaucracies to respond to change and new demands. Unlike welfare bureaucracies, which are geared toward delivering benefits, private corporations are governed by a work ethic that makes them better suited to reward employees who help welfare recipients find jobs, supporters suggest.

Private-sector boosters also predict that states and counties, whose welfare budgets will be capped under the new federal block-grant system, will be happy to embrace fixed-price contracts with large companies that can absorb the shock of government penalties, if need be. Finally, they say contracting out welfare services will help states reduce their own administrative costs.

Those who oppose privatization, however, say that profit-driven companies will use the harshest provisions of the new law to remove welfare recipients from the roles just to boost their profits. "We have people who are in tremendous need on the one hand, and on the other side we have people [private contractors] who are making a profit, and it looks like they're going to make more of a profit if they serve fewer people in need," argues Henry A. Freedman, executive director of the Center on Social Welfare Policy and Law in New York City.

The first big prize in welfare privatization will be Texas, where Lockheed, EDS and Andersen are competing for a $563 million contract to reform and administer cash assistance, Medicaid, food stamps and nutrition programs for women, infants and children.

Some smaller companies have made significant headway into the welfare-to-work marketplace. One company, America Works, has won praise from Mayor Rudolph W. Giuliani, R-N.Y., and former Gov. Mario M. Cuomo, D-N.Y., for its jobs-placement programs in New York City and Albany. It also has won accolades from admirers of its Indianapolis, Ind., program.

But Deborah A. Merrifield, commissioner of social services for the Erie County Department of Social Services in New York, predicts that if states require private enterprises to train and find jobs for all welfare clients regardless of how employable they are, the new welfare entrepreneurs are unlikely to realize huge profits.

"I think it's pretty risky business for a private, for-profit company to say, 'I shall ensure that I give someone all their benefits and get them into a job and I won't need any more [public] money,'" says Merrifield. "That's a big risk for anyone to take at this point."

---

[1] Quoted in "Welfare Reform Leader Makes Corporate Move: Ex-Official Predicts Privately Run Programs," *The Washington Post,* Sept. 17, 1996.

stitute, was quoted as declaring that President Clinton, in his generous approval of waiver requests, "can justifiably claim he has ended welfare as we know it." In effect, the waiver requests had ended the idea of welfare as a "personal entitlement."

Unlike Besharov, Mark Greenberg, a lawyer at the liberal Center for Law and Social Policy (CLASP), sees the easy waiver policy as harmful. But he agrees that it undermined the idea of strong federal action on welfare reform. "Once the Bush and Clinton administrations conveyed a willingness to grant waivers of federal requirements freely, the way to become a high-prestige state was to announce that you were departing from federal law rather than effectively implementing federal law," he says. "As all the attention shifted to whoever had submitted the most dramatic waiver, it became increasingly difficult for a state to say it was implementing welfare reform by a thoughtful implementation of the Family Support Act."

### The Clinton Plan

President Clinton may have approved so many waivers partly because of difficulties he was having resolving conflicts over welfare within his own administration. One issue was the age-old tension between a desire to help welfare recipients and a belief it would be better to get tough with them. Straddling the issue, Clinton had talked during his 1992 campaign about "empowering" Americans to leave welfare by giving them education, training and child care, and he said Americans should receive universal health insurance. But he also said welfare benefits should be cut off after a two-year transitional period.

The administration also was ambivalent about the respective roles of the federal government and the states. Harvard's Ellwood, in a December 1992 working paper on welfare reform written shortly before he joined the administration, suggested that welfare reform should be phased in gradually, beginning "in a modest number of states," and that it should be extended to others "over time." But later, Ellwood noted that gradualism would open the president to criticism that he was backing off his sweeping campaign promises. And, after travelling around the country to see what states were doing, Ellwood came to favor strong federal action. Too many states, he said, had "lost sight of the values of welfare," and the "broad framework" of a strong, national policy was needed. [22]

While wrestling with this and other issues, the administration also made a crucial strategic decision. Health-care reform, along with crime and trade legislation, would be the administration's top priority. Welfare reform would have to wait. As a result, the White House didn't even present a welfare reform proposal until June 14, 1994. And even then, it was introduced with little fanfare, and, coming just five months before congressional elections, was given little chance.

As expected, the plan would have required welfare recipients to find work within two years of accepting their benefits. To ease the transition to work, the government would spend more on job training and child care. And those who still couldn't find jobs were to be placed in federally subsidized jobs.

To control costs — Clinton had promised he wouldn't seek new taxes to pay for his plan — the administration proposed applying the plan only to people born after 1971. Even at that, it would have cost $9.3 billion more over five years than the current welfare system.

The president didn't find much support in Congress for his recommendations. Liberals were cool to the idea of a two-year limit, and to a proposal that would let states limit benefit increases to parents who had more children while on welfare. Republicans denounced the White House plan even more strenuously, complaining that it would cover only part of the welfare caseload, provide too much flexibility in administering time limits, do little to discourage illegitimate births and, unlike their own plan, continue providing welfare assistance to immigrants. [23]

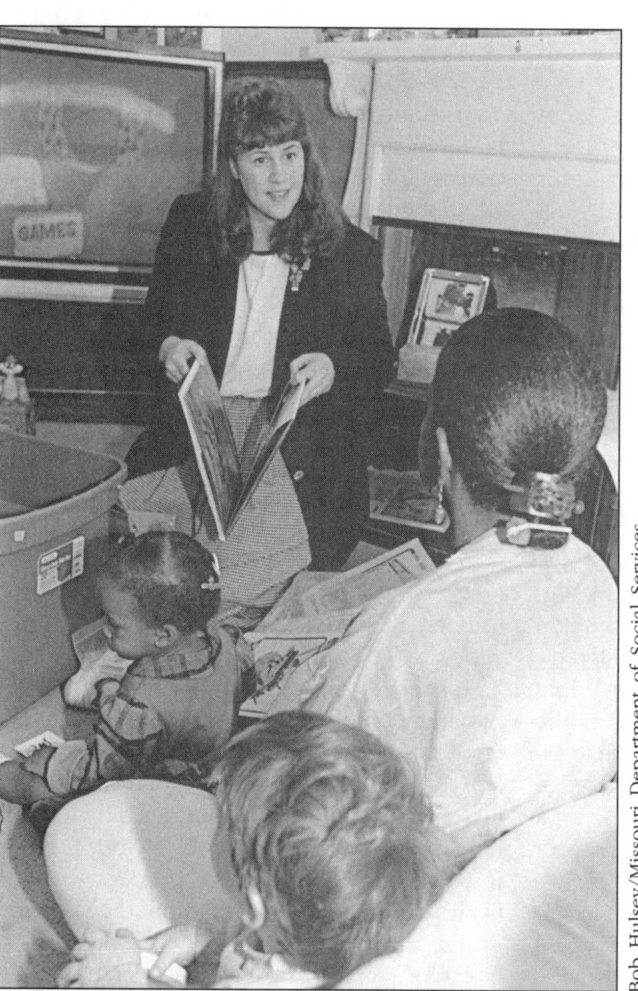


Bob Hulsey/Missouri Department of Social Services

*Educating and nurturing low-income children is a key component of Missouri's "Beyond Welfare" reform strategy.*

### *Republican Plans Vetoed*

The 1994 elections gave Republicans control of Congress, and with it, the initiative in charting federal welfare policy. The new majority brought together several disparate groups, including reformers who sought to impose tougher work requirements, states'-rights advocates who hoped to shift power from the federal government to the states [24] and budget cutters who were eager to reduce domestic social spending.

This coalition produced a welfare-reform proposal far bolder than anything the Republicans had proposed during the first two years of the Clinton administration. Earlier GOP proposals would have preserved the federal entitlement to welfare benefits while providing states more money to move welfare recipients into jobs. But the new Republican plan sought to eliminate the federal entitlement altogether and convert federal welfare spending to block grants. There was no promise of jobs for those who sought work and couldn't find it. And where the Republican welfare-overhaul legislation of 1993 would have saved taxpayers $19.5 billion over five years, the new plan would have reduced federal spending $102 billion over seven years.

President Clinton vetoed one version of the Republican welfare plan on Dec. 6, 1995, and a second one Jan. 6, 1996. But with the November 1996 elections drawing nearer, Republicans knew that Clinton would find it increasingly difficult to block welfare-reform legislation since he had promised during his 1992 campaign to "end welfare as we know it." Jack Howard, an aide to House Speaker Newt Gingrich, R-Ga., urged Republicans to send the president as tough a bill as possible because, "I believe the White House will sign just about anything we send them, so we should make them eat as much as they can." [25]

#### *'Hit by a Freight Train'*

The Republican Congress sent Clinton a third welfare reform measure in late July 1996, less than four months before the presidential election. Sen. Daniel Patrick Moynihan, D-N.Y., author of the Family Support Act of 1988 and one of the Senate's leading experts on welfare reform, watched the Republican juggernaut in dismay. The president, he said, was trapped by his own 1992 rhetoric. "He keeps his promise and he abandons his principles — or he keeps his principles and abandons his promise," Moynihan said. [26]

Clinton signed the measure on Aug. 22, 1996, despite staunch opposition from liberals, among them Children's Defense Fund President Marian Wright Edelman, a longstanding friend of the president. Edelman had said the legislation "makes a mockery of his pledge not to hurt children. . . . It will leave a moral blot on his presidency and on our nation that will never be forgotten. [27]

Ellwood decided to leave the administration after Clinton said he would sign the bill. He complained that Republicans had seized on the president's rhetoric — in particular, his pledge to "end welfare as we know it" — while ignoring the president's other pledge to provide jobs to those who can't find them. Acknowledging that the administration had lost control of the issue after the Republicans took control of Congress in 1994, Ellwood said glumly, "We got hit by a freight train, in part, of course, because our own train moved too sluggishly." [28] ■

# CURRENT SITUATION

## Maneuvering Room

As yet, it is still unclear what states will do with the newfound freedom — and responsibility — that welfare reform affords them. "I don't think there's a definitive picture of what states are going to do at this point," says Andrea Kane, senior policy analyst at the National Governors' Association. "I don't think there's any state that knows exactly what they're going to do about all the provisions."

States may have a bit of time to prepare for their new role, though. Just as a recession set back efforts to put the Family Support Act into effect, the chances of success with the new law will be improved, at least initially, by the currently strong economy.

Sustained growth and low unemployment helped push the number of families on welfare down 13 percent between 1994 and August 1996, from just over 5 million to about 4.4 million; the number of recipients, including children, dropped 14 percent, from 14.2 million to 12.2 million. (*See graph, p. 84.*) Because the new welfare block grants are based on state expenditures in the early 1990s, when caseloads were higher, that means most states actually will receive more in general welfare assistance this year than last year.

Moreover, the decline in the welfare rolls will make it easier for states to meet their initial requirements for moving welfare recipients into work. The law allows states to reduce their required work participation rate by 1 percentage point for every like decline in its total caseload. That means a state whose caseload has fallen 10 percent would have to get only 15 percent of its AFDC adults working this year, not the official 25 percent target in the law. New York, for instance, will have to have only about 20 percent of its welfare recipients working in the current fiscal year, instead of 25 percent. Mississippi, meanwhile, faces a requirement of just 15 percent — a rate it effectively has achieved already.

Because of this "caseload-reduction credit," Robert Rector, senior policy analyst at the Heritage Foundation, estimates that a typical state will have to have just 18 percent of its AFDC caseload working by 1999, not 35 percent as prescribed in the law.

Rector sees this at once as a vindication of the tough approach to welfare reform and as a "loophole" that will keep the new law from being everything it could be. "If you sincerely say that welfare will no longer be free income and that you must actually work for the benefits, all of a sudden you change the desirability of welfare, and people now have a very strong incentive to go elsewhere," he argues. "The number of people who even bother to apply to get onto welfare will go down very substantially."

Isabel Sawhill, a senior fellow at the Urban Institute, agrees that there is "anecdotal evidence" suggesting that work requirements are turning some welfare applicants away. But it's difficult to separate that effect from the impact of economic growth. For instance, while the welfare caseload in reform-minded Wisconsin dropped 37 percent between 1993 and last summer, Mississippi and Alabama, which generally aren't considered to be in the forefront of welfare reform, posted declines that were almost as substantial — 30 percent and 29 percent, respectively.

Other provisions of the law give states more room to maneuver — at least in the short run — than headlines

# At Issue:

## *Will the new federal welfare law hurt needy children?*

**MARK E. COURTNEY**
***Associate professor of social work, University of Wisconsin-Madison***

***FROM A PAPER PRESENTED AT A CONFERENCE ON CHILDREN AND WELFARE REFORM FUNDED BY THE CARNEGIE CORPORATION, OCT. 11, 1996.***

**yes**

There are a number of ways that the federal welfare reform law and its implementation at the state level could substantially increase the number of children living in poverty.

First, the Congressional Budget Office has estimated that between 2.5 million and 3.5 million children could be affected by the five-year time limit on assistance when the law is fully implemented. Second, an unknown, but potentially large, number of families will lose cash and other benefits due to non-compliance with work requirements. Third, the Urban Institute has estimated that elimination of Supplemental Security Income (SSI) and food stamp benefits for non-citizens will move approximately 450,000 children into poverty. Fourth, some parents, and future parents, will be banned from program participation for life because of drug-related crimes. This provision may have a serious impact on the child welfare system, given the large proportion of families currently involved with the system that suffer from substance abuse problems. Lastly, since the individual entitlement to support has been eliminated, some states may simply cut off benefits when economic or political circumstances result in inadequate funds to continue assistance. . . .

Growth in child poverty is likely to lead to an increase in child maltreatment and a corresponding increase in demand for child welfare services including substitute care. . . . Some families who under current law would use SSI, Aid to Families with Dependent Children and/or food stamps to house and feed their children will lose all such aid. . . .

The expansion of work requirements could also contribute to a movement of children into foster care, particularly if it is not accompanied by an adequate expansion of subsidized child care. The Congressional Budget Office estimates that by 2002 federal child care funding will fall $1.8 billion short of what will be needed to provide child care for low-income working families if states meet work participation goals by placing participants in work programs. Many parents may be faced with the choice of either losing benefits due to non-compliance with work requirements in order to care for their children or leaving their children unsupervised.

In either case, the children in these families are at increased risk of neglect. Moreover, many of the families who are most likely to be unable or unwilling to find work are, by and large, already at relatively high risk of neglecting or abusing their children. Elimination or reduction of benefits to these families will heighten that risk.

**ROBERT RECTOR**
***Senior analyst, The Heritage Foundation***

***FROM AN INTERVIEW WITH THE CQ RESEARCHER, OCTOBER 1996.***

**no**

The impact of the current welfare system on children is overwhelmingly and abusively negative. The reform has many key provisions that should reduce dependence as well as out-of-wedlock births, which are the two most harmful factors in terms of destroying children's future. By reducing dependence through work requirements and time limits, and by reducing illegitimacy through a number of incentives, the [law] should have the most profound positive effect on children's well-being.

Most of the debate on this suffers from the liberal myopia of the last 30 years, which sees the principal problem facing children as a lack of material resources and then simply tries to stuff resources into families. That approach has catastrophically failed, and everyone except the most troglodyte leftist realizes it has failed.

A child's success or well-being in future life is not really dependent upon its family's bank account status. The liberal hypothesis is if we raise family income then these kids are going to graduate from high school and the crime rate is going to go down and drug use is going to go down. But everything we've learned in the last 30 years shows that that is absolutely untrue. Trying to raise family income by giving them handouts doesn't have any beneficial consequences, but in fact has negative consequences.

If material resources were the critical reason kids fall into crime or why they drop out of school and so forth, then this country should have been awash in crime and drug abuse and so forth back in 1950, when close to a third of the population was poor. But it was not. The reality is that what's critical to children's success are the values that they receive in their communities and inside their families, not just the family's bank account level. Welfare destroys those values — the very things that are most necessary for children's success. That's why welfare harms kids.

If you can reduce dependency and reduce illegitimacy, you will actually raise the living standards of poor families. They're not getting rich by being on welfare. But that's really a secondary concern. The real problem is that the values the child acquires living in a single-parent dependent home are values that will cripple that child in its quest to become a member of American society. It's the worst environment for children that you can possibly imagine.

have suggested. For one thing, states that were operating under waivers from the old AFDC rules can continue with those programs until the waivers expire. That includes a majority of states; 43 states had waivers to conduct some 78 welfare experiments when the new law was adopted.

Besides allowing for some continuity in previously launched state welfare-reform experiments, the decision to let existing waiver arrangements continue could provide an early indication of whether provisions of the federal law will work. At least 10 states, for instance, have imposed shorter time limits on welfare benefits than the five-year limit in the federal law.

States, meanwhile, may be able to soften the impact of the federal law by using their own funds to maintain benefits for which federal money no longer can be used.

## Disparities Among States

Still, while most states are currently enjoying a windfall in their federal welfare payments, it's clear that they are beginning the new era in welfare policy with widely differing financial situations. Because the federal block grants are calculated on the basis of welfare spending in the early 1990s, states that were relatively generous, or that invested in welfare reform early in hopes of reaping benefits later, will be better off than others.

Vermont, for instance, will be in a relatively good position. Besides already having a waiver to operate its own welfare-reform program — one that focuses heavily on providing social services to needy families — the state's relatively high spending level in the past means it will collect $2,761 for every poor child in the state, according to the Center for Law and Social Policy. Texas, on the other hand, which has been considerably less generous, will get just $339 per poor child. (*See map, p. 80.*)

"States with a high level of resources have a number of alternatives, but states at the bottom have fewer alternatives because they have so much less to work with," says CLASP's Greenberg.

Supporters of the federal law say they hope that legislatures in states like Texas will be willing to make a bigger investment now. But that would require a break with their previous practices. Wisconsin, a relatively high benefit state which is operating under a series of federal AFDC waivers, illustrates the potential upfront costs that may be required.

Under its program, all welfare recipients are required to choose between four options: finding regular employment; taking trial jobs in which the state subsidizes the wages; holding community service jobs to develop the work habits and skills needed to land a private-sector job; or, for those with particularly low levels of ability, participation in "transition" work activities such as sheltered workshops.

The state expects it will have to create almost 30,000 community-service positions, roughly one for every two adults currently on welfare. Overall, it anticipates spending about 13 percent more initially under its plan, called "Wisconsin Works," than it did previously. Its child-care spending is projected to soar from $48 million to $158 million. [29]

### *Welfare Magnets*

Some analysts worry that if other states don't make comparable investments, the disparity between states could widen. That, they say, could trigger a harmful "race to the bottom," in which states feel compelled to slash benefits in order to avoid becoming "magnets" that attract poor people from other states.

"Clearly, states are going to worry more about the magnet effect," says Thomas Corbett, acting director of the Institute for Research on Poverty at the University of Wisconsin in Madison. "The fear is that compassion, however defined — it could include subsidizing employers and providing training, not just paying more in benefits — might become too costly if there's any suspicion that low-income people are being attracted to a state."

Officials in states that have been generous in the past admit privately to some concerns about becoming welfare magnets, but publicly they play the issue down. "If a governor does not make welfare reform work, it's going to be a pretty bad mark against him or her when re-election comes around," says Amy Tucci, spokesperson for the American Public Welfare Association. "So it's incumbent on legislatures and governors to make welfare reform work."

## Modest Solutions

*The New Republic* magazine predicted that the new welfare law will unleash a period of "radical state experimentation." [30] But so far, many states are looking instead at relatively modest ways to reduce their welfare rolls.

Oregon and Arkansas, for instance, are considering incentive plans that would pay bonuses to welfare recipients who find jobs. Maine is bringing back the 1960s-era idea of sending caseworkers to visit welfare applicants in their homes. New Jersey is considering consolidating transportation programs for the elderly into a single system that also helps welfare recipients get to jobs. [31]

In Kentucky, meanwhile, a task force is studying a proposal to provide "relocation assistance" to help unemployed welfare recipients move to places where jobs may be more abundant. And the Clinton administration is experimenting with ways to link inner-city people with jobs. In September, it awarded five cities $17 million to help 3,100 welfare recipients commute to suburban jobs over the next four years. Officials say they will ask for $75 million more next year to expand the program to at least 75 cities.

Utah, meanwhile, is empowering state welfare officials to intercept people with short-term problems and help them before they are forced onto welfare. That could include helping a prospective welfare applicant fix a car so he or she can continue getting to work, or paying for clothing that would improve an applicant's chances of getting a job, for instance.

At the opposite end of the spectrum, New York has initiated a large-scale public-jobs program. There, some 34,000 people already are required to work in cleanup and other jobs in exchange for their benefits. Under a new plan, the number of workfare slots could grow to 100,000 within two years. By 2002, the number may be as large as New York City's current municipal payroll — 204,000 — and could cost more than $1 billion a year. [32]

But most states may follow the lead of Iowa and others, which rather than dramatically revising their welfare programs have sought to convert them somewhat more gradually — emphasizing the importance of work and the idea that welfare is a temporary, not permanent, benefit, but taking individual circumstances into consideration.

In Iowa, for instance, caseworkers help clients develop individualized Family Investment Plans spelling out what steps they will take to become self-sufficient. The state, which stands to collect $1,161 for every poor child within its borders, even believes that it will be able to enhance its educational offerings, which have been limited in past years because of budget pressures. State welfare administrator Howard says state officials are working with community college officials on ways to provide welfare recipients with carefully targeted training.

And in Arizona, caseworkers manage portfolios on each welfare recipient, listing the benefits they receive for child care, public assistance, child support, earned income and other services. The workers then seek ways to increase clients' income and reduce their dependence on cash assistance from the government. As in Iowa and Utah, failure to comply can bring swift sanctions.

"The idea is to change behavior and get mutual responsibility going — to make sure people are living up to their contracts," says Linda J. Blessing, director of the Arizona Department of Economic Security. ■

# OUTLOOK

## Private-Sector Help?

While many state officials are relatively sanguine about the near-term prospects for welfare reform, they say the longer-term outlook is more clouded. In part, that's because current, positive trends such as declining caseloads and moderating costs could be reversed quite rapidly in the event of a recession.

"At least for the first few years, when caseloads remain low or shrink further, most states think they'll have adequate resources," says Kane of the governors' association.

The new law establishes a $2 billion contingency fund for states to tap in the event of a rise in unemployment. But that's only one-third the actual run-up in welfare costs that occurred during the last recession, from 1990 to 1992, according to the Center for Budget and Policy Priorities.

Moreover, there's good reason to believe that getting welfare recipients off assistance will become more difficult with time. States that have had the most experience with welfare-to-work efforts have found that once the most employable welfare recipients move into the labor force, caseloads will tend to become more heavily weighted with people who have the most serious obstacles to employment.

Utah, for one, already has started encountering this law of diminishing returns; it has responded by hiring more caseworkers with master's degrees in social work or counseling. "The era of rapid caseload depletions is over," warned Edward L. Schilling, director of the department of social services in Fond du Lac County, Wis. [33]

Politicians, meanwhile, are unlikely to let the welfare issue lie untouched. President Clinton, along with many Democrats, would like to reverse the steep cuts in spending on food stamps and immigrants. That may prove difficult, however, since Republicans retained control of Congress, and balancing the budget remains a major priority of both parties.

The president may have more luck with proposals designed to facilitate welfare recipients' transition to work. When Clinton signed the 1996 reform law, he sought to mollify his liberal critics by promising to seek legislation in his new term to establish a $3 billion job placement program designed to help 1 million welfare recipients find work. The president also said he would seek a $400 million tax credit for businesses that hire welfare recipients. And he promised to encourage business development in depressed urban areas by proposing more tax-favored "empowerment zones" and the creation of more community-development banks.

"Welfare is no longer a political football to be kicked around," said Clinton, who himself rode the welfare issue into office in 1992, only to find himself outflanked by Republicans two years later. "It's a personal responsibility of every American who ever criticized the welfare system to help poor people now to move from welfare to work." [34]

## FOR MORE INFORMATION

**American Public Welfare Association,** 810 First St. N.E., Suite 500, Washington, D.C. 20002; (202) 682-0100; http://apwa.org. APWA monitors federal and state legislation and regulations and disseminates information to its membership of social welfare administrators and professionals.

**Center for Law and Social Policy,** 1616 P St. N.W., Suite 150, Washington, D.C. 20036; (202) 328-5140; www.clasp.org. A public interest law firm, CLASP engages in educational activities, policy research and advocacy on behalf of low-income families.

**Center on Budget and Policy Priorities,** 820 First St. N.E., Suite 510, Washington, D.C. 20002; (202) 408-1080; www.cbpp.org. This nonpartisan research organization and policy institute conducts research and analysis on a range of government policies and programs, with an emphasis on those affecting low- and moderate-income people.

**Heritage Foundation,** 214 Massachusetts Ave. N.E., Washington, D.C. 20002; (202) 546-4400; www.heritage.org. This conservative think tank promotes the ideas of free enterprise, limited government and "traditional" American values.

**Institute for Research on Poverty,** 1180 Observatory Dr., 3412 Social Science Building, University of Wisconsin—Madison, Madison, Wisc. 53706; (608) 262-6358; www.ssc.wisc.edu/irp/. IRP is a national, nonpartisan center for research into the causes and consequences of poverty and social inequality in the United States.

Republicans, for their part, say they plan to scrutinize the administration closely to make sure officials don't seek to undermine the tough work provisions of the new law. But they, too, have further reform proposals. Sen. Daniel R. Coats, R-Ind., has proposed providing a tax credit for contributions to private charities. Others seek to relax a prohibition on providing federal funds to religious organizations that seek to help the poor.

These proposals reflect a belief that future stages of welfare reform will further diminish the role of government. "The end of poverty doesn't lie with government," says Michael Tanner, director of health and welfare studies at the Cato Institute. "No amount of restructuring, budget cutting or micromanagement of individual moral behavior can make a government-spawned welfare system work. Only a civil society, one based on voluntary cooperation and persuasion, not force or coercion — a society built upon revitalized social institutions such as the family, church and charities — can break the cycle of dependency and give the poor what they really need to become independent, whole and free."

President Clinton continues to argue for a more assertive role for government, but he concedes that, for the foreseeable future, the fate of welfare may lie more in private hands. "The most important thing," Clinton says, "is establishing a state- and then a community-based partnership with the private sector and with others who have to fill the needs of people who are trying to move from welfare to work." [35] ■

## Notes

[1] Judith M. Gueron, "A Research Context for Welfare Reform," *Journal of Policy Analysis and Management,* fall 1996, p. 548.

[2] Sheila Zedlewski et al., "Potential Effects of Congressional Welfare Reform Legislation on Family Incomes," *The Urban Institute,* July 26, 1996. p. 1.

[3] Rebecca Blank, "Outlook for the U.S. Labor Market and Prospects for Low-Wage Entry Jobs," *The Work Alternative* (1995), p. 35.

[4] *Ibid.,* p. 39.

[5] LaDonna Pavetti, "Who is Affected by Time Limits?" *Welfare Reform* (1995), p. 33.

[6] Dana Milbank, "Welfare Law's Work Rules Worry States," *The Wall Street Journal,* Aug. 5, 1996, p. A2.

[7] *The Washington Post,* Sept. 25, 1996.

[8] William Julius Wilson, *When Work Disappears: The World of the New Urban Poor* (1996), pp. xiii, 19-20.

[9] *Ibid.,* p. 53.

[10] See Marvin Kosters, "Looking for Jobs in All the Wrong Places," *The Public Interest,* fall 1996, pp. 125-131; Joe Klein, "The True Disadvantage," *The New Republic,* Oct. 26, 1996, pp. 32-36.

[11] Michael Wiseman, "State Strategies for Welfare Reform: The Wisconsin Story," *Journal of Policy Analysis and Management, op. cit.,* p. 540.

[12] Kathryn J. Edin, "The Myths of Dependence and Self-Sufficiency: Women, Welfare and Low-Wage Work," *Focus,* fall/winter 1995, pp. 1-2, published by University of Wisconsin—Madison Institute for Research on Poverty.

[13] *Ibid.*

[14] Lawrence Mishel, Jared Bernstein and John Schmitt, *The State of Working America, 1996-1997* (1996), p. 167, published by Economic Policy Institute.

[15] Gary Burtless, "Employment Prospects of Welfare Recipients," *The Work Alternative, op. cit.,* p. 89.

[16] Mary Jo Bane and David T. Ellwood, *Welfare Realities: From Rhetoric to Reform* (1994), p. 15.

[17] Quoted in *ibid.,* p. 12.

[18] *Ibid.,* pp. 20-21.

[19] *Ibid.,* p. 21.

[20] Quoted in *1993 CQ Almanac,* p. 373.

[21] For background, see "Welfare Experiments," *The CQ Researcher,* Sept. 16, 1994, pp. 793-816.

[22] Quoted in Bane and Ellwood, *op. cit.,* pp. 805-807.

[23] See *1994 CQ Almanac,* pp. 364-365.

[24] For background, see "The States and Federalism," *The CQ Researcher,* Sept. 13, 1996, pp. 793-816.

[25] Quoted in *Congressional Quarterly Weekly Report,* July 27, 1996, p. 2117.

[26] Quoted in Jason DeParle, "The New Contract with America's Poor," *The New York Times,* July 28, 1996.

[27] Quoted in *Facts on File,* Aug. 1, 1996, p. 526.

[28] David Ellwood, "Welfare Reform as I Knew It: When Bad Things Happen to Good Policies," *The American Prospect,* May-June 1996, pp. 22-29.

[29] See Mickey Kaus, "Adopt the Wisconsin Plan," *The Washington Post,* July 9, 1996.

[30] Editorial in *The New Republic,* Aug. 12, 1996, p. 8.

[31] Barbara Vobejda and Judith Havemann, "States Take Variety of Paths to Welfare Reform," *The Washington Post,* Oct. 6, 1996, p. A4.

[32] David Firestone, "New York Girding for Surge in Workfare Jobs," *The New York Times,* Aug. 13, 1996, p. B1.

[33] Quoted in "The Silent Welfare Reforms," *Business Week,* May 20, 1996, p. 73.

[34] Remarks at bill signing ceremony, Aug. 22, 1996.

[35] Remarks to the Southern Governors Association, Kansas City, Mo., Sept. 10, 1996.

# Bibliography

## *Selected Sources Used*


### *Books*

**Bane, Mary Jo, and David T. Ellwood, *Welfare Realities: From Rhetoric to Reform,* Harvard University Press, 1994.**

This collection represents nearly a decade in the work of the two experts President Clinton selected to shape his welfare proposals — and who resigned from their posts after Clinton signed the Republican-sponsored Personal Responsibility and Work Opportunity Reconciliation Act of 1996. Compiled while Bane and Ellwood were teaching at Harvard, the chapters discuss the history of welfare and set out various policy proposals.

**Murray, Charles, *Losing Ground: American Social Policy, 1950-1980,* Basic Books, 1984.**

This book played a key role in sparking the conservative revolution against government social programs that culminated in 1996 with the termination of the federal government's 61-year-old welfare experiment and the decision to turn federal welfare money over to the states.

**Nightingale, Demetra Smith, and Robert H. Haveman, eds., *The Work Alternative: Welfare Reform and the Realities of the Job Market,* Urban Institute Press, 1995.**

In this volume, based on a 1994 conference, leading authorities on welfare and labor markets explore the prospects for moving large numbers of people from welfare to work.

**Wilson, William Julius, *When Work Disappears: The World of the New Urban Poor,* Alfred A. Knopf, 1996.**

In this widely acclaimed, though controversial, book, Harvard sociologist Wilson attributes social deterioration in America's inner cities to the exodus of high-paying jobs to the suburbs. Wilson's critics say he fails to recognize how behavioral changes helped prompt the disappearance of jobs, but few question his description of the devastating consequences of widespread joblessness.

### *Articles*

**Conte, Christopher, "Will Workfare Work?" *Governing,* April 1996, pp. 19-23.**

This article describes the experience of one state, Iowa, which was among the first to convert welfare into a jobs program. Its successes have been limited by budget constraints and the near disappearance of high-paying manufacturing jobs for low-skilled workers.

**Gueron, Judith M., "A Research Context for Welfare Reform," *Journal of Policy Analysis and Management,* Vol. 15, No. 4, fall 1996, pp. 547-561.**

Gueron, president of the Manpower Demonstration Research Corp. in New York, looks at previous welfare-reform efforts and how they have sought to balance the goals of putting welfare recipients to work, protecting their children from severe poverty and controlling costs. The article is one of five in the journal that discuss welfare reform.

**"Sign It," *The New Republic,* Aug. 12, 1996, pp. 7-8.**

This article, written before President Clinton decided to sign the 1996 welfare-reform law, captures the concerns that led commentators once considered liberal to support the new block-grant approach. "The continuing agony of the underclass is destroying our cities, our race relations, our sense of civility, our faith in the possibilities of government," the magazine's editors said. "It's worth taking some risks to end it."

### *Reports and Studies*

**Edin, Kathryn J., "The Myths of Dependence and Self-Sufficiency: Women, Welfare, and Low-Wage Work," *Focus,* Institute for Research on Poverty, University of Wisconsin, fall/winter 1995; online: gopher://gopher.ssc.wisc.edu:70/11/irpgopher/publications/focus.**

Edin, an assistant professor at Rutgers University, summarizes data from interviews with welfare recipients and low-wage workers in four U.S. cities. She reports that welfare benefits in most states are so low that recipients must supplement them with other income, and that low-wage jobs don't pay enough to move families from poverty or guarantee future access to better-paying jobs. She says many unskilled single mothers use welfare as part of a broader strategy to improve their education and skills.

**Sawhill, Isabel V., ed., *Welfare Reform: An Analysis of the Issues,* Urban Institute Press, 1995; online: http://www.urban.org/welfare/overview.htm**

Written before the new welfare-reform law was enacted, this volume explores the myriad issues that surround welfare, including the federal role in maintaining a social safety net, the possibility there will be a "race to the bottom," the role of food stamps in providing a safety net and the debate over whether immigrants should receive public benefits.

**Super, David A., et al, *The New Welfare Law,* Center on Budget and Policy Priorities, Aug. 13, 1996; online: http://www.epn.org/cbpp/wconfbl2.html**

This analysis of the welfare reform act concludes that its overriding effect "is likely to be a large increase in poverty, especially among children and legal immigrants."

# 6 Social Security

ADRIEL BETTELHEIM

Like many people of her generation, Claire McGrath is a loyal defender of Social Security. The 73-year-old retired state employee from Syracuse, N.Y., relies on her $916 monthly benefit check to pay her bills and views the program as a vital safety net for the elderly. But she worries it may not be around for her grandson after politicians get through tinkering with it.

"I think we need to leave it the way it is because Social Security at least guarantees you'll receive something," McGrath says. "I know there are a lot of strains on the system, and I don't blame younger people for griping about how much they have to pay into it. But I'd hate to see them monkey with it and put us at more risk."

For decades, lawmakers who considered changing the Social Security system risked incurring the wrath of seniors like McGrath and being accused of dismantling one of America's great domestic-policy programs. So few tried that the program became known as the "third rail" of American politics; touching it meant instant death.

Lately, however, Social Security could more accurately be described as a lightning rod for far-reaching reform proposals.

Since President Clinton proposed a national dialogue on Social Security in his State of the Union address in January, Congress and Washington think tanks have been abuzz with proposals to overhaul the 63-year-old retirement system. Many plans envision "privatizing" the system by redirecting some payroll taxes from retiree benefits to individual savings plans tied to stocks and bonds. Others call for gradually raising the retirement age or even allowing the government to invest the Social Security trust fund in the stock market.

From *The CQ Researcher,* October 2, 1998. Originally published as "Saving Social Security."

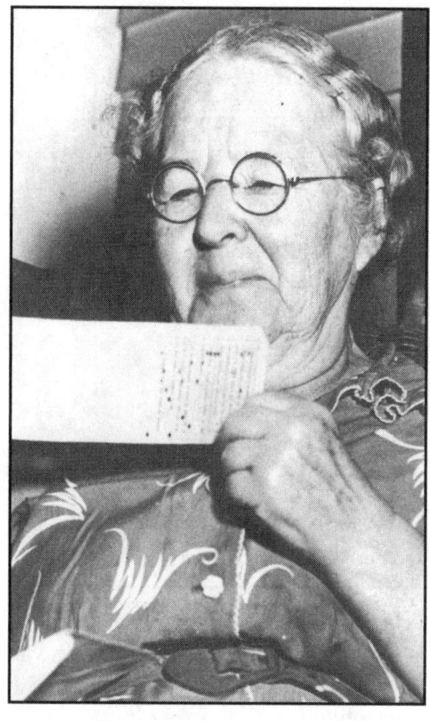

The shift in thinking is vindication for conservative and libertarian think tanks and politicians, who have long argued the present system operates like a Ponzi scheme because it relies on current workers to pay retirees more than they paid into the system. With an unprecedented 76 million baby boomers born from 1946-1964 expected to retire over the next 30 years, even some liberal Democrats concede the so-called pay-as-you-go system can't survive in its present form.

"The energy in social policy right now is to privatize," says Sen. Daniel Patrick Moynihan, D-N.Y., one of Social Security's staunchest defenders, who stunned many in March by proposing a reform plan that featured personal retirement accounts. "Any effort to keep Social Security will have to acknowledge the people who want to get rid of it, the people who are saying that government is taking your money and cheating you." [1]

Clinton and a bipartisan group of congressional lawmakers have discussed the future of the program at three town hall meetings held around the country this year. The White House, which hasn't endorsed a plan, is positioning itself to broker a compromise after the November elections and plans to host a bipartisan summit on Social Security in December.

However, recent volatility in the stock market is dampening enthusiasm for quick legislative solutions. The recent stock market gyrations tied to financial turmoil in Russia and Asia led former Labor Secretary Robert B. Reich, among others, to predict the privatization movement will stall. "Social Security was supposed to be an insurance system," he says. "The stock market is anything but an insurance system. It's more like a casino."

The calls for change are largely driven by predictions that the Social Security trust fund will face a severe financial squeeze early in the next century. According to actuarial projections, the trust fund will go broke by 2032, when benefits paid to retirees exceed revenues the system collects. The incoming money — from payroll taxes paid by current workers and their employers and the self-employed plus the interest Social Security earns on the government bonds it buys — will only be enough to pay 75 percent of all old-age, disability and survivors' benefits due. To pay the remainder, the government will have to increase taxes, cut benefits, restrict Social Security eligibility or make more drastic changes. [2]

But the reform movement is driven by more than just accounting projections. Changing public attitudes about pensions and investments have made many baby boomers and younger workers receptive to the idea of a retirement system based on accumulated wealth. The popularity of employer-sponsored 401(k) retirement plans, fueled by the bull market of the 1990s, has already tied thousands of current workers' retirement sav-

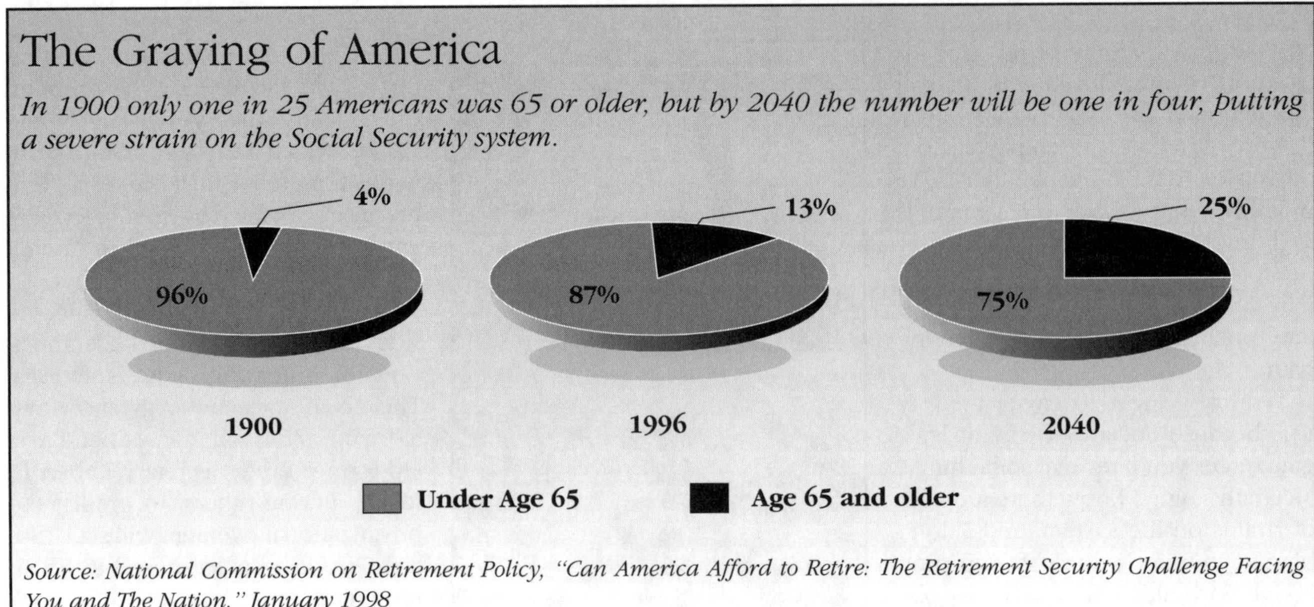


ings with personal investments. Surveys also suggest younger workers are so disillusioned with government that many don't expect Social Security to even exist by the time they retire. A 1994 poll by the youth advocacy group Third Millennium found more respondents ages 18-34 believe UFOs exist than believe they will ever receive Social Security.

"To maintain anything approximating today's opportunities for seniors in the future — and to do so without doing a massive injustice to younger people — we must make major changes in a system of public entitlements that now passes out huge windfalls regardless of need," says Peter Peterson, a former secretary of Commerce under President Richard M. Nixon and a member of the Clinton administration's Bipartisan Commission on Entitlement and Tax Reform.

Privatization advocates like Peterson argue that setting up personal retirement accounts would raise money to finance Social Security without raising taxes. The Concord Coalition, a Washington interest group that advocates policies to eliminate the federal budget deficit, estimates workers could earn 7 percent returns by investing the money they now pay into Social Security taxes in stocks instead. Currently, the Social Security taxes that aren't immediately applied to paying retirees' benefits are invested in safe but low-yielding U.S. Treasury bonds that only pay 1 or 2 percentage points above inflation. The Concord Coalition analysis assumes stocks will perform at their 75-year historical averages. [3]

However, skeptics respond there's no guarantee the stock market will continue to perform at record highs and note workers' retirement savings could be threatened by market downturns lasting several years. Additionally, placing a portion of payroll taxes into private accounts reduces the amount of money available for traditional, guaranteed monthly Social Security benefits. Privatization foes such as John Sweeney, president of the AFL-CIO, say cutting guaranteed payments would be especially harmful to low-wage workers, who have less to invest and now count on a Social Security benefit formula that is weighted in favor of people with low career earnings.

Several other proposals would attempt to reduce the strain on Social Security by raising the retirement age, which is already scheduled to increase to 67 from 65 by 2022. Raising the age further to 70, as has been proposed in several plans, means Social Security wouldn't have to start paying recipients as soon and, presumably, won't have to pay them for as long. Supporters of the idea say a higher retirement age additionally corresponds to Americans' increased longevity. In 1935, when Social Security was created, the average 65-year-old was expected to live about 12.6 more years. Today, that person is expected to live 17 additional years; by 2040 he will be expected to live at least 19 more years. [4]

Yet another reform plan would allow the Social Security system to invest its trust fund in common stocks, instead of the low-yielding government bonds. Advocates say the plan could boost the system's investment returns while preserving the core elements of the government's social safety net. However, polls show many current workers and senior citizens are skeptical about the government's ability to make the right investment decisions and worry about whether the proposal would leave Washington with too much influence on pri-

## Understanding Social Security

• Social Security, created in 1935, is the most costly item in the federal budget. The program provides old age, survivors' and disability insurance to approximately 44 million Americans. Workers and their employers fund the system by each paying payroll taxes equivalent to 6.2 percent of covered wages. Self-employed individuals pay 12.4 percent of taxable self-employment income. The Internal Revenue Service collects the taxes and deposits the money in government-administered accounts known as the Old Age and Survivors and Disability Insurance Trust Funds (OASDI).

• The payroll tax revenues are used to pay benefits to those people currently collecting Social Security pensions, a system known as pay-as-you-go. Any excess of taxes over benefit payments is invested in U.S. Treasury bonds, which earn the average rate of return on publicly traded government debt. Social Security taxes also pay for Medicare, the national health program for the elderly. The services that are funded come under Medicare Part A and include inpatient hospital care and skilled nursing care.

• Workers who accumulate enough earnings credits become eligible to receive a Social Security pension when they reach the early retirement age of 62 or become too disabled to continue working, regardless of age. A workers' dependent spouse and non-adult children can draw monthly survivors' pensions when the worker dies.

Social Security is a defined-benefit pension program, meaning each pension is based on the worker's average career earnings and on the age when the worker or worker's dependents first obtain the pension. The exact amount of the payout is determined by a formula that is codified in law and updated annually to reflect changes in wages and consumer prices.

The Social Security benefit formula is deliberately tilted in favor of workers with low career earnings, those who face an unusually high risk of becoming totally disabled and married couples with only one wage earner. It's possible to make generous payments to these groups because high-wage workers, unmarried and childless workers and dual-income married couples receive less favorable treatment under the system.

• In 1997 the Social Security system took in $457.7 billion from payroll taxes and bond interest and paid out $362 billion in benefits to retired and disabled workers and their families. Administrative costs totaled $3.4 billion. The system's assets increased $88.6 billion, to $655.5 billion, and the trust funds earned $43.8 billion on bond interest.

• The trust funds are expected to be able to cover benefits for the next 34 years. However, the 1998 Social Security trustees' report states that benefit payments will begin to exceed income in 2013, and that interest income on the Treasury bonds will be able to keep total income ahead of benefit payments only until 2021. After that, the trust funds will begin to decline until they are exhausted by 2032. At that point, tax revenue will only be able to pay three-quarters of benefit obligations.

*Sources: Social Security Administration, Brookings Institution*

vate capital markets.

Predicting whether any substantive reforms will be passed is difficult, given the timing of the debate and the ongoing legal problems surrounding President Clinton. Observers say a Democratic president who doesn't have to run for re-election and a Republican-led Congress have a brief window of opportunity next spring to enact substantial bipartisan reforms. Clinton, according to some advisers, views Social Security reform as a way of leaving a lasting legacy. But beyond next summer, the anticipated posturing in advance of the 2000 presidential and congressional elections threatens to turn Social Security into a purely political issue.

Federal officials and those close to the Social Security debate also have serious doubts about Clinton's ability to push an ambitious domestic agenda as he simultaneously deals with legal troubles stemming from his relationship with Monica Lewinsky. Should Clinton have to step down and be succeeded by Vice President Al Gore, it's unlikely that Gore would embrace a complicated, potentially divisive issue for Democrats that could threaten his chances of winning a full four-year term in 2000. Gore has already expressed serious doubts about privatizing the system.

If Clinton survives the scandal, his personal credibility with Congress may be too damaged to allow a grueling fight over a landmark social- policy program. And with financial markets around the world shaken by crises, Republicans and Democrats alike may have second thoughts about replacing the present system with individual accounts that rely on the compounded earnings power of stocks and bonds.

"Clearly there are a lot of risks to achieving reforms next year," says Social Security Commissioner Kenneth Apfel. "But the best thing for the American people is the long-term security of the Social Security system, and continuing to talk about the need for reform . . . is centrally important."

"Nobody really knows what will happen until the president weighs in," says Henry Aaron, senior fellow

## Elderly Are Fastest-Growing Group

*Due to the large number of aging baby boomers, Americans 65 and older are the fastest-growing segment of the population.*

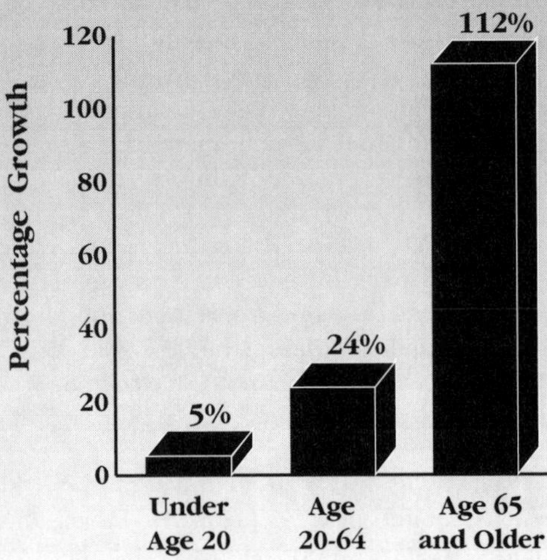


*Source: National Commission on Retirement Policy, "Can America Afford to Retire: The Retirement Security Challenge Facing You and The Nation," January 1998*

in economic studies at the Brookings Institution. "Everyone is putting [reform proposals] on the table. But it's up to the administration to really start the debate by coming up with its own plan. And making large-scale changes to social programs is often fraught with peril."

As policy-makers mull further changes to the system and debate its long-term viability, here are some questions they are asking:

***Can the existing system survive without major reforms?***

The early architects of Social Security and many liberal Democrats shake their heads at all of the recent proposals to change the system. Most believe Social Security can continue to provide a safety net for retirees and their survivors if Congress simply makes minor adjustments, occasionally raising payroll taxes or recalculating the way benefits are paid. Doing so would address concerns about the system's solvency while still guaranteeing that benefits will stay about where they are.*

"The key point is that we do not need to panic," says Rep. Jerrold Nadler, D-N.Y., who disputes the view that the system is in a financial crisis. "Social Security's status as a risk-free, guaranteed benefit program is, for millions of Americans, the sole protection against economic misfortune. That rock-solid dependability must be preserved."

Liberals like Nadler accuse reform advocates of manufacturing a crisis that pits generation against generation. They note Social Security has worked well for more than 60 years by providing a steady stream of monthly payments that beneficiaries can rely on. It also has helped lift millions of seniors out of poverty.

Robert Myers, who served as chief actuary of the Social Security Administration from 1947-1970 and deputy commissioner in 1981 and 1982, says the existing system was never intended to be an unchangeable or contractual program. Rather, its founders envisioned Congress stepping in to make gradual adjustments when demographic or accounting factors necessitated change.

"Fixing the system is easy, but finding the fix that fits both politically and socially is trickier," Myers says. "Some 80 million retirees and survivors will be drawing benefits from Social Security the year it is supposed to go broke. Having them go from a check one month to nothing the next is unthinkable. The country wouldn't stand for it."

Defenders of the system say the projected financial squeeze isn't as severe as it's being depicted. They note Social Security actuaries project the program's deficit will amount to only 2.19 percent of taxable payroll over the next 75 years. While that's a cause for some concern, program advocates argue a small tax increase could solve the problem without having to take more dramatic steps like raising the retirement age or making steep reductions in benefits.

One remedy being discussed among liberal House Democrats would increase the wage base for Social Security taxes by lifting the cap on income subject to the payroll tax. The current payroll tax is 12.4 percent (with 6.2 percent each paid by workers and employers) on salaries up to $68,400 a year. About 6 percent of all workers make more than that ceiling. Other options include extending the program to many federal government workers who are now excluded from participating in it, or means-testing the program to

* The average monthly benefit for a retired worker is $765.

## Would Women Lose Under Privatization?

The image of an elderly widow living off her monthly Social Security check is frequently evoked in debates over the retirement program. However, the push to overhaul the program is raising questions over whether older women would gain or lose under a privatized system.

Some backers of the current system contend privatization could unfairly penalize professional women and dependent spouses for a variety of reasons. First, working women typically earn less than men (71 cents for every $1, on average), and therefore have fewer funds to invest in individual savings accounts. Dependent spouses, who now are automatically entitled to 50 percent of their husband's benefits, would lose the subsidy in a system based on private accounts. Some private savings plans may also be set up to expire at death, leaving the survivor without benefits.

Women also tend to be more averse to risk when making investment decisions. A recent U.S. General Accounting Office study of women in their prime earning and saving years shows they are less likely than men to invest in potentially higher yielding but risky assets like stocks, meaning they would be at risk of having accumulated less in their private accounts at retirement. [1]

"Difficult as Social Security reform will be, our most serious challenge may be ensuring fair treatment for women," says Rep. Barbara B. Kennelly, D-Conn., ranking Democrat on the House Ways and Means Subcommittee on Social Security.

However, privatization proponents say the current system needs to be changed precisely because it cheats working women by using an outdated "model family" with a stay-at-home mom. When the program was designed, few married women worked outside the home. If benefits were to be calculated based on one's own work history, millions of widows would be left with nothing when their husbands died.

In 1939, lawmakers introduced spousal benefits that automatically entitled a woman to half of her husband's benefits, regardless of whether she had paid payroll taxes. Thus a woman who worked all of her life and paid a significant amount of taxes into the system could receive a smaller retirement benefit than a woman who never worked, even if their household incomes are identical.

The American Society of Actuaries estimates that for a family making $68,400 in pre-retirement income, a stay-at-home spouse would be entitled to a Social Security widow's benefit of $1,354 per month, compared with $1,082 for a widow who brought home half of the household income.

The disparity becomes even larger for couples who make a combined $34,200 in annual pay. The actuaries project the stay-at-home spouse would receive a monthly check of $1,082 on being widowed, while a wife who brought home half of the income draws a monthly benefit of only $674.

Cato Institute analyst Darcy Ann Olsen adds that working women typically qualify for smaller payouts under the present system because they frequently leave the work force for extended periods of time during their peak earning years to raise children. [2]

The Cato Institute endorses a system that consists entirely of individual investment accounts, in which a husband and wife split contributions and ownership of the accounts 50-50. If both spouses contributed 10 percent of earnings to the accounts, the think tank calculates all categories of women would be better off than under Social Security or hybrid plans that provide guaranteed minimum benefits and individual accounts.

Gender equity will continue to receive attention as the privatization debate pushes forward, particularly because two-thirds of working women have no other pension plan. "Too many women, minority women in particular, will find themselves about to enter a financial prison when they retire," says Jeffery Lewis, executive director of the Teresa & H. John Heinz III Foundation, a Washington public policy think tank.

[1] See U.S. General Accounting Office, "Social Security Reform: Implications for Women's Retirement," Dec. 31, 1997. For background, see Sue Kirchhoff, "Proposed Fixes Could Widen Social Security Gender Gap," *CQ Weekly*, April 25, 1998, pp. 1038-1044.

[2] See Darcy Ann Olsen, "Greater Financial Security for Women with Personal Retirement Accounts," Cato Institute Briefing Paper No. 38, July 20, 1998.

avoid paying benefits to rich retirees.

Another proposal to save the present system comes from Robert Ball, who served as commissioner of Social Security from 1962-1973. Ball believes the government can leave benefits roughly at current levels without significant new taxes as long as it finds a way to earn higher returns on its reserves. His solution would allow Social Security to invest about 40 percent of its trust funds in stocks, 30 percent in corporate bonds and the rest, as now, in government debt. A similar proposal is being prepared for House Democrats by Rep. Earl Pomeroy, D-N.D.

"There is no financial crisis in Social Security. But it does need adjustment," Ball says. He notes other federal retirement systems such as the Federal Employees Thrift Plan place their reserves in stocks without placing participants at significant risk. [5]

However, critics say such proposals ignore the fact that the program's fiscal situation is only expected to get worse as more baby boomers begin to collect benefits. Adding to the concerns are worrisome demographic

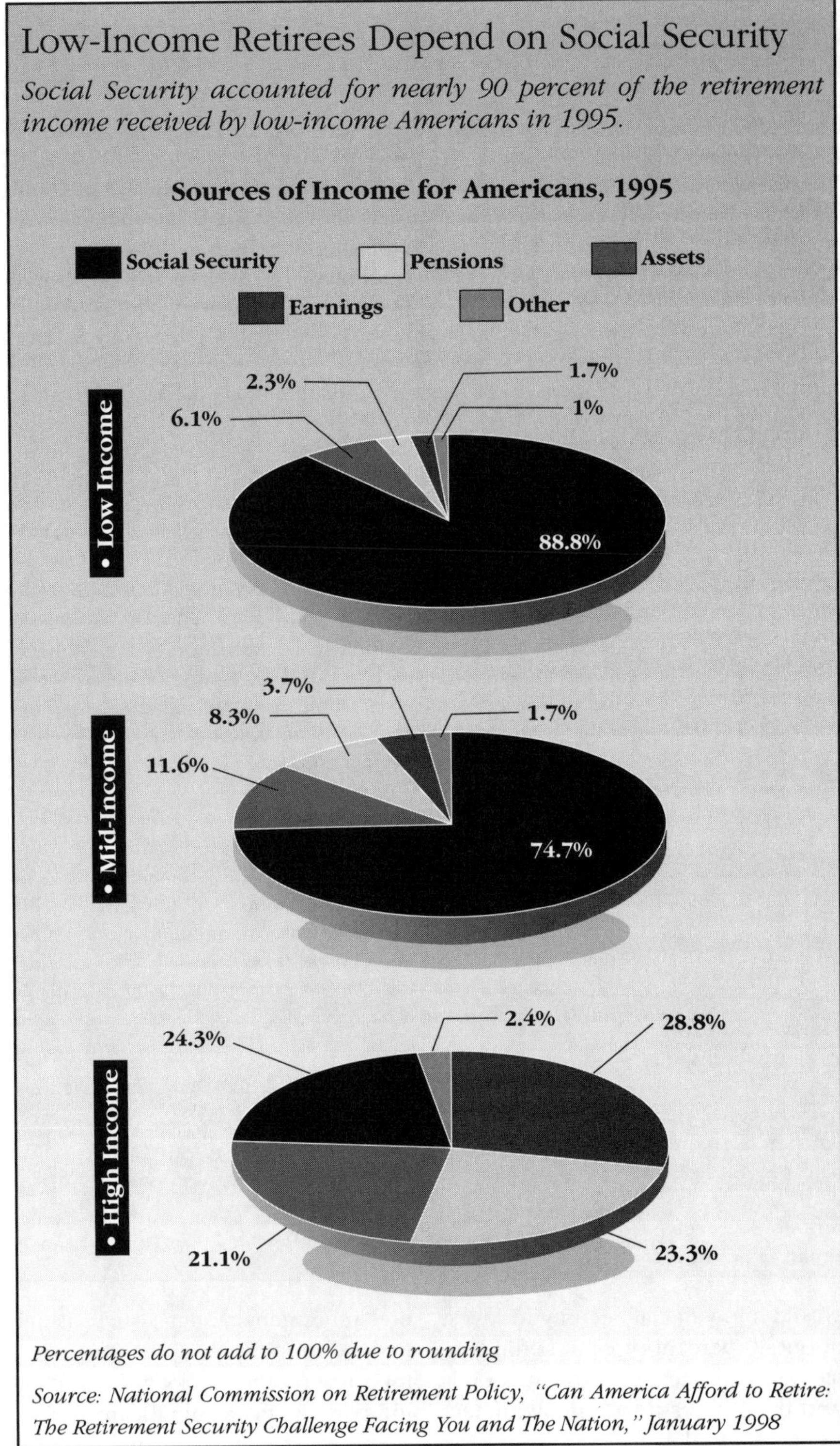

*Source: National Commission on Retirement Policy, "Can America Afford to Retire: The Retirement Security Challenge Facing You and The Nation," January 1998*

trends. Medical advances are making people live longer, meaning they will collect benefits longer. People also are retiring earlier. And the tendency toward smaller families is moving the nation closer to zero population growth, meaning there will be fewer workers in coming generations to pay taxes into the system. [6]

Daniel Mitchell, a senior fellow at the conservative Heritage Foundation, says the combined effect will be staggering liabilities for the Social Security trust funds. By 2075, the last year for which the Social Security Administration projects numbers, Mitchell calculates the trust funds will have a total shortfall of $20 trillion, adjusted for inflation. Eliminating the future deficit would require a 54 percent increase in payroll taxes, a 33 percent reduction in benefits or a combination of those approaches. Mitchell argues it would be far easier to scrap the current system of promised benefits in favor of a privatized system based on accumulated wealth.

"The important question to ask is whether the price tag for moving to a private system is smaller or larger than the amount of money lawmakers would have to find to fulfill the promises of the current system," Mitchell says.

Another important question is whether young workers are willing to pay higher payroll taxes to maintain the government's promise to retirees. Supporters of higher taxes say even a 2 percent hike will leave American workers paying less for social insurance than many Western Europeans.

However, Third Millennium Executive Director Richard Thau is alarmed by the prospect of ad infinitum payroll tax increases to keep the Social Security trust fund in balance. "The idea of raising taxes further just to fund the existing system isn't going to fly," he says. "The majority of young people believe the real challenge is to pre-fund the system and avoid the demographic tsunami that will come when the baby boomers retire."

Clinton, without endorsing a plan, has voiced concerns about raising payroll taxes. And Moynihan says long-time supporters should face up to reality and enact more forward-thinking reforms now, while the government has a balanced budget and before Social

Security's woes become overwhelming. "If we continue to treat this program as the untouchable 'third rail' of American politics, we could find one day in the not very distant future that the system has vanished," he says. [7]

### *Should individual savings accounts be included in any reforms?*

In 1981, the government of Chile decided to replace its financially strapped pay-as-you-go national pension system with a program based on individually owned, privately invested accounts. The results dramatically exceeded expectations.

By requiring all covered or dependent workers who entered the work force after 1981 to place 10 percent of their monthly earnings in a savings account, government leaders boosted the national savings rate nearly threefold and solidified the developing nation's capital and labor markets. Old-age, disability and survivors' pensions in the privatized system paid 50-100 percent more than under the old system.

The bigger payouts, combined with other free-market reforms, have more than doubled economic growth in the developing nation from its historical 3 percent annual pace to an average of 7 percent per year over the past 12 years, according to Jose Pinera, the former minister of labor and now an international consultant on pension reform. [8] Argentina, Australia, Bolivia, Colombia, Mexico, Peru, the United Kingdom and Uruguay, among others, have since shifted to pension systems that rely on private accounts. *(See story, p. 111.)*

Privatization advocates say a similar move by the United States would be economically advantageous, delivering bigger pensions to workers and helping the economy grow faster. Some believe the emphasis on personal savings would have the added feature of encouraging more individual responsibility at a time when the nation prepares for a surge in its elderly population.

## Impact of Shrinking Work Force

*There were 3.7 workers per beneficiary in the Social Security system in 1970, but by 2075 the number of workers is expected to have dropped to 1.8, providing less income for the system.*

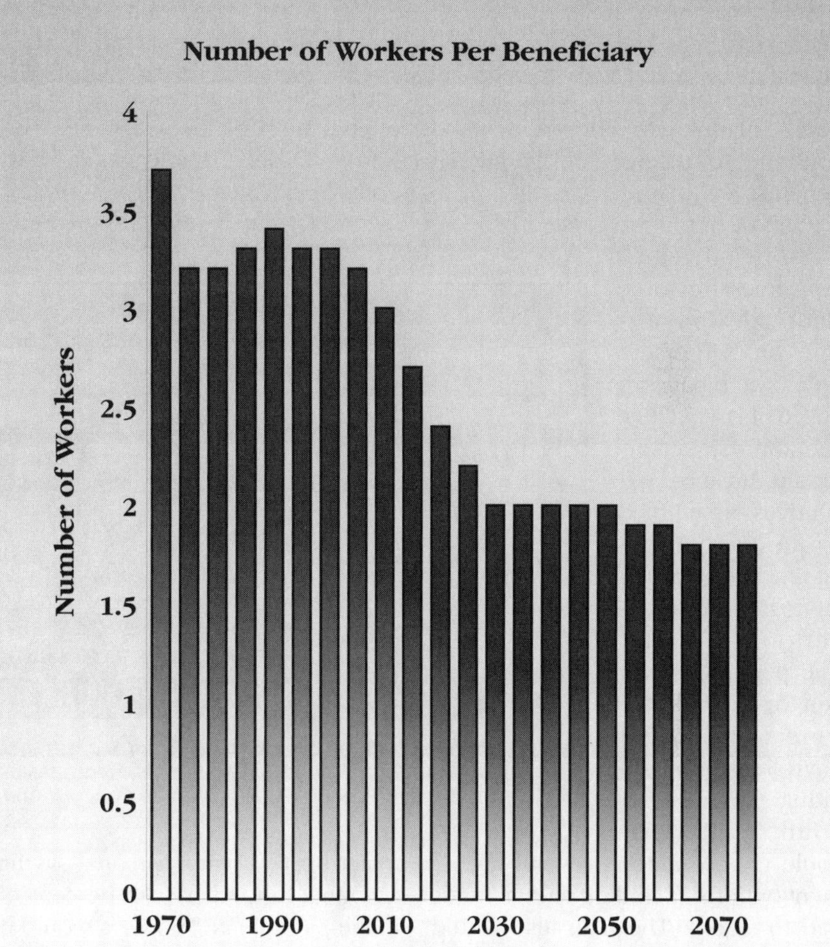


*Source: National Commission on Retirement Policy, "Can America Afford to Retire: The Retirement Security Challenge Facing You and The Nation," January 1998*

"Individual Americans should have a stake in the economy and more control over their own retirement benefits and the timing of when they retire," says Rep. Jim Kolbe, R-Ariz. "When you talk about security of the current system, it's illusory in the sense that you either have the political insecurity that exists today, or you have some kind of an economic risk that exists [in future years]."

Privatization would differ from Social Security in two important ways. First, the amount a worker receives at retirement depends entirely on how much one contributes to the savings plan and how well the investments perform. Put another way, those who set aside more and invest wisely enjoy more comfortable retirements. Secondly, pensions are paid out of an individual's accumulated savings instead of financed by taxes on active workers.

With some 44 million Americans

currently collecting Social Security, it would be impossible to immediately switch to a private system. At least a half-dozen pending proposals envision a gradual transformation that would offer young workers the chance to voluntarily invest a portion of their wages into a private system while ensuring that retirees and people planning to retire soon would continue to receive the traditional benefits.

One of the most detailed proposals to be offered so far comes from the National Commission on Retirement Policy, a bipartisan group of lawmakers, economists, actuaries and business executives assembled by the Washington-based Center for Strategic and International Studies. The plan would divert 2 percent of the current 12.4 percent payroll tax into individual savings accounts. Workers could choose among several investment options, including mutual funds tied to stocks. The plan also would increase the retirement age to 70 by 2029. The early retirement age, when people can stop working and receive reduced benefits, would increase to 65 from 62 by 2017.[9]

The presumed higher rate of return from private accounts would be offset in reduced guaranteed monthly Social Security payments. But the plan would design the cutbacks to hit the wealthy more than people with lower incomes. It also calls for a minimum benefit — 60 percent of the poverty line for people who have worked at least 20 years, rising to 100 percent for people who have worked at least 40 years — and would allow Social Security recipients to continue working without losing their benefits.

The bipartisan plan is expected to carry weight on Capitol Hill and is cosponsored by Sens. Judd Gregg, R-N.H., John B. Breaux, D-La., and Reps. Kolbe and Charles W. Stenholm, D-Texas. Another well-received centrist proposal is the plan offered by Moynihan and Sen. Bob Kerrey, D-Neb., that leaves the traditional Social Security system more or less intact but would allow workers to set up voluntary personal savings accounts funded by a 2 percent cut in the payroll tax. Workers would be given a number of investment options, all tax-deferred. While details remain to be worked out, employers would likely collect the money and send it to the Social Security Administration, which would oversee the investments.[10]

A 2 percent tax cut isn't enough for some lawmakers and public-policy experts. Rep. Mark Sanford, R-S.C., has offered the most far-reaching reform proposal, suggesting that two-thirds of payroll taxes be diverted to personal investment accounts. The plan is backed by the Cato Institute, a libertarian think tank that has been one of the prime movers behind Social Security reform.

Most budget experts agree that the economic arguments for privatization are valid but say the plans still raise troubling practical questions. One concerns "transition costs." Because money has to be found for existing pension payments at the same time workers will be asked to contribute to new private accounts, Congress would probably have to raise taxes or borrow money to keep both systems financially sound for several decades. The higher taxes would effectively replace the lost payroll taxes that were shifted into the private accounts, according to Brookings Institution senior fellows Gary Burtless and Barry Bosworth.[11]

*President Clinton discusses the Social Security system at a recent forum sponsored by the American Association of Retired Persons (AARP) and the Concord Coalition.*

Privatization critics add that the new system's reliance on market performance creates winners and losers — a radical departure from Social Security's New Deal pledge to guarantee the elderly well-defined benefits. Moreover, it could subject workers' savings to stock market volatility and high fees charged by administrators who run the investment plans.

"With all the turmoil in Asia and Russia right now, we might want to think twice about betting on go-go financial markets," says Sen. Paul Wellstone, D-Minn. "There will always be millions and millions of Americans who depend solely on Social Security for their retirement security." *(See graph, p. 104.)*

Warren B. Rudman, the former Republican U.S. senator from New Hampshire who now chairs the Concord Coalition, acknowledges the debate could be affected by recent stock market volatility. But he says steps could be taken to minimize risks to older workers, perhaps by closing any privatization plan to workers 50 years old and over.

Oddly silent in the current debate are Wall Street investment firms, which stand to gain billions of dollars in management fees if private investment accounts are adopted. Some investment firms that provide both administrative services and investment advice quietly support diverting payroll taxes into personal investments but don't want to visibly lobby and risk being accused of acting out of self-interest. [12]

Other financial service firms are equally worried about the cost of administering thousands of small new retirement accounts, fearing lawmakers will draft new regulations to lessen recipients' investment risk. The concerns have intensified as August's stock market tumble wiped out many investors' recent gains and threatened to give the high-flying mutual fund industry a black eye.

Matthew Fink, president of the Investment Company Institute, the trade group for the mutual fund industry, says investors aren't well-served by extreme proposals on either side of the Social Security debate. Investment firms support a "targeted, moderate approach" that would allow, but not require, workers to invest some portion of their Social Security tax in individual accounts, he says.

***Should the retirement age be raised?***

It took a generous buyout offer to convince Carrie Cusano to retire before age 70 from her job as a purchasing agent at Southern Connecticut State University in New Haven.

"A lot of us are just old enough to retire but young enough to work, and are quite capable of staying on," says Cusano, now 74. "Raising the retirement age is a good idea because more and more people are working longer."

Many of the plans to overhaul Social Security propose allowing workers like Cusano to remain on the job longer in order to strengthen Social Security's financial solvency. The plans assume that delaying the time when workers collect benefits means the government won't have to pay retirees for as long and can invest some of the money to build up Social Security's reserves. Brookings economist Burtless estimates even a one-year increase in the retirement age will result in approximately a 7 percent reduction in an average worker's total lifetime benefits.

**"The best thing for the American people is the long-term security of the Social Security system, and continuing to talk about the need for reform . . . is centrally important."**

***— Kenneth Apfel, commissioner, Social Security Administration***

Raising the retirement age is nothing new. In 1983, the National Commission on Social Security Reform, headed by current Federal Reserve Board Chairman Alan Greenspan, raised the retirement age as part of a package of reforms designed to save the system. The retirement age will increase in stages from 65 to 67 by 2022, while the early retirement age remains at 62. However, workers who opt out early will get only 70 percent of the full Social Security benefit.

The new bipartisan plan from the National Commission on Retirement Policy proposes taking the Greenspan commission's concept further by raising the early retirement age to 65 by 2017 and increasing the normal retirement age to 70 by 2029. The Moynihan-Kerrey plan would make similar adjustment to the normal retirement age, but not until 2073.

Such plans would reverse an early 1990s trend in which older workers like Cusano were targeted in downsizings and early retirement programs. Indeed, some companies now facing labor shortages are hiring back on a part-time basis the same workers who left several years ago. Last year, the labor force participation rate for men ages 55 to 64 was 67.5 percent, up from 65.5 percent in 1994. The participation rate for women in the same age bracket has risen steadily since the 1970s and was 50.5 percent last year. [13]

However, allowing workers to stay on the job longer could still pose problems. The U.S. General Accounting Office in July released an analysis saying millions of Americans, primarily in lower-paying blue-collar jobs, are more likely to suffer health problems well into their 60s than contemporaries in white-collar jobs. A delayed retirement age could force them to work in pain or with debilitating conditions, such as arthritis, lung disease or emotional disorders. Some might have to apply for disability benefits, increasing the cost of that program to the government. [14]

Raising the retirement age could also weigh heavily against certain ethnic groups. African-American males, for example, live nearly eight fewer years on average than white males. Raising the retirement age to 70 could prevent large numbers from drawing a pension.

There also is ample evidence that many Americans simply count on retiring early. A majority of workers, 53 percent, now start drawing Social Security benefits at 62. According to one recent analysis, America's post-World War II affluence, more generous Social Security benefits and private pension accumulations have led most workers to expect to spend, on average, one-third of their adult lives in retirement. [15]

University of Minnesota political scientist Lawrence Jacobs has analyzed public opinion polls dating to the 1970s and finds consistent opposition to raising the retirement age, sometimes exceeding 60 percent. Jacobs finds greater support for raising payroll taxes, though few are enthusiastic about that prospect. [16]

"When Americans have been asked to set spending priorities in the federal budget, they have expressed overwhelming support for maintaining or expanding the [Social Security] program," Jacobs says.

Yet Americans, perhaps paradoxically, seem receptive to working at least part of the time they are retired. Eighty percent of 2,001 baby boomers polled in June for the American Association of Retired Persons plan to work at least part time after they formally retire. Thirty-five percent said they would do it mainly for the interest or the enjoyment work provides, 23 percent wanted the money and 22 percent envisioned starting their own business or working full time at a new job or career.

Public-policy experts are trying to accommodate this desire to stay active by focusing on the earnings limits Social Security now places on its recipients. The limits — included in the original 1935 Social Security legislation as a way of making room in the work force for young, unemployed workers — penalize workers ages 65-69 by taking away $1 in Social Security benefits for every $3 they earn in excess of $14,500 in 1998. Those 62-64 lose $1 in benefits for every $2 they earn in excess of $9,120.

Legislation sponsored by Rep. Sam Johnson, R-Texas, scrapping the earnings limits has been adopted by the House GOP leadership as one of its top tax-cut ideas. Pete DuPont, the former Republican governor of Delaware and now president of the Washington-based National Center for Policy Analysis, says removing the limits would allow the United States to better tap the experience and input of its older workers.

"At a time when the country has a labor shortage and Congress is considering expanding immigration limits so more foreign workers can come to the country to fill empty jobs, doesn't it make sense to open up opportunities for the most experienced segment of the U.S. work force?" DuPont asks. "Employers need workers, and many seniors would like to work more." [17] ■

# BACKGROUND

## Belated Action

Germany's "Iron Chancellor," Otto von Bismarck, established the first social security system in 1889 to ease the financial pain of unemployment in his increasingly industrialized nation. Many historians suggest the move was less out of compassion for displaced workers than an effort to blunt Social Democratic critics of his military buildup.

Britain, Russia, France, Uruguay, Chile and Japan soon had similar versions of government-run old-age pension programs. Each nation provided elderly citizens with defined benefits based on strict eligibility rules. The programs were financed by current workers, their employers, or both.

However, retirement plans remained relatively rare in the United States during the first decades of the 20th century. Many in the country viewed social security as a socialistic European import that was out of sync with the Jeffersonian philosophy of self-reliance and minimal government. There were other more practical reasons: Most of the economy was still agricultural, and people could live off the riches of the land. In 1930, only about 15 percent of all workers were covered by any type of retirement plan. [18]

The Great Depression changed the equation. The financial crash wiped out industrial and trade union plans, leaving workers without pensions. Most seniors' savings disappeared in bank collapses. With few other means of support and a dearth of available jobs, many elderly people flocked to New York, Massachusetts and other states with old-age pension programs. Some hard-pressed state governments were forced to cut benefits or refused to accept new pensioners.

Facing mounting political pressure, Congress in 1935 passed the Social Security Act proposed by President Franklin D. Roosevelt, putting millions of retirees under a retirement plan for the first time. Originally, the program only aided retired workers age 65 and above — not their dependents — and was financed by a 2 percent payroll tax that was shared

# Chronology

## 1930s-1940s

***As part of the New Deal, President Franklin D. Roosevelt launches the Social Security system.***

**1935**
Roosevelt signs the Social Security Act, putting millions of workers under a retirement plan.

**1937**
The Federal Insurance Contribution Act (FICA) requires workers to pay taxes to support the Social Security system.

**1939**
Congress adds benefits for dependents of retired workers and surviving dependents of deceased workers.

**1940**
The first monthly benefit check is paid to Ida Mae Fuller, a retired law clerk in Ludlow, Vt.

## 1950s-1960s

***Congress increases Social Security benefits and expands the number of workers covered.***

**1954**
Coverage is extended to farm operators and most farm and domestic workers.

**1956**
Congress adds disabled workers over age 50 to the program. Women become eligible for benefits at age 62, rather than 65.

**1961**
Men become eligible to receive early retirement benefits at 62.

**1965**
Concern about the elderly leads to enactment of Medicare.

## 1970s

***Congress passes Social Security increases immediately before the U.S. economy falters.***

**1975**
Annual cost-of-living adjustments passed by Congress take effect, indexing benefits to inflation. The formula overstates the inflation rate by 25 percent, forcing the program to make larger payouts than necessary.

**1977**
Congress corrects the mistake and increases the payroll tax rate. Social Security is now thought to be actuarially sound.

## 1980s

***Social Security enters another financial crisis.***

**1982**
Inflation grows faster than wages, contrary to government projections. For the five years ending in 1982, inflation is more than 50 percent while real wages decline 7 percent. This forces the program to pay out far more than it takes in.

**1983**
Acting on the recommendations of the Greenspan commission appointed by President Ronald Reagan, Congress cuts benefits, delaying annual cost-of-living increases and gradually increasing the retirement age.

**1985**
Social Security trust funds are moved "off budget" so that the funds earmarked for the Social Security system can be tracked separately from the rest of the federal budget.

## 1990s

***Government actuaries predict current taxes are insufficient to cover Social Security benefits when baby boomers retire.***

**1994**
Social Security trustees predict the trust funds will run out of money by about 2030, seven years earlier than they projected in 1993.

**1996**
The trustees report the system will begin to run deficits in 2012. All members of a trustees' advisory panel recommend investing some or all of Social Security funds in the private sector.

**1998**
Congress and the White House continue to grapple with ways to shore up Social Security.

## 2000s

***Social Security runs out of money.***

**2011**
The first baby boomers collect benefits.

**2032**
Social Security system will no longer be able to pay all the benefits promised to retirees.

equally by employer and employee on the first $3,000 of wages.

Opposition to the payroll tax at first was intense, leading President Roosevelt to shrewdly depict the system as a kind of insurance program that was financed out of "premiums" workers paid for coverage in their old age. In fact, there were no individual accounts where workers' contributions were stashed for their own retirements. Instead, the existing work force was taxed to subsidize the benefits to current retirees. Asked about this discrepancy by an aide, Roosevelt responded, "That account is there so that those sons of bitches up on the Hill [Congress] can't ever abandon this system after I'm gone." [19]

At the time of Social Security's passage, American society was very different from today. There were many more workers than retired people, and the average American was only expected to live to 61, meaning many would never receive a single Social Security check. The result was a windfall for the very first retirees. Ida Mae Fuller, a retired law clerk from Ludlow, Vt., received the first Social Security check — for $22.54 — on Jan. 31, 1940. She had contributed only $22 to the system. At the time of her death 35 years later, her benefits totaled $22,000.

## Signs of Trouble

Between 1935-1980, Congress gradually expanded the scope of Social Security, covering more people and paying out progressively larger benefits. In 1939, Congress added benefits for dependents and survivors of a deceased worker. In 1950, the program was extended to agricultural workers, the self-employed, members of the armed forces and disabled people age 50 and above. In 1961, President John F. Kennedy pushed through Congress a 20 percent increase in benefits and an early retirement provision that offered payouts and survivor benefits to men at age 62.

The 1970s brought the first signs of trouble, as it became apparent Social Security couldn't finance all the benefits it promised. After decades of robust economic growth and low inflation, growth slowed and prices rose. Demographics also shifted; there had been 16 workers for every retiree in 1950, but by 1970 the figure had fallen to about 3.7. Adding to the problem were automatic cost-of-living increases, introduced in 1972, which indexed Social Security benefits to inflation.

By 1977, Social Security was facing a crisis. President Jimmy Carter and Congress responded by nearly doubling taxes — passing a then-record $227 billion tax increase — and slowing down the growth of future benefits. The changes were billed as long-term solutions. But when the U.S. economy took another downturn in the early 1980s, workers' wages fell and the system faced a second financial squeeze.

In 1982, President Ronald Reagan convened a bipartisan commission to discuss Social Security reforms chaired by economist Greenspan. The commission recommended delaying cost-of-living increases, taxing the benefits of higher-income retirees and gradually increasing the retirement age from 65 to 67 by 2027 — changes that were adopted by Congress in 1983.

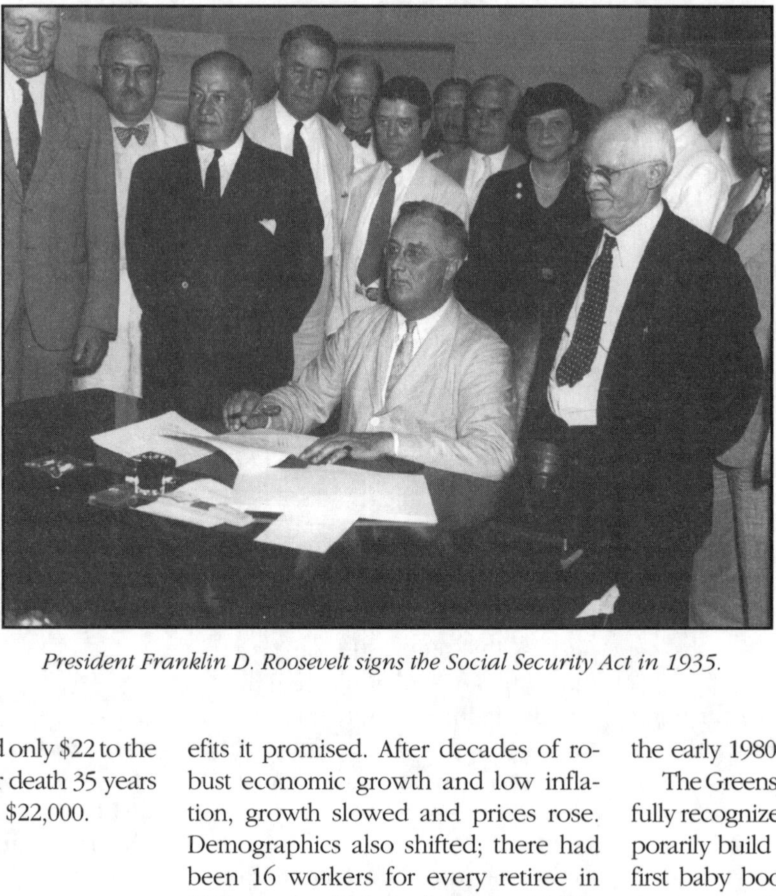

Greenspan predicted the reforms would keep Social Security solvent until at least 2068. However, Social Security's trustees now think the trust fund surplus will run out some 30 years sooner — by 2032. The trustees assume wages will grow more slowly than the Greenspan-led commission believed in 1983. Additionally, there are fewer workers and more retirees than when the commission did its work in the early 1980s.

The Greenspan commission also didn't fully recognize that surpluses would temporarily build up in the years before the first baby boomers retire, according to the Congressional Research Service. As a consequence, the opportunity to capture and invest Social Security surpluses to anticipate later deficits didn't even come up for discussion in 1983. [20]

In the late 1980s, it became evident that surpluses were indeed occurring and

Bettmann/UPI

*President Franklin D. Roosevelt signs the Social Security Act in 1935.*

## Many Nations Trying Pension Reform

At least a dozen countries have attempted to overhaul their social security systems in recent years. Here are some of the approaches that have been taken:

• **CHILE** — Gen. Augusto Pinochet installed the world's first privatized national pension system in 1981. It requires those who enter the work force after 1981 to automatically invest 10 percent or more of their wages in an individual retirement account, which isn't taxed until withdrawal. Older workers have the option of remaining in the traditional social security system.

The retirement funds had accumulated $30 billion by last year and were widely credited with solidifying the emerging nation's capital markets. However, in the past year Chile's stock market has lost more than 25 percent in dollar terms due to declining exports to Asia and falling copper prices tied to Japan's economic slowdown. The average retirement fund has declined about 5 percent over the past 12 months, and some economists fear a recession could end years of steady growth.

• **BRAZIL** — In an attempt to streamline the economy and reduce debt, President Fernando Henrique Cardoso tried to reform social security this year by offering a constitutional amendment to raise the retirement age. The Brazilian Congress rejected the proposal in May as labor unions and rivals charged the changes would have penalized manual and unskilled laborers, who tend to enter the work force at younger ages and would therefore be required to work more years.

Officials are pledging to revisit minimum-age requirements for social security after the October elections. Under Cardoso's plan, men had to work until they turned 60 and had been employed for 35 years to qualify for pensions. Women had to be at least 55 and to have worked for 30 years.

• **POLAND** — Legislation is being considered that allows creation of private pension funds with tax-deductible contributions. The criteria for granting disability allowances have also been tightened. The reform plan, similar to Chile's, is making its way through the Polish parliament.

• **GREAT BRITAIN** — A privatization plan begun by Prime Minister Margaret Thatcher in 1988 features two tiers. All workers pay into the basic government pension plan, which provides a defined benefit. But higher-income workers can leave a supplementary government plan or their employers' pension plan and invest their contributions elsewhere, presumably for higher returns.

The restructuring has allowed the British to amass more than $1 trillion in retirement savings while controlling entitlement spending. The system is credited with helping Britain remain more vibrant and economically competitive than many other European countries by providing plentiful capital for British companies through the financial markets. However, individuals have lost billions of dollars by succumbing to high-pressure sales tactics from some financial firms. Some companies are compensating them for losses, but the actions of others have sparked criminal investigations.

• **AUSTRALIA** — The Labor government in 1986 began implementing a retirement system based on mandatory private savings. By 2002, when the system is fully in place, workers will have to set aside 9 percent of their income in designated investment funds. Contributions are now taxed before they are invested in the funds. The coalition government is reviewing its tax code and studying whether it should convert to a tax-deferred system.

*Sources: Heritage Foundation,* The New York Times, *news reports.*

being used to finance the government's annual operating budget. Sen. Moynihan tried to correct this by proposing to temporarily roll back payroll taxes, then raise them again after 2015 to meet rising costs, reaching a combined employer-employee Social Security tax of 16.2 percent by 2050. However, Congress never adopted the proposal.

More recently, Social Security actuaries have predicted the payroll tax would have to be even higher than Moynihan suggested to meet costs by the middle of the next century — perhaps in the range of 18-19 percent, according to American Enterprise Institute economist Carolyn Weaver. [21] ■

# CURRENT SITUATION

## Political Football

In his 1998 State of the Union address, President Clinton urged Congress to deal with Social Security's problems before spending any projected federal budget surpluses. But most observers say the issue is far more complicated than the White House depicts.

Social Security now takes in about $100 billion a year more from payroll taxes and interest income than it pays out in retiree benefits. The big surplus is factored into federal budget forecasts and tends to obscure the deficit that actually is incurred running government programs. The Congressional Budget Office (CBO), for instance, projects an overall federal surplus of $80 billion in fiscal 1999, rising to $251 billion in fiscal 2008.

Congressional Republicans, mainly in the House of Representatives, question the wisdom of keeping such a large reserve and think a portion of the surplus ought to be used to finance tax cuts for working couples, investors and heirs to large estates. But House Democrats and a bipartisan majority in the more cautious Senate believe cutting taxes would ignore the challenge of fixing Social Security before the first baby boomers retire and the program begins to operate in the red. [22]

In reality, the surplus is part of a larger game of accounting sleight-of-hand surrounding the Social Security program. The money from payroll taxes and interest income technically is invested in Social Security's trust funds. But the government really borrows it to cover year-to-year operations. In exchange, it issues the retirement system special Treasury IOU's. When it comes time for Social Security to redeem the claims plus interest, the U.S. Treasury will have to borrow from the public or levy taxes.

As a result, some economists say there is virtually no difference between applying budget surpluses to pay down the overall national debt or using it specifically for Social Security. Many suspect Clinton was really using the Social Security message in the State of the Union to appear fiscally prudent and pressure Republicans not to pass election-year tax cuts.

White House officials disagree with the assessment, saying it is possible to strengthen Social Security's financial position by applying the surplus to it. Gene Sperling, assistant to the president for economic policy and Clinton's point man on Social Security, says the president wasn't seeking a commitment that the surplus be spent in a particular way, just that it be reserved until lawmakers have a better idea of how much is needed to save the system. [23]

"If the surpluses are drained away in the short term [via tax cuts], we're just digging ourselves in a deeper hole," adds Social Security Commissioner Apfel.

Opinion polls suggest the public would rather see the government deal with the national debt and maintain entitlements. In a recent *Wall Street Journal*/NBC News poll, 43 percent of respondents said strengthening Social Security and Medicare would be a major factor in how they vote this year, compared with 28 percent whose votes would hinge on tax cuts.

**"The energy in social policy right now is to privatize. Any effort to keep Social Security will have to acknowledge the people who want to get rid of it, the people who are saying that government is taking your money and cheating you."**

***— Sen. Daniel Patrick Moynihan, D-N.Y.***

Republicans nonetheless appear intent on defying Clinton, passing some tax cuts and using them as a marquee issue in November's elections. The GOP believes tax cuts have special appeal with its core voters, whom the party is hoping to lure to the polls for what is expected to be a low-turnout election.

House Speaker Newt Gingrich, R-Ga., says it is possible to save every penny of payroll taxes to address Social Security's problems but still apply other portions of the surplus to finance tax cuts. Gingrich has promoted legislation cutting taxes by a maximum of $70 billion to $80 billion over five years. [24]

Democrats expect to hammer the Republicans, using the argument that the GOP is endangering the Social Security system so it can pass tax cuts for the rich. But perhaps the greater danger to Republican members of Congress is relying on long-term economic forecasts to make decisions about Social Security and tax policy. Even a slightly incorrect assumption about economic growth could mean the real surplus is off by billions of dollars. And global economic instability could lead to more undesirable side effects. The CBO recently revised economic projections in light of financial turmoil in Asia and Russia, forecasting U.S. economic growth would slow from a robust 3.3 percent this year to 1.8 percent in 2000.

# OUTLOOK

## Impact on Saving

Many experts say the most enduring legacy of the Social Secu-

# At Issue:

## *Will privately invested retirement accounts relieve the financial squeeze facing the Social Security system?*

**EDWARD H. CRANE**
***President and CEO, Cato Institute, Washington, D.C.***

***FROM AN ADDRESS DELIVERED IN PARIS, DEC. 10, 1997, REPRINTED IN* VITAL SPEECHES OF THE DAY, *APRIL 15, 1998.***

### yes

I believe there is no economic issue facing the world today that is more important than converting public pension programs from pay-as-you-go government-run systems into individually capitalized, privately owned retirement systems. . . .

One of the reasons for the growing popularity of replacing a pay-as-you-go plan with an individually capped, fully funded plan is that Americans seem to intuitively know what is demonstratively true. Namely, that the returns from a privately invested retirement account will be significantly greater than the return one receives on one's alleged "investment" in Social Security. To repeat, in the United States the payroll tax is not invested, just as it's not invested in most social security systems around the world. It goes directly into payouts to current retirees, with whatever excess there may be going to help finance the federal government's deficit spending. The government leaves "Special Treasury Notes" in a so-called trust fund when it purloins these excess funds, but to see that the trust fund is a fraud, one need only consider the options facing the government whether these "bonds" are in the trust fund or not.

In the year 2010 or sooner, by our estimates, the cash flow from payroll taxes will be insufficient to meet the benefits due current retirees. Assuming the government will live up to its obligations (there is good reason to believe it will not, but for the sake of argument we will give it the benefit of the doubt), once the system's cash flow turns negative and the Social Security Administration turns to the national government for help, the government can come up with the necessary funds by: 1) increasing taxes, 2) increasing borrowing, 3) reducing benefits or 4) reducing other government spending. Now suppose the Special Treasury Notes are presented to the national government by the Social Security Administration for redemption to make up for the shortfall. The government, in order to raise the funds to redeem the bonds, is faced with precisely the same four options as if there were no trust fund at all.

Thus, when the American government officials smugly point to the approximately $2 trillion in accumulated special Treasury Bonds that are expected to be in the trust fund by 2010 and tell us that this will help finance the system until 2029 and that therefore there is no crisis, they are being disingenuous, to put it kindly. There is no trust fund in the United States and the crisis is at hand, particularly for younger workers who face the prospect of negative rates of return on their payroll taxes over their entire working lives.

**HENRY AARON**
***Senior Fellow, The Brookings Institution***

***FROM TESTIMONY BEFORE THE SENATE BUDGET COMMITTEE, JULY 23, 1998.***

### no

Advocates of private accounts have claimed that the returns to pensioners will be higher under a privatized system than under Social Security. This claim is the exact opposite of the truth for reasons that have been developed cogently in scholarly research and can be expressed simply in non-academic terms. Furthermore, private accounts would expose individual workers to risks that are now broadly shared among workers and across generations.

The logic is straightforward. Payments to support Social Security (or Social Security and private accounts) go for two purposes: to pay Social Security benefits for current or future beneficiaries that exceed reserves (the so-called unfunded liability); and to build reserves [for] future retirees.

Whether to curtail Social Security benefits for the current elderly and those soon to retire is an important issue, but it is entirely independent of the issue of privatization. Whatever decision Congress makes on this divisive issue, current workers will have to pay the same amount for those benefits, whether we retain Social Security in its current form or gradually shift to some alternative. Current workers who support benefits for the current beneficiaries derive no personal financial gain whatsoever from paying those taxes. This situation is the inescapable consequence of decisions made over the past half-century to pay larger benefits to retirees than the payroll taxes paid on their behalf could justify. Paying out those taxes as current benefits rather than retaining them as reserves produced what policy analysts call the "unfunded liability," the obligation to pay benefits to current retirees and to currently active workers in excess of accumulated reserves. We can debate whether or not it was wise to pay those benefits and build up this unfunded liability, but we cannot avoid paying it except by reneging on commitments to current beneficiaries and older workers. On this score, there is no difference at all between the return to workers under a gradual transition to privatized accounts of any kind and retention of Social Security.

Any difference between the returns workers receive under a privatized system and under Social Security must come from the taxes paid above those necessary to support current benefits and go to accumulate reserves. The average returns from similarly invested assets would be lower under private accounts than they would be under Social Security because private accounts would be more costly to administer, and these extra costs would reduce the amounts available to support pensions.

## FOR MORE INFORMATION

*If you would like to have this CQ Researcher updated, or need more information about this topic, please call CQ Custom Research. Special rates for CQ subscribers. (202) 887-8600 or (800) 432-2250, ext. 600, or E-mail Custom.Research@cq.com*

**American Association of Retired Persons,** 601 E St., N.W., Washington, D.C. 20049; (202) 434-2277; www. aarp.org. This national membership organization for persons age 50 and over monitors legislation and issues affecting older Americans and provides members with training, employment information and volunteer programs.

**Brookings Institution,** 1775 Massachusetts Ave., N.W., Washington, D.C. 20036; (202) 797-6000; www.brookings.org. This centrist-to-left-of-center think tank assesses the effectiveness of public-policy programs and is generally skeptical of sweeping plans to overhaul Social Security.

**Cato Institute,** 1000 Massachusetts Ave., N.W., Washington, D.C. 20001; (202) 842-0200; www.cato.org. This libertarian think tank advocates private-sector solutions to public-policy issues and is sponsoring a $3 million program to study privatization of Social Security.

**Heritage Foundation,** 214 Massachusetts Ave., N.E., Washington, D.C. 20002; (202) 546-4400; www.heritage.org. This conservative think tank studies Social Security privatization around the world and advocates a similar strategy for the United States.

**National Commission on Retirement Policy,** 1800 K St., N.W., Washington, D.C. 20006; (202) 775-3242; www.csis.org. This arm of the Center for Strategic and International Studies tries to foster bipartisan solutions to problems with federal entitlement programs and has crafted a centrist proposal to reform Social Security.

**Social Security Administration,** 6401 Security Blvd., Baltimore, Md. 21235; (410) 965-3120; www.ssa.gov. This federal agency administers the national Social Security and Supplemental Security Income programs.

rity debate may be a shift in the way Americans view personal savings. For decades, retirement income was likened to a three-legged stool — a leg for pension, a leg for savings and a leg for Social Security. But with the Social Security system under stress and employer-guaranteed pensions being replaced with 401(k) plans whose size depends on individuals' investment skills, more emphasis is beginning to be placed on personal savings habits.

"There seems to be a certain irrationality at work," says Stanford University economist John Shoven. "If you ask younger Americans, 'Do you think you're going to get anything from Social Security?' they answer, 'I don't think I'm going to get very much.' And if you ask them, 'Are you saving enough?' they answer, 'No. I should be saving 10 percent. I'm only saving 2 percent.' But then if you ask them, 'How well off do you think you'll be when you retire?' The answer is, 'I'll be fine.' "[25]

Indeed, studies show many members of Generation X save very little because they are busy paying off student loans and starting families. But the problem extends to other generational groups. The U.S. Department of Labor estimates that more than 50 million workers lack any kind of pension. Various academic studies show the current Social Security system actually may reduce private saving by as much as 50 percent because it promises retirement income. The studies note retirement typically is one of the main reasons people save.

Privatization advocates say the various plans to set up IRAs will change saving habits because workers will be setting aside a percentage of their wages in private accounts, instead of sending in contributions that are immediately spent on paying benefits.

But some doubt that privatization would automatically increase savings. Brookings economists Burtless and Bosworth believe setting up new accounts will probably result in workers cutting their contributions to IRAs, 401(k)s and their other existing voluntary retirement plans. Also, they note Social Security is caught in an accounting Catch 22: lowering payroll taxes to divert money to the new accounts will force the government to borrow more money from individual investors to meet its current obligations. Thus, money that would have been saved by the investors is being used to pay benefits.

"In order to boost national saving, a privatization plan must reduce someone's consumption," Burtless and Bosworth argue. They say this could only be accomplished by a privatization plan that cuts benefits to existing and soon-to-be retirees.

Clinton and other lawmakers have urged workers to save more by making a conscious decision to join 401(k) plans and other savings programs while the Social Security dilemma is worked out. Experts say that kind of forward thinking could effectively sidestep what promises to be a drawn-out debate over a volatile political issue.

Joining the plans on one's own to boost savings "is really important," says Alicia Munnell, a management professor at Boston College and former member of the president's

Council of Economic Advisers. "Life is complicated, and people have children and other immediate demands, and thinking about sitting down and saving for retirement at 30 is hard." [26] ■

## Notes

[1] See James Glassman, "Moynihan's Social Security Plan," *The Washington Post*, March 24, 1998, p. A19. For background, see Sarah Glazer, "Overhauling Social Security," *The CQ Researcher*, May 12, 1995, pp. 417-440 and Richard L. Worsnop, "Age Discrimination," *The CQ Researcher*, Aug. 1, 1997, pp. 682-705.

[2] For background, see "1998 Annual Report of the Board of Trustees of the Federal Old-Age and Survivors Insurance and Disability Insurance Trust Funds," Office of the Chief Actuary, Social Security Administration, April 28, 1998.

[3] On average, large-company stocks registered returns of 10.5 percent while smaller companies' stocks returned 12.5 percent annually.

[4] See Peter Peterson, *Will American Grow Up Before It Grows Old* (1996), pp. 21-27.

[5] For background, see Robert Ball, "A Secure System," *The American Prospect*, No. 29, November-December 1996, pp. 34-35.

[6] See Martynas Ycas, "The Challenge of the 21st Century," *Social Security Bulletin*, winter 1994, pp. 3-9.

[7] From Sen. Daniel Patrick Moynihan, "How to Preserve the Safety Net," *U.S. News & World Report*, April 20, 1998, p. 25.

[8] See testimony before the House Ways and Means Subcommittee on Social Security, Sept. 18, 1997.

[9] See Richard Stevenson, "Bipartisan Group Urged Big Changes in Social Security," *The New York Times*, May 19, 1998, p. A1.

[10] See Ronald Powers, "Moynihan Backs Social Security Privatization," The Associated Press, April 6, 1998.

[11] See Gary Burtless and Barry Bosworth, "Privatizing Social Security: The Troubling Trade-Offs," *Brookings Institution Policy Brief*, No. 14, March 1997.

[12] For background, see Brett Fromson, "A Safety Net Whets Wall St. Appetites; Social Security Proposals Could Mean Billions in Fees," *The Washington Post*, Jan. 7, 1997, p. C1.

[13] See Robert Samuelson, "Older Workers, New Patterns," *The Washington Post*, Nov. 12, 1997.

[14] For background, see U.S. General Accounting Office, "Social Security Reform: Raising Retirement Ages Improves Program Solvency but May Cause Hardship for Some," July 15, 1998.

[15] C. Eugene Steuerle, Edward Gramlich, Hugh Heclo and Demetra Smith Nightingale, *The Government We Deserve: Responsive Democracy and Changing Expectations* (1998).

[16] See Lawrence Jacobs and Robert Shapiro, "Myths and Misunderstandings About Public Opinion Toward Social Security: Knowledge, Support and Reformism," a paper prepared for the 10th Annual Conference of the National Academy of Social Insurance, Jan. 29-30, 1998, Washington, D.C.

[17] See Pete DuPont, "Punish Productive Seniors?" *The Washington Times*, Aug. 14, 1998.

[18] For background, see Peter Ferrara and Michael Tanner, "A New Deal for Social Security," Cato Institute, 1998, pp. 13-32.

[19] See Dorcas Hardy and C. Colburn Hardy, *Social Insecurity* (1991), pp. 7-12.

[20] See Congressional Research Service, "The Social Security Surplus," Nov. 21, 1988, pp. 28-31.

[21] See Carolyn Weaver, "Social Security Reform after the 1983 Amendments," paper delivered at the annual meeting of the Eastern Economic Association, Boston, Mass., March 18-20, 1994.

[22] For background, see Andrew Taylor, "Social Security Surplus Shaping Up As an Election Year Battleground," *CQ Weekly*, July 25, 1998, pp. 1999-2000.

[23] Interview in *Roll Call*, June 22, 1998, p. 3.

[24] See Robert Pear, "Wait 'Til Next Year, Gingrich Admits on Big Tax Cuts," *The New York Times*, Aug. 7, 1998.

[25] For background, see "Geezer Boom," *Hoover Digest Selections*, summer 1997, No. 3, pp. 20-23.

[26] See Jerry Morgan, "Americans Retiring Without a Stool or a Nest Egg to Sit On," *Newsday*, June 14, 1998, p. F6.

# Bibliography

## Selected Sources Used


### Books

**Steuerle, C. Eugene, Edward Gramlich, Hugh Heclo and Demetra Smith Nightingale, *The Government We Deserve: Responsive Democracy and Changing Expectations*, Urban Institute Press, 1998.**

Four respected academics illustrate how federal spending commitments made years ago are conditioning the United States' economic future. Explores how many Americans now expect to spend a significant share of adulthood in retirement.

**Peterson, Peter, *Will America Grow Up Before It Grows Old?*, Random House, 1996.**

The former Commerce secretary under President Richard M. Nixon and chief executive officer of Lehman Brothers argues that economic disaster lies ahead if the United States continues to ignore its low savings rate and unsustainable commitments to retirees.

**Carter, Marshall, and William Shipman, *Promises To Keep: Saving Social Security's Dream*, Regnery, 1996.**

Two executives at State Street Bank and Trust Co. outline a privatization plan they say will guarantee full benefits to retirees, reduce workers' taxes and cut the Social Security system's unfunded liability by 60 percent.

**Ferrara, Peter, and Michael Tanner, *A New Deal for Social Security*, Cato Institute, 1998.**

An economist and a public-policy expert trace Social Security from its inception, contending the program's problems are the result of a fundamental flaw: Social Security taxes aren't saved or invested in any way.

### Articles

**Miller, Matthew, "Rebuilding Retirement: A Dramatic Shift in Generational Politics Sets the Stage for Major Social Security Changes," *U.S. News & World Report*, April 20, 1998, pp. 20-26.**

A well-written analysis of how politicians who previously tiptoed around Social Security's problems are now offering sweeping plans to overhaul the system.

**Rankin, Robert, "Privatizing Social Security has Pitfalls, Promise," Knight-Ridder News Service, July 27, 1998.**

A good overview of rival plans to privatize Social Security and how the debate is being shaped in three White House-sponsored forums around the country.

**Wildavsky, Ben, "Working Solutions," *National Journal*, July 4, 1998, pp. 1560-1564.**

Explores how the concept of raising the retirement age has gained currency in the Social Security debate.

**Krauss, Clifford, "Social Security, Chilean Style," *The New York Times*, Aug. 16, 1998.**

Chile kicked off the push to privatize Social Security with a set of sweeping reforms in 1981. But the author says it has proven no panacea for the insecurities people feel when thinking about retirement.

### Reports

**Burtless, Gary, and Barry Bosworth, "Privatizing Social Security: The Troubling Trade-Offs," *Brookings Institution Policy Brief*, March 1997, No. 14.**

Two Brookings senior fellows argue that the supposed economic advantages of Social Security privatization require short-term economic sacrifices.

**Mitchell, Daniel, "Creating a Better Social Security System for America," *Heritage Foundation Backgrounder*, April 23, 1997.**

A senior fellow at the conservative Heritage Foundation details why Social Security is in trouble and is a bad deal for today's workers.

***Baby Boomers Look Toward Retirement*, American Association of Retired Persons, June 2, 1998.**

A Roper Starch Worldwide survey of 2,001 people born between 1946 and 1964 finds the vast majority expect to continue to work during retirement and are largely optimistic about their retirement years.

***Social Security: Why Action Should Be Taken Soon*, Social Security Advisory Board, July 1998.**

An independent, bipartisan board created by Congress and appointed by the president and Congress outlines reasons that prompt action is required to fix the retirement system.

# 7 Population and the Environment

**MARY H. COOPER**

Two hundred years ago, an English cleric named Thomas Robert Malthus wrote an essay that would forever change the secure view people had of their place on Earth. Like other animal species, Malthus wrote, humans can reproduce faster than the natural resources they require to survive. As a result, he postulated, humans eventually would overwhelm the environment, possibly resulting in their extinction.

"Famine seems to be the last, the most dreadful resource of nature," Malthus wrote. "The power of population is so superior to the power in the Earth to produce subsistence for man, that premature death must in some shape or other visit the human race." [1]

Malthus wrote his treatise in response to the prevailing optimism of the time, which saw population growth as an unqualified boon to mankind. The Marquis de Condorcet, a French mathematician and pioneering social scientist, and William Godwin, an English social philosopher, held that man was perfectible, headed toward a future free of all evil, discomfort and disease. As mankind approached immortality, Godwin predicted, population growth would cease altogether because sexual desire would be extinguished.

Two hundred years later, the debate continues — but amid profound changes. In Malthus' day, there were fewer than 1 billion people on Earth. More recently, global population has mushroomed, growing from 1.6 billion to almost 6 billion in the 20th century alone, numbers that surely would have been taken by 18th-century thinkers as confirmation of the Malthusian nightmare. But technological changes, equally unimaginable to observers at the dawn of the Industrial Revolution, have vastly increased global food supplies, giving credence to Malthus' optimistic critics. [2]

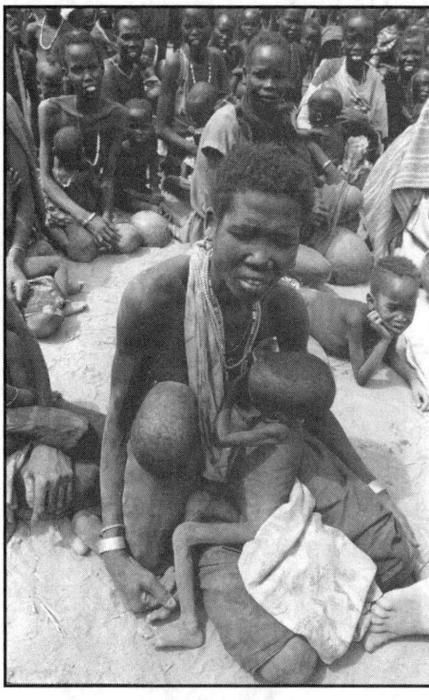

What hasn't changed over the past two centuries is the distance separating the two sides in the ongoing debate over human population. On the one side are Malthus' intellectual heirs, dubbed doomers or Cassandras. They see the continuing rise in global population as a recipe for disaster. The crash will come not only because of food shortages, they say, but because of myriad insults to the environment humans exact by their sheer numbers. *(See graph, p. 132.)*

"I certainly think we face an environmental crisis, whether it amounts to a Malthusian outcome or not," says Leon Kolankiewicz, coordinator of the Carrying Capacity Network, which promotes sustainable development. Rather than the global collapse of food supplies that Malthus envisioned, Kolankiewicz foresees any number of localized crises, similar to that which may have struck Easter Island in the Pacific Ocean, whose inhabitants are believed to have died out after exhausting the island's natural resources.

"For a time, people can exceed the long-term carrying capacity for an area, but this eventually leads to collapse," he says. "In a given region, if not the world, not only will the population collapse, but there also will be such damage to the natural capital — the resources that sustain life — that for a long time to come the environment will no longer be able to support human life."

On the other side of the debate are Godwin's successors — the boomers or Pollyannas — who say more people mean a larger pool of human ingenuity to discover new ways to thrive on planet Earth. They point to the successes of the Green Revolution, an international drive to increase crop yields in the 1950s and '60s, as evidence that humans will always come up with a technological fix to accommodate their growing numbers.

Several new developments have colored the population debate in recent years. One is the recent discovery that human activities — especially in the developed world — affect the atmosphere, long considered a relatively inexhaustible asset of Earth's environment. When scientists demonstrated that the release of chlorofluorocarbons from man-made coolants and aerosols had eroded Earth's protective ozone layer, world leaders agreed in 1992 to ban the chemicals.

More recently, scientists have concluded that burning fossil fuels may cause a gradual but potentially catastrophic warming of the atmosphere. Fear of so-called global warming resulted in last December's agreement in Kyoto, Japan, to curb the burning of oil, coal and natural gas.

Malthus' supporters point to these and other strains on the environment as signs that human population has exceeded Earth's "carrying capacity," its ability to sustain life indefinitely.

From *The CQ Researcher,* July 17, 1998.

## Childbearing Is Greatest in Africa and Asia

*The fertility rate— the average number of children that women in a country have— is generally higher in Africa and Western Asia and lower in North America, Europe and Eastern Asia. In the future, according to United Nations projections, small differences in childbearing levels will result in large differences in global population. If women average a moderate two children, population would rise to 11 billion in the 21st century and level off. If women average 2.5 children, population would pass 27 billion by 2150. But if the fertility rate fell to 1.6 children, population would peak at 7.7 billion in 2050 and drop to 3.6 billion by 2150.*

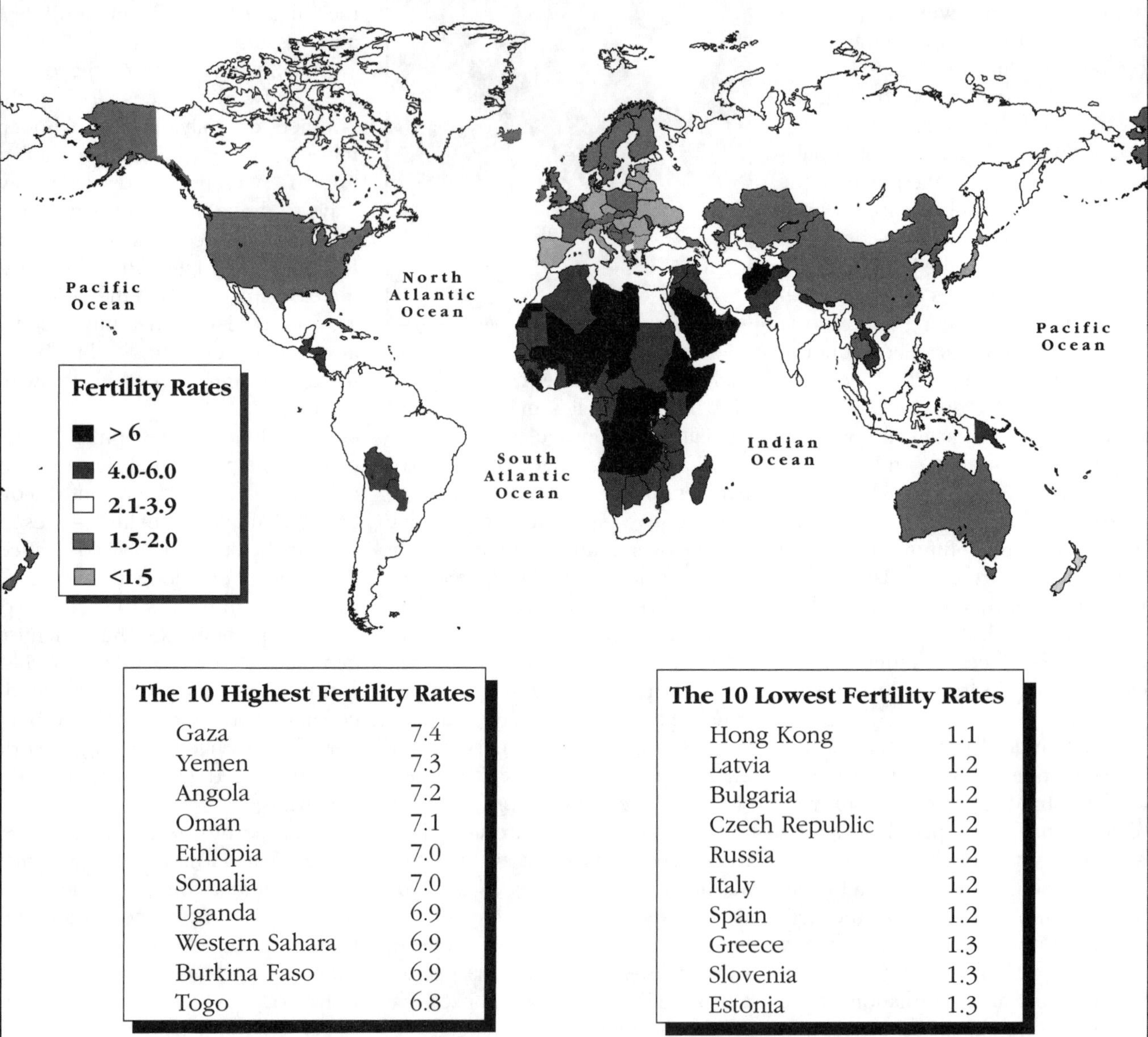


| The 10 Highest Fertility Rates | |
|---|---|
| Gaza | 7.4 |
| Yemen | 7.3 |
| Angola | 7.2 |
| Oman | 7.1 |
| Ethiopia | 7.0 |
| Somalia | 7.0 |
| Uganda | 6.9 |
| Western Sahara | 6.9 |
| Burkina Faso | 6.9 |
| Togo | 6.8 |

| The 10 Lowest Fertility Rates | |
|---|---|
| Hong Kong | 1.1 |
| Latvia | 1.2 |
| Bulgaria | 1.2 |
| Czech Republic | 1.2 |
| Russia | 1.2 |
| Italy | 1.2 |
| Spain | 1.2 |
| Greece | 1.3 |
| Slovenia | 1.3 |
| Estonia | 1.3 |

*Source: "1998 World Population Data Sheet," Population Reference Sheet*

Other signs include the rapid disappearance of plant and animal species as humans settle in once-remote parts of the world, a sharp decline in certain species of fish from overfishing, water shortages as agriculture and industry outpace existing water reserves and land degradation resulting from the relentless spread of agriculture onto land that is ill-suited to cultivation.

Although these strains have not yet precipitated a global environmental collapse, ecologists say we are living on borrowed time. "There is tremendous momentum in population growth," says Brian Halweil, a research fellow at the Worldwatch Institute, which studies global environmental problems. "Even if the total fertility rate were now at replacement level, world population growth would still be a problem." *(See map, p. 118.)* Halweil points to regions that are fast approaching a food crisis, such as the Nile River basin, whose current population of 110 million is expected to more than triple to 380 million by 2050. "With so many people being added," he says, "the per capita availability of resources will zoom down."

It's not that women are having more babies than their grandmothers. In fact, fertility rates have fallen in much of the world, especially where women have gained access to education and economic opportunities that make bearing large numbers of children less attractive. What has happened is that more children now survive to adulthood, thanks to vaccines, improved hygiene and more reliable food supplies.

Optimists in the population debate point to other statistics to refute Malthusian predictions of impending doom. While population growth continues, the rate of growth has slowed considerably in recent years as births in a growing number of countries are falling below 2.1 children per couple — the "replacement level," below which population begins to decline. This trend has forced the United Nations Population Division to lower its projections of future population growth. Under the "low" variant of its most recent projection, the U.N. agency expects human population to peak at 7.7 billion around the middle of the next century before starting a slow decline. Under its "high" variant, however, there would be 27 billion people on Earth by 2150, with no end of growth in sight.

But some optimists in the debate focus on the low numbers and conclude that the real threat today is the prospect that there will be too few people in coming decades — a virtual birth dearth.

"Predictions of a Malthusian collapse have been vastly exaggerated over the last few decades and continue in the face of new evidence that fertility rates are falling worldwide," says Steven W. Mosher, president of the Population Research Institute, in Falls Church, Va. "This is happening not only in the developed world but also in many developing countries, such as Thailand and Sri Lanka, which are already below replacement level, so that their populations will shortly be declining. The world's population will never double again."

Indeed, say optimists in the population debate, the real problem humanity faces is the coming loss of population, especially in Europe, where births have fallen far below replacement level. *(See story, p. 126.)* Ironically, Italy — homeland of the Vatican, contraception's archenemy — has the lowest fertility rate in the world: Each woman has an average of just 1.2 children in her lifetime. "If you built a fence around Europe, which has an average fertility rate of 1.35, the last European would turn out the lights in 300 years," Mosher says. "If current trends continue, the continent's population would go from 860 million today to zero."

But the Cassandras say it's too soon to start mourning the loss of European civilization. For one thing, they say, no one can predict with any certainty how many children future generations of people will choose to have. Moreover, because of high birthrates in earlier decades, the large number of women entering their child-bearing years will ensure that population continues to grow despite falling fertility rates. The fastest growth will come in the very countries that are least able to support more people — poor countries of sub-Saharan Africa and South Asia. "Population dynamics are like a supertanker," says Robert Engelman, director of the program on population and the environment at Population Action International. "They don't go from zero to 60 in 30 seconds, and they don't stop so fast either. So while total population growth has slowed more than demographers had expected, it's wrong to say the trend is irrevocable or permanent."

For 200 years, worldwide food production defied Malthusian predictions of global starvation. But now there are ominous signs that worldwide grain production will be unable to keep up with the population growth that is expected to continue for at least the next several decades. According to Worldwatch President Lester R. Brown, impending water shortages will soon force China to begin importing vast quantities of grain to feed its 1.2 billion people. This will drive up grain prices, Brown predicts, leaving developing countries in Africa and elsewhere unable to import enough to meet their food needs. The result: Malthus' nightmare.

"The jury's still out on Malthus," said Robert Kaplan, author of numerous articles on population and environmental issues. "But 200 years later, some people still agree with him. I think that's his ultimate success." [3]

In this bicentennial of Malthus' essay, these are some of the key questions being asked about population growth and the environment:

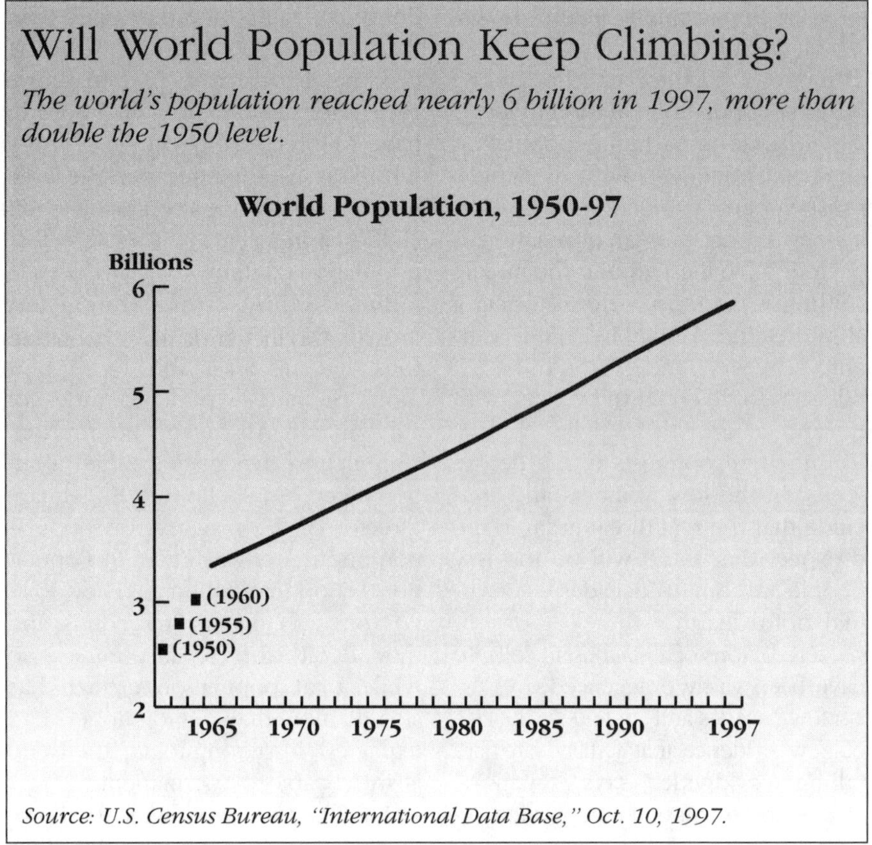

Source: U.S. Census Bureau, "International Data Base," Oct. 10, 1997.

***Can agricultural productivity increase without causing irreversible damage to the environment?***

In the 1950s and early '60s, a time of unprecedented high population growth in the developing world, demographers and policy-makers in the industrial countries realized that global food supplies — much provided by exports from developed nations — would soon fall short of demand. Agricultural researchers embarked on an urgent project to develop better-yielding grains in an attempt to avert widespread famine.

The results of this effort, later dubbed the Green Revolution, were stunning. Hybrid strains of rice, wheat and other grains were developed that produced more food per plant and shortened maturation periods so that more than one crop could be cultivated each growing season. In some instances, crop yields tripled.

The Green Revolution's success leads some experts to conclude that further advances in agronomy will suffice to feed the world's growing population. According to Mosher of the Population Research Institute, researchers at the United Nations' Food and Agriculture Organization (FAO) are confident that, even using current technology, enough food could be produced to feed as many as 14 billion people — well above most projections of Earth's population at its peak.

"There is a curious dichotomy between the world's political leaders, who are talking famine, and the researchers who are running the numbers," Mosher says. "The experts aren't being listened to by their own political bosses." In his view, the reason no one is listening to scientists who are confident in the world's ability to feed so many more people comes down to self-interest. "Population programs have been generously funded for the past 30 years, and there are a lot of researchers who have benefited from these programs and don't want to see them ended," he says. "As the Chinese would say, they don't want to see their own rice bowls broken."

While other experts agree that further improvements in food production are possible, they worry about the environmental effects of intensifying agriculture much beyond current levels. "I suspect that there is more the Green Revolution can do, that there are more opportunities to increase the yield of a set unit of land," says Engelman of Population Action International. "The important point is that almost all agricultural experts agree that the vast majority of all food will be produced on land we're now cultivating. There just isn't a whole lot of new farmland out there."

Intensifying output on existing farmland can only continue so long before the land is seriously degraded, Engelman warns. "I worry that we may not be able to increase output generation after generation without irrevocably damaging the resources we depend on for food." These include the soil, fresh water and the whole complex of systems that produce food, including organisms in the soil that facilitate the uptake of nutrients in plants.

Each year, an estimated 25 billion metric tons of nutrient-rich topsoil are blown or washed away, largely as a result of intensive agriculture. The soil that is left is denser, making it less able to retain water and allow root penetration. Irrigation produces another problem, salinization, or the buildup of salt and other waterborne minerals in the soil, which can destroy the land's productivity over time.[4] According to David Pimentel, an agricultural expert at Cornell University, soil degradation poses an even more serious threat to the environment than global warming. "It takes 500 years to produce one inch of soil," he said. "Erosion is a slow, gradual problem, but considering that 99 percent of our food comes from the land, it's one that's basic to the survival of the food system." [5]

Besides depleting the soil, irrigation and other modern agricultural techniques pose additional environmental hazards. "Inherent in Green Revolution technologies is the dependence on greater quantities of water, pesticides and fertilizers," says Kolankiewicz of the Carrying Capacity Network. "The environmental effects of this kind of agriculture are numerous and far-reaching, including pesticides that can be bioaccumulated and affect whole species and the drawdown of aquifers and depletion of stream flows by irrigation. So we're already robbing Peter to pay Paul."

Drawing on his experience as a Peace Corps volunteer in Latin America during the 1980s, Kolankiewicz also points to the damage caused as more and more marginal lands are brought into cultivation. "Very steep land is being stripped of trees because of the desperate need for food, population growth and inequitable land distribution," he says. "In many countries the best land for sustainable agriculture is owned by just a few people, who hold it idle, raise cattle on it or grow grain for export."

Some experts see a way out of this quandary through a more efficient global economy. "In an ideal, future world, there would be a number of places where people farming today would trade their labor for food produced elsewhere," says Nicholas Eberstadt, a Harvard University demographer and scholar at the American Enterprise Institute for Public Policy Research. "The environmental implications of such specialization are positive, however, because marginal lands would be under less pressure" from cultivation.

But a key condition for this outcome, Eberstadt says, is broader access to property rights. Environmental degradation occurs "when nobody feels they own a common resource, and everyone feels they can plunder it," he says, citing desertification in the Sahel in southern Sahara — caused by trying to turn marginally productive land into farmland — and severe industrial pollution in China, where property rights are severely limited. "Both a clear and rational framework of property rights and a more relaxed regimen of international trade could be facilitating mechanisms for ensuring sustainable food supplies in the future."

### *Should the U.S. government support international efforts to curb population growth?*

The United States has led the industrialized nations in funding programs that provide family-planning services to developing countries since the late 1960s. At that time, the U.N. Population Fund was set up to coordinate programs aimed at slowing rapid population growth. The federal government provides funding through the U.N. fund as well as through the U.S. Agency for International Development (AID), which helps other governments and non-governmental organizations (NGOs) in voluntary family-planning projects that provide information, services and supplies to communities throughout the world.

U.S. population assistance has been controversial, however. Anti-abortion activists charge that many overseas programs are coercive, forcing women to be sterilized or undergo abortions against their will. China's one-child policy — the toughest population-control policy in the world — has been especially criticized for allegedly forcing pregnant women who already have a child to have abortions, even late in pregnancy.

In response to the critics, President Ronald Reagan initiated the so-called Mexico City policy — named for the 1984 international population conference. Federal law already barred the use of U.S. funds to pay for abortions performed under international family-planning programs. Reagan took the ban a step further, issuing an executive order that prohibited federal funding of any NGO involved in abortion activities, even if U.S. funds were not used specifically to pay for abortions. [6]

As one of his first acts after taking office, President Clinton reversed the Mexico City policy, sparking a renewed debate over funding of international population programs. Supporters of these programs say they are largely responsible for the fall in fertility rates over the past three decades. "These programs are absolutely effective," says Carl Haub, senior demographer at the Population Reference Bureau. "A lot of countries can't get started [on cutting population growth] without outside help."

While many countries with high population growth can afford to pay for family-planning clinics, medical personnel and supplies such as birth control pills and condoms, U.S.-funded AID personnel help governments coordinate their programs, Haub says. "AID personnel provide continuity in countries with unstable local governments," he says. "They basically keep the ball rolling by providing the social marketing needed, especially in illiterate societies where it's hard to educate people on how to use birth-control methods like the pill."

Critics say that despite the existing ban on funding programs that provide abortion services or abortion-related lobbying or research, part of the $385 million AID budget earmarked for family-planning services inevitably finds its way into such programs. "Population-control programs in Third World countries involve various forms of coercion," says Mosher, who spent a year studying life in a commune in China in 1979, as the one-child policy there began to be enforced. "China is the worst case in terms of the sheer number of women who are brutalized, but it's not alone," he says. His institute has documented instances of abuse in 38 countries, including sterilizations performed

## High Fertility Means Low Development

*Regions with high fertility rates like Africa and Latin America have a lower per capita gross national product (GNP) and greater annual population increases than more developed areas, such as North America and Europe. Indeed, Europe's 1.4 fertility rate is below the replacement level, and its population is declining by 0.1 percent a year.*

**Major Regions of the World**

| | Population mid-1998 (millions) | Natural Population Increase (Annual %) | Projected Population (millions) 2010 | Projected Population (millions) 2025 | Total Fertility Rate | 1996 GNP Per Capita |
|---|---|---|---|---|---|---|
| World | 5,926 | 1.4% | 6,903 | 8,082 | 2.9 | $5,180 |
| More Developed Nations | 1,178 | 0.1 | 1,217 | 1,240 | 1.6 | 20,240 |
| Less Developed Nations | 4,748 | 1.7 | 5,687 | 6,842 | 3.3 | 1,230 |
| Africa | 763 | 2.5 | 979 | 1,288 | 5.6 | 650 |
| North America | 301 | 0.6 | 333 | 376 | 2.0 | 27,100 |
| Latin America & the Caribbean | 500 | 1.8 | 591 | 697 | 3.0 | 3,710 |
| Oceania | 30 | 1.1 | 34 | 40 | 2.4 | 15,430 |
| Asia | 3,604 | 1.5 | 4,235 | 4,965 | 2.8 | 2,490 |
| Europe | 728 | -0.1 | 731 | 715 | 1.4 | 13,710 |

*Source: "1998 World Population Data Sheet," Population Reference Bureau, 1998*

without informed consent, coerced abortions and unhygienic conditions in clinics.

"In countries like Mexico, Peru, Bangladesh and Indonesia, agents of the state are going to people's homes and telling women what they should do," Mosher says. "Imagine U.S. Health and Human Services agents coming to your home and telling you to take contraceptives. You would be outraged, yet this is the nature of population-control campaigns overseas."

But supporters of continued U.S. funding of international family-planning programs point instead to the gradual fall in fertility rates as evidence that women are voluntarily embracing the opportunity to have fewer children. "There's almost nothing rational about the debate over whether the United States is somehow contributing to abortions overseas," Engelman says. "We see the fall in fertility rates in developing countries as great news. It shows that population assistance is having the impact it was designed to have — more women are wanting fewer children."

Haub fears that the recent warnings about the dangers of population decline in the industrialized world will further erode support for U.S. funding of population programs. "This trend most definitely can have an effect on people's opinions about these programs," he says. "But fertility trends in Europe have absolutely nothing to do with trends in developing countries, which have very young populations and account for 80 percent of world population and 98 percent of the population growth."

Haub points to Mali, where the fertility rate has remained unchanged from around 7 children per woman for the past decade or more. "It's ridiculous to say that fertility rates in Africa are plummeting." Indeed, AID surveys suggest that more than 100 million married women in developing countries have an unmet need for family-planning information and contraceptives. [7]

But support for population programs remains weak in Congress, where the abortion controversy remains the primary focus of the debate on population. In April, for example, Congress added a stipulation to a State Department authorization bill (HR 1757) to pay nearly $1 billion in back dues to the U.N. that would bar U.S. aid to any international groups that lobby for abortion rights. President Clinton threatened to veto the measure. [8]

Some experts say the abortion debate in Washington undermines the progress made by family-planning efforts to date. "The U.N. estimates that if there isn't an immediate stepping up of international family planning there will be 3 billion more people in 50 years," says Halweil of Worldwatch. "That's 9.5 billion people by 2050. But reports that the population explosion is over, combined with pressure from groups that oppose abortion, are eroding domestic support for international family-planning efforts."

### *Should immigration be limited to protect the U.S. environment from overpopulation?*

Like most industrialized countries, the United States has experienced a decline in fertility rates in recent decades, as the postwar baby boom was replaced with the baby bust of the 1970s and '80s. Today, American women have, on average, 2 children. That's slightly below the 2.1 level demographers identify as replacement level fertility, since it allows for the replacement of both parents, with a small allowance for children who die before reaching adulthood.

But the U.S. population, now 270 million, is expected to grow almost 50 percent by 2050, to 387 million. [9] With fertility rates steady among native-born American women, experts say the increase is largely due to immigration. More than 800,000 immigrants legally enter the United States each year (1.1 million, if illegal immigrants are included). That level is almost triple the average annual immigration of 255,000 from World War II until 1970.

Almost as controversial as using abortion to control population growth is cutting immigration levels to slow environmental degradation. Indeed, although many environmental groups identify population growth as a threat to the environment, and most population growth in the United States today is a result of immigration, few of these organizations actually advocate capping immigration levels.

Earlier this year, the Sierra Club, one of the oldest and most respected environmental groups in the United States, ignited controversy among its members: It asked whether the group should abandon its neutrality on immigration or advocate caps on the number of people admitted each year in the interest of protecting the environment from the effects of overpopulation. When the votes were counted in April, the membership chose by a 3-to-2 margin to continue to stay out of the immigration quagmire altogether.

"This is a resounding defeat for a misguided policy," said Carl Pope, the Sierra Club executive director and a strong proponent of the group's neutral position on immigration. "Through this vote, our members have shown they understand that restricting immigration in the United States will not solve the environmental problems caused by global overpopulation. The common-sense solution to overpopulation is birth control, not border patrols." [10]

But supporters of immigration caps say the vote was little more than a politically correct cop-out encouraged by the group's leaders, who fear alienating the Hispanic and Asian immigrant population of California, its main political base. "There's no way we can stabilize population without reducing immigration," says Kolankiewicz, a Sierra Club member who was involved in the effort to bring the issue to the vote. "The Sierra Club tried to step very delicately around a very controversial domestic issue. But it's duplicitous to suggest that with continued international family-planning measures we'll be able to stabilize our population."

Over the past 45 years, Kolankiewicz says, U.S. immigration levels have quadrupled at the same time global fertility has declined by 40 percent. "We have the right and the responsibility to control our own population," he says.

While acknowledging the link between population growth and environmental degradation, some experts dispute the value of capping immigration levels in the United States. Of the 800,000 foreigners who legally enter the United States each year, all but about 120,000 gain entry because they are related to current residents or citizens. A significant reduction in immigration levels, says Haub, "would mean we'd have to tell the people who are already legal residents they can't bring over their immediate relatives. That's a political impossibility."

For its part, the Clinton administration has not taken a clear position on the issue of immigration's impact on the environment. A 1996 report by a White House task force concluded that "reducing immigration levels is a necessary part of population stabilization and the drive toward sustainability." [11] But the president recently defended immigration, calling immigrants "the most restless, the most adventurous, the most innovative and the most industrious of people."

Clinton condemned "policies and ballot propositions that exclude immigrants from our civic life" and praised the United States' tradition as an immigrant nation. "Let me state my view unequivocally," Clinton said. "I believe new immigrants are good for America." But he sidestepped the question of whether current immigration levels are appropriate. ■

# BACKGROUND

## A Radical Idea

When Malthus launched the ongoing debate over population growth in 1798, Europe was on the threshold of a radically new era. The Industrial Revolution was just getting under way, opening the way for dramatic shifts in Europe and North America from an agricultural to a modern industrial economy.

Malthus graduated from Cambridge University and later became an Anglican priest. In 1805 he became what is considered the world's first professor of political economy, a position he held at the college of the East India Company until his death in 1834.

The essay that made him famous arose from a friendly argument with his father over man's place in the world. Daniel Malthus espoused the optimistic view that prevailed at the time — no doubt inspired by the rise of democracy and technological progress — that man's ability to improve his lot is unlimited.

Two philosophers were the main purveyors of this view. In France, the Marquis de Condorcet welcomed the revolution in his country as evidence of mankind's ceaseless progress toward perfection. Even after he was imprisoned for criticizing the new Jacobin constitution, Condorcet never lost his optimism. Before starving to death in prison, he completed his writings, which were published posthumously in 1795. [12]

In England, social philosopher William Godwin shared Condorcet's views. In "An Enquiry Concerning Political Justice, and Its Influence on General Virtue and Happiness" (1793), Godwin took Condorcet's utopian thinking even further, calling for the abolition of all governmental and social institutions, including religion, school and family. All such associations, Godwin wrote, were oppressive and would no longer be needed when mankind reached its inevitable goal of perfection. At that point, he predicted, population growth would cease to be a concern. "The men who exist when the earth shall refuse itself to a more extended population will cease to propagate, for they will no longer have any motive, either of error or duty, to induce them. In addition to this they will perhaps be immortal." [13]

In refuting Condorcet and Godwin, Malthus argued that the notion that all people can live in ease and comfort defies laws of nature. Because population will always tend to grow faster than food supplies and other natural resources required for human survival, he wrote, humankind will always be afflicted with "misery and vice," such as war, famine, disease and abortion. "Famine seems to be the last, the most dreadful resource of nature," Malthus wrote. "The power of population is so superior to the power in the earth to produce subsistence for man, that premature death must in some shape or other visit the human race." [14]

Godwin's prediction that population growth will cease as people stop reproducing, Malthus wrote, defies another of the "fixed laws of our nature." "[T]owards the extinction of the passion between the sexes, no progress whatever has hitherto been made," he wrote. "It appears to exist in as much force at present as it did two thousand or four thousand years ago. . . . Assuming, then, my postulata as granted, I say that the power of population is indefinitely greater than the power in the earth to produce subsistence for man." [15]

Malthus modified his views slightly in later essays on the subject, suggesting that population growth could be slowed somewhat by delaying marriage and childbirth. But his basic thesis that there are natural limits to population growth was to greatly influence thinkers of his time and later. Charles Darwin acknowledged a debt to Malthus in devising his theory of evolution, published in 1859. Karl Marx, who published *Principles of Political Economy* the same year, denounced Malthus as a pawn of conservatives because his theory ruled out the Marxist ideal of the classless society. [16]

## 20th-Century Concerns

Record population growth in the 1960s and '70s sparked renewed interest in Malthus. The burgeoning environmental movement also raised concern about the effect of population growth on fossil fuel supplies and other natural resources. As in Malthus' time, optimists dismissed such worries, arguing that technological advances would provide for virtually limitless numbers of people.

Throughout the twentieth century, no voice has been more influential in rebutting Malthus than the Roman Catholic Church. In 1968, Pope Paul VI declared in an encyclical, "Humanae Vitae," that "each and every marriage act must remain open to the transmission of life," effectively banning all forms of birth control short of abstention. Population growth is not the problem among poor nations, the pope implied, but poor government and a lack of social justice. He called for humanity to undertake "the efforts and the sacrifices necessary to insure the raising of living standards of a people and of all its sons."

The same year the encyclical was

# Chronology

## 1700s *The debate over the impact of population growth begins.*

**1793**
English social philosopher William Godwin calls for the abolition of all governmental and social institutions as oppressive obstacles to human perfection. He predicts that population growth will eventually cease.

**1795**
Posthumously published writings by the Marquis de Condorcet, a French philosopher, argue that mankind is evolving toward perfection.

**1798**
Thomas Robert Malthus, an English cleric, warns in *An Essay on the Principle of Population* that unlimited population growth will overwhelm food supplies.

## 1950s-1960s *The Green Revolution greatly increases crop yields, quelling fears that famine will halt Earth's rapid population growth.*

**1960**
The International Rice Research Institute (IRRI) is created to increase rice yields. Research eventually leads to a doubling and tripling of yields, averting famine in Asian countries with high population growth.

**1968**
Pope Paul VI issues an encyclical entitled "Humanae Vitae," banning all artificial methods of birth control and ensuring the Roman Catholic Church's position as the most influential opponent of international population-control efforts.

## 1970s *Record population growth renews Malthusian fears, while China launches its controversial one-child policy.*

**1971**
The Consultative Group on International Agricultural Research (CGIAR) is set up to coordinate the improvement of food production worldwide. Its 16-member research organization helps boost crop and fish yields.

## 1980s *U.S. support for overseas family-planning programs wanes amid anti-abortion sentiment.*

**1980**
Stanford University biologist Paul Ehrlich bets University of Maryland Professor Julian Simon that commodity prices will rise as a result of population growth. Ten years later, Ehrlich loses the bet to Simon, who argues that technological progress will increase commodity supplies and lower prices.

**1984**
President Ronald Reagan initiates the so-called Mexico City policy — named for the population conference held there — prohibiting federal funding of any nongovernmental organization involved in abortion activities.

## 1990s *Forecasters alter their future projections in the wake of an unexpected slowing of population growth.*

**January 1993**
Shortly after taking office, President Clinton overturns the Mexico City policy.

**1996**
A White House task force calls for curbs on immigration to stabilize the U.S. population and protect the environment.

**November 1996**
The World Food Summit sets a goal of cutting in half the number of undernourished people on Earth from 800 million to 400 million by 2015.

## 2000s *Population growth is expected to continue, albeit at a slower pace.*

**2000**
After a century of rapid growth, Earth's population is expected to reach 6 billion, up from 1.6 billion in 1900.

**2050**
The population of the United States is expected to reach 387 million, up from 270 million in 1998. According to the United Nations Population Division's "middle" variant, world population is expected to peak at 7.7 billion before starting a slow decline.

## Falling Fertility Rates Threaten . . .

The population debate usually focuses on the impact of overpopulation on food supplies, health and the environment in developing countries. But scores of developed nations face an equally ominous threat: dwindling populations caused by low fertility.

Falling fertility rates have helped slow population growth throughout the world in recent years, but in some 50 countries the average number of children born to each woman has fallen below 2.1, the number required to maintain a stable population. Nearly all of these countries are in the developed world, where couples have been discouraged from having large families by improved education and health care, widespread female employment and rising costs of raising and educating children.

Conservative commentator Ben Wattenberg and others who question the value of family-planning programs have seized on this emerging trend to shift the terms of the population debate. "Never before have birthrates fallen so far, so fast, so low, for so long all around the world," Wattenberg writes. "The potential implications — environmental, economic, geopolitical and personal — are both unclear and clearly monumental, for good and for ill." [1]

According to Wattenberg, the implications are particularly dire for Europe, where the average fertility rate has fallen to 1.4 children per woman. *(See map, p. 118.)* Even if the trend reversed itself and the fertility rate returned to 2.1, the continent would have lost a quarter of its current population before it stabilized around the middle of the next century. With fewer children being born, the ratio of older people to younger people already is growing. "Europe may become an ever smaller picture-postcard continent of pretty old castles and old churches tended by old people with old ideas," Wattenberg writes. "Or it may become a much more pluralist place with ever greater proportions of Africans and Muslims — a prospect regarded with horror by a large majority of European voters." [2]

Some European governments are clearly concerned about the "birth dearth" in their midst. With fewer children being born, they face the prospect of shrinking work forces and growing retiree populations, along with slower economic growth and domestic consumption. Italy, whose fertility rate of 1.2 children per woman is among the lowest in the world, stands to suffer the most immediate consequences of shrinking birthrates. "Italy's population will fall by half over the next half-century, from 66 million now to 36 million," says Steven W. Mosher, president of the Population Research Institute. "The Italian government warns that the current birthrate, if it continues, will amount to collective suicide."

Like Italy, France and Germany have introduced generous child subsidies, in the form of tax credits for every child born, extended maternal leave with full pay, guaranteed employment upon resumption of work and free child care. Mosher predicts that the European Union will likely extend these and other policies to raise birthrates throughout the 15-nation organization in the next couple of years because all members are below replacement level.

"Humanity's long-term problem is not too many children being born but too few," Mosher says. "The one-child family is being chosen voluntarily in many European countries like Italy, Greece, Spain and Russia, which are already filling more coffins than cradles each year. Over time, the demographic collapse will extinguish entire cultures."

Although it is most pronounced in Europe, the birth dearth affects a few countries in other parts of the world as well. Mosher calculates that Japan's population will fall from 126 million today to 55 million over the next century if its 1.4 fertility rate remains unchanged. The trend is already having a social and cultural impact on the country.

"In Japan, which boasts the longest lifespans of any country in the world, it's now common for an elderly

issued, Stanford University biologist Paul Ehrlich issued an equally impassioned plea for expanded access to birth-control services in *The Population Bomb*. In this and other warnings about the dangers of population growth, Ehrlich and his wife, Anne, also a Stanford researcher, predicted that the resources on which human survival depends would soon run out. "Population control is absolutely essential if the problems now facing mankind are to be solved," they wrote. [17]

At the same time, Worldwatch's Brown began warning of an impending food crisis. "As of the mid-1970s, it has become apparent that the soaring demand for food, spurred by both population growth and rising affluence, has begun to outrun the productive capacity of the world's farmers and fishermen," he wrote in 1974. "The result is declining food reserves, skyrocketing food prices and increasingly intense international competition for exportable food supplies." [18]

The voices of alarm were dismissed by some free-market economists, who, echoing Godwin's view of man's perfectibility, asserted that human ingenuity would resolve the problems of population growth. The late Julian Simon, a professor at the University of Maryland, declared that Earth's natural resources will never be completely exhausted because human intellect, which is required to exploit them, is infinite.[19] To prove his point, Simon bet Paul Ehrlich that between 1980 and '90 the prices of several minerals would fall as technological progress raised their supply. Ehrlich bet that growing resource scarcity, stemming in part from population

## . . . Dire Consequences for Europe

person to hire a family for a day or a weekend to experience family life and enjoy interaction with young people," Mosher says. "It's sad to have to rent a family for a weekend, but this is a way of life that is no longer available to the Japanese because the country is dying."

The birth dearth has geopolitical implications, as well. "As the population plummets, you can say goodbye to Japan as a world power," Mosher says. "And this trend is very hard to reverse. Every young couple would have to have three or four kids to stop the momentum, and that's not going to happen."

Apart from encouraging childbirth, the only way governments can halt population loss is to open the doors to immigrants. In the United States, where the 2.0 fertility rate is just below replacement level, the population is growing by 160,000 people a year, thanks to immigration.

While immigration has always played a prominent, if controversial, role in the United States and Canada, it is a far more contentious issue in the rest of the developed world. Most European countries have more homogeneous societies than those of North America, and deeply entrenched resistance to immigration, especially by people from non-European countries, has fueled support for right-wing politicians like France's Jean-Marie Le Pen. Anti-immigrant sentiment has occasionally escalated into violence, such as the firebombings of housing for Turkish "guest workers" in Germany during the 1980s.

Still, immigration has become more acceptable throughout much of Europe in the past decade, and many of the "guest workers" who come from North Africa, Turkey and other places in search of jobs have stayed and even gained citizenship. "Immigrants are continuing to move to Europe, bringing their cultures and their religions with them," Mosher says. "Intermarriage also is increasing." Japan has been much less hospitable to foreigners. "Immigration is a very sensitive subject in Japan," Mosher says, "and it is unlikely to be used in the short term to address the growing shortfall of workers there."

Advocates of population-control programs dismiss the concern over shrinking birthrates. "We are delighted to see falling birthrates in our lifetimes, and will continue to encourage the trend," says Robert Engelman, director of Population Action International's program on population and the environment. "I don't want to minimize the problems associated with aging populations. But because this is a slow process, societies will have plenty of time to adjust to the economic and political stresses by increasing immigration from parts of the world where population will continue to rise for some time."

Of course, immigration will be a viable solution to depopulation only as long as humanity continues to grow in number in other parts of the world. Those who worry about falling population point to the United Nations' most conservative projections, which suggest that global population could begin to shrink as early as 2040. But others see little cause for concern.

"If world population starts to fall in 2040, so what?" Engelman asks. "Please identify the danger of population decline that starts at a level much higher than today's and at worst may bring population down to levels seen earlier in the 20th century. There's only so much fresh water, so much atmosphere to absorb the waste greenhouse gases we inject into it every day, so much forest, so much land that can be cultivated. When you consider the enormity of these problems, there's nothing to be afraid of with gradual population decline."

---

[1] Ben J. Wattenberg, "The Population Explosion Is Over," *The New York Times Magazine*, Nov. 23, 1997, p. 60.

[2] *Ibid.*

growth, would drive prices up. Simon won the bet.

## Green Revolution

Acting on concerns that rising populations in developing countries were outstripping the world's capacity to produce enough food, leaders of NGOs, foundations and national governments launched an international agricultural-research effort to avert famine. In 1960, the International Rice Research Institute (IRRI) was created to increase the yield of rice, the basic food for more than half the world's population. Within a few years, IRRI developed the first of several dwarf breeds that enabled farmers to grow more rice on limited land, using less water and fewer chemicals.

Under the leadership of the Consultative Group on International Agricultural Research (CGIAR), set up in 1971, biologists and agronomists from 16 research centers around the world have since produced hundreds of hybrid strains of staple grains, such as rice, wheat and corn. They have recently extended their efforts to improve yields of potatoes, fish and other basic foods.

These efforts have been so successful that they are known as the Green Revolution. Indeed, although world population has almost doubled since 1961, per-capita food production has more than doubled. The FAO estimates that people in the developing world consume almost a third more calories a day than in the early 1960s. As a result, experts say, there are fewer deaths from

## Population Programs Depend . . .

The International Conference on Population and Development, held in Cairo, Egypt, in 1994, laid out a formula for stabilizing the world's growing population. Adopted by 180 nations, the plan called for improvements in women's health and job opportunities and greater access to high-quality reproductive health care, including family planning.

As the following examples show, countries that embraced the Cairo conference's "program of action" are at varying stages in population planning, due to varying levels of development, status of women and religious beliefs:

**China** — In 1971 Mao Zedong acknowledged the threat posed by China's more than 850 million people and launched a family-planning policy urging later marriage, increased spacing between children and a limit of two children per couple. The policy was later intensified into the radical "one-child" policy, which attracted international condemnation for its practice of forced abortions. The policy has since been relaxed, however. According to firsthand reports, it never covered most of rural China, where many families have three or more children. Still, the fertility rate has plummeted, from 5.8 children per woman in 1970 to 2 today. China's 1.2 billion people makes it the most highly populated country in the world. [1]

**India** — In 1951 India launched the world's first national family-planning policy. Although almost half of the nation's married women use family planning, and birthrates have come down, most of the slowdown has come in the more developed southern part of the country. "The real story in the past 20 years has been in the large illiterate states of the north known as the Hindi belt," says Carl Haub, senior demographer at the Population Reference Bureau. "In Uttar Pradesh, with a population of 150 million people, women still have an average of five children." That compares with 3.9 children for the country as a whole. With 989 million people, India today is the second most populous country in the world. With an annual growth rate of almost 2 percent — twice that of China — India may surpass China by 2050. [2]

**Pakistan** — Just across India's northwestern border, Pakistan has been much less aggressive in its population program. The fertility rate has fallen only slightly, from 6.6 children per woman in 1984-85 to 5.6 children today. A number of factors have contributed to the slow fall in fertility, including official indifference, inadequate funding of population programs and the country's Islamic traditions, which grant women little status, give men the leading role in family decisions and place a high value on sons. [3]

**Bangladesh** — When Bangladesh won independence from Pakistan in 1971, it had roughly the same population — 66 million people — and the same population growth rate — 3 percent a year — as Pakistan. But the new leaders of Bangladesh, unlike Pakistan, made family planning a top priority. As a result of a sweeping education program and widespread distribution of contraceptives, the fertility rate has dropped from more than 6 children per woman to three. Today, the population of Bangladesh is 120 million, compared with 140 million in Pakistan. [4]

**Thailand** — Population-control advocates consider Thailand a major success story. Its strong government program is credited with raising contraceptive use from 8 percent to 75 percent of couples over the past 30 years. As a result, the fertility rate has plummeted from 6.2 to 2 births per woman, slightly below the replacement level of 2.1. The relatively high status of Thai women, an extensive road network facilitating access to health clinics and low child mortality are cited as reasons for the program's success. [5]

**Rwanda** — Since the bloody civil war in 1994, when as many as 750,000 Tutsis were slaughtered by rival Hutus, members of both tribes have set about what one doctor calls "revenge fertility" — a competition to procreate in

famine and malnutrition than ever before. [20] The famines that have occurred in the past 35 years, such as those in Ethiopia and Somalia in the 1980s, and now in Sudan, have been largely the result of war and civil unrest rather than scarcity of global food supplies.

A little-mentioned side effect of the Green Revolution, however, was the environmental damage that accompanied the astonishing increase in crop yields. Some of the new strains were more susceptible to insect infestation than traditional breeds. Pesticide use in rice production, for example, increased sevenfold, threatening the safety of water supplies. Some insects have developed resistance to the chemicals, resulting in yet heavier pesticide use. Green Revolution crops also require fertilizer, in some cases up to 30 times the amount used on traditional crops. With prolonged use, fertilizers can damage the soil. Finally, because many new plant strains require irrigation, the Green Revolution has been accompanied by increased erosion and water run-off, further harming land productivity.

"The reduced productivity requires added fertilizer, irrigation and pesticides to offset soil and water degradation," write David Pimentel and Marcia Pimentel of Cornell University. " This starts a cycle of more agricultural chemical usage and further increases the production costs the farmer must bear." [21] ■

## . . . On Wide Range of Factors

what is among Africa's most densely populated countries. With fertility at about 7 children per woman and population growth of 3.5 percent, the population of this impoverished country roughly the size Maryland is expected to grow from 7.2 million people today to 25 million by 2030. [6]

**Kenya** — Although it was one of the first African countries to introduce family-planning services, Kenya saw its fertility rate continue to grow for some time, from 5.3 children per woman in 1962 to 8 children per woman by 1977. In 1982, however, the government strengthened the program, providing community-based services in isolated areas that have increased the use of contraceptives among rural populations. As a result, the fertility rate has fallen to 4.5 children per woman — a rate that ensures continued population growth for decades but one that places Kenya well below the average rate of 6 children per woman in all of sub-Saharan Africa. Kenya's success in lowering fertility rates is now being mirrored in several other countries in the region, including Zimbabwe, Ghana, Nigeria and Senegal. [7]

**Tunisia** — Since 1957, Tunisia's population has doubled from 4 million to 8 million. While that's a huge increase, it pales in comparison with neighboring Algeria, which also started out in 1957 with 4 million inhabitants but now is home to 57 million. The difference, according to journalist Georgie Ann Geyer, is culture. "Thirty percent of the budget in Tunisia goes to education," she said. "Also, population control is part of the culture." [8] The government population program provides free family-planning services in most parts of the country, and mobile units serve rural areas. The program also is sensitive to religious customs: Rather than urging new mothers to use birth control methods right after delivery, for example, health personnel schedule a return visit to hospital 40 days later — the day new mothers return to society from seclusion, according to Islamic custom. [9]

**Iran** — Since the 1979 Islamic revolution, Iran's population has jumped from 35 million to 60 million, fueled in part by official encouragement for large families. In 1993, the government adopted a strict family-planning program that encourages vasectomy and other means of birth control — though abortion remains illegal in most cases — and denies subsidized health insurance and food coupons to couples with more than three children. As a result of these efforts, the population growth rate has dropped from 4 percent a year in the 1980s — among the highest in the world — to about 2.5 percent in 1996. [10]

**Peru** — To stem its 2.2 percent annual increase in population, the government of Peru in 1995 stepped up its population-control program, with the additional goal of raising the status of women in the country. Since then, the program has come under fire, as health workers are accused of offering gifts to illiterate women to undergo sterilization in often unhygienic conditions. [11]

---

[1] See Mark Hertsgaard, "Our Real China Problem," *The Atlantic*, November 1997, pp. 96-114.

[2] See "India's Growing Pains," *The Economist*, Feb. 22, 1997, p. 41.

[3] Population Reference Bureau, "Pakistan: Family Planning with Male Involvement Project of Mardan," November 1993.

[4] See Jennifer D. Mitchell, "Before the Next Doubling," *World Watch*, January/February 1998, pp. 20-27.

[5] Population Reference Bureau, "Thailand: National Family Planning Program," August 1993.

[6] See "Be Fruitful," *The Economist*, Feb. 1, 1997, p. 43.

[7] See Stephen Buckley, "Birthrates Declining in Much of Africa," *The Washington Post*, April 27, 1998.

[8] Geyer spoke at "Malthus Revisited," a conference held May 8-9, 1998, by the Warrenton, Va.-based Biocentric Institute, which studies ways to enhance the quality of life for all peoples.

[9] See Population Reference Bureau, "Tunisia: Sfax Postpartum Program," March 1993.

[10] See Neil MacFarquhar, "With Iran Population Boom, Vasectomy Receives Blessing," *The New York Times*, Sept. 8, 1996.

[11] See Calvin Sims, "Using Gifts as Bait, Peru Sterilizes Poor Women," *The New York Times*, Feb. 15, 1998.

# CURRENT SITUATION

### Population Explosion

The 20th century has seen by far the fastest population growth in human history. For the first million years or so of man's existence on Earth, global population probably did not exceed 6 million — fewer than New York City's current population. With the beginning of agriculture some 10,000 years ago, population expanded gradually until it approached 1 billion by 1700 and 1.6 billion by 1900. Population growth never exceeded 0.5 percent a year over that 200-year period. [22]

By 2000, global population is expected to reach 6 billion. The unprecedented population explosion of the 20th century peaked in the 1970s, when the growth rate reached 2 percent a year. It has since slowed, thanks to improved access to family-planning information and contraceptives and expanded educational and employment opportunities for women in developing countries.

As couples become less dependent

on children to help in the fields and take care of them in old age, the value of large families decreases. The same medical advances that helped fuel the population explosion by reducing infant mortality also enable couples to have fewer children in the knowledge that they will survive to adulthood.

As a result of these changes, fertility rates of most developing countries are following those in industrialized countries, where fertility rates have fallen dramatically in recent decades. As more people move to the cities, the cost of raising children — housing, food, clothing and schooling — is a powerful inducement to reducing family size. "Birthrates in a large number of countries in the developing world, except for Africa, Pakistan and some countries in the Persian Gulf, have come down to a degree," says Haub of the Population Reference Bureau. "The big question is whether they will come down to the 2.1 level seen in developed countries. That would bring the population growth rate to zero."

But while fertility rates are slowly falling in many developing nations, the population momentum of the earlier boom ensures that population growth will continue in these countries for years to come. While population growth rates have dropped in industrial nations, in the developing world more than 2 billion young people under age 20 are entering or will soon enter their childbearing years, according to the Population Reference Bureau. This trend is especially significant in sub-Saharan Africa, the region with the highest fertility rate in the world — an average of 6 births per woman. With 45 percent of the inhabitants of sub-Saharan Africa age 15 or younger, population growth will likely continue, no matter what the birthrate may be in the next few decades. [23]

The difference in fertility rates between industrialized and developing countries has implications for the future. Today, there are four times as many people in developing countries as in industrial countries. Because 98 percent of global population growth is taking place in developing countries, that gap is likely to widen. If current trends continue, many industrial nations will soon begin to lose population, especially young, working-age people. [24] As developing countries struggle to support and employ their growing number of youth, many more young people from the developing world may migrate to other regions, including the developed countries.

Norman Myers of Oxford University, in England, puts the number of "environmental refugees" at 25 million, primarily in sub-Saharan Africa, China, the Indian subcontinent, Mexico and Central America, who are fleeing drought, erosion, desertification, deforestation and other environmental problems.

"The issue of environmental refugees is fast becoming prominent in the global arena," Myers writes. "Indeed it promises to rank as one of the foremost human crises of our times." Myers foresees increased resistance to immigration in industrial nations. "Already migrant aliens prove unwelcome in certain host countries, as witness the cases of Haitians in the United States and North Africans in Europe. No fewer than nine developed countries, almost one in three, are taking steps to further restrict immigration flows from developing countries." [25]

## Environmental Impact

As global population continues to mount, so does the strain on the environment, as people move into previously uninhabited areas and consume ever-increasing amounts of natural resources. In recent times, the first signs of population's impact on the environment were regional food shortages in the 1960s and '70s. Initially, the Green Revolution resolved the shortages by introducing high-yield grains and innovative farming techniques. But the more intensive methods of agriculture required to boost food production in many parts of the world have since produced environmental damage of their own. "You can't fertilize crops without fresh water," says Halweil. "If you increase fertilizer use, you have to increase water use. As a result, large areas of Latin America, Africa and China are now suffering water shortages."

Another result of intensified irrigation and fertilizer use is the buildup of salt and other minerals that are left in the soil after the water evaporates. After prolonged irrigation, land also tends to become waterlogged and no longer suitable for growing plants. Even before land degradation sets in, there are certain limits to the benefits of fertilizers. "You can't just keep putting fertilizer on the land indefinitely," Halweil says. "Eventually the yield increases cease."

With economic development, more people around the world are consuming poultry, beef, pork and other meat products. As demand for such foods rises, cattle ranches are occupying land once used for agriculture, pushing farmers onto marginal lands such as steep hillsides and virgin forests. The deforestation that results, most evident recently in tropical South America and Africa, promotes erosion and has been implicated in global warming.

Biologists recently warned that a "mass extinction" of plant and animal species is now taking place, the result of human destruction of natural habitats. [26] Even the oceans are showing signs of strain from population growth. Overfishing and pollution have caused sudden decreases in fish catches, prompting temporary bans in many fisheries that only a few decades ago seemed limitless. [27]

Population growth has also been accompanied by air and water pollution. While developed countries have

# At Issue:

## *Has economic development proved Malthus wrong?*

**JAMES P. PINKERTON**
***Lecturer, Graduate School of Political Management, The George Washington University***

yes

In 1798, a 32-year-old minister from England published, anonymously, a 54,000-word "Essay on the Principle of Population." In it, he argued that "the power of population is indefinitely greater than the power in the Earth to produce subsistence for man." And so, he concluded in his famous formulation, "Population, when unchecked, increases in a geometrical ratio. Subsistence increases only in an arithmetical ratio." Neither the author nor his essay stayed obscure for long. Yet for all the renown of Thomas Robert Malthus, it is hard to think of an idea that has been simultaneously more influential and more wrong.

On the bicentennial of his famous treatise, Malthus lives on as adjective; a Nexis database search for the word "Malthusian" just in the last year found 138 "hits." Indeed, Malthusianism has become an intellectual prism for explaining the world, like Marxism or Freudianism — even for those who have read little or nothing of the original texts. Just as Marxists explain everything as a consequence of class structure or Freudians interpret behavior by identifying underlying sexual impulses, so Malthusians start with an inherent presumption of scarcity and impending doom. And so Malthus stands as the patron saint of pessimists, those who see the glass as half-empty, not half-full. As he wrote then, his view of the world had "a melancholy hue."

Interestingly, the first Malthusians were on the political right. The landed gentry from which Malthus sprang looked upon the swelling population of the big cities with fear and even loathing . . . .

Today's Malthusians, of course, are on the environmental left. Once again, the dynamic is that many among the elite look upon their fellow humans as liabilities. And once again, they have been mostly wrong.

The leading Malthusian today — if you don't count Vice President Al Gore — is Stanford Professor Paul Ehrlich. His landmark book, *The Population Bomb*, published in 1968, began with an alarm. "The battle to feed all humanity is over," he declared, predicting worldwide famine. A more recent book, *The Population Explosion* (1990), co-written with his wife Anne, carries on the same doom-gloom argument. Praising, of course, the memory of Malthus, the Ehrlichs prescribe a long list of control on virtually every aspect of human activity . . . .

Ironically, toward the end of his life, Malthus altered his views. In "Principles of Political Economy" (1820) he acknowledged that economic growth would improve the prospects of the populace. But as so often happens, the original outrageous assertion is remembered forever, while the subsequent revision, even if it is closer to the truth, fades away quickly.

**JOHN F. ROHE**
***Attorney and author of* A Bicentennial Malthusian Essay *(1997)***

no

Philosophers at the dawn of the Industrial Revolution . . . suggested that prosperity and wealth were dependent on more people. In his essay, "Of Avarice and Profusion" in 1797, William Godwin states, "There is no wealth in the world except this, the labor of man . . . ." While serving as an ordained priest in the Church of England, Thomas Robert Malthus questioned these findings. He pondered basic mathematical principles. If parents had four children, and if the population continued to double every generation, the exponential progression would be as follows: 2, 4, 8, 16, 32, 64, 128, 256, 512, 1024, 2048. The numerical surge becomes explosive. Malthus determined a finite planet could not accommodate perpetual growth . . . .

Thomas Robert Malthus unlocked the door to one of nature's best-kept and most formidable secrets. He discovered a universal law of biology. For every plant and animal, there are more offspring than the ecosystem can sustain. And we are just beginning to grapple with the ethical dilemma resulting from his humbling conclusion: This universal law even applies to us.

The view from a seemingly lofty perch on nature's food chain can be deceptive. We enjoy but a brief reprieve from universal biological principles. The prescient message of a pre-scientific era has not been rendered obsolete by modern technology.

Our planet now experiences a daily net population gain of 250,000 people (total births minus deaths), and approximately 1.3 billion go to bed hungry every night. Several hundred thousand slip beyond the brink of malnutrition every year.

While the Earth's natural capital is systematically dismantled, efforts to discredit Malthus persist. For example, Julian Simon claims the world's resources can continue to accommodate human growth for 7 billion years! By then, the unchecked human biomass would fill the universe.

Efforts to discredit Malthus do not always plummet to such overt absurdities. Subtle efforts to refute him are exhibited every time a politician promises to add more exponential growth to the GNP. Proponents of growth are implicitly found in every financial report, business forecast and economic news publication. An abiding faith in growth has become the unexamined conviction of our age. Notions of sustainability are not on the table. The talismanic affinity for growth is an implicit rejection of Malthus . . . .

We were not exempt from the laws of biology unveiled by Thomas Robert Malthus in 1798. And we are not exempt now. At the bicentennial anniversary of his essay, Malthus deserves recognition for predicting the cause of today's most pressing concerns and most challenging ethical challenges. We discredit him at our peril.

## Developed Nations Use the Most Resources

*The United States accounts for only 5 percent of the world's population but uses a third of its paper and dumps three-quarters of the hazardous waste. Similarly, other developed countries account for a small fraction of Earth's population but use the largest percentage of its metals and paper.*

**Share of Population, Waste Production and Resource Consumption**

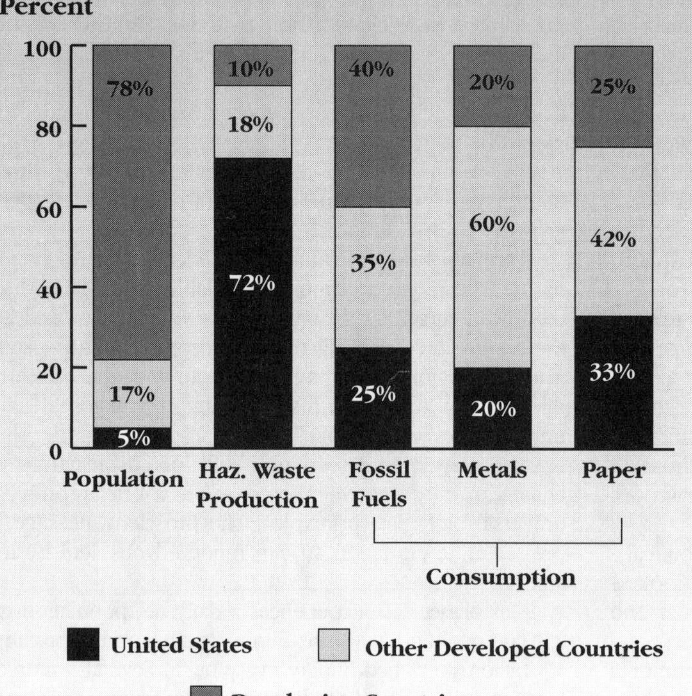


*Sources: "New Perspectives on Population: Lessons from Cairo,"* Population Bulletin, *March 1995; Natural Resources Defense Council*

have made strides in these areas, industrializing countries are facing mounting problems. China, for example, which uses coal for industry, as well as for heating and cooking, has among the worst air pollution in the world. Taiyuan, in northern China, has seven times as much particulate matter as Los Angeles, by far the most polluted city in the United States. Beijing and other Chinese cities are also blanketed by pollutants. [28]

Optimists in the population debate reject the notion that population growth by itself causes environmental damage. "I don't think there is a direct link between population and the environment," says the Population Research Institute's Mosher, who blames misguided government policies. "You can create environmental problems in a lightly populated country by failing to control pollution, just as you can have a very clean environment in a densely populated country, such as Germany, which is cleaning up the Rhine River and has greatly improved air quality. Mankind is capable of creative solutions."

Even more controversial is the link that some draw between population growth and global warming. Consumption of coal, oil and natural gas has been implicated in the gradual heating of the atmosphere that scientists fear will cause melting of polar ice caps, rising water levels and flooding of crowded coastal areas. Warming may also speed desertification and the spread of malaria and other insect-borne diseases. Although carbon-fuel consumption can be expected to continue to rise with economic development, many scientists predict that the growth in human population alone will increase demand for these fuels until cheap alternatives are developed.

But optimists in the population debate firmly reject this argument. "The odd suggestion that babies are somehow responsible for pollution tends to be the mindset of people who blame problems on the sheer number of people who exist," says Mosher, reflecting the view of many critics of the Kyoto Protocol, which was endorsed last December by the United States and 167 other countries. "But this view is wrong and was also rejected at Kyoto.

When the developed countries asked developing countries to further decrease their total fertility rates as part of the treaty, they were rejected outright, and rightly so. There is no necessary connection between the number of children being born and the level of carbon dioxide in the air."

Critics also charge that the global-warming theory rests on shaky scientific evidence. Consequently, they oppose U.S. participation in the treaty, which they say would cost more than 3 million jobs as businesses curb production to comply with its requirement to cut carbon emissions. The Clinton administration, which strongly supports the treaty, faces an uphill battle in the Senate, which must ratify it by a two-thirds majority before it will take effect in the United States. [29] ■

# OUTLOOK

## Grain Crunch?

For the past several decades, the Green Revolution has largely discredited the Malthusian prediction of imminent collapse of the global food supplies needed to feed a rapidly expanding population. But the environmental degradation that has continued apace during that time may have laid the groundwork for just such a calamity in the not too distant future. According to Worldwatch, rapid industrialization in China is reducing the supply of water farmers use to irrigate their grain crops. Because 70 percent of the grain consumed by China's 1.2 billion inhabitants comes from irrigated land, the diversion of water for industrial use may soon force the country, now largely self-sufficient, to start importing grain.

Because of its sheer size, China would quickly overwhelm the global supply of grain, driving up prices and forcing less affluent grain-importing countries, such as those of sub-Saharan Africa, out of the market. The result, Worldwatch warns, would be widespread famine. "For the 1.3 billion of the world's people who live on $1 a day or less, higher grain prices could quickly become life threatening," write Brown and Halweil. [30]

Brown has made similarly dire predictions in the past that have proved wrong, drawing the scorn of optimists in the Malthusian debate. But now, the situation he describes is sufficiently alarming to have drawn the attention of the U.S. National Intelligence Council, which calls for greater U.S.-China cooperation in agricultural production and technology. Brown and Halweil endorse the idea.

"If the world's two leading food producers can work closely together to protect their agricultural resource bases, while the world works to stabilize population," they write, "it will benefit not only each of those countries, but the rest of the world as well." [31]

Although the implications of China's water shortage are especially alarming, it is hardly the only country faced with competing demands on dwindling water supplies. According to Population Action International, some 80 percent of the world's population lives in countries facing problems with fresh water supplies. Population growth will lead to more widespread water shortages, the group predicts, heightening the risk of conflict over water supplies in areas such as the Tigris-Euphrates basin, where water rights are already a source of tension among Iraq, Syria and Turkey. [32]

Meanwhile, the CGIAR continues trying to ward off famine with further improvements in crop yields as well as fish and meat production. In an effort to halve the number of undernourished people on Earth to 400 million by 2015 — the goal set by the World Food Summit in November 1996 — the international research organization is studying the potential of bioengineering as the next weapon in its arsenal to continue the Green Revolution into the next century. [33]

## Consumption to Blame?

Today's consumer society has added a new twist to the warning issued by Malthus about inadequate food supplies. Latter-day Malthusians warn that the economic systems prevalent in most of the world today can only accelerate that end by encouraging consumption of resources without regard to its impact on the environment. In the United States, advertisements promise consumers that buying an endless array of products will bring greater happiness. With the end of the Cold War and the demise of the Soviet Union, the Western model of economic life is being pursued throughout most of the world.

Some experts say the combination of population growth and rising consumption do not threaten Earth's carrying capacity. "The long-term trend for inflation-adjusted prices of commodities has been going down, not up," Eberstadt says. "This suggests to me that natural resources are less scarce today than they were when there was less demand. In any case, we're heading toward a knowledge-and-service economy, so the direction of our development is less resource-intensive and more reliant on human skills. That gives me hope that we may be able to manage our resource demands in the future."

But many environmentalists say Malthus' nightmare will become reality that much sooner if the rest of the world adopts the consumption-based model developed in North America and Western Europe. In their view, economic growth has become a fundamental, but flawed, barometer of well-being. "Every news report, every business forecast assumes that growth is good and that more growth is better," says attorney John F. Rohe, author of the 1997 book *A Bicentennial Malthusian Essay.* "But the issue is not how we grow. It's how we can develop sustainably." *(See At Issue, p. 131)*

In this view, current efforts to protect the environment fall far short of the changes that are required to ensure sustainability. "People wonder whether the economy can continue to grow if we stop excessive consumption of oil and polluting goods," Halweil says. "They say we can shift to solar energy, fuel cells and biodegradable plastics. But the answer isn't having a hybrid-fuel car in everyone's garage. It's having fewer people driving and more taking public transportation."

The only answer to having more people on the planet, Halweil says, is to drastically cut consumption. "We are addicted to consumption, and we have to be slowly weaned off it," he says. "I don't know what it will look like, but the economic system will have to be different if the environment is to be protected." ■

## FOR MORE INFORMATION

*If you would like to have this CQ Researcher updated, or need more information about this topic, please call CQ Custom Research. Special rates for CQ subscribers. (202) 887-8600 or (800) 432-2250, ext. 600*

**Carrying Capacity Network,** 2000 P St. N.W., Suite 240, Washington, D.C. 20036; (202) 296-4548; www.carryingcapacity.org. An advocacy group that focuses on population stabilization, immigration reduction, economic sustainability and resource conservation to preserve the quality of life.

**World Bank,** 1818 H St. N.W., Suite S9035, Washington, D.C. 20433; (202) 473-8729; www.worldbank.org. The bank provides member countries with loans and technical advice for family-planning projects designed to slow population growth.

**Population Action International,** 1120 19th St. N.W., Suite 550, Washington, D.C. 20036; (202) 659-1833; www.populationaction.org. This organization promotes population stabilization through public education and universal access to voluntary family planning.

**Population Reference Bureau,** 1875 Connecticut Ave. N.W., Suite 520, Washington, D.C. 20009-5728; (202) 483-1100; www.prb.org. An educational organization that provides information on family planning and international development programs and U.S. population policy.

**Population Research Institute,** 5119A Leesburg Pike, Suite 295, Falls Church, Va. 22041; (540) 622-5226; www.pop.org. The institute focuses on human rights abuses in population programs and promotes economic development without recourse to these programs.

**Zero Population Growth,** 1400 16th St. N.W., Suite 320, Washington, D.C. 20036; (202) 332-2200; www.zpg.org. ZPG supports expansion of family-planning programs and women's access to abortion and family-planning services.

## Notes

[1] Thomas Robert Malthus, *An Essay on the Principle of Population* (1798), cited in Philip Appleman, ed., *An Essay on the Principle of Population* (1976), p. 56. For background, see "World Hunger," *The CQ Researcher*, Oct. 25, 1991, pp. 801-824.

[2] See "Population Growth," *The CQ Researcher*, July 16, 1993, pp. 601-624.

[3] Kaplan spoke at "Malthus Revisited," a conference held May 8-9, 1998, by the Warrenton, Va.-based Biocentric Institute, which studies ways to enhance the quality of life for all peoples.

[4] See Population Action International, *Conserving Land: Population and Sustainable Food Production*, April 1995.

[5] Pimentel spoke at the May conference on Malthus (see above).

[6] See "International Population Assistance," *Congressional Digest*, April 1997.

[7] See "What Birth Dearth? Why World Population Is Still Growing," *Population Action International Fact Sheet*, 1998.

[8] See "Clinton Uncaps Veto Pen As State Department Bill Clears," *CQ Weekly*, May 2, 1998, pp. 1167-1168.

[9] See James P. Smith and Barry Edmonston, eds., *The New Americans* (1997), p. 95.

[10] Quoted in William Branigin, "Sierra Club Votes for Neutrality on Immigration," *The Washington Post*, April 26, 1997.

[11] President's Council on Sustainable Development, "Task Force Report on Population and Consumption," 1996, p. iv.

[12] Condorcet's last work was *Esquisse d'un tableau historique des progrès de l'esprit humain*.

[13] Quoted in Gertrude Himmelfarb, "The Ghost of Parson Malthus," *Times Literary Supplement* (London), Jan. 23, 1998.

[14] Malthus, *op. cit.*, p. 56.

[15] *Ibid*, p. 19-20.

[16] For more information on Malthus and his time, see David Price, "Of Population and False Hopes: Malthus and His Legacy," *Population and Environment*, January 1998, pp. 205-219. See also Keith Stewart Thomson, "1798: Darwin and Malthus," *American Scientist*, May-June 1998, pp. 226-229.

[17] Paul R. and Anne H. Ehrlich, *Population Resources Environment* (1972), quoted in Appleman, *op. cit.*, p. 240.

[18] Lester R. Brown, *In the Human Interest* (1974), quoted in Appleman, *op. cit.*, p. 243.

[19] See Julian Simon, *The Ultimate Resource* (1981).

[20] See "Environmental Scares: Plenty of Gloom," *The Economist*, Dec. 20, 1997, p. 20.

[21] David Pimentel and Marcia Pimentel, "The Demographic and Environmental Consequences of the Green Revolution," *The Carrying Capacity Briefing Book* (1996), p. XII-101.

[22] *Ibid.*, p. XII-97.

[23] Population Reference Bureau, *1998 World Population Data Sheet*, May 1998.

[24] See Michael Specter, "Population Implosion Worries a Graying Europe," *The New York Times*, July 10, 1998, p. A1.

[25] Norman Myers, "Environmental Refugees," *Population and Environment*, November 1997, pp. 175-176.

[26] See William K. Stevens, "One in Every 8 Plant Species Is Imperiled, a Survey Finds," *The New York Times*, April 9, 1998.

[27] See "The Sea," *The Economist*, May 23, 1998, Survey section, pp. 1-18.

[28] See Elisabeth Rosenthal, "China Officially Lifts Filter on Staggering Pollution Data," *The New York Times*, June 14, 1998.

[29] See "Fresh Focus on Global Warming Does Not Dispel Doubts About Kyoto Treaty's Future," *CQ Weekly*, June 6, 1998, pp. 1537-1538.

[30] Lester Brown and Brian Halweil, "China's Water Shortage Could Shake World Food Security," *Worldwatch*, July/August 1998, p. 10.

[31] *Ibid.*, p. 18.

[32] See Tom Gardner-Outlaw and Robert Engelman, "Sustaining Water, Easing Scarcity: A Second Update," *Population Action International*, Dec. 15, 1997.

[33] See Consultative Group on International Agricultural Research, "Nourishing the Future through Scientific Excellence," Annual Report 1997.

# Bibliography

## Selected Sources Used


### Books

**Appleman, Philip, ed., *An Essay on the Principle of Population: Thomas Robert Malthus*, W.W. Norton, 1976.**

This volume contains not only the writings of Malthus and his contemporaries but also those of 20th-century thinkers who joined the debate over Earth's ability to support a rapidly growing population in the 1970s.

**Brown, Lester R., Michael Renner and Christopher Flavin, *Vital Signs 1998: The Environmental Trends That Are Shaping Our Future*, W.W. Norton, 1998.**

Among the trends featured are population growth and grain yields, two essential ingredients in the Malthusian prediction of famine. Though population growth has slowed, it continues, and further increases in grain yields may be hampered by dwindling water supplies.

**Easterbrook, Gregg, *A Moment on the Earth: The Coming Age of Environmental Optimism*, Penguin Books, 1995.**

The author claims that prevailing concerns over a number of environmental issues are overstated. The recent slowing of population growth, he writes, marks the beginning of an era when man's impact on the environment will be insignificant: "Human overpopulation, which environmental orthodoxy today depicts as a menace of unimaginable horror, will be seen by nature as a minor passing fad."

**Rohe, John F., *A Bicentennial Malthusian Essay: Conservation, Population and the Indifference to Limits*, Rhodes & Easton, 1997.**

The author attributes many of today's problems, from famine to road rage, to the same overpopulation that concerned Malthus 200 years ago. Compounding the problem, he writes, is the quest for economic growth regardless of its impact on natural resources.

### Articles

**Ashford, Lori S., "New Perspectives on Population: Lessons from Cairo," *Population Bulletin*, March 1995.**

The International Conference on Population and Development, held in September 1994 in Cairo, Egypt, produced a list of goals for family-planning programs. This article presents an overview of these programs around the world and identifies policies that have had the most success in reducing population growth.

**Brown, Lester R., and Brian Halweil, "China's Water Shortage Could Shake World Food Security," *Worldwatch*, July/August 1998, pp. 10-18.**

Rapid industrialization and population growth are depleting China's water supplies so fast that the country's farmers may soon be unable to meet domestic food needs. If China is forced to buy its grain, global grain prices will rise, perhaps beyond the means of poorer developing countries that depend on imports to meet their food needs.

**Hertsgaard, Mark, "Our Real China Problem," *The Atlantic*, November 1997, pp. 97-114.**

During a trip through rural China, the author found that the country's infamous one-child policy has been largely abandoned and that continuing population growth is compounding China's serious environmental pollution.

**Mann, Charles C., "Reseeding the Green Revolution," *Science*, Aug. 22, 1997, pp. 1038-1043.**

The Green Revolution prevented widespread famine in recent decades, but many scientists worry that the potential for increasing crop yields is reaching its limit. Bioengineering and other breakthroughs may provide the tools to achieve another major leap in agricultural productivity.

**Price, David, "Of Population and False Hopes: Malthus and His Legacy," *Population and Environment*, January 1998, pp. 205-219.**

The author, an anthropologist at Cornell University, presents an excellent overview of the life and times of Thomas Robert Malthus on the bicentennial of his essay on population and the relevance of his ideas to modern concerns about Earth's carrying capacity.

**Smail, J. Kenneth, "Beyond Population Stablization: The Case for Dramatically Reducing Global Human Numbers," *Politics and the Life Sciences*, September 1997.**

A Kenyon College anthropology professor opens a roundtable presentation by 17 population experts who support greater efforts to curb population growth.

### Reports and Studies

**Gardner-Outlaw, Tom, and Robert Engelman, Sustaining Water, Easing Scarcity: A Second Update, Population Action International, 1997.**

Water supplies are threatened in many parts of the world by rising population. By 2050, the authors report, at least one person in four is likely to live in countries that suffer chronic or recurring water shortages.

**Population Reference Bureau, *World Population Data Sheet: Demographic Data and Estimates for the Countries and Regions of the World*, 1998.**

This pamphlet presents a country-by-country assessment of population, fertility rates, life expectancy and other statistics that help demographers forecast future population growth trends.

# 8 Environmental Justice

MARY H. COOPER

An impoverished area of southern Louisiana has become the latest battleground in the struggle for civil rights. Only this time the goal is not desegregation or affirmative action but the right to a clean environment.

The controversy in rural St. James Parish focuses on 3,000 acres of sugar cane and a $700 million plastics plant planned by a Japanese manufacturer. The fight pits Shintech Inc. and a cadre of local supporters against environmental activists and other residents who want no part of it.

"This is our *Brown v. Board of Education*, our line in the dirt," says Robert D. Bullard, executive director of the Environmental Justice Resource Center at Clark Atlanta University. "This community is already overburdened with toxic plants."

Indeed, the parish lies along a stretch of the Mississippi River between Baton Rouge and New Orleans that is so heavily industrialized it's known as "cancer alley." More than 120 chemical plants line the 120-mile river corridor, many of which have spewed thousands of tons of dioxin and other carcinogens into the air, water and soil for decades. The parish itself is already home to 11 fertilizer and chemical plants.

Bullard and other activists argue that it is no accident that so many toxic polluters have zeroed in on the region. Throughout the country, they say, poor and minority communities are disproportionately exposed to noxious industry byproducts. Siting the Shintech plant in St. James Parish, they contend, would amount to yet another instance of environmental racism, another example of a poor community not benefiting from the nationwide improvements in environmental quality over the past three decades.

Since Bullard helped lead the call for environmental justice in the early 1980s, the movement has won high-level support. In 1994, President Clinton issued an executive order directing all federal agencies with a public health or environmental mission to make environmental justice an integral part of their policies and activities. "All communities and persons across this nation should live in a safe and healthful environment," the president's order declared. [1]

Since then, 19 federal departments, agencies and executive branch offices, from the Environmental Protection Agency (EPA) to the Federal Highway Administration, have been required to ensure that their policies do not have a disparate impact on poor and minority communities.

In February, EPA Administrator Carol M. Browner lent an even stronger endorsement to the environmental justice argument by issuing "interim guidance," or guidelines, for processing a rash of claims of environmental injustice, based on the 1964 Civil Rights Act. Title VI of the act, the country's basic civil rights law, prohibits discrimination based on race, color or national origin in programs or activities that are supported by federal funds.

Among the agencies covered by the law are state environmental commissions, which issue permits to factories and other potential polluters. According to regulations issued under Title VI, an agency violates the law if its policies or activities have a discriminatory effect, even if there was no intent to discriminate. An agency found guilty of such civil rights violations would face the loss of federal funds and be required to implement costly mitigation programs.

When Shintech proposed building the plant in St. James Parish, residents opposed to the move, together with Bullard, the Tulane University Environmental Law Clinic, Greenpeace and other environmental justice advocates lodged a formal complaint against the project. Although the state Department of Environmental Quality had already cleared Shintech to begin construction, last September Browner ordered the agency to rescind one of the project's permits and launched an investigation into charges that the choice of the site amounted to environmental racism.

Shintech joins a growing list of companies whose expansion plans have run afoul of the environmental justice movement in recent years. Since the first lawsuit of this type was filed in 1979 against a waste-dump operator in Houston, activists have turned increasingly to the courts on behalf of poor and minority communities seeking protection from pollution. [2]

Although environmental justice advocates have successfully lobbied companies to change their siting plans in a number of U.S. communities, they finally won their first legal victory in April. A Nuclear Regulatory Commis-

From *The CQ Researcher*, June 19, 1998.

sion (NRC) hearing board rejected plans to build a uranium-enrichment plant in a poor, minority community in northwestern Louisiana (*see p. 146*).

Residents of Sierra Blanca, Texas, are fighting a plan, recently approved by Congress, that would allow Vermont, Maine and Texas to dump their low-level nuclear waste at a facility to be built near their largely Hispanic community. And the EPA has agreed to study a claim of environmental racism brought by the Coeur d'Alene Indians in Idaho, who have asked the agency to designate a 1,500-square-mile area polluted by decades-old mine tailings as a vast Superfund site.

Another case has made it to the U.S. Supreme Court. Residents of Chester, Pa., a majority-black town in overwhelmingly white Delaware County, went to court to block construction of a waste facility in their community. Because there are already five such facilities in the town, and only two in the rest of the county, residents charged the decision to build yet another dump in their midst amounted to environmental racism. The court announced June 8 that it would decide whether activists can bring suits in federal court alleging environmental racism. The state claims such charges can only be filed with the EPA.

But Shintech has become what the company's controller, Richard Mason, calls the "poster child" of the environmental justice movement. He rejects the claims of environmental racism made against his company. "We did not choose that site because there were African-Americans there," he says. "We chose it because there was nobody there."

Not only is the planned location a mile and a half from the nearest residential areas, Mason says, but the company's other U.S. plant, in Freeport, Texas, has a good environmental record. "In the 24 years we have produced polyvinyl chloride (PVC) resin at the Texas plant, we have had three or four incidents, in which no one was injured and no remediation was required."

Environmental Justice Resource Center

*Residents of Chester, Pa., went to court to block construction of a waste facility in their community. The Supreme Court agreed on June 8 to decide whether the activists can bring suit in federal court alleging environmental racism.*

Shintech has promised to provide jobs and training, including opportunities for management positions, to local residents. "We've worked very hard to get to know the people there and understand their concerns," he says. "And a lot of those concerns are economic in nature."

Indeed, not all local residents are opposed to Shintech's plan. The St. James and Louisiana chapters of the National Association for the Advancement of Colored People (NAACP) are vocal supporters of the new plant, which they hope will bring jobs and economic development to a region that suffers 12 percent unemployment and where 44 percent of residents live in poverty. [3] "Poverty has been the No. 1 crippler of poor people, not chemical plants," Ernest L. Johnson, president of the Louisiana State Conference NAACP, said in a statement. "Also, the present mortality rate for African-Americans in St. James is less than the Louisiana state rate, despite the 11 previously existing petrochemical plants in the area." Johnson says an NAACP survey shows broad local support for the new plant. "Unequivocally, the residents of the 'affected community' want Shintech!"

But environmental justice advocates say jobs and other investments are inadequate tradeoffs for the health risks, noxious odors and sheer ugliness that many industrial and waste facilities impose on poor communities. "Citizens want control of their environment rather than money," says Robert Knox, acting director of EPA's Office of Environmental Justice. "The time is past when companies could come in and pay for new school buses or other amenities in exchange for locating in poor, minority communities. Everyone understands about environmental pollution now, and they are not going to accept that any more."

The Shintech case and the shift in policy that gave rise to it have created a growing backlash against the environmental justice movement. In March the Environmental Council of the States (ECOS), made up of the top appointed environmental regulators from the states, denounced the EPA's interim guidelines, claiming they were vague, detrimental to economic development and poorly devised because the state commissioners, who are EPA's partners in administering federal environmental laws, had no say in the guidelines. Furthermore, the state commissioners say the policy undermines the democratic process.

"Most decisions to locate industrial facilities are not made by bureaucrats but by locally elected officials," says ECOS member Russell J. Harding, director of the Michigan Department of Environmental Quality. "That is absolutely the way these decisions should be made in an elected democracy. The EPA guidance turns the process upside down by calling for us — the regulators who are unaccountable to local voters — to make those decisions. This is not right."

Environmental Justice Resource Center

*Children play in a park across from a Shell Oil refinery in Norco, La.*

As this latest chapter in the struggle for civil rights unfolds, these are some of the questions being asked:

### *Do poor and minority populations suffer disproportionately from exposure to toxic materials?*

"Poor and minority communities are where you find children with lead poisoning living near polluting industries, garbage dumps, incinerators, petrochemical plants, freeways and highways — all the stuff that other communities reject," says Bullard of the Environmental Justice Resource Center. "And the fact that the problem has existed for so many years seems to be still a matter of denial for a lot of people."

Statistics seem to confirm Bullard's view. A widely cited study of U.S. Census data by the NAACP and the United Church of Christ Commission for Racial Justice found that people of color were 47 percent more likely than whites to live near a commercial hazardous-waste facility. The study also found that the percentage of minorities was three times higher in areas with high concentrations of such facilities than in areas without them. Moreover, the study suggested that minorities' exposure to environmental toxins was getting worse. [4]

The EPA found similar disparities in exposure to toxins depending on income and race. Ninety percent of the nation's 2 million farmworkers, the agency estimates, are people of color, including Chicanos, Puerto Ricans, Caribbean blacks and African-Americans. Of these, more than 300,000 are thought to suffer from pesticide-related illnesses each year. Even air pollution affects minorities disproportionately, according to EPA. The 437 counties and independent cities that failed to meet air-quality standards in 1990, for example, are home to 80 percent of the nation's Hispanics and 65 percent of African-Americans but just 57 percent of all whites. [5]

Some critics of the environmental justice movement say the stunning improvements in environmental quality brought by 30 years of anti-pollution legislation benefit everyone in the United States. They also claim that the remaining environmental threats do not necessarily impact poor or non-white Americans more than anyone else.

"Since toxic air emissions, pesticide runoffs and groundwater contamination cannot neatly select their victims by race or income, the inequities visited upon minorities afflict a great many others as well," writes Christopher H. Foreman Jr., a senior fellow at the Brookings Institution. "Indeed, the range of arguably significant environmental-equity comparisons is so broad that some doubtless cut the other way: Many Native Americans, for example, breathe cleaner air than urban Yuppies and live further from hazardous waste than New Jersey's white ethnics." [6]

Activists reject this reasoning out of hand. "Sure, everyone is exposed to some level of toxins," says the EPA's Knox, "but exposure is disproportionate in poor and minority communities. He points to a black neighborhood in Gainesville, Ga., that accounts for just 20 percent of the town's population but handles 80 percent of its waste. The predomi-

## An Indian Leader Speaks Out for the Land . . .

Most instances of environmental racism that come to public attention involve black or Hispanic communities trying to keep polluting factories, sewage plants or toxic-waste dumps out of their communities. But an older and much less visible struggle is being fought by remote Indian tribes that are trying to clean up water supplies contaminated by mine tailings. Since the mid-19th century, miners and mining company executives have scoured the West for gold, silver and other minerals. They have left behind vast deposits of waste rock, or tailings, containing toxic materials. Cyanide and other chemicals used to separate some ores from rock also are left behind, usually in holding ponds. Over the years, rainwater carries these pollutants into streams and rivers, where they can be carried for miles, killing fish and contaminating drinking water.

Native Americans' pleas for environmental protection were ignored for decades, but now Indians are gaining a voice in the environmental justice movement. In what could turn out to be the most sweeping federal cleanup of pollution from mining activities ever undertaken, the Environmental Protection Agency (EPA) in February agreed to study the feasibility of designating the entire Coeur d'Alene River basin in Idaho as a Superfund site. The decision came largely as a result of the efforts of Henry SiJohn, environmental leader of the 1,600-member Coeur d'Alene tribe, whose reservation lies along the southern banks of Lake Coeur d'Alene. Staff writer Mary Cooper interviewed SiJohn by phone from his home in Plummer, Idaho.

***How long has pollution in the Coeur d'Alene River basin been a problem?***

In the 1920s and '30s, we noticed that the water potatoes, which grow along the lake, began to have a strange, metallic taste. We used to drink water from the lake, but we haven't since then.

***How did government authorities react to your complaints about the water pollution?***

The situation was different then because we were Indians, and everything was done by the superintendents of the Bureau of Indian Affairs. They had charge of us on our reservation. They said we didn't have any voice, that we couldn't buck the state or the federal government. They wouldn't do anything for us.

***Do you think minority communities like yours are exposed to more pollution than white Americans?***

I'm afraid that's true. It seems we have embedded an undercurrent of racism here in America. The Indian people have been for the longest time put into a situation whereby they were considered people who were unfamiliar with things. They couldn't participate in politics until 1924, when Congress allowed American Indians to have the vote. But even that didn't help for a long time because we

nantly black town of Chester, Pa., accounts for 11 percent of Delaware County's population but has 70 percent of the county's waste facilities. "That's clearly disproportionate," Knox says. "And it's not atypical for the country as a whole."

Some business representatives reject the notion that factory owners even look for communities of any kind to site their facilities. They say that when petrochemical companies flocked to southern Louisiana early in the century, for example, they were drawn primarily by the fact that such a long segment of the Mississippi River was deep enough to enable oceangoing barges to transport large shipments of raw materials and finished products.

"No one lived near the Baton Rouge Exxon refinery, the oldest in Louisiana, when it was built in the early 1900s," says Dan S. Borné, president of the Louisiana Chemical Association in Baton Rouge. "It and other chemical plants were built in agricultural areas, and communities literally grew toward them because that's where the jobs were. What's inferred in this debate — that people of color are targeted for chemical plants simply because they're people of color — is repugnant and ridiculous."

### *Does President Clinton's 1994 executive order provide sufficient guarantees of environmental justice?*

When President Clinton issued his 1994 environmental justice executive order, more than 10 years had passed since the first complaints of environmental racism gained public attention. In November 1992, in response to growing pressure to address the concerns of communities exposed to toxins, President George Bush created the Office of Environmental Equity within EPA to study the problem.

But it was not until Clinton's 1994 policy statement that the goal of environmental justice gained formal recognition at the federal level. "[E]ach federal agency shall make achieving environmental justice part of its mission by identifying and addressing, as appropriate, disproportionately high and adverse human health or environmental effects of its programs, policies and activities on minority populations and low-income populations," Clinton declared.

## . . . An Interview with Idaho's Henry SiJohn

had to establish our tribal government as an entity in itself and prove to people we knew what we were doing. Then we had to do assessment screenings to determine the pollution in the river basin.

***Is the government responding adequately to your requests now?***

I wish the EPA would protect the environment, especially of Indian people, through the enforcement arm of their agency. I feel they have been neglectful of punishing people that are the perpetrators of this pollution. If the Indians were the polluters, the public would have gotten up in arms and demanded that the Indians pay. However, this isn't the case. And the federal government has not protected the Indian people or the environment to the point where they enforce the law.

***Has President Clinton's support of environmental justice affected your dealings with EPA?***

By good fortune, I feel optimistic, in that someone is getting to the president of the United States with this issue. I have a lot of faith in Vice President Al Gore and his staff. I feel they truly have the interests of the environment at heart. But they can't move without the Congress of the United States. Congress is for corporate America, and corporate America is the segment of society that has dug this hole for us, and I don't know if we can escape.

***Has the environmental justice movement helped your cause?***

Environmental justice advocates are trying to help, but they don't have any idea how to go about it. I feel they and the Clinton administration could do more if they would only take a stand and tell the perpetrators they're the guilty ones.

Industry is polluting the rivers of America. People need to understand the Indian philosophy of the cycle of life. Fish have to spawn, and the spawning beds have to be protected, so they can complete the cycle of life. Because people don't understand this, they jeopardize the species to the point where they're endangered, and then we have this big to-do with the Endangered Species Act. So we have a political response rather than a natural response. Things would be different if people let animals complete the cycle of life.

***Do you think EPA will accept your request to clean up the Coeur d'Alene River basin?***

I'm very optimistic. If America doesn't wake up and take hold of things, it's going to put us all in jeopardy. People need to realize they can't survive without the environment. That's where the Indian philosophical view comes in. It perpetuates the purity of the environment. Without the natural resources of fish, animals, birds and the like we can't live. We will starve.

The agencies were not only required to correct existing problems but also had to take steps to prevent environmental injustice from occurring in the first place. Clinton gave each federal agency a year to develop and submit its strategy for achieving environmental justice and another year to report on progress in implementing the strategy.

Even though the new policy directive does not change laws currently in force, environmental justice advocates say it strengthens both the 1964 Civil Rights Act and the 1969 National Environmental Policy Act, which calls for environmental information to be made available to citizens. "We have two important pieces of legislation on the books which, if used in tandem, can be very potent weapons against environmental racism," says Bullard, pointing to several instances in which plans to build polluting facilities in communities of color were rejected after Clinton issued his executive order.

"These decisions make a lot of states nervous because they haven't really enforced equal protection when it comes to permitting," he says. "They could even lose transportation dollars because environmental justice is not just incinerators and landfills. It's also construction of highways, which have definite impacts on low-income communities and communities of color."

According to Knox of the EPA, the president's executive order has already changed the way states are dealing with the issue. At least three states — Louisiana, Maryland and Oregon — have passed executive orders on environmental justice that mirror the president's policy in order to pre-empt possible complaints of environmental racism and the loss of federal funds for highway building and other state operations. "They did this as a result of the executive order," Knox says. "They want to look at problem areas in the states so they can get ahead of the problem and make recommendations to their governors."

But some civil rights activists fear the policy may tip the scales in favor of those who want to keep industry out of poor areas at all costs, even when vital job opportunities are at stake. "In light of the executive order, environmental justice requires balancing economic benefit with environmental risks," writes Johnson of the Louisiana NAACP. "It is critical that we not succumb to outside pressure by those who have otherwise failed to promote their ideologies and now use the 'environmental race card' for their own agendas."

### *Does the focus on environmental justice distract attention from bigger health problems in poor and minority communities?*

Some observers suggest that by single-mindedly opposing industrial development in poor communities, environmental justice activists may be hurting the very people they purport to represent. "It's very common to meet people in St. James, both black and white, who say their great-great-grandfather lived here," says Mason of Shintech. "They also say they want to continue living here with their families but that there are no job opportunities that will allow them to stay. Because the base of employment there now is the parish government and the existing chemical plants, the only way to find a job is if someone quits, retires or dies."

Environmental Justice Resource Center

*Riverbank State Park was built on top of the North River Sewage Treatment Plant in West Harlem, N.Y.*

Not only are poverty and joblessness more serious problems for most minority communities than pollution, critics say, but so are a whole range of health and social ills. "Hypertension, obesity, low birthweights, inadequate prenatal care, substance abuse and violence are only some of the forces that arguably deserve pride of place in the struggle to improve the lives and health of communities of color," writes Foreman of Brookings. "That such forces are more intractable and harder to mobilize around than a Superfund site or a proposed landfill must not deter communities from asking . . . hard questions about overall health priorities." [7]

Activists say it's false logic to draw distinctions between their quest for environmental equity and these other goals of poor, minority communities. "Environmental justice is also about health," Bullard says. "The No. 1 reason why children in these communities are hospitalized is not because of drive-by shootings. It's because of asthma." The incidence of respiratory diseases has increased, especially among children and the elderly, in areas of high concentrations of ozone and particulate matter, notably urban neighborhoods close to major roadways. [8]

Bullard also points to lead poisoning as an environmental threat to health in minority communities. "The No. 1 threat to kids is lead poisoning, and this, too, is an environmental justice issue because African-American children are three to five times more likely to be poisoned by lead than are low-income white children," he says. "That's the direct result of residential segregation, so housing is another environmental justice issue."

Even crime and illiteracy can be traced to environmental racism, in Bullard's view. "There is a direct correlation between lead poisoning and learning disabilities, aggressive behavior and kids dropping out of school," he says. "So if you look at the root of many of the problems facing minority communities, both physical and environmental, you'll see they are all about health. It's no longer just a matter of a chemical plant."

Knox of the EPA agrees that environmental pollution has far-reaching effects on the quality of life in poor and minority neighborhoods. "Some people say the fight against crime should take precedence over other issues in these neighborhoods," he says. "But environmental problems only exacerbate such problems as crime and asthma in minority communities. Just because a community is poor doesn't mean the people there should not breathe clean air, drink clean water and be able to eat fruit from their gardens. You would not expect to find the same environmental quality in South Central Los Angeles that you find in Beverly Hills, but that doesn't mean that the people in South Central L.A. should not have clean air, clean water and clean soil." ■

# BACKGROUND

## Plight of the Poor

The poor have always suffered the health effects of inferior living conditions. Even before the Industrial Revolution unleashed the toxic byproducts of the manufacturing process in Europe and North America, serfs, slaves and farm laborers often lived amid farm animals in crowded, drafty hovels under unsanitary conditions that took a disproportionately heavy toll in the form of infant mortality and premature death among adults.

Industrialization added numerous new environmental threats to health and well-being that were borne overwhelmingly by the poor. As factories sprang up along the railroads and rivers in the center of towns and cities, wealthy families moved out of range of the smoke and foul odors they emitted. Lacking transportation or the money to move away from the industrial centers, poor factory workers had little choice but to live close to their places of work. Where factories sprang up in rural areas along rivers and other transportation corridors, new communities of workers and job-seekers grew up around them.

In the United States, race compounded poverty as a factor in determining exposure to industrial toxins. Beginning in the 1950s, when many black farmworkers moved to cities in the East and Midwest in search of better-paying jobs, they were drawn to downtown neighborhoods where housing was affordable and close to work. Hispanic immigrants also gravitated to low-cost, inner-city neighborhoods where manufacturing jobs could be found, or to farming communities in remote agricultural areas of the West — frequent sites of toxic-waste dumps and pesticide contamination.

Native Americans were exposed to inordinate levels of toxic waste by virtue of another historical phenomenon — the relegation of Indians to remote reservations, many of which were later found to harbor vast deposits of uranium, gold, silver and other minerals. Mine tailings exposed many tribes to toxic runoff that contaminated their water supplies.

## Birth of a Movement

The environmental plight of poor and minority communities was not an immediate priority of the modern environmental movement, which took shape in the late 1960s. [9] The first Earth Day, held April 22, 1970, marked the start of a national campaign whose main legislative victories were the 1970 Clean Air Act, the 1972 Clean Water Act, the 1973 Endangered Species Act and the 1980 Superfund legislation (the Comprehensive Environmental Response, Compensation and Liability Act).

These basic environmental laws focused on reducing the sources of pollution but basically ignored the varying impact of pollution on different income or racial groups. The first official acknowledgement that poor, non-white Americans were disproportionately impacted by environmental degradation was a statement in the Council on Environmental Quality's 1971 annual report that racial discrimination adversely affects the urban poor and the quality of their environment. [10]

That discrete communities could be disparately affected by environmental degradation became clear in 1978, when 900 families living in the Love Canal neighborhood of Niagara Falls, N.Y., discovered that their homes had been built near 20,000 tons of toxic waste. Initially rebuffed in their calls for reparations, residents demanded, and eventually won, relocation benefits. Their struggle also helped galvanize public support for federal legislation to clean up hazardous waste — the 1980 Superfund law.

Race and income were not the main issues at Love Canal. Working-class and mostly white, the neighborhood nonetheless served as a model for communities trying to ward off environmental threats. The first largely minority community to take up the challenge was in Warren County, N.C., where residents in 1982 demonstrated against a state plan to dump 6,000 truckloads of soil laden with polychlorinated biphenyls (PCBs), a highly toxic compound similar to dioxin. More than 500 protesters were arrested, calling national attention to the issue. Although the landfill was completed as planned, the protesters won agreement from the state that no more landfills would be put in their county, the state's poorest. [11]

A series of reports on environmental threats to poor and minority communities followed the Warren County protest, helping galvanize the nascent movement for environmental justice. The General Accounting Office found in a 1983 study that three of four hazardous-waste facilities in the Southeast were in African-American communities. In 1987, the United Church of Christ issued a widely cited study showing that landfills, incinerators and other waste facilities were found disproportionately in or near poor or minority communities across the country. [12]

In 1990, Bullard published the first of his four books on the subject. Like most other early works on environmental justice, *Dumping In Dixie* focused on toxic wastes and their close association with black communities in the Southeast. Bullard also called attention to the fact that black Americans are far more likely to be exposed to lead than whites, and that Hispanics are more likely to live in areas with high soot pollution. In his efforts to help impacted communities, Bullard was joined by Benjamin Chavis Jr., former executive director of the NAACP, other civil rights groups as well as mainstream environmental organizations such as Greenpeace and the Sierra Club, whose Earthjustice Legal Defense Fund works with poor communities.

The Bush administration recognized the environmental justice movement's growing clout in 1990, when then-EPA Administrator William K. Reilly established the Environmental Equity Workgroup to study the issue. Two years later, the movement gained permanent federal status with the creation of EPA's Office of Environmental Equity.

Environmental Justice Resource Center

*Residents claim that Fort Lauderdale's Wingate Incinerator, now contaminated and a Superfund cleanup site, spewed ash and soot for over 25 years on the mostly African-American Bass Dillard neighborhood.*

## Clinton's Policies

President Clinton took office in January 1993 promising to restore federal environmental protections that he said had eroded during the previous 12 years of Republican administrations. His newly appointed EPA administrator, Browner, declared that environmental justice would be a priority for the agency and renamed the Office of Environmental Equity the Office of Environmental Justice.

"Many people of color, low-income and Native-American communities have raised concerns that they suffer a disproportionate burden of health consequences due to the siting of industrial plants and waste dumps, and from exposure to pesticides or other toxic chemicals at home and on the job, and that environmental programs do not adequately address these disproportionate exposures," she said shortly after taking office.

"EPA is committed to addressing these concerns and is assuming a leadership role in environmental justice to enhance environmental quality for all residents of the United States. Incorporating environmental justice into everyday agency activities and decisions will be a major undertaking. Fundamental reform will be needed in agency operations." [13]

On Sept. 30, 1993, Browner established the National Environmental Justice Advisory Council (NEJAC), a 23-member group of representatives of environmental organizations, state and local agencies, communities, tribes, businesses and other interested parties to increase public awareness of the issue and help EPA develop strategies to ensure environmental equity. By rotating membership in NEJAC (pronounced "knee-jack," or "knee-jerk" by its critics) every three years, the agency is trying to involve as many interested parties as possible in the ongoing policy debate.

President Clinton elevated environmental justice to yet a higher plane with Executive Order 12898, which required each federal agency involved in public health or environmental matters to "make achieving environmental justice part of its mission," particularly as minority and low-income populations were affected. The order also directed Browner to create and chair an interagency working group on environmental justice to coordinate federal policies aimed at furthering environmental equity. ■

# CURRENT SITUATION

## Recent Cases

The cause of environmental justice has been advanced on several fronts since President Clinton's 1994

# Chronology

## 1960s *Job opportunities draw black workers to cities in the industrial East and Midwest and Hispanic farmworkers to agricultural areas of the West.*

**1964**
Congress enacts the Civil Rights Act, establishing the country's basic law to protect the rights of minority groups. Title VI of the law prohibits discrimination based on race, color or national origin under programs or activities supported by federal funds.

**1969**
The National Environmental Policy Act calls for information on pollutants to be made public.

---

## 1970s *The environmental movement produces major laws to curb pollution.*

**April 22, 1970**
The first Earth Day marks the start of a national campaign to improve environmental protection, starting with the Clean Air Act, passed the same year.

**1971**
The Council on Environmental Quality acknowledges that racial discrimination adversely affects the urban poor and the quality of their environment.

**1972**
Congress passes the Clean Water Act, requiring reductions in polluting runoff into the nation's waterways.

**1978**
Residents of the Love Canal neighborhood of Niagara Falls, N.Y., discover that their homes sit atop a toxic-waste dump. They demand, and eventually win, relocation benefits, establishing a model for later action by poor, minority communities.

**1979**
The first lawsuit claiming environmental racism is filed against a waste-dump operator on behalf of a poor community in Houston.

---

## 1980s *Environmental justice movement takes off.*

**1980**
The Comprehensive Environmental Response, Compensation and Liability Act creates the Superfund to pay for the identification and cleanup of severely polluted sites.

**October 1982**
More than 500 protesters are arrested after trying to block a landfill being created for soil laced with polychlorinated biphenyls (PCBs) in Warren County, N.C., the poorest county in the state. The landfill project goes ahead, but the state agrees to build no more landfills there.

**1983**
The General Accounting Office finds that three of four hazardous-waste facilities in the Southeast are in black communities.

**1987**
The United Church of Christ issues a study showing that landfills, incinerators and other waste facilities are sited disproportionately in or near poor or minority communities.

---

## 1990s *Environmental justice gains federal support.*

**November 1992**
President George Bush creates the Office of Environmental Equity within the Environmental Protection Agency (EPA).

**1993**
Newly appointed EPA Administrator Carol M. Browner renames the Office of Environmental Equity the Office of Environmental Justice and promises to promote environmental protection for all Americans.

**Feb. 11, 1994**
President Clinton issues Executive Order 12898 directing all federal agencies with a public health or environmental mission to make environmental justice an integral part of their policies.

**Sept. 10, 1997**
The EPA delays permission for Shintech Inc. to build a new plastics plant in St. James Parish, La., a highly industrialized, largely African-American area.

**Feb. 5, 1998**
Browner issues "interim guidance" to provide a framework for processing claims of environmental injustice, based on Title VI of the Civil Rights Act.

**June 8, 1998**
The U.S. Supreme Court agrees to decide whether lawsuits alleging environmental racism can be brought in federal court.

# Fighting for Environmental Justice . . .

The ongoing controversy over plans by Shintech Inc. to open a new plastics plant in St. James Parish, La., is among the most visible environmental justice cases. The following are some of the other notable battles being waged around of the country:

**Sierra Blanca, Texas** — Residents of this West Texas community, located in the 10th poorest county in the nation, fought construction of a low-level nuclear-waste facility outside the town. The facility would be the final repository for radioactive wastes from hospitals and research facilities in Texas, Maine and Vermont. Opponents complained that Sierra Blanca already is home to a large sewage sludge dump and said its selection as a dumping ground for nuclear waste amounted to environmental racism against the area's predominantly Hispanic population. Residents called on Congress to reject the three-state compact authorizing the facility. *(See "At Issue," p. 151.)* They lost their battle April 1, when the Senate approved the House-passed plan after adding amendments requiring an environmental review of the proposed site and barring other states from dumping radioactive wastes there as well.

**Brunswick, Ga.** — Contamination from lead, mercury, polychlorinated biphenyls (PCBs) and other toxins around an inactive LCP Chemicals-Georgia Inc. plant led to a $40-million, EPA-directed cleanup of this industrial area several years ago. Afterwards, the agency led a detailed area study, called the Brunswick Initiative, which failed to turn up other pollution threats to neighboring communities. But an environmental justice group called Save the People rejected the study's findings. The group and many residents of a mostly black community adjacent to another chemical plant, owned by Hercules Inc., claim that their yards are contaminated by toxaphene, an insecticide that Hercules manufactured until it was banned two decades ago.

**Oak Ridge, Tenn.** — Residents of the predominantly black neighborhood of Scarboro attribute a range of diseases in their community to the nearby Department of Energy (DOE) Y-12 nuclear weapons plant. The federal Centers for Disease Control and Prevention is investigating a possible link between the plant and respiratory illnesses in Scarboro. The DOE has offered to pay for health assessments but has not yet taken responsibility for any illnesses reported, some of which are the subject of pending litigation.

**Houston, Texas** — Three decades ago, the Kennedy Heights neighborhood was built over abandoned oil pits once owned by Gulf Oil. Today residents of this African-American community claim that leakage of oil sludge into their water supply is responsible for at least 60 cases of serious diseases found there, such as cancer and lupus, as well as hundreds of other lesser health complaints. In a lawsuit brought against Chevron, which bought out Gulf Oil, plaintiffs claim a corporate document slating the contaminated site for "Negro residential and commercial development" proves that environmental racism is at the root of their medical problems. Chevron denies that the incidence of disease in Kennedy Heights is high enough to prove a link with oil contamination. [1]

**Huntington Park, Calif.** — After four years of community opposition, the operator of a concrete recycling plant was forced to close it. Similarly, black and Hispanic residents of South East Los Angeles are organizing to get rid of the growing number of recycling facilities in their part of the city. Glass-recycling ventures spew ground glass into the air, residents say, aggravating asthma and other respiratory diseases and killing trees. Metal crushers at car- and appliance-recycling plants cause walls of neighboring houses to crack and release tiny fragments of oil and metal that contaminate the soil. [2]

**Pensacola, Fla.** — The Escambia Treating Co. ran a wood-treating facility here for 40 years, depositing highly toxic dioxin into the soil and prompting a $4 million Superfund cleanup of the site. Residents of the primarily low-income, black neighborhood adjacent to the site objected to the cleanup, saying it exposed them to an even greater health threat by bringing toxins to the surface. A local activist group, Citizens Against Toxic Exposure,

executive order. Activists cite three cases that they say set legal precedents that in the future will help reduce the incidence of environmental racism.

In northwest Louisiana in May 1997, a citizens' group blocked plans by a German-owned firm, Louisiana Energy Services, to build the first private uranium-enrichment plant in the United States. After nearly seven years of opposition, Citizens Against Nuclear Trash persuaded the Nuclear Regulatory Commission (NRC) to deny the company the required license based on evidence that race had played a part in site selection.

"The communities around that site are 97 percent black," says Bullard, who drafted a social and economic analysis of the area for the NRC. "The company didn't consider the fact that these people live off the land as subsistence hunters, fishermen and

# . . . From New Jersey to California

convinced the Environmental Protection Agency (EPA) to test the soil and, as the results proved compelling, pay for the relocation of all 358 households around the site, which is expected to cost $18 million.[3]

**Newark, N.J.** — A section of the city's East End, known as Ironbound, lies in one of the most polluted areas of the country. It is home to a garbage incinerator that serves all of Essex County and a sewage-treatment plant serving 33 municipalities and 1.5 million people. The area also contains the now-closed Diamond Alkali plant, which once produced Agent Orange, the defoliant used in the Vietnam War. The area is thought to have among the highest concentrations of dioxin in the world. When Wheelabrator Technologies tried to build a $63 million sewage sludge treatment facility there, Ironbound's residents claimed that the placement of yet another waste plant in their community, home to many poor Portuguese immigrants, blacks and Hispanics, would constitute environmental racism. The Ironbound Committee Against Toxic Waste persuaded the state Department of Environmental Protection to deny the plant's final permits.[4]

Environmental Justice Resource Center

*Responding to public health concerns in a black neighborhood in Anniston, Ala., Monsanto has begun buying out residents and relocating them.*

**Anniston, Ala.** — In the low-lying industrial and residential neighborhood of Sweet Water, production of toxic PCBs had been going on since the 1930s. In 1996, the Alabama Department of Public Health declared Sweet Water and the adjacent community of Cobb Town a public health hazard. Monsanto stopped producing PCBs at the facility in 1971, eight years before EPA banned the chemical, a known carcinogen in laboratory animals. The company also began buying out residents and relocating them, even before agreeing with the state to do so and clean up the polluted areas. But the Sweet Valley-Cobb Town Environmental Justice Task Force charges Monsanto with environmental racism against the black communities by knowingly releasing PCBs from the plant after the environmental threat became apparent in the late 1960s. About 1,000 residents have sued the company.

**Coeur d'Alene, Idaho** — Silver mining came to the pristine area around Lake Coeur d'Alene in the 1880s. By the 1920s, members of the Coeur d'Alene Indian tribe began noticing that the water and root vegetables had taken on a metallic taste. Ignored by the mining companies and governmental officials for decades, the 1,600-member tribe finally convinced the EPA in February to consider declaring the entire Coeur d'Alene River basin a Superfund site. If the agency adds the site to its list — which is strongly opposed by local businesses in this recreational area — it will become the largest federal cleanup ever undertaken, covering an area of 1,500 square miles including the Idaho Panhandle and part of western Washington, where mine tailings have also polluted the Spokane River.[5] *(See story, p. 140.)*

[1] See Sam Howe Verhovek, "Racial Tensions in Suit Slowing Drive for 'Environmental Justice,'" *The New York Times,* Sept. 7, 1997.

[2] See David Bacon, "Recycling — Not So Green to Its Neighbors," posted on EcoJustice's Web page, www.igc.org, July 28, 1997.

[3] See Joel S. Hirschhorn, "Two Superfund Environmental Justice Case Studies," posted on Ecojustice's Web page, *op. cit.*

[4] See Ronald Smothers, "Ironbound Draws Its Line at the Dump," *The New York Times,* March 29, 1997.

[5] See Michael Satchell, "Taking Back the Land That Once Was So Pure," *U.S. News & World Report,* May 4, 1998, pp. 61-63.

farmers whose water comes from wells. That plant would have been slam-dunk, in-your-face racism."

The company appealed the ruling, but a three-judge NRC panel rejected the appeal. Not only was there evidence that racial discrimination had played a role in the siting process, the judges ruled, but also that the NRC staff had failed to consider the plant's environmental and social impact on the surrounding community, as required by the executive order as well as by the 1969 National Environmental Policy Act.

"This was the first environmental justice case that we actually won in court outright," Bullard says. It was also the first time a federal agency had used President Clinton's executive order to deny a license or permit.

In Flint, Mich., last year, environmental justice activists succeeded in delaying the issuance of a permit for a power plant sited in a mostly black neighborhood. The case began after the Michigan Department of Environmental Quality issued a permit to Genesee County to build a cogeneration electric power plant fueled in part by wood scraps from building construction and demolition, which might have been contaminated with lead-based paint. The permit allowed lead emissions from the plant of 2.4 tons a year. The Flint chapter of the NAACP and other plaintiffs sued the department, charging that the surrounding community was already overburdened by lead contamination and that by issuing the permit the state had violated its mandate to protect the health of all citizens.

In response, the department reduced the allowable level of lead emissions, but the plaintiffs proceeded with the suit, charging the department with practicing racial discrimination in issuing the permit in the first place. According to Director Harding, the department agreed to comply with additional demands but refused to settle the case because the plaintiffs would not drop their charges of racial discrimination.

Both sides claimed a victory of sorts from the judgment, handed down on May 29, 1997, by Circuit Judge Archie Hayman. Plaintiffs won an injunction against future permits, pending the state's performance of risk assessments to be paid for by applicants and the holding of broader public hearings when applications for toxic facilities are made. They also won recognition that compliance with air-quality standards under the Clean Air Act does not necessarily mean that a community is not adversely affected by air pollution.

For its part, the state claimed vindication on the racial discrimination charges. "The judge said there was no racial discrimination," Harding says. "In fact, he complimented my agency, saying our overall environmental regulatory system was sufficiently protective, though he directed the agency to do more initial determinations of environmental impact."

In Chester, Pa., residents complained that their predominantly African-American city had become the main waste dump for all of largely white Delaware County. In 1996, after the Pennsylvania Department of Environmental Protection issued a permit to Soil Remediation Services Inc. to build yet another waste facility in the city, Chester Residents Concerned for Quality Living sued the agency for racial discrimination in its permitting process.

Their suit, *Chester Residents Concerned for Quality Living v. Seif,* was the first filed against a state agency under Title VI of the 1964 Civil Rights Act, which prohibits agencies that receive federal funds from practicing racial discrimination, either deliberately or by effecting "policies or practices [that] cause a discriminatory effect."

On Nov. 6, 1996, U.S. District Judge Stewart Dalzell dismissed the suit for technical reasons. On Dec. 30, 1997, however, the 3rd Circuit Court overturned the lower court, allowing the citizens' group's suit to proceed. The ruling also set an important legal precedent by enabling a low-income and minority community to pursue a charge of environmental racism regardless of whether the discrimination was deliberate. The Supreme Court has agreed to hear the case, addressing the question of whether lawsuits alleging environmental racism can be brought in federal court.

Environmental Justice Resource Center

*The Southwest Network for Environmental and Economic Justice staged a protest in Phoenix, Ariz., in 1995.*

## Pressure on EPA

The Circuit Court's ruling in the Chester case did not, however, elaborate on the question of evidence needed to mount a successful environmental justice suit against a state agency. [14] With the proliferation of charges of environmental racism in the 1990s, the EPA has come under increasing pressure to clarify the procedures for dealing with such cases. According to Knox of EPA's Office of Environmental Justice, the agency has received 49 complaints based on Title VI alone, about 20 of which are now under investigation. "EPA had to respond to a backlog of complaints," he says. "The agency had to do something to respond to this, so we issued guidelines to help identify who could bring claims and what constitutes a disparate impact on a community."

The backlogged complaints include the one in Louisiana brought against Shintech, which proposed in September 1997 to build a state-of-the-art plant to produce PVC, used to make a range of consumer products, such as plumbing pipes and shrink-wrap food wrapping. On May 23, 1997, the Louisiana Department of Environmental Quality issued three air permits for the facility. But on Sept. 10, in response to a citizens' petition, EPA Administrator Browner took the agency's first formal action on the environmental justice issue.

She canceled one of the firm's permits and directed the state agency to take environmental justice into greater consideration when reissuing the permit. In addition, she ordered further investigation of charges that the choice of St. James Parish for the plant site amounted to environmental racism. "It is essential the minority and low-income communities not be disproportionately subjected to environmental hazards," Browner wrote in her decision. [15]

The Shintech case is also the test case for the EPA's interim guidance, or guidelines. Browner issued the guidance on Feb. 5, 1998, in the wake of the Chester ruling, seeking to clarify the conditions under which a decision to issue a permit violates Title VI. The guidance describes a five-step process by which EPA must identify the affected population, primarily on the basis of proximity to the site in question, determine the race or ethnicity of the affected population and decide whether the permitted activity will impose an "undue burden" on the community. The agency will then identify any other permitted facilities in the vicinity that may compound the community's environmental threat.

S.C. Delaney/Environmental Protection Agency

*Residents of Wagner's Point, a working-class enclave in South Baltimore, link the abnormally high cancer rates in their neighborhood to emissions from a nearby wastewater treatment plant, an oil refinery and other industrial sites.*

If EPA determines that the community is impacted at a "disparate rate," the permit recipient may mitigate the environmental impact by offering other benefits to the community. Shintech, for example, has promised to spend about $500,000 for job training and small-business development in St. James Parish.

State environmental officials quickly identified what they saw as numerous flaws in the EPA's guidance, however, and asked the agency to rescind the guidance and draft a new policy together with the states. Fourteen state attorneys general and the U.S. Chamber of Commerce endorsed the environmental officials' request. "We believe the guidance is vague," says Robert E. Roberts, executive director of ECOS. "It speaks of mitigating or justifying 'disparate impacts' but doesn't make clear what such an impact is. So for those of us who have to carry out the policy, it's very difficult to know what the policy is."

Knox defends the guidance language and suggests that the state environmental officials are mainly concerned because they were left out of the drafting process. "The states are upset because they thought they should be sitting at the table," he says. "We think the guidance should work out pretty well."

Roberts says the state officials' exclusion is more than a matter of pique. "The fact that the states weren't included is important," he says, "because the state environmental departments will be making decisions that will be the basis for any environmental justice complaints that arise. Because we weren't involved in helping to craft the approach to this issue, chances are we won't do it the way EPA wants it done. At some point, we're bound to make decisions improperly because we don't know what their perspective is."

Since ECOS voiced its objections to

the new guidance, EPA has set up a special committee responsible for implementing Title VI, which also includes several state environmental officials.

## Aid for 'Brownfields'

The EPA's latest attempt to promote environmental justice may prove to be a double-edged sword. For while the interim guidance is intended to make it easier for minority and low-income communities to protect themselves from environmental threats to their health, it may also weaken economic development in these communities by discouraging companies from building new, non-polluting facilities in their midst that could provide needed employment. EPA has led an effort to convert abandoned commercial and industrial sites into productive use.

Many of these so-called "brownfield" sites scare off investors, fearful of being held liable for potential lawsuits by users of the site. While the sites are polluted, they are not polluted enough to qualify for federally funded cleanup under the Superfund program. On Jan. 25, 1995, EPA launched a program to encourage investors to build non-polluting businesses on brownfield sites, which tend to be in urban areas in or near poor or minority communities. By the end of fiscal 1997, EPA had awarded $200,000 seed-money grants to 121 brownfield restoration projects. [16]

"A lot of brownfields are in environmental justice communities," says Knox of EPA. "These communities see brownfields as providing an opportunity to get involved in the siting process and address problems in the city, an opportunity for jobs and a chance to reverse the fiscal deterioration that has drained resources from their neighborhoods. Most of all, brownfields allow communities to get their vision involved in development because they have a seat at the table."

In Knox's view, furthering environmental justice goes hand in hand with brownfield development. "The interim guidance actually helps," he says. "By ensuring that environmental justice has to be considered in the permitting process and bringing affected communities to the table, we are educating residents so they can take over their own communities and bring in clean industries."

Environmental Justice Resource Center

*Residents of this African-American neighborhood built on top of the Agriculture Street Landfill in New Orleans are petitioning the EPA to relocate them from the area, now a Superfund site. Activists call this the "black Love Canal."*

But state environmental officials predict the new guidance will be a killer for brownfield development. "The guidance enables anyone with a typewriter to stop a permit from being issued," says Harding, Michigan's environmental commissioner. "We're not opposed to environmental justice, but the guidance goes against getting brownfields going, especially in places like Detroit." Hit by widespread plant closings in the 1970s and '80s, Detroit and other Midwestern cities have many lightly polluted sites that qualify for brownfield development.

"Under the interim guidance, anybody who files an objection in an urban area can show a disparate impact," he says. "It makes it easy to make that showing and turns permitting into a nebulous process that can drag on for years."

Business representatives agree. "We're not saying there aren't concerns that need to be dealt with," says Borné of the Louisiana Chemical Association. "We are saying that with this interim guidance EPA is forever changing the landscape of development in this country. And you can forget about brownfield development because most brownfield sites are in minority communities." ■

# OUTLOOK

## Impact on Business

Industry representatives predict that EPA's policy to promote environmental justice will harm more than just brownfield development. Mason says that charging Shintech with environmental racism sends a message

# At Issue:

## *Would constructing a low-level radioactive nuclear-waste dump near Sierra Blanca, Texas, constitute "environmental injustice"?*

yes

**BILL ADDINGTON**
***Rancher, farmer and merchant, Hudspeth County, Texas***

***FROM TESTIMONY BEFORE THE HOUSE COMMERCE SUBCOMMITTEE ON ENERGY AND POWER, MAY 13, 1997.***

I speak today on behalf of Save Sierra Blanca, our citizens group, and many people in West Texas who feel run over by the state and federal governments. These people are opposed to the forced placement of this risky radioactive-waste cemetery at Sierra Blanca near the Rio Grande River. . . .

Most of the people in Hudspeth County and Sierra Blanca are poor — the median annual income is $8,000. Seventy percent of the people are of Hispanic origin, like myself. This is the reason Texas "leaders" have focused on our county for the dump site since 1983. This appeared to be the political path of least resistance. But there is strong resistance locally, regionally and internationally. There are about 3,000 people and 1,300 registered voters in the county, and every one of them who was asked signed the petition against the dump. . . .

The siting of the Sierra Blanca dump by the state legislature was a violation of environmental justice and our civil rights. . . .

If the radioactive-waste dump is approved in Sierra Blanca, it is likely that additional radioactive and hazardous facilities will follow. Westinghouse Scientific Ecology Group has entered into an option agreement to lease 1,280 acres of land adjoining the proposed Sierra Blanca site for radioactive waste processing and storage, possibly including incineration. There is also a proposal for an additional sludge dump in the community. This concentrating of hazardous facilities in communities is a characteristic of environmental injustice.

The proposed radioactive dump site is geologically fatally flawed. It is in an earthquake zone, and there is a buried fault underneath the proposed trenches. . . .

The real reason for the compact is economic — to make it cheaper for nuclear power generators to bury their waste and shift their liability. It does not "protect Texas," as has been touted. . . .

Texas began negotiations with . . . Maine in 1988, and in 1992 passed the compact. Maine's and Vermont's legislatures have approved the compact. They failed to develop their own waste sites because of heavy opposition. Maine voters approved the compact by referendum, yet people in my home are not even heard or considered. We do not get to vote on the measure or placement of the dump like Mainers, who chose to dump on us, did.

no

**SEN. OLYMPIA J. SNOWE, R-MAINE**

***FROM A SENATE FLOOR SPEECH, APRIL 1, 1998.***

As the law requires, Texas, Vermont and Maine have negotiated an agreement that was approved by each state. . . . So, we have before us a compact that has been carefully crafted and thoroughly examined by the state governments and people of all three states involved. Now all that is required is the approval of Congress, so that the state of Texas and the other Texas Compact members will be able to exercise appropriate control over the waste that will come into the Texas facility. . . .

Opponents of the Texas Compact would have you believe that should we ratify this compact it will open the doors for other states to dump nuclear waste at a site, in the desert, located five miles from the town of Sierra Blanca, exposing a predominantly low-income, minority community to health and environmental threats.

The truth is that Texas has been planning to build a facility for its own waste since 1981, long before Maine first proposed a compact with Texas. That is because whether or not this compact passes, Texas still must somehow take care of the waste it produces. . . .

The opponents of the compact would have you believe this issue is about politics. It is not about politics, it is about science: sound science. It is very dry in the Southwest Texas area, where the small amount of rainfall it receives mostly evaporates before it hits the ground. The aquifer that supplies water to the area and to nearby Mexico is over 600 feet below the desert floor and is encased in rock.

The proposed site has been designed to withstand any earthquake equaling the most severe that has ever occurred in Texas history. Strong seismic activity in the area is nonexistent. All these factors mean that the siting of this facility is on strong scientific grounds.

Our opponents say we will be bad neighbors if we pass this compact because the proposed site is near the Mexican border. In fact, the U.S. and Mexico have an agreement, the La Paz Agreement, to cooperate in the environmental protection of the border region. The La Paz Agreement simply encourages cooperative efforts to protect the environment of the region.

Any proposed facility will be protective of the environment because it will be constructed in accordance with the strictest U.S. environmental safeguards.

## FOR MORE INFORMATION

*If you would like to have this CQ Researcher updated, or need more information about this topic, please call CQ Custom Research. Special rates for CQ subscribers. (202) 887-8600 or (800) 432-2250, ext. 600, or E-mail Custom.Research@cq.com*

**Center for Health, Environment and Justice,** P.O. Box 6806, Falls Church, Va. 22040; (703) 237-2249, www.essential.org/cchw. The center helps community-based groups fend off environmental hazards. It was founded by a former resident of Love Canal, N.Y., the community built near a toxic-waste dump.

**Earthjustice Legal Defense Fund,** 180 Montgomery St., Suite 1400, San Francisco, Calif. 94014; (800) 584-6460; www.earthjustice.org. Formerly known as the Sierra Club Legal Defense Fund, this nonprofit law firm is active in cases involving environmental justice.

**Environmental Justice Resource Center,** Clark Atlanta University, 223 James P. Brawley Dr. S.W., Atlanta, Ga. 30314; (404) 880-6911. www.ejrc.cau.edu. Directed by Robert D. Bullard, a longtime environmental justice leader, the center helps communities protect themselves from pollution sources.

**Environmental Council of the States,** 444 N. Capitol St. N.W., Suite 305, Washington, D.C. 20001; (202) 624-3660; www.sso.org/ecos/. A membership group representing environmental officials of the states and the District of Columbia, ECOS opposes the EPA's new rules for handling environmental justice complaints.

**Greenpeace,** 1436 U St. N.W., Washington, D.C. 20009; (202) 462-1177; www.greenpeace.org. This research and activist group has recently become involved in several cases involving complaints of environmental racism.

**Office of Environmental Justice, U.S. Environmental Protection Agency,** 401 M St. S.W., Washington, D.C. 20460; (202) 564-2515 or (800) 962-6215; es.epa.gov. The OEJ coordinates EPA activities and provides technical assistance to communities threatened by environmental hazards.

to industry that may not be what the activists intended.

"The message is, 'You're stupid if you try to move into a community with a significant number of African-Americans, or any other racial minority,' " Mason says. "We don't want to be in a community that doesn't want us there. But this policy will deprive many people of economic opportunity, and it's bad news for economic development in general."

Some critics predict that the EPA's policy is such a deterrent to industrial development and job creation that many companies will shift production overseas.

"In the long run, this is the best economic-development program for Mexico that's ever come down the pike," Borné says. "If EPA really wants to chase our industry over the border, then this is a first-class ticket. I already see how detrimental this policy is to economic development in my state."

EPA is still investigating the Shintech case. However it is resolved, supporters of the environmental justice movement are optimistic that more aggressive steps to combat environmental racism will pay off, not only for poor and non-white Americans but also in the development of cleaner manufacturing and waste technologies.

"The movement has moved beyond the siting of facilities," Bullard says. "It's bigger than that. It embraces the full question of prevention, health and employment. We're now asking if we really need more chemicals entering the waste stream, as opposed to changing production processes to protect health and the environment. A company that produces waste is a wasteful company. So it makes sense to reduce waste so we won't need as many facilities to dispose of this stuff."

Knox agrees with Bullard's assessment and argues that the struggle for environmental justice need not be adversarial because it will benefit everyone. "If this is to be the greatest industrial society of all time, industry has to be clean," he says. "But we all have to work together to make that happen. There's a role for everybody, including business and communities. We all have to sit at the table."

Bullard says pressure from low-income and minority communities that have lodged environmental racism complaints has already spurred manufacturers to develop and adopt cleaner production processes and products, including soy-based ink for newspapers, recycled paper for packaging and pesticide-free fruits and vegetables.

"But I think the biggest impact of the environmental justice movement has not come yet," Bullard says. "That is consumers who are selective and educated about what they will buy and what they won't buy. Creating educated consumers who will start punishing companies that hurt the environment and rewarding those that adopt environmentally sound business practices will be the last civil rights battle." ■

## Notes

[1] Executive Order 12898, "Federal Actions to Address Environmental Justice in Minority Populations and Low-Income Populations," Feb. 11, 1994. For background, see "Cleaning Up Hazardous Wastes," *The CQ Researcher*, Aug. 23, 1996, pp. 752-776.

[2] In *Bean v. Southwestern Waste Management*, residents of a predominantly black subdivision in Houston charged that Browning-Ferris Industries had practiced environmental discrimination by choosing their community to site a municipal solid-waste landfill. They lost the case.

[3] For background, see "Jobs vs. Environment," *The CQ Researcher*, May 15, 1992, pp. 409-432.

[4] Benjamin A. Goldman and Laura Fitton, *Toxic Wastes and Race Revisited,* Center for Policy Alternatives, National Association for the Advancement of Colored People and United Church of Christ Commission for Racial Justice, 1994.

[5] U.S. Environmental Protection Agency, Office of Environmental Justice, *Serving a Diverse Society,* November 1997. For background, see "New Air Quality Standards," *The CQ Researcher*, March 7, 1997, pp. 193-217.

[6] Christopher H. Foreman Jr., "A Winning Hand? The Uncertain Future of Environmental Justice," *The Brookings Review*, spring 1996, p. 24.

[7] *Ibid.*, p. 25.

[8] See American Lung Association, "Health Effects of Outdoor Air Pollution," 1996.

[9] For background, see "Environmental Movement at 25," *The CQ Researcher*, March 31, 1995, pp. 283-307.

[10] See Environmental Protection Agency, Office of Environmental Justice, *Environmental Justice 1994 Annual Report: Focusing on Environmental Protection for All People,* April 1995.

[11] See Robert D. Bullard, *Unequal Protection* (1994), pp. 43-52.

[12] General Accounting Office, *Siting of Hazardous Waste Landfills and Their Correlation with Racial and Economic Status of Surrounding Communities* (1983); United Church of Christ Commission for Racial Justice, *Toxic Wastes and Race in the United States* (1987).

[13] Quoted in EPA, *Environmental Justice 1994 Annual Report, op. cit.,* p. 3.

[14] See Andrew S. Levine, Jonathan E. Rinde and Kenneth J. Warren, "In Response to Chester Residents, EPA Releases Environmental Justice Rules," *The Legal Intelligencer*, Feb. 18, 1998.

[15] See Paul Hoverten, "EPA Puts Plant on Hold in Racism Case," *USA Today*, Sept. 11, 1998.

[16] See "New EPA Report Lists Positive Effects of Agency Superfund Reform Efforts," *Hazardous Waste News*, Feb. 16, 1998.

# Bibliography

## Selected Sources Used


### Books

**Bullard, Robert D., *Dumping in Dixie: Race, Class and Environmental Quality,* Harper Collins, 1996.**

A leading activist in the environmental justice movement examines the enforcement of environmental-protection laws in the Southern United States, where poor, mostly black communities are commonly chosen as sites for waste dumps and incinerators.

**Bullard, Robert D., ed., *Unequal Protection: Environmental Justice and Communities of Color,* Sierra Club Books, 1994.**

This collection of essays describes how communities of poor and non-white Americans are disproportionately exposed to toxic wastes and other environmental hazards.

**Szasz, Andrew, *EcoPopulism: Toxic Waste and the Movement for Environmental Justice,* University of Minnesota Press, 1994.**

The author describes the environmental justice movement's evolution from grass-roots activism to federal policy. By focusing on pollution prevention rather than cleaning up polluted sites, the movement is changing the focus of environmental policy.

### Articles

**Arrandale, Tom, "Regulation and Racism," *Governing,* March 1998, p. 63.**

The Environmental Protection Agency's decision to overturn a state-issued permit to build a plastics plant near a poor, minority community in Louisiana last fall does not further the goal of environmental justice, the author writes, because it will discourage industry from bringing jobs to the very communities that are hardest hit by unemployment.

**Hampson, Fen Osler, and Judith Reppy, "Environmental Change and Social Justice," *Environment,* April 1997, pp. 12-20.**

The authors apply the tenets of environmental justice to global environmental issues, including global warming. Developed nations, which have contributed the most to this problem, should help devise solutions that reduce economic inequality between rich and developing nations, the authors contend.

**Northridge, Mary E., and Peggy M. Shepard, "Comment: Environmental Racism and Public Health," *American Journal of Public Health,* May 1997, pp. 730-732.**

The authors call for further study of the disparate impact of environmental hazards on poor, non-white communities and a broad public health initiative, similar in scope to the anti-smoking campaign, to prevent and remove toxins from these communities.

**Parris, Thomas M., "Spinning the Web of Environmental Justice," *Environment,* May 1997, pp. 44-45.**

This collection of Internet addresses provides a wealth of sources, including Environmental Protection Agency (EPA) reports and non-governmental studies, on efforts to combat pollution that affects poor and minority communities.

**Sachs, Aaron, "Upholding Human Rights and Environmental Justice," *The Humanist,* March-April 1996, pp. 5-8.**

The author reviews the international movement for environmental justice that took off after the 1988 murder of Chico Mendes, a Brazilian rubber tapper who fought for the rights of rain forest inhabitants against cattle barons who were clearing the forests for grazing land.

**Schoeplfle, Mark, "Due Process and Dialogue: Consulting with Native Americans under the National Environmental Policy Act," *Common Ground,* summer/fall 1997, pp. 40-45.**

The 1969 National Environmental Policy Act provides standards for informing Indian tribes of environmental hazards and taking steps to protect themselves from pollutants.

### Reports and Studies

**Goldman, Benjamin A., and Laura Fitton, *Toxic Wastes and Race Revisited,* Center for Policy Alternatives, 1994.**

This update of a 1987 report on the racial and socioeconomic characteristics of communities with hazardous-waste sites finds that poor and minority communities are even more disproportionately exposed to toxins than before, despite the growth of the environmental justice movement.

**National Environmental Justice Advisory Council, *Environmental Justice, Urban Revitalization and Brownfields: The Search for Authentic Signs of Hope,* December 1996.**

An EPA advisory committee finds that the development of brownfields — abandoned industrial sites that are not polluted enough to warrant federal cleanup under the Superfund program — is an important contribution to the goal of environmental justice.

**U.S. Environmental Protection Agency, Office of Environmental Justice, *Serving a Diverse Society,* November 1997.**

This pamphlet summarizes the adverse impact of air pollution, pesticides, agricultural runoff and other environmental hazards on communities of color and suggests steps communities can take to minimize exposure.

# 9 Gun Control

Kenneth Jost

When John Darrah served as a juvenile court judge in Seattle a few years ago, he handled "a steady diet" of cases involving guns. The experience left him depressed about the shattering impact of guns on young people's lives and furious with state lawmakers for not addressing the problem more forcefully.

"What I see with all these guns is that adults' selfishness in demanding their 'constitutional right' [to own and sell guns] has really destroyed the future of many children," says Darrah, a veteran King County Superior Court judge. Before guns became so accessible, he says, kids settled differences with their fists, "but now they end up in jail on very serious felonies, sometimes for life. This is foolishness." [1]

Darrah helped form a group of concerned citizens, and last November the gun-safety initiative they spearheaded appeared on the ballot. The measure required safety tests for prospective gun owners and trigger locks on all handguns sold in the state. [2]

Darrah viewed the initiative as a "modest" step, weaker than he would have preferred. But to many Washingtonians, including tens of thousands of gun owners, the proposal seemed a costly and unnecessary intrusion into their lives at best and, at worst, a threat to their safety.

"These are the same types of provisions that show up in places like Washington, D.C., and New York City, where the criminals have guns, the citizens don't and crime goes through the roof," says Jim Gordon, a computer programmer and president of an employee gun club at giant Microsoft Corp., near Seattle.

Washington state enjoys a very low crime rate, says Gordon, a self-described libertarian, because many residents carry firearms. "The criminals know that," he says, "and they don't want to take a chance."

Early polling indicated popular support for the measure, known as Initiative 676, but after a multimillion-dollar campaign by opponents — largely financed by the National Rifle Association — voters decisively rejected the measure, 71 percent to 29 percent.

Gun control supporters, who have turned in the past few years to gun safety as a politically saleable issue, responded to the disappointing defeat with a defiant attack on the NRA.

"The NRA's guerrilla tactics are the highest form of flattery," Sarah Brady, chair of Handgun Control, the nation's largest gun control organization, declared the next day. "Since when does the gun lobby have to work so hard to defeat a measure in so-called 'friendly' territory? Clearly, the tides are turning in the gun control debate."

But Tanya Metaksa, the NRA's chief lobbyist, says the defeat of the initiative represented a victory for "safety, responsibility and freedom."

"Once you explained to the Washington electorate what this was all about, they opted to be on the side of freedom vs. control," Metaksa says. "They opted to be on the side of an issue where government has less power, rather than giving it more power."

The high-powered volleys fired by Brady and Metaksa typify a debate that has raged for at least three decades amid widespread gun ownership and violence, and widespread gun regulations. The United States is believed to have more guns per capita in private hands than any country in the world — more than 235 million according to some estimates. (*See graph, p. 157.*) But the U.S. also has a complex web of some 20,000 federal, state and local gun laws — viewed by gun control advocates as helpful but inadequate and by opponents as ineffective against criminals but burdensome for law-abiding gun owners. [3]

To some observers, the gun control debate has been uninformative and deceptive. "Neither side is telling the truth generally," says author William Weir, who critiques both sides in a recent book. [4]

"In the war over guns, the first casualty was truth," says Gary Kleck, a criminologist at Florida State University who has written on gun issues for two decades.

Kleck, who describes himself as a member of liberal organizations such as the American Civil Liberties Union, is especially critical of gun control supporters' arguments. In a new book, Kleck calls much of the academic research on guns "virtually worthless." He argues that the best research suggests that the availability of guns has little impact on the level of violent crime generally and that gun control laws have not reduced gun-related crimes. [5]

Kleck also strongly defends his most controversial research finding: that defensive gun use (DGU) by crime victims is common, generally effective in preventing attack and relatively safe for the gun user. On that basis, Kleck calls laws that would "disarm" citizens a "high-risk gamble."

From *The CQ Researcher*. Originally published as "Gun Control Standoff," December 19, 1997.

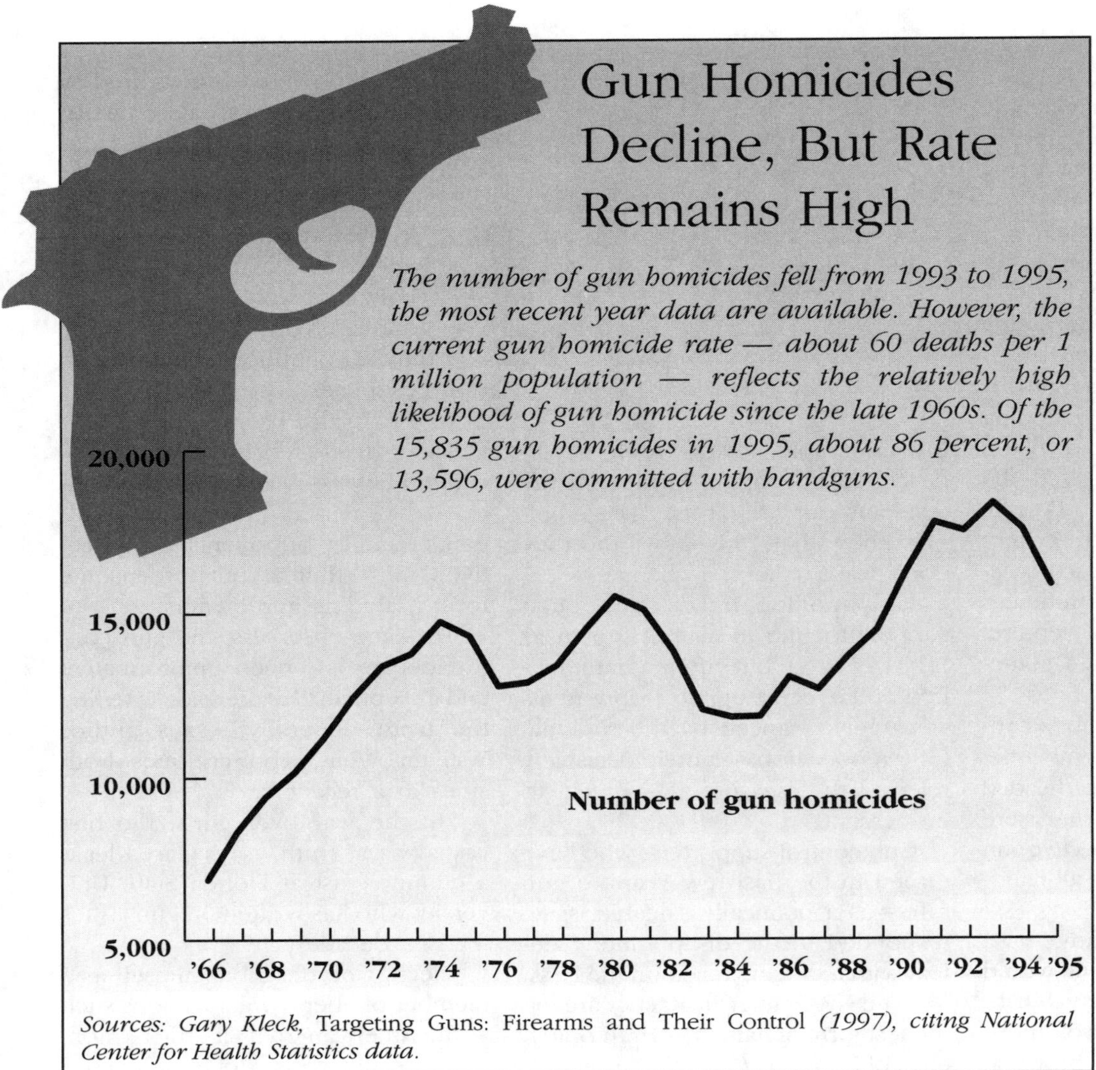


*Sources: Gary Kleck,* Targeting Guns: Firearms and Their Control *(1997), citing National Center for Health Statistics data.*

But Kleck also faults gun control opponents for some of their arguments. And he ends by proposing what he calls a "workable" gun control strategy that would include background checks on prospective gun purchasers, regulation of all private transfers of guns and stricter enforcement of laws prohibiting convicted criminals and others from carrying weapons.

Organized gun-owner groups, however, have strongly opposed most of the firearms regulations proposed since the landmark 1968 Gun Control Act was passed following the assassinations of President John F. Kennedy, Sen. Robert F. Kennedy and the Rev. Martin Luther King Jr. Author Weir, who says he belongs to both the NRA and Handgun Control, criticizes the NRA's "hysterical opposition" to any gun control. But he also faults many of the gun laws that have been enacted — including the so-called assault weapons ban, enacted in 1994 over the NRA's fierce opposition. Contrary to gun control groups' claims, Weir says the semiautomatic rifles labeled as "assault weapons" are rarely used in street crime.

The debate over gun control continues to rage despite recent statistical evidence of a declining impact from firearms. Some recent surveys found evidence that the percentage of U.S. households owning guns has fallen below 40 percent; industry figures show that gun sales are sharply down; and the number of firearm deaths fell slightly in 1995. (*See graph, p. 158.*)

"We don't have the same kind of public outcry that we had a few years ago," says Michael Beard, executive director of the Coalition to Stop Gun Violence, the lone major gun control group advocating a complete ban on handguns in the U.S.

As the gun control debate continues, these are some of the questions being asked:

### *Can gun-safety laws help prevent accidental shooting deaths and injuries?*

Kevin Gilligan was 2 years old when he became a gun victim. On the evening of March 21, 1996, Kevin's teenage half-brother Joseph fired a fatal gunshot into Kevin's head while he was playing with their father's handgun. Two other Massachusetts boys — ages 12 and 14 — died in somewhat similar accidents in the previous eight days. [6]

The deaths spurred Attorney General Scott Harshbarger, a second-term Democrat, to require safety features on all guns sold in Massachusetts. Harshbarger's action reflected recent efforts by gun control advocates to promote gun-safety initiatives. Since 1989, some 15 states have passed laws requiring adults to either store loaded guns in a place reasonably inaccessible to children or use a device to lock the gun. Adults can be held criminally liable if a child obtains an improperly stored, loaded gun.[7]

Meanwhile, gun control supporters are also pushing both the states and Congress to require that guns be sold with safety locks. Connecticut became the first state to adopt such a requirement in 1989.

Handgun control advocates applaud such moves, but the NRA is opposed. "We have an objection to anything mandatory, a one-size-fits-all mentality for everything," Metaksa says. "We believe in education. That's what we've been doing, not government mandates."

Various surveys have indicated that many, and perhaps most, gun owners don't follow basic storage safety advice. A Police Foundation study released in May, for example, found that 53 percent of long guns and 57 percent of handguns are usually kept unlocked. And 55 percent of all handguns are kept loaded.[8]

## U.S. Gun Ownership Has Risen

*Americans owned nearly a quarter-billion firearms in 1994, according to the most commonly cited figures.* Per capita ownership — about 905 guns per 1,000 population — is at the highest level ever. However, the percentage of households owning guns has hovered at around 45 percent since the 1950s, according to the most commonly cited figures, because most gun owners have two or more weapons. ***

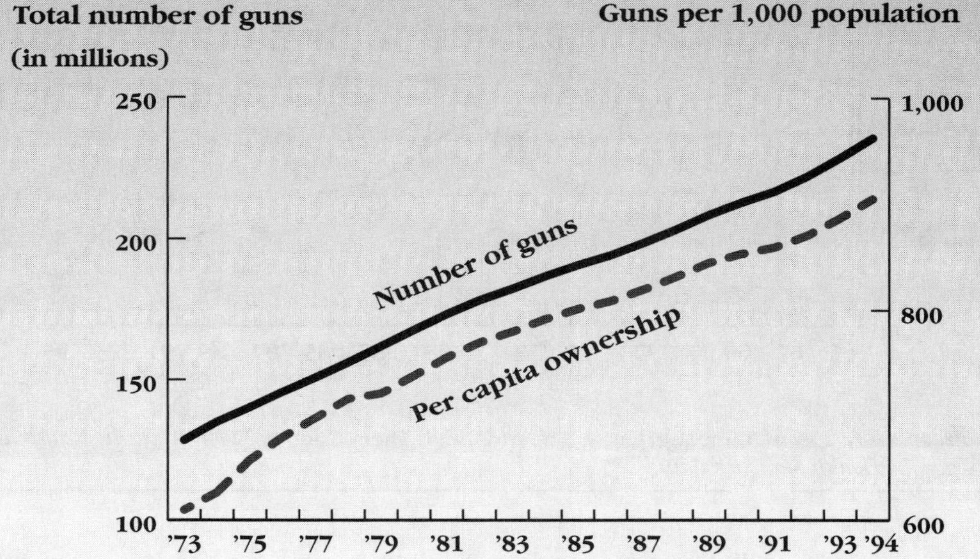


** A more recent survey by the Police Foundation estimated ownership at about 192 million guns, but some researchers suspect underreporting.*

*** Recent surveys indicate a household decline below 40 percent, but some researchers suspect underreporting.*

*Sources: Gary Kleck,* Targeting Guns: Firearms and Their Control *(1997), citing Bureau of Alcohol, Tobacco and Firearms, Census Bureau, Police Foundation*

Despite the seeming appeal of the safety issue, gun control supporters were making only slow progress at the state level, even before the defeat of the Washington state initiative. They had made even less headway at the federal level. The Consumer Product Safety Commission is specifically prohibited from regulating firearms, and safety-lock legislation failed to advance in the last session of Congress.

"This is an area of consumer protection where there's been a hole for quite a while," says Glenn Kaplan, an assistant attorney general in Massachusetts. "If the states want anything done, they have to do it themselves."

In October, however, President Clinton announced an agreement among eight domestic gun manufacturers to begin putting child-safety locks on all their handguns. By the end of next year, about 80 percent of all handguns made in the U.S. will be equipped with safety locks. But some gun control supporters minimized the importance of the move. Kristen Rand, chief lobbyist at the Violence Policy Center, says the manufacturers agreed to trigger locks only to forestall mandatory federal safety standards.

Critics of gun control doubt that

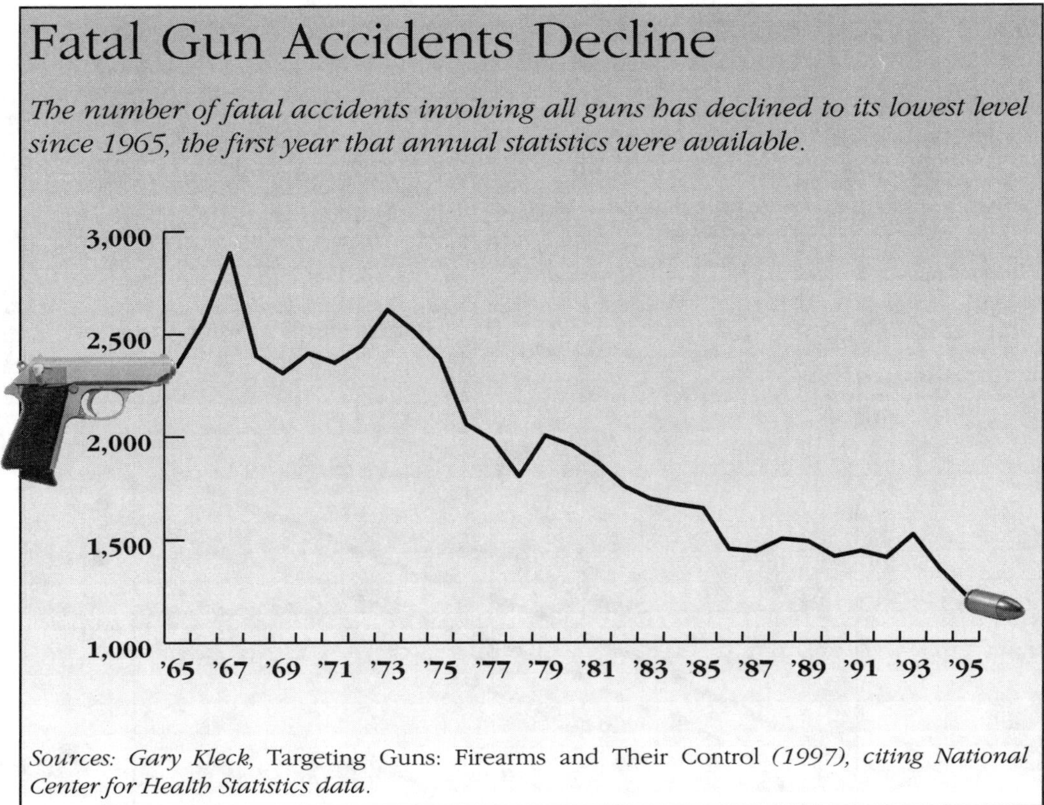


*Sources: Gary Kleck,* Targeting Guns: Firearms and Their Control *(1997), citing National Center for Health Statistics data.*

child-proof locks will have much effect. "It's unlikely to have an impact large enough that we could detect it," Kleck says. "Of course, one life is one life." [9]

But gun control supporter Philip Cook, a criminology professor at Duke University, says the safety issue indicates a strengthening gun control movement. "We've seen a new feistiness on the part of gun control advocates that has not so far accomplished a great deal," he says, "but maybe it has some prospect for the future."

### *Do laws making it easier to carry concealed weapons reduce crime?*

Gun control opponents have their own "safety" initiative: a decade-long push to enact laws allowing most adults to carry a concealed weapon without showing a special need. Florida started the trend in 1987 with a state law providing for weapons permits to be issued to all adults who seek them except convicted felons and mentally ill persons. "We're talking about allowing people to defend themselves," said the bill's sponsor, Republican state Sen. Richard Langley. [10]

Ten years later, "right-to-carry" laws are on the books in 31 states, and supporters maintain that they have helped reduce crime in Florida and elsewhere. Opponents, however, insist that the statistics are inconclusive and that the laws will contribute to gun-related violence.

The NRA, which has helped pass right-to-carry laws in more than 20 states since 1987, mostly in the South and West, says the laws "respect the right of individual citizens to exercise their fundamental right of self-defense by carrying concealed firearms for protection against criminals." Handgun Control counters that the laws "will increase the number of guns circulating in untrained hands, but will not assure increased self-defense."

Among academics, the debate has been at least as sharp, though densely statistical. [11] One study, conducted at the University of Maryland and published in 1995, found that the number of gun homicides increased after right-to-carry laws were passed in four out of the five cities they studied, including three in Florida. The researchers suggested that the fall in gun homicides in the fifth city — Portland, Ore. — might have been due to tighter gun-purchase laws enacted during the same period. [12]

In a much more detailed study first publicized in 1996, two University of Chicago researchers — John R. Lott Jr., a visiting fellow in law and economics, and graduate student David B. Mustard — reached an opposite conclusion. After analyzing crime data from right-to-carry states, they found instead a significant reduction in personal crime, including murders and rapes.

"Allowing citizens to carry concealed weapons deters violent crimes, and it appears to produce no increase in accidental deaths," researchers Lott and Mustard wrote. They estimated that if states without liberalized concealed gun provisions had enacted such laws in 1992, approximately 1,570 murders, 4,177 rapes and more than 60,000 aggravated assaults "would have been avoided yearly" — at an annual savings to society of $6.2 billion. [13]

The Lott-Mustard study spawned

# Is a Citizen's Best Defense a Gun?

For years, it has been an article of faith among gun control supporters that using a gun to ward off a criminal is both rare and dangerous. But that view was severely tested when prominent researcher Gary Kleck produced evidence that guns are used about 2.5 million times per year in the United States and that these defensive gun uses — or DGUs — help thwart many attempted crimes and only rarely result in injury to the gun user. [1]

Gun control opponents quickly seized on the finding by Florida State University criminologists Kleck and Mark Gertz, touting the statistical conclusion in fact sheets and legislative testimony. Conversely, gun control groups harshly criticized the research as unsupported and unbelievable, pointing instead to an earlier study for the Justice Department suggesting fewer than 100,000 DGUs per year.

This year, the statistical debate took another unusual turn when two pro-gun control researchers produced a report for the gun control-minded Police Foundation suggesting a figure somewhat comparable to Kleck's and then — within the same report — debunked their own finding.

Criminologist Philip J. Cook of Duke University and political scientist Jens Ludwig of Georgetown University said their estimate "is subject to a large positive bias and should not be taken seriously." "The rather frustrating conclusion," they add, "is that the available survey data leave considerable uncertainty about the 'true' number of DGUs." [2]

The statistical debate over the results of two telephone surveys conducted about a year apart has now turned into one of academic honesty as well. Cook and Ludwig, while acknowledging Kleck's methodology as "respectable," nonetheless criticize his 2.5 million estimate as "a mythical number." [3] For his part, Kleck, who initially designed the survey for the Police Foundation and was then removed from the project without explanation, says he believes Cook and Ludwig were chosen to replace him "to put the proper spin on the finding." [4]

Kleck described his research, conducted in early 1993, as the first survey ever exclusively on the question of armed self-defense. Out of nearly 5,000 people surveyed randomly by telephone, some 222 reported civilian defensive use of a gun against a human within the previous year — for a projected annual figure of about 2.5 million instances per year.

In most of the reported instances, the "defender" merely brandished the weapon; One-fourth said they fired the gun, and 8 percent said they wounded or killed the attacker. But only 5.5 percent of the defenders said they were attacked and injured after a defensive gun use, and only 11 percent said they suffered a property loss.

While conceding the number of affirmative responses was fairly small, Kleck nonetheless concluded that defensive gun uses by the "non-criminal majority" had "saved lives, prevented injuries, thwarted rape attempts, driven off burglars and helped victims save property."

Kleck also speculated that his figure was, if anything, low, because some people might be reluctant to report questionable use of a gun. And he strongly assailed the figures produced in the government's earlier National Crime Victimization Survey, saying that the technique used — face-to-face questioning by government employees — would have led many people not to mention having used a gun in the past.

In the Police Foundation study, Cook and Ludwig report that their telephone survey of about 2,500 people found 45 instances of defensive gun use within the past year — projected to be about 1.5 million instances. They call that result "comparable" to Kleck's.

Unlike Kleck, however, Cook and Ludwig argue that respondents probably exaggerated the number of defensive gun uses. Some respondents, they said, may have just been trying to "look good." Others may have been confused about their experiences. And still others, the researchers suggested, may have been "gun advocates" who "know that the number of DGUs is relevant and may be tempted to enhance that estimate through their own response to the survey."

Cook acknowledges that it was "unusual" for researchers to question the findings of their own survey. For his part, Kleck says Cook and Ludwig engaged in "very one-sided speculation about what might lead to errors in such a survey, and only about errors that might lead to overrreporting rather than underreporting."

Whatever the number, Cook and Ludwig end by questioning the value of using a gun to ward off a criminal. Access to firearms, they say, "may encourage some people to be less prudent about avoiding confrontations" or to be "less vigilant in avoiding unsafe situations." And they warn that readiness to use guns can lead to fatal accidents — though they cite no statistics on the point.

Kleck insists, however, that the evidence clearly shows that defensive gun use is common and strongly suggests that it is effective. "To disarm non-criminals in the hope that this might indirectly help reduce access to guns among criminals is a very high-stakes gamble," Kleck concludes, "and the risks will not be reduced by pretending that crime victims rarely use guns for self-defense."

---

[1] Gary Kleck and Mark Gertz, "Armed Resistance to Crime: The Prevalence and Nature of Self-Defense with a Gun," *Journal of Criminal Law and Criminology*, Vol. 86, No. 1 (fall 1995), pp. 150-187.

[2] Philip J. Cook and Jens Ludwig, "Guns in America: Results of a Comprehensive National Survey on Firearms Ownership and Use," Police Foundation, May 1997.

[3] Philip J. Cook, Jens Ludwig and David Hemenway, "The Gun Debate's New Mythical Number: How Many Defensive Uses Per Year?" *Journal of Policy Analysis and Management*, Vol. 16, No. 3 (1997), p. 464.

[4] For a more detailed critique, see Gary Kleck, *Targeting Guns: Firearms and Their Control* (1997), pp. 158-159.

## Most States Have Lax Concealed-Weapons Laws

*Nearly two-thirds of the states have lenient "right-to-carry" laws allowing most citizens to carry concealed weapons without showing a special need. Twelve states grant concealed-weapons permits under certain conditions, and seven states and the District of Columbia largely prohibit concealed weapons. **

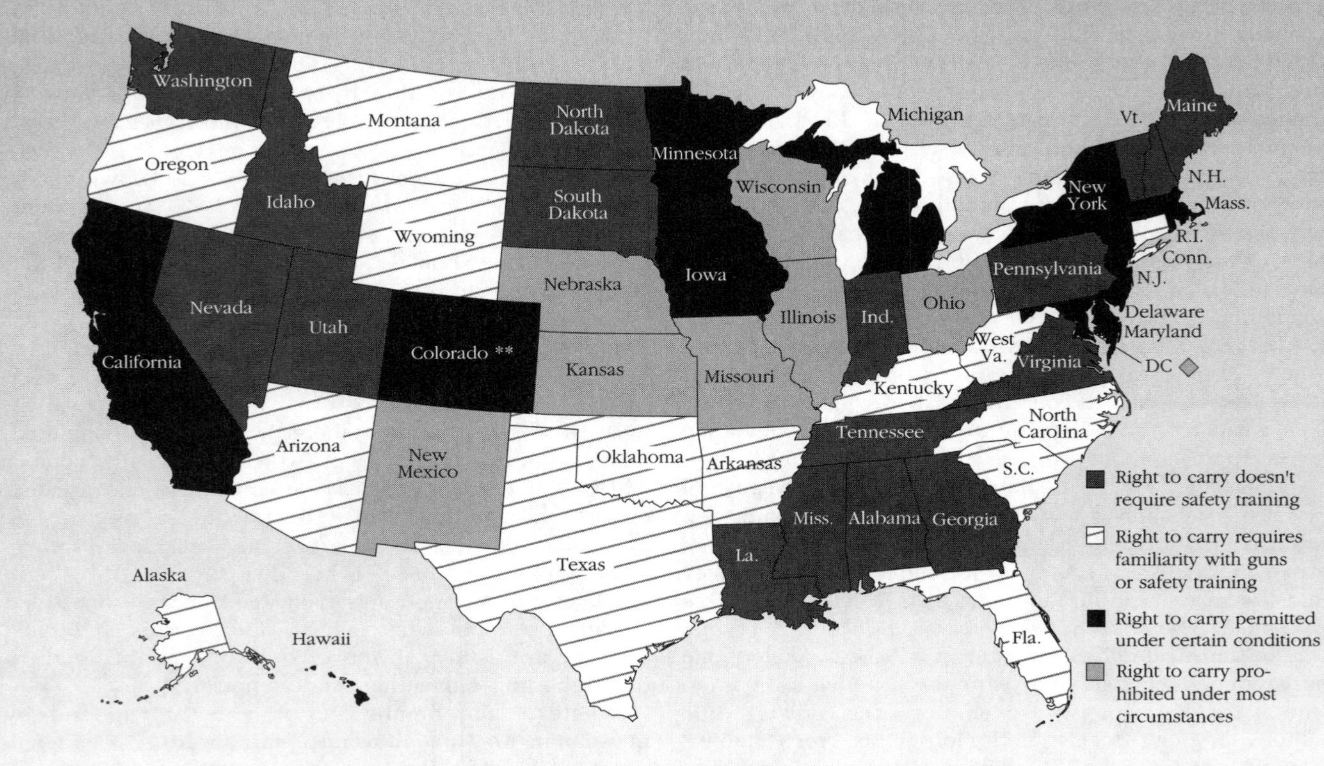


** Handgun Control characterizes Alabama and Georgia as discretionary permit states, while the NRA counts them as permissive.*

*** Colorado law allows concealed weapons, but permits are actually difficult to obtain.*

*Sources: National Conference of State Legislatures; National Rifle Association; Handgun Control Inc.*

what two critical authors have labeled "a minor cottage industry" among academics of reanalyzing the Lott-Mustard data to test — or refute — their conclusions. [14]

In one study, economist Dan Black of the University of Kentucky and criminologist Daniel Nagin of Carnegie Mellon University said Lott and Mustard used data that "provides no basis for drawing confident conclusions about the impact of right-to-carry laws on violent crime."

Black and Nagin said that the decline in homicides and rapes was almost completely attributable to data from Florida. Without Florida, they said, there was "no discernible impact." In addition, they said that the change in crime rates varied too much between states and within states to support any conclusions. "Murders decline in Florida but increase in West Virginia," they wrote. "Assaults fall in Maine but increase in Pennsylvania. . . . We doubt that any model of criminal behavior could account for the variation we observe." [15]

Other critical studies followed. Albert Alschuler, a prominent liberal professor at the University of Chicago Law School, questioned the impact of the right-to-carry laws by noting that the data showed a sharper decline in domestic homicides — presumably unaffected by carrying a concealed weapon — than in other killings. [16] Two other gun control supporters — Franklin Zimring and Gordon Hawkins — suggested that the states with right-to-carry laws were unrepresentative of crime rate trends in more urbanized states, which generally still have restrictive weapons laws. [17]

Despite the criticisms, Lott maintains that his statistical analyses all stand up and that the critics are simply wrong in some of their methodological points about the original study. "Allowing law-abiding citizens to carry concealed handguns deters violent crime and saves lives," he repeats in the opening of his response. "The results are consistent." [18]

With the academic debate continuing, some law enforcement officials appear to be backing away from their fears of the right-to-carry laws. "Some of the public safety concerns which we imagined or anticipated . . . have been unfounded or mitigated," Maj. Bill Brown of the Fairfax County, Va., police told a local reporter. [19] "It's not the old Wild West that everyone predicted," said John Russi, director of the licensing division in Florida's Department of State. [20]

Even some of Lott and Mustard's critics acknowledge that the predictions of increased gun violence have not been borne out by statistics. "I don't believe we have any good evidence one way or the other about the impact of right-to-carry laws on violent crime," Nagin says.

For its part, the NRA considers the statistical debate over — and that its side won. "You've seen a reduction in crime," Metaksa says. "You've also seen an increase in the ability of people to defend themselves."

But Joe Sudbay, director of state legislation for Handgun Control, notes that right-to-carry bills failed in a number of states during the past year, including several with Republican governors. Two governors vetoed bills after their legislatures approved them: Republican Bill Graves in Kansas and Democrat Roy Romer in Colorado.

"People are realizing that the systems in place are very weak and don't prevent non-law-abiding citizens from getting guns," Sudbay says. "We think that kind of information coming out more and more will dampen enthusiasm for changing these laws."

### *Does the Second Amendment limit the government's power to regulate individuals' possession of firearms?*

When Georgia banned the private possession of pistols in 1837, the state Supreme Court struck it down, declaring that the state Constitution protected "the right of the whole people . . . and not the militia only" to keep and bear arms. [21]

Opponents of gun control, however, have failed to win the same interpretation of the similarly worded right-to-bear-arms provision of the U.S. Constitution found in the Second Amendment. * Instead, the Supreme Court and lower federal courts have treated the amendment as limited to protection for state militias. As a result, no federal firearms legislation has been struck down on Second Amendment grounds.

Second Amendment advocates contend that the Supreme Court's only pronouncement on the issue, in 1939, is ambiguous and hope that the court may change its interpretation in the future. "I certainly believe that the Second Amendment is just like every other amendment in the Bill of Rights," Metaksa says. "It does talk about individual rights." *(See "At Issue," p. 169.)*

Supporters of gun control vigorously deny that the amendment provides no individual right to own or carry firearms. "The Second Amendment guarantees a right of the people to be armed as part of an organized state militia," says Dennis Henigan, director of the Legal Action Project at the Center to Prevent Handgun Violence. "It has nothing to do with the private ownership of guns except as a part of the organized state militia."

Henigan's confidence belies the proliferation of legal scholarship over the past 15 years examining the historical origins and meaning of the Second Amendment. *(See "Bibliography," p. 173.)* Many of the writings — including some by liberal experts on constitutional law — endorse the arguments by gun control opponents that the Second Amendment limits the federal government's power to regulate firearms. But these experts, including some staunch opponents of gun control, also generally agree that many gun laws — including bans on specific types of weapons — would pass muster under the amendment.

"The Second Amendment is relevant to federal gun control legislation in the same way that the First Amendment is relevant to legislation dealing with freedom of expression," says Sanford Levinson, a liberal professor at the University of Texas Law School in Austin. "That being said, I don't believe the First Amendment is an absolute. And I don't think the Second Amendment protects the right of every individual to own submachine guns."

Levinson, who authored a 1989 law review article entitled "The Embarrassing Second Amendment," complains that the Supreme Court and liberal legal scholars both have ignored the amendment. "The Supreme Court has simply dodged this issue, quite shamelessly," he says.

The court itself embraced the militia-protection view of the amendment in its 1939 decision *United States v. Miller* upholding the National Firearms Act, which regulated possession of machine guns. In a relatively brief and unanimous decision, the court said the law was valid because machine guns were "not part of or-

---

* The Second Amendment: "A well regulated Militia, being necessary to the security of a free State, the right of the people to keep and bear Arms shall not be infringed."

dinary military equipment" and had no "reasonable relationship to the preservation or efficiency of a well-regulated militia." Four decades later, the court refused to take up the issue when it left in place a lower court decision upholding a ban on possession of pistols enacted by the village of Morton Grove, Ill. (*see p. 165*).

Earlier this year, however, one Supreme Court justice threw out an open invitation to gun control opponents to litigate the issue. "This Court has not had recent occasion to consider the nature of the substantive right safeguarded by the Second Amendment," Justice Clarence Thomas wrote in a decision involving the Brady Act (*see p. 167*). "If, however, the Second Amendment is read to confer a personal right to 'keep and bear arms,' a colorable argument exists that the Federal Government's regulatory scheme, at least as it pertains to the purely intrastate sale or possession of firearms, runs afoul of that Amendment's protections."

"Perhaps at some future date," Thomas added, "this Court will have the opportunity to determine whether Justice [Joseph] Story was correct when he wrote that the right to bear arms 'has justly been considered, as the palladium of the liberties of a republic.' "[22]

Thomas' footnote cheered gun control opponents, but they confess they are uncertain what to do with it. "You have to find a plaintiff who wants to take the time and wait out the process for a period of years with the hope of getting to the Supreme Court," Metaksa says.

Stephen Halbrook, a Second Amendment advocate and the winning lawyer in the Brady Act case, says the amendment's impact on federal firearms laws under a personal-right theory is still "quite speculative."

"It could well be that the courts could interpret the Second Amendment to recognize individual rights, including the right to possess a handgun, but the courts could say that a background check is a reasonable regulation of that right," he says.

In the view of John Snyder, director of the Citizens' Committee for the Right to Bear Arms, a waiting period would be struck down under a broader view of the amendment. "A waiting period . . . does prevent a law-abiding citizen from defending himself or herself," Snyder says. He also thinks an assault-weapons ban would be struck down, but concedes that some bans on possession of "military firearms" probably would be upheld.

Henigan believes that few firearms laws would be ruled unconstitutional even if the Supreme Court adopted a broader view of the amendment. "It seems possible that if they did find it to be an individual right, they could still find that because of the nature of that right — access to dangerous weapons — it is subject to far greater regulation than a First Amendment right, for instance," he says. "It's so obvious that the right to be armed has more immediate implications for public safety than the right to engage in freedom of expression."

Gun control opponents say Thomas' footnote — along with a footnote by Justice Antonin Scalia in a recent collection of his lectures[23] — indicates increasing interest in the amendment at the high court. Henigan, however, emphasizes that no other justice joined Thomas' footnote. "It is Exhibit A showing the extremism of his jurisprudence," he says.

In any event, gun control opponents stop short of predicting that their view will soon prevail. "Whether the Supremes will do this issue, I have no idea," Halbrook says. "Your guess is as good as mine." And gun control supporters strongly doubt that the amendment will be used to strike down gun laws.

"It is overwhelmingly unlikely that constitutional courts will in the future interpose themselves as major barriers to federal firearms legislation," says Zimring, a professor of law at the University of California at Berkeley. "Constitutional courts are interposing themselves in fewer and fewer places to begin with. And this would be stepping into a controversy that they have managed to keep out of for the first 70 years of the modern gun control debate." ■

# BACKGROUND

## Decades of Violence

Outbreaks of crime and violence have spurred lawmakers periodically during the 20th century to try to control the use of firearms.[24] Gun owners have appealed to an American tradition of using firearms for sport and for self-defense to block those laws, or at least weaken them. The effect of the laws on crime is hotly debated, but there's no argument that they have not prevented the continuing growth of a vast private arsenal of weapons in the United States.

The modern era of gun control begins with the 1911 New York state law requiring a license to possess a pistol. The Sullivan law won overwhelming approval from lawmakers as a way to stem urban crime. Author Weir says the law has been stringently enforced, with relatively high fees for the relatively few applicants who are granted licenses. Evasion, he says, is widespread: "Most of the pistols in New York City are illegal." And he notes that New York's murder count has continued to rise despite the predictions by the law's supporters of a reduction in homicides.[25]

Two decades later, public concern about violence by organized crime prompted Congress to enact the first

# Chronology

## 1900-1950s

***Street crime prompts New York to pass trend-setting law to ban carrying of firearms; Congress passes "machine-gun" law during gangster era.***

***1911***
New York adopts Sullivan law requiring state-issued license to possess a pistol; National Rifle Association (NRA) warns the law will "disarm" good citizens.

***1934***
National Firearms Act imposes $200 excise tax on the sale of automatic weapons, short-barreled rifles and shotguns; registration provision is dropped after lobbying by NRA.

***1939***
Supreme Court upholds National Firearms Act, saying Congress can regulate firearms if regulations do not impede efficiency of state militias.

## 1960s ***Assassinations and urban violence prompt Congress to pass first broad federal gun control law.***

***1968***
Gun Control Act bans interstate sale of firearms, importing of military surplus weapons and cheap handguns and gun ownership by minors and felons.

## 1970s ***Lobbies form to push gun control, while NRA stiffens opposition.***

***1974***
Founding of Coalition to Stop Gun Violence and Handgun Control.

***1977***
NRA "hard-liners" oust moderate leadership and install new executive director, who seeks to soften group's image while taking tougher stand against gun control.

## 1980s ***Gun control supporters and opponents swap victories and defeats in the states; Congress weakens federal law.***

***1981***
Morton Grove, Ill., becomes first U.S. community to ban possession or sale of handguns; law is upheld, but goes unenforced.

***1982***
Kennesaw, Ga., passes ordinance requiring heads of household to have guns and ammunition available; it is amended later to make compliance discretionary.

***1986***
Gun Owners' Protection Act — also known as McClure-Volkmer bill — lifts ban on interstate sale of rifles and shotguns and limits requirement for license to sell firearms.

***1987***
Florida passes trend-setting state law allowing almost anyone to carry concealed weapon.

***1989***
Florida is first state to make adults liable for unsafe storage of guns in child-accident cases.

## 1990s ***Gun control proponents make gains in Congress, but are dealt setbacks by Supreme Court; more states adopt laws permitting concealed weapons.***

***Nov. 30, 1993***
President Clinton signs Brady Act, establishing five-day waiting period to buy handguns and requiring local law enforcement agencies to perform background checks on gun purchasers; act also raises fees and stiffens requirements for gun dealers.

***Sept. 13, 1994***
Clinton signs crime control bill that includes prohibition on manufacturing and importing semiautomatic assault weapons; measure survives repeal effort in Republican-controlled Congress in 1995 and 1996.

***April 26, 1995***
Supreme Court rules Gun-Free School Zones Act of 1990 unconstitutional on Commerce Clause grounds (*United States v. Lopez*).

***June 27, 1997***
Supreme Court strikes down Brady Act's background check provision on states' rights grounds (*Printz v. United States*); most police and sheriffs continue to perform background checks anyway.

***Sept. 26, 1997***
Gov. Pete Wilson, R-Calif., vetoes handgun safety bill aimed at prohibiting manufacture of cheap "Saturday night specials."

***Nov. 6, 1997***
Washington state voters reject gun safety initiative by decisive margin.

## Mass Shootings Prompt Bans Abroad

Spurred by mass shooting incidents less than two months apart, Great Britain and Australia significantly tightened their gun laws within the past two years.

In Britain, the new Labor Party government last summer pushed through Parliament a complete ban on private possession on handguns. The measure tightened a law passed by the previous Conservative Party government in February that had only banned handguns of more than .22 caliber. Both measures came in response to the deaths of 16 schoolchildren and their teacher in Dunblane, Scotland, on March 13, 1996, at the hands of a handgun-wielding assailant who then killed himself.

In Australia, federal, state and territorial governments agreed in May 1996 to ban the sale and possession of all automatic and semiautomatic firearms. The ban quickly followed the April 28 rampage by a man who used a semiautomatic rifle to kill 35 people on the island state of Tasmania.

Both countries already had tight gun laws before the most recent enactments. Other major industrialized democracies also have relatively strict firearms regulations. Japan — described as having the strictest controls in the world — bans private possession of firearms except by people who need them for official duties or by licensed hunters, shooters, athletes, dealers or collectors. Canada, which has had regulations somewhat comparable to those in the United States, will begin next year requiring licensing of all gun owners and registration of all firearms. [1]

Gun control supporters in the United States have long pointed to the strict gun laws in other countries — and the relatively low gun death rates in those countries — as demonstrating the need to tighten restrictions in this country. Handgun Control notes that in 1992 handguns were used to murder 13 people in Australia, 33 in Great Britain, 60 in Japan, 128 in Canada and 13,495 in the United States.

But the National Rifle Association (NRA) and other gun control opponents insist that the foreign laws are too restrictive and, in any event, cannot be imported into the United States. As for the British and Australian laws, the NRA's chief lobbyist says both laws are overreactions.

"The bans would not have stopped people who are criminally inclined or mentally deranged from creating the carnage that they created," says Tanya K. Metaksa. "But they're symptomatic of a knee-jerk reaction to a tragedy to ban the firearm rather than to take care of the people who have perpetrated the problem."

[1] For background on laws in other countries, written by an opponent of gun control, see David B. Kopel, *The Samurai, the Mountie, and the Cowboy: Should America Adopt the Gun Controls of Other Democracies* (Prometheus, 1992). Kopel is an environmental lawyer in Denver and an associate policy analyst with the Cato Institute, a libertarian think tank.

significant federal controls on firearms. The National Firearms Act of 1934 curtailed civilian ownership of machine guns, sawed-off shotguns, silencers and other "gangster-type" weapons through a federal registration requirement and a $200 per weapon tax. A broader pistol registration requirement was dropped in the face of opposition from the National Rifle Association. Five years later, Congress followed with the Federal Firearms Act, which established federal licensing of manufacturers, dealers and importers of weapons involved in interstate trade.

### Gun Control Act

The broadest federal law, however, was put on the books in 1968, when the country was reeling from the assassinations of three national leaders — John F. Kennedy, Robert F. Kennedy and Martin Luther King — as well as urban riots and a rising crime rate. To try to stem gun-related violence, Congress passed an omnibus measure, the Gun Control Act of 1968, that remains today as the framework for federal firearms regulation.

The law included provisions that:

- Banned the interstate sale of handguns or long guns — aiming at the kind of mail-order purchase that Lee Harvey Oswald made of the gun police say he used to kill President Kennedy in 1963.
- Prohibited the importation of guns not readily adaptable for sporting purposes — aiming at the "Saturday night specials" regarded as the prime weapon for street criminals.
- Barred felons, minors and persons with mental illness from owning any firearms.
- Prohibited any private ownership of so-called destructive devices, such as bazookas and submachine guns.
- Required persons who sold more than a very few guns to obtain licenses from the federal government as dealers and comply with various controls and record-keeping requirements.

Today, the law's basic provisions are no longer in great dispute, but the partisans in the gun control debate differ sharply on their impact. Gun control supporters say the web of laws has helped keep guns out of the hands of criminals, made it harder for potential criminals to obtain guns and made it easier for law enforcement authorities to track the sale of firearms. "We believe we can save lives by regulating the sale of firearms," says Henigan of the Center to

Prevent Handgun Violence, "and we believe there's more than adequate proof of that."

But opponents say the laws have had little effect on criminals, but a significant impact on gun owners and dealers. "It has made it more difficult for commerce in firearms," Metaksa says. "I don't think it's had any effect on crime."

Academic experts also divide on the issue, but one gun control supporter suggests both the benefits and the costs of the laws are being exaggerated.

"If I had to guess, I would say they are making a difference at the margin, and they're doing it with a relatively small imposition on the American public," Cook says. "The history of the laws is a history of fairly modest restrictions on individual freedom to own and use guns, with fairly modest results, results in the right direction."

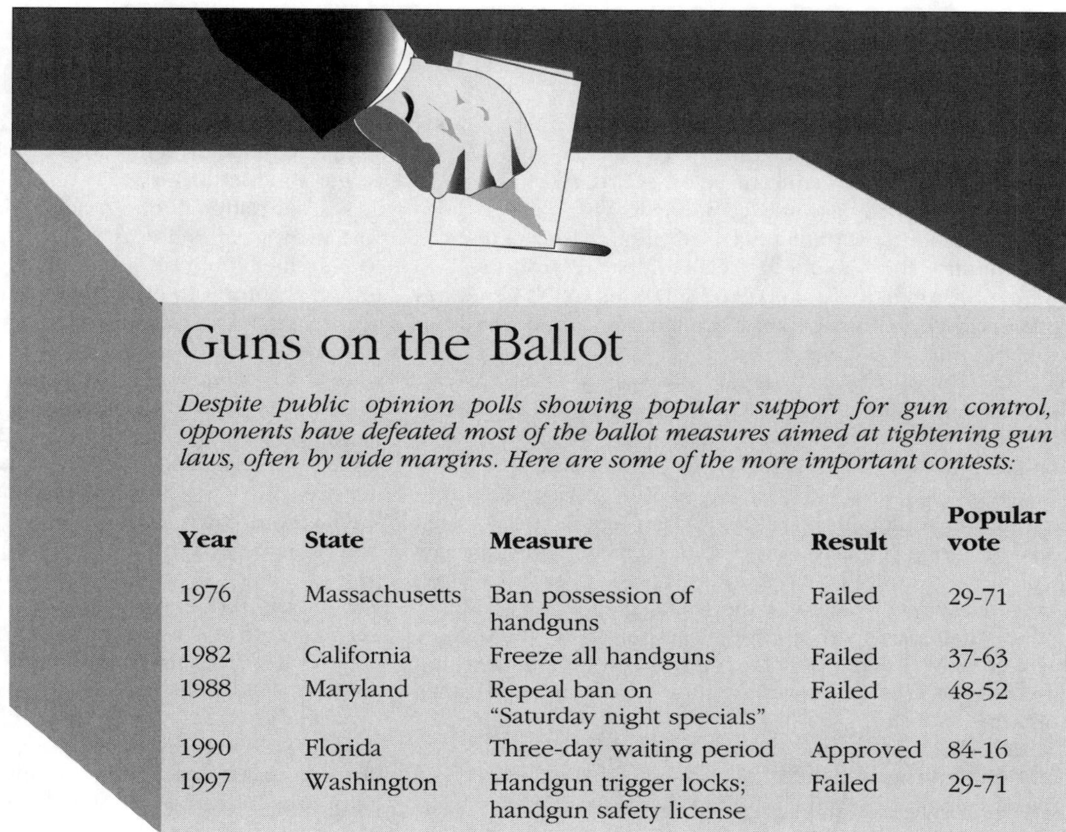

## Guns on the Ballot

*Despite public opinion polls showing popular support for gun control, opponents have defeated most of the ballot measures aimed at tightening gun laws, often by wide margins. Here are some of the more important contests:*

| Year | State | Measure | Result | Popular vote |
|---|---|---|---|---|
| 1976 | Massachusetts | Ban possession of handguns | Failed | 29-71 |
| 1982 | California | Freeze all handguns | Failed | 37-63 |
| 1988 | Maryland | Repeal ban on "Saturday night specials" | Failed | 48-52 |
| 1990 | Florida | Three-day waiting period | Approved | 84-16 |
| 1997 | Washington | Handgun trigger locks; handgun safety license | Failed | 29-71 |

## Swapping Victories

Tiny Morton Grove, Ill., became the first U.S. municipality to completely ban handgun possession. Village trustees approved the ban in 1981 amid clamorous opposition from NRA members bused in for the meeting. Later, the ban survived a legal challenge when the federal appeals court in Chicago ruled, 2-1, that it did not violate the Second Amendment. [26]

Gun supporters responded in kind. In 1982, Kennesaw, Ga., required every head of household to keep a gun and ammunition available. Town officials credit the law with reducing home burglaries, although it has since been amended to allow anyone with serious objections to the law to ignore it.

Nearly two decades later, both ordinances have gone completely unenforced, according to Weir. But they did have the effect of dramatizing the wide gulf in the gun control debate. And they ushered in a decade-plus of back and forth on the issue, with the opposing sides swapping victories and defeats in Congress and in the states.

Opponents of gun control scored their biggest victory in Congress when they persuaded lawmakers to weaken the 1968 gun control law. Most significantly, the Gun Owners' Protection Act — also known as the McClure-Volkmer bill, after its sponsors: Sen. James A. McClure, R-Idaho, and Rep. Harold L. Volkmer, D-Mo. — legalized the interstate sale of rifles and shotguns. The 1986 bill also limited the number of people who were required to get licenses to sell firearms and imposed some limits on federal enforcement against dealers.

The bill was a major victory for the NRA, but supporters of gun control managed to retain the existing ban on the interstate sale of handguns. They also added provisions that barred the importing of barrels used in making "Saturday night specials" — the 1968 law banned importation of most firearms, but not parts — and outlawed the further manufacture or import of machine guns for civilians. [27]

Gun control supporters also scored two quick victories in Congress afterward. Later in 1986, lawmakers approved a ban on armor-piercing

# Critics From All Sides Fire at the ATF

The agency responsible for enforcing federal firearms laws has a budget of only $534 million, with half of the money devoted to three other areas. It has a mere 240 inspectors to monitor compliance with federal laws and regulations by 80,000 licensed firearms dealers across the country. But, despite its relatively small size, the U.S. Bureau of Alcohol, Tobacco and Firearms (ATF) generates giant-size controversies among advocacy groups on both sides of the gun control issue. [1]

Gun control opponents regard the agency as an abusive, overzealous police force guilty of small-scale harassment of gun owners and dealers and large-scale fiascos like the botched raid on the Branch Davidian headquarters in Waco, Texas, in 1993, in which a tank assault, tear gassing and fire killed 75 adults and children. The agency "has been manufacturing criminals for decades, creating phony gun law violations to justify its existence," writes Wayne R. LaPierre, executive vice president of the National Rifle Association. [2]

For their part, gun control supporters view the agency as ineffective in enforcing federal firearms laws and, within the past two or three years, guilty of cozying up to the firearms industry.

"ATF has not done their job," says Kristen Rand, chief lobbyist for the Violence Policy Center. "They've become the lap dog of the gun industry."

Accustomed to drawing flak from gun control opponents, ATF made headlines last month when White House aides blasted the agency for laxness in enforcing the ban on imported assault weapons. The aides leaked stories that a "rogue operation" within ATF had accelerated approval of import permits for 150,000 modified assault weapons despite President Clinton's clear intent to keep such guns out of the country. Clinton stepped in the next day to suspend previously issued permits and freeze applications for any more pending a Treasury Department study. [3]

"ATF had enough indications that the administration wanted the ban enforced," Rand says. "The ATF basically gave a roadmap to the industry on how to modify weapons to get them allowed in."

But the National Rifle Association (NRA) says the agency was merely enforcing the law fairly. Tanya Metaksa, the NRA's chief lobbyist, says the guns that Clinton is trying to ban "conform in every way" to the criteria permitted by the 1994 law that banned certain types of assault weapons.

The NRA has toned down its rhetoric toward the agency since 1995, when an NRA fund-raising appeal described ATF agents as "jack-booted government thugs." That remark prompted former President George Bush to publicly renounce his NRA membership. Today, Metaksa says, "We've found that there are always good agents and bad agents in enforcing the law, and we've found both at the ATF."

ATF traces its history back to 1791, when Congress passed a tax on distilled spirits that led to the Whiskey Rebellion. It operated as part of the Internal Revenue Service until 1972, when it became a separate bureau within the Treasury Department. The budget for fiscal 1998 of $534 million represents an 8.5 percent increase over the previous year's figure of $492 million.

In past years, the agency budget was broken out into its four major functions: firearms, accounting for about half of the budget; alcohol, its second-largest area; tobacco and explosives. This year, however, the president's budget dropped those categories and instead showed that the agency was to devote about three-fourths of its budget to "reducing violent crime."

---

[1] For background, see Stephen Labaton, "How A.T.F. Became a Demon," *The New York Times*, May 14, 1995, "Week in Review," p. 5.

[2] Wayne R. LaPierre, *Guns, Crime, and Freedom* (1994), p. 197.

[3] See *Los Angeles Times*, Nov. 13, 1997, p. A1; *The Washington Post*, Nov. 14, 1997, p. A18; *The New York Times*, Nov. 15, 1997, p. A1.

bullets — popularly called "cop-killer" bullets. And in 1988, Congress approved a law requiring guns to contain a minimum amount of metal — a provision intended to prevent the manufacture of so-called plastic pistols that could defeat metal detectors. But Weir mocks both laws. He says that the company that manufactured armor-piercing bullets had already stopped making them by the time of the ban. And he says there never was a plastic pistol: The controversy stemmed from a German-made pistol that had a plastic frame but still contained 19 ounces of metal and could be observed by metal detectors. [28]

Meanwhile, gun control opponents were scoring significant victories in the states. The NRA responded to the Morton Grove ban by urging states to pass laws pre-empting local regulation of firearms — and thus blocking any further local bans. By the end of the decade, some 39 states had passed such laws. In addition, the NRA pushed through the first of the new laws liberalizing provisions for carrying concealed weapons. A few states followed Florida's 1987 action over the next few years. Then came 10 more states in the 1995-1996 legislative sessions — bringing the total number to 31.

Gun control supporters did win one significant state-level victory when Maryland banned "Saturday night specials" in 1988. Opponents of the measure qualified a ballot measure to repeal the ban, but it survived, 52 percent to 48 percent, after a nasty campaign marked by pamphlets in Baltimore's African-American neighborhoods depicting the ban as an effort to disarm black people. Earlier that same year, though, California voters decisively rejected a proposal to freeze the number of handguns in the state. [29]

## Action in Congress

Bill Clinton's election in 1992 brought a gun control supporter to the White House for the first time in 12 years. With a Democratic-controlled Congress, Clinton helped push through two major pieces of legislation: the Brady bill in 1993 and the assault weapons ban in 1994. But the Republicans' capture of both houses of Congress in 1994 effectively eliminated the possibility of further legislative gains for gun control supporters. And the Supreme Court weighed in with two rulings that struck down gun control provisions on federalism grounds.

Adoption of the Brady Act in 1993 capped a nine-year lobbying drive spearheaded by Sarah Brady, who was an effective spokeswoman for gun control, especially when she appeared at rallies with her wheelchair-bound husband Jim. * Both the House and the Senate had approved the bill in 1991, only for Senate Republicans to block final action in 1992. The logjam was broken with Clinton's strong support in 1993, and Jim Brady was at the president's side when he signed the measure into law on Nov. 30.

A year later, Clinton again had to lobby hard for inclusion of the assault weapons ban in the omnibus anti-crime bill working its way through Congress. Gun control supporters had lobbied for a ban on semiautomatic assault weapons for years, blaming them for such mass shooting incidents as the 1989 killing of five children and wounding of 29 others in a Stockton, Calif., elementary school. The NRA and other opponents ridiculed the proposal, arguing that the weapons being prohibited in fact were rarely used in crimes.

The House had rejected the proposal by 70 votes in 1991, but gun control supporters redoubled their efforts and — with last-minute lobbying by Clinton and several Cabinet members — won the critical House vote on May 5, 1994, by the slimmest of margins: 216-214. Despite last-minute efforts to kill the measure, it stayed in the crime bill that Clinton signed into law in September. The provision banned the further manufacture or import of 19 semiautomatic weapons by name and other weapons if they included certain features — such as folding stocks for rifles and shotguns or, for a pistol, a magazine that attaches outside the grip.

Gun control opponents believe the ban actually contributed to the Republican victory in the 1994 congressional elections by helping defeat some 20 Democrats who had voted for the ban. Clinton himself voiced that view in 1995 when he blamed the Democrats' loss of Congress in part on the NRA. [30] But Handgun Control President Robert J. Walker disagrees. He insists that almost all of the Democrats who lost after voting for the assault weapons ban were from marginal districts anyway and that some supporters of the ban used the issue to help win their campaigns — notably, Rep. Robert G. Torricelli, a New Jersey Democrat who was elected to the Senate.

Whatever the electoral impact, many House Republicans came to Congress committed to repealing the assault weapons ban. The House did approve a repeal measure in March 1996, by a vote of 239-173, but public opinion appeared to be against the move. Senate GOP leader Bob Dole of Kansas, headed toward the Republican presidential nomination, said he would not bring the issue to a vote in the Senate.

Still, gun control opponents continue to insist the measure has done nothing to reduce crime. But a study done for the Justice Department by the Urban Institute estimates that the ban had reduced gun murders by 6.7 percent in 1995. [31]

## Supreme Court Rulings

Meanwhile, the Supreme Court was creating problems for gun control supporters. In 1995, the justices ruled, 5-4, that a 1990 law making it a federal crime to possess a firearm near a school exceeded Congress' power to regulate interstate commerce (*United States v. Lopez*). Two years later, in a more significant case, the court struck down a key part of the Brady Act by the same 5-4 margin. The court's conservative majority declared that the provision requiring local police to conduct background checks on gun purchasers violated state sovereignty. [32]

Gun control supporters tried to minimize the two rulings. Congress approved a slightly revised version of the gun-free school zone law in 1996, circumventing the court's 1995 ruling by requiring prosecutors to prove an impact on interstate commerce as an element of the offense. The law has yet to be tested. As for

* James S. Brady was President Ronald Reagan's press secretary and was shot and seriously wounded during the March 30, 1981, assassination attempt on Reagan.

the Brady Act, its supporters emphasized that most of the provisions, including the mandatory five-day waiting period, were unaffected by the ruling. They also said that most police and sheriffs' departments would continue to do the background checks either voluntarily or because of state law requirements. And they cited Justice Department figures to claim that the law had blocked more than 250,000 sales to people not eligible to buy firearms during its three years on the books. [33]

Not surprisingly, the NRA disputed claims that the law was preventing unauthorized purchases of firearms by pointing to the relatively small number of criminal prosecutions brought under the law. They also said that a better method of enforcing the purchase restrictions was the instant computerized verification system that the law mandated the federal government to institute by the end of 1998.

In both decisions, the majority justices steered clear of any substantive pronouncement about gun control except for Thomas' invocation of the Second Amendment in his controversial footnote. As for the dissenting justices, they argued in both cases that the court should have deferred to Congress' judgment about the need for legislation to control gun violence.

Most legal commentators viewed the decisions as significant for their impact on federalism rather than on gun control. But David Williams, a professor at Indiana University School of Law, says the justices may be preparing to take on the right-to-bear-arms issue. "I don't think it's a coincidence that they're taking all of these federalism decisions [concerning] guns," he says. "They're thinking about federalism and guns together." ■

# CURRENT SITUATION

## Washington State Loss

With about a month before the Nov. 4 election, supporters of the gun safety initiative in Washington were optimistic. Their polls showed 62 percent support for the measure, Initiative 676, which required trigger-locking devices on all handguns sold in the state and handgun safety licenses.

But voters rejected the initiative by 697,000 votes — 71 percent to 29 percent. What happened is a matter of sharp dispute between the opposing sides in the gun control debate.

Opponents of the initiative say they organized an effective grass-roots campaign, with 13,000 in-state contributors, 27,000 volunteers, 83,000 yard signs and 600,000 "door hangers" distributed the weekend before the balloting. "We outworked them in the critical weeks of the campaign," says Alan Gottlieb, director of Washington Citizens Against Regulatory Excess — dubbed WeCARE.

Supporters of Initiative 676 blame their defeat not on a grass-roots campaign but on more than $2 million they say the NRA contributed to help pay for last-minute billboards, print ads and radio and television commercials.

"You can't take that kind of barrage and expect any other result," says Tom Wales, a federal prosecutor who was co-chairman of Washington Citizens for Handgun Safety. "We simply did not have the resources to keep our voice from being drowned out."

The opponents' advertising campaign undercut the initiative's early support by claiming the measure's licensing provisions would entangle gun users in red tape and unnecessary safety training. They also claimed that the measure would expose gun users' medical records to law enforcement agencies and eliminate an existing provision for stalking victims to get expedited processing for gun permits.

Wales says the latter two issues were particularly effective in eroding support among women, its strongest constituency. The initiative's supporters argued in vain that the allegations were false. They said the initiative made the same provision as existing law to require disclosure if a gun permit applicant had been committed to a mental institution. As for stalking victims, they said that local police could still grant waivers of the waiting period if necessary.

Gottlieb says that opponents of the initiative had already started to turn the corner by mid-October, before the big advertising blitz. Polls then showed the measure behind, 46 percent to 49 percent. Opponents continued to gain momentum. All but five Washington newspapers opposed the initiative, as did the influential Washington State Council of Police Officers and the state's association of firearms instructors.

In retrospect, national gun control leaders faulted the initiative's supporters for creating an overly complex measure — eight pages long — and for failing to enlist law enforcement support at the outset. But Wales says supporters met with local law enforcement officials and were convinced there was no way to gain their support. "I'm not sure that doing anything differently would have made any difference," he says.

### *Setback in California*

The defeat came only six weeks after gun control proponents had suffered

# At Issue:

## *Does the Second Amendment guarantee an individual right to keep and bear arms?*

yes

**Tanya K. Metaksa**
***Chief lobbyist, National Rifle Association***

Our Founding Fathers did not create our civil liberties. They safeguarded them in the Bill of Rights, and we all know it's true. Diminish freedom of the press, and we diminish democracy. Usher out the right of the people to peaceable assembly, and we usher in a police state. Abandon the safeguard against unreasonable searches and seizures, and we abandon our homes.

Then there's that Second Amendment.

Second Amendment opponents say the right belongs to states, but consider the words of Yale law Professor Akil Amar. "The ultimate right to keep and bear arms belongs to 'the people' not 'the states.' . . . '[T]he people' at the core of the Second Amendment are the same 'people' at the heart of the Preamble and the First Amendment, namely citizens."

Finding others who concur is hardly difficult. Professor Glenn Harlan Reynolds of the University of Tennessee summed it up by saying that scholars adhering to an individual-rights interpretation, "dominate the academic literature on the Second Amendment almost completely."

Second Amendment opponents say the courts are hostile to this right. Yes, certain jurists have an aversion to certain rights, and no one should be surprised. It's the Murphy's Law of American civil rights.

Duke University's William Van Alstyne argues, "[T]he essential claim advanced by the NRA with respect to the Second Amendment is extremely strong . . . . The constructive role of the NRA today, like the role of the [American Civil Liberties Union] in the 1920s with respect to the First Amendment, ought itself not to be dismissed lightly."

Van Alstyne is saying that while First Amendment jurisprudence didn't begin until the 1920s, no one argues there were no First Amendment rights then, and no one should argue there are no Second Amendment rights now.

Second Amendment opponents say the NRA won't take this right to the Supreme Court, but it is they who fear such a case. When the NRA sought a decision by the Supreme Court in the *Morton Grove* handgun ban on Second Amendment grounds, it was Handgun Control that urged the court not to hear the case.

Half the households in the United States exercise this right. This right empowers Americans to use firearms to thwart crime 2.5 million times annually. This right is why 71 percent of Washington state voters rejected a draconian gun owner registration scheme in the 1997 elections, and why the national trend is toward policies like right to carry.

For indeed, the Second Amendment preserves the greatest human right — the right to defend one's own life.

no

**Dennis A. Henigan**
***Director, Legal Action Project, Center to Prevent Handgun Violence***

*A well regulated Militia, being necessary to the security of a free State, the right of the people to keep and bear Arms, shall not be infringed.*
(Second Amendment to the U.S. Constitution)

In 1991, former Chief Justice Warren Burger referred to the Second Amendment as "the subject of one of the greatest pieces of fraud, I repeat the word 'fraud,' on the American people by special interest groups that I have ever seen in my lifetime." The NRA, Burger said, had "misled the American people and they, I regret to say, they have had far too much influence on the Congress . . . than as a citizen I would like to see — and I am a gun man."

The "fraud" denounced by the chief justice is the inexcusable failure of the gun lobby to acknowledge the full text of the Second Amendment and its consistent interpretation by the courts. The Second Amendment is the only provision in the Bill of Rights with an express statement of its purpose. The grant of the right "to keep and bear arms" is preceded by a preamble the NRA chooses to ignore: "A well regulated Militia, being necessary to the security of a free State. . . ."

The federal courts have unanimously held that the amendment grants the people the right to be armed only in connection with service in state militias. As the Supreme Court has written, the "obvious purpose" of the Second Amendment was "to assure the continuation and render possible the effectiveness" of the state militia, adding that the amendment "must be interpreted and applied with that end in view." And the "well regulated Militia" is not a self-appointed army of "patriots" training for armed resistance to government policies they oppose. Twice the Supreme Court has held that the modern version of the constitutional "militia" is the National Guard.

If the NRA's Charlton Heston is right, and the Second Amendment confers our most important constitutional right, then why did the NRA attack the Brady Act in court as a violation of the Tenth Amendment, but not the Second Amendment? And why doesn't the NRA's lawsuit against the federal assault weapon ban even mention the Second Amendment? Because the NRA is well aware that never in our nation's history has a gun law been struck down on Second Amendment grounds. On this issue, the NRA is not only guilty of fraud, but of hypocrisy as well.

Gun violence is not a constitutional issue; it is a public health and safety issue. The constitutional debate is phony. The 35,000 Americans fatally shot every year are real.

another setback. In the face of strong opposition from the NRA, gun control advocates had pushed a bill through the California Legislature requiring tough safety standards for U.S.-made "Saturday night specials" — more than 80 percent of which are manufactured in the Los Angeles area.

But California's Republican governor, Pete Wilson, vetoed the measure in September, saying it would deprive law-abiding people of a chance to buy inexpensive protection from crime.

Gun control supporters can count some victories during the past year, including the gun-safety regulations in Massachusetts and the defeat of concealed weapons bills in several states. Handgun Control's Sudbay says the group will continue to push for safety legislation in several states, including a bill in New Jersey to require the manufacture of so-called "smart" or personalized handguns that can only be operated by an authorized user. But he concedes that in many other states gun control supporters will be "in a defensive posture," seeking to block passage of concealed weapons laws.

Metaksa says the decisive defeat of the Washington state initiative should thwart efforts to enact similar legislation in other states. "I mean, this wasn't a squeaker," she says. "This was a blowout."

## Standoff in Congress

Even as the Brady Act was being challenged in court, gun control supporters drew up an omnibus gun control bill dubbed Brady II that, among other things, sought to require federal licensing of handgun owners and registration of handgun transfers, raise the minimum age for possession of handguns to 21 and prohibit "Saturday night specials." But political realities forced them to concentrate their efforts on less ambitious goals, like mandatory trigger locks and "one-gun-a-month" limits on handgun purchases to thwart street criminals.

On the opposite side, gun control opponents still want to repeal the assault weapons ban but have likewise bowed to political reality in putting that issue on a back burner. Instead, they spent the past session resisting or trying to undo initiatives from the other side. Early in the session, for example, they unsuccessfully sought to weaken or repeal a provision enacted late in 1996 that barred possession of firearms or ammunition by anyone who had been convicted of a domestic violence offense.

Gun control supporters had the initiative during most of the session. President Clinton endorsed the trigger-lock provision in his State of the Union message. But House GOP leaders kept the provision out of an administration-backed juvenile justice bill, in part to keep any gun issues out of the legislation. After the House approved the bill, supporters of the trigger lock provision were still hoping to add it to the measure in the Senate. But the agreement by the major domestic gunmakers to include trigger locks in newly manufactured guns has all but killed the prospect of congressional legislation.

Apart from the trigger-lock issue, the only other fights over firearms issues were minor skirmishes. Gun control supporters counted as a victory a provision earmarking a modest $1.3 million add-on for the Bureau of Alcohol, Tobacco and Firearms (ATF) to help trace guns used by juveniles in crimes. (*See story, p. 166.*) They also claimed victory in defeating an effort by gun owners' groups to exempt from the assault weapons ban certain U.S. military surplus weapons that had been given to foreign governments and then modified to include features covered by the ban. But supporters of the move succeeded in requiring a study of the issue. "They'll be back," says Handgun Control lobbyist Marie Carbone.

The NRA, still licking its wounds from the setbacks in President Clinton's first term, had no victories to boast of during the past congressional session. But Metaksa took credit for bottling up any gun control initiatives, like the trigger-lock requirement or one-gun-a-month proposal. "So far we've been able to hold off those kinds of proposals both in the House and the Senate," she says.

From her perspective, Carbone says that gun control opponents have a numerical edge in Congress but have been reluctant to use their advantage. "Probably the other side starts out ahead, but they haven't really done anything with that," she says. "I think that shows that basically the American people support our position, and [gun control opponents] have been a little bit reluctant to do things with the [congressional] support that they have." ■

# OUTLOOK

## Unchanging Debate

In a new book, longtime gun control advocates Zimring and Hawkins argue that the overall U.S. crime rate is comparable to the crime rate in other industrialized countries. But the United States does have a significantly higher rate of fatal crimes, they say. And they blame the high death rate on one factor in particular: the distinctly American high level of gun ownership and gun availability.

"The use of firearms in assault and robbery is the single environmental factor of American society that is most clearly linked to the extraordinary death rate from interpersonal violence in the United States," they write. [34]

Gun control supporters have long made that point their central premise: that guns cause crime and that restricting their availability will reduce crime. The NRA and other gun owner groups have a succinct response: "Guns don't kill people, people kill people," they say. The solution to gun crime, they say, is getting tough with criminals, not with gun owners.

Gun control skeptic Kleck dismisses both arguments as simplistic fallacies. Longer prison sentences and other get-tough crime policies, he says, have not been effective in reducing crime levels overall. But gun controls have not been shown by the evidence to have much impact on crime, except for a weak effect on a few specific categories of offenses.

Gun control supporters achieved significant victories in the first two years of the Clinton administration but have been stymied since by an anti-gun control leadership in the Republican-controlled Congress. The safety initiatives being pushed by gun control groups on Capitol Hill and in state capitals represent an end-run around the opposition. Kleck and Zimring both say the efforts are worthwhile, but minimize their long-term significance. "It's an interesting new wrinkle," Zimring says, "but I would be terribly surprised if it became the center of controversy over the next decade."

Politically, the major advocacy groups disagree sharply about the trend on the issue. The NRA's Metaksa says that despite President Clinton's strong support, gun control advocates "have had a harder time over the last few years."

"The momentum is shifting to freedom and to people being responsible for their own actions," she says. "When that happens, I think you will see the proposals by our opponents have less credibility and less support."

"I think they're completely and absolutely wrong," says Handgun Control's Walker. He says most Americans continue to favor moderate gun controls and that support for gun control is generally a plus in political campaigns.

"It's fair to say now that there are as many one-issue voters on our side as there are one-issue voters on the other side," Walker says. "When guns are an issue, a hot issue in the race, we believe that the winner in the vast majority of races is going to be the pro-gun control candidate."

Still, gun control supporters are also pursuing a non-political strategy. "Some people I talk to in the gun control movement say their best hope is through litigation," says Duke's Cook. "They have seen what the attorneys general have done through the tobacco litigation, and they see that as a model of what they can do in terms of the kinds of guns or types of ammunition that can be marketed. That gives them the possibility of a big win without having to go through the state legislatures or Congress."

So far, however, gun control ad-

## FOR MORE INFORMATION

**American Shooting Sports Council,** 1845 The Exchange, Suite 150, Atlanta, Ga. 30339; 770-933-0200; www.assc.org. The trade association represents gun manufacturers, retailers and distributors.

**Bureau of Alcohol, Tobacco and Firearms,** Department of the Treasury, 650 Massachusetts Ave., N.W., Suite 8100; Washington, D.C. 20226; (202) 927-7970; www.atf.treas.gov/. The ATF enforces federal gun laws.

**Citizens Committee for the Right to Keep and Bear Arms,** 12500 N.E. Tenth Pl., Bellevue, Wash. 98005; 425-454-4911; www.ccrkba.org. The committee, founded in 1974, claims about 600,000 members and supporters.

**Coalition to Stop Gun Violence,** 1000 16th St. N.W., Suite 603, Washington, D.C. 20036; 202-530-0340; www.gunfree.org. The coalition is the successor organization to the National Coalition to Ban Handguns, founded in 1974, and continues to favor the ultimate goal of banning all handguns in the United States.

**Gun Owners of America,** 8001 Forbes Place, Suite 102; Springfield, Va. 22151; 703-321-8585; cgibin.erols.com/crfields. Founded in 1975, the group claims about 180,000 members.

**Handgun Control Inc.,** 1225 I St. N.W., Suite 1100, Washington, D.C. 20005; 202-898-0792; www.handguncontrol.org. Founded in 1974 as the National Council to Control Handguns, this is the largest of the gun control advocacy groups, claiming 400,000 members.

**National Rifle Association,** 11250 Waples Mill Rd., Fairfax, Va. 22030; 703-267-1000; www.nra.org. The NRA, founded in 1871 and with a current claimed membership of 3 million, has been a powerful lobbying force against firearms regulations since the 1930s.

**Police Foundation,** 1201 Connecticut Ave. N.W., Suite 200, Washington, D.C. 20036; 202-833-1460. The foundation is a privately funded, independent organization established by the Ford Foundation in 1970 for the purpose of supporting improvements in policing; it supports gun control.

**Violence Policy Center,** 1350 Connecticut Ave. N.W., Suite 825, Washington, D.C. 20036; 202-822-8200; www.vpc.org. The center was founded in 1988 as a research and advocacy group on gun control issues.

vocates have not won final rulings imposing liability on gun manufacturers or dealers for gun injuries or deaths. Still, gun manufacturers are sufficiently concerned that they have lobbied Congress to include protective provisions in pending product liability overhaul bills.

Meanwhile, the central issues remain much the same today as they have been for decades. "The core concerns of the gun debate may never change," Zimring says. "They haven't changed in a generation."

"What you've had here for a long time is a yin and yang thing, more back and forth," says author Weir. "I think it's a controversy that will probably be around for a long time." ■

## Notes

[1] For background, see "Juvenile Justice," *The CQ Researcher,* Feb. 25, 1994, pp. 169-192.

[2] For detailed background on the initiative, see Barbara A. Serrano, "Gun Measure Isn't as Simple as It Seems," *The Seattle Times,* Oct. 26, 1997, p. A1. See also *The New York Times,* Oct. 13, 1997, p. A1.

[3] For background, see "Gun Control," *The CQ Researcher,* June 10, 1994, pp. 505-528.

[4] See William Weir, *A Well Regulated Militia: The Battle for Gun Control* (1997).

[5] Gary Kleck, *Targeting Guns: Firearms and Their Control* (1997). The book is an updated and less technical version of Kleck's earlier book, *Point Blank: Guns and Violence in America* (1991).

[6] See *The Boston Globe,* March 22, 1996.

[7] The states are California, Connecticut, Delaware, Florida, Hawaii, Iowa, Maryland, Minnesota, Nevada, New Jersey, North Carolina, Rhode Island, Texas, Virginia and Wisconsin.

[8] Philip J. Cook and Jens Ludwig, "Guns in America: Results of a Comprehensive National Survey on Gun Ownership and Use," Police Foundation, May 1997, pp. 20-21.

[9] Quoted in *USA Today,* Oct. 10, 1997. See also *The New York Times,* Oct. 9, 1997, p. A1.

[10] Quoted in *St. Petersburg Times,* May 13, 1987.

[11] See *The Washington Post,* March 23, 1997, p. C5.

[12] See David McDowall, Colin Loftin and Brian Wieresma, "Easing Concealed Firearms Law: Effects on Homicides in Three States," *Journal of Criminal Law and Criminology,* Vol. 86 (fall 1995), pp. 193-206. See also *The New York Times,* March 15, 1995, p. A23. The other cities studied were Jacksonville, Miami, Tampa and Jackson, Miss.

[13] See John R. Lott Jr. and David B. Mustard, "Crime, Deterrence, and Right-to-Carry Concealed Handguns," *Journal of Legal Studies,* January 1997, pp. 1-68. See also John R. Lott Jr., "More Guns, Less Violent Crime," *The Wall Street Journal,* Aug. 28, 1996, p. A13.

[14] See Franklin Zimring and Gordon Hawkins, "Concealed Handguns: The Counterfeit Debate," *The Responsive Community,* spring 1997, p. 55.

[15] Dan A. Black and Daniel S. Nagin, "Do 'Right-to-Carry' Laws Deter Violent Crime?" *Journal of Legal Studies,* January 1998 [forthcoming]. The Black-Nagin study was first circulated in October 1996.

[16] Albert W. Alschuler, "Two Guns, Four Guns, Six Guns, More Guns: Does Arming the Public Reduce Crime," *Valparaiso University Law Review,* Vol. 31 (1997), pp. 1-9.

[17] Zimring and Hawkins, *op. cit.,* pp. 45-60. Zimring is a professor of law at the University of California at Berkeley; Hawkins is a retired professor of criminology at the University of Sydney, in Australia.

[18] See John R. Lott Jr., "The Concealed Handgun Debate," *Journal of Legal Studies,* January 1998 [forthcoming]. See also John R. Lott Jr., *More Guns, Less Crime: Understanding Crime and Gun Control Laws* (University of Chicago Press, April 1998) [forthcoming].

[19] Quoted in *Fairfax Journal,* July 9, 1997, p. 1.

[20] Quoted in Ellen Perlman, "Living With Concealed Weapons," *Governing,* February 1996, p. 34.

[21] The case is *Nunn v. State* (1846), cited in Weir, *op. cit.,* p. 37.

[22] The case is *Printz v. United States.* Story's reference came from his book *Commentaries* (1833).

[23] See Antonin Scalia, *A Matter of Interpretation: Federal Courts and the Law* (1997), pp. 136-137 n. 13 ("It would also be strange to find in the midst of a catalog of the rights of individuals a provision securing to the states the right to maintain a designated 'Militia'.")

[24] Much of the historical background is drawn from Weir, *op. cit.*

[25] *Ibid.,* p. 41.

[26] The case is *Quilici v. Village of Morton Grove.*

[27] See *1986 Congressional Quarterly Almanac,* pp. 82-86.

[28] See Weir, *op. cit.,* pp. 100-104 ("cop-killer bullets"), pp. 105-107 ("plastic pistols").

[29] See Weir, *op. cit.,* pp. 221-222.

[30] *Cleveland Plain Dealer,* Jan. 14, 1995, p. 1A. ("The NRA's the reason the Republicans control the House," Clinton was quoted as saying.)

[31] Urban Institute, "Impact Evaluation of the Public Safety and Recreational Firearms Use Protection Act of 1994," Feb. 19, 1997.

[32] See Kenneth Jost, *Supreme Court Yearbook, 1994-1995,* pp. 43-46; *Supreme Court Yearbook,* 1996-1997, pp. 45-49.

[33] See U.S. General Accounting Office, "Implementation of the Brady Handgun Violence Prevention Act," January 1996.

[34] Franklin E. Zimring and Gordon Hawkins, *Crime Is Not the Problem: Lethal Violence in America* (1997), p. 122.

# Bibliography

## *Selected Sources Used*


### *Books*

**Davidson, Osha Gray, *Under Fire: The NRA and the Battle for Gun Control*, Henry Holt, 1993.**
Davidson provides a critical journalistic account of the history and role of the National Rifle Association (NRA) in the gun control debate. The book includes an 11-page bibliography.

**Kleck, Gary, *Targeting Guns: Firearms and Their Control*, Aldine de Gruyter, 1997.**
Kleck, a professor of criminology at Florida State University, argues with detailed statistical evidence that the availability of guns has no net impact on violent crime rates and that gun control laws have not been shown to produce net reductions in gun-related crimes. The book includes a 33-page list of references.

**LaPierre, Wayne R., *Guns, Crime, and Freedom*, Regnery, 1995.**
LaPierre, executive vice president of the NRA, strongly argues against gun control measures on constitutional and policy grounds. The book includes source notes and a list of law review articles on both sides of the issue.

**Weir, William, *A Well Regulated Militia: The Battle Over Gun Control*, Archon, 1997.**
Weir, who says he is a member of both Handgun Control and the National Rifle Association, accuses both sides in the gun control debate of pushing "shocking" amounts of misinformation and ignoring deeper causes of violence in the United States. The book includes detailed source notes and a 14-page bibliography.

**Zimring, Franklin E., and Gordon Hawkins, *The Citizen's Guide to Gun Control*, Macmillan, 1987.**
Zimring and Hawkins provide a "non-technical" guide to the issue. Zimring is director of the Earl Warren Legal Institute at the University of California at Berkeley; Hawkins, now retired, was director of the Institute of Criminology at the University of Sydney. In their new book, *Crime Is Not the Problem* (Oxford University, 1997), they argue that the United States' distinctive crime problem is gun violence rather than overall crime.

### *Reports and Studies*

**Cook, Philip J., and Jens Ludwig, "Guns in America: Results of a Comprehensive National Survey on Firearms Ownership and Use," Police Foundation, May 1997.**
The 94-page summary report is most noteworthy for a controversial section that reports — and then criticizes — a survey finding indicating widespread defensive gun use in the U.S.


**The Second Amendment: A Bibliographical Note**

A committed group of scholars has forcefully argued that the Second Amendment protects an individual's right to own and use firearms, while gun control proponents defend the established judicial view that the amendment protects only the right of the states to maintain a militia.

For two book-length expositions of the individual-right thesis, see Joyce Malcolm, *To Keep and Bear Arms: The Origins of an Anglo-American Right* (Harvard University Press, 1994), and Stephen P. Halbrook, *That Every Man Be Armed: The Evolution of a Constitutional Right* (University of New Mexico Press, 1984). Malcolm is a professor of history at Bentley College; Halbrook, a Fairfax, Va., attorney, argued the successful challenge to the Brady Act before the Supreme Court, though not on Second Amendment grounds.

The first major law review article to set forth the individual-right thesis is Don B. Kates Jr., "Handgun Prohibition and the Original Meaning of the Second Amendment," *Michigan Law Review,* Vol. 82, 1983, pp. 204-273; Kates is a San Francisco attorney. Two liberal constitutional experts have adopted, at least in part, the individual-right view: Sanford Levinson, "The Embarrassing Second Amendment" (*Yale Law Journal,* Vol. 99, 1989, pp. 637-659); and William Van Alstyne, "The Second Amendment and the Personal Right to Arms" (*Duke Law Journal,* Vol. 43, 1994, pp. 1236-1255). Levinson is at the University of Texas Law School, Van Alstyne at Duke Law School.

The major law review articles refuting the individual-right thesis include two authored or co-authored by Dennis A. Henigan, director of the legal action project of the Center to Prevent Handgun Violence: "Arms, Anarchy and the Second Amendment," *Valparaiso University Law Review,* Vol. 26, 1991, pp. 107-129; and "The Second Amendment in the Twentieth Century: Have You Seen Your Militia Lately?" *University of Dayton Law Review,* Vol. 15, 1989, pp. 5-58 (co-authored with Keith A. Ehrman, a San Francisco lawyer).

David C. Williams, a law professor at Indiana University, criticizes the contemporary relevance of the "citizen militia" in his article "Civic Republicanism and the Citizen Militia: The Terrifying Second Amendment," *Yale Law Journal,* Vol. 101, 1991, pp. 551-615. Historian Gary Wills sharply challenges the historical accuracy of the Second Amendment advocates' thesis in "To Keep and Bear Arms," *New York Review of Books,* Sept. 21, 1995, pp. 62-73.

# 10 Internet Privacy

**DAVID MASCI**

Every day, millions of on-line consumers turn to the Internet to find everything from tips on travel to advice on healthy eating.

Many click on the popular GeoCities site. Not surprisingly, GeoCities wants something in return: marketable personal information. To encourage visitors to fill out questionnaires and reveal their names, incomes and other personal data, GeoCities offers them free E-mail accounts and their own Web home page.

In the past, GeoCities promised that the personal information being collected would not be shared "with anyone without your permission." But on Aug. 13, 1998, the Federal Trade Commission (FTC) accused GeoCities of breaking its promise.

"GeoCities has misled its customers, both children and adults, by not telling the truth about how it was using their personal information,"said Jodie Bernstein, director of the FTC's Bureau of Consumer Protection, in a statement released that day.

According to the commission, GeoCities shared information about more than 2 million of its Web users with outside parties without receiving or even asking for permission. The data was used to create advertisements and solicitations personalized to appeal to the original GeoCities visitors.

"GeoCities was collecting all this sensitive information and the people [who had completed questionnaires] didn't realize what was going on," says Deirdre Mulligan, staff counsel at the Center for Democracy and Technology. "They didn't know what they were giving away."

Of course, much of the Internet, almost by definition, is not private.

From *The CQ Researcher,* November 6, 1998.

Indeed, the new medium connects people around the world in a way that few could have dreamed about. Created by the Pentagon in the 1970s as an alternate means of communication during wartime, the net now offers tens of millions of ordinary people access to an amount of information that would dwarf what is stored in the Library of Congress.

The Internet has been hailed as the most important communications development since Guttenburg invented movable type more than 500 years ago. As with the advent of printing, the creation of the Internet has led to an information explosion that is rapidly transforming almost every sphere of life, from education to communications to retail commerce.

The number of people on-line is growing exponentially. Just four years ago, there were only about 3 million Internet users around the world, mostly in the United States. At the beginning of this year, the number had ballooned to nearly 60 million in the U.S. alone and more than 100 million worldwide. [1]

Along with an increase in the number of people on-line has come a corresponding growth in commercial use. Established retailers and a host of newcomers have created Web sites to hawk everything from rare books to sex toys. By the end of last year, 10 million people worldwide had purchased a product or service on-line. [2]

But the Internet, like most new technologies, presents challenges as well as tremendous opportunities for society. Every day, millions of Americans disclose personal information about themselves when they buy goods or services from an on-line business or simply visit Web sites. In many cases, companies that operate these sites offer few or no assurances as to how this information will be used. Many, in fact, trade or sell consumers' names and addresses and other data to retailers and marketers. Other companies have sprung up solely for the purpose of collecting and selling personal information.

The growth of such on-line enterprises has prompted many policymakers and others to question whether they have the right to acquire and, more importantly, pass on personal data to third parties. And if so, should the Web sites be required to tell consumers what they intend to do with the birth dates, E-mail addresses and telephone numbers they are collecting?

According to an FTC study released on June 4, only 14 percent of commercial Web sites publicly disclosed their privacy policies. At the same time, 92 percent, collected personal information from users who visited them. [3] Another survey, conducted by *Business Week* in March, found that non-users of the Internet cite privacy concerns as their main reason for not going on-line. [4]

For its part, GeoCities acknowledged no wrongdoing and paid no fine. Yet, as part of a settlement with the FTC, it did agree to establish and enforce a new privacy policy. Now, when on-line consumers complete the GeoCities' questionnaire, they are told that the information will be released to outside parties.

Indeed, the FTC could not force GeoCities to stop passing on personal information. It is only empowered to act against what it sees as "deceptive

## Most Web Sites Collect Personal Information

*The vast majority of Web sites collect personal information from on-line consumers, and most collect several types of information, such as name, address, Social Security number and birth date.*

**Percent of Web Sites Collecting Personal Information**

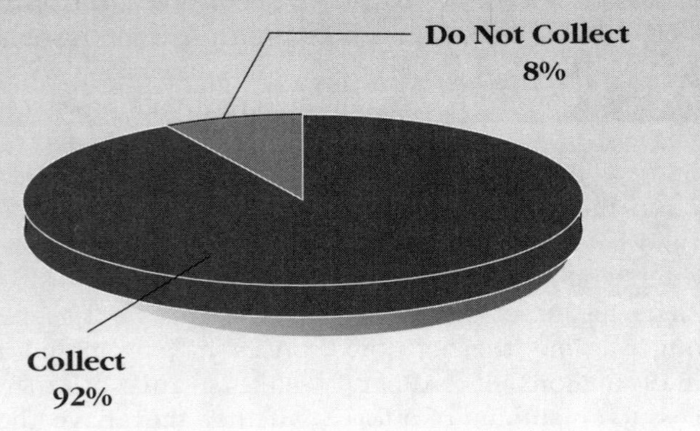


*Source: "Privacy Online: A Report to Congress," Federal Trade Commission, June 1998.*

practices," such as claiming you're not passing on private information when you actually are. "We are not trying to tell them what their privacy policies ought to be," said Toby Levin, staff counsel at the FTC. [5]

That's part of the problem, say many privacy advocates. They point out that because there is no law protecting privacy on-line, Web sites are not obligated to do so. In fact, say some, the GeoCities case may end up doing more harm than good. "It has had a perversely undesirable effect in that it has convinced companies on-line not to post privacy policies so as to avoid any [FTC] scrutiny," says Jason Catlett, president of Junkbusters Corp., a New Jersey on-line-privacy protection firm. In other words, if there is no posted policy, there can be no deceptive practices.

Privacy advocates like Catlett say that the current system, where Web sites establish and enforce their own privacy policies if at all, is terribly flawed. They are urging the Clinton administration and Congress to step in with legislation aimed at protecting consumer privacy on-line. "We need to lay down some rules, simple do's and don'ts, for on-line privacy," says Jerry Berman, executive director at the Center for Democracy and Technology, a civil liberties group that focuses on technology issues. Among other things, such rules would give consumers the right to see the information collected about them and the ability to stop its dissemination to third parties.

In addition, Berman and others favor the creation of a privacy agency within the federal government to enforce the new rules and advise businesses on how to establish effective privacy policies. The FTC, they say, does not have the staff to police the Internet for evidence of deceptive practices (its current mandate), let alone enforce new privacy laws. [6]

Privacy advocates admit that there are Web sites, usually created by large businesses, that do have adequate privacy policies. But the majority of on-line sites offer consumers little or no protection when it comes to maintaining the confidentiality of personal information.

The computer and retail industries argue, however, that government regulation is unnecessary and unrealistic. To begin with, they say, the Internet is still taking shape, making talk of rigid rules on privacy unrealistic. "At this stage, trying to nail down some policy with legislation might not work and could end up retarding the growth of on-line commerce," says Russ Bodoff, the general manager for the Better Business Bureau On-line, an industry group that aims to make self-regulation work.

Bodoff says that his organization and others like it have helped hundreds of Web sites create and enforce privacy standards. Already, supporters of self-regulation say, most of the biggest and most well-known sites have privacy policies. "With a little bit of guidance, self-regulation can be as effective as legislation," Bodoff claims.

Finally, self-regulation boosters argue, the on-line industry has an interest in guaranteeing privacy since consumers who feel abused by Web sites won't visit them again. Says Chet Dalzell, a spokesman for the Direct Marketing Association: "Marketers and retailers on-line know that they have to extend a certain amount of privacy and make sure transactions are secure in order to ensure that customers will visit or shop at their Web site."

As Dalzell suggests, privacy doesn't just entail creating a policy or rules to protect the confidentiality of information. Transactions and other communications must be secure from those who do not want to follow any rules that might be set.

Computers, as well as phones and other communications tools, secure the transfer of data by using encryption technology. Encryption software protects information by scrambling it into

## Few Sites Disclose Information Policy

*Less than 15 percent of the Web sites that collect personal information tell consumers who is collecting the information and how it will be used.*

**Percent of Web Sites With an Information Disclosure**

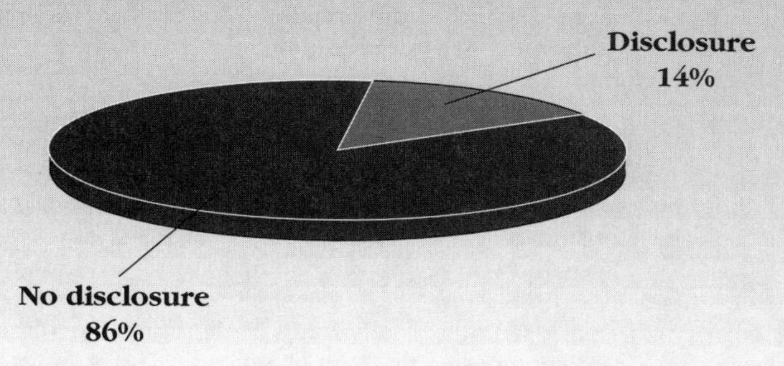


*Source: "Privacy Online: A Report to Congress," Federal Trade Commission, June 1998*

an unreadable code at its source and unscrambling it when it is received.

Encryption is already widely used on-line in the United States to protect everything from sensitive E-mail to credit card numbers. But the intelligence and law-enforcement communities are wary of the potential for the misuse of this technology.

Currently, the United States bans the export of powerful encryption technology. The intelligence community argues that such controls are needed to keep powerful technology out of the hands of America's enemies, who would use it to thwart U.S. intelligence-gathering efforts.

"If this were easily obtainable, our ability to keep apprised of what terrorists and other enemies were doing would be severely hampered," says Dan Smith, chief of research for the Center for Defense Information, a pro-defense think tank. The ban should be kept in place even if it only delays states like Iraq and Libya from acquiring sophisticated encryption technology. "At least we have more time . . . to stay one step ahead of them," he says.

At the same time, the law-enforcement community is pressing Congress to require software makers to install a "key" or "back door" in their encryption programs, making it possible for state and federal officers to decode encrypted data. "When we obtain a court-ordered warrant, we should be able to access the encrypted information, just like we can wiretap phones and search homes today," says Charles Barry Smith, a special agent and encryption expert at the FBI. Most programs today contain no such key, often making data retrieval difficult if not impossible.

Smith and others say that criminals and terrorists are increasingly using computers to store information and to communicate with each other. And, they claim, strong encryption programs are already hampering law enforcement's efforts to conduct surveillance and gather evidence in many cases.

But privacy advocates and the computer industry oppose both existing and proposed limits on encryption technology. To begin with, they argue, export controls are merely hurting American companies, which are losing this segment of the overseas software market to European and Asian corporations. "By hamstringing U.S. companies, we've simply created an opportunity for foreign firms to take over a market that should be ours," says Solveig Singleton, director of information studies at the CATO Institute. Some of this advanced, foreign encryption is available to America's enemies, defeating the purpose of the export limits in the first place.

In addition, privacy advocates argue, the proposed "key" to allow law enforcement to unlock encrypted information defeats the whole purpose of protecting your data. "It doesn't make any sense: Why would you want encryption that could be opened by a third party?" asks Marc Rottenberg, director of the Electronic Privacy Information Center, which promotes on-line privacy and other civil liberties.

Questions concerning encryption or the regulation of Web sites will take on increasing importance as more and more people spend more and more time on-line. Other privacy concerns also have come to the fore. For instance, many experts, including some in the business community, supported the recent successful effort in Congress to enact legal protections for children's privacy on-line. Many of the same people also favor some sort of special protection for medical records and other very sensitive information.

As these and other issues are debated, here are some of the questions Internet experts are asking:

### *Should the federal government set privacy standards for the Internet?*

On Friday, July 31, Vice President Al Gore delivered what was dubbed as a "major" speech on Internet pri-

## Data-Collection Business Is Booming

In today's hyperconnected world, it's not difficult to find personal information about someone. Most search engines have "people finders" or "personal locators" that supply telephone numbers, street addresses, and even directions to people's houses. For a little money, say $25, one can obtain someone's Social Security number, previous addresses and possibly their driving record.

And that's just the tip of the iceberg. "Most people don't realize how much information about them is out there," says Deirdra Mulligan, staff counsel at the Center for Democracy and Technology.

"We should be worried about this," agrees Mary Griffin, counsel for the Consumers Union of the United States. "People just don't know how little privacy protection they have when it comes to this stuff."

Particularly worrisome, say privacy advocates like Griffin, are the hundreds of companies in the United States today that devote themselves to collecting an unfathomable amount of information about almost everyone in the country. Some can provide detailed financial histories, including information about bank accounts, credit card balances and loans. Others offer employment records or track buying habits.

"They have gone on an information-collecting binge," says Charles Morgan Jr., chief executive for Arkansas-based Acxiom Co., one of the largest information-collection firms in the country. "There's just this insatiable appetite for more information to make better decisions." [1]

The information these firms collect is used for a variety of purposes, from running credit checks to creating marketing campaigns. And the data comes from a huge number of sources. When someone fills out a credit-card application, registers with a club, completes a survey or enters a contest, there is a good chance that the information they have given will end up with one or more of these firms. Much of the information also comes from government agencies. "With so much public information on-line, it's easy to find out a lot about someone," says Pamela Rucker, a spokeswoman for the National Retail Federation.

There has long been a wealth of information available about Americans. After all, the United States has always been a consumer-driven and legalistic society. But until recently, there was no affordable way to collect, store and retrieve this data. Computers — and later the Internet — changed that. "The information was always there, but it took technology to enable them to use it properly," Rucker says.

And the opportunities offered by technology have led to an explosion of new data-collection firms. In the last five years alone — the period paralleling Internet growth — the number of firms has increased by a factor of 10. Today, there are more than 1,000 companies collecting and selling information. [2]

Many observers complain that the rush to collect personal information that has followed the computer and Internet revolutions has not been accompanied by proper efforts to protect privacy. "Technology is clearly ahead of policy here," Griffin says. Jason Catlett, president of Junkbusters Corp., a privacy-protection firm, agrees. "What we have is really a form of surveillance."

Griffin and others think that anyone who collects information from a consumer should be required to give the consumer the option of prohibiting disclosure to outside parties. For example, she says,"When you filled out a credit-card application, there would be a box you could check giving you the right to stop the transfer of that information to others."

But those who collect and use the information counter that the services they provide are integral to the flow of modern commerce in the Information Age. For example, they say, when people apply for credit cards or auto insurance, credit checks can be run almost instantaneously. Consumers may value their privacy, but they value convenience even more. "Consumers don't want it tomorrow, they want it now or yesterday," Rucker says.

[1] Quoted in Robert O'Harrow, "Data Firms Getting Too Personal?" *The Washington Post*, March 8, 1998.

[2] *Ibid.*

vacy at the White House. Gore, who has long had an interest in the Net and is the administration's point man on technology issues, addressed computer industry executives, privacy advocates and others. "Privacy is a basic American value — in the Information Age and in every age," Gore said. "And it must be protected." [7]

The vice president went on to say that the nation needed a "Privacy Bill of Rights," so as to guarantee that Web sites do not acquire and use information in ways that are unfair to consumers. "You should have the right to choose whether your personal information is disclosed," Gore said. "You should have the right to know how, when and how much of that information is being used; and you should have the right to see it yourself."

But while Gore called for new legislation to protect children's privacy on-line, he stopped short of asking Congress to codify his Bill of Rights. Instead, he urged the on-line industry to step up its efforts at self-regulation, a policy long supported by the Clinton administration. [8]

For many privacy advocates in attendance that day, like the Electronic Privacy Information Center's Rottenberg, Gore's speech "came up short." According to Rottenberg and others, the vice president should have used the address to call for comprehensive privacy legislation. "The time has come to establish certain privacy protections in law, period," Rottenberg says.

Rottenberg and others argue that legal protections are needed because the on-line industry has shown — after being given years to establish and enforce effective privacy standards — that it is incapable of policing itself. "The industry is clearly not doing enough on its own," says Berman of the Center for Democracy and Technology.

While Berman admits that there are "some companies, usually big, established ones, that play by the rules, many don't recognize privacy concerns at all." A lot of these bad actors are "small start-ups that aren't aware that they have a responsibility to consumers." Like Rottenberg, Berman argues that "we will probably need some legislation to establish some minimum privacy benchmarks."

Those benchmarks, Berman says, include the protections mentioned by Gore: the right to choose whether your personal information can be disseminated and, if permission is given, to know how the data will be used. In addition, Berman says, "there has to be accountability, some sort of punishment for [the site] or remedy for the individuals" who have had their privacy violated.

Finally, opponents of self-regulation say, there should be an agency or office to oversee and, if necessary, enforce privacy protections. "You need an office with some staff and resources and authority to make some decisions," Rottenberg says, adding that the president could appoint a "privacy czar" patterned after the drug czar, a position created in 1987 to coordinate the war against illegal narcotics.

Currently, the FTC has a role in overseeing privacy issues on-line. But while the agency has studied the issue and made recommendations, it has no authority to regulate the fair use of information on the Internet. Indeed, all it can do is prosecute deceptive or fraudulent practices. In the case of privacy, that means that if a Web site posts a policy but does not follow its own rules, the agency can prosecute it for deceiving the site's users.

But, says Beth Givens, director of the Privacy Rights Clearinghouse, a privacy advocacy group in San Diego, even in the deceptive-practices arena, the agency does not have the resources to prosecute any but the most egregious cases. "If the FTC gets enough complaints about someone, they may eventually decide to do something," she says. "But if Jane or John Q. Grievance wants redress, the FTC is not strong enough to help."

The FTC's weakness points to the need for a new privacy agency, she and others say. It would not only enforce new privacy laws but also represent the United States in the international arena. "This is something that could actually be good for business," says Robert Gellman, a privacy consultant in Washington, D.C., who opposes comprehensive privacy legislation but favors a privacy agency. For instance, he says, such an office could negotiate with the European Union as it begins implementing the on-line privacy directive that it put into effect in October. *(See story, p. 182.)* "Right now, we really have no one to speak for us on this issue except the FTC, and they're only interested in privacy when they get a headline out of it," Gellman says, adding that most other developed countries already have a privacy agency or office.

But many supporters of self-regula-

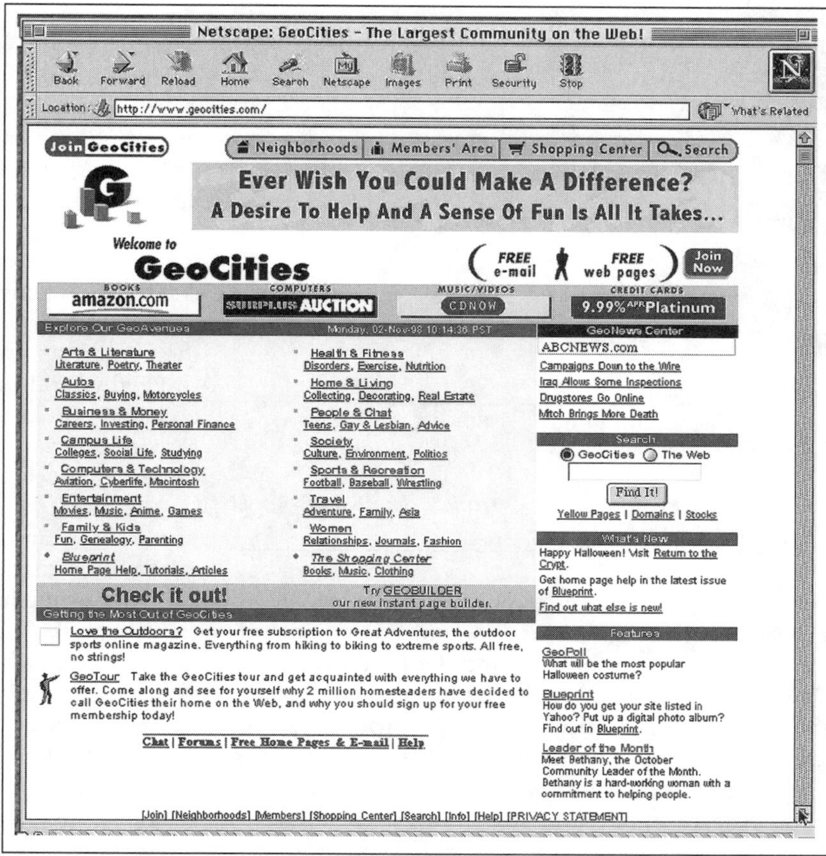

*After the Federal Trade Commission accused the popular GeoCities Web site of misleading on-line visitors, it agreed to disclose that it releases personal information about visitors to outside parties.*

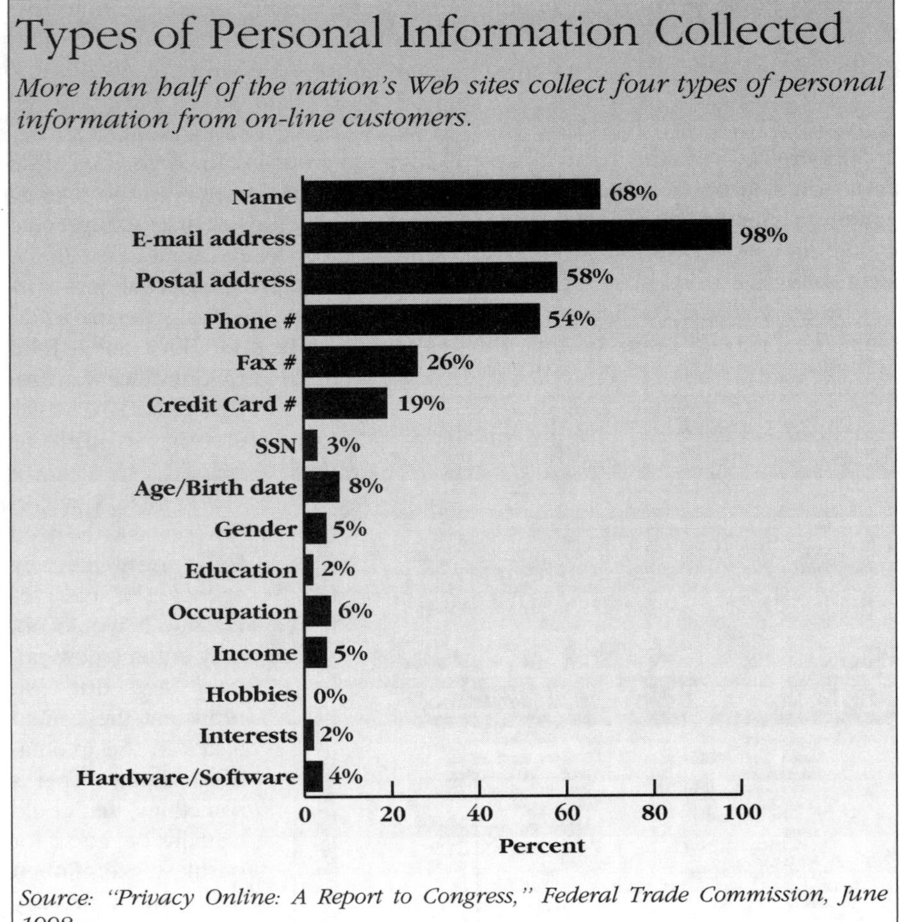

*Source: "Privacy Online: A Report to Congress," Federal Trade Commission, June 1998*

tion claim that privacy agencies and laws would be nothing less than Orwellian. "The government shouldn't try to be big brother," said Ira Magaziner, one of President Clinton's leading advisers on the Internet. Regulations, Magaziner said recently, are "a knee-jerk reaction of the industrial age, when government was expected to protect you. In the digital age, there are new paradigms; one of them is to empower people by giving them the tools to protect themselves." [9]

Others who oppose government action point out that most Web sites are now trying to post and enforce privacy policies. "The majority of Web sites where there is shopping and things like that have privacy policies posted," says Dalzell of the Direct Marketing Association (DMA). Indeed, several organizations, including the DMA and the Better Business Bureau (BBB), have created privacy guidelines for members. Some groups, like the BBB, even have a "seal of approval" for sites that meet their standards.

Supporters of self-regulation also point out that Web sites will protect consumer privacy if for no other reason than it's good business. "Consumers will only go where they feel comfortable, and businesses on-line and elsewhere know that," says Mark Uncapher, vice president of the Information Technology Association of America, an industry group. "That fact, more than anything else, will drive self-regulation."

Other opponents of government action argue that privacy restrictions might put many sites out of business, since the personal information they receive is sometimes a substantial source of revenue, especially for less well-established businesses. According to CATO's Singleton, people who favor protecting privacy sometimes forget that it also "entails limiting the kind of information businesses can exchange with each other," she says. "Now that may not sink a big company, but many businesses on the Web are small and not profitable," she adds.

For example, Singleton says, many magazines are trying to stay afloat by selling targeted advertising, which appeals to the specific interests of each user. "Regular banner ads aren't lucrative," she says. But in order to sell targeted adds, the site must know something about the users, such as their interests, age and education.

Finally, and perhaps most important, self-regulation boosters argue, it is premature to talk about privacy regulation because the Internet is still in its infancy. "E-commerce was born just a few years ago, so this is a new area where marketers are still learning and struggling to determine the right formula," Dalzell says.

Gellman, while less optimistic about the promise of self-regulation, agrees that a comprehensive law on privacy would be hard, if not impossible, to write for the Internet at this or any time. "It's so hard to distinguish between industries, types of records and other things that writing rules would be very difficult," he says. "I mean, should the rules for access to medical records be the same as those for pizza delivery records?"

Uncapher agrees, adding that even if effective rules for today could be drafted, it would be counterproductive at this stage in the Internet's development to try to pin down a lasting policy. "The medium is growing so quickly," he says, "that it's impossible to come up with hard-and-fast rules on something like privacy."

But privacy advocates counter that the Internet is not beyond the grasp of effective regulation. "That argument is a cop-out because no change that would come, no growth in the Net, would obviate the need for basic protections, like requiring [Web sites] to disclose how they're using the information they gather," Givens says.

Rottenberg agrees that the argument against regulation is specious. "They don't think it's possible to enact legal safeguards for privacy because the technical changes are coming too fast," he says. "But they do believe in legal safeguards for copyrights and patents, which also concern fast-changing technology."

In addition, Givens, Rottenberg and others argue, consumers alone will not drive privacy policy. For one thing, they say, many people don't think or care about privacy issues. Others are simply not aware that their personal information is being taken and used by the Web sites they visit. "We could do all the best consumer education in the world," Givens says, "but there will always be people who will be vulnerable to abuse and deception."

### *Should encryption technology be free from export and other restrictions?*

A recent television advertisement depicts a man working at a computer while his wife reads the newspaper. "Hon, do we have encryption software on our computer?" she asks. "Yeah," he says. "That makes it safe to do our bills on here. Encryption locks our private information." His wife then points out that "Washington" wants to acquire the "key" to encryption programs, making everyone's sensitive information open to possible government scrutiny. "Should we trust Washington bureaucrats with the key to our private lives?" she asks. [10]

The commercial is reminiscent of the famous "Harry and Louise" spot, in which another anxious husband and wife worried about President Clinton's plans to overhaul the nation's health-care system. That advertisement is credited with helping kill the health-reform initiative.

**Today, with millions of shoppers using credit cards on-line and millions more sending important information via E-mail, encryption has become a major tool of commerce.**

The fact that "Harry and Louise" are now talking about encryption at all is testament to how far the Information Age has penetrated daily life. Until the 1990s, encryption technology was largely the provenance of the national-security community, a technology used to protect sensitive data from the Soviet Union and other unfriendly powers. Today, with millions of shoppers using credit cards on-line and millions more sending important information via E-mail, encryption has become a major tool of commerce.

Encryption software protects data by scrambling it into an unreadable code. Only someone with companion software can decode the message and read the data. As the husband in the television commercial says, this allows consumers to send their credit card number or a sensitive document on the Internet, secure in the knowledge that it will be seen only by those authorized to see it.

And security is important. When someone sends an E-mail message or purchases something with a credit card on-line, the information is often routed through a number of computers — sometimes more than a dozen. At any one of these junctures, the data can be intercepted and downloaded by a third party without anyone else's knowledge.

Currently, there are no limits on the use of encryption technology in the United States. Any person or company can buy the most powerful program available. Indeed, many companies that have a presence on the Web are employing powerful encryption programs to ensure that transactions are secure.

But export controls limit the sale of much of the more powerful encryption programs overseas, even to America's closest allies in Europe and Asia. These controls, which have been in place for decades, are meant to keep the technology out of the hands of America's enemies by keeping it close to home. Less powerful encryption programs can be exported. Indeed, the Clinton administration recently eased up on some of these export restrictions. Still, the most powerful, and hence popular, U.S. encryption products are generally not available overseas.

In addition to export controls, the law-

## Europe Protects On-line Privacy

While policy-makers in the United States debate the need for formal on-line privacy protection, their counterparts in the European Union (EU) have already embraced it.

The Directive on Personal Data Protection has been hailed as a model for the United States. It incorporates the basic principles espoused by American privacy advocates, giving individuals significant control over the use of sensitive personal information about them, such as health and financial records.

The directive gives EU citizens the right to see any information a Web site has collected about them. It also requires data collectors to inform citizens how the information will be used and empowers individuals to prohibit sites from passing on data to third parties.

But American businesses, and others, argue that the EU directive could severely hamper both traditional and Internet commerce in Europe and the United States. In particular, American companies complain about a provision in the law prohibiting the export of sensitive information to countries, like the U.S., that do not have similar privacy protections.

If that provision were enforced and the United States did not enact its own privacy-protection law, the flow of credit card numbers, addresses and similar information from Europe could grind to a halt, and with it much transatlantic commerce. "The potential for disruption here is enormous," says Chet Dalzell, a spokesman for the Direct Marketing Association.

Hoping to avoid a trade war, U.S. Commerce Department officials have proposed what is known as a "safe harbor" approach, allowing continued export of information to those U.S. companies with in-house privacy policies that meet EU standards. "We say, 'Let's create a situation where, if companies agree to follow certain data practices, they can be held harmless under the new directive,' " says David Aaron, under secretary of Commerce.

But, so far, U.S.-E.U. negotiations have produced no agreement. European officials call the safe harbor approach impractical. "The prevailing message from Brussels right now is that the EU is unwilling to do a deal with each American company," says Jason Catlett, president of Junkbusters, an on-line privacy-protection firm based in Green Brook, N.J. Catlett and others say that the Europeans hope that the United States will enact its own Internet privacy law.

Officials in both camps say that for the time being, no action is likely to be taken against American companies and others on-line. For one thing, the new directive, which went into effect on Oct. 25, still must be approved by the legislatures in each of the 15 member states of the European Union. So far, only two countries, Greece and Portugal, have formally ratified the directive, although, according to the European Union, 10 others are in the process of doing so presently.

Still, many predict, there could be trouble as early as next year if no agreement is reached. "I don't think the EU would cut off American Web sites, because we so dominate the Web right now," Catlett says. "But I do think they would pursue big, individual companies like Citibank or IBM and force them to shut down a large part of their Web traffic to and from Europe."

enforcement community, led by the FBI, has been pushing for new laws that would allow government officials to unscramble encrypted data, so long as they obtained a search warrant. Many existing programs allow only those who have purchased the encryption software to unscramble the data. Not even the manufacturer of the program has the means to decode what its customers have encrypted. The law-enforcement community wants encryption makers to be required to include a "key" or "back door" that would allow the company to unscramble data encrypted by its product in cases where the authorities obtained a valid search warrant.

Many high-technology companies and privacy advocates argue that restrictions on encryption of any kind — both existing and desired — are unnecessary and harmful. To begin with, they say, the current export restrictions are shortchanging consumers who buy encryption programs either alone or bundled into a software package. This is done to ensure that the software can be exported to other markets.

"If they installed stronger encryption features in the software, they would have to repackage these things for export," Rottenberg says. In other words, companies are intentionally "dumbing down" encryption protection to ensure that it is not affected by the export controls.

As a result, Rottenberg and others say, many on-line consumers and businesses are now much more vulnerable to an invasion of privacy, even though the technology to better protect them is readily available. Indeed, they point out that the Justice Department estimates that computer security breaches cost American companies and consumers $7 billion in 1997.

Intentionally putting weak encryption into larger software packages is also hurting the software makers, who are losing markets to companies in other technologically sophisticated countries in Europe and Asia. These foreign software makers are already filling the niche in the encryption market left open by the absence of competition from the United States. "Other countries are happy to use U.S. export controls as an excuse to outsell U.S. companies in this field," says CATO's Singleton.

In addition, opponents argue, export controls are not preventing the technology from falling into the wrong hands. "Today there are companies in other countries with strong encryption technology, much of it developed by software engineers who were educated in the United States," Singleton says. "So it's foolish to think that preventing strong encryption from leaving the United States is going to stop people from getting their hands on this technology."

But others disagree, arguing that America's strong encryption technology is still the world's best and thus should not be fully exportable. "It's clear that this technology could do great harm if it fell into the wrong hands, and so must be controlled," says Eugene "Red" McDaniel, president of the American Defense Institute.

McDaniel worries that the U.S. intelligence community would be unable to keep track of the nation's enemies if encryption technology were exported. "It could be devastating," he says.

The Center for Defense Information's Smith agrees. "This stuff could severely hamper our efforts to collect foreign intelligence by making it hard to nearly impossible to listen in on what our enemies are doing," he says.

Smith acknowledges that other companies in other nations undoubtedly are working on strong encryption and that American export controls may only delay the technology from falling into the wrong hands. Still, he argues, delay is reason enough to maintain the tight controls.

"We are clearly the most advanced in this area, and so even if we only delay the wrong people from getting hold of strong encryption," he says, "something good will have come from the [export] restrictions. If, say, Iraq doesn't get good encryption for a few more years because of these controls, at least the NSA [National Security Agency] has more time to come up with ways to crack these stronger [encryption] codes."

Others point out that American industries that need strong encryption, like banking, are able to buy the best in the world. And, says the FBI's Smith, echoing the industry argument, since most ordinary people don't buy software solely for encryption, export controls will be less likely to hurt software companies. "You buy Lotus Notes for what it does, not because it has strong encryption," he says, referring to a popular IBM software program. "The U.S. dominates about 70 percent of the world software market, not because it makes good encryption but because of the quality of the software and what it does."

And if some consumers get weaker encryption protection as a result of the export laws? "That's a small price to pay for our keeping this stuff away from potential enemies," says Smith of the Center for Defense Information.

Similarly, the FBI's Smith and others in the law-enforcement community argue that their proposal to require all encryption technology to have a "back door" is a small price for businesses and consumers to pay for protection against society's dangerous criminals. FBI Director Louis Freeh told the House Select Committee on Intelligence in September 1997 that without "a viable key management infrastructure that supports immediate decryption capabilities for lawful purposes, our ability to investigate and sometimes prevent the most serious crimes and terrorism will be severely impaired." [11]

Freeh and others point out that gaining access to computer records has helped solve or prevent countless crimes. For example, he says, World Trade Center bomber Ramsey Youseff used a computer to store his plans to destroy 11 U.S. airliners. If the information had been protected by a strong encryption program, it might not have been recoverable.

Now, they say, commercially available encryption technology is beginning to thwart investigations. "We're starting to see its use in the area of terrorism, where both domestic and international terrorists are using commercially available encryption software to encrypt stored files and E-mails, and we're being frustrated at being able to gain plain-text access," Smith says. "In some of these cases, we don't know what they're talking about," he adds.

Law enforcement officials say that being prevented from accessing encrypted information upsets the balance between the need for privacy and the legitimate needs of the police. "We have the right to engage in a reasonable search after showing probable cause and pursuant to a warrant," Smith says. "This takes that away from us."

But privacy advocates argue that providing a "key" to encryption programs defeats the whole purpose of securing information in the first place. "The idea that you regulate encryption because it might cause the FBI problems is nonsense," Rottenberg says. "It's like saying that we should regulate typewriters because they may be used in a criminal act."

CATO's Singleton agrees, adding that requiring software makers to include a "key" to access encrypted messages in "real time," or as they're being sent, could be terribly burdensome for the software maker. "To allow the intercept of real-time communications is a technical feat that would require a lot of money and work," she says. ■

# BACKGROUND

## Early Privacy Efforts

The value of privacy, or the right to be left alone, has long been recognized in the United States as a fundamental right. The U.S. Constitution's Bill of Rights recognizes privacy a number of times when it prohibits what it terms "unreasonable" search and seizure and allows defendants to refuse to incriminate themselves. Today, there is large body of statute and common law aimed at safeguarding individuals from unreasonable state interference.

But, according to privacy advocates, statute and common law have not kept apace with technological change. "There basically is no right to privacy on the Internet," Givens says. Still, there are principles that have come down during the last 25 years governing the fair use of a person's personal information or data.

The first glimmer of recognition that some sort of fair-use standards were needed came in 1973, when the Department of Health, Education and Welfare (HEW) created a task force to study the effect that computerization of medical records would have on privacy. The task force produced a "Code of Fair Information Practices," which set down several basic principles aimed at safeguarding personal privacy, including:

- Ensuring that the existence of personal databases is publicly known;
- Providing ways for people to learn what kind of information about them is in a database and how it is being used;
- Ensuring that individuals can check the accuracy of information about themselves and prevent the administrators of the database from using that information for purposes other than those for which it was collected;
- Providing guarantees that the information will not be misused. [12]

The HEW principles have formed the basis for later efforts to protect information privacy. For instance, Congress largely codified them when it passed the Privacy Act of 1974. Although the act's title implies broad, sweeping privacy coverage, it actually only applies to federal agencies when they collect data from individuals.

In 1980, the HEW principles were again largely incorporated in another set of privacy standards, this time drafted by the Organization of Economic Cooperation and Development (OECD). The Paris-based organization, which is a forum for some of the world's richest countries (including the United States), adopted "Guidelines on the Protection of Privacy and Transborder Flows of Personal Data." The guidelines did not have the force of law and instead were developed to aid nations in harmonizing their privacy policies. [13] They have been influential, most notably within the European Union, which issued its Directive on Protection of Personal Data in June 1995.

## The 'Cookie' Monster

According to privacy advocates like Rottenberg, the phenomenal rise of Internet use has not been accompanied by a corresponding increase in the level of privacy awareness. "It hasn't kept pace with the technology," he says. Mulligan of the Center for Democracy and Technology agrees, adding: "A lot of people, when they're typing this stuff into their computers, think it's private, like they're using a typewriter or something."

But what exactly happens when someone logs on and begins "surfing the Net?" Just as there is a lack of consumer awareness of the extent to which personal data may be used by third parties, there is often a corresponding fear that by simply visiting a Web site one forfeits one's E-mail address and other confidential information.

In fact, when users visit a Web site, their browser usually releases very little detailed, personal information about them. From the visitors' Web browser, the site can determine what kind of computer and Web browser is being used. The visitors' browser also reveals the last site they visited and, if they're at work, the name of their company. [14]

In addition, someone's browser releases its host E-mail address, such as aol.com or nyu.edu. With this information, the Web site could send an E-mail to everyone at the host address, a technique known as "spraying."

Not revealed is what would be considered more personal information: someone's name, phone number and home address. In almost all cases, E-mail addresses also remain confidential, unless the visitor is using a very old Web browser, some of which do reveal the user's E-mail in full.*

But Web sites do have ways of extracting a little more information about on-line users without asking anyone to disclose anything. For instance, the site can deposit a small amount of code in the user's hard drive, known as a "cookie." While a cookie cannot pry a person's name or E-mail address from them, it can track everything they do each time they're on the site.

The cookie allows the site to determine if the user is a return visitor and, if so, what they have done each time they have visited. So, for instance, Yahoo or another commonly used search engine might know that, say, user No. 8954 reads the Bible, has an interest in sailing and checks the stock price of IBM each day. This, in turn, allows the site to select specific advertisements to suit the particular user's interests. [15]

"People pick up all kinds of cookies all the time and immediately begin collecting all kinds of information about you," says Catlett, comparing them with parasites.

---

*There are a number of special programs capable of retrieving some E-mail addresses, but they are not commonly used.

# Chronology

## 1960s-1980s

***Early computer networks created by the military and universities eventually evolve into the Internet. The federal government and others begin considering privacy rights in the Information Age.***

***1969***
Pentagon's Defense Advanced Research Projects Agency (DARPA) establishes ARPANET, a precursor to the Internet.

***1973***
A privacy task force created by the Department of Health, Education and Welfare (HEW) develops basic principles to safeguard personal health information stored on computers.

***1974***
Congress passes the Privacy Act, which applied the HEW task force's principles to government records.

***1980***
The Organization of Economic Cooperation and Development establishes privacy standards based largely on the HEW principles.

***1984***
Pentagon gives up control of the Internet.

## 1990-2000

***The increased use of personal computers and modems leads to the dramatic growth of Internet use. Privacy advocates begin calling for legal protections for Internet users.***

***1991***
The Center for Media Education is founded.

***1992***
The Privacy Rights Clearinghouse is founded.

***1994***
There are 3 million Internet users worldwide.

***1995***
The European Union (EU) adopts the Directive on Personal Data Protection.

***1996***
Congress passes the Health Insurance Portability Act, which requires new federal standards to protect health records to be in place by August 1999.

***1997***
According to the FTC, Internet businesses spent almost $1 billion for on-line advertising.

***March 1997***
FBI Director Louis J. Freeh urges a Senate committee to set limits on encryption software.

***December 1997***
An estimated 10 million people have purchased something over the Internet.

***January 1998***
The number of Internet users is estimated at 60 million in the United States alone.

***June 1998***
The FCC releases a report to Congress on Internet privacy.

***August 1998***
The FCC settles with the Web site GeoCities for alleged privacy violations.

***Oct. 21, 1998***
Congress passes legislation aimed at protecting children's privacy on-line.

***Oct. 25, 1998***
The EU's Directive on Personal Data Protection takes effect.

***1999***
Deadline for Congress to enact new standards to protect health records.

***2000***
FTC estimates that Internet advertising spending will total $4.35 billion.

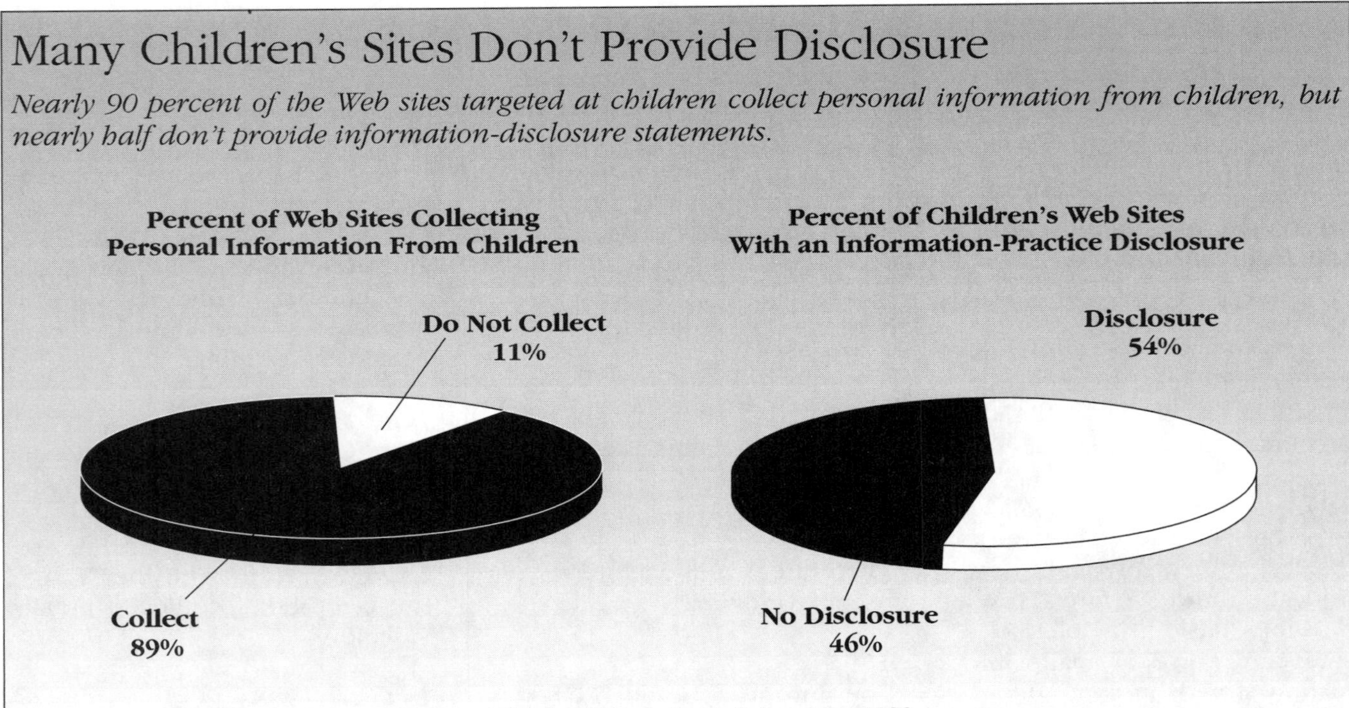


But there are ways to fight back. A program offered free by the Junkbusters Corp. prevents cookies, blocks out banner ads and protects attempts to pry an E-mail address from the user.

Some Internet experts say that the obsession with on-line confidentiality is misplaced. "What are we protecting consumers from, free coupons?" asks CATO's Singleton. "Targeted advertisements are actually an advantage to consumers because they speak to their interests."

But Catlett says the idea that consumers are being so closely tracked on-line is scary. "They're building these enormous profiles of where people are browsing and what they're looking at, that can be used to hurt them," he says. For example, Catlett predicts, on-line browsing records will be subpoenaed. "You know, it's like leaving behind radioactive material that can be traced," Catlett says. "The only reason it exists is because it's a windfall for the marketers." ■

# CURRENT SITUATION

## Medical Records

A family member is suddenly hospitalized while on vacation, thousands of miles from home. Instead of calling hometown doctors and hospitals in a search for relevant health records, the treating physician simply pulls up the patient's medical history on the Internet.

If the scenario sounds a little farfetched, it shouldn't. Health-care providers, insurance companies and others are already putting personal medical information on-line. Indeed, there are companies that provide secure sites on the Web where individuals can store medical information for themselves and their families. "Because my kids have allergic reactions to medication, I have always been concerned over what would happen if they needed care when I wasn't available," says Leslie Lee, a housewife from Menlo Park, Calif., who recently put her family's health records on-line. [16]

For many consumers like Lee, online access to health records is a valuable and worthwhile service. But privacy advocates worry that using the Internet to store and access sensitive medical information could lead to profound breaches of privacy. "Many health-care providers and others already sell or give medical records away," Rottenberg says, pointing out, for example, that a lot of pharmacies sell prescription lists to pharmaceutical companies. "The Internet, of course, raises a host of new privacy concerns," he adds.

These concerns range far and wide. For instance, epidemiologists have recently expressed interest in tapping medical record databases for research purposes. Should they gain access and, if so, how would the information be controlled? And what rules would govern access for law-enforcement officials?

Computer-industry representatives say that while there are legitimate concerns, the situation should not turn into a privacy nightmare. "There is already a consensus today that parties that have no role in the person's health-care process — basically if they're not in the payment stream — shouldn't have access to the records." says Uncapher of the Information Technology Association.

Today, the presence of medical records on-line is still small, but growing fast. For instance, while only 16 percent of the nation's hospitals use the Internet to store and access patients' records, the number is almost double what it was two years ago.[17]

Currently, there are no nationwide laws to protect the confidentiality of medical records, although some states, like California, offer limited privacy protections. That is likely to change in the near future. In 1996, Congress passed the Health Insurance Portability Act, which among other things, mandated new federal standards to protect the confidentiality of medical records by August of 1999. If Congress doesn't act by that date (and so far it hasn't), the law authorizes the Department of Health and Human Services (HHS) to do the job for them via regulations.

In August, HHS announced standards that it would like to see either passed by Congress or promulgated as regulations. Among the proposals put forth by the agency were requirements that companies lock access to records, train employees in privacy standards and develop a security plan to ensure medical-record safety.

"Electronic medical records can give us greater efficiency and lower cost, but those benefits must not come at the cost of loss of privacy," said HHS Secretary Donna Shalala.

## Protecting Children

Children who visit the Liberty Financial Company's Web site for young people can learn a number of things about managing money, from how to open a savings account to the rudiments of investing. The site also offers kids a chance to win prizes, but only after they complete a survey that asks their E-mail address, age, sex and whether they own any stocks, bonds or other forms of wealth.

Peter P. Morgan, senior vice president for Liberty, says that the survey allows his company to better tailor the site to children's needs and that the information is not sold or even saved. "From our perspective, this site was meant to be an educational site for the benefit of kids and parents who want to teach [them] about economics,' " he says.[18]

But others see tremendous potential for sites like Liberty's to violate a child's privacy. "Children are so easily manipulated and their good will can be abused," says Katharina Kopp, a senior policy analyst at the Center for Media Education, a children's advocacy group. "When it comes to protecting their privacy, they cannot make rational decisions and are incapable of protecting their rights," she adds.

AP/Callie Lipkin

*The Federal Trade Commission says 89 percent of all children's Internet sites collect personal information on children, but only 23 percent advise children to get a parent's permission before releasing information. Above, sixth-graders log-on in DeepHaven, Minn.*

Kopp and other children's advocates say that there are a huge number of sites directed at kids. Some, like the Liberty site, are owned by companies that don't generally sell products or services to children. So why worry about them? According to Kopp, "marketers have long realized that kids can influence purchases, not only of children's items but adult purchases too." For instance she says, oil giant Chevron has created a Web site for children because the company knows that kids can convince their parents to buy their gasoline. In addition, she says, sites like Chevron's can acclimate children to a company brand so that when they become adults they will choose Chevron over other products."

Currently, about 10 million children under age 18 use the Internet regularly, more than five times more than in 1995. A recent survey by the Westin group found that 97 percent of parents oppose the selling or use

## Protecting Yourself On-Line

Many Web sites post privacy policies aimed at allaying any concerns that on-line visitors might have. But others don't have such policies or, if they do, don't post them. Still, privacy advocates say, there are some things that Internet users can do to protect their privacy, such as:

- Check to see if the Web site you are visiting has a posted privacy policy. If it doesn't, there is no way of knowing how the information you give will be used. If a site does post a policy, check to see the limits it places on their ability to transfer your information to others.
- Download one of the many privacy-protection programs available on the Internet. They can block attempts to "steal" your E-mail address or shield your hard drive from "cookies," the code that many Web sites use to track someone's past and present activity on the site. Some, like the Junkbusters program cost nothing.
- Clean out your Web browser's memory cache after each session. The cache keeps a record of the Web sites you've visited, making it easy for others to trace your steps. Your browser's Preference folder should offer the option to empty the cache.
- Encrypt your on-line messages. Intercepting and reading E-mail is not that difficult. A good encryption program can make snooping much harder.

of information gathered from children. In the same survey, 80 percent of parents objected to Web sites requesting a child's name and address, even if that information is only going to be used internally. [19]

In a report released in June, the FTC determined that 89 percent of all children's sites it surveyed collected information on children. Of these, only 23 percent advised children to get their parents' permission and fewer than 10 percent attempted to require such permission. [20]

In the same report, FTC Chairman Robert Pitofsky called on Congress to act to protect children's privacy. "The Commission recommends legislation that would place parents in control of the on-line collection and use of personal identifying information from their children," he wrote. He went on to recommend that Web sites receive parental consent before getting information from children 12 and under. For older children, the commission recommended that the site notify parents before taking any information.

Pitofsky's call did not go unheeded on Capitol Hill. In October Congress added language that closely paralleled the FTC proposal to its fiscal 1999 omnibus spending bill. That measure was signed into law on Oct. 21. ■

# OUTLOOK

## Will Government Act?

Most privacy advocates predict that legal protection will eventually be extended to personal information on-line. "It is generally the case that when a new technology comes along, it takes time to sort the rules out," Rottenberg says. "But we usually end up with some sort of privacy protection, and I think that will be the case here."

Congress already has acted to protect children's privacy. Some action on medical record privacy is expected in the near future.

But Rottenberg and others also believe that more comprehensive privacy protections may be enacted soon. Their optimism stems in part from a belief that the Clinton administration is slowly shifting its position on Internet privacy from one of self-regulation to at least limited government oversight. "I think Gore may be in the process of changing his mind," Rottenberg says. "His hope is still that self-regulation will work, but that we should prepare for something else if it doesn't."

Givens of the Privacy Rights Clearinghouse agrees that government is likely to soon lose patience with industry attempts at self-regulation. "The government is starting to say, 'We've given you a chance and it hasn't worked out all that well,' " she says. Indeed, in testimony in July, FTC Chairman Pitofsky told a House Commerce subcommittee that Congress should give the on-line industry until the end of 1998 to have an effective privacy policy in place. "If it does not work out, we believe Congress should seriously consider legislation," he said.

Others think that the European Union's new directive on on-line privacy may prod the business community into focusing more closely on privacy protection. "U.S. [on-line] firms may face some fines as the [EU] member states begin implementing the directive, and that might get them on board in favor of some sort of privacy regulation," Rottenberg says.

But others say that talk of imminent regulation is premature. "I think for now, legislative energy will be focused on protecting children and medical records," says Uncapher of the Information Technology Association. "I think the government is going to give self-regulation more of a chance, give it more time."

# At Issue:

## *Should the federal government set privacy standards for the Internet?*

yes

**Deirdre Mulligan**
***Staff counsel, Center for Democracy and Technology***

***FROM TESTIMONY BEFORE THE SENATE COMMERCE, SCIENCE AND TRANSPORTATION SUBCOMMITTEE ON COMMUNICATIONS, SEPT. 23, 1998.***

The Center for Democracy and Technology (CDT) believes that it is time for Congress and relevant stakeholders to develop a bipartisan, national privacy policy for the Internet. While efforts at self-regulation continue, and are a necessary component of the electronic marketplace, legislation will speed the adoption of Fair Information Practices across the market, provide a level playing field, and ensure that bad actors are deterred.

Toward this end, CDT has called for legislation enabling the Federal Trade Commission to develop rules to protect the privacy of both adults and children. . . .

The Federal Trade Commission Report "Privacy Online: A Report to Congress" found that, despite increased pressure from the White House to develop meaningful self-regulation and growing public anxiety about privacy on the Internet, companies continue to collect personal information on the World Wide Web without providing even a minimum of consumer protection. . . .

While self-regulation is a necessary part of any effective privacy regime on the global Internet, structural flaws in a purely self-regulatory system and specific difficulties that arise from the nature of the Internet suggest that self-regulation alone will result in incomplete protection. The four primary shortcomings of industry self-regulation in the privacy area have been: 1) the failure to incorporate core elements of fair information practice into substantive guidelines; 2) the lack of oversight and enforcement; 3) the absence of legal redress to harmed individuals; and, 4) the inability to set enforceable limits on government access to personal information.

Self-regulatory efforts to provide privacy protections on the Internet, to date, continue to exhibit these structural flaws. . . .

If Congress acts soon, it can protect privacy, build upon and improve the ongoing activities in the private sector, establish a level playing field and create a structure for oversight and enforcement of privacy practices on the Internet. Failure to act will result in continuing consumer distrust of the Internet, inadequate attention to individual privacy in the marketplace, and a legal framework that in some instances actually punishes those moving in the right direction while creating no incentive for self-regulatory activities. . . . However, we must also recognize that legislation will not on its own provide complete privacy protection. Privacy protection must build upon the strengths of existing efforts — self-regulatory and technical — but fold them into a comprehensive system of enforceable privacy protections.

no

**Steven J. Col**
***Senior vice president and general counsel, Council of Better Business Bureaus Inc. and BBBOnline Inc.***

***FROM TESTIMONY BEFORE THE HOUSE COMMERCE SUBCOMMITTEE ON TELECOMMUNICATIONS, TRADE AND CONSUMER PROTECTION, JUNE 21, 1998.***

The question posed so frequently in recent weeks by many in the executive and legislative branches, probably including some committee members, and by others closely following the on-line privacy-protection issue, is "has self-regulation of online privacy worked?" . . .

The better question for the subcommittee and the Congress as a whole to ask itself is not whether self-regulation of on-line privacy "has" worked, but rather whether self-regulation of on-line privacy "can" work, and is it "likely" to work sooner and better than other alternatives?

Let me explain. The Internet is moving at warp speed. What we know now about the technology, the type and number of content and marketing and advertising providers, the marketing techniques used, consumer access to and use of the medium and the extent to which privacy is jeopardized and is protected, is very, very different than the state of our knowledge just a year ago. . . .

Add to this equation the fact that the so-called Internet industry is many industries, and is not the cohesive force some would suggest. It is ISPs and browsers, and software companies, and on-line "cookie" companies and stockbrokers, and auto dealers, and computer sellers, and so on. Users are equally diverse, including sophisticated computer users, mainstream novices, business personnel, grandmothers and children.

Expectations that this environment would produce in this, the consumer Internet's infancy, a cohesive, organized, fully developed, comprehensive, ubiquitous and completely effective and funded program to protect and enforce on-line privacy may be naive. The point is, we are all learning, and we are developing techniques and responses to emerging issues as our learning progresses.

And, make no mistake about it, an exclusive legislative alternative to a self-regulatory approach is no better, and maybe is much worse. It won't be speedy and it won't have the nimbleness required to respond to the changing technology and cast of players. I dare say that had the Congress passed an omnibus privacy-protection law last year, covering all aspects of the Internet marketplace as it existed at that time, we would be testifying today before an oversight committee to discuss whether the government has adequately enforced the law, or whether the law required substantial change to accomplish its purposes.

CATO's Singleton agrees, adding that government attempts to enact comprehensive privacy regulation on the Internet would be fiercely resisted. "For years and years, businesses have enjoyed tremendous freedom in this area," she says, "and they're not going to let it go easily." ■

# FOR MORE INFORMATION

*If you would like to have this CQ Researcher updated, or need more information about this topic, please call CQ Custom Research. Special rates for CQ subscribers. (202) 887-8600 or (800) 432-2250, ext. 600, or E-mail Custom.Research@cq.com*

**Business Software Alliance,** 1150 18th St. N.W. Suite 700, Washington, D.C. 20036; (202) 872-5500; www.bsa.org. This organization of software companies promotes the growth of the software industry worldwide.

**Center for Democracy and Technology,** 1634 Eye St., N.W. Suite 1100, Washington, D.C. 20006; (202) 637-9800; www.cdt.org. The center lobbies for civil liberties, including the right of privacy, in the computer and communications media.

**Center for Media Education,** 1511 K St., N.W. Suite 518, Washington, D.C. 20005; (202) 628-2620; www.cme.org/cme. The center promotes the responsible use of new technologies for children.

**Electronic Privacy Information Center,** 666 Pennsylvania Ave. S.E. Suite 301, Washington, D.C. 20003; (202) 544-9240; www.epic.org. The center conducts research on the impact of the computer revolution on civil liberties, such as privacy.

## Notes

[1] Figures cited in Federal Trade Commission Associate Director David Medine's testimony before the House Judiciary Subcommittee on Courts and Intellectual Property, March 26, 1998.

[2] *Ibid.*

[3] Federal Trade Commission, "Privacy On-Line: A Report to Congress," June 1998, p. 23.

[4] Medine, *op. cit.*

[5] Quoted in Joel Brinkley, "Web Site Agrees to Safeguards in First On-Line Privacy Deal," *The New York Times,* Aug. 14, 1998.

[6] For background, see "Regulating the Internet," *The CQ Researcher,* June 30, 1995, pp. 561-584.

[7] Quoted in Ed Murrieta, "Gore: Protect Privacy," *Wired News,* July 31, 1998.

[8] Quoted in *Ibid.*

[9] Quoted in Deborah Scoblionkov and James Glave, "Magaziner: Back Off, Big Brother," *Wired News,* July 22, 1998.

[10] Quoted in Rajiv Chandrasekaran, "Harry and Louise Have a New Worry: Encryption," *The Washington Post,* July 28, 1998.

[11] Testimony before the Senate Judiciary Subcommittee on Technology Terrorism, and Government Information, Sept. 3, 1997.

[12] Beth Givens, "A Review of the Fair Information Principles: The Foundation of Privacy Policy," Privacy Rights Clearinghouse, October 1997.

[13] *Ibid.*

[14] Elizabeth Weise, "Revealing Secrets About Privacy on the Web," *USA Today,* June 24, 1998.

[15] *Ibid.*

[16] Quoted in "Doctors and Patients Now Access Medical Records On-Line," *Business Wire,* Aug. 24, 1998.

[17] Milt Freudenheim, "Medicine at the Click of a Mouse; On-Line Health Files are Convenient. Are They Private?" *The New York Times,* Aug. 12, 1998.

[18] Quoted in Pamela Mendels, "Internet Sites for Children Raise Concerns on Privacy," *The New York Times,* July 4, 1998.

[19] Cited in testimony by David Medine, associate director, FTC, before the House Judiciary Subcommittee on Courts and Intellectual Property, March 26, 1998.

[20] FTC Report, *op. cit.*

# Bibliography

## *Selected Sources Used*


### *Books*

**Brin, David, "The Transparent Society: Will Technology Force Us to Choose Between Privacy and Freedom?" Addison Wesley (1998).**

Brin, known more as a science fiction writer than a social commentator, argues that it is not possible to protect privacy in our technologically advanced society. But instead of limiting the ability of technology to guard privacy, the author proposes what he calls "reciprocal transparency," or complete openness. If companies or the government can collect information about citizens, Brin argues, they should fully know what that information is and where it's going.

### *Articles*

**Clark, Charles S., "Regulating the Internet," *The CQ Researcher*, June 30, 1995.**

Clark's piece, while a bit dated, is an excellent introduction to the debate over Internet policy, including privacy protection.

**Clausing, Jeri, "Critics Contend U.S. Policy on the Internet Has Two Big Flaws," *The New York Times*, June 15, 1998.**

Clausing outlines the problems privacy advocates and others have with the Clinton administration's decision not to push for formal privacy protections on-line. This passivity, they say, will ultimately slow the commercial growth of on-line commerce.

**Freudenheim, Milt, "Medicine at the Click of a Mouse; On-Line Health Files Are Convenient. Are They Private?" *The New York Times*, Aug. 12, 1998.**

The article discusses the privacy implications of putting people's health records on-line.

**Glover, K. Daniel, "Do You Have the Right to Be Left Alone?" IntellectualCapital.com, Aug. 27, 1998.**

This on-line article gives a good overview of some parts of the basic debate over privacy protection in the Information Age.

**Gruenwald, Juliana, "Who's Minding Whose Business on the Internet?" *CQ Weekly*, July 25, 1998.**

Gruenwald chronicles recent efforts in Congress to regulate privacy on-line. She writes that lawmakers are facing increasing pressure to do something to guard consumer privacy, especially with regard to children.

**Hansell, Saul, "Big Web Sites to Track Steps of Users," *The New York Times*, Aug. 16, 1998.**

Hansell describes how big Web sites like Lycos-Tripod are collecting and storing information about Internet users' likes and dislikes in order to produce targeted advertisements.

**O'Harrow Jr., Robert, "Data Firms Getting Too Personal?" *The Washington Post*, March 8, 1998.**

O'Harrow gives a detailed and well-researched account of the data-warehousing industry. The article makes clear how easy it is for data-collection firms to collect even very personal information about almost anyone.

**Mendels, Pamela, "Internet Sites for Children Raise Concerns on Privacy," *The New York Times*, July 4, 1998.**

The article chronicles the growing concern over the potential for Web sites to violate the privacy of minors. Particularly worrisome for privacy advocates are those sites directed specifically at young people.

**Quittner, Joshua, "No Privacy on the Web," *Time*, June 2, 1997.**

Quittner gives a good summary of the debate over whether to regulate privacy on-line.

**Weise, Elizabeth, "Revealing Secrets About Privacy on the Web," *USA Today*, June 24, 1998.**

Weise provides an easy-to-read account of what can and cannot be learned about someone when they visit a Web site.

### *Reports and Studies*

**Federal Trade Commission, "Privacy On-Line: A Report to Congress," June 1998.**

An exhaustive examination of on-line privacy issues by the closest thing the United States has to a privacy agency. In particular, the report details concerns regarding the privacy of children on the Internet.

**Smith, Robert Ellis, "War Stories: Accounts of Persons Victimized by Invasions of Privacy," *Privacy Journal*, 1997.**

Smith, publisher of the journal, has collected hundreds of tales of privacy invasions, both on- and off-line.

# 11 Drug Testing

KATHY KOCH

For Julie Izard, just married and looking for part-time work, organizing social activities at her apartment complex in Alexandria, Va., sounded perfect. Since the pay was minimal and the job only involved a few evenings a week, she viewed it almost as a volunteer position.

So she was surprised when she was sent to a nearby laboratory for a drug test. "I thought it was kind of funny," Izard says, since it wasn't a high-security job and she wouldn't be in charge of people's safety.

Drug testing has become a prime weapon in the nation's war on drugs, and more and more typical citizens like Izard — not just drivers, pilots, train operators and high-security government employees — are being asked to provide urine samples.

Nearly three-quarters of America's biggest companies hand job applicants a plastic cup as part of the recruiting process. A decade ago, only 21 percent of U.S. companies drug-tested recruits.

Most companies only test job applicants. Others screen both applicants and "safety-sensitive" employees — such as those who operate machinery. Still others test any employees who appear to be using drugs.

Increasingly, however, employers are requiring random testing of all employees — raising the hackles of some employees, unions and civil libertarians.

Momentum for the exponential growth in drug testing has come from several sources:

• The federal government — Transportation and Defense Department rules require drug testing for certain safety-sensitive jobs in both the public and private sectors; and the 1988 Drug-Free Workplace Act requires federal contractors or grant recipients to maintain drug-free workplaces.

• Courts — A series of decisions recognizes private employers' right to test employees and applicants.

• Insurance companies — Insurers favor testing as a means of reducing accident liability and controlling health-care costs.

• Testing laboratories — Laboratories aggressively market their testing services to companies, schools and government agencies.

But clearly, much of the momentum for drug testing has come from Congress. "Over the past 15 years, Congress has passed laws requiring workplace drug testing of more than a tenth of the work force, or about 12 million individuals," says J. Michael Walsh, who designed the federal employee drug-testing regime.

Yet the same Congress has refused to undergo drug testing itself. Judges and political candidates are also exempt from mandatory drug testing, the courts have said (*see p. 206*).

Meanwhile, federal, state and local governments are widening their drug-testing net to cover even more citizens. Besides government employees, drug tests are now given to welfare mothers, prisoners, college-loan recipients and, sometimes, students wanting to join school clubs. And at the urging of President Clinton, Congress and some states are considering requiring all teenagers applying for a driver's license to be tested.

Some experts predict that eventually anyone receiving public money of any sort will have to be tested. Louisiana already requires random drug testing of anyone who receives anything of economic value from the state — and those who balk can lose their job, license, loan, scholarship, contract or public assistance.

Local school boards also are expanding drug testing. For years, middle- and high-school athletes have undergone testing. [1] Now some school districts are requiring anyone participating in extracurricular activities to be tested. A few districts test any student who parks a car on school property. A handful of private schools have tested their entire student bodies, something public schools so far have been prohibited by the Constitution from doing, although at least two Texas school districts are toying with the idea.

Perhaps nowhere are the "bladder cops" — as some critics call drug testers — more prevalent than in the scandal-plagued sports world. (*See story, p. 202.*)

Civil libertarians and privacy advocates complain that the ever-widening drug-testing net dangerously erodes Americans' constitutional rights. While polls show most people agree that testing workers in safety-sensitive positions is appropriate, the trend toward testing new groups is "an evisceration of the Fourth Amendment in the name of the drug war," says Ethan Nadelmann, director of the Lindesmith Center, a drug- policy think tank.

Other critics call drug testing "chemical McCarthyism" because an improperly administered test could yield a false-positive result from the use of legitimate prescription drugs or even eating a poppy-seed bagel. Innocent job seekers or employees can lose their jobs. Sixty percent of companies fire an employee who tests positive for drugs; only 23 percent retain them, referring them for drug treatment.

If fired for a positive drug test, an employee usually cannot collect unemployment insurance. And employees who are injured on the job and test positive after the accident will probably

From *The CQ Researcher*, November 20, 1998.

## Marijuana Was Most Frequently Detected

*More than half of the employees who tested positive for drugs in 1997 had used marijuana.*

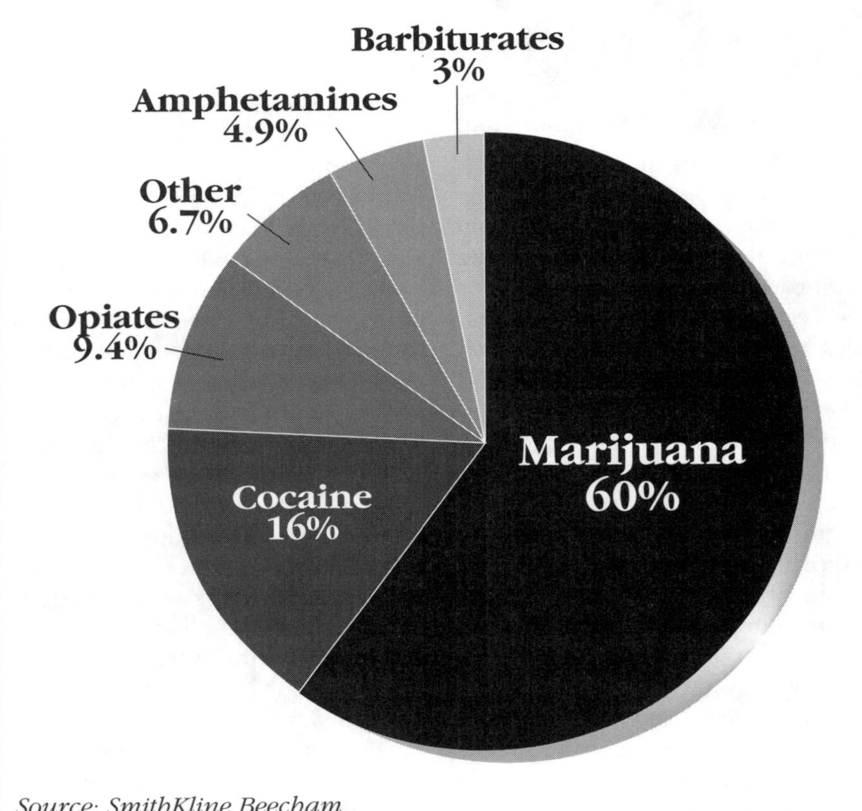


*Source: SmithKline Beecham*

be fired and become ineligible for health benefits, workers' compensation or unemployment insurance.

Critics complain workplace drug testing gives employers unprecedented police power over what employees do during off-duty hours and unfairly targets those who use marijuana, which can remain in the system weeks longer than other "hard" drugs.

Proponents, however, say the magnitude of the nation's drug-abuse problem, and the cost of drug abuse to society — in lost productivity, workplace accidents, tardiness, absenteeism, workplace theft and increased health-care costs — justifies testing, even if it infringes on individual privacy rights. [2]

"This problem is bleeding America," says Mark de Bernardo, executive director of the Institute for a Drug-Free Workplace, a coalition of businesses, business organizations and individuals. "The United States is the world's leader in substance abuse. We have 6 percent of the world's population, but we engage in 60 percent of the world's illicit drug use."

Last year, 13.9 million Americans — 6.4 percent of the population — used illicit drugs on a regular basis, a 10 percent increase from the 1992 record low of 5.8 percent. But the current rate is about half the 25 million who used illicit drugs in 1979, when drug use in America reached its peak and began declining, a decade before drug testing came into vogue.

Drug-testing advocates argue that because 74 percent of illicit drug users are employed, the workplace is an excellent place to catch them. "Employers have the most effective weapon in the war on drugs," de Bernardo says. "If your job is contingent on your being drug-free, it creates a powerful incentive for you to get off and stay off drugs.

Moreover, de Bernardo says, "Once an employer has a drug-testing policy, fewer drug abusers apply, and some [abusing] employees voluntarily leave."

Many abusers then seek work in small companies, he says, because only 3 percent of small firms — which employ half the nation's work force — have drug-testing programs. But twice as many employees in small firms use illegal drugs as in large firms.

To close the small-business "escape hatch," Congress last month appropriated $10 million for the Drug-Free Workplace Act of 1998 to encourage small companies to establish testing programs.

Polls show employees generally accept drug testing as a necessary evil, although there are still those who chafe at what they see as an unwarranted invasion of their privacy. Employees have filed dozens of court suits in the last 15 years, along with a handful of students, even though most students and parents favor drug testing because it gives students an excuse to resist peer pressure to use drugs. (*See story, p. 196.*)

These are some of the questions being asked by those debating this issue:

### *Does drug testing deter drug use?*

"There are lots of books and research to show that drug testing deters drug use," de Bernardo says. "Individual companies have seen dramatic decreases in positive drug-test rates."

He is quick to add that drug testing alone isn't a deterrent. It must be accompanied by a comprehensive substance-abuse prevention program that includes four other components: a written anti-drug policy, an anti-drug education program, rigorous enforcement and a treatment program for addicted employees.

Drug-testing proponents often cite a 1988 U.S. Navy study showing that drug use among enlisted men went down from 48 percent in 1980 to 5 percent in 1988 after a comprehensive substance-abuse prevention program with random drug testing was instituted. [3]

Indeed, a 1987 Navy personnel survey showed 83 percent considered random testing the Navy's strongest deterrent to drug abuse. "Significantly, 27 percent also said that they would resume their use of illicit drugs if the Navy discontinued its drug-testing program," according to the Institute for a Drug-Free Workplace. [4]

Another study showed a 50 percent drop in positive drug tests — from 22.9 percent to 11.6 percent — at the Southern Pacific Railroad after a year of "reasonable-suspicion" drug testing. [5]

## Americans' Drug Use Is Rising

*Americans' drug use has been rising since 1992, but it was still 35 percent less in 1997 than it was in 1979, when U.S. drug use reached an all-time high.*

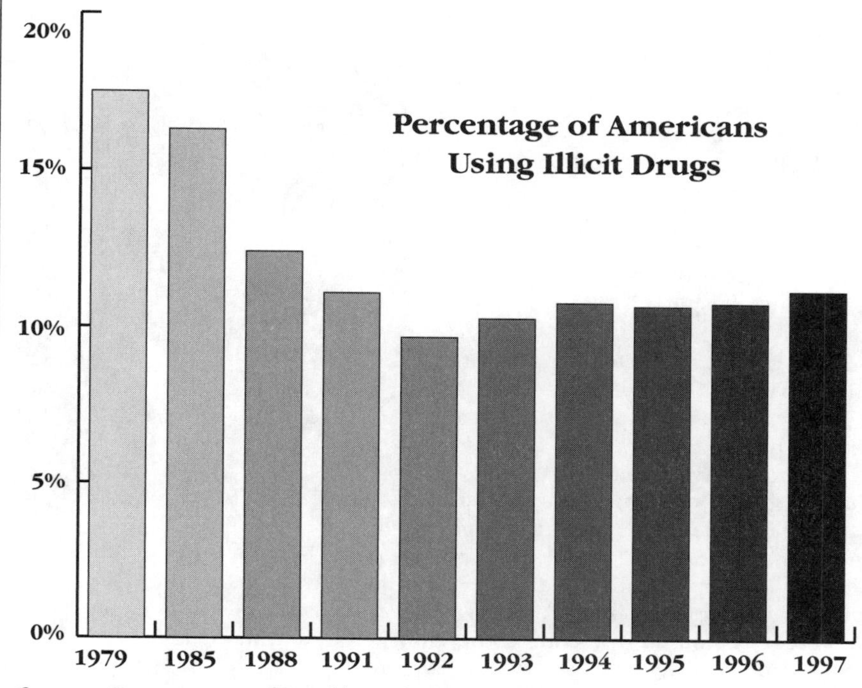


*Source: Department of Health and Human Services, "National Household Survey on Drug Abuse," 1997*

Walsh says drug testing "keeps mainstream working folks from casual recreational use."

Workplace drug testing will deter drug use among those recreation users, most of whom are employed suburbanites, said Rep. Gerald B.H. Solomon, R-N.Y., as he argued for the bill to encourage small businesses to start drug testing. "If we were to solve that problem," he said, it would eliminate U.S. demand for drugs, "and in Colombia they would be making bathtubs instead of [exporting] drugs into this country."

Proponents also point to American Management Association (AMA) statistics showing the percentage of employees testing positive for drugs declined from 8.1 percent in 1989 to 1.9 percent in 1995. [6]

But Eric Greenberg, AMA's director of management studies, says the declining figures do not prove drug use is actually declining. That's because employers have been expanding the total pool of persons tested to include all employees, not just those suspected of drug use. If you test more employees who show no obvious signs of drug use, "Naturally, the test-positive ratios will go down," he says.

"When companies didn't expand the pool of employees covered, the percentages stayed the same," he says. "This is why I say those statistics do not show that drug testing is a deterrent."

Lewis Maltby, director of the Office of Workplace Rights at the American Civil Liberties Union (ACLU), which opposes random drug testing, agrees. "When you go from suspicion-based testing to random testing, the number of hits are going to go down," he says.

Maltby argues that anti-drug education programs may be more of a deterrent. Companies that combine drug testing with education programs consistently have lower test-positive ratios than firms that rely solely on testing.

But some companies are cutting both their drug-education and supervisor-training programs, which teach

# They Decided to Fight the System . . .

Hollister Gardner is hardly a rebellious teenager. He maintained an "A" average while serving as president of the National Honor Society, drum major in the band and treasurer of Future Farmers of America (FFA) at his West Texas high school.

But Gardner rebelled last year when he was told that he would have to pass a drug test to keep participating in such extracurricular activities.

Having never been involved in drugs, he chafed at the implication that he was guilty unless proven innocent. He believes the Fourth Amendment of the Bill of Rights protects U.S. citizens from such warrantless searches without "reasonable suspicion" that someone is guilty.

So he never signed the consent form. His 12-year-old sister, Sarah, and his 13-year-old cousin Molly also refused to sign theirs.

When the school notified Hollister that he could no longer attend after-school activities, he sued the Tulia Independent School District board, whose members include his father, Gary, the only board member who opposed drug testing when it was instituted. Representing himself in federal court, Hollister argued the board's drug-testing policy is unconstitutional.

*Hollister Gardner*

"The school district can't test just because they feel like testing," he said. "People fought and died for these rights, and they are not to be given up to the Tulia School Board just because they think they can take them from you." [1]

The elder Gardner agreed with his son's decision. "To my eyes, it's almost a duty," he says. "It was something he just had to do." No trial date has been set in the case, which is pending in Amarillo's federal court.

The school district contends its policy is legal because in 1995 the U.S. Supreme Court upheld the Veronia, Ore., school district's policy of randomly testing all high school athletes. In that case, the court said random, suspicionless drug tests were justified because the drug crisis in the Veronia district had reached "epidemic proportions."

Gardner, now a sophomore at Angelo State University, says the drug problem in rural Tulia was not severe enough to justify warrantless searches. "I don't use drugs," he told a newspaper reporter at the time, "and no one I know in my organizations uses them." [2]

Tulia School Superintendent Mike Vinyard says the school board instituted drug testing after a 1994 survey showed 27 percent of students in grades 7-12 had used drugs at least once, and 10 percent said they had used marijuana prior to the survey. Six percent of junior high kids said they had smoked marijuana before class.

Although the survey showed Tulia's drug use was below the state average, Vinyard says, "We think any drug use is serious." He said "about a dozen students" have tested positive since the program began in January 1997.

Most parents like the policy, he says, because fear of random testing gives students an excuse to resist peer pressure to use drugs. "The Gardner family is really the only critic of the program," Vinyard says. "Most parents would like to randomly test all students rather than only those in extracurricular activities."

At least two other Texas school districts apparently feel the same way. The Texas Association of School Boards has reviewed at least two proposals from school districts wanting to require all students to be randomly drug tested. Shellie Hoffman, the association's director of legal services, would not reveal the names of the districts.

If adopted, they would become the first public school districts in the country to test all students. The policy would undoubtedly be challenged legally, says Jim Harrington, director of the nonprofit Texas Civil Rights Project. "The Supreme Court has made it very clear that drug testing can only be applied in certain cases, such as where there is a pervasive drug culture, violence or physical danger for athletes, or where students are considered role models," he says.

Hollister says that while parents may favor drug testing, many students supported him. "I had quite a few people come up to me and thank me for sticking up for their rights," he says.

But standing up for one's rights is costly, he says. Not unexpectedly, he and his family have paid emotionally,

managers to spot drug abuse — a policy that could prove "penny-wise but pound-foolish," Maltby says. Only 6 percent of surveyed companies rely only on drug testing, says the AMA report.

Drug-testing opponents say there are no peer-reviewed, scientific studies to show that drug testing deters drug use. "The decline in drug use in this country began in 1979," says Maltby. "Nobody was doing drug testing in 1979."

"The era of drug testing began in 1985-1986, yet since 1991, drug use

# . . . When Ordered to Take Drug Tests

academically and financially for their stand. "I warned him if he refused to sign, he would get more flak than he ever thought about, and that they might not even let him graduate," remembers Hollister's father.

Hollister was not allowed to show his pig at the agricultural fair with other members of his FFA group, and his sister Sarah was told she could not play in the band. The school later allowed protesting students to stay in after-school activities until the case is settled.

The family also paid about $6,000 for transportation, court fees and administrative costs, says Gary Gardner, who calls himself "just a small dirt farmer." The costs were especially burdensome because of the huge losses Texas farmers suffered due to bad weather this year. "Any other year it wouldn't have been so bad," he says.

Hollister has even greater respect for the Constitution now. "Our family has always understood what the Constitution meant," he says. "Now I've really developed a love for it."

A lifelong love for the Constitution also led Georgia history teacher Sherry Hearn to stand up against drug testing. And she, too, has paid a high price.

Three years away from retirement, the award-winning Savannah, Ga., high school teacher lost her job — and nearly lost her pension — when she refused to take a drug test on demand.

For 27 years Hearn, who was her county's Teacher of the Year in 1994, had taught her American history students that the Fourth Amendment protects citizens against unreasonable searches and seizures by police. Not surprisingly, she had been an outspoken critic of her district's policy of allowing "lockdowns," or periodic, unannounced, schoolwide searches — using drug-sniffing dogs — to ferret out illegal guns or drugs. Many school districts, including 400 in Texas alone, use drug-sniffing dogs to search school grounds.

During the two-hour lockdowns in Savannah, students and teachers must stand in the hallways, while dogs search each room, bookbag and purse, and students are scanned with metal detectors.

Hearn maintains such searches without specific information that someone may possess drugs or weapons are an invasion of constitutional rights and a dreadful message to be sending students. She had opposed the tactics at faculty meetings, to her principal, the school board and to police officers who conducted the lockdowns.

Then during a lockdown on April 4, 1996, police say they found a partially smoked marijuana cigarette in Hearn's car. But police refused to show her the evidence, claiming it had been accidentally destroyed. Hearn refused to submit to a drug test without first seeing her lawyer, especially since the officers had searched her car without her permission, in clear violation of the school's written policy.

School board officials claim Hearn was fired for insubordination. She claims she was targeted by police because she had objected to the lockdowns.

No action was taken against the officers who searched her car without permission. And the school board never investigated a tip police received giving them the initials of a student who had bragged to classmates that he had "planted" the marijuana in Hearn's car.

"The board feels very strongly about its drug-free workplace policy, and we feel equally strongly that we can't pick and choose who gets to follow the rules," Chatham County School Board President Karen Matthews told The Associated Press. [3] Hearn's case is pending before the U.S. District Court in Atlanta.

Since she was fired, Hearn has been unable to find a full-time job at any Georgia public school. She believes she was blackballed for standing up for her rights. "How else would you explain someone with my qualifications not being able to find a job, when we have a teacher shortage in Georgia?" she asks.

She finally was hired at a juvenile detention center, and is enrolled again in the state's pension program.

Knowing how much standing up for her rights has cost her, if she had to do it over again would she take the test? She hopes not. "It would endanger my credibility with my students, which I spent 27 years building up."

More important, she says, "I would be voluntarily surrendering my rights. Anytime you accept any sort of violation — no matter how minor — of your basic liberties there are those who will take increasing liberties. Eventually, you won't have any left."

[1] Allan Turner, "Defending his rights; Student risking all to oppose drug testing," *The Houston Chronicle,* Feb. 2, 1997.

[2] *Ibid.*

[3] John Cheves, "Fired Chatham teacher sues," *Florida Times-Union,* April 17, 1997.

among teenagers has been going up," points out Allen St. Pierre, executive director of the NORML Foundation, which wants to legalize marijuana.

Critics like St. Pierre claim the statistics used to "prove" that testing deters drug abuse are "twisted and manipulated" by proponents, many of whom are connected to the testing industry.

"It's really hard to prove that drug testing is a deterrent in itself," says William Sonnenstuhl, professor of industrial labor relations at Cornell University. "If you look at the railroad industry, the first industry in which drug testing was implemented, they were not successful until the unions started educating their members to stop drinking and covering up for members who used alcohol or drugs on the job."

"I don't think drug testing deters anyone, except for the novices," Sonnenstuhl continues. "Skillful drug users know how to beat the tests. It just becomes a game they have to play."

In 1994, the National Academy of Sciences (NAS) reviewed all of the literature on drug testing and found "no conclusive scientific evidence from properly controlled studies that employment drug-testing programs widely discourage drug use or encourage rehabilitation." [7]

Drug-testing opponents say that rather than testing teenagers for drug abuse, it is cheaper to teach them how to say no to drugs.

"There are lots of peer-pressure resistance classes available to schools," says Jim Harrington, director of the Texas Civil Rights Project. "And they are much cheaper than drug testing."

Proponents say the "tough love" zero-tolerance approach encourages abusers to get treatment.

But skeptics point out that when an applicant fails a drug test, 98 percent of large employers reject his application, and 63 percent fire existing employees who test positive, rather than referring them to a company-supported drug rehab program. [8] Those fired workers are then usually ineligible for unemployment or health benefits, as well as workers' compensation if they were injured on the job before testing positive. Thus, say critics, most can't afford to join a drug-treatment program.

The "dumping" of drug abusers back into the community, unemployed and without benefits, "encourages their entry into illegal economies," says Paul M. Roman, research professor of sociology and director of the Center for Research on Deviance and Behavioral Health at the University of Georgia.

Workplace testing also misses those most seriously addicted to drugs who are usually unemployed, say critics. Other argue that some drug abusers merely substitute alcohol or harder drugs, such as heroin or cocaine, that are more difficult to detect through urinalysis because they only stay in the body for a few hours.

Nadelmann says, "If you want to get bombed on Saturday night now, and you need to be 'clean' on Monday morning, instead of smoking a joint, which will stay in your system longer, you'll switch to cocaine or heroin."

### *Does drug testing protect worker and public safety?*

Proponents say companies with drug-testing policies have safer workplaces, better overall job performance, reduced liability for accidents and injuries and reduced medical and insurance costs.

"Without question, substance abusers account for higher rates of accidents in the workplace," says de Bernardo. "Lots and lots of studies link illicit drug use to impairment, and impairment to safety and health concerns."

"No one doubts that employers with effective substance-abuse policies have fewer workplace accidents," said Thomas J. Donohue, president of the U.S. Chamber of Commerce. As a result they have fewer workers'-compensation claims. Several states, he said, now offer employers who have such programs discounted rates on insurance premiums. [9]

In addition, "Employers consistently report reduced rates of employee violence and crime" after implementing a comprehensive substance-abuse policy, Donohue added.

Dan Wurzburg, corporate safety director for Sordoni Skanska construction-management firm in Parsippany, N.J., said, "In the construction industry, having a drug-free workplace program means that the company can absolutely be assured that it will have a better safety record, and fewer accidents mean lower costs and lower insurance premiums."

According to data in the recent bill to encourage small businesses to set up workplace drug-testing programs, accidents involving drug users are 300-400 percent higher than among non-users.

In the Southern Pacific Railroad study, personal injuries and accidents dropped dramatically after drug testing was implemented. Personal injuries, for instance, dropped from 2,234 in 1983 to 322 in the first six months of 1988. Train accidents caused by human error decreased from 911 to 54 during the same period. [10]

But opponents question the statistics used by advocates to show that drug abusers cause more workplace accidents. For instance, the claim that 47 percent of workplace accidents are caused by drug abusers — used by Congress in October to justify spending $10 million to encourage workplace drug testing in small companies — "is absurd on the face of it," Sonnenstuhl says. "Such statistics are based on a series of assumptions "inferring causation where what has been shown is only correlation."

Workplace accident reports show that most accidents result from "a series of management or supervisory decisions that create or tolerate unsafe work environments, equipment and practices," Sonnenstuhl says.

"To blame drug users is to shift focus and remedial efforts from a strategy that has been proven successful [i.e., reducing hazards and educating workers about workplace safety] to one of dubious assumptions, merits and promise," sociologist Staudenmeier says.

Sonnenstuhl says drug testing is being sold to employers and employees as a question of job safety. But

# Experts Question Hair Testing

New drug-testing techniques being introduced are considered less invasive than urinalysis and almost impossible to "beat." Hair testing, for instance, can detect drug use as far back as three months. By comparison, urinalysis only detects heroin and cocaine within hours or days of use, and marijuana for up to 70 days.

Not surprisingly, some of the new techniques raise thorny questions about accuracy, privacy and the purpose of drug testing.

Ethan Nadelmann, director of the Lindesmith Center, a drug-policy think tank, argues that testing hair, sweat and saliva is more — not less — invasive because it delves more deeply into one's past history. And because hair and saliva contain DNA, they reveal information about medical conditions and genetic makeup that some employees may not want to reveal to their bosses.

"Hair testing opens the door to genetic testing by employers," says Lewis Maltby, director of the Office of Workplace Rights at the American Civil Liberties Union (ACLU), noting that companies could refuse to hire someone based on inherited medical conditions, which the applicant may not even know about. Although hair testers claim they wouldn't look at DNA, the procedure stirs controversy on several other fronts.

In hair testing, a snippet of hair from the back of the neck (or the armpit of a bald person) is tested for drug residues. The developer of the technique, Boston-based Psychemedics Corp., says it detects four times more drug users than urinalysis.

Florida entrepreneur H. Wayne Huizenga, founder of Blockbuster Entertainment and Waste Management Inc. and owner of the Miami Dolphins, is a major stockholder in Psychemedics and helped raise the company out of debt in 1989. With Blockbuster and Waste Management as major clients, the firm has grown to more than 1,400 clients today, including General Motors and The Sports Authority.

"Hair testing will continue to grow dramatically," says company General Counsel William Thistle. "It's inevitable once companies see the advantages."

Sales have more than doubled in the last five years, as more firms adopted the process. Several police departments have signed on as well, including New York City and Chicago. At least 40 private schools have begun testing students' hair, among them De la Salle High School in New Orleans, which randomly tests its entire 860-member student body.

(Public schools are generally thought to be prohibited by the Fourth Amendment from testing entire student bodies.)

Psychemedics has lobbied Congress to require the Health and Human Services Department (HHS) to adopt hair testing for all federal employees, but so far the agency has resisted.

"We in the federal government are not confident of it at this time," says Donna Bush, chief of drug testing for the Substance Abuse and Mental Health Services Administration (SAMHSA).

The National Institute on Drug Abuse, the Food and Drug Administration, the College of American Pathologists and the Society of Forensic Toxicologists are all concerned that hair testing may be unfairly biased against persons with coarse black hair, such as African-Americans, Asians or Hispanics. Some tests have shown that coarse hair shows much higher concentrations of drugs than lighter hair after ingestion of the same amount of drugs.

"There is no study, any time, any place, anywhere, that shows that Psychemedics' testing procedures have a racial bias," Thistle says. "I've been involved in hair testing since 1989, and at no time has there been a racial-discrimination lawsuit on the grounds that hair testing is racially biased."

Other scientists claim hair testing doesn't differentiate between drugs absorbed into the hair from environmental contamination, such as being at a concert where marijuana is smoked.

For these reasons, the ACLU strongly opposes hair testing. "Every reputable scientific organization in America rejects the use of hair testing for employment purposes," Maltby says.

Thistle says the ACLU should favor hair testing because it is not biased against marijuana users like urine testing. "With a urine test, the chances of finding a marijuana user are greater than finding a cocaine or heroin user," he says. "With hair testing, all drug users are uniformly caught."

Further, he says, the company's special decontamination procedure, which includes washing hair samples in various solutions for nearly two hours before conducting the tests, eliminates contamination due to passive absorption.

While Psychemedics' decontamination procedures may be carefully performed, critics say no one knows whether other hair testing labs are being as careful, because hair testing is unregulated. There are no national standards for hair analysis as there are for urinalysis.

John Baenziger, special commissioner of toxicology at the College of American Pathologists, says his group does not support hair testing yet because it is "not being done uniformly" and the procedures being used in labs "are not being looked at in a critical fashion."

more and more, all employees are being tested, including clerks and receptionists. As a result, "drug testing becomes just a moral cover for 'You shouldn't be using drugs.' "

Critics argue vociferously that drug testing does not test one's current fitness for duty, especially in the case of marijuana, which can show up in the urine for up to 70 days after consumption, long after the effects of the drug have worn off. Meanwhile, other drugs and alcohol are washed out of the system within a few hours, they point out. And cocaine doesn't show up immediately after being ingested.

Because of these discrepancies, "Most people who fail tests are totally sober, and most who are stoned pass," Maltby says.

"We've got reams and reams from the government itself that show urinalysis doesn't test impairment," St. Pierre says. "All the testimony before Congress has said that having marijuana metabolites in your urine does not prove impairment."

"So drug testing is not done to protect the public health, it is mainly done for the symbolism," he says. "Logic has totally been thrown out the door, as it has for most of this war on drugs."

If companies really wanted to protect workplace safety, they would go after alcohol use, say critics. "The biggest problem regarding workplace safety, bar none, is alcohol," St. Pierre says. Most urinalysis does not check for alcohol levels.

"Alcohol is an enormous problem," de Bernardo acknowledges. "Any employer who addresses drug abuse and not alcohol is foolish."

Critics of drug testing often favor impairment testing as the best way to protect public safety. "There are better ways to protect the public safety than to invade somebody's privacy," Maltby says. "It is absolutely clear that impairment testing protects the public safety better than urine testing."

Impairment testing, also called performance testing, involves using computerized video programs to test eye-hand coordination by requiring the employee to use a "joy stick" to keep a cursor in the middle of a screen. An employee takes several practice tests to establish his "baseline" capability, and then is tested randomly — or daily for those with safety-sensitive positions — to see whether he is impaired.

Yet, Donna Bush, chief of drug testing for SAMHSA, says, "At this time we've not seen evidence in the peer-reviewed scientific literature that impairment testing works." "Performance testing is easily manipulated," says de Bernardo.

Walsh agrees. "There's not much data to show that it really works. And there's no data at all to show that it would detect drug use. If I'm an illicit drug user, I would have every incentive not to do well on the baseline."

Walsh and de Bernardo say such tests do not detect illegal drug use because they do not differentiate as to whether someone is impaired because he has been using drugs or he is merely fatigued because he was up all night with a sick child.

"Performance testing doesn't determine whether someone is engaged in illegal behavior," says de Bernardo. "It protects people's jobs who don't deserve that protection."

For that reason, urinalysis advocates also do not favor another method being used by police officers in some states to test driver impairment. They use new devices shaped like binoculars, which test the reactions of the pupils to flashes of light. "It shows if you are under the influence of something," says Maltby, but it doesn't determine whether it's alcohol or illegal drugs. ■

# BACKGROUND

## War on Drugs

In 1971, President Richard M. Nixon declared the nation's first "war on drugs." But drug use continued, especially among youths, until it peaked in 1979.

By then, drugs like marijuana and cocaine had become socially acceptable in many quarters. For instance, in 1979, 19 percent of Americans 18-25 had used cocaine in the preceding twelve months, according to the National Institute on Drug Abuse. [11] As marijuana became regarded as a "soft drug" like alcohol and tobacco, eleven states decriminalized possession of small amounts, one legalized it and twenty-nine others made possession of small amounts a misdemeanor, writes Beverly Potter, co-author of *Drug Testing at Work.* In 1977, President Jimmy Carter even called for decriminalization of marijuana possession.

In 1978-79, as drug use was reaching its peak in America, an anti-drug backlash developed, led by the "parents movement," which later became the Atlanta-based anti-drug group National Families in Action. In 1980-81, the military vowed to clean up its ranks and began random, suspicionless drug testing.

By 1982, President Ronald Reagan had declared a second "war on drugs," and drug testing outside the military came into vogue. In 1986, the president and his senior advisers submitted urine samples to be screened for the presence of illegal drugs. The symbolic gesture was designed to encourage private employers to test their workers, and to reduce employee opposition to testing.

Sociologist Staudenmeier calls Reagan's push for private employers to do drug testing "privatized social control." The Fourth Amendment prohibits the government from requiring the general population to provide urine samples, he points out. "We find the president of the United States appealing to employers to use their power to accomplish what the state cannot: widespread urine testing of American citizens," he wrote. [12]

But there was scant public outcry as companies increasingly began ask-

# Chronology

## 1960s

***Marijuana, hallucinogens and other drugs become widespread among middle-class youth during the counterculture revolution. Drug use becomes rampant among Vietnam soldiers.***

***1968***
Mandatory drug testing in the military begins as addicted Vietnam vets begin returning home.

## 1970s

***Marijuana and cocaine become socially acceptable in many quarters, even as the country launches its first "war on drugs."***

***1971***
President Richard M. Nixon declares the first "war on drugs."

***Aug. 3, 1977***
President Jimmy Carter calls for decriminalization of marijuana possession.

***1979***
Drug use peaks. Eleven states decriminalize possession of small amounts of "pot," one legalizes it and 29 others make possession a misdemeanor. Anti-drug backlash develops, led by the "parents movement."

## 1980s

***Cocaine becomes the drug of choice among urban professionals. Crack cocaine, a highly addictive form of cocaine, causes skyrocketing crime rates. Only 5 percent of high-school seniors smoke marijuana daily, compared with 10 percent in 1978.***

***1982***
President Ronald Reagan declares a second "war on drugs."

***July 1985***
Arkansas court rules that "the excessive intrusive nature" of drug testing student athletes without reasonable suspicion is not justified by its need.

***1986***
In a symbolic gesture, Reagan and his senior advisers submit urine samples to be screened for the presence of illegal drugs. In September Reagan issues Executive Order 12564, calling for a "drug-free workplace" in all federal agencies.

***November 1988***
Congress passes Drug-Free Workplace Act, requiring federal contractors or grant recipients to maintain drug-free workplaces. Many employers set up voluntary testing programs. Employees begin suing, claiming drug testing is a violation of individual privacy rights. Courts allow suspicionless drug testing.

***1989***
President George Bush unveils his National Drug Control Strategy, encouraging comprehensive drug-free workplace policies in the private sector and in state and local government. In *National Treasury Employees Union v. Von Raab* decision, Supreme Court upholds random drug testing when a "special need" outweighs individual privacy rights.

## 1990s

***President Bush expands the federal drug-testing program to include all White House personnel. Clinton expands the Reagan-Bush drug-testing policies. Drug use increases.***

***1991***
Congress passes the Omnibus Transportation and Employment Testing Act, extending drug and alcohol testing to 8 million private-sector pilots, drivers and equipment operators.

***1992***
Drug use begins increasing. Clinton is elected president.

***1995***
In *Veronia School District v. Acton*, the Supreme Court rules that random urinalysis of high school athletes is justified because the drug crisis in the school district has reached "epidemic proportions."

***1996***
Marijuana arrests are up 80 percent, mostly for possession. Teenage drug use becomes a hot campaign issue. Just before the election, Clinton proposes mandatory drug tests for all teens seeking driver's licenses.

***1998***
In June Congress rescinds federal student loans to any student convicted of a drug charge. In August Congress refuses to order tests for members of Congress and their staffs. In October the Supreme Court lets stand a rural Indiana high school's policy of testing all students in extracurricular activities and passes the Drug-Free Workplace Act of 1998.

# Athletes vs. Drug Testers

Athletes have long been subjected to drug testing for performance-enhancing drugs, which are often dangerous to an athlete's long-term health and give users an unfair advantage over athletes that don't use them. [1]

But the use of banned performance-enhancing drugs appears to be on the rise, despite stepped-up testing. Athletic drug testing has become a constant cat-and-mouse game, as athletes continually try to outsmart the drug testers, and the laboratories keep improving their detection technology.

This year several drug-testing scandals have rocked the sports world, including:

- In July the top team in the prestigious Tour de France bicycle race was disqualified amid news that some cyclists were using the banned synthetic hormone EPO. The hormone, which increases the red blood cell count, gives athletes greater endurance by putting extra oxygen into the blood. But it is extremely dangerous and has been blamed for dozens of athletes' deaths.
- Irish swimmer Michelle de Bruin was banned for four years from swimming competitions after manipulating a test sample.
- Chinese swimmer Yuan Yuan was arrested at Sydney airport on her way to the World Swimming Championships in Perth. She was carrying 13 vials of human growth hormone, which her coach later said were his. He was suspended for 15 years.
- In February Canadian snowboarder Ross Rebagliati's Olympic gold medal was taken away after he tested positive for marijuana; it was returned after he appealed, claiming it was due to secondhand smoke.

Closer to home, controversy swirled around Mark McGwire, the record-breaking St. Louis Cardinals slugger who broke Roger Maris' single-season home-run record on Sept. 27. McGwire was using the controversial performance enhancer androstenedione, a testosterone-boosting precursor to anabolic steroids developed by East Germany's state-sponsored athletic drug program in the 1970s.

"Andro" rapidly elevates testosterone levels, producing a temporary energy surge described by East German swimmer Raik Hannermann as a "volcanic eruption." [2] It is sold in U.S. health food stores as a nutritional supplement.

Because andro is allowed in Major League Baseball (MLB), McGwire was cheered on to victory while taking the drug. But Olympic shotputter Randy Barnes was banned for life by the International Amateur Athletic Federation (IAAF) in July after he tested positive for the same substance, which some scientists say is extremely dangerous.

Because experts disagree over whether androstenedione should be considered an anabolic steroid and thus be banned because it is available only by prescription, sports organizations treat it differently. The IAAF, the International Olympic Committee (IOC), the National Football League and the National Collegiate Athletic Association have all banned it. But MLB and the National Basketball Association have not, and the National Hockey League prohibits only illegal drugs. [3]

Such dramatic inconsistencies in athletic drug testing have led many to call for reform of international drug-testing laws so they are clear, consistent and enforceable.

Complicating the situation was the U.S. government's loosening of laws governing food supplements in 1994, which allowed products like androstenedione to be marketed in the U.S. as a food. Such products were not available over-the-counter under old Food and Drug Administration rules. Now, foreign athletes come to the United States shopping for banned performance-enhancers.

Other supplements, like the muscle-building amino acid creatine, are now widely used by high school and professional athletes alike. Creatine hit the headlines last summer, when both McGwire and his closest home run competitor, Sammy Sosa of the Chicago Cubs, admitted using it. Creatine is considered safe, but the long-term effects are unknown.

With new "natural" performance drugs and masking agents constantly being developed, drug testers have difficulty figuring out how to detect the new substances, and deciding whether they should be legal.

"In today's world, athletes who are determined to cheat know that natural substances are the way to go," said Don Catlin, a professor of medicine and pharmacology at the University of California at Los Angeles and a member of the IOC medical commission. The new substances, including androstenedione, are popular with athletes because they are currently undetectable through testing, and so new that many leagues have not formed policies about their use, he said. [4]

The IOC has called for establishment of an independent international agency to coordinate drug testing for Olympic athletes. The proposal will be discussed at a sports drug summit in February in Lausanne, Switzerland.

The Association of Professional Team Physicians recently called on MLB to ban androstenedione. Even if it does, there will probably be other questionable supplements on the market soon.

"There's a whole cornucopia of other things right behind it," said Catlin. "That's where things are going." [5]

---

[1] See Richard L. Worsnop, "Athletes and Drugs," *The CQ Researcher*, July 26, 1991, pp. 513-536.

[2] Quoted in Scott M. Reid, "Special Report: Slugger's drug widely banned," *The Denver Post*, Aug. 25, 1998

[3] Under federal law, anabolic steroids are a controlled substance, available only by prescription.

[4] Kirk Johnson, "Mac's use of drug raises issues beyond sports," *The* (Charleston, S.C.) *Post and Courier*, Sept. 1, 1998.

[5] *Ibid.*

ing employees for urine samples. Following a barrage of press articles in 1986 about crack cocaine and babies born addicted to crack, public attitudes about drugs took a sharp right turn. A *Time*/CBS survey found that 72 percent of full-time workers said they would voluntarily submit to drug testing, and 25 percent of full-time factory workers said they had a colleague who used drugs. [13]

Several high-profile accidents in the 1980s involving drugged or drunken drivers and pilots added fuel to the national anti-drug sentiment. In 1981, a Navy pilot, apparently high on marijuana, crashed into the deck of the U.S.S. *Nimitz*, destroying several planes and causing more than $100 million in damages. Marijuana was also implicated in the 1987 Conrail-Amtrak train collision in Maryland, which killed 16 people. And alcohol was blamed for the 1989 *Exxon Valdez* accident in Alaska, which caused one of the worst oil spills in U.S. history. [14]

The public began to demand that those responsible for the safety of others — such as pilots, surgeons and police officers — be drug-free. In addition, the highly publicized deaths of University of Maryland basketball star Len Bias and Cleveland Browns' footfall player Don Rogers led to a public outcry about drug use among sports stars. Drug testing was touted as part of the solution to both problems.

Meanwhile, with increased availability bringing lower costs, cocaine had became the drug of choice among successful young urban professionals. Crack cocaine had also entered the picture, a highly addictive form of free-base cocaine, blamed for skyrocketing urban crime rates.

In the late 1980s, then-Attorney General Richard L. Thornburgh called drug testing by employers the moral thing to do. "That's really what started this whole process and has been driving it all along," Sonnenstuhl says. "The responsibility has to be put at the foot of the federal government for inciting all of this stuff."

Despite all the hysteria about skyrocketing drug use in the 1980s and Reagan's push for drug testing, total drug use nationwide had begun a steady decline in 1979 that continued until 1992. Cocaine and crack use continued to flourish in the 1980s among a small percentage of the population, but marijuana use, particularly among students, declined. By the late 1980s, for instance, only 5 percent of high-school seniors smoked marijuana every day, compared with 10 percent in 1978. [15]

## Workplace Testing

Nonetheless, in September 1986 President Reagan issued Executive Order 12564, calling for a "drug-free workplace" in all federal agencies and ordering that employees in "sensitive positions" be tested for illegal drug use. The rule allowed anyone who tested positive to be fired after a single offense, but mandated that second offenders must be fired. President George Bush later expanded the program to include testing for all White House personnel. Today, 1.7 million employees in 111 federal agencies are tested, with those in safety-sensitive positions usually tested on a random basis.

Congress expanded the drug testing net with the Drug-Free Workplace Act of 1988, which required federal contractors or grant recipients to maintain drug-free workplaces. Although drug testing wasn't mandated, many employers set up testing programs.

In 1989, President Bush unveiled his National Drug Control Strategy. It said the federal government "has a responsibility to do all that it can to promote comprehensive drug-free workplace policies."

Two years later, Congress passed the Omnibus Transportation and Employment Testing Act of 1991, which extended mandatory drug and alcohol testing to 8 million private-sector pilots, drivers and equipment operators.

President Clinton has expanded the Reagan-Bush drug-testing policies to prisons, where those "who commit a lion's share of the crimes in this country are in a controlled environment," said White House senior adviser Rahm Emanuel. "We have to slam shut the revolving door between drugs and crime. Through mandatory testing, you will force a change in their behavior that will break the link." [16]

Arguing that most drug offenders get arrested sooner or later, the administration pushed through Congress a law requiring states to test and treat prisoners and parolees for drugs before they can receive federal prison-construction funds. It also increased the number of residential treatment centers in federal prisons and more than tripled the number of inmates being treated for substance abuse. [17]

Critics say the administration's anti-drug policies are nothing more than a war on casual marijuana users, because they are the ones most often "caught" with current drug-testing methods.

"Despite criticism that this administration is soft on drugs, FBI data clearly demonstrate that Clinton's war on marijuana smokers is the toughest ever waged in our nation's history," says St. Pierre of the NORML Foundation. Marijuana arrests have risen 80 percent since 1990, according to the FBI. Nearly 642,000 people were arrested for marijuana offenses in 1996, St. Pierre says, 85 percent for possession.

## Legal Challenges

As soon as drug tests began appearing in schools and workplaces, individuals, unions and the American Civil Liberties Union (ACLU) began challenging the practice in court. Plaintiffs typically claimed drug testing violated individual privacy rights or Fourth Amendment protections against unreasonable search and seizure by government agents.

Until the mid-1980s, the lower courts had consistently ruled that — except in the military — it was unconstitutional to randomly drug test without "reasonable suspicion" that someone was using drugs.

But in the mid-1980s, as the "war on drugs" gained momentum and public attitudes toward drugs shifted, courts began allowing suspicionless drug testing when the state was seen to have an administrative interest that overrode an individual's right to privacy. This "administrative exception" was applied to jockeys, prison guards, nuclear plant employees, public school teachers and Customs Service employees.

In a precedent-setting 1989 case involving customs inspectors — *National Treasury Employees Union v. Von Raab* — the Supreme Court for the first time allowed random, suspicionless drug testing when there is a "special need" that outweighs the individual's privacy rights. The courts spent the next decade defining "special need."

Civil rights scholars viewed the *Von Raab* ruling as a major departure for the court because it was holding individual privacy rights as less important than the state's interest in winning the war on drugs. [18]

The decision is tantamount to jettisoning the need to establish probable cause before searching private homes because the state has a strong interest in eliminating crime, argued law scholar Jeannette C. James. [19]

But perhaps no case shocked civil libertarians more than *Veronia School District v. Acton*, in which the Supreme Court ruled in 1995 that suspicionless, random urinalysis of high-school athletes was justified because the drug crisis in the school district had reached "epidemic proportions." Yet the Veronia district had found only 12 positive drug tests in four and a half years. Just 10 years earlier the court had struck down as unreasonable a New Jersey school's athlete drug-testing program in a school district where 28 students tested positive for drugs in a single year.

Justice Antonin Scalia — who had written a scathing dissent in *Von Raab* — wrote the majority opinion in the *Veronia* case.

Scalia argued that student athletes have even less privacy rights than the general student body because they are role models and because they dress and shower in close proximity to one another. He also said that school drug testing was a response to drug usage by athletes.

"Obviously his view of the evils of drugs had changed between 1989 and 1995," says Paul Armentano, publication director of NORML. ■

# Current Situation

## Teen Drug Use Rises

After the *Veronia* ruling, more school districts instituted random drug testing of athletes, driven in part by new national surveys showing that declining teen drug use had suddenly reversed itself in 1992 and was rising steadily.

Indeed, drug use among teenagers became a hot campaign issue in 1996, after the annual "National Household Survey on Drug Abuse" showed that teen drug use had more than doubled during Clinton's first term. [20] Republican presidential candidate Bob Dole blamed Clinton for the upswing, pointing out that he had slashed funding for the White House drug-policy office (which Clinton later restored) and had hired employees who had used drugs in the past.

Clinton pointed out that the increase in teen drug use was a multiyear trend that started before he was even sworn into office. Administration officials also noted that from 1992-1995 Congress consistently cut anti-drug education funds administered under the Safe and Drug-Free Schools program. Critics have called the program ineffective because there are few restrictions on how the money is spent, and it is allocated on a per-capita basis, rather than targeted at districts with severe drug problems.

Officials in the White House Office of National Drug Control Policy also pointed to opinion polls showing student attitudes about the dangers of marijuana had begun to change in 1990. Clinton's drug czar, Barry R. McCaffrey, said that from 1990-1993, the percentage of high-school seniors viewing marijuana use as risky fell. [21]

Joseph A. Califano, Jr., president of the National Center on Addiction and Substance Abuse at Columbia University, blamed the increased teen drug use on baby boomer parents' complacency about drugs. Califano released a survey showing that two-thirds of babyboomer parents who used drugs in their youth expected their children to do the same, and 40 percent felt they had little influence over their teenagers' decisions about drugs.

"What is infuriating about the attitudes revealed in this survey is the resignation of so many parents to the present mess," Califano said. [22]

Shortly before the election, Clinton proposed encouraging states to impose mandatory drug tests for all teens seeking driver's licenses. "Our message should be simple: no drugs, or no driver's license," Clinton said in his weekly radio address. Republicans called the proposal an election-year gimmick.

Since the 1996 election, teen drug use has continued rising, even as more schools have implemented or expanded testing programs. The percentage of youths ages 12-17 using illicit drugs increased from 9 percent to 11.4 percent from 1996-1997, still far below 1979's record high of 16.3 percent. Teen drug use had dropped to an all-time low of 5.3 percent in 1992.

Perhaps even more worrisome for parents and officials are the latest statistics showing that drug use among 12- and 13-year-olds increased from 2.2 percent to 3.8 percent from 1996-97. [23]

Some schools have responded to rising teen drug use by requiring testing not only for athletes but also for all students participating in extracurricular activities, such as band, drama and student council. Other schools test students who drive to school.

## Privacy Issues Raised

Parents generally like testing programs, and some even want all students tested.

"The majority of kids support drug testing because it gives them an excuse to say 'no' to drugs," says Robert Weiner, spokesman for the White House Office of National Drug Control Policy. "The administration has been strongly supportive of giving schools that tool," he says.

But some parents and teenagers have sued their local school boards, claiming testing is an unconstitutional invasion of privacy.

However, on Oct. 5 the Supreme Court let stand a rural Indiana high school's policy of requiring mandatory drug testing for all students in extracurricular activities. After a concerned parent sued the Rush County School Board, an Indiana appellate court had ruled that the policy does not violate students' privacy rights, even though the school district is not experiencing a serious drug problem. [24]

"We're getting closer to that line where you can expect to be tested just because you show up at school," said Kenneth J. Falk, an attorney for the Indiana Civil Liberties Union, which represented the plaintiffs. [25]

On the other hand, "Kids now can say, 'I can't experiment because my number may come up,' " said Rush County School Board lawyer Rodney V. Taylor. [26]

Although the court's inaction is not a precedent-setting decision, the ruling it left in place remains binding in Indiana, Illinois and Wisconsin. Critics say it opens the door for similar policies in other states. Several school districts had been waiting for the court to decide the case before they expanded their testing programs.

Civil libertarians and some editorial writers were stunned by the court's inaction.

"Drug abuse among teenagers is alarming, but so is the ease with which the Rehnquist court has disregarded fundamental constitutional protections guaranteed to citizens under the Fourth Amendment," said a *St. Petersburg Times* editorial. "Historically, suspicionless searches have been deemed to violate personal privacy and the protection against unreasonable searches and seizures. There may be compelling reasons to allow such searches, such as when public safety mandates it. But that's certainly not the case here." [27]

Critics point out that besides infringing on the Constitution, such programs target the wrong kids. High achievers who spend their free time playing in the band are not likely to be using drugs, they argue.

## Politicians Not Tested

In other recent Supreme Court action on drug testing, the court last March 2 denied an appeal by two government economists who balked at taking random drug tests because they have access to the Old Executive Office Building next-door to the White House.

But the court has rejected drug testing for judges and politicians. The justices struck down a Georgia law requiring candidates for state office to take drug tests. Because urinalysis intrudes on a person's right to privacy, it should be used only when the risk to public safety "is substantial and real," the high court said. [28]

Meanwhile, lawmakers in the last two years introduced more than 60 bills requiring drug testing in one form or another; most were never acted upon.

The law providing $10 million to help small businesses establish drug-free workplaces was the only major drug-testing legislation approved. It also ordered the Small Business Administration to study the extent and costs of drug use in the workplace.

While Congress pushed for more small businesses to do drug testing, it refused to submit to drug testing for congressmen and their staffs, claiming it was too undignified and possibly unconstitutional.

"It's not fair to require more and more Americans to undergo drug testing, when the same Congress that passed the laws expanding the practice over the last 15 years won't submit to the same level of scrutiny themselves," St. Pierre says.

On the opening day of the 105th Congress, the House had passed a rules package requiring all representatives and their staffs to undergo random drug testing. But the rule was never implemented, due to opposition from both Republican and Democratic leaders, some of whom feared that the results of positive drug tests might be used against them by a political opponent.

"Of course, the information would be used against them," St. Pierre says. "That's exactly the way drug testing is being used across the country. We deny welfare mothers custody of their children, we deny students access to student loans, we deny employees access to workers' compensation or health benefits. Everybody is being punished for positive drug tests except the people who forced these laws on the country. It's rank hypocrisy."

"We have a few well-placed people who don't want this," said Rep. Joe L. Barton, R-Texas, who co-sponsored the bill with House Rules Committee Chairman Solomon. [29] ■

# OUTLOOK

## Questions of Fairness

Under the Drug-Free Workplace Act of 1998, more small companies are expected to begin asking their employees for urine samples. Some fear that cash-strapped firms may cut corners by only performing the one-step screening test, which is more likely to turn up false-positives. Congress recommended that the more comprehensive two-step testing be done, but many employers already reject job applicants based solely on the single-screening tests.

In large companies, drug testing is here to stay, predicts de Bernardo of the Institute for a Drug-Free Workplace. "There will be no retreat on drug testing," he says. "The numbers of companies testing increases every year." He predicts more large companies will expand their "for-cause" testing programs to include universal random testing.

"It's by far the fairest type of testing you can do," he says. "It is inherently objective and has a greater deterrent impact." Testing only for "reasonable suspicion" is inherently subjective and open to abuse by an employer with a grudge, he adds.

But as employers expand their testing, they may run into a new obstacle: hemp seed oil. Sold in health food stores, hemp oil reportedly lowers cholesterol, fights viruses, increases calcium absorption and reduces inflammation. Because it comes from the same family as the marijuana plant, hemp oil can cause a user to test positive for marijuana.

Observers predict that marijuana smokers will start using the supplement to mask their marijuana use.

Others worry that as drug testing becomes more widespread, the confidentiality of the results may be compromised. "This information will become part of student records, insurance records and other databases, regardless of the reason that someone tested positive and how long ago it happened," says Alexander Robinson, public policy director of the Drug Policy Foundation.

Questions about fairness are already being raised about new tests using hair, sweat and saliva. The new techniques are considered less intrusive than urinalysis, and thus less subject to legal challenge. They are also expected to detect more drug users, because they are almost impossible to "beat."

Some say the expanding use of hair and urine testing is leading the country closer to a police state.

"You have a police-state mentality," Robinson says. "Incentives have been established in schools rewarding students who turn in other students. State and local ordinances reward kids who turn in their parents."

At the White House, Weiner acknowledges that a "vocal few" see drug testing as moving toward a police state.

"People are making a huge deal out of this *horrendous* violation of individual rights," he says, "but it's also a violation of civil liberties to go through an X-ray machine at an airport, or to wear a seat belt. Their concerns about Americans' civil liberties are important, but the law has to support the general good. There's nothing wrong with drug testing when you have a national consensus."

Some opponents hope for a public backlash. "The hope is that proponents will go so far there will be some backlash," Nadelmann says. If not, drug testing could lead a desensitized public down "a slippery slope to greater and greater loss of freedom. Bit by bit, we are slowly getting used to greater and greater intrusion."

Some observers are concerned that so many students nationwide have acquiesced to drug testing without thinking much about its long-term impact on their privacy rights.

"As these students, now inoculated with an intolerant attitude, take power, invasions of privacy will become more widely implemented because they will be seen as prime American values," wrote Arnold Trebach and Scott Ehlers of the Drug Policy Foundation. [30]

Cornell's Sonnenstuhl argues that rather than curtailing constitutional rights, invading privacy and turning employers into policemen, "The best way to prevent alcohol and drug abuse in the workplace is for supervisors to do the job they were hired to do — monitor job performance and use discipline to encourage abusers to get treatment," he says. "Most large corporations are not training their supervisors to do their jobs."

But at a steel foundry in Portland, Ore., Pat Bishop has no doubts about testing. "We've been randomly testing everyone in the company for the

# At Issue:

## *Is workplace drug-testing effective?*

**Michael Walsh**
***President, the Walsh Group, P.A., a Bethesda, Md., research and consulting firm, and former executive director of the President's Drug Advisory Council.***

***FROM HR NEWS, APRIL 1996.***

**yes**

In 1994, the National Academy of Sciences (NAS) issued a report, "Under the Influence: Drugs and the American Workforce," in which the principal finding was that there is little or no data in the scientific literature to demonstrate the effectiveness of drug-free workplace programs in reducing substance abuse.

My colleagues at the American Civil Liberties Union have taken this to mean that these programs don't work. The fact is that the NAS found no evidence that the programs don't work either; there simply wasn't conclusive evidence one way or the other.

But from a national perspective, there are positive signs of success. Since the widespread implementation of drug-free workplace programs in the mid-1980's, we have seen a significant decline in the use of drugs by employed individuals. Data from the "National Household Survey on Drug Abuse" (conducted by the National Institute on Drug Abuse and, more recently, by the Substance Abuse and Mental Health Services Administration) indicate that the number of full-time workers that are current users of illegal drugs has dropped by more than 6 million over the last 10 years.

Over the last 15 years "employee drug testing" has become a standard business practice in the American workplace. A recent survey conducted by the American Management Association (AMA) indicates that nearly 80 percent of surveyed firms test employees for drugs.

Since 1987, company drug testing in the United States has increased by more than 300 percent. With the increased prevalence of illegal drug use, most executives believe that the absence of pre-employment testing would be an open invitation to drug users. The approximately 80 "Forensic Urine Drug Testing" laboratories certified by the U.S. Department of Health and Human Services are currently processing about 60,000 specimens a day, and many employers who conduct employee testing programs use labs certified by other organizations or use on-site test procedures.

This phenomenon of workplace drug testing evolved slowly over more than a decade. During that time policies, procedures, and technology have changed considerably. In general, most organizations don't have "drug-testing programs." Rather, "testing" has become the foundation for a comprehensive programmatic approach to substance abuse. Prevention and deterrence are the key concepts of most workplace programs, not detection, but when a worker develops a problem the standard practice is to get the substance-abusing employee into treatment, and back to work.

**Lewis L. Maltby**
***Director, American Civil Liberties Union National Task Force on Civil Liberties in the Workplace.***

***FROM HR NEWS, APRIL 1996***

**no**

Mounting evidence suggests that drug testing does not work, or at least that the claims of those who make their living selling testing are greatly exaggerated.

The most important evidence comes from the National Academy of Sciences. The academy's Institute of Medicine recently released a report which examines all the major studies regarding drugs and the workplace and summarizes the state of our knowledge. This report casts doubt on the effectiveness of drug testing. The critical assumption on which all drug-testing programs are based is that those who use illegal drugs are less productive than other employees.

The academy, after reviewing all the evidence, found no consistent relationship between drug use and the quality of an employee's work. No relationship was found between drug use and productivity, or between drug use and the rate of workplace accidents. In some areas, drug use did make a difference. Drug users had slightly higher rates of absenteeism.

The ultimate question for an employer is whether urine testing is cost-justified. Here, too, the academy found little support of the industry's claims. Some studies found that drug testing was not cost-effective. Others reached the opposite conclusion, but were described by the academy as "deeply flawed." Overall, the academy concluded that, "decisions by organizations to adopt such programs have often been made without a well-grounded consideration of the likely benefits."

One reason the expenses of drug testing are so hard to justify is that few drug users are ever identified. According to the National Institute on Drug Abuse, only 3 percent of all random drug tests are positive. When one considers the cost of programs required to identify these few people, serious questions emerge. The federal government recently found that the average cost of a confirmed positive test result is $77,000. Is it really worth this much money to learn that a file clerk is smoking marijuana on a Saturday night?

Non-testing employers do not ignore the problem of drug abuse. They simply choose to deal with it differently. Many companies rely on careful employee selection and thorough performance evaluation and quality-control systems to create a high-quality workforce, avoiding those with any performance-impairing problems, including drug abuse.

The truth is that there are many strategies for dealing with employee drug abuse. Urine testing is one strategy, but is not the only one. There are other approaches, and mounting evidence from impartial sources indicates that urine testing may not be the best way.

# The Marijuana Debate Goes on

Discussions about drug testing invariably turn to marijuana and the age-old questions: Is it harmful? Addictive? Does it act as a "gateway" to harder drugs? Marijuana residues stay in the body longer than other drugs, thus causing more marijuana users to get "caught" by urinalysis than users of other drugs.

"Drug testing is all about marijuana," says John P. Morgan, professor of pharmacology at City University of New York Medical School, who supports legalization of marijuana. "It's a critical weapon in the government's war on recreational marijuana users," he adds, noting that more people have been arrested for possession of marijuana during the Clinton administration than any other.

Critics like Morgan say drug testing should focus on more dangerous and addictive drugs like cocaine and heroin, or alcohol and tobacco, rather than "pot."

But testing proponents contend that marijuana is dangerous, addictive and a gateway to harder drugs and that cracking down on marijuana will indirectly stem the demand for heroin and cocaine.

"It's easy for people to underestimate the impact that marijuana has,"says Mark de Bernardo, executive director of the Institute for a Drug-Free Workplace, which promotes workplace testing. "There are a lot more casual users of alcohol, who don't get addicted, than there are users of illicit drugs" who don't get addicted."

According to a recent report by the National Center on Addiction and Substance Abuse (CASA) at Columbia University, teens 12-17 who use marijuana are 85 times more likely to use cocaine than non-marijuana users. [1]

CASA President Joseph A. Califano contends that the gateway effect means that recent increases in marijuana use among teens will translate into 820,000 more children who will try cocaine in their lifetime, of whom 58,000 will become addicts. Califano wrote that the statistical link between smoking pot and using harder drugs presents "a convincing case for a billion-dollar-a-year investment to move biomedical research on substance abuse and addiction into the big leagues at the National Institutes of Health, along with heart disease, cancer and AIDS." [2]

But Morgan calls the addiction and gateway arguments the "Big Lie" being promulgated by "more and more people, including urine testers and prevention, treatment and education specialists, whose livelihoods depend on the war on marijuana."

"For the large majority of people," Morgan says, "marijuana is a terminus rather than a gateway drug. More than 72 million Americans have tried marijuana at some point in their lives," including the president, the Speaker of the House and the secretary of Health and Human Services, he points out. "Yet in the over-30 population, only 0.8 percent of the population is continuing to use marijuana on a daily or even near-daily basis." [3]

"The lies and exaggerations about marijuana's dangers do little to discourage young people from trying marijuana, and may even have the opposite effect," Morgan writes in his new book, *Marijuana Myths, Marijuana Facts, A Review of the Scientific Evidence.*

Co-authored with Lynn Zimmer, associate professor of sociology at Queens College, the book analyzes the data supporting each of 20 arguments against marijuana used by government agencies and drug testing proponents. "Over and over, we discovered that government officials, journalists and even many 'drug experts' had misinterpreted, misrepresented or distorted the scientific evidence," wrote the authors.

The gateway theory tries to establish a causal relationship when only a statistical association exists, Morgan says. "Most people who ride a motorcycle have ridden a bicycle," he writes. "However, bicycle riding does not cause motorcycle riding."

Regarding marijuana dependence, Morgan cites a study by two pharmacologists who independently ranked the dependence potential of caffeine, nicotine, alcohol, heroin, cocaine and marijuana. Both ranked marijuana and caffeine as the least addictive, and one said marijuana was less addicting than caffeine. [4]

However, treatment specialists report anecdotal evidence of psychological dependence on marijuana, especially by heavy marijuana users. [5] But drug-testing opponents contend that almost all heavy marijuana users are also heavy alcohol users, who probably self-medicate to deaden pre-existing emotional pain.

A study released last March by the National Institute on Drug Abuse (NIDA) apparently supports that finding. It found that teenagers with prior serious anti-social problems are at high risk for marijuana dependence. "This study provides additional important data to better illustrate that marijuana is a dangerous drug that can be addictive," said Alan I. Leshner, director of the institute. [6]

Yet in its "Facts Parents Need to Know" fact sheet on its Web site, NIDA concedes that "Most marijuana users do not go on to use other illegal drugs."

The government also says marijuana is "a hugely significant cause of car crashes," and that marijuana users are "jamming hospital emergency rooms and drug treatment centers," according to White House Office of National Drug Control Policy spokesman Robert Weiner.

"Those are all absolutely false statements," Morgan says. "There's no scientific basis for them." He cites a 1993 Department of Transportation study that said, "Of the many psychoactive drugs, licit and illicit, that are available and used by people who drive, marijuana may well be among the least harmful." [7]

In the largest such study ever undertaken, Australian

researchers at the University of Adelaide found that drivers using marijuana were no more likely to be involved in an accident than those who were drug-free.[8]

Morgan concedes that "inexperienced marijuana users and inexperienced drivers, in particular, may be unable to drive safely even after small doses of marijuana."

Weiner's claim that hospital emergency rooms are "jammed" with marijuana users is based on federal Drug Abuse Warning Network (DAWN) statistics showing recent increases in the number of patients mentioning marijuana in hospital emergency rooms.

Morgan points out that marijuana use is on the increase, and inexperienced users may suffer acute anxiety the first time they use it. But, he says, even though marijuana is the most widely used illicit drug in America, it is mentioned in emergency cases less often than most other illicit drugs, and less than over-the-counter drugs. For instance, in 1993, 47 percent of the drug "mentions" by adolescents were for over-the-counter pain medications, compared with about 8 percent for marijuana.

In addition, he points out, marijuana is rarely mentioned alone. About 80 percent of the marijuana "mentions" also involved alcohol use, he says. "When a patient mentions marijuana, it does not mean marijuana caused the hospital visit," Morgan writes.

Out of more than 500,000 drug-abuse episodes reported by emergency rooms in 1994, only 1.6 percent — or slightly more than 8,000 — involved only marijuana. "And none of the marijuana-only mentions were hospitalized," he says.

Further, he says, evidence of marijuana use was found in only 587 of the 8,426 drug-related deaths in 1993. "In all of those cases, other drugs were found as well," he says. "Marijuana did not cause a single overdose death."

But, argues de Bernardo, "Today's marijuana has 22 times the THC[9] that it had in the 1960s. It's much stronger, more addictive and more dangerous."

After examining statistics from the University of Mississippi's Potency Monitoring Project (PMP), Morgan concludes, "There is no reason to believe that today's marijuana is stronger or more dangerous than the marijuana smoked during the 1960s and '70s."[10]

Independent analyses of marijuana in the 1970s showed an average purity of 2-5 percent. Since 1980, average marijuana potency has fluctuated between 2-3.5 percent, he writes, with no consistent upward or downward trend. But comparing potency data across the 1970s and '80s is misleading, he says, because PMP samples in the '70s were typically from low-potency sources. Improved storage practices and measurement methods in the '80s may have increased the amount of THC detected.

Even if today's marijuana were more potent than in the 1960s, it would not necessarily be more dangerous or produce more intense effects on the body, Morgan says.

"There is no possibility of a fatal overdose from smoking marijuana, regardless of THC content," he writes. In fact, he says, since the main danger from marijuana is damage to the lungs, higher-potency marijuana may be slightly less harmful than lower-potency marijuana, because users tend to smoke less of it to achieve the same "high."

The NIDA Web site points out that marijuana smoke contains the same cancer-causing ingredients as tobacco, sometimes in higher concentrations. "Studies show that someone who smokes five joints per week may be taking in as many cancer-causing chemicals as someone who smokes a full pack of cigarettes every day," it says.

Morgan concedes that marijuana smokers are at risk because they inhale more deeply and retain smoke in their lungs longer than tobacco smokers, and "joints" are not filtered. But he says there are no epidemiological studies showing higher rates of lung cancer in marijuana smokers than in tobacco smokers, probably because they inhale less smoke overall than cigarette smokers. But, he wrote, heavy smokers of both marijuana and tobacco possibly "have an increased risk of lung cancer."[11]

Drug-testing proponents also point out that about 100,000 people seek treatment for marijuana dependency each year. Morgan argues that many of those were referred to treatment centers by employers or courts, after they tested positive for marijuana. Most do not meet the official definition for "dependency," Morgan says, but either the court or the boss has given them the choice of seeking treatment, being fired or serving time, he says.

"Which would you choose?" he asks.

---

[1] "Cigarettes, Alcohol, Marijuana: Gateways to Illicit Drug Use," Center on Addiction and Substance Abuse, Columbia University, October 1994.

[2] From an editorial written by Califano in September 1997 and distributed to several newspapers.

[3] Morgan's statistics come from the "1994 National Household Survey on Drug Abuse, Population Estimates," Substance Abuse and Mental Health Services Administration, 1995.

[4] P.J. Hilts, "Is Nicotine Addictive? It Depends on Whose Criteria You Use," *The New York Times*, Aug. 2, 1994.

[5] For background, see Sarah Glazer, "Preventing Teen Drug Use," *The CQ Researcher*, July 28, 1995, pp. 666-689.

[6] Thomas Crowley, et. al, "Cannabis Dependence, Withdrawal and Reinforcing Effects Among Adolescents with Conduct Symptoms and Substance Use Disorders," *Drug and Alcohol Dependence*, spring 1998.

[7] H. Robbe and J. O'Hanlon, "Marijuana and Actual Driving Performance," Department of Transportation, 1993, p. 107.

[8] See C.E. Hunter et. al., "The Prevalence and Role of Alcohol, Cannabinoids, Benzodiazepines and Stimulants in Non-fatal Crashes," University of Adelaid, Department of Forensic Science, 1998; Robbe, *op. cit.* (Netherlands study).

[9] THC is the chief psychoactive ingredient in marijuana.

[10] The PMP has been monitoring the potency of marijuana samples submitted by law enforcement agencies since the early 1970s.

[11] Marijuana smokers are only 3 percent more likely than non-smokers to visit doctors for respiratory illnesses like bronchitis, according to researchers at the Kaiser Permanente Medical Care Program, he says.

past five years, and during that time the percentage of employees testing positive has gone down from about 5 percent to 1," says Bishop, manager of health services for ESCO Corp.

"We work with molten metal, and our employees support drug testing overwhelmingly. No one wants to work with someone who is drug-impaired." ■

## FOR MORE INFORMATION

*If you would like to have this CQ Researcher updated, or need more information about this topic, please call CQ Custom Research. Special rates for CQ subscribers. (202) 887-8600 or (800) 432-2250, ext. 600, or E-mail Custom.Research@cq.com*

**Center for Addiction and Substance Abuse, Columbia University,** 152 West 57th St., New York, N.Y. 10019; (212) 841-5200. CASA conducts research on drug and alcohol abuse and prevention; it considers marijuana a "gateway" drug.

**Drug Policy Foundation,** 4455 Connecticut Ave., N.W., Suite B-500, Washington, D.C. 20008-2302; (202) 537-5005; www.dpf.org. This nonprofit research organization studies alternatives to the nation's drug war, including legalization.

**Institute for a Drug-Free Workplace,** 1225 Eye St., N.W. Suite 1000, Washington, D.C. 20005; (202) 842-7400; www.drugfreeworkplace.org. This business-oriented coalition seeks to improve productivity and safety through detection and treatment of drug and alcohol abuse.

**National Clearinghouse for Alcohol and Drug Information,** P.O. Box 2345, Rockville, Md. 20847-2345; (800) 729-6686; www.health.org. Provides publications, videotapes and educational materials to help parents talk to their children about drug use.

## Notes

[1] For background, see Richard L. Worsnop, "High School Sports," *The CQ Researcher*, Sept. 22, 1995, pp. 825-858.

[2] For background, see Richard L Worsnop, "Privacy in the Workplace," *The CQ Researcher*, Nov. 19, 1993, pp. 1021-1044.

[3] "Winning the War on Drugs — Check the Military," *The Drug-Free Workplace Report*, fall 1990, p. 4.

[4] Marci M. DeLancey, "Does Drug Testing Work?" Institute for a Drug-Free Workplace, 1994.

[5] Robert W. Taggart, "Results of the Drug Testing Program at Southern Pacific Railroad," *Drugs in the Workplace: Research and Evaluation Data*, National Institute on Drug Abuse, 1989.

[6] "Workplace Drug Testing and Drug Abuse Policies: Summary of Key Findings," American Management Association, 1996.

[7] "Under the Influence? Drugs and the American Work Force," National Academy of Sciences, 1994.

[8] American Management Association, *op. cit.*

[9] Chamber of Commerce press release.

[10] Taggart, *op. cit.*

[11] Beverly A. Potter and Sebastian Orfali, *Drug Testing at Work: A Guide for Employers and Employees (1990).*

[12] William J. Staudenmeier Jr., "Urine Testing: The Battle for Privatized Social Control During the 1986 War on Drugs," from *Images of Issues, Typifying Contemporary Social Problems*, Joel Best, ed. (1989).

[13] Potter, *op. cit.*

[14] *Under the Influence? Drugs and the American Work Force*, National Research Council, 1994.

[15] Potter, *op. cit.*

[16] Quoted in Christopher S. Wren, "Clinton to Require State Efforts to Cut Drug Use in Prisons," *The New York Times*, Jan. 12, 1998.

[17] *Ibid.*

[18] Paul Armentano, "A Look at the Historical Legal Basis for Urine Testing," *NORML Reports*, December 1995.

[19] Jeannette C. James, "The Constitutionality of Federal Employee Drug Testing," The *American University Law Review*, fall 1988.

[20] The survey is published each year by the Substance Abuse and Mental Health Services Administration.

[21] For background, see Sarah Glazer, "Preventing Teen Drug Use," *The CQ Researcher*, July 28, 1995, pp. 674-697.

[22] Quoted in Roberto Suro, "Boomers expect teen drug use, survey finds," *The Washington Post*, Sept. 19, 1996.

[23] Substance Abuse and Mental Health Services Administration.

[24] The case is *Todd v. Rush County Schools*.

[25] Ouoted in Frank J. Murray, "High court declines to debate school drug testing," *The Washington Times,* Oct. 6, 1998.

[26] *Ibid.*

[27] "Opening the way to drug tests," *The St. Petersburg Times*, Oct. 13, 1998.

[28] Joan Biskupic, "Court allows drug tests for OEOB pass holders," *The Washington Post*, March 3, 1998.

[29] Quoted in "Different Sauces for Geese and Ganders?" The Associated Press, Aug. 7, 1998.

[30] Arnold Trebach and Scott Ehlers, "The war on our children: destroying the rights of America's youth to save them from drugs," "The Playboy Forum"; *Playboy*, February 1997. Trebach is a professor at American University and editor-in-chief of *The Drug Policy Letter*, published by the Drug Policy Foundation; Ehlers is associate editor.

# Bibliography

## *Selected Sources Used*


### *Books*

**Holtorf, Kent, *Ur-ine Trouble*, Vandalay Press, 1998.**
Holtorf, a physician, has spent years reviewing the scientific data about drug testing. He describes how poorly trained personnel in uncertified laboratories can erroneously cause a job seeker to test positive for drugs and how common foods and medicines can cause false-positive test results.

**Jacques Normand, et al., *Under the Influence? Drugs and the American Work Force*, National Academy of Sciences, 1994.**
This National Academy of Sciences analysis of all the studies done before 1994 on the effectiveness of workplace drug testing found that "there is as yet no conclusive scientific evidence from properly controlled studies that employment drug-testing programs widely discourage drug use or encourage rehabilitation."

**Potter, Beverly A., and Sebastian Orfali, *Drug Testing at Work, A Guide for Employers and Employees*, Ronin Publishing, 1990.**
The authors describe how tests work, the civil rights issues involved, how to set up a program and how employees can protect themselves from false-positive results.

**Zimmer, Lynn, and John P. Morgan, *Marijuana Myths, Marijuana Facts,* Lindesmith Center, 1997.**
The 241-page book, published by billionaire George Sorros' drug-law reform think tank, includes more than 60 pages of bibliography and footnotes listing scores of studies on marijuana and its effects on the human body. Each chapter deals with one of the arguments against marijuana use.

### *Articles*

**Armentano, Paul, "A Look at the Historical Legal Basis for Urine Testing," *NORML Reports,* December 1995.**
The publications director for the National Organization to Reform Marijuana Laws (NORML) writes about the legal history of drug testing, reviewing major court decisions and how the Supreme Court's position on privacy rights has shifted.

**DeLancey, Marci M., "Does Drug Testing Work?" Institute for a Drug-Free Workplace, 1994.**
This 116-page report by the institute — a coalition of businesses and individuals that promotes workplace drug testing — provides pages of statistics about the prevalence, cost and effectiveness of alcohol, drug and substance abuse. It also offers testimonials from companies that have established drug-testing programs.

**James, Jeannette C., "The Constitutionality of Federal Employee Drug Testing," *The American University Law Review,* fall 1988.**
James, a lawyer, focuses on the controversial Supreme Court decision in *National Treasury Employees Union v. Von Raab*. She contends the decision was tantamount to jettisoning the need to establish probable cause before searching private homes because the state has a strong interest in eliminating crime.

**Murray, Frank J., "High court declines to debate school drug testing," *The Washington Times*, Oct. 6, 1998.**
The author discusses the controversial Oct. 5 decision by the court to let stand a rural Indiana high school's policy of requiring mandatory drug-testing for all students in extracurricular activities, regardless of whether they are suspected of using drugs.

**Staudenmeier, William J., Jr., "Urine Testing: The Battle for Privatized Social Control During the 1986 War on Drugs," from *Images of Issues, Typifying Contemporary Social Problems*, edited by Joel Best, 1989.**
Sociologist Staudenmeier calls President Ronald Reagan's push for private employers to start drug testing "privatized social control." The Fourth Amendment prohibits the government from requiring the general population to be tested for drugs, he points out.

**Trebach, Arnold, and Scott Ehlers, "The war on our children: destroying the rights of America's youth to save them from drugs," *Playboy*, February 1997.**
Two Drug Policy Foundation editors argue that current U.S. drug-testing policy is indoctrinating several generations of children with the belief that venerable constitutional privacy guarantees are less important than the need for drug control.

### *Reports*

***National Household Survey on Drug Abuse*, Substance Abuse and Mental Health Services Administration, 1997.**
The annual survey shows that teen drug use has been climbing since 1992.

**Taggart, Robert W., *Results of the Drug Testing Program at Southern Pacific Railroad*, Drugs in the Workplace: Research and Evaluation Data, National Institute on Drug Abuse, 1989.**
This study showed a 50 percent drop in positive drug tests after a year of "reasonable suspicion" drug testing.

# 12 Antitrust Policy

KENNETH JOST

It has been called the most valuable square foot of real estate in the world, and it's at the center of a bitter fight between the world's richest man and most powerful nation.

The fight heated up last month when the U.S. government and 20 states launched antitrust suits against Bill Gates' giant Microsoft Corp. At issue is control of that little piece of "real estate" — the first screen that personal computer users see when they boot up machines powered by Microsoft's ubiquitous Windows operating system.

Microsoft chairman and co-founder Gates says the icon-filled screen opens the door for computer users to vast storehouses of information and countless opportunities for enhanced productivity. But Microsoft, he says, should hold the key to that door: His company designed it, sells it and can best be relied on to continue improving it.

Government lawyers say that Windows — used in 90 percent of the world's personal computers — is essentially "the on-ramp to the information superhighway," and no single company should control it. Moreover, they say, Microsoft has abused its power through a host of allegedly anti-competitive practices to boost its business at the expense of rival firms.

The Justice Department's lawsuit, Assistant U.S. Attorney General Joel I. Klein declared on May 18, "seeks to put an end to Microsoft's unlawful campaign to eliminate competition, deter innovation and restrict consumer choice."

Two hours later, an amiable but unyielding Gates answered the charges in a news conference at the company's Redmond, Wash., headquarters. "Federal and state regulators have taken the unprecedented step of trying to intervene in America's most successful and growing industry," Gates said. "This is a step backwards for America, for consumers and for the personal computer industry that is leading our nation's economy into the 21st century." [1]

From *The CQ Researcher,* June 12, 1998.

The lawsuits came in the week that Microsoft was scheduled to ship the latest upgrade of its PC operating system, Windows 98, to computer manufacturers in advance of a scheduled release to customers this month.

The suits stop short of seeking to block the release of Windows 98. But they ask a federal judge in Washington, D.C., to order a major change in Microsoft's operating system. The Justice Department and the states are seeking a preliminary injunction to require all future versions of Windows that include Microsoft's Internet Explorer software for browsing the Internet also to include a competing software developed by a rival firm, the Netscape Navigator. [2]

Allowing Microsoft to "bundle" its browser with its monopoly operating system without including Netscape's, Klein told reporters, "could well cause irreversible harm to competition by letting Microsoft unlawfully achieve a second monopoly, this time in Internet browsers."

To back up its charges, the Justice Department included in its 53-page complaint seemingly damaging quotes from internal Microsoft messages and documents suggesting a conscious plan to use its Windows monopoly to "leverage" its new browser and displace Netscape's earlier — and market-leading — product.

"Pitting browser against browser is hard since Netscape has 80 percent market share, and we have [less than] 20 percent," Microsoft Senior Vice President James Allchin was quoted as telling a colleague in January 1997. "I am convinced we have to use Windows — this is the one thing they don't have."

But Gates and other Microsoft executives depicted the proposed remedy as a punishment for the company's success and a disservice to customers. "Forcing Microsoft to include Netscape's competing software in our operating system is like requiring Coca-Cola to include three cans of Pepsi in every six-pack it sells," Gates said.

As for the internal communications quoted in the Justice Department complaints, Gates and others insisted they were taken out of context. Gates also branded as "absolutely false" the most damning allegation — that he had personally met with Netscape executives in May 1995 to divide up the market, offering to keep Microsoft out of the browser market if Netscape promised not to try to produce a rival operating system. [3]

The lawsuit immediately conjured up images of some of the country's most historic antitrust actions — from the early 20th-century suit that broke up John D. Rockefeller's Standard Oil trust to the more recent litigation that split up AT&T in the 1980s. Microsoft executives offered a less flattering comparison. They likened the suit to the Justice Department's failed antitrust suit against IBM, which lasted for 13 years before the government dropped the case in 1982 for lack of evidence.

The suit against Microsoft comes at a time of increased antitrust activity both at the Justice Department and the Federal Trade Commission (FTC).

## Antitrust Activity Has Increased

*In the past 10 years, the number of planned corporate mergers rose 35 percent while antitrust investigations quadrupled and cases filed more than doubled.*

**Premerger Notifications**

| | 1988 | 1997 |
|---|---|---|
| *Received* | *2,747* | *3,702* |
| *Investigations initiated* | *56* | *220* |
| *Cases filed* | *6* | *14* |

*Source: Justice Department, Antitrust Division*

Antitrust enforcement peaked in the 1960s and early '70s, when many policy-makers viewed corporate size as an inherent economic and political problem. But antitrust laws went out of favor in Washington under President Ronald Reagan, who filled key antitrust posts with avowed advocates of big business and determined skeptics of antitrust laws except in limited circumstances.

President Clinton has not been especially vocal on antitrust issues, but his appointees — Klein and his predecessor at the Justice Department, Anne Bingaman, and Robert Pitofsky as FTC chairman — view antitrust enforcement more positively than their counterparts from the Reagan-Bush era. "It seems to be far more robust than what we had seen earlier," says E. Thomas Sullivan, dean of the University of Minnesota Law School.

"There's a revived interest," says Irwin Stelzer, director of regulatory policy studies at the American Enterprise Institute in Washington. "You've got two good people — Klein and Pitofsky — and they're doing a very good job. They're not crazy like some of the old 'big is bad' people."

The increased interest in antitrust action stems in part from a wave of corporate mergers in the United States and around the world over the past few years. The consolidations — last year's were valued at more than $1 trillion in assets — affect everything from banking and telecommunications to pharmaceuticals and office supplies.[4] *(See chart, p. 228.)*

The Justice Department and FTC have approved some of the mergers while blocking others. "It's hard to accuse the Clinton administration of being either a pushover for transactions or relentlessly hostile," says William E. Kovacic, who teaches antitrust law at George Mason University School of Law in Fairfax, Va.

Some of the biggest deals are still awaiting review, in some cases by other independent agencies. The proposed merger of Citicorp and Travelers is being reviewed by the Federal Reserve Board, while the Federal Communications Commission will study the planned acquisition of MCI Communications by British-based WorldCom Inc. Meanwhile, the Justice Department already had one major antitrust case in court before the Microsoft suit: an effort to block the merger of two giant defense contractors, Lockheed Martin and Northrup Grumman *(see p. 226.)*

As Microsoft's Sept. 18 trial date approaches, here are some of the major issues being debated:

### *Have antitrust laws been good or bad for the economy overall?*

The Supreme Court once called the nation's first antitrust law, the 1890 Sherman Act, the "Magna Carta of the free enterprise system" — in effect, a fundamental guarantee for the right of all businesses to fair competition in the marketplace.[5] In the 108 years since then, Congress has periodically reaffirmed that commitment by expanding antitrust laws to cover other business practices besides classic monopolies and cartels. *(See chart, p. 216.)* And the federal government has repeatedly invoked those laws to break up or control business monopolies — generally to public approval.

Some experts and advocates say the laws have served the country well by promoting and preserving competition. Others maintain that antitrust laws and antitrust enforcers have proved to be too weak to prevent anti-competitive abuses and the growth of giant corporations that wield undue economic power. But still others say that the antitrust laws have been bad for the U.S. economy, even bad for competition — punishing successful companies, protecting inefficient ones and in the end hurting rather than helping consumers.

"It's been an uneven 100 years," says Rudolph Peritz, a professor at New York Law School and author of a recent history of antitrust policy. "Antitrust enforcers and policy-makers have done better at some times and worse at others."

Peritz says the early focus of antitrust laws in breaking up monopolies like the Standard Oil and tobacco trusts established a pattern of generally preventing the creation of single-company industries. But he says the laws have been less effective in dealing with "oligopolies" — industries in which a small number of producers control the market and, according to antitrust advocates, provide less than complete competition.

The more centrist Kovacic says antitrust laws have served an important purpose by committing the federal government to free markets rather than central planning as a central economic principle. "The [Justice Department] antitrust divisions have historically been a voice for promoting private enterprise and rivalry," he says.

More concretely, Kovacic says the laws have discouraged the formation of "producer cartels" — agreements between rival firms to set prices or divide the market. But he notes that price-fixing agreements persist — citing, for example, the recent prosecution of Archer Daniels Midland Inc. that last fall cost the agriprocessing firm a then record $100 million fine for fixing prices on two products. (A price-fixing case against Ucar International, the nation's leading manufacturer of graphite electrodes, a key component in electric arc furnaces, produced a new record fine of $110 million in April.) [6]

Some conservative and libertarian antitrust experts, however, see little but negative effects from the government's use of antitrust laws. In his influential book, *The Antitrust Paradox*, published in 1978, Robert Bork complained that the antitrust laws had evolved into "rules that significantly impair both competition and the ability of the economy to produce goods and services efficiently." [7] Bork, a Yale law professor at the time and later a federal judge and unsuccessful Supreme Court nominee, was one of the leading members of the so-called "Chicago school" that advocated a more strictly economic approach to antitrust issues (*see p. 223*).

Robert Levy, a senior fellow in constitutional studies at the libertarian Cato Institute, says the overall effect of the antitrust laws has been "deleterious."

"I don't think that antitrust laws ever had any legitimate functions," Levy says, "and I don't think they have any legitimate function now given the dynamism of today's markets."

Unlike Levy, most conservatives accept the idea that antitrust laws should prohibit what one of Bork's disciples — federal Judge Frank Easterbrook Jr.— once labeled "plain-vanilla cartels and mergers to monopoly." [8] But they criticize the expansion of antitrust to two other business practices.

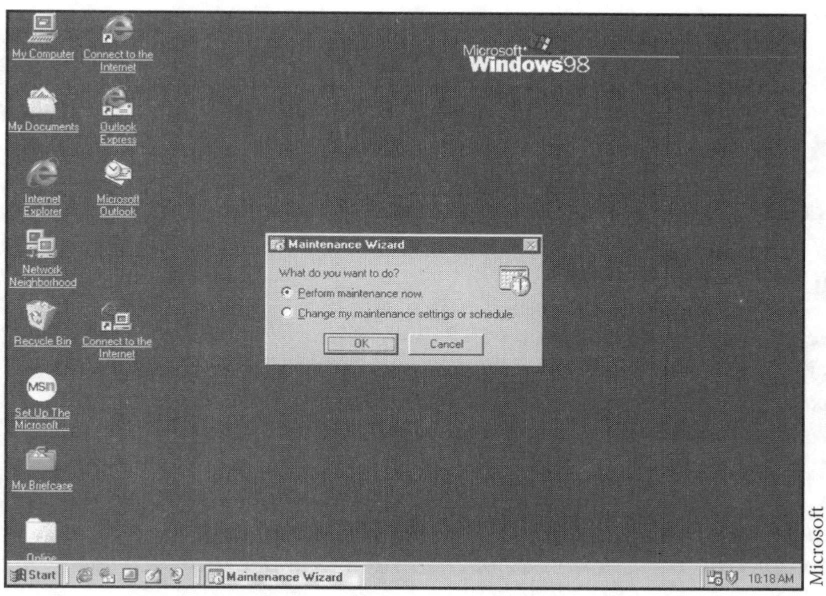

Microsoft

*Antitrust suits against Microsoft Corp. contend that it should not require computer makers to include Internet Explorer, Microsoft's browser software, as a condition of using its Windows 98 operating system. Microsoft says Explorer is an integrated feature of Windows that can't be lopped off.*

First, they say that antitrust laws should generally not apply to so-called vertical mergers between, for instance, a manufacturer and a retailer, or to vertical "restraints" — such as a restriction by a manufacturer on a dealer's ability to set prices or expand outside a specified territory. Second, they generally defend the legality of so-called "tying" arrangements that condition the sale of one product on the buyer's agreement to purchase a second product. And they believe that the antitrust laws were often enforced too rigorously, particularly in the 1950s and '60s, against so-called horizontal mergers — combinations between firms producing the same product or service. Conservatives viewed many of these mergers as likely to produce greater efficiencies without adverse effects on competition.

Some more liberal-leaning experts today agree that the Supreme Court under Chief Justice Earl Warren was too strict in disallowing any mergers that would result in increased concentration in the industry. "In retrospect, the antitrust policies of the Earl Warren era were excessive in the way they defined markets," Sullivan says.

For their part, conservatives say that the Supreme Court and lower federal courts have become more sophisticated in handling antitrust issues because of the growing influence of the Chicago school since the late 1970s.

"If the federal government wants to challenge a merger, it has to define a relevant market and then show how the concentration in that market rises to a troublesome level and show why there are barriers to entry," says John Lopatka, a professor at the University of South Carolina Law School. "And if the defendants raise the issue, the government is going to have to explain that the mergers do not generate efficiencies — that is, cost savings — all of which is a proper analysis."

But the emphasis on so-called microeconomics — the study of firm behavior — discomforts liberal antitrust experts. "Microeconomics is a

## Major Federal Antitrust Laws

**Sherman Act (1890)** — *Prohibits any "contract, combination or conspiracy . . . in restraint of trade" (section 1) or monopolizing or attempting to monopolize interstate or foreign trade or commerce (section 2); Justice Department authorized to bring criminal cases or civil suits; criminal violations punishable by up to a year in prison and $5,000 fine; individuals may bring civil suits, with triple damages allowed.*

**Clayton Antitrust Act (1914)** — *Prohibits price discrimination (section 2), exclusive dealing and "tying" contracts (section 3), and stock acquisitions of other companies (section 7) where effect "may be to substantially lessen competition or tend to create a monopoly in any line of commerce."*

**Federal Trade Commission Act (1914)** — *Prohibits "unfair methods of competition" and "unfair or deceptive acts or practices" (section 5); creates FTC as independent agency with authority to issue cease-and-desist orders to enforce law.*

**Robinson-Patman Act (1936)** — *Outlaws "unjustified" price discounts that result in injury to competition (section 2(a)); buyers seeking unjustified price discounts also subject to liability (section 2(f)).*

**Celler-Kefauver Act (1950)** — *Strengthens Clayton Act's provision against anti-competitive mergers to cover acquisition of assets as well as stock of another company and to cover merger with firms in different line of commerce.*

**Antitrust Procedures and Penalties Act (1974)** — *Changes price-fixing and other violations from misdemeanors to felonies; raises maximum fines to $1 million for companies and $500,000 for individuals; increases maximum prison sentence to three years. Also requires public disclosure and judicial review of case settlements negotiated by Justice Department.*

**Hart-Scott-Rodino Antitrust Improvements Act (1976)** — *Requires merging companies above specified size to notify Justice Dept. and FTC before completing transaction; establishes mandatory waiting period for completing transaction or beginning joint operations.*

*Source: Ernest Gellhorn and William E. Kovacic,* Antitrust Law and Economics in a Nutshell *(1994).*

narrow lens that can tell us at best about one particular kind of economic power: market power," Peritz says. "But firm size reflects another kind of economic power. You can have a merger between two multibillion-dollar companies, like Nynex and Bell Atlantic, that will fly through antitrust scrutiny because they are in different 'markets,' but we all know from our experience that there [was] an increase in economic power of all sorts when those two companies merged."

### *Is the current wave of mergers good or bad for consumers?*

When the government divided AT&T into seven regional telephone companies and a separate long-distance carrier, it hoped to be ushering in an era of wide-open competition that would improve service and lower rates. Long-distance service has become a heartily competitive market, but local telephone service remains a monopoly. Now, some of the so-called Baby Bells are getting back together and promising — in the face of consumer-group skepticism — that the mergers will enhance competition and bring customers better service and lower prices.

The developments in the telephone industry encapsulate a debate that has raged since the beginning of U.S. antitrust policy: whether corporate mergers help consumers by lowering costs and thereby prices or hurt consumers by reducing competition and thereby the incentives to keep prices low. Despite 100 years of argument and reams of academic research, the issue continues to sharply divide policy-makers, interest groups and experts.

Chicago school experts stoutly insist that most mergers do benefit the economy. "The presumption is that the merger is going to be beneficial," Lopatka says. "If one wants to interfere with the market, one has to prove that interference with the market is going to produce greater benefits than allowing the market to work."

"You can't stop every merger, and it would be bad if you did," says Stelzer, a conservative who does not count himself in the Chicago school.

But Peritz maintains that the view that large firms will be more efficient is overstated. "Efficiency and large size do not correlate so simply," Peritz says. "Large firms are much, much bigger than they need to be to take advantage of economies of scale in production."

The Clinton administration's record on mergers draws mixed reviews. Critics on the right say the administration has been too aggressive. "There's a long list of anti-merger activity," says the Cato Institute's Levy. As one example, he describes the opposition to the planned merger between the two giant office-supply chains, Staples and Office Depot, as "plain silliness."

"There was no evidence at all that there was any monopoly power being exercised by those two companies," Levy says. "There were plenty of competitors in the office-supply market."

Critics on the left, however, say the administration has been too timid in challenging corporate combinations. "The antitrust officials have not been as aggressive in challenging transactions until it gets to an extreme level of concentration," says Gene Kimmelman, co-director of the Washington office of Consumers Union. "I would not call that aggressive enforcement."

A number of experts, however, including several self-described conservatives, give the administration generally good marks in merger cases. "My impression is that they're applying the law pretty consistently," says Thomas Kauper, a professor at the University of Michigan Law School.

Stelzer agrees. "I think they've got it about right," he says. But Stelzer does fault Klein for not opposing the merger last year of two Baby Bells serving the Eastern and Mid-Atlantic states: Bell Atlantic Corp. and Nynex Corp.

Lopatka also declines to criticize the administration's stance on mergers. He specifically notes that he came to agree with the FTC's opposition to the Staples-Office Depot merger despite his initial skepticism. "They had pretty strong empirical evidence that when the two firms were not competing with each other, the price went up," Lopatka says.

For his part, though, Peritz regrets the reduced concern about corporate growth that dates from the Reagan-Bush presidencies and continues today. One reason for the changed attitude, he says, is that policy-makers have come to focus more on increasing shareholder value than on protecting consumers.

"What's not happening is a sufficient concern for what's happening to consumers, suppliers, and others who deal with these now even more enormous firms," Peritz says.

### *Should the federal government and the states have filed antitrust suits against Microsoft?*

From the moment the suits were filed — indeed, in the several weeks leading up to the filing — the antitrust case against Microsoft was being played out in the political and public relations arenas as much as in court. Members of Congress and newspaper editorials weighed in on opposite sides of the dispute. So did other computer executives.

The suit also drew sharply divided reactions among antitrust experts. Supporters of the suits maintain that they are well-grounded in established antitrust doctrines and that the requested remedies were both appropriate and modest. Critics see the allegations against Microsoft as weak, both factually and legally, and predict either a defeat for the government or at most a fairly weak settlement.

"It was important that the suit was filed," Peritz says. "The remedies that the Justice Department and the state attorneys general are asking for are reasonable, and consistent with the kind of anti-competitive behavior they're claiming Microsoft is engaged in."

"This is an old-time antitrust case in which Bill Gates is trying to establish that high-tech industries are so different from the rest of the world that antitrust laws shouldn't apply," Stelzer says in agreement. "It's a pretty straightforward tying case, a straightforward abuse of monopoly-position case."

But in Lopatka's view, "It's not a very strong complaint, not a very strong theory." Each of the government's theories, he says, presents difficult problems of proof under existing antitrust precedents. "I think the government is going to lose," he concludes.

The Justice Department has already battled Microsoft in court twice, with limited results. It ended its first investigation in July 1994, when Microsoft agreed to a consent decree requiring it to change some of the restrictions in its contracts with PC manufacturers and other software makers. Today, the decree — formally issued in August 1995 after one judge balked at approving it — is widely regarded as weak. "They proposed solutions that became obsolete in a hurry," George Mason's Kovacic says.

Then, last October, the Justice Department returned to court, claiming that Microsoft was violating the 1995 decree by forcing computer makers to include its Internet Explorer browser as a condition of selling Windows 95. U.S. District Judge Thomas Penfield Jackson granted an injunction in December requiring Microsoft to allow computer makers to unbundle the browser. But

## *United States v. Microsoft* ... The Main Event

**1990**

- *Microsoft introduces Windows 3.0 on May 22, using point-and-click system first developed by Apple Computer*
- *Federal Trade Commission (FTC) opens investigation of Microsoft, without public announcement*

**1991**

- *Microsoft confirms FTC investigation on March 11; depicts probe as "technical"*

**1992**

- *FTC investigation continues*

**1993**

- *FTC on Feb. 5 deadlocks, 2-2, on seeking court order to force Microsoft to cease manufacturing software incompatible with rivals' operating systems*
- *FTC deadlocks again July 21; closes probe, but turns file over to Justice Department*
- *Justice Department opens antitrust investigation in August*

**1994**

- *Microsoft reaches settlement July 16 with Justice Department and European authorities, agreeing to change contracts with computer makers and eliminate some restrictions on other software makers*

**1995**

- *Federal Judge Stanley Sporkin on Feb. 14 rejects settlement as "not in the public interest"*
- *Federal appeals court in Washington on June 16 overturns Sporkin's decision; assigns case to new judge, to be picked at random*
- *Federal Judge Thomas Penfield Jackson approves settlement on Aug. 21*
- *Windows 95 launches retail sales Aug. 24*

**1996**

- *Microsoft discloses on Sept. 19 that Justice Department had opened new antitrust probe*

**1997**

- *Bill Gates listed in* Forbes *(July 28 issue) as world's richest private individual, with estimated net worth of $36.4 billion*
- *Justice Department files petition on Oct. 20 charging Microsoft with illegally coercing computer makers to equip PCs with Internet Explorer browser software*
- *Judge Jackson issues order on Dec. 11 requiring Microsoft to allow PC makers to offer Windows 95 with or without Internet Explorer*

**1998**

- *Federal appeals court hears Microsoft's appeal of Jackson's order, on April 21*
- *Justice Department and the states put off plans to file broad antitrust suit on May 14 as Microsoft asks for talks aimed at settlement; talks collapse on May 16*
- *U.S., states file suit May 18, seeking preliminary injunction to force Microsoft to change restrictive contracts and to include Netscape Navigator, competing browser software, in Windows 98*
- *Judge Jackson on May 22 schedules trial for Sept. 18 on U.S., states' motion for preliminary injunction*
- *Windows 98 to be made available to customers on June 15*

when the federal appeals court in Washington heard Microsoft's appeal of the injunction in April, the government conceded that no computer maker had exercised that option up to then. [9]

The appellate judges appeared skeptical of the government's case in the April 24 arguments. In any event, the case concerned only Windows 95

# U.S. v. Microsoft: The Lines Are Drawn

**U.S. Assistant Attorney General Joel I. Klein**
*Comments accompanying filing of antitrust suit against Microsoft by the Justice Department, May 18, 1998*

In essence, what Microsoft has been doing, through a wide variety of illegal business practices, is leveraging its Windows operating system monopoly to force its other software products on consumers. This is like having someone with a monopoly in CD players forcing consumers to take its CDs in order to get the machine. We believe most Americans would prefer to choose their own CDs and, for their matter, their own software products as well. . . .

Microsoft is unwilling to compete fairly and on the merits; rather, it prefers to leverage its Windows monopoly 'to make people use' its browser. The antitrust laws take a very different view of the way the marketplace should work: those laws are premised on the belief that . . . people should be able to choose for themselves what products they use.

. . . [N]othing we are doing here will or should prevent Microsoft from innovating or competing on the merits. What cannot be tolerated — and what the antitrust laws forbid — is the barrage of illegal, anti-competitive practices that Microsoft uses to destroy its rivals and to avoid competition on the merits. That, and that alone, is what this lawsuit is all about.

**Bill Gates**
*Chairman, Microsoft*
*Comments following filing of federal antitrust suit, May 18, 1998*

Forcing Microsoft to include Netscape's competing software in our operating system is like requiring Coca-Cola to include three cans of Pepsi in every six-pack it sells. The changes the government is demanding on the boot-up screen is like telling Coca-Cola that it must remove its name from every can of soda. And saying that we must remove Internet technology from Windows is like telling Coca-Cola that it must take something out of its formula. . . .

Computer users today have more choices than ever before. PC users can already choose between Microsoft's Internet Explorer and any other Web browser, and computer manufacturers are free to install Netscape browsers on any computers they sell. . . . Computer manufacturers choose to configure the first screen differently. They choose to add any browsers. They choose to market whatever productivity software they want. . . .

We believe an antitrust lawsuit is counterproductive, costly to the taxpayers, and ultimately will be unsuccessful in the courts. . . . I am confident that in the end, America's judicial system will uphold our right to innovate on behalf of consumers. I look forward to presenting our case in court and continuing to create great software for our consumers.

and was already being overshadowed by the broadening investigations of Microsoft.

The government's lawsuit includes four allegations that also appear in the states' complaint. The first charges that Gates and other Microsoft executives unsuccessfully tried to persuade Netscape to divide up the browser and operating-system markets. The government quotes Netscape Executive Vice President Marc Andreesen as describing the no-compete proposal in a meeting between executives of the two companies in June 1995. Gates has vehemently denied the allegation.

The three other claims involve ongoing Microsoft activities: the bundling of Internet Explorer with Windows; restrictions on computer manufacturers' discretion to alter the initial Windows boot-up screen; and Microsoft's agreements with Internet service and content providers that the government says are aimed at promoting Microsoft services and excluding those of competing firms. The states add one other claim in their lawsuit: a contention that Microsoft is also trying to monopolize the market for office-services software through similar tying arrangements and exclusionary contracts.

Peritz says the evidence of antitrust violations is strong. "Microsoft has tried to achieve a monopoly in applications," Peritz says. "They've done that by taking applications and integrating them into the operating system." As for the remedy, he agrees with the government's effort to force Microsoft to include the Netscape browser in its Windows programs — but prefers the states' request that a third browser be included as well. "Just as we don't want Microsoft to dominate that field," he says, "we don't want Microsoft and Netscape to dominate it either."

Lopatka, however, doubts the government's evidence is strong enough to prevail in court. And, if so, he believes the suits are a mistake.

"We have a market that's certainly functioning well, in terms of generating lots of benefits for consumers," The University of South Carolina's Lopatka says. "I don't think you want to interfere with the market on a hunch." ■

# BACKGROUND

## Trust Busting

Congress passed the first of the federal antitrust laws in 1890 with bipartisan support at a time of rapid industrial consolidation and rapacious business practices. Four times since then — in 1914, 1950, 1974 and 1976 — Congress approved major revisions of the law aimed at tightening the prohibitions against monopoly power and adding new curbs on unfair business practices. But the executive branch and the federal courts have followed an uneven course in enforcing and interpreting the laws, alternating between periods of somewhat stricter and laxer antitrust enforcement. [10]

The Sherman Act bears the name of Sen. John Sherman, a Republican from Ohio — home of the biggest industrial trust of the late 19th century, John D. Rockefeller's Standard Oil of Ohio. Actually, though, Sherman's original proposal to ban any practices that restrained "full and fair competition" was amended in favor of narrower language prohibiting any contracts or combinations "in restraint of trade." The amended bill passed Congress overwhelmingly in July 1890 and was signed into law by a Republican president, Benjamin Harrison.

Today, Congress' intent in passing the law is one of the major points of disagreement. Bork and others in the so-called Chicago school argue that Sherman himself and Congress as a whole had one goal in mind: "consumer welfare," by which they mean lower prices. "The touchstone of illegality is raising prices to consumers," Bork wrote in an influential law review article in 1966. [11]

Most experts, however, say Bork's thesis ignores the substantial evidence that Congress also wanted to preserve and promote smaller businesses for social and political as well as economic purposes. "His view is far too narrow," says Thomas Sullivan. [12]

## Supreme Court Rulings

Whatever Congress' intent, the Sherman Act had a mixed initial reception in the courts. The Supreme Court took a literalist approach in some of its earliest cases — for example, breaking up a rate-fixing agreement in 1897 among 18 freight railroads that lower courts had ruled legal. This literalist approach also led the court to cite antitrust law in curbing the powers of labor unions — an interpretation that Congress eventually put to rest by declaring that labor was not a "commodity" for purposes of antitrust law. At the same time, though, the high court narrowed the scope of the law by ruling in the 1895 "sugar trust" case that the act applied only to "commerce" and not to manufacturing — a doctrine that the court itself repudiated in the late 1930s.

The court created a more durable limitation on the law in 1911 in two decisions that nonetheless broke up Rockefeller's Standard Oil trust and James Duke's American Tobacco trust. Viewing the law as a limitation on constitutionally protected freedom of contract, the court's conservative majority declared that those trusts were illegal only because they were created through "unnatural and wrongful" acts. [13] This so-called Rule of Reason approach to the law prevailed for the next two decades. It then yielded to a more literal "per se" interpretation of the law, but re-emerged in the mid-1970s to become what is now the accepted method for applying the law.

Congress responded to the decisions three years later with a new law expressly aimed at reversing what one senator called the court's "deadly blow to trust litigation." [14] The Clayton Antitrust Act added a laundry list of specifically prohibited business practices, including price discrimination, tying agreements and stock acquisitions, where the effect might be "to substantially lessen competition or tend to create a monopoly." A separate law created a new regulatory agency, the Federal Trade Commission (FTC), with broad power to identify and enjoin unfair commercial conduct.

Despite the Clayton Act's broad language, the Supreme Court again weakened the law through judicial interpretation.

By 1950, antitrust-minded lawmakers determined the law needed revision if it was to prevent anti-competitive mergers. The Celler-Kefauver Act strengthened the law in two ways: first, by extending the act's prohibition against mergers achieved through stock acquisitions to the purchase of a competitor's assets as well; and second, by extending the law not only to mergers between competitors but to all corporate mergers with anti-competitive effects.

The law has blocked relatively few of these so-called conglomerate mergers. But the provision is nonetheless very controversial between liberals, who applaud Congress' effort to restrict corporate growth, and conservatives, who see no benefit in restraining mergers between non-competing companies.

A quarter-century later, Congress acted again to stiffen antitrust laws. In 1974, it substantially raised penalties for antitrust violations. Then in 1976 it passed a law, the Hart-Scott-Rodino Antitrust Improvements Act, requiring any company with more

# Chronology

## 1890-1950

***Congress passes antitrust laws aimed at preventing anti-competitive business practices.***

**1890**
Sherman Act prohibits any "contract, combination or conspiracy . . . in restraint of trade" or monopolizing or attempting to monopolize interstate or foreign trade or commerce.

**1911**
Supreme Court upholds government's effort to break up Standard Oil trust, but ruling softens Sherman Act by allowing "reasonable" restraints of trade.

**1914**
Clayton Antitrust Act prohibits a number of anti-competitive practices, including exclusive dealing and "tying" contracts. In the same year, Congress creates Federal Trade Commission (FTC) with power to bar "unfair" competition.

**1936**
Robinson-Patman Act outlaws "unjustified" price discounts that result in injury to competition.

**1941**
Report by Temporary National Economic Committee questions economic benefits of mergers.

**1945**
Appeals court upholds government's antitrust suit against Aluminum Co. of America (ALCOA).

**1950**
Celler-Kefauver Act strengthens Clayton Act's provision against anti-competitive mergers.

## 1950s-1960s

***Supreme Court adopts strict stance against mergers.***

**1962**
Supreme Court, in *Brown Shoe Co.*, bars manufacturer from acquiring Kinney Shoe Co.; acquisition would have given firm 5 percent of retail market.

**1968**
Justice Department guidelines call for challenging mergers if four firms would have more than 75 percent of market.

## 1970s

***Antitrust laws are strengthened by Congress but sharply challenged by members of "Chicago school."***

**1974**
Antitrust Procedures and Penalties Act raises penalties for price-fixing and other violations.

**1976**
Hart-Scott-Rodino Act requires large companies to report planned mergers.

**1978**
Robert Bork's *The Antitrust Paradox* sharply criticizes antitrust laws.

## 1980s

***Reagan administration severely restricts antitrust enforcement.***

**1982**
Assistant Attorney General William Baxter announces settlement of seven-year-old antitrust suit against AT&T, with agreement for divestiture of local telephone companies; divestiture is completed in 1984. On same day, Baxter announces government is dropping 13-year-old suit against IBM; action is "without merit," Baxter says. Later in year, Justice Department adopts new merger guidelines, raising standard for challenging corporate combinations.

## 1990s

***The Clinton administration adopts stricter antitrust policies; wave of domestic and global mergers begins in mid-decade.***

**1993**
Anne Bingaman appointed assistant attorney general for antitrust; doubles number of mergers challenged by division in two years in office.

**1995**
Robert Pitofsky appointed FTC chairman; leads commission in challenging mergers or forcing concessions before mergers are approved.

**1997**
Joel I. Klein named to head Justice Department Antitrust Division; wins Senate confirmation despite criticism for approving Bell Atlantic-Nynex merger.

**1998**
Justice Department and 20 states file antitrust suits against Microsoft Corp.; FTC launches major antitrust action against Intel Corp. on June 8; both agencies have other major antitrust cases ready for trial.

## Private Antitrust Suits Allow Big Awards

Pepsi vs. Coke may sound like a consumer taste test, but it's actually a court case: a high-stakes effort by second-ranked Pepsi Cola to use federal antitrust laws to gain on the long-time industry leader, Coca-Cola Co.

Pepsico Inc. filed suit in federal court in New York last month claiming that Coke was illegally monopolizing the soft-drink market in violation of the Sherman Antitrust Act. The 16-page suit claimed that Coke improperly bars food-service distributors — the companies that supply products for restaurants, theater chains, stadiums and the like — from providing Pepsi products to their customers if they already handle Coke.

A Coca-Cola spokeswoman immediately branded the May 7 suit as "totally without merit." But in a motion to dismiss the complaint, filed on May 28, Coca-Cola acknowledged the heart of the complaint while maintaining that it was perfectly legal to insist that distributors handle only Coke products. Pepsi, the motion said, was "seeking to force Coca-Cola to allow its distributors also to carry the brands of its main competitor."

The court fight between the two soft-drink giants rests on Congress' decision in passing the 1890 Sherman Act to provide for enforcement of the law both by the government and by private individuals and companies. In the century since then, private antitrust suits have allowed consumers and companies injured by anti-competitive conduct to recover big damage awards: Successful plaintiffs can collect three times the amount they lost because of the antitrust violations plus punitive damages and attorney's fees.

In addition, private suits have sometimes pushed the government into taking action on its own. Most notably perhaps, an antitrust suit filed in March 1974 by an upstart long-distance carrier, MCI, against AT&T helped pave the way for the government suit eight months later that eventually forced the breakup of the telephone monopoly.

More recently, competitors of Microsoft Corp. were first to bring unfair competition claims against the computer giant while the Justice Department was still investigating. And the Federal Trade Commission's June 8 complaint against Intel Corp. stems in part from an antitrust claim against the microprocessor manufacturer by a manufacturer of computer work stations.

Private antitrust suits "have had a big impact," says William E. Kovacic, a professor at George Mason University Law School in Fairfax, Va. But he notes that since the mid-1970s the Supreme Court has issued a number of rulings creating substantive or procedural obstacles for antitrust plaintiffs. The trend continues. In October the high court issued a unanimous ruling making it harder for a dealer to challenge a maximum-price requirement imposed by a manufacturer or supplier.

Thomas Kauper, a professor at the University of Michigan Law School, agrees that Supreme Court rulings helped curb private antitrust suits after the boom period of the 1960s and early '70s. But he thinks litigation is now picking up. "My impression is that over the last seven or eight years, we're seeing a good deal more private litigation," Kauper says.

Joe Sims, a private antitrust lawyer in Washington, D.C., agrees, but he also sees a change in the kinds of suits being filed. In the past, Sims says, the most common kinds of suits were class actions brought on behalf of consumers injured by price-fixing or other anti-competitive conduct, or suits by dealers challenging restrictions imposed by manufacturers or suppliers. But Supreme Court rulings have made distribution suits more difficult, Sims says, while class actions have become too expensive to justify the risk.

Instead, Sims says there is an increase in what he calls "strategic litigation" — like the Pepsi-Coke suit. "It's big company vs. big company," Sims explains. "One big company is trying to deal with a business problem by invoking the antitrust laws. That's becoming reasonably common."

Whether brought by the government or by a private company or individual, antitrust litigation is expensive, time-consuming and dicey. But the payoff can be well worth the expense — as MCI's success in the telecommunications industry since 1974 shows. As for Pepsi, Sims says the cost of its antitrust suit is "not very relevant."

"Say it costs you $2-$3 million in legal fees to generate one of these cases," Sims says. "Two or three million dollars in the context of an important business issue is peanuts. If the result of what they do is they gain one or two or three market-share points, that completely overwhelms that expense."

than $100 million in assets or sales to give the Justice Department and FTC advance notice of any merger valued at more than $15 million. The law also gives state attorneys general power to file civil antitrust suits on behalf of consumers — the provision being used in the states' antitrust suit against Microsoft. [15]

### The Politics of Antitrust

The first great "trust-busting" president was a Republican: Theodore Roosevelt, who led the fight to break up Frank Harriman's Northern Pacific trust in 1904 and later bolted from the GOP because of what he saw as weakness on the issue on the part of his successor, William Howard Taft. Since then, support for antitrust enforcement has tended to be stronger in Democratic than in Republican administrations. That partisan split deepened with the conservative shift on antitrust issues during the Reagan and Bush administrations.

The Supreme Court continued to slow antitrust enforcement for a quarter-century after its Standard Oil decision. In 1918 and 1920, for example, the court rejected efforts to break up two giant companies, United Shoe Corp. and U.S. Steel Corp., despite evidence that each controlled more than 80 percent of its industry and had been guilty of questionable business practices. In the 1920s, the court also gave its blessing to the creation of industry trade associations despite concerns among some antitrust advocates that the groups could facilitate price-setting and market divisions among competitors.

President Franklin D. Roosevelt reinvigorated antitrust policy after a failed effort in his first term to link government, business and labor in the National Recovery Administration as a means of lifting the country out of the Great Depression. In his second term, he appointed Yale law Professor Thurman Arnold to head the Justice Department's antitrust division. Arnold viewed antitrust as a tool to eliminate "bottlenecks" that prevented full competition and increased prices to consumers.

His pragmatic approach disappointed some business critics, but it bore fruit in a number of consent decrees reshaping industry practices and some significant court victories after his departure from government — such as a celebrated 1945 decision curbing the Alcoa Co.'s monopoly power in unprocessed aluminum.

Roosevelt also had a lasting impact on antitrust policy through his appointment of liberal justices to the Supreme Court, two of whom — William O. Douglas and Hugo L. Black — each served for more than 30 years. The court's more favorable attitude toward government regulation did not produce an immediate change in antitrust doctrine. In 1947, for example, it issued an important decision rejecting the government's effort to prove a conspiracy to monopolize because of parallel-pricing policies followed by major film studios vis-a-vis independent theater owners. And in 1956 it rejected an effort to break the duPont chemical company's monopoly on cellophane, reasoning that other wrapping materials competed with duPont's product.

By the 1960s, however, Black and Douglas, along with Chief Justice Earl Warren and others, provided a somewhat reliable liberal majority that produced some of the court's furthest extensions of antitrust law. In the most controversial ruling, the court in 1962 upheld the government's effort to block the merger of Brown Shoe Co., the country's largest shoe manufacturer and third-largest retailer, with another major retailer, Kinney Shoe Co. Together, the two companies would have controlled only 5 percent of the retail market, but the court agreed with the government that the merger would violate the Celler-Kefauver Act by hastening concentration. Most controversially, Warren's opinion declared that the law called for the protection of small businesses even if it meant higher prices for consumers. [16]

The pro-small-business philosophy — derided by critics as "big is bad" — was seen in other court rulings in the decade that broke up mergers in industries that by today's standards would not have been viewed as concentrated. For its part, the Justice Department in 1968 adopted somewhat more lenient merger guidelines that nonetheless promised to oppose combinations even of relatively small firms in industries that were already "highly concentrated" — defined as four or more firms controlling 75 percent of market share.

Outside Washington, however, antitrust doctrine was shifting out from under the government's control. A band of scholars at the University of Chicago was shaping a new view of antitrust law that would displace the Jeffersonian rhetoric of protecting small businesses with a single-minded focus on economics and a predisposition to permit all but the most evidently anti-competitive mergers and business practices. By the 1980s, this so-called "New Learning" would come to dominate not only academic debate about antitrust issues but also policy decisions by the government and in the courts.

## The Chicago School

The so-called Chicago school of antitrust traces its origins to works in the 1950s and '60s by University of Chicago law Professor Aaron Director and economists George Stigler and Ronald Coase. But the two Chicago scholars best known for propagating its tenets are Bork and Richard Posner. [17]

Posner, now a federal appeals court judge, set out what he regarded as a "scientific" theory of economic efficiency — one based on empirical study, not ideology — in two books: *Economic Analysis of Law* (1973) and *Antitrust Law: An Economic Perspective* (1976). [18] In Posner's view, competition was a means to an end — efficiency — rather than an end in itself. On that basis, he argued that "whenever monopoly would increase efficiency, it should be tolerated, indeed encouraged." In addition, as Peritz points out in his critical analysis, Posner focuses solely on maximizing production — "productive efficiency" — and dismisses any concerns about distribution of wealth as "political" or "social" rather than economic.

Bork's *The Antitrust Paradox* followed in 1978 with an even stronger denunciation of antitrust laws and the Supreme Court's decisions interpreting the laws. Antitrust law, he declared, was a "policy at war with itself" because of "mutually incompatible goals." Instead of focusing on the "only legitimate goal . . . the maximization of consumer welfare," antitrust law, he said, was primarily used to protect "the survival or comfort of small business." [19]

With surprising speed, the Chicago school displaced the previously dominant Harvard school of antitrust analysis, which had viewed the growth of large industrial organizations as a problem rather than a natural or even salutary feature of the economy. [20] Bork's book is acknowledged today even by its many critics as perhaps the most influential work on antitrust ever. Chicago school adherents take credit for ushering in an antitrust "revolution" with their emphasis on free-market economics. And, in fact, the Harvard school has all but disappeared, at least in name: The competing intellectual camp today is called the "post-Chicago school."

The Chicago school's anti-regulatory views matched the philosophy that Ronald Reagan brought to the White House after his election as president in 1980. Reagan appointed Chicago school disciples to key policy-making posts: William Baxter to head the antitrust division, James Miller to chair the FTC. Baxter took office saying that he would not consider "industry concentration" as a factor in decision-making. The Justice Department issued new merger guidelines in 1982, significantly relaxing the test for objecting to a combination; through the 1980s, the department challenged only 28 out of the 10,000 merger notifications filed. [21] Reagan also named Bork, Posner and many other Chicago school disciples to the federal bench, where they helped reorient the courts' interpretation of antitrust statutes. [22]

## New Court Philosophy

For its part, the Supreme Court had already begun to take a more relaxed stance on antitrust issues by the mid-1970s. In one important decision, the court in 1974 approved a merger of two coal producers that resulted in a company with 50 percent market share; the opinion was written by Justice Potter Stewart, a dissenter from the court's stricter merger rulings in the 1960s. Three years later, the court in 1977 gave manufacturers leeway to impose restrictions on dealers, such as territorial franchises, even if the result was reduced competition among retailers. In the same year, the court made it somewhat harder for private companies to prove injury in antitrust suits. [23] The high court's conservative trend continued through the 1980s, especially after the Reagan-appointed justices forged a somewhat solid conservative majority under Chief Justice William H. Rehnquist.

The conservative trend did not completely supplant stricter antitrust views. Despite his general orientation, for example, Baxter presided over the completion of the breakup of AT&T in 1984 — and proudly took credit for his role. [24] The Supreme Court in 1985 issued a ruling, little noticed outside the antitrust bar, adopting the view that firms with monopoly power may violate antitrust law by refusing to let competitors use "essential facilities" — a doctrine with potential application to the Microsoft case. [25] Still, by decade's end, conservative antitrust perspectives had clearly come to dominate both the executive branch and, perhaps more significantly, the federal judiciary as well.

## Antitrust Revival?

President Clinton gave encouraging signals to antitrust advocates by picking liberals for the government's two top antitrust posts at the FTC and Justice Department. But as a self-styled New Democrat, Clinton was also interested in reassuring both Wall Street and Main Street that the administration was not reflexively pro-regulation or anti-business. In addition, the administration inherited the Reaganized federal judiciary, skeptical of expansive antitrust enforcement, as well as an increasingly globalized economy in which antitrust barriers were widely viewed as anachronistic and counterproductive.

To head the Justice Department's antitrust division, Clinton in 1993 appointed Bingaman, a former law professor and antitrust litigator with a Washington law firm. In her first two years in the antitrust post, Bingaman, the wife of New Mexico's Democratic senator, doubled the number of division cases challenging, restructuring or blocking proposed mergers. [26] But she also presided over one of the division's most embarrassing courtroom defeats when a federal judge in fall 1994 threw out a high-profile criminal price-fixing case against General Electric Co. on grounds the evidence was too weak.

When the term of holdover FTC Chair Janet Steiger expired in 1995, Clinton nominated Robert Pitofsky, a staunch liberal who had served two tours of duty at the agency and gone on to be a professor and dean of Georgetown University Law Center in Washington. Like Bingaman, Pitofsky brought to his post a more skeptical attitude toward mergers that helped thwart a number of proposed combinations submitted to the agency for review in his first year — for example, a $1.8 billion merger between two big drugstore chains, Rite Aid Corp. and Revco D.S. Inc. [27] But some mergers went through even after a hard look from the agency, most notably the 1996 telecommunications marriage of Time Warner Inc. and Turner Broadcasting System Inc. [28]

Klein won Senate confirmation to the Justice Department post last summer, but only after weathering some congressional criticism for approving the Bell Atlantic-Nynex merger while holding the position in an acting capacity. [29] While he continues to say he has no ideological predisposition against mergers, his more activist stand in recent cases has won over some skeptics. "Klein is underrated," Peritz says. "I certainly underrated him until recently." Sen. Ernest F. Hollings, a South Carolina Democrat who criticized Klein over the Bell Atlantic merger, said he "has done a fine job" so far. [30]

The antitrust division's statistics reflect an increase both in corporate marriages and in the Justice Department's scrutiny of the deals. In 1997 the division received 3,702 premerger notifications — more than double the number in the early years of the decade and one-third more than in 1988, the last full year of Reagan's presidency. The department initiated investigations in 220 of the cases in 1997 — nearly four times the 56 investigations begun in 1988. *(See graph, p. 214.)*

Congressional Quarterly/Douglas Graham

*Software executives testify during a March 3, 1998 Senate Judiciary Committee hearing on competition and antitrust issues; from left: Bill Gates, Microsoft; Scott McNealy, Sun Microsystems; and Jim Barksdale, Netscape Communications.*

So far this year, the Justice Department has moved in court against two big deals: the Lockheed-Northrup Grumman merger and the plan by a satellite TV company jointly owned by MCI and Rupert Murdoch's News Corp. to merge with one owned by major cable TV companies. In announcing the satellite TV suit on May 12, Klein said, "unless this acquisition is blocked, consumers will be denied the benefits of competition — lower prices, more innovation and better services and quality."

In the same week, Justice Department attorneys and state attorneys general were putting the final touches on their lawsuits against Microsoft. Plans were set for a news conference to announce the suit on Thursday, May 14. But Gates, who had met with Klein privately the week before, made an eleventh-hour bid to try to settle the case without litigation. The suits were put on hold while lawyers on both sides met on Friday and Saturday. But the sessions ended with nothing but recriminations.

After the suit was filed, Gates said he had tried to settle the case, but the government had presented Microsoft with "non-negotiable demands" that were designed to benefit its competitor, Netscape, at consumers' expense. For his part, Klein told reporters that Microsoft had not gone far enough to respond to the antitrust issues in the case. "What they put on the table would not by any means have benefited consumers or eliminated the anti-competitive practices that are alleged in the complaint," Klein said. ■

# CURRENT SITUATION

## 'Aggressive Competitor'

Until recently, Microsoft has enjoyed the kind of reputation that cannot be bought. In much of the public's mind, the company went from start-up to multibillion-dollar giant in less than two decades on the basis of nothing more than American-style work, smarts and entrepreneurship. "Microsoft should be celebrated as a hero," says James K. Glassman, a senior fellow at the American Enterprise Institute and columnist for *The Washington Post.*

Within the computer industry, however, another image of Microsoft formed in the past few years: that of a greedy monopolist that grew by imitating innovations by other companies and maintained its dominance through hardball negotiations with its partners and ruthless business practices toward its rivals.

"Microsoft is a very aggressive competitor," says James Love, director of the Consumer Project on Technology at the Center for the Study of Responsive Law, founded by Ralph Nader. "They use every conceivable weapon at their disposal to destroy their competitors."

The federal and state suits filed May 18 will give the government and Microsoft an opportunity to air those opposing views of the company in a federal court this fall. Microsoft asked for a seven-month delay before a hearing on the motions for a preliminary injunction, saying it needed time to study the allegations in the suits and the evidence already gathered by the Justice Department and the states. But federal Judge Thomas Penfield Jackson gave Microsoft a first-round defeat by cutting the requested delay nearly in half.

Jackson said he was concerned that a longer delay would allow Microsoft too much time to market Windows 98 without a ruling on the government's effort to force inclusion of Netscape's competing browser software. "By the time you propose to be ready," Jackson said at a May 22 hearing, "16-18 million horses will already be out of the barn, and that's too late."

Heading the Justice Department's team of lawyers at the hearing was David Boies, until recently a star litigator on Wall Street who years earlier led IBM's successful defense of the government's antitrust suit. [31] "This will be resolved very expeditiously," Boies said outside the courtroom.

For his part, Microsoft lead attorney William Neukom told reporters, "We will use the time the court has provided to . . . present a very powerful case."

The dueling press conferences on the day of the suits' filing, along with the complaints themselves and the Justice Department's accompanying 71-page legal memorandum, hint at the arguments both sides will make in the fall.

The most damning accusation — that Gates offered to divide the operating-system and applications markets with Netscape executives in 1995 — was backed up by depositions from Netscape officials. But Gates called the allegation "absolutely false." And Lopatka at the University of South Carolina says that even if the accusation is proved, the government may be entitled to nothing more than an injunction against any collusion in the future. "That doesn't amount to much," he says.

Lopatka says Microsoft will be able to convince the judge that Microsoft's bundling of the browser software, limits on changing the Windows boot-up screen and restrictive agreements with Internet service and content providers all have sufficient business reasons or consumer benefits to offset any adverse effects on competition.

Other experts view the government's chances more positively, but still hedge their bets. "This is a pretty powerful complaint as complaints go," says AEI's Stelzer. "It's got a lot of good documentary evidence, but you can't say who's going to win."

Meanwhile, the FTC is preparing its own antitrust action against another computer industry giant: Intel Corp., which manufactures the Pentium microprocessing chip used in an estimated 80 percent of PCs. In a complaint filed with an FTC administrative law judge on June 8, the commission charged Intel with abusing its monopoly power by refusing to share technical information with three other computer companies that were both customers and potential competitors: Compaq Computer Corp., Digital Equipment Corp. and Intergraph Corp. The complaint charged that Intel was retaliating against the three companies for their actions in connection with patent-related disputes with Intel. In a statement, Intel denied that it had violated any laws, but executives reportedly acknowledged in interviews many of the facts alleged in the FTC complaint. [32]

## The Urge to Merge

Supporters and critics of big business have sharply divergent views of the reasons for the current wave of corporate mergers and their likely effects. Supporters say the combinations stem from a desire to increase efficiencies in production and enhance opportunities, all to the ultimate benefit of consumers. Critics, however, say the mergers typically stem from an effort to reduce competition or take advantage of undervalued stock, benefiting corporate managers and shareholders but rarely producing the claimed benefits for consumers.

Many disinterested observers doubt the claims for consumer benefits. "There is scant hard evidence that mergers, hostile or friendly, have in fact generated the promised efficiencies," writes Peter Passell, an economics columnist for *The New York Times* who is generally sympathetic to business. [33]

Nonetheless, supporters of mergers appear to be dominating the current debate over the issue both in Washington and among the public at large. When Chrysler Corp. and the German automaker Daimler-Benz AG made the stunning announcement of their planned merger on May 6, hardly anyone was heard raising concerns about the effects on competition or consumers. *The Wall Street Journal*, the first newspaper to disclose the planned merger, reported after the announcement that antitrust lawyers in Europe as well as the United States — not specifically identified — expect the deal to be approved "because it wouldn't create a dominant player in the industry." [34]

Critics and observers did raise some concerns a month earlier when two giants in the financial-services industry, Citicorp and Travelers Group Inc., announced their planned merger on April 6. Still, most observers expect the deal to be approved. And the House of Representatives narrowly voted a few weeks later, on May 13, to repeal the federal Glass-Stegall Act, which limits the ability of banks to merge with securities firms. [35]

There is some evidence, however, of an increased willingness in Washington to question or challenge some mergers. The Justice Department's lawsuit filed March 23 to block the

# At Issue:

## *Are antitrust enforcers right to be going after Microsoft?*

***The New York Times***

***From an Editorial, May 19, 1998.***

yes

In their sweeping antitrust suit against Microsoft, the Justice Department and 20 state attorneys general have made reasonable demands to preserve competition in the world of computers and the Internet. Bill Gates needs to respond with something better than disingenuous countercharges that his company is being punished for its success. Instead of forcing a protracted court battle over remedies, Microsoft should work with federal and state lawyers to reshape the marketplace to help consumers obtain the products they may want. . . .

Much will now depend on whether the Justice Department and attorneys general can prove their charges of illegal anti-competitive conduct. One of the most explosive charges disclosed yesterday was that Microsoft first tried to cut a deal with Netscape, makers of the main rival to its Web browser, to carve up the browser market. Only when that approach failed, said the department, did Microsoft shift tactics and try to muscle Netscape out of the market, fearing that its success on the Internet would supplant Microsoft's dominance in the operating system business. In response, Microsoft says that its conversations with Netscape were innocent and that every one of its decisions was a legal effort to serve its customers.

For all its heated language, the Justice Department stepped back from trying to block the shipment of Microsoft's Windows 98 operating system. . . . Instead, the government wants Microsoft to unbundle its own browser, Internet Explorer, from Windows 98 or to include the rival Netscape browser along with it. The government also wants Microsoft to stop giving preference to its own software products on the screen that first comes up when customers turn on their computers.

Microsoft maintains that everything it is being asked to do is impractical. That is for the courts to decide. But Mr. Gates must know better than to assert that the government's demands are the equivalent of asking Coca Cola to include cans of Pepsi in all its six-packs. Coca Cola is not a monopoly, but Microsoft's operating system is. It would be better if Mr. Gates recognized that reality and stopped behaving as if his company were still a struggling upstart. As he said yesterday, the world awaits an era of accelerating change in computers, with undreamed-of products in voice recognition, artificial intelligence and Internet commerce. The Justice Department and the attorneys general are right that the inventors of products in these areas must be allowed to market them to consumers free of a stranglehold by Microsoft.



***The Rocky Mountain News***

***From an Editorial, May 20, 1998.***

no

If the Justice Department's antitrust action against Microsoft is justified — and we emphasis if — it is because the law, as interpreted by the U.S. Supreme Court, prohibits a dominant company in any industry from engaging in ruthless restraint of trade and anti-competitive acts. And while it has yet to be ruled on in court, Microsoft at least appears to have taken occasional unfair advantage of the fact that it's the producer of 90 percent of all computer operating systems in place in this country. . . .

The difficulty for anyone inclined to support the government's lawsuit on those limited grounds is that the Justice Department has much broader and more dubious motives for its lawsuit. While government lawyers apparently don't envision breaking Microsoft up, in the manner of Standard Oil and AT&T, they are intent on regulating the content of Microsoft's products. This is bad business, bad economics and utterly perverse public policy. Federal and state prosecutors must recognize that Microsoft became as dominant as it is through business savvy and ingenuity and because consumers want its products. It is nothing short of alarming that prosecutors should insist that Microsoft either exclude its own browser from its new Windows 98 software or include Netscape's. . . .

The government has no business prescribing what such a product might be like, and becomes something as bad as anti-competitive when it does. It becomes anti-innovative. There are many other extraordinary software features that could soon be coming around the bend, and Microsoft technicians should have an incentive to develop them and stick them in Windows. In what other instance has a firm been told it must diminish what it sells or promote and sell a competitive product? An equally disturbing aspect of the government's case is its focus: the most dynamic sector of the U.S. economy. After all, it is hard to identify the victims of Microsoft's alleged predatory activities. Netscape? Perhaps, although it retains a healthy share of the browser market. Consumers? Hardly. The price of software and other computer products has continued their 20-year plunge. If Microsoft were exploiting consumers and stifling innovation — the classic profile of a monopolist — then a government lawsuit might be more understandable. Instead, Microsoft leads a sector of the economy that is the envy of the world. The truth is that Microsoft represents just a small fraction of all software business and is far from immune to a competitor who has better ideas.

## U.S. Mergers Add Up to $Billions

*Here are some of the major corporate mergers proposed recently involving U.S. firms:*

| | Companies | Date Proposed | Value | Status |
|---|---|---|---|---|
| PENDING | *American Home Products Corp., Monsanto Co.* | *June 1, 1998* | *$35 billion* | *Likely to be reviewed by the Federal Trade Commission(FTC)* |
| | *Citicorp, Travelers Group Inc.* | *April 6 , 1998* | *$70 billion* | *Pending review by Federal Reserve Board, Comptroller of the Currency* |
| | *Daimler-Benz AG, Chrysler Corp.* | *May 7, 1998* | *$38 billion* | *Being reviewed by U.S., European authorities* |
| | *Lockheed Martin Corp. Northrup Grumman Corp.* | *July 3, 1997* | *$2.9 billion* | *Justice Dept. opposing merger in court* |
| | *McKesson Corp., AmeriSource Health Corp.* | *Sept. 23, 1997* | *$1.7 billion* | *FTC opposing merger in court, as well as merger of two other wholesalers: Cardinal Health, Inc., and Bergen Brunswig Corp.* |
| | *NationsBank Corp. BankAmerica Corp.* | *April 13, 1998* | *$30 billion* | *Pending review by banking regulators* |
| | *SBC Communications Inc., Ameritech Corp.* | *May 11, 1998* | *$56.2 billion* | *Pending review by Federal Communications Commission (FCC), Justice Dept., state regulators* |
| | *WorldCom Inc., MCI Communications Corp.* | *Nov. 10, 1997* | *$37 billion* | *Pending review by Justice Dept., European Union (EU) Commission* |
| APPROVED | *Bell Atlantic Corp., Nynex Corp.* | *April 21, 1996* | *$23 billion* | *Approved by FCC in August 1997, with some pro-competitive conditions; Justice Dept. decided in April 1997 not to oppose deal* |
| | *Bertlesmann AG, Random House Inc.* | *March 23, 1998* | *$1.5 billion* | *Approved by FTC May 29; FTC initiated "second request" review* |
| | *Boeing Co., McDonnell Douglas Corp.* | *Dec. 15, 1996* | *$13 billion* | *Completed July 1997 after FTC decision not to oppose deal; some concessions to win approval of European Union* |
| | *Thomson Corp., West Publishing Co.* | *Feb. 26, 1996* | *$ 3.4 billion* | *Justice Dept. approved merger, June 1996, after firms agreed to license products, sell some publications* |
| FAILED | *SBC Communications Inc., AT&T Corp.* | *May 1997 (talks disclosed)* | *$50 billion* | *Merger talks called off June 27 because of business disagreements, likely opposition from FCC* |
| | *SmithKline Beecham PLC, American Home Products Corp.* | *Jan. 20, 1998 (talks disclosed)* | *$60 billion (estimate)* | *British firm called off talks to pursue merger with Glaxo Wellcome PLC; those talks also failed* |
| | *Staples Inc., Office Depot Inc.* | *Sept. 4, 1995* | *$3.4 billion* | *Merger blocked after federal judge upheld FTC bid to enjoin deal, June 30, 1997* |

*Source: Facts on File*

Lockheed Martin-Northrup Grumman merger surprised many observers because it had failed to move against previous mergers among defense contractors in the past several years, including the $13.4 billion merger between Boeing and McDonnell Douglas last August.[36]

FCC Chairman William Kennard similarly took a tougher line than the agency's previous stance on mergers when SBC and Ameritech announced their planned merger on May 11. The two companies will have "a high burden" to prove that the merger is in consumers' best interest, Kennard told the *Chicago Tribune* the day after the announcement. He said that in approving the Bell Atlantic-Nynex merger and SBC's earlier acquisition of Pacific Telesis, the commission "didn't contemplate further mergers" between the so-called Baby Bells.[37]

Some lawmakers also were raising questions about reduced competition in other industries. The day after American Airlines and US Airways announced plans for a so-called marketing alliance on April 23, Senate Commerce Committee Chairman John McCain, an Arizona Republican, criticized the move and called for legislation to remove what he called "institutional impediments to competition" in the airline industry.

Still, most industry observers appear to expect most of the proposed mergers to win approval either in whole or in part. One recent trend has been for companies to announce merger plans and then gain regulatory approval by making concessions — for example, selling off some parts of one or the other company or agreeing to certain conditions aimed at promoting competition.[38] MCI Communications was following that strategy when it announced plans on May 28 to sell off its Internet facilities in order to win approval from European regulators of its merger with the British-based telecommunications giant, WorldCom. ■

# OUTLOOK

## 'Hundred Years' War'

When it recently surveyed the history of the U.S. market system in the 20th century, *The Wall Street Journal* prepared a chart with major events characterized either as "promoting" or "restricting" markets. Most of the economic regulatory statutes on the list — like the Food and Drug Act of 1907 or the National Labor Relations Act of 1937 — were shown as restricting markets. But as the century's first important event promoting markets, the newspaper listed, "[Theodore] Roosevelt begins 'trust-busting' campaign."[39]

The view of antitrust laws as an important, even essential, element of a free-market system has lasted for more than a century and still has a powerful hold on the views of policymakers and the public at large. "In the long run, the enormous productivity and wealth of the American economy depends on keeping competitive forces powerful," says the AEI's Stelzer.

But that favorable assessment of antitrust policy has never gone unchallenged. Today, the criticism of antitrust enforcement is gaining strength in some quarters even as the federal government shows greater interest in flexing its muscles to promote competition in the marketplace. "Given innovation, technology and dynamic markets, it's hard to imagine that there is such a thing as a sustainable monopoly absent governmental barriers" to competition, says Levy at the Cato Institute.

The spurt of antitrust enforcement by the Justice Department and the FTC over the past year has been depicted — sometimes positively, sometimes not — as an antitrust "revival." "The temperature is rising," Stelzer says.

But some consumer advocates say that even with the increased activity and interest, both the administration and Congress are too weak in promoting and protecting competition.

"This administration has been in the last few years extremely modest and timid to the point of endangering the emergence of competition in key industries," says Kimmelman of Consumers Union. "And Congress and state and federal regulators have eliminated a lot of ownership restrictions and permitted a lot of consolidations to take place."

Federal courts are also less receptive toward antitrust cases than they had been in the past, chiefly from the late 1930s through the mid-'70s. "In the modern era, when the government has been forced to litigate, their track record has not been particularly good," George Mason's Kovacic says.

The likely outcome of the administration's current major antitrust cases is very much uncertain. The Supreme Court precedents on illegal tying arrangements that the administration cites in its suit against Microsoft are viewed by some legal observers as inconclusive. As for the mergers, the high court has not issued a ruling in the area for 25 years. And Kovacic believes one reason for the gap is that the Justice Department has been loath to appeal merger cases to the court for fear of getting a ruling that would raise the standard for blocking corporate combinations.

In his history of "competition policy," Peritz characterizes the period since passage of the Sherman Act as a "hundred years' war" between two competing visions of freedom: freedom from private economic power or freedom from government power. "Because we dread domination — both political and economic — we have called for policy that limits both kinds of power, policy that satisfies commitments to both individual liberty and rough equality," he writes.[40]

"Antitrust policy has been almost a Rorschach test" for social and political values, Peritz adds today. "Has it been successful in serving the dominant interests at the time? Yes. Has there been historical consistency? No, but I don't know that historical consistency is something that we should demand." ■

## Notes

[1] The cases filed in U.S. District Court in Washington, D.C., are *U.S. v. Microsoft Corp.*, 98-1232, and *New York v. Microsoft Corp.*, 98-1233.

[2] The states filing suit were California, Connecticut, Florida, Illinois, Iowa, Kansas, Kentucky, Louisiana, Maryland, Massachusetts, Michigan, Minnesota, New Mexico, New York, North Carolina Ohio, South Carolina, Utah, West Virginia, and Wisconsin. The District of Columbia also joined the suit. See *The Wall Street Journal,* May 28, 1998, p. A24. For background on the Internet, see "Regulating the Internet," *The CQ Researcher,* June 30, 1995, pp. 561-584.

[3] For background on Microsoft and Gates, see Stephen Manes and Paul Andrews, *Gates: How Microsoft's Mogul Reinvented an Industry — And Made Himself the Richest Man in America* (1993), James Wallace and Jim Erickson, *Hard Drive: Bill Gates and the Making of the Microsoft Empire* (1992), and, for a sharply critical account, Jennifer Edstrom and Marlin Eller, *Barbarians Led by Bill Gates: Microsoft from the Inside* (1998).

[4] For background on antitrust policy and professional sports, see "The Business of Sports," *The CQ Researcher,* Feb. 10, 1995, pp. 121-144.

[5] The quote comes from the decision in *United States v. Topco Associates Inc.* (1973).

[6] For background on Archer Daniels Midland, see *The Wall Street Journal,* Oct. 16, 1996, p. A4. The Decatur, Ill.- based company pleaded guilty to two criminal counts for fixing prices with foreign producers of lysine, a livestock-feed additive, and citric acid, an ingredient in numerous foods and beverages. For background on Ucar International, see *The Washington Post,* April 8, 1998, p. C13. Ucar allegedly conspired with unnamed co-conspirators to set prices and production levels in the world market.

[7] Robert H. Bork, *The Antitrust Paradox: A Policy at War With Itself* (1978), p. 4.

[8] Frank H. Easterbrook, "Workable Antitrust Policy," *Michigan Law Review,* Vol. 84, p. 1701 (1986).

[9] Packard Bell NEC Inc. became the first PC maker to take advantage of the option when it announced on May 29 that it would block access to Microsoft's browser in a new line of notebook computers about to be unveiled.

[10] Much of the background is drawn from Rudolph J.R. Peritz, *Competition Policy in America, 1888-1992: History, Rhetoric, Law* (1994).

[11] Robert H. Bork, "Legislative Intent and the Policy of the Sherman Act," *Journal of Law and Economics,* Vol. 9, pp. 7-48 (1966). See also Bork, *The Antitrust Paradox,* op. cit., pp. 50-71. Bork, now a fellow at the American Enterprise Institute, emerged in spring 1998 as a supporter of the government's antitrust actions against Microsoft. Bork said his stance was consistent with his previous views but also acknowledged that he was working as a paid consultant to Microsoft's rival, Netscape. See Robert H. Bork, "What Antitrust Is All About," *The New York Times,* May 4, 1998, p. A19.

[12] For differing interpretations of Congress' intent in passing the Sherman Act, see Robert H. Lande, "Wealth Transfers as the Original and Primary Concern of Antitrust: The Efficiency Interpretation Challenged," *Hastings Law Journal,* Vol. 34 pp. 68-151 (1982), excerpted in Sullivan, *op. cit.,* pp. 71-84; and David Million, "The Sherman Act and the Balance of Power," *Southern California Law Review,* Vol. 61, pp. 1219-92 (1988), excerpted in Sullivan, *op. cit.,* pp. 85-115.

[13] The decisions are *Standard Oil v. United States* and *United States v. American Tobacco Co.* See Peritz, *op. cit.,* pp. 50-52.

[14] The speaker was Sen. James Reed, a Missouri Democrat; quoted in *ibid.*, p. 65.

[15] See *1976 Congressional Quarterly Almanac*, p. 431-438, and *1974 Congressional Quarterly Almanac*, pp. 291-292. For assessments of the impact of the premerger notification rule and other provisions of the law, see "Symposium: Twenty Years of Hart-Scott-Rodino Merger Enforcement," *Antitrust Law Journal,* Vol. 65, spring 1997, pp. 813-927.

[16] The decision is *Brown Shoe Co. v. United States.*

[17] For background, and a critical interpretation, see Peritz, *op. cit.,* pp. 236-245. Peritz cites as a seminal article Ronald Coase, "The Theory of Social Cost," *Journal of Law & Economics,* Vol. 3, 1960, pp. 1-44.

[18] For a summary of Posner's views, contrasted with those of the "Harvard school," see Richard A. Posner, "The Chicago School of Antitrust Analysis," *University of Pennsylvania Law Review,* Vol. 127, pp. 925-948 (1979), excerpted in Sullivan, *op. cit.,* pp. 193-209.

[19] Bork, *op. cit.,* pp. 3-11.

[20] The classic Harvard school text is Carl Kaysen and Donald Turner, *Antitrust Policy: An Economic and Legal Analysis* (1959). For an excerpt, see Sullivan, *op. cit.,* pp. 181-192.

[21] See Peritz, *op. cit.,* p. 278.

[22] See William E. Kovacic, "Reagan's Judicial Appointees and Antitrust in the 1990s," *Fordham Law Review,* Vol. 60, 1991, pp. 49-124.

[23] The cases, in order, are *United States v. General Dynamics* (1974); *Continental T.V., Inc. v. GTE Sylvania, Inc.* (1977); and *Brunswick Corp. v. Pueblo Bowl-O-Mat, Inc.* (1977). See *ibid.*, pp. 97-98.

[24] For an account of the AT&T case, see Steve Coll, *The Deal of the Century: The Breakup of AT&T* (1986).

[25] The case is *Aspen Skiing Co. v. Aspen Highlands Skiing Corp.* (1985).

[26] For background, see *The New York Times,* Oct. 22, 1995, sec. 3, p. 1.

[27] See *The New York Times,* April 25, 1996, p. D1. For biographical background, see *The Washington Post,* April 13, 1995, p. D12.

[28] See *The New York Times,* Sept. 13, 1996, p. D1.

[29] For a profile, see *The Wall Street Journal,* May 18, 1998, p. A1.

[30] *The Washington Post,* March 24, 1998, p. C5.

[31] For a profile of David Boies, see Amy Singer, "A Firm Of His Own," *The American Lawyer,* May 1998, p. 62.

[32] See *The New York Times*, June 9, 1998, p. A1; *The Wall Street Journal*, June 9, 1998, p. A3.

[33] Peter Passell, "Do Mergers Really Yield Big Benefits?", *The New York Times,* May 14, 1998, p. D1. See also Peter Passell, "When Mega-Mergers Are Mega-Busts," *The New York Times,* May 17, 1998, p. E18.

[34] *The Wall Street Journal,* May 7, 1998, A10.

[35] See *CQ Weekly,* May 16, 1998, p. 1301. Senate action is regarded as less likely.

[36] See *The Washington Post,* April 7, 1998, p. C2.

[37] *The Chicago Tribune,* May 13, 1998, p. A1.

[38] See *The Wall Street Journal,* March 4, 1997, p. A1.

[39] *The Wall Street Journal,* May 14, 1998, p. A10.

[40] Peritz, *op. cit.,* p. 3.

# Bibliography

## Selected Sources Used


### Books

**Bork, Robert H., *The Antitrust Paradox: A Policy at War With Itself,* Basic Books, 1978.**
Bork, a Yale law professor at the time, helped provoke a thorough re-examination of antitrust doctrine with his controversial thesis that antitrust laws have no justification except to promote "consumer welfare" — defined in terms of productive efficiency. The book includes detailed source notes.

**Gellhorn, Ernest, and William E. Kovacic, *Antitrust Law and Economics in a Nutshell,* West Publishing, 1994.**
This primer, written for a legal audience, covers the major topics in antitrust law, including horizontal and vertical restraints, mergers, price discrimination and so forth. It includes the text of the key parts of the Sherman and Clayton acts as well as a table of cases. Gellhorn, a former law school professor and dean, is an attorney in Washington; Kovacic is a professor at George Mason University School of Law.

**High, Jack C., and Wayne E. Gable (eds.), *A Century of the Sherman Act: American Economic Opinion, 1890-1990,* George Mason University Press, 1992.**
The book includes 17 articles — most of them critical of antitrust policy — written by leading economists dating from the early 20th century through the mid-1980s. High and Gable are professors at George Mason University.

**Peritz, Rudolph J.R., *Competition Policy in America, 1888-1992: History, Rhetoric, Law,* Oxford University Press, 1996.**
Peritz, a professor at New York Law School, synthesizes the history of antitrust law with other political, economic and intellectual trends from the adoption of the Sherman Act in 1890 through the Reagan and Bush presidencies. The book includes detailed source notes. For a number of articles discussing and critiquing the book, see "Symposium: Provocations and Reflections Upon Competition Policy in America," *The Antitrust Bullet,* Vol. 42, No. 2 (summer 1997), pp. 239-456.

**Shenefield, John H., and Irwin M. Stelzer, *The Antitrust Laws: A Primer* [3d ed.], American Enterprise Institute Press, 1998 [forthcoming].**
This 142-page primer, written for a business audience, provides a compact overview of antitrust laws, agencies and concepts. It includes a two-page suggested list of further readings. Shenefield, a former assistant attorney general for antitrust, is now a Washington lawyer; Stelzer, an economist, is director of regulatory policy studies at the American Enterprise Institute in Washington.

**Sullivan, E. Thomas [ed.], *The Political Economy of the Sherman Act: The First One Hundred Years,* Oxford University Press, 1992.**
This anthology includes 15 excerpted articles by leading scholars and policy-makers representing major developments in the political, economic and intellectual debates about antitrust policy. Sullivan is dean of the University of Minnesota law school. He is also co-author with Herbert Hovenkamp of the University of Iowa law school of an antitrust casebook, *Antitrust Law, Policy, and Procedure* (Michie Publishing, 3d ed., 1994).

### Articles

**Lowenstein, Roger, "Trust in Markets: Antitrust Enforcers Drop the Ideology, Focus on Economics," *The Wall Street Journal,* Feb. 27, 1997.**
The 3,350-word article gives an excellent overview of the development of antitrust policy from passage of the Sherman Act in 1890 through President Clinton's first term. The article was part of a series entitled "Amalgamated America." A later article analyzed enforcement policies by antitrust agencies. See John R. Wilke and Bryan Gruley, "Merger Monitors: Acquisitions Can Mean Long-Lasting Scrutiny by Antitrust Agencies," *The Wall Street Journal,* March 4, 1997, p. A1.


## FOR MORE INFORMATION

*If you would like to have this CQ Researcher updated, or need more information about this topic, please call CQ Custom Research. Special rates for CQ subscribers. (202) 887-8600 or (800) 432-2250, ext. 600, or E-mail Custom.Research@cq.com*

Information and documents about the antitrust suit against Microsoft Corp. and the company's response can be found at the following world wide web sites: **Justice Department**, www.usdoj.gov/atr; **states** [National Association of Attorneys General], www.naag.org; **Microsoft**, www.microsoft.com.

**Cato Institute,** 1000 Massachusetts Ave., N.W., Washington, D.C. 20001; (202) 842-0200; www.cato.org. The libertarian think tank has published a number of monographs critical of government regulation of the marketplace.

**Center for Responsive Law,** P.O. Box 19367, Washington, D.C. 20036; (202) 387-8030; www.essential.org. The center's Consumer Project on Technology studies competition issues in the computer industry.

**Consumers Union,** 1666 Connecticut Ave., N.W., Suite 310, Washington, D.C. 20009; (202) 462-6262; www.consunion.org. Consumers Union, publisher of *Consumer Reports,* lobbies on a range of consumer issues.

# 13 Privatizing Government Services

**RICHARD L. WORSNOP**

Shortly after Stephen Goldsmith became mayor of Indianapolis in 1992, he fired many of the city's middle-managers. But trimming the municipal payroll wasn't his main purpose, he says. Nor was he planning to contract out city services to private-sector firms. "My goal," he told local business executives at the time, "is to produce the most efficient service at the lowest cost, maybe by government, maybe by some of you in the room." [1]

Goldsmith is widely credited with making good on his promise. Over the past four years, he has shaved the city's operating budget by $26 million while still investing more money in public safety and infrastructure improvements than any other Indianapolis mayor.

As things turned out, many of the cost savings and service improvements did come from privatization. At the same time, city government departments are encouraged to bid for the contracts themselves. In 1995, for example, Indianapolis city workers bested three national firms to win a three-year, $16-million maintenance contract for city vehicles. The winning bid featured "a combination of reductions in management costs, greater worker productivity, a reduced work force and age-and-benefit concessions," noted the Reason Foundation, a leading advocate of privatization. [2]

According to Deputy Mayor Charles "Skip" Stitt, Indianapolis officials prefer to call their approach competition rather than privatization. "We allow, encourage and facilitate city employees to compete against private vendors for the right to do work that has historically been done by cities," he says. "We're always going to try to provide better service at lower cost, with competition as our chief tool."

From *The CQ Researcher,* August 9, 1996.

Stitt acknowledges that privatization carries with it "an enormous amount of baggage — some good, some very bad." In fact, he says, "moving from a traditional public-sector monopoly to a private-sector monopoly is only going to be marginally more efficient at best. When we examined our goals, we realized we wanted continual competition — much like any private business experiences every day. We do some privatization, yes, but it's not our main objective."

Indianapolis' approach to privatization is one of many variations in use throughout the country at the local, state and federal levels. In the most common form, known as contracting out, the government hires a private supplier to provide a specific service, such as processing Medicaid claims or operating publicly owned recreational facilities. Other forms of privatization involve selling public assets, such as dams, schools and hospitals, to private purchasers; lease-back arrangements, under which private parties buy or build public facilities that are then leased to government agencies; and vouchers, which consumers may use like cash for food, housing, education and other needs.

Sales of public assets to private interests have been relatively infrequent in the United States, at least at the federal level. In contrast to many other nations, the United States has no tradition of government ownership of the economy — railroads, airlines, telecommunications, mining, the steel industry and so on. (*See story, p. 242.*)

The fundamental structure of the federal government also accounts for the relative lack of action, suggests Reason Foundation President Robert W. Poole Jr. "We don't have a parliamentary system with strict party discipline, as in Britain," he says, "where [Prime Minister] Margaret Thatcher was able to push her ambitious privatization program through in the 1980s over Labor Party objections."

"It's not that we don't have things to privatize" at the federal level, Poole adds, among them the often-criticized air traffic control system. And though efforts to privatize federal prisons and big power-generating networks like the Tennessee Valley Authority have faltered in recent years, the battle surely isn't over. For instance, a new company comprised of several hundred employees from the Office of Personnel Management was awarded a contract this spring to conduct background investigations on prospective federal employees and officials (*see p. 248*).

In addition, a House subcommittee recently completed hearings on a bill that could allow privatization of the U.S. Postal Service. And Congress this year may pass legislation allowing private-sector companies to pay royalties to use national park sites for advertising or movies. Bill sponsors cite the parks' $4 billion backlog of maintenance and repair needs and estimate the measure could generate $100 million annually. There even has been talk, by President Clinton and others, about a "test" of partial

## Collective Bargaining Barred for Many Public Employees

*State and local public employees in more than half the states (white and gray areas) have limited or no rights to union representation and collective bargaining. Union officials argue that without the right to bargain, workers fear losing their jobs to the lowest bidder and thus don't perform at peak efficiency.*

*Source: "Working Together for Public Service: Report of the U.S. Secretary of Labor's Task Force on Excellence in State and Local Government Through Labor-Management Cooperation," U.S. Department of Labor, May 1996*

privatization of the Social Security system to help bolster its shaky finances. [3] *(See story, p. 238.)*

For the most part, though, state and local governments have been the nation's privatization leaders over the past decade or so. "Nearly 40 percent of cities [surveyed] told us they had entered into new contracts to provide municipal services in the past year," said Donald J. Borut, executive director of the National League of Cities. [4]

And the trend continues. Late last year, privately financed toll roads — the first in the U.S. in a century — opened in Northern Virginia and Los Angeles. In April, moreover, Gov. Pete Wilson, R-Calif., issued a report arguing that privatization could help California cope with its "limited resources." Wilson proposed to "eliminate the obsolete, consolidate the overlapping, sell the surplus, privatize the independent and turn over to local government or nonprofits those tasks that don't require state-level intervention, along with the resources to fund them." [5]

But even though Republicans control the state Assembly, Wilson "faces formidable barriers to privatization," the Reason Foundation noted. "California's constitution and personnel code severely limit contracting out in most instances, and pro-privatization reforms are unlikely to make their way out of the Democrat-controlled Senate." [6]

Foreign governments have far outstripped the United States in privatizing infrastructure projects, which are viewed in this country as primarily the responsibility of states and localities. Overall, Poole told lawmakers in February, "some 980 specific [privatization] projects [worth] almost $700 billion are in some stage of active consideration by governments in 95 countries. Unfortunately, only a handful of these projects — and only a small fraction of this massive investment — is taking place in the United States. While the World Bank and [the Agency for International Development] are telling governments worldwide why they should privatize major infrastructure, the United States itself relies primarily on government finance, ownership and operation for airports, highways, seaports, water supply and waste-disposal facilities." [7]

Poole and other privatization advocates contend that private operation of government services, if properly planned, almost invariably brings significant cost savings and service improvements. Skeptics, notably officials of public-employee unions, challenge those claims. "Many . . . would have us believe that government usually fails and that the answer is not to try to correct its failings but to turn to the private sector," Al Bilik, president of the Public Employee Department of the AFL-CIO, told a House subcommittee last year.

"But when looking for ways to improve government, we cannot afford to forget our history," Bilik continued. "We must remember the countless scandals and stories of fraud, political corruption and unreliable services that flooded newspapers in the early decades of this century, inspiring the public to insist that government hire workers directly to collect garbage, maintain roads and infrastructure, police our neighborhoods, treat the ill and teach our children. We must remember how private-sector promoters reaped hundreds of millions of dollars at the taxpayers' expense from Sam Pierce's ill-advised privatization schemes at the U.S. Department of Housing and Urban Development just five years ago." [8]

As the privatization debate continues, these are some of the questions being asked:

### *Does privatization cut costs and improve service?*

Poole contends there is "a very powerful case that private ownership of major infrastructure will generally lead to greater efficiency, wiser investment decisions and greater customer friendliness. Those types of infrastructure where the United States has relied primarily on the private sector — electricity and telecommunications — are the world standard in their field. But the same cannot be said about the quality of our airports, our highways, our seaports, our water supply, or our waste-disposal facilities," which are not privatized. [9]

Professor Charles W. Thomas, director of the Private Corrections Project at the University of Florida, makes a similar claim on behalf of privately operated prisons. (*See story, p. 244.*) Contracting out the construction of a correctional facility, Thomas told a House subcommittee last year, can save 15-25 percent on site acquisition and preparation, architectural design and furnishings and equipment. Another plus, he said, is that "contracting out allows government to decrease the total number of public employees, or at least to decrease the rate of growth in the number of public employees." [10]

**"No earnest, hard-working employee whose position has been eliminated but wants to keep working for the city" would be denied a job.**

***— Mayor Stephen Goldsmith Indianapolis, Ind.***

Critics often seize on such remarks to support their claim that privatization's cost savings and productivity gains come at the expense of workers. H. George Frederickson, a professor of public administration at the University of Kansas, says, "Every detailed assessment of privatization that I've seen concludes that, where money is saved, it is ordinarily not saved as a consequence of efficiencies and better management [but] through lower wages. Either that, or by decertifying unions, not having unions, or moving to part-time or flextime. To put it crudely, these economies come out of the hides of the workers." [11]

Frederickson also believes that support for privately operated prisons will quickly fade after the first major riot. "If that happens, then somebody's going to say, 'Hey, who's responsible here?' It's a little like the ValuJet crash. Who was responsible for that? Was it Sabre, which was on contract to ValuJet to do plane maintenance? Was it ValuJet itself? Or was it the Federal Aviation Administration?"

Louis G. Albano, president of the New York City Civil Service Technical Guild, disputes the notion that free-market competition can revitalize government services.* "Competition for government contracts exists more in theory than in practice," he testified in 1995. "When competitive bids are opened to the private sector, frequently only one or two companies make a bid. In a typical year, New York City awards more than $1 billion in contracts to companies that were sole

* The guild is a local affiliate of the 1.3-million-member American Federation of State, County and Municipal Employees, the nation's largest union of government workers.

## Federal Enterprises Offer Tempting Targets

*The sale of federal enterprises ranging from the Tennessee Valley Authority to the Corporation for Public Broadcasting would yield more than $75 billion, according to the Reason Foundation, which promotes privatization.*

| Federal Enterprise | Estimated Revenue If Sold ($Billions) | Estimated Annual Savings ($Billions) |
|---|---|---|
| Tennessee Valley Authority | 12.0 | ? |
| 5 Power Marketing Administrations (PMAs)* | 14.0 | 2.0 |
| Dams | 20.0 | ? |
| General Services Administration, Veterans Administration and Department of Defense energy facility | 10.0 | ? |
| U.S. Postal Service | 8.1 | -- |
| Air Traffic Control System | -- | 1.8 |
| Global Positioning System** | 7.0 | |
| National Weather Service | 2.5 | 0.4 |
| U.S. Geological Service | 0.5 | 0.6 |
| 4 NASA Aeronautics Labs | 1.5 | 0.3 |
| Amtrak | -- | 1.0 |
| Corporation for Public Broadcasting | 0.3 | 0.3 |
| **Totals** | **76.9** | **6.2** |

* *PMAs generate and distribute electricity. The 5 PMAs are the Bonneville PMA, Western Area PMA, Southwest and Southeast PMAs and the Alaska PMA, which was privatized this year.*

* *The global positioning system is an Air Force satellite-tracking system.*

*Source: "Privatization 1996: A Comprehensive Report on Privatization of Government Assets, Enterprises and Public Services," The Reason Foundation, 1996*

bidders. And even when competitive bidding takes place at the time a contract is first awarded, it rarely occurs at renewal time."

Albano went on to assert that, "Private contractors must find a way to sustain their profit margin, and that often comes at the expense of quality. These companies either hire low-wage, temporary and often unqualified workers or slash costs on the services they provide." [12]

Bilik of the AFL-CIO raised a related point before the same panel. "[I]n both the public and private sector," he said, "when employees ... do not have the security of a collective-bargaining agreement, when they are under constant threat that their jobs could be given away at any point to the lowest bidder, when employers do not invest in training or skills development, you will find little commitment to excellence. A high-skill, high-performance workplace is not built on contingent, part-time workers earning poverty-level wages. Excellence depends on committed, career public employees." [13]

Indianapolis officials respond that public employees need not feel threatened when municipal services are subjected to competition from private vendors. No rank-and-file city workers have lost their jobs since Mayor Goldsmith's initial purge of middle management. Indeed, Goldsmith pledged that "no earnest, hard-working employee whose position has been eliminated but wants to keep working for the city" would be denied a job. [14]

Training programs aimed at creating a skilled, flexible work force enable Indianapolis workers to shift jobs within the city government. Even so, some employees remained skeptical. "When management of the waste-water treatment program was privatized, some layoffs were expected," a recent Labor Department task force report noted. "However, this was avoided by a combination of efforts developed with the new contractor and in a 'safety net' provision negotiated into the city's collective-bargaining contract" with the American Federation of State, County and Municipal Employees (AFSCME). These provisions, the report stated, "contribute to employment security in a way that provides cooperation toward service efficiency." [15]

Goldsmith, as always, attributes Indianapolis' privatization successes to the competitive process itself. In "every one of our competitions, the quality of the service has gone up, not down, as we have competed out and lowered the cost," he said last fall. "We have not yet had a competition where the quality did anything other than go up. . . . And the reason quality goes up is because these competitions force a focus on the customer." [16]

Nonetheless, some privatization tools, such as vouchers, are seen as double-edged. "While vouchers can increase efficiency, they do nothing to control overall expenditure levels," wrote William D. Eggers, director of the Reason Founda-tion's Privatization Center. "Vouchers in and of themselves have no rationing mechanism. . . . In fact, [when] the quality of government-financed services [is improved], vouchers will likely increase demand for the service. The result: Reductions in unit costs generated by competition may be overwhelmed by rising program caseloads." [17]

Most privatization advocates concede that government should never relinquish control of some core functions. "Services can be contracted out or turned over to the private sector," said the authors of the 1992 best-seller *Reinventing Government*. "But governance cannot. We can privatize discrete steering functions, but not the overall process of governance. If we did, we would have no mechanism by which to make collective decisions, no way to set the rules of the marketplace, no means to enforce rules of behavior." [18]

According to Stitt, such limits are guiding principles of privatization in Indianapolis. "Police officers on the beat and fire department workers who actually fight fires are not subject to competition," he says. "Nor are the folks who make zoning and land-use decisions. We don't believe it is appropriate, in any circumstance, to contract out policy-making, rule-making or contract-management responsibility. Regardless of whether it is a private or a public entity delivering the service, the city is responsible for ensuring that it is delivered. And that responsibility never goes away."

### *Should the U.S. Postal Service be privatized?*

Privatization backers point to many federal programs that they claim would benefit from outside competition, including the National Weather Service, Amtrak, government-owned hydroelectric dams and the air traffic control system. But to many true believers, the most tempting target of all is the U.S. Postal Service (USPS), which employs more workers than any other civilian unit of the federal government.*

The chief reason for privatizing USPS, the Reason Foundation argues, "is not to raise money but to improve the organization's ability to survive. The USPS has already lost large market segments in the area of packages and express delivery to more efficient private-sector competitors. It continues to internally cross-subsidize its weaker operations with its monopoly [on first- and third-class mail delivery]. This monopoly status amounts to a pair of 'golden handcuffs.' Until USPS gives up its statutory monopoly, it will not be free to compete." [19]

**Giving private delivery firms access to mail boxes would "lead to a glut of unwanted materials and destroy the security and sanctity of the mail."**

***— Moe Biller, President American Postal Workers Union***

But the powerful labor unions that represent USPS employees are sure to resist any moves to repeal the statutes mandating the postal monopoly on first- and third-class mail. They recall what happened after the USPS monopoly on express mail was lifted in 1979. Federal Express, Purolator Courier and other private carriers quickly seized the lion's share of the overnight-delivery market.

"Once monopoly status was removed from express service, we saw the private postal sector blossom, to the great benefit of the public," says David F. Linowes, chairman of the President's Commission on Privatization during the Reagan administration. "The Postal Service had to cut its own express mail rates to stay competitive," he adds. "But USPS should be exposed to more outside competition. If it turns out that industry cannot compete effectively, OK, so be it, and let USPS continue to provide the service."

Linowes, a professor of public policy at the University of Illinois, says he is "not arguing for a massive turnover of USPS to private enterprise." But he contends that the postmaster general wouldn't dare introduce a delivery service as innovative as Federal Express "because he wouldn't have the authority to take a dramatic step like that. We're living in a technological age where you have to be able to make dynamic decisions expeditiously, and government — even a quasi-government entity like the Postal Service — just isn't geared for that type of response."

A bill introduced June 25 by Rep. John M. McHugh, R-N.Y., chairman of the House Postal Service Subcommittee, would take USPS a few steps further down the road to privatization. Among other provisions, the measure would:

- Create a new system for setting the price of stamps and other services;
- Allow the postal service to negotiate volume discounts with bulk mailers, such as L.L. Bean, J.C. Penney and even the federal government itself;
- Authorize an experiment allowing private delivery companies to use the mail boxes now reserved for the U.S. mail;

* With more than 845,000 workers, the USPS has moved ahead of the Defense Department's civilian work force as the government's biggest employer of non-military workers.

## Fixing the Social Security System

For the U.S. Social Security system, the day of reckoning will arrive in 2013. That is when experts say the federal pension system will begin going broke, to put it bluntly. In financial terms, the year marks the point when outlays for retirees' pensions will exceed the retirement system's income from payroll tax revenues and taxes on Social Security benefits.

To postpone what some worried observers are calling doomsday for the retirement system, economists have proposed a number of reforms, including proposals to partially privatize the system.[1]

In fact, an upcoming report by the Social Security advisory council will recommend the need for changes to the system, changes that Democrats and Republicans alike acknowledge are necessary. President Clinton jumped into the fray at the end of July, suggesting that a "test" of changes in the system might be possible, though he said he favored studying the issue closely "before we made a big sweeping decision."[2] Meanwhile, a Cato Institute study released July 23 said low-wage workers would be among those who would gain the most from privatization of Social Security.[3]

One of the most widely discussed privatization "solutions" calls for investing some of the billions of dollars in Social Security Trust Funds in corporate stocks and bonds. Historically, private-sector equities have provided substantially higher rates of return than Treasury bonds, in which Social Security revenues are currently invested. The system would still run out of money eventually, but it would remain solvent longer.

Under one privatization scenario, the government would make private-sector investment decisions for each taxpayer. Alternatively, taxpayers themselves would place a percentage of their payroll contributions in tax-deferred savings accounts of their choice, much as millions now do under 401(k) plans at their workplace.

The individual investment approach already has earned high marks in Chile. Starting in 1981, the Chilean government required workers to place 10 percent of their earnings in a government-regulated retirement account. Retirement benefits ultimately would depend on the returns from those accounts, with a minimum benefit guaranteed by the government. In addition, Chilean workers are required to pay an additional 3 percent of wages for commercial life and disability insurance.

So far, the benefit-to-contribution ratio of Chile's privatized system is substantially higher than yields from the old, publicly managed system.

Still, some experts caution that privatizing the U.S. Social Security system would entail drawbacks that could offset the advantages. Lawrence J. White, an economics professor at the New York University School of Business, recently warned that "any diversion of the . . . Trust Funds' assets or future surpluses into equity investments would increase the federal government's [overall] deficit on the remainder of its operations," since Social Security funds in hand are used in budget calculations. "In turn, this would mean that the government would have to borrow more money from the general public by selling bonds; raise taxes; and/or reduce other expenditures by a commensurate amount."[4]

White also suggested that letting the Social Security Administration (SSA) decide where to invest trust fund money would have political repercussions. "For example, a decision to restrict the SSA's investments to equity shares in the [Standard & Poor's] 500 is a policy that favors large companies over small ones and equity security investments over all others," he asserted. "Is this politically appropriate? An improved risk-return position can be achieved by having the SSA devote 20-30 percent of its equity portfolio to foreign companies. Is this politically appropriate?"[5]

Adopting the Chilean model also would pose problems, according to John B. Shoven, a Stanford University economics professor. To begin with, he noted recently, "Chileans had a much, much more favorable set of initial conditions for change than we do. We have 3.2 workers [contributing funds] for every retiree; they had 9. They have an extremely young society, and . . . it's easier to change the retirement system when you don't have many retired people or people nearing retirement."

Chile also benefited from having a large budget surplus, which enabled the government to pay for the existing retirement system's liabilities out of general revenues. "Obviously, we can't do that here," wrote Shoven. "We do not have a large federal government surplus. Finally, Chile had a strong dictatorship, which . . . may have some disadvantages, but it certainly makes a radical change simpler to implement."[6]

---

[1] For background, see "Overhauling Social Security," *The CQ Researcher*, May 12, 1995, pp. 417-440.

[2] "Social Security: A private matter?" *U.S. News & World Report*, July 29, p. 53.

[3] Cato Institute, "Privatizing Social Security: A Big Boost for the Poor," July 26, 1996.

[4] Lawrence J. White, "Investing the Assets of the Social Security Trust Funds in Equity Securities: An Analysis," *Investment Company Institute Perspective*, May 1996, p. 2. (The institute is the mutual fund industry's trade association.)

[5] *Ibid.*, p. 15.

[6] John B. Shoven, "The Coming Crisis in Social Security," *Investment Company Institute Perspective*, April 1996, p. 13.

- Use antitrust laws to open the USPS to outside competition; and, in addition,
- Limit the Postal Service monopoly on letter mail to items bearing postage of $2 or less.

Postal union leaders lost little time voicing their displeasure with the bill. In a letter to McHugh dated June 27,

President Moe Biller of the American Postal Workers Union complained that giving private delivery firms access to mail boxes would "lead to a glut of unwanted materials and destroy the security and sanctity of the mail." He also said it would "open the door to privatization of the Postal Service — a concept to which we are adamantly opposed."

The proposed $2 ceiling on letter-mail delivery was blasted as a betrayal of the American principle of "universal postal services at reasonable and uniform prices. Over time, Biller predicted, "this $2 cap would allow private carriers to skim away more and more profitable, easy-to-serve areas of letter delivery and leave unprofitable areas for the Postal Service. . . .This is another unacceptable step toward privatization of letter-mail service."

Kenneth Vlietstra, executive director of the National Association of Postmasters of the United States, shares Biller's misgivings about partially lifting the USPS monopoly on letter mail. "Ever since the Continental Congress founded our postal system, the aim was to provide essentially the same service to all Americans no matter where they lived — whether in metropolitan or rural communities. In my opinion, the only way we can continue to provide that total, universal service at reasonable cost is through retention of the statutes that give the Postal Service the exclusive right to handle certain classes of mail."

Like Biller, Vlietstra also believes that private delivery companies would shed unprofitable routes. "United Parcel Service [UPS] used to go to Alaska," he notes. "And then, a couple of years ago, they pulled out, because it just wasn't profitable for them. UPS likes to say, 'We go everywhere.' But the truth is, they don't."

American Postal Workers Union

*With more than 845,000 employees, the U.S. Postal Service is the nation's largest civilian employer.*

In sharp contrast to Biller and Vlietstra, Poole contends the McHugh bill doesn't go nearly far enough toward privatizing USPS. McHugh's proposals "probably are worthwhile tinkerings" with the existing system, he says, but "we need competition across the board to spur the kind of accountability, innovation and cost reduction that postal customers deserve. And we're not going to get that without real deregulation of the whole postal field."

In Poole's view, the Postal Service "has to become a private enterprise to compete effectively" in the open market. After cutting its ties to the government, USPS could "go to the capital markets for the money it needs to modernize in a major way."

Above all, Poole says the Postal Service "needs total freedom to revamp its work force. That means doing away with the Civil Service protection that stands in the way of deciding which people do which jobs, and so on. You've got to take a radical approach to achieve true reform. Other countries are doing that, and the McHugh bill doesn't come close."

### *Is labor-management acrimony over privatization easing?*

In areas where public-employee unions are strong, efforts to privatize government services typically run into fierce opposition. However, the Labor Department's task force report suggested that confrontation increasingly may be yielding to cooperation. [20]

In the public workplace of the future, the report stated, traditional approaches to service delivery, workplace communication and collective bargaining "will not be sufficient." Recognizing this, "many state and local governments" have started "depending upon the participation of employees."

Workplace cooperation, the task force added, "requires that the confrontational rhetoric be lowered and that elected officials, union leaders and workers focus on their common tasks." This approach, in turn, can be "a doorway to reducing confrontation in collective bargaining relationships that have had a history of conflict." [21]

The task force cited numerous examples of labor-management cooperation in the delivery of government services. In Peoria, Ill., for example, health-care costs were climbing 9-14 percent a year at a time when municipal revenues were falling. To control costs, the city and the unions agreed in 1993 to take health care off the bargaining table and entrust it to a joint labor-management panel. The next year, health-care costs for city workers were $1.2 million less than the projected amount of $6 million. As a further "bonus," no health-care decisions in Peoria have gone to arbitration since the joint panel was formed. [22]

In Phoenix, Ariz., long at the forefront of local privatization efforts, labor-management détente brought similar results nearly 20 years ago. The opportunity arose in 1978, when a new fire chief and new president of the firefighters local took office and resolved to end almost 40 years of labor-management strife. "They initiated annual planning retreats, during which labor and management jointly develop annual plans for addressing problems and seeking improvement," the task force noted. "Arbitration has not been used in Phoenix for 10 years." [23]

Poole is among the privatization experts who question whether a broad nationwide trend can be extrapolated from these and other examples scattered through the task force report. "That's the public-employee union party line," says Poole. "But, 'Where's the beef?' I'm a skeptic waiting to be persuaded by the evidence."

Donald F. Kettl, a political science professor at the University of Wisconsin in Madison, believes that worker fear colors the privatization decisions made in both government and private industry. "There is more cooperation today, for sure, than there had been in the past on many fronts," he says. "But on the other hand, tensions are rising in the private sector because of management pressure to contract out and outsource work. And in the public sector, you'll find a mood bordering on panic at the prospect of contracting out more government work to private companies. It's fair to say that government employees are deeply worried about the threat that privatization poses for their job security."

Meanwhile, where privatization has bolstered efficiency, both labor and management often claim the credit. Stitt, for example, believes that the cooperation model touted in the task force report clearly applies to Indianapolis.

"We started out really at odds with our AFSCME union" when Goldsmith became mayor, he says. "Part of the problem was that we weren't communicating as well as we needed to. Another part concerned focus. When we made it clear that our goals were to lower the cost of government services while improving their quality, the local union leadership came to us and said, 'We believe we've got a vital role to play in that effort. And assuming there's a level playing field, we're interested in competing head-to-head for these services that you're thinking about moving into the private sector.' That was a key turning point. From that point on, we worked much more collaboratively than we did initially."

Stitt cites a recent example of such collaboration to illustrate his point. "When we solicited proposals for the operation of our sewer-collection system, our union partnered with a private vendor in going after the contract. When you contrast that with where we were four years ago, it's safe to say we've come a long way. That is, we and they together have come a long way."

The AFL-CIO's Bilik, who served on the Labor Department task force, views the Indianapolis experience from a rather different perspective. When Goldsmith became mayor, Bilik says, he soon realized he couldn't fulfill his pledge to privatize many of the non-uniformed services of the city government.

"So he cast about for a fallback position and said, 'I'm going to try to get our city employees to compete against private contractors, and see who can do the job most effectively. And we'll give it to whoever submits the best offer.'

"Once he started to do that, he forced the employees into a bidding process," Bilik continues. "But it has since become clear that the city workers do the best job. They do it much more cheaply, and more effectively, than any private contractor can. Even before Goldsmith became mayor, the union in fleet maintenance and the department director got together and started to work cooperatively without any threat of privatization. And they did a tremendous job."

That should have surprised no one, says Bilik, because "Working people, by and large, want to do a good job; they don't have to be threatened or whacked into submission. All they need is some recognition, appreciation and involvement. And they want to be asked what they think.

"To me, that's the essence of the whole thing. We encourage the leaders of all our unions to recommend to their members, and to the managers with whom they deal, that there be free and open entry into cooperative relations, with all issues discussed and with full effort made to improve the quality of service. That's our position as a labor organization, and it's shared by the leaders of all our unions." ■

# BACKGROUND

## Progressives' Reforms

Public-private partnerships have existed in the United States since the early days of the Republic. "It simply made no sense for the government to produce all of its own goods and services when private suppliers stood ready to do business with the government," Kettl wrote.

The suppliers ranged from naval "privateers" — non-governmental agents who took in customs duties at sea for a commission — to the original Secret Service, which was operated by the Pinkerton detective agency. Almost until 1900, the federal government

# Chronology

## 1900s-1910s *Progressive reformers seek to impose government controls on railroads and corporations.*

***1903, 1906***
The Elkins and Hepburn acts ban free passes and rebates on rail-roads and strengthen the authority of the Interstate Commerce Commission.

***February 1918***
The U.S. Railroad Administration begins operating the nation's railroads. Private control returns two years later.

—— • ——

## 1920s-1930s *In the heady economic climate after World War I, government regulation of private enterprise loses support. During the Depression, President Franklin D. Roosevelt revives the old Progressive program of the New Deal to spark the ailing economy.*

—— • ——

## 1950s *Business finds a friendlier climate in Washington during the post-war Eisenhower administration.*

***1955***
A Bureau of the Budget directive states, "The federal government will not start or carry on any commercial activity to provide a service or product for its own use if such product or service can be procured from private enterprise through ordinary business channels."

## 1960s *Privatization is suggested for the Tennessee Valley Authority (TVA), one of the proudest achievements of the New Deal.*

***1963***
Sen. Barry Goldwater of Arizona, the 1964 Republican presidential nominee, proposes that the federally owned TVA be sold to private interests.

—— • ——

## 1980s *President Ronald Reagan and British Prime Minister Margaret Thatcher promote privatization.*

***1981***
Congress privatizes the National Consumer Cooperative Bank.

***November 1984***
The British government sells its 50.2 percent stake in British Telecommunications Plc (British Telecom) for $4.8 billion.

***1986***
By prohibiting the use of tax-exempt financing, accelerated depreciation and investment tax credits for environmental infrastructure projects, the Tax Reform Act makes water and waste-water-treatment facilities less attractive as candidates for full private ownership.

***March 26, 1987***
Conrail, the federally owned freight carrier, is sold to the public for $1.65 billion.

***1987***
The British government sells the former British Airports Authority for $2.5 billion. BAA's properties included the three main London airports and four airports in Scotland.

—— • ——

## 1990s *State and local governments turn increasingly to privatization to trim costs and improve services.*

***Dec. 18, 1991***
President Bush signs the Intermodal Surface Transportation Efficiency Act, permitting states to impose tolls on non-Interstate highways, bridges and tunnels, or even sell them to private enterprises.

***1991***
Gov. William F. Weld, R-Mass., voices interest in selling the Massachusetts Turnpike.

***February 1992***
Gov. Mario M. Cuomo, D-N.Y., says he will entertain offers from private interests wishing to buy the New York State Thruway.

***April 30, 1992***
Bush signs an executive order aimed at helping state and local governments sell or lease to private interests such publicly owned "infrastructure assets" as roads, bridges and airports.

***September 1995***
A 14-mile toll road links Dulles International Airport and Leesburg, Va. It is the first private toll road to be built in the United States in a century. Three months later, a private toll highway opens in suburban Los Angeles.

***June 25, 1996***
The Postal Reform Act of 1996 would allow the Postal Service to negotiate volume discounts with bulk mailers and to give private delivery companies access to residential mailboxes.

# The Growing Global Privatization Club

The global privatization club keeps growing. In a July 11 address at the New York Stock Exchange, Israeli Prime Minister Benjamin Netanyahu invited U.S. business to invest in his country. "I'm committed to privatize just about all of the government firms and many of the government services," he said, "and we are eagerly seeking out experiences from other countries."

There are plenty of examples to choose from. Britain led the way toward privatization in the 1980s, as Prime Minister Margaret Thatcher sold off numerous government-owned enterprises to private business. Today, Latin America and the formerly communist countries of Eastern Europe are the pacesetters.

If experience elsewhere is any guide, Israelis probably will have mixed feelings about privatization. "Russians are unhappy about the spectacle of the state transferring potentially fabulous assets on the cheap to a coterie of rapacious insiders," *The Economist* noted last winter. "And Britons appear to be less cross about privatization in principle than about a handful of not obviously deserving utility bosses turning themselves into millionaires on the way" from public to private ownership.[1]

Nowhere, perhaps, has the privatization process been more difficult than in Eastern Europe. According to United Nations information officer Christopher McIntosh, the obstacles "include lack of a free-market culture; confusion over who owns the enterprises and how much they are worth; poor physical infrastructure, which discourages foreign investment; the absence of a legal framework governing the conduct of business; and shortage of investment capital."[2]

In such a climate, problems are almost sure to arise. For example, noted McIntosh, "when a government sells a viable enterprise, the profits go to investors, who tend to be wealthier than the average taxpayer. Thus, income disparities are increased. Other consequences can include higher prices for basic goods and services, large-scale layoffs, loss of national assets to foreign buyers and the possible closure of vital industries."

Nonetheless, privatization continues to advance throughout the region, including Russia. By July 1, 1994, when the first phase of Russia's privatization program ended, two-thirds of the nation's industry was in private hands, and 40 million Russians owned shares in privatized companies. Today, more than 75 percent of the country's work force is employed in the private sector. In addition, the Federal Property Fund, one of Russia's main privatization agencies, announced in June that it would sell stakes this year in six oil firms and the nation's biggest power producer. Boris Yeltsin's July 3 election to a second term as Russia's president signaled that his free-market reform program likely would remain on course.

Similar reforms are making inroads in Latin America. Last year, for example, the Brazilian Congress voted to end the government monopolies of telecommunications, oil refining and exploration, mining and coastal shipping. The purpose was to attract urgently needed foreign investment. Neighboring Argentina, meanwhile, reinvigorated its energy industry by auctioning off individual state-owned units to private investors, including North Carolina's Duke Power Co. and Louisiana's Entergy Corp. The privatization program brought improved service, sharply lower prices and escalating demand for electricity.

Mexico already has undergone widespread privatization, but there is resistance to privatizing one of the country's most sacred cows. In February, Mexican Energy Minister Jesus Reyes Heroles said he did not favor privatizing Petroleos Mexicanos (Pemex), the state oil monopoly. Three foreign energy companies had proposed a natural-gas development project in which they would share in the profits but not ownership of the gas reserves. Such an arrangement, they argued, would be permissible under the Mexican constitution.

Reyes disagreed. "Let's not lose time trying to come up with schemes to go around the law," he said. "We want to say loud and clear: 'Here is the line. It won't move.' "[3]

Meanwhile, Canada this summer will join 16 other countries that have privatized air traffic control systems, according to the Reason Foundation, which supports privatization. "They've shifted it out of being a government department, funded by taxes, and made it a stand-alone corporation funded by user fees," says foundation President Robert W. Poole Jr. "A new user-owned corporation, owned by the various segments of aviation, will buy the Canadian system from the government for $2 billion."

[1] "Selling the State, Contd.," *The Economist*, Dec. 9, 1995, p. 14.

[2] Christopher McIntosh, "To Market, to Market," *The Futurist*, January-February 1994, p. 24.

[3] Quoted in *The Wall Street Journal*, Feb. 20, 1996, p. A14.

jailed federal prisoners through contracts with state and local governments, which often allowed private companies to use the prisoners' labor.[24]

At the turn of the twentieth century, the Progressive Movement spurred demands for government action to check the social upheaval that was caused by industrialization after the Civil War. During the 1890s, for example, reform mayors such as Hazen Pingree in Detroit, James Phelan in San Francisco and Samuel Jones in Toledo, Ohio, were elected on platforms pledging municipal ownership of public utilities.

Urban reformers often were thwarted, however, because state legislatures, largely controlled by railroads and big corporations, blocked municipal agitation for greater control over their own local affairs. Consequently, progressives shifted their attention to gubernatorial politics. Their most noteworthy success was the election of Robert M. La Follette, who served as governor of Wisconsin from 1901 to 1906.

Among his achievements, La Follette won from the Legislature a state banking-control measure and an anti-lobbying law aimed at big corporations. Furthermore, corporate taxes were raised, a railroad commission was formed to set rates and a conservation commission was established. Similar laws and policies came into force in other states where progressives attained positions of power.

As progressives gained strength at the state level, they began to seek comparable influence in national politics. Some headway was made against the great corporate trusts during Theodore Roosevelt's presidency, when Congress approved two important laws regulating the railroads. (*See "Chronology," p. 241.*) Meanwhile, a series of exposés by muckraking journalists led to the passage of federal laws such as the Pure Food and Drug Act and the Meat Inspection Act (both 1906), which sought to combat abuses in the food industry.

William Howard Taft, who succeeded Roosevelt as president, staunchly opposed progressivism. But Woodrow Wilson, who followed Taft, endorsed many progressive measures, among them the Federal Reserve Act (1913), which reformed the currency system; the Clayton [Antitrust] Act (1914) and the Federal Trade Commission Act (also 1914), which extended government regulation of big business; and the Keating-Owen Act (1916), restricting child labor.

## Railroad Experiment

With one notable exception, U.S. entry into World War I effectively ended the short but intense period of progressive reform in the United States. As a war-emergency measure, railroads were placed under the control of the United States Railroad Administration (USRA), headed by Treasury Secretary William G. McAdoo. President Wilson had taken possession of the railroads on Dec. 26, 1917, using a provision of the Army Appropriations Act of 1916. In doing so, he sought to achieve enough railroad efficiency to meet wartime transportation demands. Government operation of the railroads began in February 1918.

Under the new Federal Control Act of 1918, the president could guarantee the carriers annual compensation not to exceed the average of their net operating incomes in the three previous years. No carrier was to pay dividends in excess of its regular rate during the test period. The president was empowered to fix passenger fares and freight rates, subject to modification by the Interstate Commerce Commission (ICC), and to require carriers to make additions and improvements to their equipment.

In one sense, the experiment proved successful: The entire rail system became far more efficient than at any time previously. Accumulation of traffic at terminals had reached a peak in May 1917, when there was a nationwide "shortage" of 164,000 freight cars. At war's end in November 1918, the shortage had been virtually eliminated, despite an enormous surge of freight traffic in the intervening period. The reduction, however, was effected in part through such costly expedients as moving empty boxcars to areas where they were needed, sometimes across the country.

Walker D. Hines, who succeeded McAdoo as director general of USRA in January 1919, computed the average annual cost of operating the railroads under federal control at $4.4 billion, or 83 percent more than the average annual operating cost of $2.4 billion during the three-year period before the war. Hines pointed out, however, that the rise in operating costs was not out of line with increases in costs in private industry during the war. Moreover, he noted that the system of wartime government control did not have the advantage of permanency, which facilitates long-range planning.

While public opinion favored private ownership of the railroads after the war, organized labor and various farm organizations began campaigning for continued public operation. A proposal advanced in February 1919 by Glenn E. Plumb, counsel of the Associated Railway Employees of America, called for operation of the carriers by a National Railways Operating Corporation, managed by a board representing rail employees, rail management and the public. The federal government was to buy the railroad properties and lease them to the corporation, while the ICC was to retain power to regulate rates. A bill embodying the so-called Plumb Plan was introduced in the House in August 1919, but it never came to a vote. Six months later, in February 1920, the nation's railroads returned to private operation.

## Policy Seesaw

In fact, the 1920s saw the resurgence of big business and conservative Republicanism on a major scale. In the heady postwar economic climate, government regulation of private enterprise no longer commanded broad popular support. The Progressive Party's last hurrah at the national level came in 1924, when La Follette ran as its presidential candidate and was able to carry only his home state of Wisconsin.

However, popular opinion shifted once more as the Great Depression worsened in the early 1930s. Hoping to spark the ailing economy, Presi-

## The Big Business of Private Prisons

As recently as the early 1980s, "not a single privatized jail or prison [existed] either within or beyond the boundaries of the United States," writes Charles W. Thomas, director of the University of Florida Private Corrections Project. [1] What a difference a decade makes. At the end of 1995, 104 privately run adult correctional facilities with a combined rated capacity of 63,595 inmates were operating in this country.

Today, private firms manage correctional facilities in 18 states, the District of Columbia and Puerto Rico. [2] Overseas, private correctional facilities are operated in Australia and Britain. But the story doesn't end there. Last year, 10 states arranged to house some of their prison inmates in privatized facilities in other states. [3]

Prison privatization disturbs some policy-makers, who cite the potential for abuse of inmates when operators implement cost-trimming measures. History provides some justification for worry, Thomas told a House Judiciary subcommittee last year. He noted that Alabama and Florida "were involved in convict lease arrangements with private firms" until the 1920s. These deals "yielded significant financial benefits to both the firms and the coffers of the jurisdictions." [4]

Thomas went on to note that courts long maintained an arm's-length posture with respect to prison management. An 1891 Virginia Supreme Court decision, *Ruffin v. Commonwealth*, summed up the prevailing attitude for decades afterward: "[A prisoner] has, as a consequence of his crime, not only forfeited his liberty, but all his personal rights except those which the law in its humanity accord him. He is, for the time being, the slave of the state."

The situation today is quite different, Thomas testified: "[Correctional] facility contracts — whether by statute, contractual provisions or a combination of the two — prohibit private corrections management firms from deriving financial benefits either by charging prisoners a fee for the services they receive or by exploiting the labor of prisoners for their own [personal] benefit. In and of itself, this change in the relationships [that] contracts establish between government, private management firms and prisoners reduces the probability of many of the abuses that characterized private involvement in corrections previously."

From 1991 through 1995, the rated capacity of all privately operated adult correctional facilities grew at an average rate of 35.11 percent a year, according to Thomas. Recognizing that, "Nothing can continue to compound out at an annual average rate of growth of 35 percent," Thomas calculated that the rate would drop by 3 percent a year starting in 1996, eventually plateauing at 19 percent. Thomas projects a total inmate population of 236,036 in 2001.

At the start of 1995, 19 firms operated U.S. prisons; 17 remained at year's end. The two dominant companies are Corrections Corp. of America (CCA) and Wackenhut Corrections Corp., which together account for about 75 percent of the market.

Though Thomas feels that additional companies will enter the private corrections field, he senses a trend toward further consolidation. "The competitive and economic advantages of size are too consequential. Thus, the real question is not whether there will be more consolidation. Instead, it would appear to be a matter of who will merge with or acquire whom." [5]

---

[1] Charles W. Thomas and Dianne Bolinger (project assistant), *Private Adult Correctional Facility Census*, ninth edition, March 15, 1996, p. i.

[2] The 18 states with privatized prisons are Arkansas, California, Colorado, Florida, Kansas, Kentucky, Louisiana, Mississippi, Nevada, New Mexico, Oklahoma, Pennsylvania, Rhode Island, Tennessee, Texas, Utah, Virginia and West Virginia. Georgia is scheduled to join the list later this year.

[3] The 10 states that send inmates to prisons in other states are Alaska, Colorado, Hawaii, Missouri, New Mexico, North Carolina, Oklahoma, Oregon, Utah and Virginia.

[4] Testimony before House Judiciary Subcommittee on Crime, June 8, 1995.

[5] Thomas and Bolinger, *op. cit.*, p. v.

dent Franklin D. Roosevelt revived and expanded the old progressive program under the banner of the New Deal. Legislative and policy proposals issued by the White House during the "Hundred Days" after FDR's inauguration left no doubt that the federal government intended to play a pivotal role in guiding the nation's economy. Congress and the Supreme Court generally went along, though often with great reluctance.

World War II sent progressivism into hibernation yet again. And with the 1952 election of Dwight D. Eisenhower — the first Republican to occupy the White House in 20 years — opposition to government interference in the economy began to mount. In 1955, the Bureau of the Budget (now the Office of Management and Budget, or OMB) issued a policy directive discouraging federal agencies from producing any "product or service [that] can be procured from private enterprise through ordinary business channels."

That policy has remained in force ever since. However, conservatives complain that it is honored more in the breach than in the observance. Joseph R. Wright Jr., former deputy director of the OMB, noted that a revised version issued in 1960 allowed for exceptions in cases where "procurement from commercial sources involved higher costs." [25]

As conservatives began to displace moderates as the Republican Party's dominant force during the 1960s, calls for privatization of government programs became more insistent. Sen. Barry Goldwater of Arizona, who was to be the 1964 GOP presidential nominee, made waves when he suggested in an Oct. 28, 1963, letter to Rep. Richard Fulton, D-Tenn., that the Tennessee Valley Authority (TVA) be sold to private interests. Goldwater argued that the massive public power network "would be better operated and . . . of more benefit for more people if it were part of private industry." He added that "it would be a benefit and a great boon to Tennessee to have TVA placed on the tax rolls."

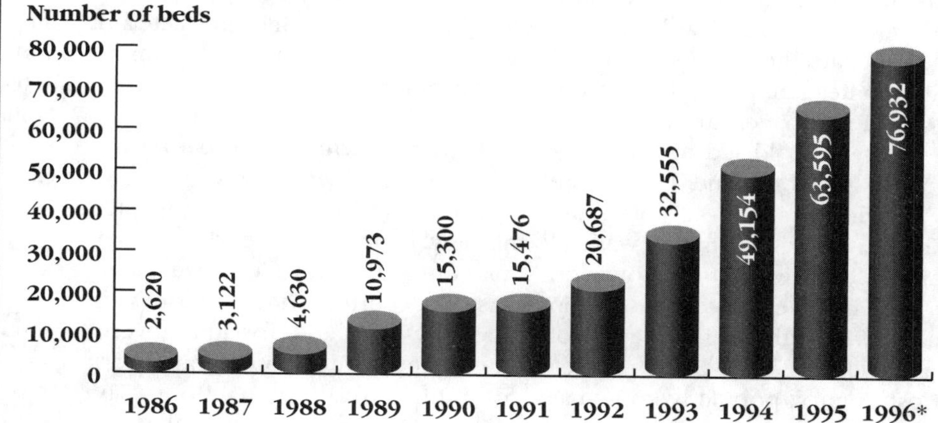


Goldwater's proposal would raise no eyebrows today. In 1963, however, it came under fire even from Southern Republicans, who recognized that TVA was politically sacrosanct in the region it supplied with low-cost electricity and recreational waterways. Nonetheless, Goldwater would not yield. In a February 1964 news release, he said he meant only to turn "a federal white elephant into a more productive and useful part of our economy — without in any ways penalizing the people of the Tennessee Valley or taking anything away from them."

Because he lost the 1964 election to incumbent President Lyndon B. Johnson, Goldwater never got the chance to put his ideas about privatization into practice. Indeed, the term had yet to emerge. Peter F. Drucker, the celebrated business writer and consultant, is credited with originating the term in his 1969 book *The Age of Discontinuity*. The fledgling concept got an additional boost when Anthony H. Pascal, a Rand Corp. analyst, examined the private delivery of public services in a much-noted study published three years later. [26]

## Reagan's Impact

By the time Ronald Reagan became president in 1981, privatization had become a prime domestic goal of the Republican Party. A 1988 OMB report summed up the general philosophy: "Competition is the driving force behind quality and economy of operations in the private sector. Private-sector managers are continually challenged by competitors who may force them out of business if they do not operate in the most efficient manner. This constant competitive pressure forces managers to be innovative and flexible as they promote performance-based management to serve their customers."

On the other hand, the report said, "Government managers, in normal operations, do not encounter the same pressures for efficiency that private sector managers do. . . .-Competition with the private sector can highlight these inefficiencies and consequently help identify the changes necessary either to streamline the government operation or to determine whether the private sector can more efficiently perform the service." [27]

One of the Reagan administration's first efforts to privatize government assets involved the sale of millions of acres of federally owned land, mostly in Western states. "I want to open as much land as I can," Interior Secretary James G. Watt said. "The basic difference between this administration and the liberals is that we are market-oriented. We are trying to bring our abundant acres into the market so that the market will decide the value." [28]

The land-sale proposal was hailed by private industries that stood to benefit from it and by economic analysts who shared the administration's view that private enterprise can manage a large-scale land program more competently than government. However, the plan alienated many ranchers, who dreaded losing access to land they had long used for grazing. And real estate speculators and state land managers feared that massive sales of public land would depress property prices throughout the region for years to come.

When the dust settled, the opponents of land sales had carried the day. In July 1983, Watt withdrew lands controlled by the Interior Department from the sale program. Department officials said he had come to regard the plan as a political liability to Reagan, particularly in the West. Outrage over an insensitive joke Watt had told led to his resignation in October, and little more was heard of the land-sale program.

The Reagan administration was still committed to privatization, however. The issue returned to center stage in January 1984 with the final report of the President's Private Sector Survey on Cost Control, popularly known as the Grace commission.* The blue-ribbon panel cited numerous "random examples of bureaucratic absurdity" and predicted the federal government would post annual deficits of $1 trillion or more by the end of the century unless spending was brought under control. The antidote to such a financial debacle, the commission said, was the adoption of private-sector management practices.

The Grace commission's chief privatization proposal concerned the government's policy of selling federally subsidized electricity to customers in the Northwest at one-third the private-market rate. If the federal power were sold at market prices, the panel stated, revenues over three years would increase $4.5 billion.

The administration, meanwhile, was pursuing other privatization opportunities. In 1981, Reagan signed legislation directing the Treasury to dispose of its stock in the National Consumer Cooperative Bank by the end of the year. The bank was left to function as a private entity without further government assistance.

Then, in 1987, during the second Reagan administration, the government sold its 85 percent stake in Conrail, the federally owned freight carrier, for $1.65 billion — a deal that Transportation Secretary Elizabeth H. Dole called "the largest privatization in U.S. history." She predicted it would "break ground for more privatizations to come."

* The commission was chaired by J. Peter Grace, chairman of W.R. Grace & Co.

### *Report of the Commission on Privatization*

Later that year, Reagan directed his newly appointed President's Commission on Privatization to evaluate past and current privatization ventures by U.S. and foreign governments and to develop a framework for future privatization efforts. The commission's report, released March 18, 1988, went well beyond previous Reagan attempts to trim the size of the federal government and sell off many of its assets.

In presenting the report, Linowes of the University of Illinois, the commission's chairman, described federal agencies as "muscle-bound to the point of paralysis when it comes to considering more effective alternatives." Government, he added, "should not be in the business of business."

The panel's 78 recommendations included:

- Repealing the statutes that give the Postal Service a monopoly on delivering letter mail;
- Selling Amtrak, the government-owned passenger rail network;
- Selling the federal government's $250 billion portfolio of housing, business, agricultural and educational loans;
- Converting airport traffic-control to private operation, with the federal government continuing "to regulate the national airspace" and to remain responsible for air safety; and
- Converting U.S. military commissaries and federal, state and local correctional facilities to private management.

"Our report," Linowes said, "is not about money, budgets or political ideologies. It is about programs and services and restoring to the American people their basic rights and obligations upon which our nation has been built." [29]

The report was issued at the start of the 1988 presidential campaign season, and there was no time to implement it before Reagan left office the following January. But privatization remained a key White House concern under George Bush, Reagan's successor.

## Bush Carries On

In December 1991, for example, Bush signed into law the Intermodal Surface Transportation Efficiency Act (ISTEA), which reversed 70 years of federal opposition to toll roads. The law permits federal highway funds to be funneled into a variety of user-fee projects, including construction of new toll highways, bridges and tunnels and rebuilding of existing toll facilities. (*See "At Issue," p. 247.*)

Such projects may be privately owned under ISTEA, provided the state transportation agency has a contractual relationship with the private operator. The law also permits the federal matching share to run as high as 80 percent.

ISTEA's supporters predicted it would help states deal more effectively with the mounting problem of "crumbling infrastructure." Instead of scrambling for more tax revenue to finance bridge and road repairs, state governments could turn the job over to private enterprise and also realize a one-time windfall.

President Bush gave further encouragement to the privatization movement in an executive order issued April 30, 1992. Its aim was to help cities and states privatize "infrastructure assets" ranging from roads, power plants and rail systems to air-

# At Issue:

## *Is privatization the best way to solve the nation's highway congestion problems?*

**Peter Samuel**
***Author of 1995 Cato Institute policy paper, "Highway Aggravation: The Case for Privatizing the Highways"***

**FROM *INSIGHT ON THE NEWS*, OCT. 9, 1995.**

yes

Our cities are choking on traffic, and the gas-tax system of paying for highways has to go. . . .

The Federal Highway Administration estimates that the United States is spending $32 billion a year on roads overall but needs to spend $46 billion to maintain current conditions and $14 billion a year on top of that to overcome current deficiencies during the next 20 years. That kind of money isn't going to be generated from increased taxes because the American people won't stand for it. We need a radical reform of the way we run and fund our highways. . . .

Financing highway use by means of a federal gas tax is a crude, one-size-fits-all straitjacket. It charges automobile drivers far too much for the use of uncongested highways and far too little for the use of scarce rush-hour congested highway space in the big cities. The diesel-fuel tax on trucks needs overhauling as well: It bears no relation to the damage that trucks do to highway pavement and provides no incentive to truckers to configure their vehicles (with lighter loads or more axles) so as to minimize pavement damage. Tolls that could be varied by level of congestion, time of day and truck-axle weight would be a far more sensitive pricing instrument than fuel taxes, since they would reflect more closely the cost imposed by the user's use of the highway. . . .

The beauty of the market mechanism of tolls over the crude gas/diesel tax and hand-down system we currently suffer is that it provides the right incentives to the various participants. A state highway authority relying on increased gas taxes for its activities has an incentive to make life miserable for motorists, since frustrated drivers in stop-and-go traffic are most likely to support the state agency's higher funding. So, the state highway superintendent on that repaving job may ponder: Why rush to remove those cones closing off two out of three lanes well before the evening rush hour begins? By contrast, a for-profit toll company will lose its customers to "free" roads or competing toll facilities whenever it doesn't provide free-flowing conditions. . . .

And with time-variable tolls in rush hours (congestion pricing) there will be an incentive to a proportion of motorists to rearrange their trips out of the rush-hour highway lanes (rescheduling them, carpooling, taking transit or rearranging where they live, work, shop or visit), lessening the tendency for the facility to become overloaded and reducing the highway expansion required.



**William D. Fay**
***President, Highway Users Federation for Safety and Mobility***

***FROM INSIGHT ON THE NEWS, OCT. 9, 1995.***

no

Peter Samuel argues that, because traffic congestion is so annoying, roads should be sold off piecemeal to the highest (private) bidder, who would charge drivers for use. Because new technologies would make paying the tolls almost effortless, Samuel implies, no one would mind the charges. Congestion would end because drivers magically would find new routes to the workplace or be able to change their work schedules so that no one else would be on the road at the same time.

. . . Our roads do have problems, but congestion — while bad — isn't the worst of them. Our nation's highway system is the economic envy of the world. But it's falling apart. . . .

When Americans are asked to name programs in which government should be involved, they invariably name highways. When asked which roads are the best, they point to the federally funded interstates. They also believe the federal gas tax is justified if it goes toward road and bridge improvements. With so many other less popular candidates for privatization, why change the one that people applaud?

The Highway Users Federation supports a dialogue on federal vs. state roles, innovative financing and privatization. While there is a real need for more private capital in road construction, operation and maintenance, a federal highway program remains essential to meeting America's interstate commerce and national defense needs. There are better solutions to the problems threatening our nation's highways, including full funding of highway programs and more public-private partnerships. . . .

The Cato Institute's remedy to charge on a sliding scale according to road congestion adds up to a new tax on drivers. Instead of pushing people off the road and onto welfare, why not encourage companies to develop telecommuting programs, flextime and compressed work-weeks?

If roads were owned by companies instead of government, the theory goes, private operators would rush to fix every pothole to keep customers. In exchange for their vigilance, drivers would pay happily to drive on these roads. Private investors are building roads for public use today in a few densely populated urban areas. These projects, if successful, will provide much-needed congestion relief, profiting both the investors and commuters.

But privately owned highways are not, and never will be, a substitute for the most successful transportation-development project history: the federal highway program. Among the most fundamental responsibilities of the federal government today is providing the financial wherewithal to maintain a coast-to-coast and border-to-border network of highways.

ports, housing, schools and hospitals.

The order greatly eased a financial regulation that had blocked many state and local privatization initiatives. It required states or cities that sold facilities built with federal aid to repay the amount originally contributed to the project by Washington.

Bush allowed state and local governments selling infrastructure assets to recoup their project costs first. If any money remained, the federal government would then get its share. Any remaining funds would be kept by the seller. Taxpayers "still come out ahead" under the Bush executive order, Poole declared. "The facilities will remain in use by the public, so the [federal] grants will have accomplished their intended purpose. And the privatized facilities will begin paying federal corporate income taxes." [30] ■

# CURRENT SITUATION

## Overcoming Obstacles

Four years later, it appears that the Bush executive order did little to bring about the sale or leasing of publicly owned infrastructure properties. According to the National Center for Public-Private Partnerships, the repayment requirement and difficulties in valuing such facilities have "virtually precluded efforts" to dispose of public assets. [31] To break the impasse, the center has urged that the power to sell government enterprises be codified in legislation and that the repayment provision be abolished.

Reimbursement provisions are by no means the sole obstacles to privatization at the federal level. For example, three Agriculture Department agencies — the Farmers Home Administration, the Agricultural Stabilization and Conservation Service and the Soil Conservation Service — must maintain minimum employment levels. This limits opportunities to save money by contracting out work to private companies.

Similarly, the Defense Department is barred from contracting out security and firefighting services, and the executive branch is prohibited from using appropriated funds to pay commercial firms to produce government publications. The publications ban is designed to protect the turf of the Government Printing Office (GPO), the congressional agency that publishes the *Congressional Record* and numerous federal reports, catalogs and documents. However, on occasion GPO itself invites bids from commercial suppliers on a wide variety of printing and binding services.

Despite all the roadblocks, privatization of federal programs creeps forward. On July 6, for example, the Office of Personnel Management (OPM) allowed employees in its Office of Investigations Service to form a profit-oriented private company to conduct background and security checks on federal job applicants. The new company, called U.S. Investigations Services Inc., was sold to the employees under an employee stock ownership plan (ESOP), a device that originated in the private sector. OPM Director James B. King called the initiative a "unique" arrangement "that no one else has done" in the federal government. [32]

Similarly, Poole told lawmakers last year, giving postal workers partial ownership of a privatized Postal Service would be the best way to reassure postal workers and their unions that privatization "is truly in their interest. Turning workers and managers into shareholders is one of the best-known ways to change the corporate culture of a bureaucratic enterprise, giving every individual a tangible stake in its success as a profitable private enterprise." He added, "Privatizing USPS could involve the creation of the world's largest employee stock ownership plan." [33]

However, privatization advocates doubt that Congress will approve so sweeping a change in the foreseeable future. Poole himself concedes he is frustrated by the lack of progress toward privatizing federal power generating and distribution systems. "It's fine that the Alaska PMA [power marketing administration], which is tiny, was privatized this year," he says, "but what about TVA [and] the other major enterprises owned and operated by the federal government that make it the largest single provider of electricity in the United States?

"Everybody else is getting out of electricity. It's being privatized in Italy, Germany, Britain, Argentina, Brazil and Australia, among other countries. Why isn't this happening in the United States? It's very bizarre that the issue is not even seriously on the national policy agenda."

The University of Florida's Thomas, likewise, is disappointed that privatization of federal prisons seems to be on indefinite hold. He says he was "surprised" by the Justice Department's recent announcement that the Bureau of Prisons (BOP) "is not going to privatize one or more of its facilities, as Clinton proposed in his fiscal 1996 budget message. The president recommended the privatization of four BOP facilities then being built, plus a majority of all future pretrial- detainee and low- and minimum-security facilities."

But when the proposal came before the House Appropriations Committee, Thomas notes, "the Republican-dominated panel said, in effect, 'This may be a little too much, too soon.' So the committee targeted a 2,000-bed facility under construction in Taft, Calif., and said, 'Let's use that as a pilot project.' And then the BOP decided it didn't want to go along with the idea."

## Local-Level Progress

Why does the federal government continue to drag its feet on privatization, while many state and local governments eagerly embrace it? Linowes believes it's a question of perspective. "Generally, in all matters of this type, local administrators can function much more expeditiously than national administrators," he says. "They have freedom to experiment more. And they can see for themselves any improvements in areas such as garbage collection and water supply."

Another advantage, Linowes says, is that "the risks aren't as great in local government, and unions usually aren't as strong. On the national level, though, unions can be a major impediment to change." By the same token, state legislatures "are much more responsive to new ideas" than Congress is. "They're more receptive to requests by private industry to take over a government function, and they can get in and out of a privatization deal much more rapidly than federal officials can."

In Kettl's view, state and local governments are more comfortable with privatization than the federal government is because they were the first to feel acute fiscal stress. He notes that seven years separate Proposition 13, the tax-limitation initiative that California voters approved in 1978, and Gramm-Rudman, the mandatory deficit-reduction legislation that Congress passed in 1985.

As a result, state and local governments "got on the privatization bandwagon earlier," Kettl says. The jump-start, he says, nurtured a new kind of leadership at the state and local level — "mayors and governors who staked their reputations on trying much more aggressively than their predecessors did to improve government's performance."

Finally, says Kettl, "state and local governments simply provide more direct services than the national government. Most of what the national government does is write checks and manage contracts. If you're already contracting out a lot, as the federal government is, it's hard to contract out even more. The national government, in fact, has contracted out and relied on privatization strategies far more extensively than its critics realize." ■

# OUTLOOK

## More Opportunities?

Kettl anticipates no turning back from privatization gains made to date. "I expect privatization to continue at all levels of government," he says, "because the experience of cities such as Indianapolis and Phoenix shows not only a potential for saving money and improving services but also an opportunity to build political capital. Again and again, we've seen state and local officials squeeze political juice out of this."

At the national level, Kettl believes the country is "only at the first stage of a lengthy debate over what the federal government should do and how it should do it. [Vice President] Al Gore's National Performance Review and [House Speaker] Newt Gingrich's "Contract With America" were just the opening salvos of that battle."

Linowes also sees privatization gaining ground, "because it has proved its effectiveness. There will be slip-ups here and there. But by and large, government institutions will have to develop a sense of entrepreneurship if they want to continue functioning effectively."

At the same time, Linowes believes, private industry will continue to try to outperform government. "That will produce a healthy, marketplace situation in which the party that delivers the products or services more effectively — be it public or private — wins out in the long run. Only after we abandon the myth that government *must* provide certain services will government be able to meet the needs of the people more effectively than private industry can."

The University of Kansas' Frederickson also envisions further privatizing of government programs, but he is not enthusiastic at the prospect. What bothers him is that privatization's failures, notably in elementary and secondary education, often are blamed on unions. "People aren't willing to say, 'Hey, isn't it possible that privatization wasn't a good idea to start with?'

"The real issue, in my opinion, is how much people are willing to pay for quality services. I'll readily grant that abuses occur in government; and some terrible things go on in the public sector. But I'm pretty sure they won't be solved by privatization."

In Deputy Mayor Stitt's opinion, the ongoing fiscal squeeze and limited opportunities to engage in deficit spending assure that state and local governments will continue to embrace privatization. "In Indianapolis, we're entering our eighth consecutive year of a property-tax freeze," he says. "Even so, our citizens are still demanding that we do a better job. We hope to rise and meet that challenge."

Even in communities skeptical of the contracting-out process, Stitt believes, "people will find it tougher and tougher to get by without capturing the savings that privatization brings. I have heard mayors and staff people from around the country say, 'We really ought to focus on these issues now, before we get into a situation where we have to lay off lots of city workers.' "

## FOR MORE INFORMATION

**Investment Company Institute,** 1401 H St. N.W., 12th floor, Washington, D.C. 20005-2148; (202) 326-5800; www.ici.org. ICI, the mutual fund industry's trade association, frowns on the diversion of Social Security Trust Fund revenue to equity mutual funds.

**Reason Foundation,** 3415 S. Sepulveda Blvd., Suite 400, Los Angeles, Calif. 90034; (310) 391-2245; www.reason.org. The foundation promotes privatization of government programs in the United States and overseas and publishes books and journals on the issue.

**Private Corrections Project,** Center for Studies in Criminology and Law, University of Florida, Gainesville, Fla. 32611-5950; (904) 392-1025; web.crim.ufl.edu/pcp. The corrections project tracks developments at the state and local levels.

**Public Employee Department,** AFL-CIO, 815 16th St. N.W., Washington, D.C. 20006; (202) 393-2820; www.aflcio.org/ped. The department represents unions of public workers at all levels of government.

Indianapolis' privatization experience, says Stitt, is notable for "the scope, the intensity and the pace at which we've pursued competition as a core strategy. It's not that we were a city in trouble to begin with. In fact, there was a good deal of opposition initially from folks who said, ' We're not a city in crisis. Why should we do this?'

"But the mayor encouraged us not to look two or four years down the road, but 20 years. As we did that, we saw potential trends that concerned us, such as slowing or even diminishing population growth, disparities in income between suburban and urban residents and continuing flight of wealth and economic opportunity from the community.

"So, we asked ourselves, 'How can we create wealth in our community, rather than redistributing it?' And privatization, or whatever you want to call it, was one of the strategies we chose."

But to New York City union President Albano, better management, not privatization, is the answer to increased efficiency. "Our most successful companies treat their frontline workers as assets, not expendable parts," he told lawmakers last year. "These companies have transformed themselves by replacing the hierarchical workplace of old with one that respects workers' knowledge and experience. . . . If we were to begin with this assumption, I believe we would be asking ourselves a different question today. Not how do we find ways to privatize more public services, but rather what is the mission of government and what kind of work force is necessary to carry out that mission.

"[I]n the case of our own experiences with engineering and architectural services in New York City . . . we would save money and improve the quality of service . . . if more of this work were done in-house." [34] ■

## Notes

[1] Address to Indianapolis Chamber of Commerce, Indiana Convention Center, Jan. 30, 1992.

[2] Reason Foundation, "Privatization 1996: A Comprehensive Report on Privatization of Government Assets, Enterprises, and Public Services," 1996, p. 7.

[3] See "Social Security: A private matter?" *U.S. News & World Report,* July 29, 1996, p. 53.

[4] Quoted in Reason Foundation, *op. cit.,* p. 1.

[5] Gov. Pete Wilson, "Competitive Government: A Plan for Less Bureaucracy, More Results," April 1996, p. 14.

[6] Quoted in Reason Foundation, *op. cit.,* p. 6.

[7] Testimony before the Joint Economic Committee, Feb. 5, 1996.

[8] Testimony before House Government Reform and Oversight Subcommittee on Government Management, Information and Technology, March 14, 1995.

[9] Testimony before the Joint Economic Committee, Feb. 5, 1996.

[10] Testimony before House Judiciary Subcommittee on Crime, June 8, 1995.

[11] For background, see "Labor Movement's Future," *The CQ Researcher,* June 28, 1996, pp. 553-576.

[12] Testimony before House Government Reform and Oversight Subcommittee on Government Management, Information and Technology, March 14, 1995.

[13] *Loc. cit.*

[14] Quoted in U.S. Labor Department, "Working Together: Report of the U.S. Secretary of Labor's Task Force on Excellence in State and Local Government Through Labor-Management Cooperation," May 1996, p. 37.

[15] *Loc. cit.*

[16] Stephen Goldsmith, "The Politics of Privatization," in "Privatization 1996," *op. cit.,* p. 12.

[17] Quoted in Reason Foundation, *op. cit.,* p. 25.

[18] David Osborne and Ted Gaebler, *Reinventing Government: How the Entrepreneurial Spirit Is Transforming the Public Sector* (1992), p. 45.

[19] Reason Foundation, *op. cit.,* p. 3.

[20] The 14-member task force was headed by Mayor Jerry Abramson of Louisville, Ky., and former Gov. James J. Florio, D-N.J., and also included labor and management representatives and academics.

[21] U.S. Labor Department, *op. cit.,* p. 3.

[22] *Ibid.,* p. 4.

[23] *Ibid.,* p. 5.

[24] Donald F. Kettl, *Sharing Power: Public Governance and Private Markets* (1993), p. 7.

[25] Joseph R. Wright Jr., "Let's Get the Feds to Use the Private Sector," *The Privatization Review,* winter 1987, p. 28.

[26] Anthony H. Pascal, "Clients, Consumers and Citizens: Market Mechanisms for the Delivery of Public Services," paper presented at the Conference on Centrally Planned Social Change, Quail's Roost, N.C., April 1972.

[27] Office of Management and Budget, "Enhancing Governmental Productivity Through Competition: A New Way of Doing Business Within the Government to Provide Quality Government at Least Cost," August 1988, p. 1.

[28] Quoted in *The New York Times,* July 3, 1982.

[29] Press release accompanying report of the President's Commission on Privatization, March 18, 1988.

[30] Robert W. Poole Jr., "Invest in Infrastructure — Privatize," *The Wall Street Journal,* May 5, 1992.

[31] Statement submitted to House Government Reform and Oversight Subcommittee on Government Management, Information and Technology, March 14, 1995.

[32] Quoted in *The Washington Post,* April 14, 1996, p. A4.

[33] Testimony before House Budget Committee, March 1, 1995.

[34] Testimony before House Government Reform and Oversight Subcommittee on Government Management, Information and Technology, March 14, 1995.

# Bibliography

## Selected Sources Used


### Books

**Kettl, Donald F., *Sharing Power: Public Governance and Private Markets,* The Brookings Institution, 1993.**
Shifting from public to private operation does not automatically make a government program less expensive and more efficient, writes Kettl, a political science professor at the University of Wisconsin. "Market competition substitutes one set of problems, revolving around conflicts of interest and monitoring, for the manifest problems of direct government administration. The problems associated with the market must be managed, not chanted away with the competition mantra."

**Osborne, David, and Ted Gaebler, *Reinventing Government: How the Entrepreneurial Spirit Is Transforming the Public Sector*, Addison-Wesley, 1992.**
"Privatization is one arrow in government's quiver," argue Osborne and Gaebler. "But just as obviously, privatization is not the solution. Those who advocate it on ideological grounds — because they believe business is always superior to government — are selling the American people snake oil."

### Articles

**McIntosh, Christopher, "To Market to Market: Navigating the Road to Privatization," *The Futurist*, January-February 1994.**
This survey of privatization efforts in foreign countries concludes that "Legal and physical infrastructures tend to be more conducive to privatization in the developed market economies than in the developing countries or in the transitional economies. Nevertheless, some very poor countries have had successes in their privatization programs."

**Pulley, John, "U.S. Air Force Inc.: The Privatization of Newark AFB, Ohio," *Federal Times*, July 8, 1996.**
Pulley describes the hard choices facing longtime employees of Ohio's Newark Air Force Base, which has been bought by Rockwell International Corp. and is scheduled this fall to become a private operation called Rockwell Guidance Repair Center.

**Shenk, Joshua Wolf, "The Perils of Privatization," *The Washington Monthly*, May 1995.**
Many of the complaints about inefficient, unresponsive government stem from shoddy contracting practices, writes Shenk. "Without clear guidelines, good information on what [private] contractors are doing and the ability to fire them when they screw up, government often ends up spending much more than it would cost to do the work with its own employees."

### Reports and Studies

**Investment Company Institute, *Investing the Assets of the Social Security Trust Funds in Equity Securities: An Analysis,* May 1996.**
This study by the ICI, which represents publicly traded investment funds, examines proposals to head off a Social Security funding crisis by investing part of the money in the Trust Funds in U.S. corporate stocks and bonds. It concludes that such a course would entail more risk and, possibly, less return than proponents believe.

**Reason Foundation, *Privatization 1996*, 1996.**
In its 10th annual report on privatization, the Reason Foundation, a leading advocate of privatization, reviews notable 1995 developments at the local, state and federal levels as well as in foreign countries.

**U.S. Department of Labor, *Working Together for Public Service: The Secretary of Labor's Task Force on Excellence in State and Local Government Through Labor-Management Cooperation,* May 1996.**
The task force argues that "cooperative workplace partnerships" between management and labor hold the key to service improvement in the future. "A focus on service with employee participation can also be a doorway to reducing confrontation in collective bargaining relationships that have had a history of conflict," the task force notes.

**House Government Reform and Oversight Subcommittee on Government Management, Information and Technology, *Hearing on The Federal Role in Privatization* (published proceedings of hearings on March 14, 1995).**
Proponents and critics of privatization air their views on what the federal government should and should not do to clear the path for private operation of government programs.

**Thomas, Charles W., and Dianne Bolinger, *Private Adult Correctional Facility Census,* Ninth edition, March 15, 1996.**
Thomas, director of the University of Florida's Private Corrections Project, reviews 1995 developments in prison privatization.

**House Committee on the Budget, *Privatization* (published proceedings of hearings on Feb. 28 and March 1, 1995).**
Privatization supporters, including Rep. Scott L. Klug, R-Wis., University of Illinois Professor David F. Linowes and Reason Foundation President Robert W. Poole Jr. explain why government, private enterprise and taxpayers all would benefit if more public programs were privately operated.

# 14 High-Tech Labor Shortage

KATHY KOCH

Recruiters flew Andrew F. Stark to the West Coast three times last month. Since September he has been wined and dined by firms around the country. One suitor even gave him a bird's eye tour of their city — via helicopter.

After considering a dozen offers, some with hefty signing and performance bonuses, Stark made his choice — a Wall Street financial services firm. He won't say how much he's getting, but salaries in his league typically top out at $75,000 per year. Not bad for a 23-year-old engineering and computer science graduate student fresh out of MIT.

It's a sellers' market for talented techies, as the information revolution seems to gobble up all the brain power in sight. America's transformation from an industrial to a knowledge-based economy has created robust demand for computer workers, especially in California's Silicon Valley.

"A year and a half ago, we had a Ph.D. who was making $95,000," says John Rohde, president of FirsTel Co., a Silicon Valley firm that develops operating systems for telephone companies. "He went to work for somebody else for $115,000 and we just got him back by offering him an additional $10,000, plus stock options."

FirsTel expects to double its labor force every year for the next five years, but not with Americans. "It'll be done in India and in Northern Ireland," Rohde says. "We can't get the computer engineers we need quickly enough in this country." Indeed, his small company can hardly compete with titans like Microsoft, which has more full-time recruiters (80) than he has employees.

To woo prospective systems analysts, computer scientists, Internet specialists and other high-tech wizards, some companies are offering $20,000 signing bonuses and $5,000-$15,000 finders' fees to employees for referrals. Some recruiters are even signing up teenage techies still in high school. *(See story, p. 260.)*

And to retain existing employees, companies are offering enticements ranging from stock options and flextime to subsidized laundry service and day care. One company arranges white-water rafting trips for workers.

The computer industry's voracious labor needs have been intensified by the emergence of hundreds of new software companies in recent years, plus the explosive growth of the Internet. Last year, $10 billion in goods and services were traded on-line, according to the Commerce Department. In five years, the amount could exceed $400 billion. In fact, in less than 15 years, a fifth of the world's population — more than a billion people — will be linked by the Internet, said Secretary of Commerce William M. Daley.

"We are in the midst of the most far-reaching technology revolution we have ever known," Daley said. "There is a very real threat that technology could overwhelm us — that it could move faster than our ability to train our people to manage it." [1]

The problem, many government and business leaders say, is that America isn't producing enough information technology (IT) workers to fight the revolution. The shortage of IT professionals "threatens the growth of the entire U.S. economy, our global competitiveness and the wage stability that is the bedrock of this country's low inflation," says Harris N. Miller, president of the Information Technology Association of America (ITAA).

But skeptics like Rep. Ron Klink, D-Pa., charge that industry allegations of a labor shortage "have no credibility in the world of labor statistics" and amount to a "conspiracy" to convince Congress that "the doors to foreign workers must immediately be flung wide open." [2]

In response, 14 high-tech CEOs told the Senate Judiciary Committee in a letter dated March 31, "We are not interested in academic or theoretical disputes about the methodology of surveys. We live and work in the real world. Failure to address current and future worker shortages could mean a loss of America's high-technology leadership in the world."

In fact, the CEOs added, shortages of qualified American workers could force U.S. firms to locate future factories abroad, taking thousands of U.S. jobs with them.

Such grave predictions catch Washington's attention. "In this new economy, technology is our engine of growth," Daley said. High-tech accounts for 40 percent of America's annual gross domestic product growth, and Silicon Valley is "as vital to our economy as Detroit or New York." [3]

The Hudson Institute predicts that if left unaddressed, the labor shortage could result in a 5 percent drop in economic growth — $200 billion in lost output.

The Commerce Department pre-

From *The CQ Researcher,* April 24, 1998.

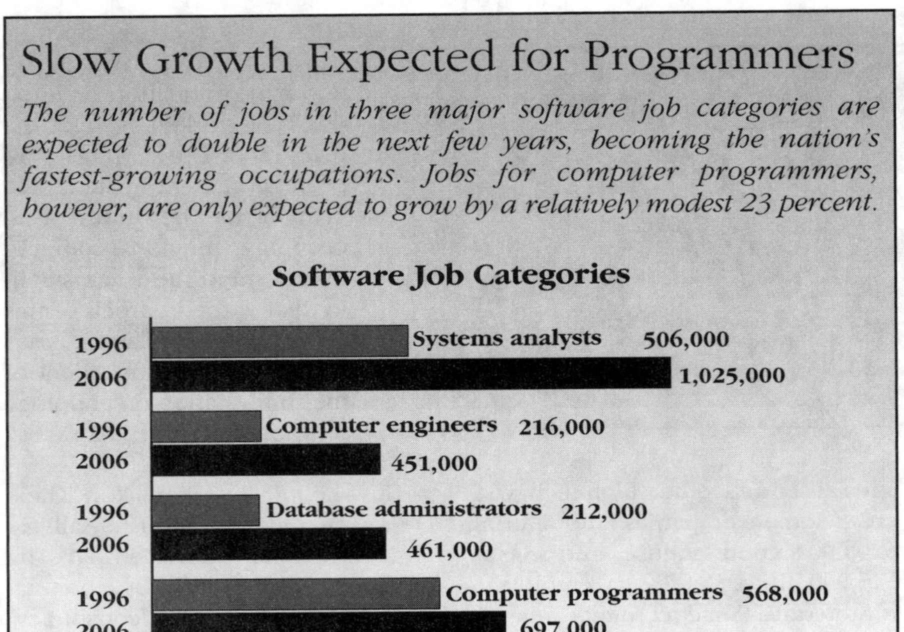


## Slow Growth Expected for Programmers

*The number of jobs in three major software job categories are expected to double in the next few years, becoming the nation's fastest-growing occupations. Jobs for computer programmers, however, are only expected to grow by a relatively modest 23 percent.*

*Source: "National Software Alliance Report to the Nation," January 1998*

dicts that the U.S. will need 1.3 million new computer workers in the next 10 years — or about 138,000 a year. Sen. Spencer Abraham, R-Mich., says part of the solution is to loosen immigration laws to admit up to 115,000 additional temporary workers each year. Abraham's proposal is awaiting Senate action; a House subcommittee held hearings on a similar proposal on April 21.

In Abraham's home state, meanwhile, computer science classes are swamped at Michigan State University, and lab space and graduate teaching assistants are in short supply. "All our classes are full to capacity," says department Chairman Anil K. Jain, adding that since 1994, enrollments have skyrocketed 58 percent.

"It's a nationwide problem," Jain says. "Every major university in the country is looking for computer science professors." And it's not just computer majors packing the classes. Of the more than 6,600 students taking computer classes at Michigan State last year, only 584 were computer science and engineering majors.

Computer science and engineering enrollments nationwide rose about 40 percent in 1996 and '97, following a decade in which they declined or stagnated. University officials predict a significant rise in the number of computer science graduates, starting in 1999. [4]

Community colleges and private computer-training schools report a similar upsurge in enrollments. However, most experts predict the supply of home-grown computer workers won't catch up with demand anytime soon.

Exacerbating the talent crunch is the so-called "Year 2000" (Y2K) problem posed by the impending end of the millennium. Thousands of programmers with knowledge of older computer languages like COBOL are needed to painstakingly rewrite billions of lines of code so the nation's older mainframe computers can seamlessly switch from the 1900s to the 2000s. To find them, recruiters are beating the bushes from Sun Belt golf courses to Russia and Asia. *(See story, p. 264.)*

American recruiters in talent-rich countries like India, Ireland and the Philippines are beginning to stumble over European recruiters competing for the same programmers, not only for their own Y2K problems but also to convert Europe's computers to the Euro monetary system.

With U.S. unemployment at 4.7 percent and the economy increasingly relying on computers, the skills gap goes beyond high-tech industries.

"We're not just talking about a shortage of qualified engineers and scientists for our top software [and] semiconductor firms," Daley added. "Every nook of our economy now depends on technology." [5]

In past periods of low unemployment, U.S. companies typically responded by raising wages. But in today's global economy, business executives say they cannot hike prices and stay competitive with foreign companies paying lower wages.

For computer workers, real wages remained essentially flat from 1988 until 1996, when they began rising, according to the Bureau of Labor Statistics (BLS). But the high-tech industry says the BLS statistics are low because they don't include benefits like stock options.

The introduction of cheaper computers — they are now available for under $1,000 — has also helped to keep high-tech wages down.

Since 1990, American high-tech firms have increasingly tapped overseas talent and outsourced lower-end programming work overseas to keep costs down. Partly as a result, the number of programming jobs in America remained constant from 1988-1996, while jobs for all other professionals expanded by nearly 30 percent, according to Robert I. Lerman, director of the Urban Institute Human Resources Policy Center. [6]

But now the tight labor market is apparently ratcheting high-tech wages upward. A variety of studies indicate that since 1996 wages have risen from an average of 7 percent to as much as 20 percent for some skills, especially computer scientists and systems analysts. Wages for programmers — the high-tech equivalent to assembly-line jobs — aren't rising as fast.

Similarly, jobs for computer scientists and engineers are expected to grow by 114 percent in the coming decade, but programming jobs by only about 23 percent. Unless significant numbers of new workers are produced, however, the national skills gap may widen.

"By the turn of the century, 60 percent of our nation's jobs will demand skills currently held by only 20 percent of the population," Daley said.

As the high-tech debate continues, these are among the most frequently asked questions:

### *Is the labor shortage a myth?*

"An enormous amount of anecdotal evidence from the business community" indicates there is a tight labor market, said Kelly Carnes, deputy assistant Commerce secretary for technology policy. "No one disputes the BLS estimate that we will need more than a million new information-technology workers in the next 10 years. But there are not a lot of good statistics on the supply" of workers. [7]

Skeptics charge that the high-tech industry has exaggerated the severity of the problem to frighten Congress into loosening restrictions on foreign workers.

Industry claims of a "desperate software labor shortage" are a myth, according to Norman Matloff, a computer science professor at the University of California, Davis. "Access to cheap labor is the 'hidden agenda' behind ITAA's campaign to develop an image of a software labor shortage in the public consciousness," he charges in an online report on the controversy. [8]

Those claiming that there is a labor crisis base their arguments on two controversial studies, one by ITAA, the other by Commerce.

"Nothing I've read from either the Commerce Department or the ITAA has any credibility whatsoever," says Lawrence Mishel, director of research for the Economic Policy Institute.

The American Engineering Association (AEA) charged in February that both reports were "grossly unscientific and very biased toward the conclusion that there is a critical shortage of IT workers."

But, ITAA's Miller responds, "The only people calling this shortage a myth are unions and think tanks — the same people who run around saying the Earth is flat. The reality is that this economy is red hot, and jobs are very hard to fill."

In its initial report in January 1997, the ITAA said there were 190,000 high-tech job openings in the United States in 1996. In a January update, the group estimated that computer and non-computer companies actually had 346,000 vacancies for programmers, systems analysts, computer engineers and scientists. [9]

ITAA's findings are based on an "unacceptably low" response rate and thus cannot be generalized to the national level, said the General Accounting Office (GAO) in a March 23 report. [10]

"We would never equate the number of vacancies in any occupation with saying that means there's a shortage of X number of people," Carnes said.

Miller says his group's vacancy figure is actually "undercounted" because it only estimated job openings in companies with more than 100 employees, and small businesses create most of the nation's new jobs.

The report also narrowly defined high-tech workers as those in only four categories, he added. "We could have included lots of other types of computer workers, like those who work on technology 'help' desks, those who install systems, routers and wires, etc," he says. The study also did not count job vacancies in the nonprofit sector, or in federal, state and local governments, he points out.

Indeed, 90 percent of the nation's software workers are employed in non-software companies and by government agencies, says the National Software Alliance (NSA). "These jobs . . . pay less and [thus] are often more difficult to fill," said the NSA. [11]

The Commerce Department stopped short of calling the situation a "shortage," labeling it a "skilled-worker deficit." Drawing on BLS figures, Commerce said last September that between 1994 and 2005 the United States would need 95,000 new workers each year to fill a million newly created computer jobs. [12]

In January, however, the department updated its figures and said 137,800 new workers a year would be needed to fill a total of 1.3 million new high-tech jobs. [13] In making its case for a worker deficit, the department noted that only 24,553 students had graduated with a bachelor's degree in computer and information science in 1994.

The GAO cited "serious analytical and methodological weaknesses" in Commerce's findings, chiefly that it understated the number of technically skilled Americans available for high-tech jobs. Focusing only on the number of bachelor's degrees awarded in computer science and engineering does not prove a worker shortage, the GAO said, because computer workers traditionally come from a variety of educational backgrounds. In reality, only 29 percent of computer scientists, programmers and systems analysts have computer science degrees, according to the National Science Foundation.

"Some of the most high-tech jobs

## Computer Jobs Attracted Most Foreign Skilled Workers

*Computer workers comprised only a quarter of the 312,563 temporary foreign workers in the United States in 1995, but by 1997 the percentage had grown to nearly half the total.* At the same time, physical therapists, the biggest group of skilled foreign workers in 1995, dropped to a quarter of the total in 1997.*

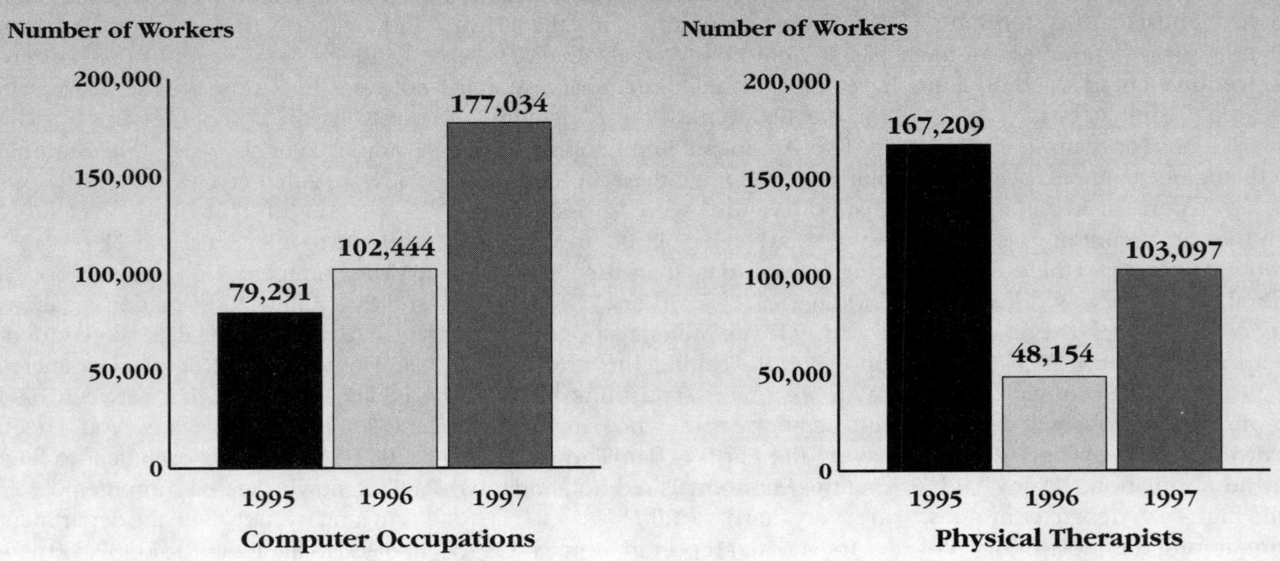


**Note: Includes H-1B and other categories of skilled temporary workers.*

*Source: Department of Labor, 1998*

out there just don't require college degrees," says Gordon Brace, network engineer at the American Geological Institute (AGI).

The NSA study pointed to an obviously much larger pool of qualified employees available than just those with computer-science degrees. "Since 1993, the number of [computer-science] graduates has remained flat. However, over this same period, the number of software workers increased 62 percent," the NSA added.

"Workers from many fields, with a variety of degrees, are pouring into software jobs," the NSA said.

Klink contends that the United States produces 810,000 bachelor's, master's and Ph.D. degrees in all categories of engineers and in all the hard and soft sciences. "Any one of these degrees could be used to develop a career in information technology," he says.

Brace, a 14-year computer-industry veteran, recently took a six-month, $8,000 course to become a Microsoft-certified systems engineer.

"Out of the 20 people in my class, only one or two had a computer-science or engineering degree," he says. "And the database manager here at AGI has a music degree."

Focusing only on four-year computer-science degrees also ignores the more than 15,000 high-tech graduates turned out each year by community colleges, as well as thousands of others coming from vocational and technical schools.

"There's not been enough attention paid to that group," Miller acknowledges. "We need to look more at short-term educational programs as a way of dealing with the work force problem."

A complete picture of the available high-tech labor pool should also include unemployed or underemployed skilled workers, the NSA said.

Skeptics also charge that if there were a true shortage, wages would be going up disproportionately in the computer field. "We have not been able to discern a shortage in our review of the wage data," said EPI's Mishel.

But BLS statistics do not reflect the lucrative benefit packages being offered, such as signing bonuses, say proponents of higher quotas for foreign computer workers.

"That's absurd," Matloff says. "The vast majority of new workers do not get signing bonuses" nor benefit packages like those being offered to graduates of schools like MIT and Stanford. "And of course employees who are already working don't get them either."

Matloff also notes that if companies were desperate, they would not be rejecting 98 percent of their applicants. "The fact that employers can be so picky demonstrates an oversupply of labor," he says.

Employers, on the other hand, say that many of those who send in résumés do not have the skills they need. It's a "skill shortage" rather than a shortage of warm bodies, they say.

So is there a true shortage?

"Markets are tight," Carnes concluded. "Whether or not there's a shortage, and you can say it's 190,000 or 350,000 [jobs], we don't think is really the relevant question," she said. "The relevant question is, 'How can we prepare Americans to have the skills needed to go out and get those 1.3 million new jobs?'"

### *Should the United States import more temporary foreign computer workers?*

The supercharged debate over foreign workers boils down to two key questions: How will they affect American jobs and wages? And will they discourage more Americans from entering the computer field?

The computer industry wants Congress to increase the number of skilled temporary workers who can enter the country using H-1B visas, now capped at 65,000 workers. The controversial visas were designed to allow employers to quickly fill urgent vacancies on a temporary basis. Last August, for the first time since the cap was established in 1990, all the H-1B visas were issued just before the Sept. 30 end of the fiscal year. This year all the visas are expected to be gone by June, just before the graduation hiring crunch.

Businesses say they must be able to hire the "best and brightest" from American universities. About a third of the new engineering graduates Microsoft hires each year are foreign students, Microsoft Vice President Michael Murray told the Senate Immigration Subcommittee in February. Nearly 40 percent of the electrical and computer engineering master's and Ph.D. students at American universities are foreign-born, he pointed out.

Denying U.S. industry a crack at the brightest foreign graduates is like "sending the first-round draft choices of the high-tech world to play on other countries' teams," writes T.J. Rodgers, president of Cypress Semiconductor Corp. [14]

No one objects to U.S. companies hiring creative geniuses, regardless of their nationality. But as immigration experts have been telling Congress since 1993, that's not the majority of H-1B workers.

"The geniuses are only a tiny fraction of the H-1Bs," says Michael Teitlebaum, a demographer at the Alfred P. Sloan Foundation and former vice chairman of the National Commission on Immigration Reform. "Most H-1Bs are programmers being brought in several hundred at a time. They are code writers [and] they are doing the kind of things any well-educated American with the proper training can do."

Following a series of well-publicized abuses of the H-1B system in 1993 and 1994, then-Labor Secretary Robert B. Reich told the Senate Judiciary Committee in 1995 that some employers bring in hundreds of foreign workers at a time to work in relatively low-level computer-related and health-care occupations.

"These employers include job contractors — some of which have a work force composed predominantly, and even entirely, of H-1B workers — [who] then lease these employees to other U.S. companies or use them to provide services previously provided by laid-off U.S. workers," Reich told the committee.

The H-1B law does not prohibit employers from replacing American workers with foreign temporary workers. Nor does it require an H-1B employer to show that he first recruited domestically or that there is a shortage in the United States of the type of workers being imported. The Labor Department has been asking Congress since 1993 to close these loopholes; industry has opposed such moves.

The latest Immigration and Naturalization Service (INS) figures show that the 11 companies that imported the most H-1B workers last year each brought in more than a hundred workers. The top importer was Mastech, a Pittsburgh, Pa., labor contractor who imported 672 workers and whose clients include AT&T and Citibank as well as the Department of Defense and the Federal Aviation Administration.

Matloff contends that huge numbers of American employees have been displaced by foreign workers. Pointing out that while the number of foreign computer professionals arriving on H-1B visas increased more than 450 percent from 1988 to 1995, new programming jobs increased by only 35 percent during roughly the same period, according to the NSA.

But Cypress' Rodgers told the Senate Immigration Subcommittee in 1996 that it is "preposterous" to worry that foreign workers will displace American workers. "Each Cypress engineer creates jobs for six additional people who make or administer or sell the products developed" by those engineers.

Not raising the cap will cost Americans jobs, he said. When the cap was reached last August, Cypress had to lay off workers awaiting final visa approval, "delaying the sale of millions of new chips and the cre-

## High-Tech Wages Rank Near Top

*The average American high-tech worker earned nearly $50,000 in 1996, or 73 percent more than the average private-sector wage earner (top). Salaries for workers in software services led the high-tech field (bottom).*

**Wage Comparisons**

| Sector | Average Wage |
|---|---|
| Securities and Commodities | $103,786 |
| Total High-Tech | $49,586 |
| Health Care | $30,830 |
| Construction | $30,341 |
| Private Sector | $28,582 |
| Education | $27,976 |

**Leading High-Tech Industries**

| Industry | Average Wage |
|---|---|
| Software Services | $61,500 |
| Computer Manufacturing | $57,300 |
| Defense Electronics | $56,700 |
| Semiconductor Manufacturing | $54,900 |
| Photonics | $52,200 |

*Source: "Cybernation," The American Electronics Association and NASDAQ; U.S. Bureau of Labor Statistics*

ation of hundreds of manufacturing jobs." Many H-1B applicants are already working for U.S. companies — usually on student visas — as they await their H-1B visas.

Rodgers said that because he has been unable to find as many American computer engineers as he needs, his company has opened offices in Ireland and India, where he employs 60 engineers. "We are being forced by government policy to fill the jobs offshore that we cannot fill here," he said.

Several executives have told the Senate subcommittee that not being able to import foreign workers forces them to cut back on programming projects, delay new products and trim expansion plans. Two-thirds of the companies surveyed by the ITAA said that the labor shortage was the biggest barrier to growth for their companies.

Rohde explains that he often needs to hire someone quickly or he will lose out on a contract. "Let's say I get a big project, and it needs to be done in six months, but I'll need 10 more engineers. I know it will take me six months just to find the engineers in the U.S. But in India I can find them in 10 days."

A major concern of American labor unions is that the H-1B program depresses American wages. "It is imperative that the H-1B visa program be reformed to eliminate employer abuse, which has resulted in the displacement of U.S. workers and depression of wages," AFL-CIO President John J. Sweeney said in a March 26 statement.

To prevent undercutting of Americans' salaries, the law requires employers of foreigners to pay at least 95 percent of the "average prevailing wage" in a region. But unions say that the law in effect provides a 5 percent "discount" for employers who rely on foreign labor. Further, they say, the law allows employers to simply lay off higher-paid, mid-career American workers and bring in foreign workers at entry-level "prevailing" wages.

Proponents of raising the cap say such abuses are a thing of the past that wouldn't happen in a tight labor market. "A company today that doesn't pay prevailing wages won't get employees," says Chuck Rudisill, director of investor relations for Mastech. "We always pay by the book."

Besides, says ITAA's Miller, competitors would complain. "They watch each other like a hawk. If a company saw a competitor paying less than prevailing wage, it would go ballistic."

"We have one pay scale, no matter whether a person's name is Sanjay or Jack," says William Bold, director of government affairs for Qualcomm, a major San Diego, Calif., wireless phone manufacturer.

A Labor Department official who asked

not to be quoted by name says that despite the current tight labor market, "We're still receiving complaints at about the same steady rate as always." About 90 percent of the H-1B employers that the department investigates are paying less than the prevailing wage, he says.

The official noted that complaints come from competitors more than from the H-1B employees because the employee is usually being sponsored for permanent resident status by his boss. "They have a lot of incentive not to complain," he notes. About half of the immigrants approved for permanent status entered the country as H-1B workers, he says.

While some critics say dependency on employees makes H-1B workers "indentured servants," Rohde disagrees. "People on H-1B visas come and go all the time. The days of slavery in this country are long past. We've even had people in the middle of the green card process who have been hired away." In order to keep his foreign engineers from jumping ship, he says, he is constantly upgrading their benefits.

The Labor official says it's not quite that simple, however, because if the worker leaves his job he loses his visa. "These folks are not free to move in the labor market," he says, "because they have to first find another employer willing to start the H-1B process all over again."

But Matloff argues that being able to constantly increase the labor pool with temporary workers depresses Americans' wages. "Even if employers pay the foreign workers the prevailing wage," he says, "the temporary nature of the H-1B visa means they can continually replace workers as they rise in the salary scale."

Immigration experts Demetrios G. Papademetriou and Stephen Yale-Loehr agree that immigrants depress wages but say that in the long run they end up creating other jobs. "It is true that immigrant labor has probably moderated wage inflation among U.S. engineers, scientists and other highly qualified professionals," they write. "This has provided U.S. business with a key competitive advantage internationally, thus helping them to prosper and, in the long run, to create more and better jobs." [15]

Critics of raising the cap fear that admitting more foreign computer workers will discourage America's own "best and brightest" from going into the field.

"People thinking about going into the computer industry are not stupid," Teitlebaum says. "If they see this is how government responds to rising salaries in the computer industry, they will go into law or medicine."

The critics also claim that raising the cap would relieve the pressure for companies to retrain existing employees in "hot" new skills. "Too many employers are using the H-1B program to avoid their responsibility to train U.S. workers for high-tech jobs," Reich told the Senate committee in 1995.

Raising the cap will also interfere with the natural workings of the labor market, which is already adjusting, critics point out. "What you have is an industry that has been boom and bust," Teitlebaum says. "It was bust five years ago. It's been booming since. It takes time for the market to adjust. But they don't want to wait."

Indeed, industry says that the high-tech world moves too fast to wait. In the fast-paced high-tech industry, "this deficit of skilled workers will lead to lost business opportunities, slower innovation and an erosion of the dominance of U.S. high-tech companies in the world market," Kenneth M. Alvares, a Sun Microsystems vice president, told lawmakers in February.

### *Are industry recruitment and labor practices to blame for the tight labor market?*

Much of the high-tech industry's tight labor situation is "self-inflicted," the AFL-CIO charges, "created by shortsighted human-resource practices" and insufficient training and education programs. Lifting the cap removes any pressure for the industry to alter its labor practices, the group said. Its executive council said in a March 26 statement that rather than raising the cap the high-tech industry should do more to:

- Retain and retrain experienced workers;
- Recruit more women and people of color;
- Hire and retrain older, downsized workers who are unemployed or underemployed;
- Pay higher salaries; and
- Improve working conditions.

The labor group's complaints were echoed in six government-sponsored ITAA task force reports released in January, which explored ways the industry can increase the pool of available workers.

One task force found that high-tech companies subtly discriminate against older men and women with families because they are perceived as "less available for the overtime, night and weekend work."

As one Silicon Valley manager said: "The top management in our company has directed us to focus our hiring on new or recent graduates only. These are people who have no family and can work long hours. Yes, salary is a major factor. . . . You work the young ones for five years and then replace them." [16]

"I call it the vampire industry," says a congressional staffer who works on the H-1B issue. "Every day they need fresh, new blood."

Software management consultant Edward Yourdon noted the trend toward the disappearance of mid-career software professionals in his 1996 book: "I've visited organizations that used to have 100 software people [and] then returned two years later to

## Teenage Techies Win Praise ...

Can't find a programmer? Desperate software companies are advertising in high school newspapers these days — and they're hitting pay dirt. Teenage techies win praise for their passion, time and energy — things many older workers don't have.

"Passion is the key," says Grady Ogburn, a manager at Datametrics Systems Corp., in Fairfax, Va. "You have to be passionate about the new things the technology is capable of doing. You have to be a techno-geek, because it's easy for people who love the technology to stay on top of it."

Two summers ago, Ogburn hired Brent Metz, then 15, as an intern. He turned out to be an extremely valuable Unix programmer for Datametrics, which develops software to help clients manage mainframe performance. Brent joined 15,000 other American youths 16-19 who worked as either programmers or systems analysts last year — up from 4,000 in 1994, according to the Bureau of Labor Statistics.

Teens have time to surf the Worldwide Web and keep up with what's happening in technology, Ogburn points out.

"Older workers have jobs — they're working to put bread on the table," Ogburn says. "They can't surf the Web all day, and they certainly don't go home at night and play on the Web, which is what these kids do."

While kids are surfing, they're also learning, says Travis Riggs, president of Creative Edge Software, in Sterling, Va., who hired 16-year-old Seth Berger to help develop video games.

"Kids have time to try new things, like learning how to do all the graphics," Riggs says. "Most of what Seth knows he learned on his own. Somebody in their mid-20s doesn't have that kind of free time to learn new things." In fact, said Riggs, some of his older graphic artists sometimes turn to Seth for help.

Teenagers also have the energy needed to work the "crazy hours" required to get a new company off the ground, says Elliott Frutkin, president of four-year-old Ideal Computer Strategies, of Washington, D.C. Last summer, Frutkin hired Josh Foer to help develop Web pages for clients. He was astonished at what the 14-year-old could do — like integrating a database to a Web site using the new "Cold Fusion" program.

"That's one of the really big skills people are looking for right now," he says. Josh had learned it while playing around on the Web.

"He had also surfed enough Web sites to know the difference between a professionally done Web page and a homemade one," Frutkin says, unlike most of the applicants who come to him when he advertises in the regular classified ads.

"Ninety-nine percent of the people who answer classified ads are not qualified," he says. They are mostly "old

find that the staff had been reduced to a dozen younger and less expensive people." [17]

But computer-firm executives say their highly competitive industry requires long hours. "If you want to succeed, that's what you have to do," Rohde said. "Are you telling me doctors and lawyers work less hours?"

The industry's reputation for working young employees grueling hours and then nudging them out after a few years to make room for entry-level or foreign workers discourages prospective employees interested in a career with longevity, the task force said.

"The half-life of a programmer is six years," says AEA President Bill E. Reed. "That's a hell of a waste of an education. What about the other 30 years of their lives? The companies should be retraining them, at their own expense."

Rohde says he pays for his employees to keep their skills current. "We have people in school all the time," he says. "We pay 100 percent of their education costs if they want to go to night school."

Miller denies that the industry discriminates against older workers or women. "If companies are practicing all this age and sex discrimination, where are all the lawsuits?" he asks.

"It's not an age-discrimination thing," says an industry lobbyist. "It's a skills thing. We need people right away with the latest skills."

Many industry critics complain that recruiters often can't find workers because they focus too narrowly on finding someone with the "hot" skill-of-the-month, rather than searching for those with talent and aptitude.

"You could train a person who is literate in computer programming but doesn't know a particular language, and he can become proficient in about a month," Teitlebaum says. "But when you say you'll only take people with two years' experience in Java, when Java is such a new language, you're not going to find them."

For instance, he suggests, there is a "gold mine" out there of technically oriented Ph.D.s in related fields — such as unemployed mathematicians and physicists — who could become systems designers with minimal retraining.

Rohde says he would hire any Ph.D. who walked into his office as long as he had some computer experience. "Why should I train a new employee?" he said. "If people want to find a job they have to re-educate themselves and then come to you for a job."

The AFL-CIO claims that because

## . . . And Big Bucks for Their Passion

school Cobol programmers" trying to pick up new skills. "They're definitely not as on top of the technology as Josh was," he says.

Does he feel that employers discriminate against older programmers, as some industry critics have alleged?

"I don't care if someone is 15 or 50, if they have one of the hot skills I need," he says. He advises anyone looking for a job in Web site development to teach themselves one of the new database-to-Web integration programs.

Both Ogburn and Frutkin said they do not understand why industry executives are complaining that the country is not producing enough graduates with four-year computer science degrees to fill all the country's high-tech job vacancies.

"You don't need a four-year degree to do a lot of this stuff," Ogburn says. "You can't get a degree in passion for technology."

He concedes that a four-year degree shows that a person has perseverance and diligence, and can prioritize and use time wisely. "But when I see a 4.0 [grade-point average] from Carnegie Mellon [University]," he says, "all that means is I have to pay them more."

"Sure, we have people who learned their skills in the classroom," Frutkin says. "But we also need tons of people who didn't get them that way."

Frutkin has concluded that the best way to develop a long-term staff is to recruit college interns and give them on-the-job training. "We're trying to work with people who are less developed in their skills, less set in their ways. It takes new ways of thinking to be able to market effectively on the Internet."

Some teens find their summer or part-time jobs so appealing they drop out of high school or decide not to go to college at all. Seth is seriously considering skipping college because he fears he will fall behind on his skills, and says he can gain more experience working.

Besides, the next video project he's scheduled to do for Riggs could net him a six-figure check. If he gives all that up and then shells out for college tuition, "That's over a quarter of a million dollars it would cost me to learn stuff I already know," he says.

Computer-science teacher Donald Hyatt gets calls all the time from recruiters looking for summer interns or prospective employees among his students at prestigious Thomas Jefferson High School of Science and Technology in suburban Washington. He advises all his students to stay in school and go on to college.

"Most students realize that they need a long-term education, not just a few skills," Hyatt says. "These kids could leave school right now and make $70,000 a year. It's hard to tell them not to do it. After all, after 29 years of teaching, I'm not making that much myself."

the industry is beginning to rely more and more on temporaries, part-timers and contractors, it lacks incentives "to make crucial investments" in training its work force.

On the contrary, ITAA says, high-tech companies spend $210 billion a year on employee training of all kinds.

The biggest problem is that the technology changes faster than either schools or employers can train workers in the new skills. To stay competitive, companies say they need employees already trained in the newest technology who can hit the ground running.

With technology changing every 15-18 months, companies say they cannot afford to train somebody in the latest program. Besides, employers fear that as soon as they train someone, they'll be hired away. Some companies ask employees to sign a contract promising to repay the company for training costs if they accept another job within two years.

The Clinton administration is urging the industry to spend more on training. "You should be as active as we are in the development of a well-trained work force," Daley told a group of business leaders. "Invest time and resources in [your employees], and it will pay off." [18]

Finally, critics say, if the industry really wanted to retain good employees, it would upgrade salaries across the board, rather than giving employees a patchwork of stock options and benefits.

"If high-tech workers are so important to the development of the economy over the next 20 years, then you would expect their salaries to reflect that," says Paul Kostek, president of the U.S. branch of the Institute of Electrical and Electronics Engineers.

Microsoft's Murray pointed out in his Senate testimony that the average software job pays $60,000, more than double the $28,000 paid to the average private-sector employee. *(See graph, p. 258.)*

Rohde scoffed at complaints that salaries aren't high enough. "The average [experienced] engineer's salary in Silicon Valley is $75,000-$80,000, and going up $10,000 a year," he said. "That's not enough?"

According to the annual salary survey by *Computerworld* magazine, however, the salaries of new computer science graduates with a bachelor's degree had increased to an average of $36,666 in 1997, while experienced programmers received from $45,000-$75,000. ■

# BACKGROUND

## Skills Gap or Glut?

The roots of the current skills gap lie partly in the high-tech industry's boom-bust cycles over the past two decades. The resultant periodic gluts of scientists and engineers kept salaries low, encouraging America's own "best and brightest" to choose more lucrative fields, like law or medicine, some analysts say. Science and engineering wages also have been depressed in part because immigration policies enacted by Congress in 1990 resulted in a huge influx of overseas scientists and engineers, according to engineers' unions.

"This is the third 'crisis-level shortage' of high-tech professionals in the last two decades we have heard about from corporate America," says the AEA's Reed. "In each of the first two instances, the shortage never materialized. We do not believe this one will either."

Reed notes that in the early 1980s predictions by the high-tech industry of a coming shortage of skilled workers were followed by an oversupply of computer engineers and scientists, after a record number of degrees were awarded in 1986.

Then in the late 1980s — in an unpublished report that was nonetheless widely circulated and roundly criticized — the National Science Foundation (NSF) predicted imminent shortages of scientists and engineers. The 1990 Hudson Institute's "Workforce 2000" report seemed to bolster the NSF prediction.

Congress cited the two studies when it amended immigration law in 1990, substantially increasing the number of skilled workers allowed to immigrate to the United States each year. The Immigration Act of 1990 increased the number of permanent, work-based admissions allowed each year from 54,000 to 140,000 and created tens of thousands of slots for various types of temporary skilled workers, including 65,000 under the controversial H-1B program.

Immediately thereafter, the Soviet Union broke up, defense spending was slashed and the aerospace and other industries were aggressively downsized. Not surprisingly, the job market for scientists and engineers once again collapsed. Still, from 1990-1993, the United States produced 50 percent more bachelors' degrees in computer science, math and engineering than it needed. The unemployment rate reached 12 percent for Ph.D.s in mathematics and physics, forcing many into low-paid, "post doctoral" positions, Lawrence Richards, then executive director of the Software Professionals' Political Action Committee, told lawmakers in 1995. [19] Growth in wages stagnated.

Despite the oversupply of domestic engineers and scientists, more than 314,000 foreign scientists and engineers entered the country on a variety of temporary visas between 1991 and 1995, said immigration researcher and former Labor Department official David S. North. And another 100,000 became permanent residents, he said.

"Government and industry may be reducing their investments in science and engineering; unemployment may be growing in both fields; but the government keeps admitting more and more non-immigrants in science and engineering," North told the Senate Judiciary Committee in 1995.

In a book outlining his research, North concluded that the presence of numerous highly skilled and hard-working foreign scientists and engineers had "soothed the establishment" in government, industry and academia. However, he concluded, they also had depressed wages, led indirectly to more unemployment, hastened the retirement of middle-aged, native-born scientists and engineers and reduced incentives to increase the number of female, black, Hispanic and Native American scientists and engineers. He also concluded that the low number of Americans choosing science and engineering careers was due to lower salaries. [20]

In a lengthy 1996 report for Empower America, author Stuart Anderson challenged North's findings. "No evidence exists that foreign-born engineers in the high-technology field have lowered the earnings or harmed the employment prospects of native-born American engineers as a group," he wrote." [21]

Indeed, Anderson found that median earnings for engineers in electronics, electrical machinery and computers, seven years after they obtained their bachelor's degrees, increased by 43.4 percent from 1975-1995, compared with 12.6 percent for the average American worker.

## H-1B Controversy

In 1993 and 1994 the TV news shows "60 Minutes" and "48 Hours" revealed that labor contractors had brought in hundreds of programmers on H-1B visas to replace Americans being laid off. In one infamous case, the workers being fired had to retrain their replacements. One of the contractors bringing in guest workers told "48 Hours" that he had been unable to find enough Americans to do the jobs.

"What he did not mention was that his guest workers were earning $10,000-$20,000 a year less than the laid-off Americans," Richards told lawmakers. The Labor Department said that because of loopholes in the H-1B law, companies were increasingly using it to bring in lower-end programmers en masse and as a quick first step for importing skilled foreign workers on the way to

# Chronology

## 1970s

***Revolutions in microchip technology, including the invention of the microprocessor, drastically reduce the cost of the thousands of electronic components required in a computer.***

**1971**
American engineer Marcian E. Hoff combines the basic elements of a computer on one tiny silicon chip, which he calls a microprocessor.

**1974**
The first affordable desktop computer designed specifically for personal use, the Altair 8800, is sold by Micro Instrumentation Telemetry Systems.

**1977**
Tandy Corp. becomes the first major electronics firm to produce a personal computer. Soon afterward, a small company named Apple Computer, founded by engineer Stephen Wozniak and entrepreneur Steven Jobs, begins producing a superior model.

---

## 1980s

***The high-tech industry predicts a shortage of skilled workers, followed by an oversupply of computer engineers and scientists, after a record number of degrees are awarded in 1986. Later in the decade, the National Science Foundation (NSF) predicts imminent shortages of scientists and engineers.***

**1981**
IBM introduces the "Personal Computer," or PC. Competition from the makers of "clones" (computers modeled after IBM PCs), drives down the price of PCs.

---

## 1990s

***The job market for scientists and engineers collapses following the collapse of the Soviet Union and widespread defense and aerospace downsizing in response to global competition. The unemployment rate for engineers more than doubles by 1994. Yet more than 314,000 foreign scientists and engineers enter the country on a variety of temporary work visas between 1991 and 1995. Another 100,000 become permanent immigrants during the same period.***

**1990**
The Hudson Institute's "Workforce 2000" report seems to bolster the NSF prediction of an impending skilled-labor shortage. Congress cites the two studies when it amends immigration law, increasing from 54,000 to 140,000 the number of permanent, work-based admissions allowed each year and creating myriad other skill- and profession-based visas for foreign nationals coming to study, work and conduct business on a temporary basis. The controversial H-1B program, allowing up to 65,000 skilled workers to enter the country each year, is born.

**April 8, 1992**
The House Committee on Science, Space and Technology holds a hearing blasting the earlier NSF study as seriously flawed.

**1993 and 1994**
Several high-profile cases reveal that companies are using H-1B visas to bring in hundreds of workers to replace American programmers being laid off.

**January 1995**
The Labor Department tries to implement new regulations to plug some H-1B loopholes. The department is sued by the National Association of Manufacturers. Congress convenes hearings partly because of the negative publicity about the H-1B program.

**1996**
In May, the Labor Department's inspector general finds that the H-1B program "is broken and needs to be fixed." Bills are introduced slashing some of the entry slots for skilled workers, but after intense lobbying by a coalition of industry, university administrators and immigration lawyers' associations, no reforms are enacted. In July, a court strikes down the new Labor Department rules.

**1997**
The Commerce Department and Information Technology Association of America (ITAA) declare a severe shortage of skilled high-tech workers and set up six task forces to study the problem.

**1998**
In January, the task force reports are released and the administration announces a $28 million program to boost skilled-worker training. In April the Senate Judiciary Committee agrees to increase the H-1B cap to 95,000 this year and up to 115,000 in subsequent years.

## The 'Year 2000 Problem' . . .

Predictions about the impact of the so-called "Year 2000 Problem" range from apocalyptic havoc to a mere blip on the computer screen. Doomsayers say it could resemble a Hollywood disaster film: chaotic international money markets, inaccessible bank vaults, blank air-traffic control screens, blacked-out power grids, crippled missile defense systems. Not to mention non-functioning telephones, ATMs and elevators.

Others say it will be the biggest non-event in history. To show how safe the skies will be, Federal Aviation Administrator Jane F. Garvey plans to board a plane at midnight on December 31, 1999, and fly from Washington, D.C., across three time zones to California.

Whether one subscribes to the big bang or the big yawn theory, the cost of fixing the problem, nicknamed Y2K, will be steep — from $200 billion to $600 billion at last count, says the Gartner Group, a Stamford, Conn., computer consulting firm. But that doesn't include hundreds of billions more in potential litigation costs if calendar-challenged computer systems aren't brought up to date.

All because of two little digits. The Y2K millennium bug was born in the early days of programming, when mainframe memory was precious. To save memory space, dates were abbreviated to two digits, without the 19; thus 1999 would appear as 99. But computers weren't programmed to deal with the year 2000. So on Jan. 1, 2000, it is feared that computers may go haywire. Some could shut down; some might just hiccup; some might roll back the date to 1900, invalidating much of the date-sensitive data they store.

It's a digital nightmare with a grindingly boring and time-consuming solution. Literally billions of lines of computer code must be painstakingly scanned for any dates, then rewritten to recognize the new century. A lengthy testing phase then follows. One estimate says the problem will take 700,000 person years to fix. Because the bug lurks mostly in mainframes, it requires knowledge of old computer languages, like COBOL, which today's young PC programmers never learned.

But the bug also lives in millions of embedded chips found in just about every electronic device — from elevators to coffee makers — with time- or date-sensitive mechanisms. Repairing these is particularly maddening for manufacturers, many of whom were late in waking up to the Year 2000 problem. They must find millions of these computerized devices hidden among their production equipment, such as machine tools, measuring instruments and computerized valves. General Motors is already encountering "catastrophic problems" in every one of its plants, said chief information officer Ralph J. Szygenda.[1]

Most experts think it could take months or even years to work out all the bugs in repaired systems. Moreover, many companies and governments targeted only their most critical systems to repair first, leaving the others until later. Some fear that when a repaired system interacts with an unrepaired system, it could transmit the problem back to the bug-free system — much like a computer virus — wiping out years of repairs.

Many companies are already feeling the bug's effects. In a survey released in March, the Information Technology Association of America (ITAA) found 44 percent of member companies had experienced failures under actual operating conditions, and 67 percent reported failures under test conditions.

The ITAA and industry executives blame the nationwide shortage of high-tech workers, at least in part, on the Y2K problem, saying that thousands of key personnel have been diverted to sort out Year 2000 problems. But companies that supply commercial clients with Y2K workers say business is slow. The ITAA surveyed its members last July and found that only 4 percent had all the business they could handle. More than 80 percent said they could easily provide more Year 2000 workers if needed.

Edward E.Yardeni, chief economist at Deutsche Morgan Grenfell, a New York investment bank, says the low demand for Y2K workers means "there isn't enough alarm about it." Yardeni sees as much as a 60 percent chance that the lack of Y2K preparedness could trigger a severe global recession. European countries have not focused on the problem to a large extent because they have been busy trying to convert to the Euro by next year, and Japanese companies have been distracted by their own economic problems.

"The time has come to act as though we are preparing for a war," Yardeni told representatives of the global banking community on April 7 at a "Year 2000" symposium organized by the Bank for International Settlements (BIS) in Basle, Switzerland. He recommends establishment of a multinational Year 2000 Alliance, with a commander in chief to organize a global militarylike campaign to increase public awareness, develop fail-safe systems to prevent an accidental nuclear missile launch and make sure vital utilities and

becoming permanent residents.

As written, the law "amounts to nothing more than a way for employers to obtain cheap labor and to drive down the wages of native workers," Richards said in his Senate testimony.

The industry not only brings in large numbers of foreigners to do code-writing but also exports a lot of it, particularly to India. New developments in satellite technology allow companies here to work closely with employees abroad.

The trend toward foreign workers was predicted by Yourdon in his 1992 book, *Decline and Fall of the American*

# . . . Titanic Disaster or Big Yawn?

telecommunications are secure. "Measures must be taken to thwart terrorists, hackers and other malevolent opportunists from taking advantage of any Y2K chaos," he told the group.

Meanwhile in the U.S., Yardeni says, although larger U.S. companies have been working on Y2K for years, the government and smaller companies are not panicked enough. Many computer labor market experts echo the same sentiment.

"Companies aren't desperate enough yet," says Bill Payson, who runs Senior Staff 2000, a job clearinghouse aimed at linking retired COBOL programmers with companies needing Y2K repair work. Payson says he has plenty of experienced programmers willing to work on Year 2000 problems, but they want to telecommute.

Most of them live in Sun Belt states. "They say to me, 'I'm damned if I'm going to leave this golf-course community and come live in a hotel in Chicago to pull their chestnuts out of the fire, when I told them 20 years ago that this was going to be a problem,' " Payson says.

"But most employers won't even consider letting them telecommute," he says. "They're not quite panicky enough to be innovative. But when they realize they have to choose between letting a critical program literally collapse or use these folks living near the golf course, they'll see the light."

Yet other companies are willing to outsource at least some of their Year 2000 work — via satellite — to job shops in India and other nations.

"We get solicitations from Indian firms at least two or three times a week," says Dave Ehlke, of Y2K Plus, which provides Y2K swat teams for a dozen companies and government agencies around the country. "Their general pitch is that they can get us people 20 percent cheaper than Americans," he says. "But I'm not going to hire somebody just because they are cheaper. You really have to know the people you hire."

Industry lobbyists deny that labor contractors are bringing in computer workers who are being paid less than Americans. In the current tight labor market, they say, such lower-paid workers would immediately be hired away by another firm offering them more.

Even the Russians are coming to the rescue of American companies. Russia is a rich source of COBOL and mainframe programmers, although they are not as familiar with business applications as programmers from more capitalistic economies. "A tremendous number of Y2K remediation shops in New York City are staffed by Russians," says Bruce Grant, president of Resource Solutions International, in Herndon, Va.

Grant's company recruits at industries in the Midwest, and among downsized and retired military personnel, especially those in the Washington, D.C., area.

"The military is about a quarter the size it was during Desert Storm," he says. "There's a large amount of talent still out there."

Many experts say that most firms won't be ready on Dec. 31, 1999, because of the "industrial chain reaction" effect.

Large companies and governments depend on independent suppliers for critical goods and services, notes Stephanie Moore, senior analyst for Giga Information Group, a Stamford, Conn., consulting firm. "Even if you fix all your systems internally, if somebody you rely on for supplies hasn't fixed all theirs, it can cause a domino effect — breaking the supply chain and putting people out of business."

Even if all the banks and financial institutions around the world have debugged their own computers, it could all crash if the hundreds of telecommunications and electrical power systems they rely on haven't been repaired, the BIS warned on April 9.

The domino effect also could affect government agencies that depend on each other. Rep. Steve Horn, R-Calif., chairman of the House Oversight Subcommittee on Government Management, Information and Technology, recently reported that only nine out of 24 federal agencies are expected to finish all their critical Year 2000 conversion work on time. In fact, the Defense Department has converted only 24 percent of its 2,915 critical systems and is not expected to finish until 2009, he said, calling the situation "intolerable."

John Koskinen, who was appointed by President Clinton on Feb. 4 to spearhead the government's conversion program, is convinced that all 7,850 critical systems within the government will be completed on time. "There is not an agency in the government that is not devoted to solving this problem," he says.

Koskinen says his team must perform the "delicate balancing act" of increasing worldwide awareness of how urgent the problem is while not "creating panic and precipitous, counterproductive activity."

[1] Gene Bylinsky, "Industry Wakes Up to the Year 2000 Menace," Fortune, April 27, 1998.

*Programmer*. "During the 1990s," Yourdan wrote, "software development may well move out of the U.S. into software factories in a dozen countries whose people are well-educated, less expensive and more passionately devoted to quality and productivity."

Those in favor of raising the cap say it makes more economic sense for those jobs to be done by foreigners here. "The work's got to be done. It will either be done here or overseas. Why not bring the foreigners here to do it?" asks a Senate staffer who works on the legislation. "Then we get the economic benefit of those jobs being done here — and all the support jobs they create."

In addition, executives argue, having the drudge work done wherever it is cheapest frees up money for higher-paid programmers and systems designers who do the more creative work.

If you look at labor strictly as a commodity, says Cato Institute economist Stephen Moore, bringing in foreign engineers is a "great deal" for America. "It costs about $150,000 to educate an engineer. If we let the Indian government pay for the education, then we get that benefit for free. In a sense, we're really robbing that country of its investment. The Indians are the ones who should be upset about this, not the Americans."

During 1995 and 1996, Congress worked on several reform proposals. Reich had asked for more effective investigatory and enforcement authority to prevent employers from abusing the program. Bills were introduced slashing some of the entry slots for skilled workers, and hearings were held on Capitol Hill. However following intense lobbying by a coalition of industry, university administrators and immigration lawyers' associations, none of the reforms was enacted.

In 1995, the Labor Department tried to implement new regulations to plug some of the H-1B loopholes. The new rules would have allowed the department to launch an investigation without first having to receive a complaint; reduced from six years to three the maximum time an employee could remain under an H-1B visa; and required companies to provide more evidence that they were paying the going rate in their region. The department was sued by the National Association of Manufacturers, which said the department had not given sufficient public notice, and that the new regulations were "onerous and anticompetitive."

In July 1996 the court struck down the new rules as having been insufficiently advertised. Also that year, the Labor Department's inspector general found that the H-1B program "is broken and needs to be fixed." It does not protect U.S. workers' jobs and salaries, largely because the department's role is limited by law to no more than "rubber stamping" employers' applications, said the report. [22]

To illustrate this weakness in the law, Richards had told the Senate committee, he applied to the Labor Department for permission to hire 40 foreign programmers at $4.50 an hour. "This application was approved and sent back to me in nine days," he said. [23]

## Focus on Education

Annual caps on enrollment in university computer science departments also add to the current shortage of home-grown computer experts. "Competing for a finite number of dollars, enrollment is limited in computer science and other popular fields to force enrollment in less popular ones," said the NSA report. "Because private and public research dollars are often awarded to less popular fields (e.g., physics, chemistry, biosciences), these departments hold a financial advantage over other fields. This gives them a political edge in faculty employment and in holding enrollment down in other fields in favor of theirs."

The Michigan State experience reflects that dilemma. "The department budget doesn't get influenced by how many students are in the classes," says Chairman Jain, who had to impose grade-point cutoff criteria in order to limit the number of students entering junior-year computer science programs. "That's one way we are handling the increased demand for classes."

Other computer department heads noted that because of tenure limitations, universities are not free to hire and fire professors as demand fluctuates from year to year.

Besides, says Jain, there aren't a lot of Ph.D.s in computer science hanging around looking for jobs. "We have to compete with major research labs like Lucent Technologies and IBM, which are hiring a large number of Ph.D.s," he says. "Private industry can offer much larger salaries than we can."

Even graduate assistants are hard to find, he said, because the private job market is so good. "It's so easy for graduate students to go out and get a good-paying job right now in private industry."

Industry says the roots of the current problem lie in the failure of America's education system. American high schools don't provide world-class math and science curricula and universities teach too much theory and not enough applied technology, they say.

"When we are looking for engineers we turn a lot of people away because they don't have the right skills," says FirsTel's Rohde. But when he recruits in India or China, he finds qualified people "in droves," he adds. "The engineers we get out of Ireland, Scotland, China and India are more disciplined, they work harder, they are more dedicated and they are better trained."

"Why don't American educators go over there and find out what they're doing right?" he asks. Many companies, resigned to the apparent inability of the education system to provide capable workers, have established training centers to bring new graduates up to speed, not only in technology but also in basic skills and literacy.

In the latest international rankings in math and science, U.S. high school seniors were nearly last among students from 21 participating nations. Even America's academically elite students — who take physics or advanced math courses in high school — scored last in physics and second from the bottom in high-level math.

The rankings were from the Third International Mathematics and Science Study (TIMSS), which periodically tests fourth-, eighth- and 12th-graders from 40 nations.

# At Issue:

## *Should more foreign high-tech workers be allowed into the United States?*

**yes**

**William T. Archey**
***President and CEO, American Electronics Association***

***WRITTEN FOR THE CQ RESEARCHER, APRIL 1998.***

**I** speak on behalf of the entire high-technology industry when I say legal immigrants play a critical role in the high-technology industry. A cap on the number of temporary, employment-based visas, or H-1B visas, is a cap on our industry's growth.

The high-tech industry is experiencing tremendous growth and is a driving force in this nation's economy. From 1995 to 1996 alone, the high-tech industry created more than 240,000 jobs. We are the single largest exporter of manufactured goods in the country, exporting $150 billion worth of goods last year.

However, to continue this level of growth, we need to ensure there are enough qualified workers in the United States. In other words, we need to ensure that the supply satisfies the demand. Our companies, therefore, invest millions of dollars per year retraining our U.S. work force.

Unfortunately, after exhaustive searches in the United States, native workers are sometimes not available. And sometimes the position requires a culturally diverse background. Despite popular opinion, there is no financial advantage to hiring highly skilled legal immigrants. Relocation fees, visa processing costs, legal bills and the much-in-demand talents of individuals being recruited frequently make the process more expensive than hiring a U.S. worker.

Legal immigrants play a small but critical role in addressing the short-term needs of the industry. Although constituting an infinitesimally small percentage of the overall high-tech work force, their innovative expertise creates intellectual property and products in the United States, which in turn creates jobs for U.S. workers. Without legal immigrants, the world leadership position the U.S. high-tech industry enjoys today would be undermined.

Opponents of increasing the cap on H-1B visas call on industry to train, retrain and recruit existing U.S. workers. We are doing that, and then some. Many of the problems in producing qualified U.S. workers are also a function of the inadequacies of the U.S. educational system, particularly grades K-12. Our companies are very involved in educational reform, but that reform is a long-term proposition. Our companies cannot cease hiring highly skilled legal immigrants while waiting for these reforms to take hold. Indeed, many of those legal immigrants will make the kind of contributions that will help assure future generations of American workers opportunities for high-skilled, high-paying jobs.

**no**

**Norman Matloff**
***Professor of computer science, University of California at Davis, and former software developer in Silicon Valley***

***WRITTEN FOR THE CQ RESEARCHER, APRIL 1998.***

**T**he information technology (IT) industry is using the H-1B work visa program far in excess of its intended function, which is to deal with temporary, spot shortages. The number of visas requested by employers for computer specialists increased by 352 percent from 1990-1995, during which time the number of jobs in the field increased by only 35 percent.

An audit conducted by the Department of Labor found rampant abuse in the visa program. Several independent studies have confirmed that the foreign-national computer programmers and engineers are paid on average 15-30 percent less than comparable U.S. workers.

IT employers claim a desperate labor shortage, yet wages for computer programmers went up by only 7 percent last year. If you were an employer who was desperate to hire, wouldn't you be willing to pay a salary premium of more than 7 percent?

Industry lobbyists claim that H-1Bs are needed because few of our nation's young people have the interest and ability to go into computer science and related fields. That claim is false; computer science enrollment has doubled in the last two years. Yet one wonders why the industry wants more graduates when it is not even bothering to recruit many of them. Even the Information Technology Association of America, which is leading the lobbying effort to increase the H-1B cap, concedes that most IT employers recruit new graduates at only a small number of colleges.

The IT industry is not making good use of the labor pool of experienced workers either. Most firms in the industry, large and small, hire only about 2 percent of their applicants for IT positions. Age discrimination is widespread, with an unemployment rate of 17 percent among computer programmers over age 50. Most don't make it that far. Only 19 percent of those with a computer science degree are still in the field 20 years after graduation, compared with 52 percent for civil engineering. Sun Microsystems, a firm vociferously demanding a higher H-1B quota, classifies as "senior" anyone with six years of experience, say at age 28.

The sky won't fall if the H-1B program is not expanded. On the contrary, without this pool of imported labor to rely on, the industry would be forced to take a closer look at the workers who are already here.

An education task force set up by the ITAA and the Commerce Department has recommended a wide range of improvements in elementary and secondary education, including:

• Requiring all middle and high school math and science teachers to have at least a bachelor's degree in math or science;

• Requiring four years of physics for all high school students and more advanced mathematics in grades four through eight; and

• Increasing corporate donations for public K-12 education; boosting teacher salaries, to make the profession more appealing, and having teachers take extra math, science and computer courses.

Educators who have compared the United States with high-performing countries have found that American schools cover too many subjects on a superficial level. For instance, American textbooks are encyclopedic in size, compared with small paperback textbooks used in high-performing countries. Other countries also encourage more independent thinking and group problem-solving, researchers say.

Meanwhile, a plethora of public and private efforts are under way across the country to bring technology to the nation's elementary and secondary schools, many of which don't have the hardware, software or teacher training to make wide use of high-tech. ■

# CURRENT SITUATION

## Action in Congress

The congressional debate over the cap on foreign temporary workers pits a powerful coalition of computer companies, immigration lawyers and university administrators against labor unions and engineers' groups.

The measure ran into only token opposition in the Senate Judiciary Committee earlier this month, unlike two years ago when former Sen. Alan K. Simpson, R-Wyo., tried to make it harder for employers to import foreign workers. After industry complaints that it would cripple their global competitiveness, Simpson abandoned his efforts, calling the claims "hype and hysteria." [24]

At the time, Simpson was joined by Sen. Edward M. Kennedy, D-Mass., with strong support from then-Labor Secretary Reich. Now Simpson and Reich are out of the picture, and Kennedy's once strong attempts to reform the H-1B program appear tempered.

Caught between his usual labor constituency and strong pressure from high-tech companies back home, Kennedy offered an alternative measure jointly with Sen. Dianne Feinstein, D-Calif., whose constituency includes Silicon Valley. Their measure was supported by the Clinton administration, which said it "strongly opposes" a measure sponsored by Sen. Spencer Abraham, R-Mich., to raise the cap.

The Kennedy-Feinstein alternative, which was rejected on an 8-10 vote along party lines, would have raised the cap to 90,000 but limited the visas to three years. It included most of the enforcement enhancements the administration has sought for five years, including requiring employers to first try to recruit Americans and making it illegal to lay off Americans to hire foreigners.

Sen. Abraham at the last minute presented an amended version of his original bill, raising the cap to 95,000 this year and 105,000 each year from 1999 through 2002. In 2003, the number would drop back down to 65,000. Up to 10,000 additional workers could be admitted each year after 1999, if those slots were not used up by physical therapists the previous year. [25]

In an effort to garner bipartisan support, Abraham added provisions sought by both Kennedy and the administration. One would make it illegal to lay off Americans within six months before hiring foreign workers or 90 days afterward. In addition, the Labor Department would be allowed to conduct spot inspections — without waiting for a complaint — but only of employers who had previously violated the law.

The measure was approved 12-6 on April 2, with Democrats Feinstein and Herb Kohl, Wis., joining the panel's 10 Republicans.

The bill provides $50 million in federal matching grants for 20,000 scholarships a year for low-income students studying mathematics, engineering or computer science. Another $10 million would be authorized to train unemployed Americans in new high-tech skills, and $8 million would be used to set up a job bank on the Internet. The money for scholarships, training and the job bank were designed to appease the White House, which had already proposed similar initiatives.

Nonetheless, the administration still opposes Abraham's bill, says Sally Katzen, deputy director of the National Economic Council.

"They made a modest step," she says. "But there's a lot of work that needs to be done. We've been very clear that having employers both recruit and retain U.S. workers is very important."

One of the alternatives suggested by the administration is to require employers to "simply check off a box" attesting that they had tried to hire Americans before recruiting foreign workers, she says. "We believe that request is not unreasonable." The industry staunchly opposes such a requirement because it fears it could delay hiring for years while the Labor Department defines what kind of a recruitment effort employers would have to make.

Katzen points out that the Abraham bill only authorizes money for scholarships and training, without specifying where the money would come from. The

Kennedy-Feinstein bill would have required employers to pay a $250 application fee, raising $100 million, of which $90 million would be used for loans to workers needing training. The other $10 million would be used to develop "regional skills alliances" between government and industry to identify local labor market needs and develop regional strategies for meeting them.

As the Abraham bill awaits full Senate action, the House Immigration Subcommittee was scheduled to hold hearings on the issue April 21. Subcommittee Chairman Rep. Lamar Smith, R-Texas, has promised to propose legislation to raise the cap, but "with safeguards."

Meanwhile the administration recently announced $28 million in new initiatives to bring technology to underserved communities, retrain laid-off workers from other industries and create a Web site listing high-tech job vacancies. ■

## FOR MORE INFORMATION

*If you would like to have this CQ Researcher updated, or need more information about this topic, please call CQ Custom Research. Special rates for CQ subscribers. (202) 887-8600 or (800) 432-2250, ext. 600, or E-mail Custom.Research@cq.com*

**American Electronics Association,** 601 Pennsylvania Ave. N.W., North Bldg., Suite 600, Washington, D.C. 20004; (202) 682-9110; www.aeanet.org. This trade association represents more than 3,000 U.S.-based companies in the software, electronics and information technology industries.

**American Engineering Association,** P.O. Box 820473, Fort Worth, Texas 76182-0473; (817) 280-8106. The AEA represents 1,000 scientists, engineers, designers and programmers throughout the country.

**Information Technology Association of America,** 1616 N. Ft. Myer Dr., Suite 1300, Arlington, Va. 22209-3106; (703) 522-5055; www.itaa.org. This trade association monitors legislation and regulations for the computer and software industry.

**Institute of Electrical and Electronics Engineers — United States Activities,** 1828 L St., N.W., Suite 1202, Washington, D.C. 20036-5104; (202) 785-0017; www.ieeeusa.org. This professional and technical society is the U.S. arm of an international organization representing 219,000 electrical, electronics and computer engineers in the United States.

# OUTLOOK

## More Foreign Workers?

Even if Congress raises the cap on foreign workers, it will probably only be the latest round in the eventual globalization of high-tech industry jobs.

"The foreign technical worker has become the drug of choice for American industry," says AEA's Reed. "Make no mistake about it, they are addicted. Within the next four years, they will be back asking for more."

"I don't understand why we should have a quota at all on very high-skilled talent," FirsTel's Rohde says.

"It's an international world now, and this is an international industry. Eighty percent of my revenues come from outside the U.S. If we couldn't hire internationally and if we couldn't sell internationally, we couldn't survive. This is the wave of the future," says Rohde. "Having an insular mentality about jobs in the U.S. is crazy."

But hiring foreign workers may get harder and costlier, as international competition for foreign workers intensifies, say industry analysts.

"The rest of the world is waking up to the same demand and the same shortages," Gale Fitzgerald, CEO of Computer Task Group, of Buffalo, N.Y., told National Public Radio in February. "I think we should attract as many qualified people [from overseas] as we possibly can to help U.S. industry, but that's a short-term fix. That's not the long-term answer to the U.S.'s problem."

Barring any catastrophic fallout from either the Asia crisis or the Year 2000 computer glitch, most expect the industry's explosive growth to continue for the foreseeable future. Thus most see the current robust job market for high-tech workers continuing unabated.

"I think the demand will be this way for a number of years," said Harvey Shrednick, professor at Arizona State University's College of Business. "Because technology is a continuously changing, continuously competitive environment." [26]

Others are more cautious. They point to skyrocketing computer enrollments at universities, community colleges, technical and vocational schools, as well as increasing internships and computer vocational classes at the high school level. Industry is constantly striving to invent labor-saving software, they say, and if Asia's economic troubles worsen it could spur an exodus of Asian high-tech talent to the United States.

"On top of those pressures, you're going to have all those people who have been diverted to fix the Year 2000 problem out on the labor market in a couple of years," says a Labor Department official. "I worry that when all these kids studying computer science come out on the other end, there isn't going to be anyplace for them to go."

ITAA's Miller dismisses such fears. "The administration needs to get those Neanderthals over at the Labor Department on board."

## Model Programs

As the tight labor market becomes a worldwide problem, U.S. companies are investing more in the nation's education infrastructure, and partnerships between industry and educational institutions are proliferating. A number of model programs around the country, including several highlighted in the ITAA task force report, show how industry, academia and government can work together to solve the problem:

- Cisco Systems Inc., of San Jose, Calif., has launched an $18 million program to train more than 1,000 students for entry-level networking positions via a rigorous two-year academic and hands-on training program in 57 high schools and junior colleges.
- Syntel Inc., a Michigan-based computer labor contractor has launched an eight-week "technology boot camp" to provide metropolitan Detroit with well-trained junior software programmers.
- The Tech Corps, a national organization with chapters in 40 states, recruits IT professionals to volunteer in their local schools to help install and integrate new technologies into the curriculum.
- Microsoft has teamed up with the nonprofit Green Thumb organization in a pilot program to provide IT training to low-income older workers in three cities. Microsoft has also committed $7 million plus software and technical assistance to 25 community colleges over a five-year period to train unemployed or underemployed workers, welfare recipients, single parents, legal immigrants and the disabled in IT skills.
- Omaha's Applied Information Management Institute is perhaps the most comprehensive example of regional coordination. The institute is a consortium of 34 businesses, 10 colleges and universities, the chamber of commerce and the state government. It helps develop IT curriculums, sponsors publicity campaigns encouraging students to consider computer careers and offers paid internships at local businesses.

The institute also established an on-line mentoring project pairing students with professional advisers, sponsors an on-line Virtual Career Fair and holds a one-week summer Cyber Camp for middle and high school students. The group also gave scholarships to 22 elementary and secondary teachers to develop technology-oriented curricula to share with other Nebraska teachers.

"The good news is that there's a lot of stuff going on," Miller says "The marketplace is responding. I see a lot of good old-fashioned American ingenuity trying to solve the problem."

It will also take a collaborative effort, says Secretary Daley. "We are at an economic crossroads, and we have to work harder until education catches up with innovation. That will require a strong partnership between government, the private sector, labor groups, high schools, trade schools, community colleges and academia." [27] ■

*Kathy Koch is a freelance writer in the Washington, D.C., area.*

## Notes

[1] From a speech to the Third Annual Technology for Learning Summit, Los Angeles, Calif., June 25, 1997.

[2] Testimony before Senate Judiciary Immigration Subcommittee, Feb. 25, 1998.

[3] Speech to the Commonwealth Club and San Jose, Calif., Chamber of Commerce, June 26, 1997.

[4] Dexter Kozen and Stu Zweben, "Undergrad Enrollments Keep Booming, Grad Enrollments Holding Their Own," *Computing Research News*, March 1998.

[5] Technology for Learning Summit, *op. cit.*

[6] Testimony before Senate Judiciary Immigration Subcommittee, Feb. 25, 1998.

[7] Carnes spoke on National Public Radio's "Science Friday," Feb. 27, 1998.

[8] Norman Matloff, "Debunking the Myth of a Desperate Software Labor Shortage," University of California, Davis, 1998.

[9] "Help Wanted: A Call for Collaborative Action for the New Millennium," Information Technology Association of America and Virginia Polytechnic Institute and State University, 1998.

[10] "Information Technology: Assessment of The Department of Commerce's Report on Workforce Demand and Supply," General Accounting Office, March 23, 1998.

[11] Jack A. Bobo and Susan Tinch Johnson, "Software Workers for the New Millennium: Global Competitiveness Hangs in the Balance," National Software Alliance, 1998.

[12] "America's New Deficit: The Shortage of Information Technology Workers," Department of Commerce, September 1997.

[13] "Update: America's New Deficit," Department of Commerce, Office of Technology Policy, January 1998.

[14] T.J. Rodgers, "Give Us Your Tired, Your Poor — and Your Engineers," *The Wall Street Journal*, March 9, 1998.

[15] Demetrios G. Papademetriou and Stephen Yale-Loehr, *Balancing Interests: Rethinking U.S. Selection of Skilled Immigrants*, Carnegie Endowment for International Peace, 1996.

[16] Quoted in Matloff, *op. cit.*

[17] Edward Yourdon, *The Rise and Resurrection of the American Programmer*, 1996.

[18] From remarks to the Chicago Economic Club, Dec. 18, 1997.

[19] Testimony before Senate Judiciary Committee, Sept. 28, 1995.

[20] David S. North, *Soothing the Establishment: The Impact of Foreign-Born Scientists and Engineers on America* (1995).

[21] Stuart Anderson, "Employment-Based Immigration and High Technology," *Empower America*, 1996.

[22] "The Department of Labor's Foreign Labor Certification Programs: The System Is Broken and Needs to Be Fixed," Office of Inspector General, Department of Labor, May 1996.

[23] Quoted in the *Los Angeles Times*, July 15, 1996.

[24] Quoted in *CQ Weekly Report*, March 30, 1996.

[25] Until last year, the largest users of H-1B visas were hospitals importing physical therapists. Last year, for the first time, computer companies became the largest user of H-1B visas.

[26] Quoted in Rochelle Garner, "Pressure Gap: Transforming the IT Workforce," *Computerworld*, Feb. 2, 1998.

[27] Technology for Learning Summit, *op. cit.*

# Bibliography

## Selected Sources Used


### Books

**North, David S., *Soothing the Establishment: The Impact of Foreign-Born Scientists and Engineers on America*, University Press of America, 1995.**
A former Labor Department official studies the economic impact of the steady growth in the number of foreign-born scientists and engineers on graduate schools, university faculties and industry. He concludes that they have depressed wages and thus discouraged native-born students from pursuing engineering and science careers.

**Papademetriou, Demetrios G., and Stephen Yale-Loehr, *Balancing Interests: Rethinking U.S. Selection of Skilled Immigrants*, Carnegie Endowment for International Peace, 1996.**
Two analysts with the International Migration Policy Program of the Carnegie Endowment for International Peace examine U.S. policy regarding both permanent and temporary immigration of skilled workers.

**Yourdon, Edward, *Decline and Fall of the American Programmer*, Yourdon Press, 1992.**
Software industry expert Yourdon warns that American programmers may be replaced by talented and much cheaper programmers in India, Russia, Brazil, Singapore and Manila. To survive, the American software industry must restructure and re-engineer itself, increasing productivity and quality at the same time.

**Yourdon, Edward, *Rise and Resurrection of the American Programmer*, Prentice Hall, 1996.**
Software industry expert Yourdon revisits his previous dire predictions about the decline of the American software industry, and says that higher-paid American programmers have been "saved" from competition from cheaper overseas programmers by the introduction of visually oriented software development tools, which helped boost productivity.

### Reports and Studies

**Anderson, Stuart, "Employment-Based Immigration and High Technology," *Empower America*, 1996.**
The author, who wrote this report before becoming director of immigration research and analysis for the Senate Judiciary Subcommittee on Immigration, argues that immigrants are a catalyst for economic growth and do not displace American workers or depress American wages. Instead, immigrants create jobs, the author argues.

**Bobo, Jack A., and Susan Tinch Johnson, "Software Workers for the New Millennium: Global Competitiveness Hangs in the Balance," *National Software Alliance*, Arlington, Va., January 1998.**
This in-depth look at the computer industry contends that America can't produce enough computer workers to fill the current shortfall without importing more workers. The authors argue that more effort should be made to recruit and train/retrain American workers.

**Department of Commerce, Office of Technology Policy, "America's New Deficit: The Shortage of Information Technology Workers," September 1997.**
The Department of Commerce concluded that the growth of high-tech jobs exceeds America's ability to produce enough skilled workers to fill those jobs. To boost that argument, it says the country will need 95,000 new high tech workers a year in each of the next ten years, but that U.S. universities only awarded 24,553 bachelors' degrees in computer and information science in 1994.

**Department of Commerce, Office of Technology Policy, "Update: America's New Deficit," January 1998.**
This study, which updates the department's September study (above), finds that the country will need 137,800 new computer workers a year between 1996 and 2006.

**Information Technology Association of America and Virginia Polytechnic Institute and State University, "Help Wanted: A Call for Collaborative Action for the New Millennium," 1998**
This study by the information technology industry trade association contends there are 346,000 vacant IT jobs in the United States, representing a "severe shortage" of skilled workers.

**Matloff, Norman, "A Critical Look at Immigration's Role in the U.S. Computer Industry," University of California at Davis, August 1997.**
The industry critic and computer science professor examines computer hiring and employment practices. Matloff says the industry casts aside mid-career professionals in order to hire foreign nationals because they will work for less in order to get the employer to sponsor them for permanent immigrant status.

**Matloff, Norman, "Debunking the Myth of a Desperate Software Labor Shortage," University of California at Davis, 1998.**
The computer professor who has become a thorn in the side of the computer industry argues that there is no shortage of software workers, but that the computer industry is trying to scare Congress into allowing more foreign nationals into the country.

# 15 Promoting Democracy in Asia

KENNETH JOST

When political change came to the world's fourth most populous nation this spring, it arrived with stunning speed.

On May 20, an estimated 1 million Indonesians, mostly youths, rallied in the central square of Yogyakarta, a large university city on the south Javan coast. They listened to speaker after speaker call for the resignation of President Suharto, the country's autocratic, longtime leader.

"We expected that the struggle could linger on for several months before we could push Suharto," recalls Mohtar Mas'oed, an activist and senior lecturer at Gadjah Mada University, who attended the rally.

Less than 20 hours later, however, the former general went on television and abruptly ended his 32-year rule over the sprawling chain of islands.

"It was very surprising for us when he decided to step down by himself," Mas'oed says.

In truth, Suharto had little choice. He had amassed billions of dollars for himself, his family and his political cronies after taking power in a 1965 coup. But as he hunkered down in the presidential palace in Jakarta, the capital, members of parliament and his Cabinet deserted him, along with the leader of Indonesia's powerful military.

A turbulent year of economic collapse and political turmoil — climaxed by the killing of six students at Jakarta's Trisakti University eight days earlier — had left Suharto, at age 76, with virtually no support.

The killing of the students sealed Suharto's fate, says Nasir Tamimi, deputy chief editor of the newspaper *Republika*. "People were very angry," he recalls. Five hundred people were killed in rioting in Jakarta over the next three days — forcing Suharto to cut short a trip to Egypt in a fruitless effort to calm the country and keep his office.

From *The CQ Researcher*. Originally published as "Democracy in Asia," July 24, 1998.

But William Liddle, a professor at Ohio State University and an expert on Indonesia, says that Suharto's demise was due more broadly to public discontent over the collapse of the economy in the wake of the financial crisis that swept Asia beginning last July. [1] The economic woes also heightened public resentment about the system of corruption and cronyism that had allowed Suharto and his family to amass a fortune estimated at $30 billion to $40 billion in a country with an annual state budget in 1997 of about $30 billion.

"It's the economy, stupid," Liddle says, recalling the slogan from President Clinton's 1992 campaign. Suharto "really did depend on that economic base. And there was the family favoritism: He just let [his children] do whatever they wanted."

Suharto yielded the presidency to his vice president, B.J. Habibie, a Western-educated aeronautical engineer, who removed some of Suharto's close associates from the Cabinet and promised to institute political reforms. But he also disappointed the country's unseasoned reform movement by announcing an election schedule that called for parliamentary balloting in mid-1999 and the election of a new president at the end of the year.

"Some observers think he's not going fast enough," says Donald Emmerson, a professor of political science at the University of Wisconsin in Madison who visited Indonesia in June. Even so, Emmerson says that Habibie is "comfortable with the ideology of democracy" and has been "extremely adroit" in managing a delicate political situation.

But Emmerson and other experts stress that Indonesia's path of political reform depends most on Habibie's ability to manage a dire economic situation. Poverty and unemployment have soared in the year since Indonesia's rupiah first plunged in value last July. Last year, the International Monetary Fund (IMF) put together a $43 billion bailout package only to see Suharto balk at its terms. Now the IMF estimates that Indonesia's gross national product will decline 10 percent this year — in stark contrast to the 6.6 percent average annual growth between 1985 and 1994.

Political reform in Indonesia would represent a major gain for advocates of democracy in Asia. But the uncertainty about the outcome matches the mixed assessments that human rights advocates in the United States make about the path of democratization in the region.

"There have been major gains in the past year, but I wouldn't say this is an overall trend," says Mike Jendrzejczyk, Washington director for the Asia division of Human Rights Watch.

Charles Graybow, an Asia specialist at the conservative-leaning human rights group Freedom House, sees both "bright spots" and "setbacks" in Asia

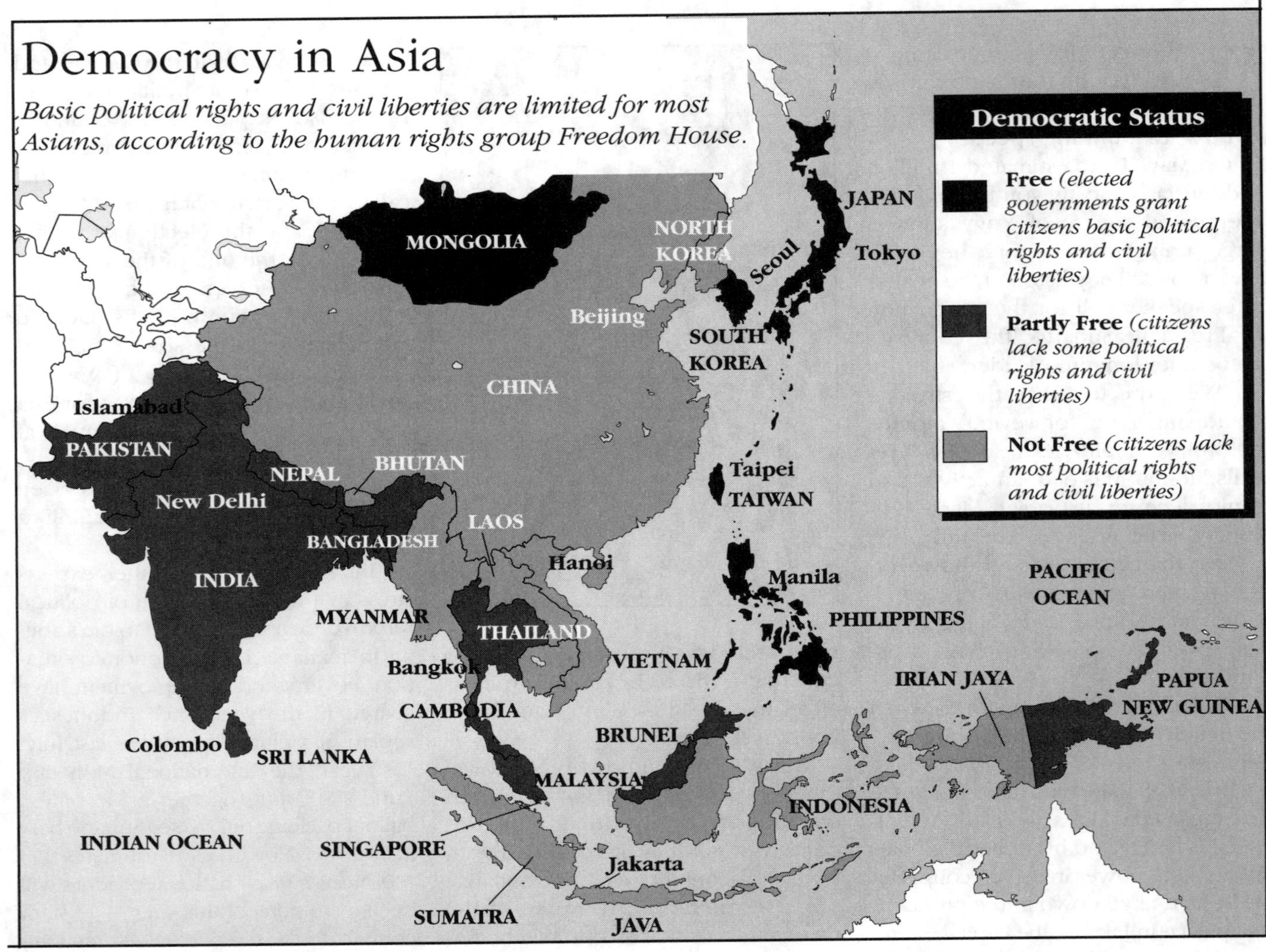


over the past decade. Many countries with formal democratic processes, he says, still have "weak" institutions, such as political parties, labor unions, business groups and so forth.

On the plus side, advocates of democracy point to moves toward freer political systems in such countries as South Korea, Taiwan and Thailand in East and Southeast Asia and in Bangladesh, Nepal and Pakistan in South Asia. *(See chart, p. 276.)* But the military regime in Myanmar, the former Burma, remains intractable; the elections being held in Cambodia on July 26 are widely viewed as rigged by the country's dictator, Hun Sen; the "dominant party" democracies in such countries as Malaysia and Singapore show few signs of welcoming free political competition; and political change is expected to be slow, at best, in China, much less in the region's other communist countries. [2]

Still, one former Clinton administration official is optimistic about the long-term prospects for reforming Asia's undemocratic political systems. "Political liberalization is definitely spreading in Asia," says Catharin E. Dalpino, a guest scholar at the Brookings Institution who served as deputy assistant secretary of State for human rights in President Clinton's first administration.

On the other hand, Larry Diamond, editor of the *Journal of Democracy* and a senior research fellow at the Hoover Institute at Stanford University, is less optimistic. "I see, frankly, a region where there's maybe growing popular aspirations but not a rising tide that would be likely to lead to new democratic transitions," says Diamond, who spent the last year as a visiting scholar at the Academia Sinica in Taiwan.

The goal of democracy — pushed by human rights groups and the United States — is not universally shared. Over the past two decades, a few Asian leaders and Western scholars have contended that democratic government may be incompatible with Asian culture and economic growth.

Human rights advocates scoff at this so-called "Asia-values" debate. "It's said that ordinary Asian citizens prefer order and stability and that they're not really interested in participating in politics," Graybow says. "But what we've seen is that when Asian citizens have the opportunity to participate, they do. The voter turnout, when citizens feel that there is a choice, tends to be very high."

Amartya Sen, an Indian economist, also debunks the claimed linkage between economic growth and closed political systems. "If you look merely to economic growth, there's nothing to indicate in general that authoritarian governments do better than non-authoritarian countries," says Sen, a former professor at Harvard University and now master of Trinity College, Cambridge University, in England.

As experts debate the impact of President Clinton's recent trip to China, and the chances for political reform in Indonesia, these are some of the questions being asked:

### *Does "Western-style" democracy conflict with "Asian values"?*

Since gaining independence from British colonial rule, Malaysia and Singapore have had governments that were democratic in form but widely viewed as undemocratic in practice. Both countries have been ruled continuously by a single political party or coalition, and both governments place what the U.S. State Department calls in Singapore's case "formidable obstacles" in the path of political opponents. [3]

Despite the criticism — or perhaps because of it — the longtime leaders of the two countries have helped spark an international debate over the role of democracy in Asia. In speeches, writings and interviews, Malaysia's prime minister, Mahathir bin Mohamad, and Singapore's Lee Kuan Yew, who served as prime minister for 31 years and since 1990 has continued to wield influence as "senior minister," have defended their countries' political system as better suited for "Asian values" than so-called Western-style democracy.

"Asian societies are unlike Western ones," Lee remarked in one widely noted interview. In Lee's view, Western societies exalt individual interests over the collective good while Asian culture looks more to the best interests of society as a whole. A free-for-all-democracy, he told *The Wall Street Journal*, would produce a "tinderbox kind of society" for Singapore. Malaysia's Mahathir has similarly warned against the risk of allowing "pedantic notions of democracy" to result in "an excess of freedom." "To Asians," Mahathir says, "democracy does not confer a license for citizens to go wild." [4]

Human rights advocates in and outside Asia insist that the supposed tension between democracy and Asian values reflects a misunderstanding of both concepts. Asian cultures are not as hostile to democracy as the theory assumes, they say, and Asian peoples have demonstrated in many countries that they are willing to work and sacrifice for popular self-government.

"It would be a mistake to think that in Asia people haven't been willing to sacrifice a great deal to have democracy established and guaranteed," Professor Sen says.

Sen says that ancient Hindu and Buddhist writers emphasized the importance of individual freedom and tolerance and that the common depiction of Confucianism as valuing administrative efficiency over individual freedom is oversimplified. In recent history, he says, Asians in many countries have demonstrated "a strong commitment" to democracy — despite resistance first from colonial powers and then from homegrown authoritarian governments.

Still, some political scientists do see a distinctive Asian model of democratic government — a so-called dominant party system that minimizes political competition for the sake of social order and economic growth. In his influential book, *The Third Wave*, Harvard political scientist Samuel Huntington called it "democracy without turnover" and said it represented "an adaptation of Western democratic practices, to serve not Western values of competition and change, but Asian values of consensus and stability." [5]

Lucian Pye, a political scientist at the Massachusetts Institute of Technology, likens the current dominant-party systems in Asia to China's Nationalist Party in the early 20th century, which envisioned a "tutelary role" for itself in creating democratic government. Today, Pye says at least some of the dominant-party systems — including South Korea's and Taiwan's — deserve credit for promoting both economic growth and democratic development. [6]

Asia's economic growth during the past two decades, in fact, created a receptive climate for the "Asia-values" theory. Growth was particularly strong in countries that limited political rights, like Indonesia, Singapore, South Korea and Taiwan. With an economic crisis sweeping through Asia over the past year, however, advocates of democracy are arguing with renewed vigor that semiauthoritarian governments actually threaten economic development.

"This has really spelled the death knell for the Asia-values argument," says Freedom House's Graybow, "because it shows that authoritarian governments may have brought some illusion of stability, but in the long run you need openness and accountability to have sustainable economic growth."

Singaporean leaders defend their political system as democratic and bristle at the recurrent criticisms from the State Department in its annual human rights report, and from human rights groups. "What Asians object to

## Democracy Eludes Many Nations in Asia

| Country and Population | Type of Government | Political Conditions |
|---|---|---|
| **East Asia** | | |
| **China** *1.2 billion* | *Communist one-party* | *Chinese Communist Party "holds absolute power, has imprisoned nearly all active dissidents, uses the judiciary as a tool of state control and severely restricts freedoms of speech, press, association and religion."* |
| **Japan** *125.8 million* | *Parliamentary democracy* | *Liberal Democratic Party government weakened by economic crisis, but no credible opposition party.* |
| **Mongolia** *2.3 million* | *Presidential-parliamentary democracy* | *Formerly communist Mongolian People's Revolutionary Party recaptured presidency in June 1997 because of discontent with economic "shock therapy" program enacted by reformist coalition elected in 1996.* |
| **North Korea** *23.9 million* | *Communist one-party* | *"Most tightly controlled country in world"; Kim Jong Il, son of the late longtime leader Kim Il Sung, formally assumed leadership in October 1997* |
| **South Korea** *45.3 million* | *Presidential-parliamentary democracy* | *Election of opposition leader Kim Dae Jung as president in December 1997 caps decade-long political liberalization; National Security Law still used to curb contacts with North Korea.* |
| **Taiwan** *21.4 million* | *Presidential-legislative democracy* | *Democratic transition consolidated by 1996 elections, but ruling Kuomintang Party maintains political advantages through control of media, business interests.* |
| **South Asia** | | |
| **Bangladesh** *119.8 million* | *Parliamentary democracy* | *June 1996 elections were freest in country's history, despite violence and irregularities; but parliamentary boycotts and other confrontational political tactics make normal legislative operations impossible.* |
| **Bhutan** *0.8 million* | *Traditional monarchy* | *King wields absolute power; government arrested monks and civilians in 1997 to curb support for pro-democracy movement* |
| **India** *942 million* | *Parliamentary democracy* | *Fairest elections in country's history in 1996 produced fractured parliament with no consensus on major issues; weak rule of law and social tensions contribute to widespread violations of civil liberties.* |
| **Nepal** *23.2 million* | *Parliamentary democracy* | *Parliamentary government in place since end of absolute monarchy in 1991 is fragmented, but human rights conditions have improved* |
| **Pakistan** *133.5 million* | *Presidential-parliamentary democracy* | *Nawaz Sharif led Pakistan Muslim League to victory in February 1997 election, then consolidated power in showdown in December with president, supreme court; democratic institutions weak, corruption widespread.* |
| **Sri Lanka** *18.7 million* | *Presidential-parliamentary democracy* | *Political institutions "severely tested" by civil war, ethnic tensions, partisan violence; government put forth proposal in 1997 to end ongoing civil war with Tamil separatists.* |
| **Southeast Asia** | | |
| **Brunei** *0.3 million* | *Traditional monarchy* | *Sultan serves as prime minister and, along with inner circle of relatives, holds "absolute power."* |
| **Cambodia** *10.9 million* | *Monarchy, constituent assembly* | *Co-premier Hun Sen regained total power after 1997 coup; "bleak" prospects for fair vote in 1998 elections* |
| **Indonesia** *207.4 million* | *Dominant party (military-dominated)* | *"Turbulent year" in 1997 included violent parliamentary election campaign, crackdown on dissidents and student leaders, ethnic and sectarian violence due to frustration over corruption, and financial crisis; [President Suharto was forced out of office in 1998 and was replaced by Vice President B.J. Habibie].* |

| Country and Population | Type of Government | Political Conditions |
|---|---|---|
| **Laos**<br>*5 million* | *Communist one-party* | *One-party state controlled by Lao People's Revolutionary Party; some elements of state control relaxed in recent years.* |
| **Malaysia**<br>*20.6 million* | *Dominant party* | *Government has "significant control" over media, uses security laws to limit freedom of expression and chill political activity; judiciary subject to government influence in sensitive cases.* |
| **Myanmar**<br>*46 million* | *Military* | *"Effectively a garrison state ruled by one of the most repressive military regimes in the world."* |
| **Papua New Guinea**<br>*4.3 million* | *Parliamentary democracy* | *Elections marred by irregularities and violence; democratic institutions tested by fiscal pressures, corruption and challenge of nation-building in diverse country.* |
| **Philippines**<br>*72 million* | *Presidential-legislative democracy* | *Free elections marred by vote-buying and fraud; official corruption rampant; populist Vice President Joseph Estrada was front-runner in presidential race [elected, May 1998]* |
| **Singapore**<br>*3 million* | *Dominant party* | *Authoritarian People's Action Party crushed opposition in January 1997 election; government chills dissent through civil defamation suits, security laws and other harassment of opponents and journalists.* |
| **Thailand**<br>*60.7 million* | *Parliamentary democracy (military-influenced)* | *New constitution adopted in September 1997 aimed at rooting out corruption and establishing greater accountability in wake of public protests over economic crisis; new prime minister in office since November heads eight-party coalition.* |
| **Vietnam**<br>*76.6 million* | *Communist one-party* | *Vietnamese Communist Party rules nation as Leninist state with "tight control of all political, economic, religious and social affairs"* |

*Source:* Freedom in the World: the Annual Survey of Political Rights and Civil Liberties, 1997-98, *Freedom House; updates from news accounts are bracketed*

is U.S. arrogance and self-righteousness," says Tommy Koh, an ambassador-at-large in Singapore's Ministry of Foreign Affairs and executive director of the Asia-Europe Foundation.

Sen acknowledges that the Asia-values debate reflects anti-Western, anti-imperialist feelings among some Asians. "There was a tendency," he says, "to reject your rule, reject your authority and reject your values, too." But he says the persistent efforts by democracy movements throughout Asia show that democracy has universal appeal.

"The fact that people continue to agitate for political rights and individual freedom indicates that people do have an intrinsic interest in freedom without regard to economic development," Sen says. "That applies as much to Asia as to anywhere else."

### *Should the United States do more to encourage democracy in Asian countries?*

When Secretary of State Madeleine K. Albright attended last year's meeting of the Association of Southeast Asian Nations (ASEAN), she urged Asian leaders to join the United States in pressuring Myanmar's military government to allow political reforms. "We must insist that we work together to promote conditions that will lead toward true democracy," Albright told the nine-nation group on July 27.

The response was polite but noncommittal. "It is for ASEAN to decide what we will do," said Malaysia's foreign minister, Abdullah Ahmad Badawi, "and we will bear in mind the views of Ms. Albright and others." [7]

The tepid reaction to the call for pressuring an evidently authoritarian regime in a relatively small country gives one measure of the difficulties the United States faces in trying to encourage democratization in Asia. The United States' professed commitment to democratic change is simply not shared by countries in the region — not by the communist regimes of China, North Korea and Vietnam; not by countries that themselves have less than completely democratic political systems; and not even by the big democracy that is the United States' major ally in the region, Japan. [8]

Meanwhile, human rights advocates and Republican lawmakers give the Clinton administration no more than middling grades for its efforts to promote democracy in the region. The administration, in the view of these critics, was slow and half-hearted in adopting economic sanc-

tions against the Myanmar regime, has given little emphasis to human rights in other countries and has simply abandoned any pretense of pressuring China to grant political and human rights to its 1.2 billion people.

"The administration's track record in Asia on human rights and democracy is very mixed," says Jendrzejczyk of Human Rights Watch. "In some ways, the administration has positioned itself to keep human rights and democracy issues very much in the background while focusing very much on economic and security concerns."

Clinton's policy of "engagement" with China has drawn criticism from human rights groups on the left and the right. "The administration hasn't made a powerful push for the rule of law in China," Graybow says. "It's possible to promote human rights and commercial interests at the same time," he says.

Elsewhere in the region, the administration manages to draw flak alternately for being too timid in pushing human rights issues or for being too assertive. Jendrzejczyk, for example, criticizes the administration's belated decision to impose economic sanctions on Myanmar. "They waited until the very last minute when pressure from Congress became almost unbearable," he says.

Some Indonesia experts, however, say Albright made a mistake by publicly calling on Suharto to step down prior to his resignation. "Indonesians are very nationalistic," Liddle says. "It's a very delicate situation."

In any event, the U.S. influence on events in Asia is easy to exaggerate. With the exception of Jendrzejczyk, most observers say the U.S. sanctions on Myanmar — which no U.S. allies have supported — are having little, if any, effect. "We either have to persuade our European allies to go along and isolate the Burmese regime," Diamond says, "or else we need to pursue other means of pressuring for change in Burma."

The United States can take some credit for helping bring democracy to Asian countries in the past. The U.S. put the Philippines on a slow path toward self-government after seizing the islands as a colony from Spain at the turn of the century. It introduced democracy into occupied Japan after World War II and pressured European powers to yield up their colonies — for example, in Indonesia.

Today, however, the impetus for democratization comes from Asian peoples themselves. "It's inaccurate to imply that we jump-started any of these transitions," Dalpino says. "The Asians jump-started them themselves, which is the way it ought to be."

### *Is Indonesia on the road to a successful transition to democracy?*

On May 23, in his first speech to Indonesians after assuming the presidency, Habibie sent ambivalent signals about his commitment to political change by promising to undertake "gradual and constitutional reforms." [9] Habibie's background was itself ambivalent. He was an engineer who had attended school and worked in Europe but also advanced politically and prospered financially under Suharto.

Since taking office, Habibie has instituted some significant changes — for example, permitting new political parties and freeing some political prisoners. But Indonesians and outside observers are divided about Habibie's commitment to thoroughgoing changes — and about his own prospects for holding on to power.

"He is now perceived as going with the reformists," Tamimi says. "He has established a style where a president is just like any other citizen."

But Muhammed Hikam, a political scientist at the Indonesian Institute of Sciences, is less impressed. "Unfortunately, Habibie can do only so much," Hikam remarked during a visit to the United States last month with other members of the International NGO [non-governmental organizations] Forum on Indonesian Development.

Hikam says Habibie and his family are still linked to the corruption and favoritism of the Suharto regime. "He is not talking about reform within himself," Hikam says, "so he's still lacking moral credibility."

U.S. experts on Indonesia have similarly mixed views about Habibie. Emmerson calls him "extremely cosmopolitan" and "able to bridge gaps." Liddle is more critical. "He is a very arrogant person," he says.

Even so, Liddle credits Habibie with a real commitment to reform. "I think he's serious," Liddle says, "because without it he simply can't govern. He has to get some kind of political legitimacy."

The prospects for change are also clouded by weaknesses within Indonesia's reform movement, which has only limited political experience and no unifying platform or individual leader. "The problem of the reform movement is basically structural," Hikam says. "It has had no real political platform that is shared by all reform groups in Indonesia, including the students."

Liddle also fears that pro-democracy sentiment might fade if the government is unable to right the economy and restore political order. "These people are not used to the typical to-and-froing of democracy," he says. "If it looks to most of the middle class that the new government is not able to control the forces erupting in society, people will turn to the military very quickly again."

Other observers fear the military may unilaterally intervene to slow or prevent political changes. "The fragmented pro-reform forces and the economic disaster will bring new temptation for the military to step in," says Goenawan Mohamad, an editor of the pro-democracy newspaper *Tempo*.

For his part, though, Tamimi believes both the government and pro-democracy groups are on a path toward reform. "People and the government are starting to talk with each other," he says. "That didn't happen for 40 years."

As for Habibie, the economy may hold the key to his political fortunes. "The economy is bad and unlikely to get better," Emmerson says. "Whoever is president is likely to suffer, and that is going to hurt Habibie."

On the other hand, Tamimi says, "If Habibie's successful in making democracy a reality, and if he's successful in establishing the economic situation, people will follow him."

Despite the problems and uncertainties, observers and advocates in Indonesia and the United States voice a measure of cautious optimism about the prospects for democracy there.

"Now people are starting to make a program, to talk with each other," Tamimi says. "It will take time, but I think we are on the right track."

"There's a golden moment of opportunity here," Liddle says. "Indonesia could create a democracy here if it just seizes the moment." ■

# BACKGROUND

## East Meets West

Asians had relatively little experience with democracy before the arrival of European explorers, traders and colonizers in the 15th century. Asian societies — from sophisticated China and Japan to the less developed kingdoms and sultanates of the Indian subcontinent, the Malay Peninsula and the East Indies — were mostly hierarchically organized and governed. Asia has been late to develop the kind of representative assemblies, popular elections and written constitutions that comprise what is sometimes called "Western-style" democracy.

Hierarchical tendencies were reinforced by the region's dominant religions: Buddhism and Hinduism, both of which predated Christianity, and Islam, which spread through much of Asia beginning in the seventh century. Some scholars find democratic strains in Buddhism and Hinduism by focusing on the rulers' obligation in both religions to govern wisely and with the consent of his subjects. But historically, both Buddhism and Hinduism have been associated with elitist, authoritarian ruling systems. Similarly, Confucianism, the Chinese school of political thought that dates from the sixth century before Christ, contains some germs of democratic theory — for example, the right of the people to depose an unjust ruler. In practice, however, it, too, came to be associated with authoritarian rulers. [10]

The European powers also did little to prepare their Asian colonies for self-government until the very end of the colonial period. Spanish and Portuguese sailors were the first Europeans to explore the region, followed by Dutch traders in the 17th century, the British in the 18th and the French in the 19th. Developing trade was the first and most important objective; ruling colonies was an afterthought and nation-building did not make the agenda until the 20th century, if then. [11]

Of the major European colonies, only India had begun to take shape as a nation by 1900. France ruled what is now Vietnam as two disconnected colonies: Tonkin in the north, Cochin-China in the south. Britain had "organized" the Malay Peninsula into federated states, unfederated states and the "Straits Settlements." The Dutch East Indies was a geographic location, not a political entity. The 20th century saw some moves toward education and self-government in Asia — so-called enlightened policies — but they were typically limited. In Indonesia, for example, only 230 native-born Indonesians had college educations in 1942. [12]

Asia's largest countries that escaped colonization — China and Japan — did make some early moves toward democracy. In 1890 Japan adopted a constitution modeled on the Prussian charter, with a bicameral Diet including an elected lower house and a Cabinet of advisers to make decisions to be issued in the emperor's name. Competitive political parties developed by the 1920s, and the prime minister and Cabinet became responsible to the Diet. But in the 1930s the military took power, repressed democratic processes and led the nation into war first in China and then throughout East Asia.

In China, Western-trained Sun Yat-sen led a revolutionary movement that sought to unify China under a federal republic. But democratic impulses proved weaker than warlordism and communism. The Nationalist Party — the Kuomintang or KMT — emerged as the leading power in the elections of 1912 but came to be dominated by local warlords more interested in protecting their power bases than in establishing democracy. The Chinese Communist Party split from the KMT in the 1920s, joined in unsteady alliance during the war with Japan but then gained power after a four-year civil war following the Japanese surrender in 1945.

It was the Japanese who ousted the European powers from most of their Asian colonies, embarrassing the white rulers with their easy conquests of the East Indies, Indochina and the British-ruled territories, including the supposedly impregnable Fortress Singapore. The Japanese occupiers encouraged anti-imperialist and pan-Asian sentiment even while subjugating the native peoples. At war's end, the colonial rulers expected to return. As author John Keay writes, however, the colonies were "reoccupied" but "never retaken." [13]

## Paths of Independence

Nationalist movements gained strength in Asia before and during World War II and immediately challenged the European powers' attempt to return after the war's end. Over the next two decades, the British, Dutch and French were ousted and independence was won in India (1947), Burma (1948), Vietnam (1954) and Malaya (1957, renamed Malaysia in 1963). Meanwhile, the United States had imposed a U.S.-style constitution on the defeated Japanese. Democratic government took hold in Japan, but elsewhere across Asia ethnic, religious, economic and ideological divisions stunted the growth of democracy and helped bring authoritarian regimes to power. [14]

India's democratic movement began with the formation of the National Congress Party in 1875, which first advocated self-government, then independence from Britain. The movement came to be led by Mohandas Karamchand Gandhi, an Indian lawyer whose masterful political organizing and strategy of civil disobedience forced Great Britain to cede independence after the end of World War II. The movement toward independence, however, unleashed violence between the majority Hindus and minority Muslims, resulting in partition and the establishment of Pakistan as a Muslim homeland. Burma, ruled by Britain as part of India, had been moving toward separation before the war and gained its own independence in 1948.

In Indonesia, a nationalist movement also had been forming under Sukarno, who founded the Indonesian National Party (PNI). He encouraged strikes and non-cooperation with Dutch authorities and was imprisoned or exiled for most of the 1930s. During the war, he collaborated with the Japanese while other nationalists opposed the occupiers. As the war was ending, Sukarno and his colleagues declared Indonesia's independence. [15]

During four years of fighting and diplomatic maneuvering, the Dutch sought to preserve their rule by decentralizing power through a federal structure. The nationalists rejected the idea and fought a guerrilla war that, combined with diplomatic pressure from the United States and the United Nations, forced the Dutch to yield. Queen Juliana gave her formal assent to independence in December 1949. The new constitution called for a parliamentary democracy, with the first post-independence national elections to be held in 1955. In defiance of nationalist sentiments, the Dutch remained on the eastern half of New Guinea while Portugal still ruled the eastern half of the smaller island of Timor.

In Indochina, the nationalist movement was led by Ho Chi Minh, who (under the name Nguyen Ai Quoc) had pre-

# Chronology

## Before 1945

***Asia has limited experience with democratic forms before colonialism; European powers do little to prepare their colonies for self-government.***

**1890**
Japan establishes democratic constitution, the first in Asia.

**1935**
Britain provides limited self-government for India, but move does not satisfy independence movement.

## 1945-1965

***Era of European colonialism ends; most of the newly independent nations adopt some form of parliamentary democracy, but many come to be dominated by one party or yield to military rule.***

**1947**
Japan adopts U.S.-style constitution, providing for parliamentary democracy under constitutional monarch; India gains independence from Britain; Pakistan is established as Muslim homeland.

**1949**
Indonesia gains independence from the Netherlands; Communists come to power in China.

**1954**
France is ousted from Indo-China; Vietnam is partitioned between communist and pro-West governments.

**1963**
Malaysian Federation is established as independent nation, ending British colonial era in Southeast Asia; Singapore is ousted from federation two years later.

## 1965-1989

***U.S. fights protracted war in Vietnam but fails to prevent communist victory; Cold War politics shapes U.S. ties with authoritarian regime.***

**1965**
Sukarno is ousted in Indonesia; Suharto comes to power.

**1979**
U.S. recognizes People's Republic of China, downgrades relations with Taiwan.

**1986**
Philippines President Ferdinand E. Marcos ousted, succeeded by human rights activist Corazon Aquino.

**1989**
Chinese military suppresses pro-democracy rally at Tiananmen Square, killing hundreds.

## 1990s

***With end of Cold War, democratization gains prominence in U.S. diplomatic agenda; democracy activists step up efforts in Asia, with uneven results.***

**1990**
Burmese military government nullifies election won by National League for Democracy.

**1991**
Burmese pro-democracy leader Aung San Suu Kyi awarded Nobel Peace Prize; military coup in Thailand; king forces coup leader to resign in 1992, paving way for return of democracy.

**1993**
Cambodia holds first election under 1991 Paris peace agreement, resulting in coalition government; Japan's Liberal Democratic Party yields power after losing parliamentary election.

**1995**
U.S. and Vietnam re-establish diplomatic relations; Malaysia's ruling coalition wins electoral landslide, with opposition party reduced to nine seats in parliament.

**1996**
Congress Party defeated at polls in India, but Hindu nationalist party falls short of majority; Taiwan holds first popular election for president; Bishop Carlos Belo and Jose Ramos-Horta, activists for East Timorese self-determination, are awarded Nobel Peace Prize.

**1997**
Singaporean opposition parties reduced to two seats after parliamentary elections; Hong Kong reverts to China; opposition leader Kim Dae Jung elected president of South Korea.

**1998**
Hindu nationalist party again leads coalition government, but wins only one-fourth of seats in Indian parliament; Suharto is ousted in Indonesia; his successor as president, B.J. Habibie, promises reforms, elections in 1999; President Clinton visits China; Cambodian elections, scheduled for July 26, are widely criticized as weighted in government's favor.

## Indonesia's Year of Living Turbulently

**May 1997** Ruling Golkar party wins sixth consecutive victory in parliamentary elections on May 29; more than 200 people die in riots before balloting.

**July 1997** Rupiah closes down 5 percent on July 21 (about 2,500 to the dollar) in the wake of the July 2 devaluation of the Thai bhat.

**October 1997** International Monetary Fund (IMF) announces three-year, $33 billion loan package to stabilize Indonesia's economy; accord follows President Suharto's agreement to institute reforms in banking and elsewhere.

**Suharto**

**January 1998** Rupiah plunges to more than 9,000 to the dollar, prompting panic-buying for food and staples; Suharto, in new accord with IMF, promises Jan. 15 to end system of patronage favoring his children and friends.

**March 1998** IMF delays first $3 billion installment of aid package on March 6 as Suharto balks at reforms; Suharto re-elected president March 11 by People's Consultative Assembly; after swearing-in, as many as 10,000 students protest at Gadjah Mada University in Yogyakarta, burning an effigy of the president.

**May 1-10, 1998** Suharto is quoted May 1 as ruling out reform before end of five-year term in 2003; student protests held throughout Indonesia next day; rioting follows on May 5 as fuel and energy prices rise after government cuts subsidies.

**May 11-20, 1998** Six students killed May 12 after police open fire on protesters at Jakarta's Trisakti University; 500 people die in rioting over next three days concentrated in Jakarta's wealthy ethnic Chinese neighborhoods; Suharto, after returning from Egypt May 15, announces May 19 he will hold new elections and not run for president again; behind the scenes, military chief Gen. Wiranto pressures Suharto to step down immediately.

**May 21-31, 1998** Suharto announces immediate resignation May 21; Vice President B.J. Habibie is sworn in as successor; Gen. Wiranto removes Suharto's son-in-law from military command May 22; Habibie drops key Suharto associates in new cabinet named May 23 and promises "gradual and constitutional reforms," but says on May 25 that elections may not be held before mid-1999.

**Habibie**

**June 1998** IMF commits additional $4-$6 billion to aid package June 24; Habibie announces five-year action plan on human rights on June 25; the next day he proposes to release East Timorese rebel leader Jose Xanana Gusmao in exchange for recognition of Indonesian sovereignty; Gusmao says no deal.

**July 1998** National Golkar party conference July 9-11 elects Habibie-backed candidate Akbar Tanjung as party leader in secret ballot; rupiah drops to more than 14,000 to the dollar.

sided over the founding meeting of the Vietnamese Communist Party in Hong Kong in 1930. The French responded to a campaign of hunger marches and commandeering of local estates with an air and ground offensive; many party activists were arrested, and Ho himself was later held by British authorities in Hong Kong. He was reported to have died in detention, but in fact escaped, eventually to Moscow, and returned to lead the nationalist movement during World War II. The French, like the Dutch, had expected to resume their colonial rule, but — despite fitful U.S. support — left Indochina after the 1954 defeat at Dien Bien Phu. Two decades later, Vietnam was unified under communist rule after the U.S. failed in its efforts to preserve a pro-American regime in the south.

The nationalist movement was weaker in what became Malaysia, in part because of the mix of native Malays and ethnic Chinese Malayans. Britain also proved more adroit in countering a communist-dominated insurgency with a mixture of military and political responses. With the insurgency deemed defeated, Britain granted independence to Malaya in 1957 while continuing to hold Singapore and its possessions on the island of Borneo: the sultanates of Sabah and Sarawak. Singapore, with its majority-Chinese population, was added to what became the Malaysian Federation in 1963 — balanced by the addition of the predominantly Malay populations of Sabah and Sarawak. But the Malay-dominated government ousted Singapore two years later out of concern that its Chinese population would threaten the ethnic Malays' political control.

## Asian-Style 'Democracy'

Democratic forms, including regular elections and representative assemblies, took hold in most of the non-communist Asian countries after the colonial period ended. But from India to Japan and in most of the smaller countries in between, the political systems were dominated by single parties. Political rights were generally protected in some of the countries, including India and Japan, but less so in many others, including Indonesia, Malaysia, Singapore, South Korea and Taiwan.

Indonesia, according to Huntington, was the most authoritarian of these supposedly democratic countries. [16] The only free election in the nation's history, in 1955, gave four parties roughly comparable power in the parliament: Nationalists, Communists and two Muslim parties. Four years later, Sukarno, who served in the largely ceremonial role of president, joined in a coup with the military, which also chafed under the political fragmentation and its own limited role. The coup returned Indonesia to the strong presidential system of the short-lived 1945 constitution. "Guided democracy," Sukarno called his new system. "Far more guided than democratic," Emmerson says.

Sukarno, according to Liddle, sought to reduce his dependence on the military by aligning himself domestically with the communists as he also took on a leading role internationally as spokesman for the non-aligned nations. Communist-instigated unrest climaxed in the assassination of six Indonesian generals in 1965, most likely by leftist officers. The coup enabled Maj. Gen. Suharto to assume control of the military and lead a crackdown on the communists, depicted later by the film "The Year of Living Dangerously."

Suharto began his 32-year rule by restating the five principles that Sukarno had proclaimed in 1945 — monotheism, humanitarianism, unity, democracy and justice. He also eventually reduced the number of recognized parties to just three: the governing Golkar party and two opposition parties. Suharto was assured of re-election by the People's Consultative Assembly, since he effectively controlled 500 of its 1,000 seats. And the army buttressed Suharto's power by suppressing any signs of political opposition.

Elsewhere in East and Southeast Asia, one-party rule proved almost as durable despite somewhat greater political freedom. In Malaysia, the ruling National Front has dominated every election since 1971. In Singapore, Lee's People's Action Party has held even greater sway.

Meanwhile, South Korea and Taiwan also were effectively ruled by single parties, thanks in part to periods of martial law justified by the threats posed by their communist neighbors, North Korea and mainland China. In Thailand, a period of relative democracy in the 1970s produced a degree of political disorder that a military-dominated government sought to control in the 1980s with authoritarian measures. In neighboring Burma, on the other hand, the military strongman Gen. Ne Win crafted a new constitution in 1974 that made his Burma Socialist Program Party the only recognized party.

Of the former European colonies, India was the most auspicious in its early years of democracy. Its first prime minister, Jawaharlal Nehru, an ally of Gandhi's in the independence struggle, also proved skillful in the practical politics of democracy. But his daughter, Indira Gandhi, who succeeded to the post in 1966, stirred harsh criticism when she assumed virtually dictatorial powers from 1975 to 1977 and was widely blamed for politicizing the judiciary and civil service and permitting corruption to flourish at the local level. Her son, Rajiv, showed even less political talent in his years as prime minister after his mother's assassination in 1984. Throughout, however, India continued to hold regular national elections, and the Congress Party peacefully yielded power when it failed to maintain its majority position in 1977 and 1989.

## 'People's Power'?

Over time, Asia's authoritarian and semiauthoritarian governments bred domestic pro-democracy and human rights movements. In some countries they gained sufficient strength to challenge the regimes at the polls; elsewhere, they had to focus on mass protests, court challenges and pleas for international support. Meanwhile, the collapse of the Soviet Union and the end of the Cold War freed both the United States government and conservative U.S.-based groups to give greater emphasis to human rights and democracy as a diplomatic and political goal abroad.

The first demonstration of the potential impact of these Asian pro-democracy movements came in the Philippines, where longtime President Ferdinand E. Marcos was forced from office in 1986. Marcos, elected in 1965, imposed martial law in 1971 and ruled with an iron hand for the next 15 years. The assassination of opposition leader Benigno Aquino in 1982 helped galvanize the "People's Power Movement," which rallied behind his widow, Corazon. By 1985, when Marcos had all but lost his grip on power, President Ronald Reagan passed the word that there would be no U.S. intervention for its longtime ally. Marcos went into exile in Hawaii, and Corazon Aquino was installed as president and later elected in her own right. [17]

Events in the Philippines may have inspired challenges to the military regime in Burma, too, but the effort backfired. The military in 1988 installed a new ruling body, the State Law and Order Restoration Council, which proceeded simultaneously to suppress popular dissent and set elections for 1990. When the opposition National League for Democracy emerged as the winner — despite the house arrest of its leader, Nobel Peace Prize-winner Aung San Suu Kyi — the government ignored the results. [18]

Other military-dominated regimes

# Indonesia's Troubled Rule Over East Timor

Indonesia invaded and then annexed East Timor 22 years ago to eliminate a potential threat to its stability. Instead, Indonesia's often violent rule over the tiny former Portuguese colony fueled an independence movement and eventually became a major diplomatic embarrassment for President Suharto.

Now, with Suharto's resignation, some observers see the possibility of resolving the issue. "The political transition in Indonesia has opened up the political middle ground," says Donald Emmerson, a political scientist at the University of Wisconsin in Madison.

Indonesia's new president, B. J. Habibie, is willing to discuss some measure of autonomy for East Timor, whose 600,000 residents occupy the eastern half of an island about the size of Maryland.

East Timorese independence advocate Jose Ramos-Horta, who shared the 1996 Nobel Peace Prize, has suggested that a referendum on East Timor's status could be held not immediately — as the movement has demanded — but five years from now.

Emmerson, a longtime student of Indonesian politics, thinks that a delayed vote offers something to both sides in the dispute. "The independence movement is realizing that it makes no sense politically to insist on a referendum tomorrow," he says. As for the Indonesian government, he continues, "the longer the time before the referendum, the more time Indonesia has to build a sense among the East Timorese that they belong in Indonesia."

The current-day dispute is a legacy of arbitrary boundaries drawn by European colonial powers centuries ago.[1] Portugal and the Dutch East India Trading Company established trading posts on opposite ends of the island, which lies near the coast of Australia at the southern end of the major chain of Indonesian islands.

The Indonesian national revolution after World War II brought the Dutch-ruled western half of the island into the new nation, but Portugal retained control of its colony — which, unlike Muslim-dominated Indonesia, was predominantly Roman Catholic. Portugal began to decolonize only decades later, in the 1970s, when a long-ruling dictatorship fell to a socialist-led opposition.

By then, the East Timorese people were themselves divided between three forces: an avowedly leftist independence movement, Fretilin (the Revolutionary Front for Independence of East Timor); the more elitist Timorese Democratic Union (UDT), which favored gradual independence and some continuing ties to Portugal; and a group favoring incorporation within Indonesia: the Timorese Popular Democratic Association, known by the acronym Apodeti.

Fretilin, with the largest amount of support, stirred fears in Jakarta and in Washington of a communist stronghold in the Indonesian archipelago. When a civil war broke out in August 1975, Portugal sided with Fretilin, Indonesia with Apodeti. On Dec. 7, Indonesia invaded East Timor. Historian M.C. Ricklefs says the invasion — supported by the U.S. — may have resulted in as many as 60,000 civilian casualties.

Indonesia formally annexed East Timor in July 1976, as Fretilin retreated to the hills. William Liddle, a political scientist at Ohio State University who visited East Timor in January, says the Suharto government brought "a lot of material progress" to the island — roads, schools, health centers and so forth. But the military presence remained — and continued to exact a heavy toll in deaths and injuries. "There was an awful lot of random, wanton killing," Liddle says.

In the worst such incident, Indonesian troops killed up to 200 East Timorese at the funeral of a separatist sympathizer in 1991. Subsequently, Fretilin rebel leader Xanana Gusmao was sentenced to 20 years in prison.

Awarding the Nobel Peace Prize to Ramos-Horta and Bishop Carlos Belo in 1996 helped gain international support for East Timor. U.S. policy, however, continued to recognize East Timor as part of Indonesia.

Liddle thinks Habibie's offer to talk about autonomy may only embolden the independence movement. Emmerson, however, thinks the East Timorese may be cautioned by the current economic crisis in Indonesia and the region.

The political calculations in Jakarta are also multisided. Resolving the issue may appeal to Habibie, Emmerson says, but he also has bigger political problems.

Catharin E. Dalpino, former deputy assistant secretary of State for human rights, notes that any change in East Timor could encourage anti-Jakarta sentiment in other areas, notably Irian Jaya. Indonesia incorporated Irian Jaya, which occupies the western half of the former New Guinea, in 1969 after administering the former Dutch colony for the United Nations for seven years.

For now, Dalpino thinks Habibie's willingness will encourage more pro-independence demonstrations on East Timor. "It will kick up more dust," she says. But, she adds, "there's probably more hope for a mid-term to long-term solution."

[1] For background, see M.C. Ricklefs, *A History of Modern Indonesia since c. 1300* (2d ed., 1993); *The Washington Post*, July 10, 1998, p. A27.

in East Asia, however, did yield to domestic pressure or outside events during the 1980s and '90s.

In South Korea, the government, on the eve of hosting the Olympic Games, agreed to a new constitution and popular elections in 1988; the balloting left the governing Democratic Justice Party in shaky control and boosted the opposition Party for Peace and Democracy. Today, the longtime opposition leader Kim Dae Jung — imprisoned or exiled for years by the military government — serves as the country's president after a narrow election victory in December.

Taiwan began a decade-long path toward democracy in 1986 when its president, Chiang Ching-kuo decided to lift martial law, ease press censorship and permit political parties. After his death in 1988, constitutional reforms were carried forward by his successor, Lee Teng-hui, who went on to win Taiwan's first popular election for president in 1996.

In Thailand, the military upset a fragile balance between democracy and authoritarianism by seizing power from the elected government in 1991. After parties aligned with the military won a narrow victory in elections in March 1992, the leader of the coup, Gen. Suchinda Kraprayoon, tried to put the prime minister's post under military control. Public protests followed, and eventually King Bhumibol Adulyadej forced Suchinda's resignation and a new beginning of democratization.

## Suharto's Final Days

There were few signs of democratization in Indonesia, however, as late as last year. Suharto's hold on power appeared secure, thanks to a rigged electoral system, the military's support and impressive economic growth. Leading up to the May 1997 parliamentary election, Suharto had engineered the ouster of the head of the Indonesian Democratic Party (PDI) and banned any discussion of a possible alliance with the other recognized party, the Muslim United Development Party. The result: The governing Golkar political bloc secured its largest majority ever — about 73 percent of the vote. [19]

When the rupiah fell last July, however, Asia's economic crisis caught up with Indonesia — and Suharto. The IMF eventually pledged up to $43 billion in bailout aid but insisted on stringent fiscal conditions that included eliminating subsidies on critical consumer goods. When the rupiah fell further in January, Indonesians took to the streets to protest rising prices; by spring, pro-democracy students were calling for Suharto's ouster.

Suharto might have survived, nonetheless, but for the deaths of six students at Jakarta's Trisakti University on May 12. The shootings fueled more unrest and destroyed any remnant of Suharto's credibility with key military and political leaders. Publicly, armed forces chief Gen. Wiranto criticized the calls for Suharto's resignation, but privately he was scripting his removal. Suharto on May 19 promised to hold new elections and step down at some unspecified future date. But two days later, deserted by the military and by his Cabinet, Suharto announced his resignation on television "as of the reading of this statement." He named Habibie as his successor. [20] ■

# CURRENT SITUATION

## Building Democracy

Four days after taking office, Habibie announced a "national action plan" on human rights. The plan called for the government to ratify international human rights accords, publicize human rights policies and give "top priority" to implementing human rights provisions.

The initiative was "very big news" to journalist Tamimi, who attended the session. "I'm satisfied because he has signed all these international agreements on human rights," Tamimi says. "So now Indonesia has joined the rest of the world."

But in the two months since Habibie's accession, both the government and its opponents have found that the path to political change is treacherous.

Habibie has drawn criticism both within and without Indonesia for the new election schedule. "The longer you have Habibie in power without democracy, the Indonesian crisis will be worse and worse," says political scientist Hikam.

"International confidence will be increased by holding an election for the Indonesian people to choose both a president and a representative assembly — and much sooner than the schedule" outlined by Habibie, says Human Rights Watch's Jendrzejczyk.

For its part, the reform movement appears unprepared to offer the country a unified platform or a strong alternative to Habibie. "It's been 40 days now, and we still don't know what to do with this," Mas'oed, the Gadjah Mada lecturer and activist, remarked recently.

Habibie scored a significant political victory earlier this month with the election of his executive secretary, Akbar Tanjung, to head the ruling Golkar party. Akbar was elected by secret ballot, 17-10, at the end of the party's special three-day conference July 9-11 in Jakarta; he defeated a Suharto-backed candidate, Edy Sudrajat, a former armed services chief. After winning, Akbar told reporters he would reform Golkar and "rid it of nepotism, corruption, and collusion." [21]

Tamimi says the party gathering was a "big victory for democracy" because of the first-ever direct election of the chairman. He also believes that Akbar himself rather than Habibie may prove to be the long-run winner from the meeting. "It pushes him toward being a prominent political figure," Tamimi says. "If Indonesia is becoming a real democracy, he will be in the best position to put himself forward as a candidate for president."

Habibie continues to gain generally positive reviews from Indonesian and U.S. observers. "Habibie has without a doubt surprised his critics," Emmerson said after the Golkar meeting. Tamimi, however, is more cautious about Akbar. "He was a part of the Suharto system," Tamimi says. Asked if he doubts Akbar's commitment to reform, Tamimi pauses before answering: "We should give him the benefit of the doubt."

Among the government's opponents, the prevailing picture is disarray. More than 30 political parties had registered as of mid-July, stirring fears of electoral fragmentation. Tamimi, however, expects the opponents to sort themselves out by next year's elections. He sees five major opposition parties: two predominantly Muslim parties, one modernist, the other traditional; a nationalist party; a party for Christians and other religious minorities; and a social democratic party. None of the parties is likely to win a majority, Tamimi says, and the opponents could gain enough strength to put together a coalition to deny Golkar a role in a new government.

Meanwhile, the economy remains the dominant issue for Habibie. In his speech to Golkar, Habibie conceded that the government's economic reforms had yet to yield "concrete results." [22] But even after acknowledging the country's lackluster financial markets and other problems, Habibie was optimistic. "In reality, the country has huge natural resources, manpower, experience, institutions and strong determination to come out of the crisis," he said.

## Democracy in India

Fifty years after India became the world's most populous democracy, President K.R. Narayanan called the anniversary "a golden moment in the history of India and the world." But Narayanan also acknowledged that democracy's record in India has been mixed. [23]

"I am painfully aware of the deterioration that has taken place in our country ... in recent times," Narayanan said on Aug. 15, 1997. He pointed to the ill treatment of women and low-caste Indians; the lack of adequate education, health care and clean water; and the "criminalization of politics."

Throughout India, the anniversary turned into "a very somber celebration," recalls Sumit Ganguly, an Indian political scientist at Hunter College of the City University of New York. "People focused more on India's shortcomings. There was a great deal of soul-searching."

Political events have also raised concerns about India's democracy outside the country. The rise of Hindu nationalism as a political force has rekindled worries about the sectarian divisions in Indian society. The Hindu nationalist Bharatiya Janata Party (BJP) emerged as the leading vote-getter in parliamentary elections in 1996 and early this year but fell short of a majority. Today, the BJP's leader, Atal Behavi Vajpayee, leads a shaky coalition government. Some observers fear that the government decided to test nuclear weapons in May in part to strengthen its domestic political support.

Ganguly acknowledges concerns about the commitment to democracy among some BJP members. "There are some people who have some fascist orientation, and I don't use that term loosely," he says. But he also says that "countervailing forces" limit the influence of the party's more extreme elements. Freedom House's Graybow agrees. "Hopefully, [the party] will be moderated by having to form a coalition with others," he says.

India's commitment to democracy has also been tested by the secessionist movement in predominantly Muslim Kashmir. Ganguly, author of a new book on the problem, says the Indian government has practiced "calibrated but ruthless" repression against the insurgents; the U.S. State Department similarly cites what it calls "serious human rights abuses" by government forces in Kashmir and neighboring Jammu. [24]

Despite those shortcomings, Sunil Khilnani, an Indian who teaches politics at Birkbeck College, University of London, says democracy has taken root in the Indian consciousness. "As an idea, it's been an enormous success," says Khilnani, author of a new book assessing Indian democracy. "There's no one in India today who questions democratic politics, whether they're on the right or left, rich or poor. There's a general feeling that democracy is the only way for India." [25]

## Conflicted Democracies

India's neighbors, however, have had less success with democracy. Pakistan has had military rule for more than half its half-century of independence. [26] Democracy was restored in 1988, but the military still wields great influence. In addition, Islamic fundamentalists pressure the government on religious issues, ethnic and regional divisions run deep and political and economic corruption persist. The country's president resigned in December after complaining that Prime Minister Nawaz Sharif had politicized the judiciary while defending himself against corruption charges.

Bangladesh, the former East Pakistan, also has had frequent periods of military rule since independence in 1971. But Graybow lists Bangladesh among emerging democracies in the 1990s, and the State Department credits the country with a relatively free multiparty system.

Sri Lanka, on the other hand, had a strong tradition of democratic prac-

# At Issue:

## *Has the Clinton administration done a good job of promoting democracy in Asia?*

**Catharin E. Dalpino**
***Guest Scholar, The Brookings Institution, former deputy assistant secretary of State for human rights***

***WRITTEN FOR THE CQ RESEARCHER, JULY 21, 1998.***

yes

Crafting effective U.S. strategies to promote democracy in Asia is difficult in today's policy environment. The lingering sense of triumph over the collapse of Soviet communism has encouraged a Eurocentric approach to political change and an exaggerated estimate of the power of external actors, even superpowers, to direct democratic transitions. Moreover, some politicians and the press recall only the moments of dramatic resolution — the fall of the Berlin Wall — and therefore view democratization as a sprint. In reality, it is a marathon.

The strength of the Clinton administration's approach to Asia is its willingness to play a strong supporting role in helping Asians find their own democratic solutions to political problems, despite domestic pressure at times for more dirigiste or high-decibel policies.

U.S. assistance programs in the Philippines to decentralize power and strengthen civil society have helped that country stay the democratic course. In Mongolia, democracy-assistance programs paid off in 1996 when parliamentary elections turned the communists out of power. Equally important, the defeated party took its place on the back bench without protest.

Clinton administration support to Indonesia's struggling non-governmental sector and to the National Human Rights Commission has helped to build the foundation for a democratic transition with Suharto's departure.

The administration's response to democratic backsliding in Cambodia last July was firm, but appropriately nuanced. Support was increased to Cambodian human rights organizations while aid to the government itself was suspended. U.S. pressure has kept the Cambodian seat vacant at the United Nations, pending a democratic resolution to the conflict. With U.S. urging, the Association of Southeast Asian Nations (ASEAN) pressed Hun Sen to agree to elections.

The success of the most important Clinton administration policy in Asia — to promote political liberalization in the Leninist states — can't be measured for years. Requests in the fiscal year 1999 budget, for programs such as the president's Rule of Law Initiative for China, are realistic first steps that will help to change the relationship between state and society in these countries. Paradoxically, our ability to encourage eventual democratization in China and its Leninist neighbors will depend upon our willingness to leave Cold War models and methods behind.

**Mike Jendrzejczyk**
***Washington Director, Human Rights Watch, Asia Division***

***WRITTEN FOR THE CQ RESEARCHER, JULY 21, 1998***

no

The Clinton administration has tried to balance competing agendas in Asia, generally placing the highest priority on economic and security interests rather than on human rights and democratization. The results are decidedly mixed.

While enthusiastically promoting an agenda of free trade and open markets, the administration has been slow to see the linkage between the meltdown of Asian economies and growing aspirations in many countries for more open, accountable governance, the rule of law and an end to corruption. And in countries like China and Vietnam, it has been willing to abandon potentially effective policies and sources of leverage, relying instead on the market to eventually produce political change.

Indonesians trying to jettison repressive institutions and a political culture created over more than 30 years are now eager for change. They are clearly looking for U.S. support that goes beyond aid to non-governmental organizations or humanitarian assistance, as vital as that may be. They want U.S. support for a speedier transition and creative help in solving longstanding human rights problems such as East Timor.

Citizens of Burma and Cambodia, struggling under military rule or trying to restore democracy, believe that by withholding legitimacy — and funding by international financial institutions — the U.S. can create the political space they urgently need. They've already waited years to peacefully exercise their basic rights and feel they can ill afford to wait much longer.

Next week's meeting of the Association for Southeast Asian Nations (ASEAN) in Manila will provide an interesting window on the shifts under way in the region. Thailand and the Philippines have publicly called for the abandonment of "constructive engagement" (i.e. not interfering in the internal affairs of other nations) as an outmoded approach. They propose instead a policy of "flexible engagement" in order to deal with destabilizing problems, including the lack of progress in democratization.

In this rapidly evolving environment, the United States should not place its major emphasis on long-term rule-of-law programs alone, or on the instincts of "visionary" leaders such as Jiang Zemin, as Clinton called the Chinese president. And while being careful not to impose "American values" or solutions, the Clinton administration should clearly articulate more effective bilateral and multilateral policies that can aid Asia's crucial transitions.

# Putting Myanmar on the Political Map

When U Zarni came to the United States 10 years ago, he expected to get a degree in education and return to his native Burma. But today he leads a coalition of other Burmese expatriates working within the United States for economic sanctions against his country. Their goal is to pressure the military government to permit the restoration of democracy.

"We put Burma on the map of international politics," Zarni says of the Free Burma Coalition, which he founded in 1995. "We as a grass-roots campaign brought Burma to American and international households."

The effect of the coalition's work, however, is sharply disputed. In 1997, Congress passed and President Clinton signed into law an economic-sanctions bill prohibiting U.S. companies from making new investments in Myanmar, as the military government renamed the country. Zarni says one state — Massachusetts — and 20 municipalities have passed broader sanctions measures that cut off trade with any companies operating in Myanmar. [1]

Zarni and other human rights advocates believe the sanctions are having an effect. "The junta itself admitted that they are reeling from the effects of American sanctions," says Zarni, now a graduate student at the University of Wisconsin in Madison.

As evidence, Zarni cites recent comments by a member of the ruling council, Brig. Gen. D.O. Abel, to *Leaders* magazine, an international business-oriented publication. Abel said that American companies are "holding off" investing in Myanmar because of the sanctions and that the sanctions are having an effect on other multinational companies. "Any Japanese companies that are operating here in Myanmar cannot operate in the state of Massachusetts," Abel said. "They and other multinational companies don't want to invest here because they are afraid of retaliation from the United States."

Zarni says the sanctions have led some 25 multinational companies — including Pepsico, Texaco, Heineken, Levi Strauss, Liz Claiborne and Eddie Bauer — to pull out of Myanmar. Two big U.S.-based oil companies — Arco and Unocal — are still there, however. Unocal is joint-venturing with a French and a Thai company on a $1.2 billion gas pipeline.

Policy-makers and foreign policy experts generally dismiss the effects of the sanctions as minimal. "We don't have sufficient leverage on Myanmar to force change from the outside," says Catharin E. Dalpino, a guest scholar at the Brookings Institution and former deputy assistant secretary of State for human rights in the Clinton administration. "And we haven't been able to get our allies, both Asian and European, to join with us."

Clearly, though, Zarni's group has raised awareness of Myanmar's military government inside the United States. The coalition operates an Internet site (www.freeburma.org) with up-to-date news and pro-democracy information. The coalition also used its boycott of Pepsi Cola to good effect. "Third-graders were boycotting Pepsi because their teachers were teaching them about human rights," Zarni says. [2]

Some other Asian expatriate groups also have lobbied within the United States to try to influence U.S. policy toward their native countries — most notably Chinese groups, such as the Independent Federation of Chinese Students and Scholars. The Washington-based group has helped organize protests in the United States against the Chinese government.

Generally, though, the groups' impact on policy appears to be relatively minimal. Until recently, at least, Asian-Americans have tended to shy away from domestic U.S. politics, and their numbers have been too small to have much influence except in a few areas. The influence of expatriate groups is inherently limited by their divided attention between the United States and their home country. An earlier Burmese group, for example, the Committee for Restoration of Democracy in Burma, is less visible in the United States because it concentrates on helping students and others inside Burma. And, as U.S. policy toward China illustrates, partisan politics and broad economic interests usually carry more weight in government decision-making than pro-democracy lobbying from ethnic or expatriate groups.

Zarni cut off ties with his family still in Myanmar — parents and seven siblings — to protect them from repercussions from his work in the United States. He has been granted political asylum in the United States, but he still hopes to return. "When the country is free," he says, "I intend to go back."

---

[1] For background, see *The Christian Science Monitor*, Jan. 29, 1998, p. 6.

[2] For further background, see *The New York Times*, April 8, 1997, p. A18, and *The Chronicle of Higher Education*, Feb. 14, 1997, p. A43.

tice predating its independence from Britain in 1948 that has been tarnished by protracted ethnic violence between the Sinhalese majority, mostly Hindu, and the predominantly Buddhist Tamil minority. The government's refusal to grant Tamil demands for more autonomy sparked a civil war that has raged since 1983. A measure of political order returned in the 1990s, but the government has yet to craft a political settlement acceptable to the separatist Tamils.

Meanwhile, Japan — arguably the region's most successful democracy — is in turmoil. "The Japanese political leadership is floundering," says Ellis Krauss, an expert on Japan at the University of California-San Diego. The Liberal Democratic Party (LDP) fell from power in 1993, regained control of the government in 1996, but — in the midst of an economic recession — suffered a stinging rejection at the polls in elections earlier this month. Prime Minister Ryutaro Hashimoto immediately resigned.

Even before Japan's economic problems surfaced, however, the government gave the United States only scant encouragement in efforts to promote democracy in Asia. "Japanese foreign policy is far more pragmatic" than U.S. policy, Krauss says. "It tends to be based on a more narrowly defined self-interest." ■

# OUTLOOK

## Change and Resistance

When he ended his nine-day trip to China earlier this month, President Clinton emphatically predicted the eventual rise of democracy in Asia's largest country. But Clinton also acknowledged "powerful forces resisting change" in China. And he dodged a reporter's question asking whether he expected to see democracy in China in his lifetime. [27]

Similarly, in most of Asia's non-democratic countries. There are stirrings of democracy, but the democratic forces face strong resistance from well-entrenched governments — whether they be communist, military or one-party regimes.

"We see growing pressure for democratic change" in Asia, says the Hoover Institute's Diamond. In most of the region, though, "it's hard to discern movement" toward democracy, he says.

Other U.S. observers and advocates are somewhat more optimistic. Brookings' Dalpino predicts "a series of quiet watersheds" in several Asian countries over the next few years. Daniel Steinberg, director of the Asia studies program at Georgetown University, even sees gradual political liberalization in Asia's most authoritarian countries.

"We're talking about the rise of alternative centers of power, which means the state is less centralized than it once was," Steinberg says. "That's happening even in China. And on the economic side, you're getting people making economic decisions without reference to the state."

The likelihood of democratic change in China remains sharply disputed. The government is encouraging villages to hold elections for local offices, but there is no movement toward electing leaders at the national level. When the *Journal of Democracy* gathered 10 experts earlier this year to offer predictions about the potential for democratization in China over the next decade, the optimists outnumbered the pessimists, but they all hedged their bets. [28]

Among Asia's other communist regimes, Vietnam and Laos have both adopted some market-oriented reforms, and both countries held national elections last year. But the State Department reports little progress toward political liberalization. In North Korea, the government has ruled out any political or economic liberalization.

Myanmar's military regime similarly shows no easing up. "Nothing's changed there," says Steinberg, who visited Myanmar earlier this summer. "They will have a civilian government at some point in the indefinite future, but it will be militarily controlled." Malaysia's and Singapore's dominant-party governments also show no signs of liberalizing political rights or, for now at least, losing popular support.

On the subcontinent, Pakistan continues to have elements of repression and arbitrary rule despite democratic forms. Bangladesh witnessed a peaceful change of government after elections two years ago, but political violence and electoral fraud persist. And Sri Lanka's civil war continues to mar its record in democratic government.

The bright spots for advocates of democratization are relatively few, but significant. "We've seen some nice consolidation of democracy in Thailand, in the Philippines, in South Korea," Dalpino says. Nepal has held four relatively free elections since political parties were legalized in 1990. Mongolia is making what the State Department calls good progress toward democracy in its transition from a communist regime. And India and Japan remain relatively secure in their democracies despite domestic political turmoil.

The U.S. role in encouraging democratic developments, most observers say, is limited but still significant. Diamond, for example, credits the Clinton administration with standing behind the Thai government as it instituted political reforms. He and others also stress the importance of the less visible U.S. support, including financial assistance, for associations, labor unions, human rights organizations and other elements of so-called civil society. "These are micro-type linkages," Diamond says, "part of the ongoing, more prosaic process of building democracy."

Many of these organizations are funded through the National Endowment for Democracy, which Diamond notes has a difficult time getting funding every year on Capitol Hill. "It's been one of the great success stories of U.S. foreign policy," he says, "but it has to fight for its existence every year."

Meanwhile, the biggest question mark for the moment is Indonesia, which must institute political reform and economic revival simultaneously. Mas'oed fears the economic problems may temper popular support for reform. "The common people tend to think more about food than about the reform movement now," he says.

"That's a problem."

After watching the Golkar conference, however, Tamimi was optimistic about the prospects for democracy. "This is very good for democracy," he says. "If the ruling party gives this good example, others will follow. When you disagree, there is no other way but through voting — no more manipulation." ■

## Notes

[1] For background, see Christopher Conte, "Deflation Fears," *The CQ Researcher*, Feb. 13, 1998, pp. 121-144.

[2] For background, see David Masci, "China After Deng," *The CQ Researcher*, June 13, 1997, pp. 505-528, and Patrick G. Marshall, "New Era in Asia," *The CQ Researcher*, Feb. 14, 1992, pp. 121-144.

[3] U.S. Department of State, *Country Reports on Human Rights Practices for 1997*, March 1998, p. 900.

[4] Fareed Zakaria, "Culture Is Destiny: A Conversation with Lee Kuan Yew," *Foreign Affairs*, March/April 1994, pp. 109-126; *The Wall Street Journal*, June 25, 1996, p. A1; Mahathir Mohamad and Shintaro Ishihara, *The Voice of Asia: Two Leaders Discuss the Coming Century* (1995), pp. 82-83.

[5] Samuel P. Huntington, *The Third Wave: Democratization in the Late 20th Century* (1991), p. 306.

[6] Lucian Pye, "Dominant Party Democracies in Asia," in *Democracy in Asia and Africa* (1998), pp. 69-72. For background, see Kenneth Jost, "Taiwan, China and the U.S.," *The CQ Researcher*, May 24, 1996, pp. 457-480.

[7] See *The New York Times*, July 28, 1997, p. A3; *The Washington Post*, July 30, 1997, pp. A1, A19. ASEAN includes Brunei, Indonesia, Laos, Malaysia, Myanmar, the Philippines, Singapore, Thailand and Vietnam.

[8] For background, see Mary H. Cooper, "U.S.-Vietnam Relations," *The CQ Researcher*, Dec. 3, 1993, pp. 1057-1080.

[9] For excerpts, see *The New York Times*, May 23, 1998, p. A8.

[10] See Yoneo Ishii, "Buddhism"; Werner Menski, "Hinduism"; and Winberg Chai and May-klee Chai, "Confucianism," in *Encyclopedia of Democracy* (1995).

[11] Some background is drawn from John Keay, *Empire's End: A History of the Far East from High Colonialism to Hong Kong* (1997).

[12] Donald K. Emmerson, "Indonesia," in *Democracy in Asia and Africa* (1998), p. 86.

[13] Keay, *op. cit.*, p. 212.

[14] Background drawn in part from individual country articles in *Democracy in Asia and Africa* and Keay, *op. cit.*

[15] For background, see Emmerson, *op. cit.*; Keay, *op. cit.*, pp. 32-35, 247-269.

[16] Huntington, *op. cit.* For background, see Emmerson, *op. cit.*; William Liddle, "Indonesia," in *Comparative Governance* (1992); M.C. Ricklefs, A *History of Modern Indonesia Since c. 1300* (1993).

[17] For a detailed account, see Raymond Bonner, *Waltzing with a Dictator: The Marcoses and the Making of American Policy* (1987).

[18] See Aung Cin Win Aung, *Burma: From Monarchy to Dictatorship* (1994).

[19] See State Department, *op. cit.*, pp. 784-785.

[20] For accounts of Suharto's fall, see *Far Eastern Economic Review*, June 4, 1998, pp. 21-26; *Newsweek*, June 1, 1998, pp. 34-43; *Time*, June 1, 1998, pp. 60-63.

[21] Quoted in *The New York Times*, July 12, 1998, p. A8.

[22] Quoted in *The Washington Post*, July 10, 1998, p. A31.

[23] See *The New York Times*, Aug. 15, 1997, p. A13. For a retrospective on India's 50 years of independence, see John F. Burns, "India's Five Decades of Progress and Pain," *The New York Times*, Aug. 14, 1997, p. A1.

[24] State Department, *op. cit.*, p. 1637. See Sumit Ganguly, *The Crisis in Kashmir: Portents of War, Hopes of Peace* (1998).

[25] See Sunil Khilnani, *The Idea of India* (1998).

[26] For background, see John F. Burns, "Pakistan's Bitter Roots, and Modest Hopes," *The New York Times*, Aug. 15, 1997, p. A1.

[27] For edited transcript of the Clinton news conference, see *The Washington Post*, July 4, 1998, pp. A20-21.

[28] "Will China Democratize?" *Journal of Democracy*, January 1998, pp. 3-64.

# Bibliography

## Selected Sources Used


### Books

***Democracy in Asia and Africa*, CQ Books, 1998.**
This reference work includes articles by leading Asia scholars assessing the status of democracy in Asia and Africa. Each article includes a short bibliography. Additional articles on Buddhism, Hinduism and Confucianism can be found in *The Encyclopedia of Democracy* (CQ Books, 1995).

**Ishida, Takeshi, and Ellis S. Krauss (eds.), *Democracy in Japan*, University of Pittsburgh Press, 1989.**
Essays by 13 experts evaluate political, social and economic democracy in Japan as of the end of the 1980s.

**Keay, John, *Empire's End: A History of the Far East from High Colonialism to Hong Kong*, Scribner, 1997.**
Keay, a British scholar, provides a readable survey of Dutch, English, French and American colonialism in East Asia beginning in the 17th century but focusing on the period 1930-1975.

**Khilnani, Sunil, *The Idea of India*, Farrar Straus Giroux, 1998.**
Khilnani, a political scientist at the University of London's Birkbeck College, provides an evocative picture of Indian political culture since independence. The book includes a 25-page bibliographic essay.

**Liddle, William, "Indonesia," in Philip Shiveley (ed.), *Comparative Governance*, McGraw-Hill, 1992.**
Liddle, a professor of political science at Ohio State University, contributes an overview of Indonesian politics and government to this political science text.

**Ricklefs, M.C., *A History of Modern Indonesia Since 1300* (2d ed.), Stanford University Press, 1993.**
This authoritative history traces events in Indonesia from the arrival of Islam in the 14th century and colonization by the Dutch in the 17th century through independence and the Sukarno and Suharto eras. The book includes detailed source notes, maps and a 25-page bibliography. Ricklefs is a history professor at the Australian National University in Canberra.

**Steinberg, David I., *The Future of Burma: Crisis and Choice in Myanmar*, University Press of America, 1990.**
Steinberg, now a professor at Georgetown University, wrote this account of the 1988 military coup and its aftermath immediately before the national elections in 1990, which were nullified by the military regime. The book includes a short list of suggested reading, including Steinberg's *Burma: A Socialist Nation of Southeast Asia* (Westview Press, 1982). For more recent books by a pro-democracy Burmese journalist now living in the United States, see Aung Chin Win Aung, *Burma: From Monarchy to Dictatorship*, Eastern Press, 1994; *Burma and the Last Days of General Ne Win*, Yoma Publishing, 1996.

**Tharoor, Shashi, *India: From Midnight to the Millennium*, Arcade Publishing, 1997.**
Tharoor, a United Nations official who has lived outside India for most of his life, writes what he describes as a "paean" to India that nonetheless sharply criticizes the country's political system for producing corruption and instability. The book includes a four-page chronology covering 1947 through April 1997 and a seven-page glossary.

### Reports and Studies

**Freedom House, *Freedom in the World, 1997-1998*, 1998.**
The 610-page volume includes country-by-country assessments of political and economic freedoms covering events through Jan. 1, 1998. The volume includes a global overview essay and regional essays on East Asia and South Asia.

***Human Rights Watch World Report 1998: Events of 1997*, December 1997.**
Human Rights Watch's most recent annual report, covering events through 1997, includes featured essays on 10 Asian countries.

**U.S. Department of State, *Country Reports on Human Rights Practices for 1997*, March 1998.**
The State Department's most recent annual report provides detailed country-by-country assessments of human rights, civil liberties, political rights, protections against discrimination and workers' rights.


### FOR MORE INFORMATION

*If you would like to have this CQ Researcher updated, or need more information about this topic, please call CQ Custom Research. Special rates for CQ subscribers. (202) 887-8600 or (800) 432-2250, ext. 600, or E-mail Custom.Research@cq.com*

The **U.S. State Department's** annual *Country Report on Human Rights Practices* can be found online at www.state.gov.; (202) 647-2492.

Here are private organizations that follow human rights issues in Asia:

**Freedom House,** 1319 18th St., N.W., Washington, D.C. 20036; (202) 296 5101; 120 Wall St., 26th floor, New York, N.Y. 10005; (212) 514-8040; www.freedomhouse.org. The human rights organization publishes a biennial volume, *Freedom in the World*, with country-by-country assessments of political and economic freedoms.

**Human Rights Watch,** 350 5th Ave., 34th floor, New York, N.Y. 10018; (212) 290-4700; 1522 K St. N.W., Suite 910, Washington, D.C. 20005; (202) 371-6592; www.hrw.org. The human rights organization publishes periodic reports and an annual volume, *Human Rights Watch World Report.*

# 16 U.S.-Russian Relations

**David Masci**

On April 30, the Senate did something that would have been unthinkable just 10 years ago: It voted to admit three former Soviet-bloc nations into the North Atlantic Treaty Organization (NATO), the very alliance created to rebuff Soviet aggression.

In an age that has seen the Berlin Wall fall and a McDonald's open in Moscow, admitting Poland, Hungary and the Czech Republic to NATO may seem anticlimactic. After all, the countries of Eastern Europe, once locked in a forced alliance with the Soviet Union, have been free for almost a decade. The Soviet Union itself decon-structed more than six years ago into Russia and 14 other independent countries. Moreover, Russia, once the epicenter of world communism, is now struggling to become a capitalistic democracy.

Indeed, by most reckonings Russia is no longer a mighty superpower but a basket case — weak economically, militarily and politically.

Hoping to help, the United States and its Western allies have provided advice and billions of dollars in aid since Russia became an independent state in December 1991. [1] For its part, Russia has tried to reform its economic and political systems along Western lines. It has also supported some key American foreign-policy initiatives, notably in Bosnia.

At the same time, Russia has shown that old, totalitarian habits sometimes die hard, as in President Boris N. Yeltsin's forcefully shutting down the Duma, or legislature, in 1993, and supporting pugnacious former Soviet clients, like Iraq.

Such Soviet-era behavior reflects the paradoxical nature of U.S.-Russian relations. While the two countries have grown closer since the Soviet Union's dissolution, they are still not the allies that some had predicted they would become. "There was this assumption after the Cold War that Russia and the U.S. would be pals, and that hasn't always panned out," says Anne Phillips, an assistant professor at American University's School of International Service. In fact, in the last few years relations between Russia and the United States increasingly have been characterized by friction.

Only time will tell whether the tension will increase or fade. The issue certainly was at the heart of the debate on the Thursday night that 80 senators voted to enlarge NATO. Indeed, to many Americans the enlargement debate boils down to one question: How far can the United States trust Russia?

Many supporters of NATO enlargement argue that the alliance must be maintained and strengthened to guard against the very real possibility that Russia not only will become powerful again but also aggressive. As columnist Charles Krauthammer recently wrote: "[J]ust because Russia is no longer an ideological rival doesn't mean that it has ceased to be a Great Power rival." Moreover, he added, "a country that expanded at the rate of one Belgium every two years [for] 300 years does not easily learn the virtues of self-containment." [2]

Others argue that it's not just a question of trusting Russia but of giving countries formerly dominated by the Soviet Union the freedom to choose whether or not to ally with the West.

"After all those years of living in effective slavery, [the Russians have] turned to us and said, 'We have the opportunity to express our national will, to be free,' " said Sen. Joseph I. Lieberman, D-Conn., during the Senate debate.

And, Lieberman and others say, bringing the new democracies of Eastern Europe into the world's largest and most powerful military alliance will promote stability in an unstable region. "We're not just collecting new countries here," says Sen. Richard G. Lugar, R-Ind., the second-ranking Republican on the Senate Foreign Relations Committee and a staunch NATO expansionist. "It's in our interest to create a larger sphere of security and stability, and that's what NATO expansion will do."

Finally, Lugar and others say, expanding NATO's zone of stability eastward is in Russia's interest too, since it will reduce the possibility of conflict in the region. There are even those who predict that Russia itself will join NATO someday.

But others say that NATO expansion will do little more than exacerbate already-existing tensions between Russia and the West, increasing rather than reducing the prospect for conflict. To begin with, they claim, Russia's weakness makes the need for an expanded NATO almost laughable. And yet, anti-expansionists say, the United States and its allies are sacrificing good future relations with Russia for an unnecessary alliance. "We're poisoning our relations with Russia for nothing," says Ted Galen Carpenter, senior vice president for defense and foreign policy at the Cato Institute.

At the same time, Carpenter and others argue, expanding NATO into Eastern Europe only loads more secu-

From *The CQ Researcher,* May 22, 1998.

## NATO's New Look

*The 16-member North Atlantic Treaty Organization will be expanded for the first time in 15 years when Poland, Hungary and the Czech Republic are formally admitted in 1999. Nine other countries in Eastern Europe are seeking admittance to the alliance.*

*Source: Congressional Budget Office, "The Costs of Expanding the NATO Alliance,"* CBO Papers, *March 1996.*

rity commitments onto a U.S. military that is already overextended. And, they add, the new countries are militarily weak and able to contribute little to collective security, requiring the Western European allies to shoulder more burdens for almost no benefit.

Expansion opponents also point out that Russia, its conventional forces cash-starved and virtually disintegrating, will rely more heavily on nuclear weapons to counter the greater NATO presence. Concern about nuclear weapons, already realized to some degree, is especially intense because of questions about Russia's control over its nuclear arsenal.

Some worried experts view the accidental launch of a Russian missile or some other nuclear catastrophe as highly possible, even likely. "It's the greatest national security threat the United States faces today," says Bruce Blair, a senior fellow at the Brookings Institution.

Blair and others claim that Russia's nuclear weapons are on "hair-trigger" alert, or ready to be fired the instant a possible attack is detected. Even more frightening, they say, parts of the old Soviet early-warning system are either off-line or improperly maintained.

But others are less concerned about accidental firing, noting that, unlike regular soldiers, the troops who guard and operate Russia's nuclear arms are still a disciplined, coherent force.

In addition, they say, if Russia's early-warning system were no longer adequate, the Americans who help maintain the Russians' nuclear arsenal would undoubtedly voice concern. "[American] specialists have confidence that there is no danger," says Vladimir Petrov, a professor emeritus of international affairs at The George Washington University.

Experts may debate the effectiveness of Russia's command and control over its nuclear arsenal, but there is wide agreement that the nuclear brinkmanship that once characterized the Cold War has subsided, at least for now. Still, some Russia-watchers say that competition between the two countries in the international arena remains intense. Some argue that Russia still views its relations with the United States as a zero-sum game — that they win each time the Americans lose, and vice versa.

According to proponents of this view, a number of recent events prove Moscow's ill intentions. For instance, it is noted that Russia worked diligently to thwart U.S. efforts to punish Iraq for not cooperating with United Nations weapons inspectors. According to Jeff Gedmin, a research fellow at the American Enterprise Institute (AEI), Russia's behavior in the case of Iraq was designed to obstruct what the Russians saw as another example of U.S. global hegemony. "They look for ways to block us as a way to increase their own stature," he says.

But others argue that Moscow is simply pursuing its own interests, as any country would. "Russia's resistance to some U.S. moves around the world is no longer a balance of power or ideological contest but is driven by national prestige and national interest," says Leon Aron, a senior fellow at the AEI. For instance, in Iraq, Russia has very important interests, Aron and others point out. For starters, they say, the Iraqis, as a former client state of the Soviet Union, borrowed billions for weapons purchases that they have never repaid.

Differences over Iraq, or NATO for that matter, illustrate the complexity of relations between the U.S. and Russia. As policy-makers and academics try to understand and improve this all-important relationship, here are some of the questions they are asking:

### *Does Russia's firm opposition to NATO expansion justify slowing or stopping new members from joining?*

Since its founding in 1949, NATO has been the world's premier military alliance. Anchored in Western Europe and held together by American military might and leadership, NATO was the West's primary bulwark against Soviet aggression. And for more than 40 years, millions of NATO troops (including, at one time, 500,000 Americans) guarded the frontiers of Western Europe, from the frozen fields of Norway above the Arctic Circle to the warm Mediterranean waters off Turkey.

Still, although the borders of the alliance stretched across Europe, its hub and the focus of most of its activity was in the heart of the continent, in West Germany. The great war that never came between the forces of East and West, capitalism and communism, would have been fought there, in the heart of Europe. Hence it is not surprising that the first new members admitted to NATO were Poland, Hungary and the Czech Republic.* Not only are they the most politically and economically advanced of the former Soviet-bloc countries, but they also are just to the east of Germany, right in Europe's center. More specifically, they give the alliance another layer of protection against its old (and perhaps future) foe: Russia. Or, as columnist Krauthammer wrote recently in *The Washington Post*: "NATO . . . is expanding in the service of its historic and continuing mission: containing Russia." [3]

Not surprisingly, Russia has objected to this first round of NATO expansion. But it has accepted the entry of its three former allies as a fait accompli. For one thing, there was little it could do about the expansion, except scream from the sidelines. Russia, with its economy and military in ruins, is largely powerless to oppose the West these days.

Now other countries — from the Baltic states in the north to Ukraine in the center to Romania and Bulgaria in the south — are trying to enter the NATO alliance, a prospect that makes political and military planners in Moscow furious (*see p. 304*).

Many say that NATO should welcome new members, regardless of Russia's objections. To start with, they say, after decades and, in many cases, centuries under Russia's yoke, the states of Central and Eastern Europe should be free to build economic, political or military links with the West and, in particular, the United States. "These are newly free states, and they should be able to decide on their own whether they want to apply for NATO membership without being dictated to by the Russians," says Gedmin of the AEI.

And, Gedmin and others argue, by bringing these states into NATO, the West is helping to promote much-needed stability in the region. In particular, they say, NATO brings American influence and prestige to the new member countries, which can be a force for resolving local disputes and coaxing them closer together. "NATO offers Central and Eastern Europe America as an umpire or fair broker, a role that Russia, Germany and other powers of Europe cannot play for reasons of history," Gedmin says.

Supporters also argue that NATO is a defensive alliance and not, in any way, threatening to Russia. "No one, anywhere, honestly believes that NATO is going to attack Russia," says John Tedstrom, a research leader in Russian, Ukrainian and Eurasian affairs at the Rand Corp. The problem, Tedstrom and others say, is one of Russian perceptions, not any credible threat from the West.

---

*Poland, Hungary and the Czech Republic are expected to be formally admitted into NATO at the alliance's 50th anniversary meeting on April 4, 1999.

## What Is Boris Yeltsin Up to?

Boris Yeltsin's behavior has often confounded his allies and adversaries alike. Over the years, the Russian president has sometimes appeared confused and, at times, even inebriated in public. Coupled with his heart problem and other ailments, Yeltsin's strange comportment has prompted regular speculation about his mental and physical health.

But Yeltsin-watchers were working overtime recently when the Russian leader fired his prime minister of five years and the entire Cabinet without warning or obvious reason. Yeltsin further stunned observers by naming a relatively unknown 35-year-old politician, Sergei Kiriyenko, to replace Victor Chernomyrdin.

Even though Yeltsin's March 24 move does not seem to have backfired — Kiriyenko was confirmed by the usually hostile Duma — many speculate that the Cabinet shakeup is a sign that after years of erratic behavior, the president has finally come totally unhinged.

This is not the first time Yeltsin has been written off. In addition to his repeated erratic behavior, the president has faced several serious health scares — including a quintuple coronary-artery by-pass in 1996 — only to re-emerge from convalescence with his hands still firmly holding the reins of power.

Still, many question how much longer Yeltsin will be able to carry on. "There's a lot of evidence that he is increasingly in his dotage, in a general state of incipient senility with moments of lucidity and energy," says Frank Gaffney, director of the Center for Security Policy. As a result, he says, "we're increasingly seeing a stage-managed presidency with more scripted events."

Gaffney and others point to a number of recent incidents that, in addition to the Cabinet firing, leave one wondering about Yeltsin's overall condition. For example, during the most recent standoff between the United States and Iraq, Yeltsin warned President Clinton that military action against Saddam Hussein's regime would lead to a "world war." Others talk of his now famous offer (subsequently withdrawn) during a December trip to Sweden, to reduce Russia's nuclear forces by one-third.

One of the president's closest confidants, business tycoon Boris Berezovsky, has publicly worried about Yeltsin's alleged incapacity. Berezovsky, who virtually bankrolled Yeltsin's 1996 presidential campaign, admitted that "the president's health prevents him from doing practical, political work every day." [1]

Many wonder how Yeltsin has lasted this long — politically and otherwise. At 67, he has already exceeded the average life expectancy for a Russian male by a decade. Add to this a lifetime of rumored heavy drinking and political intrigue, and Yeltsin's condition might not seem so surprising.

But other observers note that many, including the president's predecessor, Mikhail Gorbachev, have underestimated Boris Yeltsin, only to be surprised later by his resiliency and determination. In fact, some say, far from being a sign of mental instability, the recent Cabinet firing was a bold stroke.

"It seems it wasn't the irrational move we all thought it was at first," says Leon Aron, a resident scholar at the American Enterprise Institute. Bringing in a new team may actually help to jump-start the now moribund economic-reform process, he says.

Blake Marshall, executive vice president of the U.S. Russia Business Council, agrees, arguing that Chernomyrdin, a centrist with presidential ambitions, was too afraid of offending business interests and other powerful elites to make bold and necessary moves on the economy. Kiriyenko, on the other hand, is a liberal reformer who doesn't have the same ties to the powers that be in Russia. Consequently, he has a lot less to lose if he steps on toes to get things done, Marshall says.

Others perceive another, more political motive in Yeltsin's recent actions. By denying Chernomyrdin the high-profile post of prime minister, Yeltsin is dampening his former colleague's chances in the presidential election of 2000.

Does that mean that the Russian leader is contemplating another run for the presidency? In spite of Yeltsin's health problems and Russia's constitutional two-term limit, many feel that he wants to keep his job when his second term ends in 2000. "Like most revolutionary politicians," Aron says, "he feels that his staying in power is what is needed for the country and what the people really want."

[1] Fred Coleman, "Who's Running Russia?" *USA Today*, April 6, 1998.

Moreover, Tedstrom and others contend, NATO is good for Russia, even if it doesn't yet know it. "If we want Russia to complete its transformation into a modern European power, the last thing we should do is to act as if Central Europe is still a Russian sphere of influence," Secretary of State Madeleine K. Albright wrote recently in *The New York Times*. [4]

On the other hand, supporters of expansion say, enlarging and strengthening NATO is a good way to ensure that Europe and the United States will be ready for any unforeseen threats that may arise in the future if Russia doesn't remain a friendly state. "Russia isn't a threat today, but it's possible that a new Russia — a hard-line communist state or nationalistic state — could emerge," says Gedmin.

But others argue that NATO has lost it's raison d'être since the breakup of the Soviet Union and should, at the very least, not be expanded. Opponents of broadening NATO membership point out that the new Russia is smaller in both area and population than the Soviet Union was. Moreover, its economy is in a weak, almost anemic, state. In addition, they say, the country is no longer the communist state that once sought to spread its influence — and Marxist revolution — around the globe.

And, opponents of expansion point out, Russia's conventional forces have shrunk and decayed dramatically. No longer the fearsome steamroller of the Cold War, the country's military could not even pacify the small, breakaway province of Chechnya, let alone threaten a big country like Poland.

More important, these opponents say, expanding the alliance now is like taunting an injured animal, a stupid and dangerous act that could lead to a backlash. "It's very unwise to crowd a great power, especially one that's in distress," argues the CATO Institute's Carpenter. Not surprisingly, Carpenter and others say, NATO expansion has only made the Russians more paranoid and jumpy, at a time when their nation is in chaos and their military is falling apart.

Petrov of The George Washington University, agrees, adding that Russia's paranoia is not entirely unfounded. "These arguments from the West about building stability and the other things are hypocrisy," he says. "NATO is directed against Russia, period."

As a result, Petrov and others say, a new, stronger alliance may well create a more unstable and aggressive Russia — just the result the West wants to avoid. According to Grigory Yavlinsky, leader of the reformist Yabloko party, NATO expansion is a vote of no-confidence in Russia that could well become a self-fulfilling prophecy. "The most important message of NATO expansion for Russians . . . is that the political leaders of Western Europe and the United States do not believe that Russia can become a real Western-style democracy within the next decade or so," he writes in a recent issue of *Foreign Affairs*. [5]

Indeed, opponents argue, Russia's anxiety over NATO has already produced undesirable results. Most notably, in 1997, the Russians moved more of their tactical nuclear weapons closer to their western border in an effort to beef up their sagging conventional forces close to Europe. "Since they can't match NATO conventionally, they're relying more and more on nuclear weapons," Carpenter says. "No one really wants that," he adds, referring to the greater likelihood that a catastrophic accident or mistake will occur.

In addition, Carpenter and others claim, expansion has pushed Russia closer to non-Western powers like China and Iran. "By forcing them to accept this, we're pushing them into the arms of others instead of building closer and better relations with them," Carpenter says.

Finally, opponents argue, NATO expansion isn't going to make the alliance stronger, because the nations of Central and Eastern Europe are not militarily powerful. "Having small powers as allies doesn't strengthen but weakens you because you incur obligations to defend these countries and get nothing for it in return," Petrov says.

Reuters/Gleb Garanich

*Russian soldiers in Belarus guard the last Soviet-era nuclear missile outside Russia in December 1996, just before it was shipped to Russia.*

### ***Does Russia currently have adequate control over its nuclear arsenal?***

On Jan. 25, 1995, a scientific rocket launched from Norway threw Russia's nuclear forces into a state of high alert. Early-warning stations had reported that the projectile was heading for Russian territory and was probably an American nuclear missile fired from a Trident submarine. Within minutes, President Yeltsin had opened the briefcase containing the launch codes for Russia's nuclear weapons. Twelve minutes after first detecting it, the military informed the president that the rocket was now heading out to sea and ended the alert. [6]

The false alarm sent shivers through many in the arms-control and military communities and, for some, highlighted the potential weaknesses in Russia's command and control over its nuclear weapons. Many analysts, like the Brookings Institution's Blair, say that Russia's lack of control over

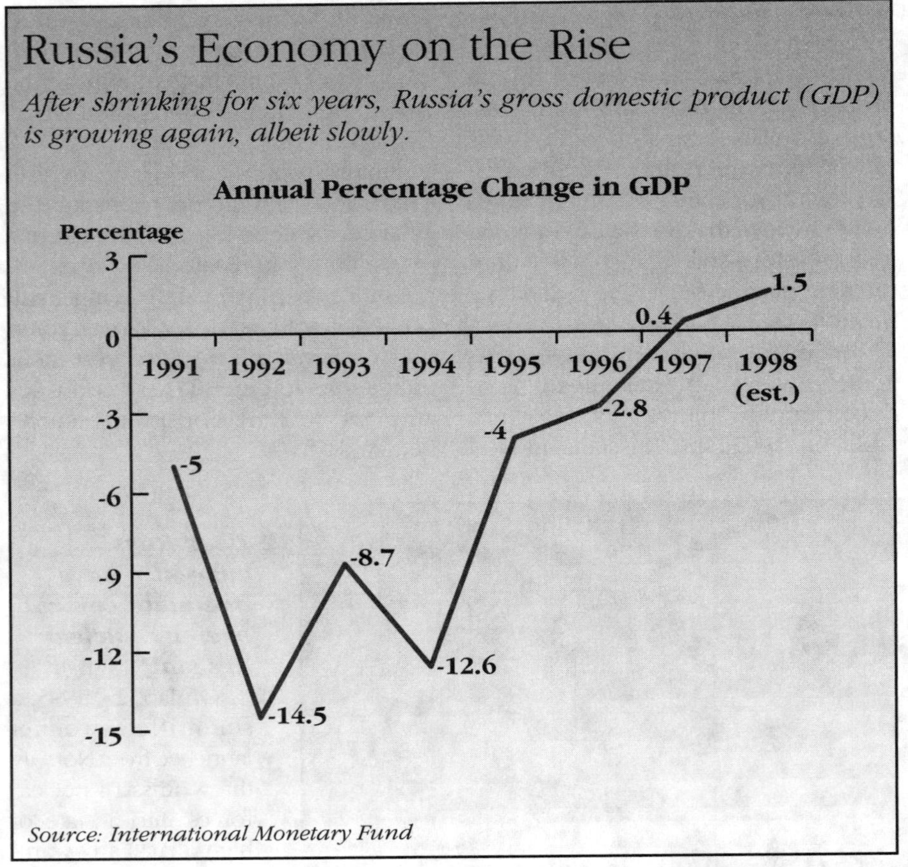


**Russia's Economy on the Rise**

*After shrinking for six years, Russia's gross domestic product (GDP) is growing again, albeit slowly.*

*Source: International Monetary Fund*

its nuclear arsenal is America's No. 1 national-security problem.

Even though nuclear forces in Russia have been reduced significantly since the heyday of the Cold War in the 1970s and '80s, the country still maintains about 6,000 warheads mounted on 1,300 missiles. And while the START II treaty (ratified by the U.S. Senate but not the Russian Duma) would bring the numbers of missiles and warheads down much further, many say Russia's control over these weapons is inadequate to ensure that an accidental or unauthorized launch will not occur. *(See story, p. 304.)*

To begin with, Blair argues, Russia maintains its nuclear forces on "high alert," meaning that it will fire its missiles if there is evidence that an enemy nuclear attack is in progress. This "hair-trigger" setting makes the prospect of an accidental launch much more likely.

Pessimists like Blair maintain that having nuclear forces on high alert is even more troubling when one considers that the country's early-warning system (which detects incoming attacks) has degraded significantly since the 1980s, making it more likely that Russia will mistake non-military missile launches (like the one from Norway) as aggressive actions.

The reasons for the degradation of the warning system are twofold. First, due to a lack of funds, Russia's spy satellites are not being replaced when they stop operating. Hence the country no longer has as many "eyes" in space as it once did. Second, many of the early-warning radar stations are located in former Soviet republics that are now independent countries. Some of these new states, like Ukraine and Latvia, no longer allow the Russians to use the facilities on their territory. "This has left some gaping holes in the system," says Sherman Garnett, a senior associate at the Carnegie Endowment for International Peace. And, Garnett says, those facilities still controlled by the Russians (both in and out of their country) are not operating at peak performance levels. "The system is breaking down, and there simply is no money to fix it," he says.

In addition, the pessimists say, more than machinery is deteriorating. The Strategic Rocket Forces, those personnel charged with guarding and operating the land-based nuclear arsenal, have suffered from the same decline in money, training and moral that has affected the rest of the military. "They're still better than the average military units," Blair says. But, he adds, due to a decline in proper training, "they are less proficient than they once were in handling nuclear weapons." In addition, he says, "they are much less motivated to adhere to safety standards than they used to be because their housing and food are less than adequate."

But others argue that Russia's control over its nuclear forces, while far from perfect, is not the catastrophe waiting to happen that many claim it to be. "The command and control system is reliable," says Dmitri Simes, a former adviser on Russia to President Richard M. Nixon and president of the Nixon Center for Peace.

Simes and others point out that Russia has put great value in its nuclear forces in the last decade as its conventional capability has declined. "It's the one area where there is still parity with the United States and so, even with the deterioration of the rest of their military, the nuclear weapons are still relatively well-maintained," Petrov says.

As for the Strategic Rocket Forces, optimists say, there is still adequate unit cohesion and acceptable moral. "They've deteriorated less [than other Russian units] because they've gotten special budgetary treatment, in part because the Russians are relying on nuclear weapons more and more," says Bruce Parrott, director of Russia Area and East European Studies at the Brookings Institution.

Optimists also point out that American officials who have unprecedented access to Russia's nuclear forces have not expressed deep concern about command and control. "We have hundreds of people over there, and they are not screaming that the sky is falling," Petrov says. And, optimists like Petrov point out, the situation is going to get better as overall conditions in Russia improve. "The worst is over because the economy is going to begin improving, and they will have more money to put into things like this," Simes says.

### *Does Russia, in the spirit of past Cold War rivalry, often oppose American foreign-policy initiatives to prevent the United States from growing too strong internationally?*

Late last year, Saddam Hussein expelled United Nations weapons inspectors from his country, prompting the United States to prepare an aerial barrage against Iraq that would have rivaled the firepower used in the Persian Gulf War. Into this tense standoff stepped Russian Foreign Minister Yevgeni Primakov.

Near the end of November, Primakov met with the Iraqis and convinced them to allow weapons inspectors back into the country. The deal was grudgingly accepted by the United States, and the conflict, at least for a short while, was avoided.

Many view Primakov's efforts as a triumph of diplomacy over force. But others argue that the Russian's actions allowed Saddam to thwart the United Nations for a time without ultimately paying any price. "[The Russians] were running interference for a bad guy," says Frank Gaffney, president of the Center for Security Policy.

More important, Gaffney and others say, Primakov's actions in Iraq are part of a broader foreign-policy strategy whose primary goal is to obstruct American initiatives wherever possible. For example, they point to Russia's continued sales of nuclear reactors to Iran in spite of vociferous U.S. objections. In addition, they say, Russia has blocked or has tried to block other American initiatives, from NATO expansion to U.S. efforts to build oil pipelines in the former Soviet republics of the Transcaucasus, such as Azerbaijan, Armenia and Turkmenistan.

Reuters/Desmond Boylan

*Secretary of State Madeleine K. Albright and Russian Foreign Minister Yevgeni Primakov met for talks in Spain in January in an effort to resolve the conflict over U.N. weapons inspections in Iraq.*

Indeed, these analysts say, Russia largely views its relations with the United States as a zero-sum game. In others words, according to AEI's Gedmin, Russian policy-makers "think that whenever America loses, Russia wins."

Gedmin and others argue that Russia's view of the United States is driven by a number of factors, including a desire to restrain what they see as America's immense and unique global power. "They are keen on ensuring that the United States doesn't have a free hand to do whatever it wants," Gedmin says.

Much of the sentiment against the United States is left over from the days of superpower competition. "There's a continuity between the foreign policy of the communists and the current government's position," says Chandler Rosenberger, a research fellow at the Institute for the Study of Conflict, Ideology and Policy in Boston. "The U.S. is still the enemy."

Anti-American sentiment is also viewed as a product of the effort to restore Russia to the status of a great power. "They think that Russian greatness can only be restored at our expense," Gaffney argues. And since Russia currently cannot project power in the same way that the old Soviet Union once did, "thwarting the United States is the only way at this stage of the game to put Russia back on the map," he says.

Indeed, defying the United States is a popular course of action in many parts of the world today. Many countries, from regional powers like France and China to developing nations like Malaysia, regularly question Washington's wisdom on a variety of issues.

But, those suspicious of Moscow argue, Russia is perhaps the most active player in this drive to curtail what is seen as American hegemony. "Primakov looks at the map and finds countries that are in trouble and tells them that they're not going to be pushed around any more," Rosenberger says. He points to a recent speech the foreign minister gave before a summit of East Asian nations in which he criticized the United States for pressuring them to make painful economic reforms. "Of course, he's a hit when he does this."

But other scholars say that it is unnecessarily alarmist to view Russia as an enemy or even with unusual suspicion. "There isn't a zero-sum game anymore," George Washington University's Petrov says. "That's ridiculous."

Petrov and others point out that the country, while no longer a super power, is still a great power, with legitimate interests outside their borders. "As the Russians have gotten back on their feet a little, they have begun to define their interests," says the Nixon Center's Simes. "And of course, there are genuine differences in interests and perspectives."

And yet, Simes says, these "differences" are not a sign of some plot or strategy to undermine the United States. "They are not driven by some ideology or desire to oppose the U.S. like they were in the old [Soviet] days," he says, noting that France and other traditional U.S. allies often have serious policy disputes with Washington. "It is natural."

Simes and others point out that in Iraq, for instance, the Russians have their own interests, which, when examined, make their recent actions understandable. For one thing, Iraq is much closer geographically to Russia than it is to America and was, for many years, a close ally of the Soviet Union. In addition, the country still owes the Russian government close to $8 billion for past purchases of weapons and other items, which largely explains Primakov's desire to diffuse the crisis and restore a more "business as usual" atmosphere.

And, George Washington's Petrov points out, Russia was joined by most of the rest of the world in its Iraq policy. "We shouldn't view Iraq as some sort of betrayal [by the Russians]," he says. "Except for the British, we were alone in our policy."

Petrov, Simes and others argue that Washington needs to understand that Russia will not blindly follow the United States simply because it won the Cold War, nor should it. Such unrealistic expectations stem, in part, from Moscow's behavior in the year or so just before and after the fall of the Soviet Union, Parrott contends. "We got into a situation where they gave us everything we wanted," he says, referring to Russian support for the Persian Gulf War and other American initiatives. "That sort of spoiled us."

In addition, he argues, the United States still often approaches Russia as a vanquished foe instead of a potential ally. "There is a certain triumphalism at work here on our part," he says. "The Russians are tired of hearing that we won the Cold War."

Finally, Petrov and others point out, Russia has played ball with the United States on the big issues that are important to Washington. For instance, they say, Moscow has cooperated with the United States in Bosnia, where Russian troops currently work alongside NATO peacekeepers. Even on the first round of NATO expansion, they say, Russia bowed to the inevitable without kicking up too much of a fuss.

"When we are firm with the Russians and let them know that it's something important, like NATO expansion or Bosnia, they come around," says AEI's Aron. ■

# BACKGROUND

## 'Honeymoon' Days

The United States greeted the collapse of the Soviet Union and the birth of the new Russian Republic in 1991 with a burst of goodwill and optimism. Almost overnight, the focus of nearly 50 years of American fears was replaced by a seemingly friendly, pro-democratic government. In a Christmas Day speech to the American people that year, President George Bush reflected the upbeat mood, welcoming "the emergence of a free, independent and democratic Russia led by its courageous president, Boris Yeltsin." [7]

Of course, Soviet-American relations had improved dramatically under Yeltsin's predecessor, Mikhail S. Gorbachev. Indeed, roughly a year before Bush's speech, the Soviets had supported the United States and its allies against Iraq in the Persian Gulf War, which would have been inconceivable just a few years earlier. Still, the emergence of the dozen-plus independent, former Soviet republics signaled definitively that the Cold War was officially over.

Almost immediately after the Soviet breakup, the Bush administration began working with Russia and other new states on a plan to safeguard the USSR's nuclear weapons. In particular, the Americans wanted Russia to retain control over not only its own warheads but also over those deployed in other former republics. Bush did not want to create a host of new nuclear powers.

By May 1992, the three new states that also had nuclear weapons — Ukraine, Belarus and Kazakhstan — all agreed to give them to Russia. (Ukraine delayed transferring its nuclear weapons in an apparent effort to extract more American aid, but it eventually abided by the agreement.)

The following month, Bush and Yeltsin agreed to reduce their strategic nuclear forces by 50 percent more than the cuts called for in the original START treaty that had been negotiated during the Soviet era. The new agreement became the basis for

# Chronology

## 1990-1991

***The Soviet Union dissolves, leaving Russia and 14 other independent countries in its place.***

**1990**
Boris Yeltsin wins a seat in the Russian Duma, or parliament, returning to the political arena three years after being forced out of the ruling Politburo.

**August 1991**
As the new president of the Russian Federation, Yeltsin successfully leads the resistance to a hard-line coup against Soviet President Mikhail Gorbachev. Although Gorbachev is returned to power, Yeltsin's role in resisting the coup leaves him as the most powerful man in Russia.

**December 1991**
Gorbachev resigns, and the Soviet Union dissolves. Congress passes the Nunn-Lugar Cooperative Threat Reduction Act, which aims to help the Russians and others dismantle nuclear weapons.

## 1992-1994

***Russia and the United States work closely on arms control and other issues.***

**April 1992**
The Group of Seven (G7) industrial democracies announce a $24 billion aid package for Russia and other former Soviet republics.

**May 1992**
Under pressure from the United States, Ukraine, Belarus and Kazakhstan give up their nuclear weapons, leaving Russia as the only former Soviet republic with a nuclear arsenal.

**January 1993**
President Clinton and Yeltsin sign the START II (Strategic Arms Reduction Talks) agreement in Moscow.

**October 1993**
Yeltsin orders an artillery attack on the White House, site of the Congress of People's Deputies, after members refuse his order to leave. He earlier had disbanded the legislature after it voted to end economic reforms.

**January 1994**
Russia agrees to join the Partnership for Peace, a group of former Soviet-bloc countries affiliated with NATO.

**Dec. 11, 1994**
Yeltsin orders Russian troops to attack separatist rebels in Chechnya.

## 1995-1999

***Relations between Russia and the United States are strained over NATO expansion and other issues.***

**January 1996**
Senate ratifies the START II treaty.

**July 1996**
Yeltsin is re-elected for a second four-year term.

**March 1997**
Clinton and Yeltsin meet in Helsinki to discuss Russia's concerns over NATO expansion.

**May 1997**
Clinton and Yeltsin sign the NATO-Russian Founding Act in Paris, which gives Russia an advisory role in NATO decision-making.

**July 1997**
Hungary, Poland and the Czech Republic are invited to join NATO.

**December 1997**
Foreign Minister Yevgeni Primakov brokers a last-minute deal with Iraq over United Nations arms inspections, delaying U.S. military action against Iraq.

**March 1998**
Yeltsin sacks his entire Cabinet, including Prime Minister Victor Chernomyrdin. His new choice for premier, Sergei Kiriyenko, is approved by the Duma in April.

**April 1998**
Senate ratifies the resolution adding Hungary, Poland and the Czech Republic to NATO.

**Summer 1998**
Duma is expected to vote on START II.

**April 1999**
NATO is expected to formally admit Poland, Hungary and the Czech Republic.

## Race for Space Now a Team Effort . . .

Many people think that cooperation in space between Russia and the United States began only after the Soviet Union collapsed in 1991. But the famous link-up between America's *Apollo* and Russia's *Soyuz* capsules occurred in 1975, more than a decade before the Cold War ended.

Still, today the two countries are working together in space in a way that previously would have been unimaginable, even during the height of detente in the 1970s. The focus of U.S.-Russian efforts is a new International Space Station (ISS), which is scheduled to begin operation in 2004. The project is being headed by the United States, which has been the world's premier power in space since it landed a man on the moon in 1969. But the Russians are playing a crucial role in the development and construction of the new station.

Russia now has the only permanent space station in orbit. *Mir* (which means "peace" in Russian) may be 12 years old and over the hill, but it is still flying and has been used by a string of American astronauts in the last few years to prepare them for the long stays in space that will come when ISS is aloft.

In addition, Russia is helping to build parts of the station, including a crucial service module. The cylindrical, 43-foot-long component will contain some of the station's living quarters and its life-support system.

Space exploration was one of the hottest areas of competition between the United States and the then-Soviet Union during the Cold War. The launching of *Sputnik* in 1957 began the "space race." And until the mid-1960s, Russia seemed to be winning, racking up one triumph after another. In 1960, it became the first nation to send a human, Yuri Gagarin, into orbit. Over the next few years, the Russians passed a number of other milestones, including the first woman in space and the first space walk.

But in May 1961, President John F. Kennedy, in a now famous speech before Congress, committed the United States to putting the first man on the moon before the end of the decade. During the next eight years, the United States poured tens of billions of dollars into developing the technology needed to achieve Kennedy's dream. America's deep pockets and ingenuity paid off in July 1969, when Neil Armstrong and Buzz Aldrin landed on the moon. A similar Russian effort had become mired in problems and was abandoned.

The 1970s saw a warming in relations between the two countries. And just as intense Cold War competition had led to the space race, detente brought a new spirit of cooperation, culminating with the *Apollo-Soyuz* link-up. The Soviet invasion of Afghanistan in 1979 and the election of cold warrior Ronald Reagan the following year sidelined any future plans for cooperation in space.

Things are different now. Russia's space program, suffering from low budgets and low morale, is dependent on the United States, which provides much-needed funding. In fact, the U.S. provides about one-sixth of the $600 million budgeted by Russia for its work in space in exchange for permission to put American astronauts aboard *Mir*.

But some American analysts question whether the United

START II, which was signed in Moscow in January 1993. *(See story, p. 304.)*

In addition to helping the former Soviet republics sort out their nuclear weapons, the United States and its Western allies also attempted to aid Russia and the other members of the new Commonwealth of Independent States (CIS) in jump-starting their moribund, statist economies. On April 1, 1992, the U.S. and its primary allies, the largest industrial nations known as the Group of Seven (G7)*, announced a $24 billion aid package to help Russia and the other CIS states.

As it turned out, much of the announced aid was in the form of previously pledged assistance; other chunks of it came in the form of loans. In short, the $24 billion figure was greatly inflated, leading the Russians to refer to it as "The April Fool's Day Gift." [8]

Still, American assistance was not insignificant. From 1991-1995, the United States gave about $4 billion to Russia and another $4.7 billion to other former Soviet republics. Much of the aid came in 1992 and '93, when U.S. goodwill toward its former enemy was running high. By 1996, however, aid to all former Soviet republics had dropped to $640 million, or a quarter of what it had been just a few years before. [9]

### Clinton's Initiatives

The early summit meetings between Bush and Yeltsin were more than just politically productive. In addition to hammering out agreements on arms control and other matters, the two leaders had established, in three summits spread over a year, a publicly warm relationship. But in November 1992, Bush lost the presidency, leaving Yeltsin to face a new American chief executive the following year.

Like Bush, Bill Clinton believes in the need to establish close personal ties with other world leaders. At his first meeting with Yeltsin in Vancouver, Canada, in 1993, the new

* Members of the G7 are France, Germany, Italy, Great Britain, Canada, Japan and the United States. The group has since been expanded to include Russia.

# . . . But Uncle Sam Is at the Helm

States is getting its money's worth by investing in and relying on Russia's space program. They say that sending American astronauts to *Mir* for long stays has largely been a waste of time and money because it is so old and poorly maintained that the astronauts spend most of their time keeping it operational instead of engaging in learning and experimentation. Indeed, last year, *Mir* suffered a number almost devastating accidents and problems, including a collision with another Russian space vehicle that almost forced two cosmonauts and an astronaut on board to abandon ship.

Others argue that America's investment in Mir has been worthwhile. "The training and knowledge we've gotten from *Mir* will prove useful," says Henry Hertzfeld, a senior research scientist at The George Washington University's Space Policy Institute. In particular, Hertzfeld says, the station's problems may have provided invaluable lessons for the Americans. "You learn when things go wrong," he says. "Even if the problems on ISS turn out to be different, we will have learned a lot about managing problems from our experience on *Mir*."

Another criticism of U.S-Russian cooperation revolves around the service module that Russia is building for ISS. In late April, NASA announced that the launch date for the first part of the station, originally set for June, would be pushed back into the fall. The reason, the space agency said, is that its Russian counterpart is behind schedule in the delivery of the service module. The Russian space agency in turn blames Moscow for the delay, pointing out that the central government has not put up all of the funding promised for the project. A similar delay occurred a year before for the same reasons. [1]

Many analysts say that including Russia in the ISS project was a mistake because the country lacks the financial wherewithal and political stability to honor commitments. Indeed, the Russian government currently owes its space agency $45 million in funding for the module. Moreover, the recent change in cabinets has left everyone wondering whether the new prime minister, Sergei Kiriyenko, will be more or less effective at finding money to fulfill Russia's ISS obligations. [2]

But Hertzfeld and others say that Russia's problems are not atypical, pointing out that lack of funding and indecision on the part of the United States has delayed the space station numerous times. "No project of this magnitude comes in on time and at cost," he says.

In addition, Hertzfeld argues, giving space-station work to Russia serves another important purpose: keeping its scientists from working on missiles and other weapons for unfriendly regimes, such as those in Iran and Iraq. "They have a highly trained labor force with a lot of experience and no money," he says. "If we can benefit from that experience and, at the same time, ensure that it isn't used by the wrong kind of country, then everyone wins."

[1] "The Space Station: No Business, as Usual," *The Economist*, May 2, 1998.

[2] *Ibid*.

president succeeded in establishing a good rapport with his counterpart. A few months later, a joint commission was established by their seconds, Vice President Al Gore and Russian Prime Minister Viktor Chernomyrden. The new body was to meet every six months in an effort to maintain a continuous dialogue on important issues.

The close relationship between Clinton and Yeltsin has paid handsome dividends for the Russian leader. Clinton refused to criticize Yeltsin when he disbanded and then bombed the Duma in 1993. And, the American president remained silent the following year, when Russia invaded Chechnya, causing the deaths of tens of thousands of civilians.

In Clinton's first term, a variety of agreements were signed. At the Moscow summit in January 1994, the two leaders agreed to de-target their nuclear missiles, previously aimed at each other. Moreover, several arms-control treaties were extended or enacted, including the Chemical Weapons Convention in 1993, the non-proliferation treaty in 1995 and the 1996 Comprehensive Nuclear Test Ban.

Progress was also made with regard to conventional forces. The process had begun in 1990 (just before the Soviet Union's breakup) with the Conventional Forces in Europe Treaty, which required both sides to significantly reduce their military presence in Europe. Further progress was made in 1994, when Russia joined the "Partnership for Peace," an organization created by NATO to foster military cooperation among NATO members and former Soviet-bloc states.

Under the partnership's auspices, Russia and the United States held joint military exercises in 1994 for the first time. Repeated in 1995, the exercise culminated in Russia's participation in peacekeeping operations in Bosnia at year's end. Even more surprising, the Russians agreed to place their forces in Bosnia under overall U.S. command.

The relationship between the two countries was growing in other ways, as well. In 1992, Russia agreed to participate in the American-led effort to build a space station. And by 1996, American astronauts were training

## Progress Predicted on Nuclear Weapons

The second Strategic Arms Reduction Treaty (START II) has yet to be ratified. But officials in both the United States and Russia are already thinking about START III and even IV.

START II, which would radically cut nuclear warheads in both countries, was agreed to in early 1993 at the last summit meeting between Presidents George Bush and Boris Yeltsin. The U.S. Senate ratified the treaty in 1996. But Russia's counterpart, the Duma, has yet to consider the agreement, a political hot potato in Russia.

Currently, both countries have roughly 8,000 deliverable strategic warheads. Many are mounted on ground- and submarine-based missiles. Others would be delivered aboard strategic bombers.

If ratified by the Duma, START II would reduce each country's nuclear arsenal to about 3,000 warheads. The proposals put forth for START III would bring that number down to about 2,000 or just 20 percent of the arsenal each nation had during the height of the Cold War.

President Yeltsin resubmitted an amended version of Start II to the Duma on April 13. The change, approved by the United States, would extend the deadline for destroying all warheads covered under the agreement from Jan. 1, 2003, to the end of 2007. Russia requested the extra time, claiming that it needed to allow them to spread out the cost of dismantling and destroying the weapons.

Guessing political outcomes in Russia is a difficult proposition. But many predict that the president, who just scored a victory in the Duma by getting his new prime minister, Sergei Kiriyenko, approved, will win on the START treaties as well. "There's a sense in Moscow right now that they will grudgingly get done," says Sherman Garnett, a senior associate at the Carnegie Endowment for International Peace.

"Grudgingly," because powerful, nationalistic politicians in Russia see START II as another step in the country's long slide into obscurity on the world stage. They point out that Russia's nuclear forces are the only vestige remaining of its former superpower status. According to Victor Ilyukhin, the Communist chairman of the Duma's Security Committee, START II is "beneficial only for the United States and NATO, but not for Russia, which may lose its last defense shield if this document is ratified."

But many experts, including the top brass of Russia's armed forces, argue that the treaty will be good for the country, even from a chauvinist's viewpoint. Almost all agree that the country's nuclear arsenal is deteriorating at an alarming rate. Some argue that many of Russia's existing missiles may not even work anymore, due to age or lack of maintenance. That number is expected to grow dramatically in the coming decade, they say. "These weapons are expensive to maintain and upgrade, and Russia simply doesn't have the money to do that anymore," says John Tedstrom, a researcher at the RAND Corp.

Bruce Blair, a research fellow at the Brookings Institution, agrees. "The whole system is in a tailspin," he says. And so, Blair, Tedstrom and others say, Russia's nuclear arsenal will be reduced through attrition, regardless of whether they ratify the treaty or not. "STARTs II and III are the only chance they have to maintain some sort of nuclear parity with the United States," Tedstrom says.

Supporters of the treaty have something else working in their favor: The Americans have let it be known that final negotiations on START III cannot begin until START II is ratified. "We think it would be better for me to go to Russia after the Duma ratifies START II, because then we can work on START III," President Clinton said last December.[1]

Still, the two countries have already worked out a broad outline for START III. And officials in both countries, including Duma Foreign Affairs Committee Chairman Vladimir Lukin, predict that, at this stage, the details could be ironed out quickly if the presidents were to meet.[2]

Some are even looking beyond START III. According to a recent report in Jane's Defense Weekly, Clinton administration officials have raised the prospect of a fourth START agreement that would reduce warhead levels among all declared nuclear powers, not just Russia and the U.S.[3]

Of course, thinking two treaties ahead may be premature when the fate of START II has yet to be resolved. Still, anxious arms-control officials may not have to wait much longer. The Duma is expected to take up START II before the summer ends.

---

[1] Quoted in "Clinton Ready to Go to Russia After Duma Ratifies START II," Agence France Press, Dec. 16, 1997.

[2] David Hoffman, "START II Approval Imperiled, Russian Says," *The Washington Post*, Dec. 7, 1997.

[3] Barbara Starr, "New U.S.-Russian Arms Control Talks Imminent," *Jane's Defense Weekly*, March 11, 1998.

aboard *Mir*.[10] *(See story, p. 468)* In addition, a barrage of American products — from movies and music to Coke and McDonald's — opened a window into life in the United States.

### NATO Expansion

During the first few years of the U.S.-Russian "honeymoon," Moscow desperately sought guidance and help, and Washington eagerly obliged. In recent years, however, the relationship often has been strained.

NATO enlargement has been a particular sore point. In 1994, the United States and its Western European partners began their campaign to include some former Warsaw Pact nations in the alliance. While Yeltsin had previously expressed little concern over the prospect of expansion, he and Primakov began a campaign to stop former Soviet allies from joining. Many analysts say that Yeltsin's change of heart grew out of his perceived need to insulate himself from more nationalist politicians like Vladimir Zhirinovski, who view an expanded alliance as a threat. [11]

Still, Yeltsin undoubtedly knew that he was ultimately powerless to stop at least the first round of enlargement — adding Hungary, Poland and the Czech Republic. In spite of their loud protests, Russian officials knew the West was far more powerful than Russia and that a larger NATO was, in Clinton's view, a question of "not if, but when." [12]

In March 1997, Yeltsin met Clinton in Helsinki, Finland, to discuss, among other things, accommodating Russia's concerns before the new members joined in July. The talks led to a new agreement signed by the two leaders in Paris in June, along with other NATO officials. The so-called "Founding Act" gave Russia assurances — if not airtight promises — that NATO would not place nuclear weapons or large numbers of troops on the territory of its new members. In addition, the act established a joint council to give Moscow an advisory role in all NATO decisions. The new council would allow the Russians to be heard, but not to vote, at alliance meetings. [13]

Friction over NATO enlargement is unlikely to end. President Clinton and other Western leaders have stated publicly that the alliance plans to take in more members in the future. Some of these candidates, such as the Baltic republics and Ukraine, were once part of the Soviet Union, and Russia has called NATO membership for them unacceptable. "If they took in the Baltics, that would be different for the Russians, since it was once theirs," Simes says. He warns that admitting former Soviet republics into NATO could make Russia less friendly and more obstructionist to the West.

But NATO has not been the only sore point between the two countries. The United States has been troubled by Russia's apparent indifference to arms proliferation. American policy-makers have often chided Moscow for its willingness to sell weapons or nuclear technology — from ballistic-missile technology for India to nuclear materials for Iran — with little seeming regard for the potential consequences.

For its part, Russia has been angered by what it considers excessive U.S. unilateralism. Lately, Moscow has been exercised over America's unwillingness even to consult with Russia when planning to use force against a former Soviet ally or client. "Thus, United States air strikes against Libya in 1993, Serbs in Bosnia in 1994 and Iraq in 1995 and 1996 brought Russian protests," writes Raymond L. Garthoff, a retired senior fellow at the Brookings Institution. [14] ■

## 'Connections' Called Key to Success

*A recent survey in Russia shows that citizens are deeply cynical about how to get ahead in the new capitalistic economy.*

**What are the reasons for:**

| **Poverty** | | **Wealth** | |
|---|---|---|---|
| *Economic system* | 82%* | *Connections* | 88%* |
| *Laziness and drinking* | 77 | *Economic system* | 78 |
| *Unequal possibilities* | 65 | *Dishonesty* | 76 |
| *Discrimination* | 47 | *Good possibilities* | 62 |
| *Lack of effort* | 44 | *Talents* | 50 |
| *No talents* | 33 | *Luck* | 42 |
| *Bad luck* | 31 | *Hard work* | 39 |

** Percentage of respondents agreeing to each reason*

*Source:* The Economist, *Nov. 22, 1997; Interfax-AIF*

# CURRENT SITUATION

## Troubled Economy

Even as he was firing the entire Cabinet on March 24 in an effort to stimulate efforts at economic reform, President Yeltsin was declaring those selfsame reforms to be "irreversible." But many economists are uncertain that Russia will continue on the reformist or, as some cynics say, the quasi-reformist, path toward a free market.

Of one thing there is no doubt: The average Russian has been through tremendous economic pain in the last decade. Moreover, many economists assert, most Russians are worse off today than when they were Soviet citizens. Indeed, real income has fallen by one-third over the last decade, leaving almost one-quarter of all Russians living below the poverty line. Not surprisingly, 41 percent of the Russians polled recently chose former Soviet President Leonid Brezhnev as their favorite leader. Yeltsin, by contrast, received top votes from only 14 percent. [15]

Hardships were expected when the Soviet Union collapsed and newly independent Russia began to transform its state-run economy. But Yeltsin has been in power for nearly a decade, some economists argue, and the near future looks no better than the recent past. "The problem is not only that the majority of Russians remain worse off than before the economic transition but that they cannot become better off," writes economist and Duma member Grigory Yavlinsky. [16] Yavlinsky and others argue that improvements in the nation's standard of living will not come until certain structural impediments to the economy are removed, notably a small but powerful group of wealthy businessmen who run much of Russia's economy. Much like America's 19th-century "Robber Barons," they own vast conglomerates engaged in a variety of enterprises. [17]

Most of Russia's tycoons are believed to be profoundly corrupt, having benefited more from insider connections and bribery than business acumen. Predictably, many influential businessmen exercise tremendous influence within the government and oppose reforms to the system which has benefited them so handsomely. [18] According to Yavlinski, "their market of insider deals and political connections stands in the way of an open economy that would benefit all Russian citizens." [19]

Another impediment to market-oriented reforms is the broader, more general corruption that pervades the country. "Everything in Russia is for sale. Everything can be bought," Potter says. Yavlinsky agrees. "Graft permeates the country, from street crime to Mafia hits to . . . rigged bids for stakes in privatized companies." [20] As a result, contracts and the rule of law in general are often not enforced, making it much harder to conduct legitimate business.

Understandably, the rampant corruption has made Russians cynical. According to a November 1997 poll taken by Russia's Interfax-AIF news agency, 88 percent of those surveyed said that a person needs "connections" to get ahead. Almost as many respondents, 78 percent, said that "dishonesty" is also crucial to success. "Hard work" was deemed an important factor for only 39 percent of those polled. [21]

Reuters/Sergei Karpukhin

*Russian Foreign Minister Yevgeni Primakov, left, meets with his Iranian counterpart, Kamal Kharrazi, in Moscow in February. Critics point to such encounters as evidence of Russia's increasing belligerance toward the U.S.*

At the same time, millions of government pensioners and employees, as well as those from state-owned enterprises, are owed months of back pay. The arrearage has largely been caused by the failure of the government to enforce the tax laws. Some experts estimate that Russians owe an astounding $100 billion in back taxes — roughly one-quarter of the nation's gross domestic product (GDP). [22]

## Helping Hands

Still, the economic news out of Russia is not all bad. The GDP, after shrinking for nearly a decade, has slowly begun to grow. Many economists say that the economy has "bottomed out," pointing to last year's 0.4 percent increase and a projected growth rate of 1.5 percent in 1998. Other key economic indices also leave some room for cautious optimism. Industrial production grew 1.4 percent last year. And inflation, the bane of many developing economies, was only 11 percent in 1997. [23]

Much of the good news comes on the heels of success in reforming the economy. A cornerstone of the reform program is the effort to privatize state-owned businesses. So far, tens of thousands of state companies and small businesses — about 75 percent of the economy — are now in private hands. In addition, the country has a small, but growing, stock market. And soon it is likely to also have a new, streamlined tax code that experts think will create a fair and effective tax-collection system.

Many economists and others argue that the United States and other advanced countries can best help Russia along the path to economic reform by encouraging the continued development of the institutions needed to

# At Issue:

## *Should the United States be more sensitive to Russia's concerns about NATO expansion?*

**yes**

SEN. BYRON L. DORGAN, D-N.D.

*WRITTEN FOR THE CQ RESEARCHER*

Russia's opposition to NATO expansion does not itself justify slowing down or stopping other countries from joining the alliance. Russia should not have a veto over this policy.

However, America's relationship with Russia is among the most important in the world, and we need to manage it in a way that makes America more secure. No matter how well-intentioned NATO expansion may be, I believe it will harm our relationship with Russia and jeopardize some of our highest diplomatic priorities.

Only Russia can destroy its nuclear weapons in accordance with arms-control agreements. Only Russia can control the thousands of tactical nuclear warheads that it retains. Only the Russian Duma can ratify START II and lock in new strategic nuclear weapons reductions. And only Russia can negotiate further reductions with the United States, to culminate in a possible START III accord.

NATO expansion — particularly expansion to include the Baltic states — will likely cause Russia to rely more, not less, on nuclear weapons. Russia's military planners will have to plan for defense the same way NATO's planners always have — by judging a potential adversary's capabilities, not its intentions. With NATO tanks on Russia's borders, Russian planners will be less likely to want further reductions in their stockpile of nuclear weapons.

NATO enlargement also threatens the cooperation with Russia in other areas, including crisis management in the former Yugoslavia, control of weapons technology and responses to rogue regimes. Since the administration's policy to expand NATO became clear, Russia has opposed military action against Iraq, has sought to block sanctions against Serbia over the crisis in Kosovo and has boosted its weapons sales to Iran. Further expansion of NATO will likely lead to further examples of Russia countering American diplomatic efforts.

This is frustrating because the end of the Cold War presented us with an historic opportunity to draw Russia to the West, to integrate it into the family of democratic and capitalistic nations. Rather than repeating the mistakes of the World War I peace settlement, which humiliated a defeated Germany and alienated it from the international community, we should repeat the successes of the World War II peace settlement, in which we aided Germany and Japan following the war and won their lasting friendship by welcoming them into international institutions.

**no**

SEN. RICHARD G. LUGAR, R-IND.

*WRITTEN FOR THE CQ RESEARCHER*

Central and Eastern European stability is as much in Russia's interest as America's. NATO enlargement provides an opportunity for the alliance to be proactive in shaping peace and stability, and lessens the chances of U.S. involvement in a regional conflict.

NATO enlargement neither punishes nor isolates Russia. There is nothing inconsistent between a healthy U.S.-Russian relationship and an expanding NATO. Russia has accepted, in the NATO-Russia Founding Act, the rights of neighbors to choose their security arrangements.

NATO members will continue to have both common and divergent interests with Russia, whether NATO enlarges or not. There will be areas of collaboration and discord in the relationship. Distinctions will be determined by differences in geography, history and economic standing, not by Cold War ideology or NATO enlargement. Managing coincidental and conflicting interests will be done by building bridges where possible and drawing lines where necessary.

Some critics believe that NATO enlargement somehow condemns the START II Treaty and cooperative U.S.-Russian nuclear dismantlement activities to the dustbin of history. But Russia's recent ratification of the Chemical Weapons Convention would indicate that the linkage between NATO enlargement and arms control is more political than strategic.

Russian tardiness in arms-control matters has more to do with internal Russian politics surrounding the Russian budget than defense policy planning. Although the Russian Duma continues to drag its heels in deliberations on the START II Treaty, it should be remembered that they began this practice long before NATO enlargement. Recently, Duma Speaker [Gennady] Seleznev has said that START II would be ratified by the Duma before it adjourns this summer because it "meets Russia's interests." NATO enlargement does not change the fact that START II, and a potential START III, is in their security interests.

In my recent trips to Russia it has been clear that NATO enlargement is unlikely to affect our cooperation with Russia to reduce the threat from weapons of mass destruction.

NATO enlargement and deeper NATO-Russian relations both have immense value for the United States and Europe. They are complementary and reinforcing objectives. The best outcome for the United States and Europe is success for both tracks.

establish a market economy. "We ought to be emphasizing the kinds of things that allow the economy to grow fairly, like the rule of law, effective regulation and standardized practices," Rosenberger says.

According to Blake Marshall, executive vice president of the U.S.-Russia Business Council, "We need to be there to offer advice and answer questions when these reforms are taken up by the Duma." In addition, Marshall says, American officials and business executives need to "rally public support [for reform] by explaining that these changes will bring benefits."

Another way to encourage change would be to facilitate meetings, both in Russia and the United States, between business people and government officials. "We need to foster more human-to-human contact so that [the Russians] can see how we do things," says Herman Pirchner Jr., president of the American Foreign Policy Council.

Very few Russia-watchers think that U.S. aid is having much of an impact on Russia's economy. "It's basically a drop in the bucket," Pirchner says, referring to the roughly $250 million Russia received last year.

Moreover, Pirchner and others argue, large dollops of assistance, such as the International Monetary Fund's (IMF) current $10 billion loan to Russia, often can do more harm than good. "The payments they're receiving from the IMF often have the effect of postponing needed structural reforms," he says, "because they give the Russians enough cash to get by."

In the end, Pirchner and others say, the IMF, the United States and other would-be friends of Russia can only have so much impact because the drive for reform must come from the Russian people. "Whatever we do will be on the margins because 150 million Russians are going to have a far greater impact on their economy than will the rest of the world," Pirchner says. ■

# OUTLOOK

## Rising Nationalism

Winston Churchill once called Russia "a riddle wrapped in a mystery inside an enigma." The country has become more open and arguably less Byzantine since Britain's wartime leader used the evocative description in a 1939 BBC radio address. But Russia nonetheless remains difficult to fathom even today, making attempts to predict the future particularly daunting.

And yet, divining the future in Russia is important, experts say, because the nature of its relations with the United States will depend more on what happens in Moscow than in Washington. So much hinges on Russia, they say, because it, unlike the United States, is in the midst of a profound transformation.

Most scholars agree that if Russia moves toward market reforms and democracy, it will forge closer ties to the West and the United States. But if it drifts back toward authoritarian and nationalistic policies, it will probably have more troubled relations with Washington.

For some, the future looks bright. "Russia is heading toward greater democracy, even if it isn't quite what we think of as democracy in the West," says American University's Phillips, who notes that Japan and other Asian countries have unique democratic institutions that work well for them.

Phillips offers two reasons for her optimism. First, she argues, the IMF and other Western institutions and countries are using the promise of loans and other benefits to nudge Russia toward becoming a more market-oriented, democratic society. "We're using carrots and sticks to push Russia in the right direction," she says.

In addition, Phillips says, Russia is naturally moving toward democracy. "There's been a real decentralization of authority there," she says, referring to the growing independence of the country's many regions and states. "This is a democratic movement in a sense."

Sen. Lugar, who shares Phillips' optimism, sees another hopeful sign. "When you look at the young people, who are the future, you realize that they don't want to go back to the old ways," he says. "That's one reason why, with all the back and fill, I think the trend in Russia is positive."

But Gaffney and others see a more ominous trend. "When democracy tries to exist with quasi-authoritarianism, as is the case there now, one always prevails over the other," he says. "Given Russia's tradition of the strong hand and ruthless repression, it seems quite likely that authoritarianism will prevail."

Rosenberger agrees, comparing Russia's post-Soviet history with that of Yugoslavia over the last decade. "In both countries you see a shift from the nationalism of communism to plain nationalism," he says. Indeed, he argues, the nationalist card is a good one for people like Yeltsin and Serbian leader Slobodan Milosevic to play, since it is very appealing in countries (like Serbia and Russia) where the people feel frustrated and resentful over their nation's reduced economic and political power. "A lot of [Westerners] have a hard time believing this, but many people in both countries are supportive of the strong nationalist position," Rosenberger says.

And "nudging" from the IMF and others is only going to make things worse, he warns. "This well of resentment will grow even bigger as long as we push our own free-market determinism on Russia," he says.

If a stronger and more nationalistic Russia emerges, the United States could have a much harder time getting Moscow to cooperate. "If you look at their aggressive foreign policy now, when they're so weakened," Gaffney says, "you realize that it will get much worse as they become more armed and powerful in coming years."

Can the United States prevent the emergence of an aggressive, nationalistic Russia? Many argue that the West, and the United States in particular, must be firm with Russia's leaders when they begin acting like their Soviet predecessors.

"It doesn't help the cause for reform in Russia when we roll over and don't do anything when they do something wrong . . . like invade Chechnya and kill tens of thousands of civilians," Rosenberger says. "Out of fear of not offending the Russians, we go soft, which of course only encourages the nationalists, who think their room to maneuver against the West has expanded."

Reformer and Duma member Yavlinsky agrees. "[T]he West should hold those in power in Russia accountable for undemocratic deeds, in much the same way it is willing to criticize its allies," he writes. "Western leaders should apply to Russia the same criteria for evaluating the health of its democracy and the strength of its market economy that they apply to themselves." [24] ■

## FOR MORE INFORMATION

*If you would like to have this CQ Researcher updated, or need more information about this topic, please call CQ Custom Research. Special rates for CQ subscribers. (202) 887-8600 or (800) 432-2250, ext. 600*

**American Enterprise Institute,** 1150 17th St. N.W., Washington, D.C. 20036; (202) 862-5846; www.aei.org. This research and educational organization studies a wide range of policy issues.

**Brookings Institution,** 1775 Massachusetts Ave. N.W., Washington, D.C. 20036; (202) 797-6111; www.brook.edu. This think tank sponsors research on domestic and international economics and other areas.

**Carnegie Endowment for International Peace,** 2400 N St. N.W., Washington, D.C. 20037; (202) 483-7600; www.ceip.org. The endowment is an international-affairs research organization with an affiliate office in Moscow.

**Center for Security Policy,** 1250 24th St. N.W., Suite 350, Washington D.C. 20037; (202) 466-0515; www.security-policy.org. The center is an educational institution that focuses on defense and arms-control policy.

**Council on Foreign Relations,** 58 East 68th St., New York, N.Y. 10021; (212) 434-9400; www.foreignaffairs.org. This foreign policy think tank has several Russia scholars.

## Notes

[1] For background, see "Aid to Russia," *The CQ Researcher*, March 12, 1993, pp. 217-240, and "Russia's Political Future," *The CQ Researcher*, May 3, 1996, pp. 385-408.

[2] Charles Krauthammer, "Good Geopolitics," *The Washington Post*, April 17, 1998. For background, see "Expanding NATO," *The CQ Researcher*, May 16, 1997, pp. 433-457.

[3] Krauthammer, *op. cit.*

[4] Madeleine K. Albright, "Stop Worrying About Russia," *The New York Times*, April 29, 1998.

[5] Gregory Yavlinsky, "Russia's Phony Capitalism," *Foreign Affairs*, May/June 1998.

[6] Bruce W. Nelan, "Nuclear Disarray," *Time*, May 19, 1997.

[7] Quoted in Raymond L. Garthoff, "U.S. Relations with Russia: The First Five Years," *Current History*, October 1997.

[8] *Ibid.*

[9] *Ibid.*

[10] "The Space Station. No Business as Usual," *The Economist*, May 2, 1998. For background, see "Space Program's Future," *The CQ Researcher*, April 25, 1997, pp. 361-384.

[11] Robert Service, *A History of Russia in the Twentieth Century* (1998), pp. 533-534.

[12] Quoted in Melinda Liu, "Eastward Expansion," *Newsweek*, May 26, 1997.

[13] *Ibid.*

[14] Garthoff, *op. cit.*

[15] Cited in "Russia's Part-Time President," *The Economist*, Feb. 14, 1998.

[16] Yavlinsky, *op. cit.*

[17] David Hoffman, "Russia's 'People's Capitalism Benefiting Only the Elite," *The Washington Post*, Dec. 28, 1997.

[18] *Ibid.*

[19] Yavlinsky, *op. cit.*

[20] *Ibid.*

[21] "Russia's Reforms in Trouble," *The Economist*, Nov. 22, 1997.

[22] Daniel Williams, "Russia's Ever Mounting Back Taxes," *The Washington Post*, Dec. 26, 1997.

[23] Statistics from the World Bank's Web site.

[24] Yavlinski, *op. cit.*

# Bibliography

## Selected Sources Used


### Books

**Mandelbaum, Michael, *The Dawn of Peace in Europe*, Twentieth Century Fund, 1996.**
Mandelbaum, a professor at Johns Hopkins University's School of Advanced International Studies, argues that NATO is still necessary for Europe's security, even in a post-Soviet world. At the same time, he says, Russia's interests must be constantly considered if new security arrangements are to be lasting.

**Service, Robert, *A History of Twentieth-Century Russia*, Harvard University Press, 1998.**
Service, a professor of Russian history and politics at the University of London, chronicles Russia's history from the days of the czars to President Boris Yeltsin's re-election in 1996. His analysis of communism and the Communist Party in post-Soviet Russia is particularly insightful.

### Articles

**Albright, Madeleine, K., "Stop Worrying About Russia," *The New York Times*, April 29, 1998.**
The secretary of State argues that NATO enlargement will not produce an aggressive and hostile Russia as many predict. In fact, she says, expanding the alliance is the best way to encourage democracy in Russia. "If we want Russia to complete its transformation into a modern European power, the last thing we should do is to act as if Central Europe is still a Russian sphere of influence," she writes.

**Cooper, Mary, "Expanding NATO," *The CQ Researcher*, May 16, 1997.**
Cooper's excellent overview of the NATO enlargement debate looks at the issue from a number of important angles, including NATO's continued usefulness and the validity of Russia's concerns.

**Garthoff, Raymond, "U.S. Relations with Russia: The First Five Years," *Current History*, October 1997.**
Garthoff details the ups and downs of relations between the United States and Russia. In particular, he chronicles the many summits and agreements that make up the brief history of the relationship.

**Hoffman, David, "Russia's 'People's Capitalism' Benefiting the Elite," *The Washington Post*, Dec. 28, 1997.**
Hoffman documents the rise of Russia's "tycoons," a small group of wealthy, well-connected businessmen who are squeezing out smaller, more legitimate businesses in their quest for complete control of the country's economy.

**Bruce W. Nelan, "Nuclear Disaster," *Time*, May 19, 1997.**
Nelan describes the sorry state of Russia's still enormous nuclear arsenal. He argues that a number of scenarios, from a political crisis to the misidentification of a non-threatening, foreign rocket, could lead to the use of nuclear weapons.

**Rosenberger, Chandler, "Russian Roulette," *National Review*, Jan. 26, 1998.**
Rosenberger, a research fellow at the Institute for the Study of Conflict, Ideology and Policy, argues that Russia's foreign policy is guided by a desire to block the United States at every turn. He notes that Russian Foreign Minister Yevgeni Primakov has spent the last few years whipping up anti-American sentiment among Russia's allies in Europe and Asia while at the same time opposing U.S. actions against rogue regimes like Iraq and Iran.

**Yavlinsky, Grigory, "Russia's Phony Capitalism," *Foreign Affairs*, May/June 1998.**
Yavlinsky, a reformist member of the Duma, claims that Russia is at a crossroads, both politically and economically. To make sure the country moves in the right direction, he writes, Western nations "should apply to Russia the same criteria for evaluating the health of its democracy and the strength of its market economy that they apply to themselves."

**Zakaria, Fareed, "Can't Russia Join the Club Too?" *Newsweek*, May 4, 1998.**
Zakaria presents a number of arguments in favor of admitting Russia to NATO, including this one: "If one of NATO's new goals is to strengthen democracy, then surely its place lies with the most important democratic experiment taking place on the European continent — in Russia."

### Reports and Studies

**Kober, Stanley, "NATO Expansion and the Danger of a Second Cold War," The Cato Institute, Jan. 31, 1996.**
Kober, a research fellow at the Cato Institute, presents a host of arguments against expanding NATO. He predicts, among other things, that enlarging NATO will create a more nationalist Russia that is suspicious of the West.

# Index

# INDEX

# INDEX

# INDEX